bones.axp
bubbld.axp
bubble.axp
comet.axp
disint.axp
dust.axp
explod.axp
expvol.axp
firewk.axp
flame.axp
flock.axp
lghtng.axp
magic3.axp
magic4.axp
manim.axp
mapbox.axp
mshres.axp
pcloud.axp
plasma.axp
rain.axp
refrac.axp
rings.axp
sincos.axp
skin.axp
snow.axp
spurt.axp
stbrst.axp
vapor.axp
vortex.axp
aurora.axp
bones.axp
bubbld.axp

3D Studio IPAS Plug-In Reference

Tim Forcade

New Riders Publishing, Indianapolis, Indiana

3D Studio IPAS Plug-In Reference

By Tim Forcade

Published by:
New Riders Publishing
201 West 103rd Street
Indianapolis, IN 46290 USA

Printed in the United States of America 1 2 3 4 5 6 7 8 9 0

```
Forcade, Tim
    3D studio IPAS plug-in reference / Tim Forcade.
       p.    cm.
    Includes index.
    ISBN 1-56205-431-7
    1. Computer animation. 2. Autodesk 3D studio. 3. Computer
  graphics.   I. Title
  TR897.7.F67  1995
  006.6—dc20                                                95-16740
```


Warning and Disclaimer

This book is designed to provide information about the 3D Studio computer program. Every effort has been made to make this book as complete and as accurate as possible, but no warranty or fitness is implied.

The information is provided on an "as is" basis. The author and New Riders Publishing shall have neither liability nor responsibility to any person or entity with respect to any loss or damages arising from the information contained in this book or from the use of the disks or programs that may accompany it.

Publisher	Don Fowley
Associate Publisher	Tim Huddleston
Product Development Manager	Rob Tidrow
Marketing Manager	Ray Robinson
Managing Editor	Tad Ringo

Trademark Acknowledgments

Dedication

To Betsy, the love of my lives.

About the Author

Building on an education in traditional fine arts that stressed drawing, painting, sculpture, and graphic design, Tim Forcade's art work has advanced through optical, kinetic, and electronic media. This has resulted in numerous works utilizing photography, digital electronics, and video as well as the invention of electronic image processing systems of his own design.

Concurrent with his art work, Tim has over two decades of practice as a commercial artist, designer, and studio photographer. In 1977 Tim formed Forcade & Associates as a graphic resource to the commercial and professional communities. His experience extends from illustration and publication design, through photography and 3D visualization, to computer animation and multimedia. Tim's project experience includes work for clients including the University of Kansas, Spiegel, Kimball International, and the National Collegiate Athletic Association.

Tim's work has been exhibited and published in the United States, Canada, Europe, and Japan. He has written and presented extensively on the subjects of applied 2D and 3D computer graphics and animation. He is a contributing editor to *Computer Graphics World* and *Computer Artist* magazines.

Acknowledgments

I want to thank Terry Gilbert (GizmoKing), whose combination of outstanding technical expertise, organization, and dedication was absolutely essential to this project. I also want to thank the other essential contributors, Betsy Forcade (Princess of the Plains) for her invaluable opinions and editing; Mark Anderson (IPASavant) for his creativity, tenacity, and humor; and Guy Stephens (AniMinion) for the hard work between sound checks and sessions.

Thanks to Gary Yost and his Group, for their blue flame crania and their willingness to spread it around. Thanks to Bob Bennett and Autodesk for ongoing access and quality day-to-day data since 3DS day one.

Thanks to all the IPAS programmers, vendors, and tech support people not only for their fantastic cooperation but for developing all this incredible software.

Thanks to Jim LeValley, John Kane, Tim Huddleston, Steve Weiss, Stacey Beheler, Kevin Coleman, et al at NRP for the trust and the work.

Finally, thanks to Maggi and Wayne.

Credits

Acquisitions Manager
Jim LeValley

Software Specialist
Steve Weiss

Production Editor
John Kane

Marketing Copywriter
Tamara Apple

Acquisitions Coordinator
Tracey Turgeson

Publisher's Assistant
Karen Opal

Cover Image
Copyright Virgin Interactive Entertainment, Inc., 1995, created by Mechadeus

Cover Designer
Karen Ruggles

Book Designers
Tim Forcade
Kim Scott
Sandra Stevenson-Schroeder

Production Team Supervisor
Laurie Casey

Graphics Image Specialists
Jason Hand
Laura Robbins
Craig Small
Todd Wente

Production Analysts
Angela D. Bannan
Bobbi Satterfield
Dennis Clay Hager
Mary Beth Wakefield

Production Team
Gary Adair
Dan Caparo
Kim Cofer
Erika Millen
Gina Rexrode
Beth Rago

Indexer
Bront Davis

Contents at a Glance

Table of Contents

CONTENTS

New Riders Publishing

The staff of New Riders Publishing is committed to bringing you the very best in computer reference material. Each New Riders book is the result of months of work by authors and staff who research and refine the information contained within its covers.

As part of this commitment to you, the New Riders reader, New Riders Publishing invites your input. Please let us know if you enjoy this book, if you have trouble with the information and examples presented, or if you have a suggestion for the next edition.

Please note, though: New Riders staff cannot serve as a technical resource for 3D Studio or for related questions about software- or hardware-related problems. Please refer to the documentation that accompanies 3D Studio or to the applications' Help systems.

If you have a question or comment about any New Riders book, there are several ways to contact New Riders Publishing. We will respond to as many readers as we can. Your name, address, and phone number will never become part of a mailing list or be used for any purpose other than to help us continue to bring you the best books possible. You can write us at the following address:

New Riders Publishing

Attn: Associate Publisher

201 W. 103rd Street

Indianapolis, IN 46290

If you prefer, you can fax New Riders Publishing at (317) 581-4670.

New Riders Publishing is an imprint of Macmillan Computer Publishing. To obtain a catalog or information, or to purchase any Macmillan Computer Publishing book, call (800) 428-5331.

Thank you for selecting *3D Studio IPAS Plug-In Reference*!

bones.axp
bubbld.axp
bubble.axp
comet.axp
disint.axp
dust.axp
explod.axp
expvol.axp
firewk.axp
flame.axp
flock.axp
lghtng.axp
magic3.axp
magic4.axp
manim.axp
mapbox.axp
mshres.axp
pcloud.axp
plasma.axp
rain.axp
refrac.axp
rings.axp
sincos.axp
skin.axp
snow.axp
spurt.axp
stbrst.axp
vapor.axp
vortex.axp
4dots_i.ixp
afchk_i.ixp
afdiv_i.ixp
afdiv4_i.ixp

IPAS Plug-Ins: A Virtual Image Synthesizer

Beginning in the late 1960s and continuing into the early 1980s, I designed and built a number of analog image synthesizers that I called light machines. Light machines began as manually controlled, incandescent and fluorescent display devices designed for the purpose of creating expressive light and color compositions. The early manual-control devices evolved through multichannel, sound-driven light arrays into a series of light machines that used semiconductor chaos to synthesize, colorize, and animate 3D "sonic objects."

Most of the light machines had one essential notion in common: they were designed for use as a series of discrete image processing modules that could be controlled with numerous switches and dials as well as patched together in any combination. My fascination with analog image synthesis was centered on devising new ways of creating, connecting, and adjusting these numerous modules to reveal and manipulate complex color imagery. Interestingly, after years of experimentation I never saw the same object twice.

This is the essence of 3D Studio IPAS plug-ins. They give you the ability to create an endless variety of unique animated imagery using your own custom image synthesizer—an image synthesizer that you design, on the fly, each time you apply one or more IPAS plug-ins to your 3D Studio illustrations and animations. Instead of knob twiddling and numerous patch cord connections, you can adjust IPAS plug-ins using an interface consisting of multiple sliders and radio buttons. Furthermore, IPAS plug-ins are considerably more robust and predictable than light machines, which could occasionally take hours to visualize anything more than a single white dot.

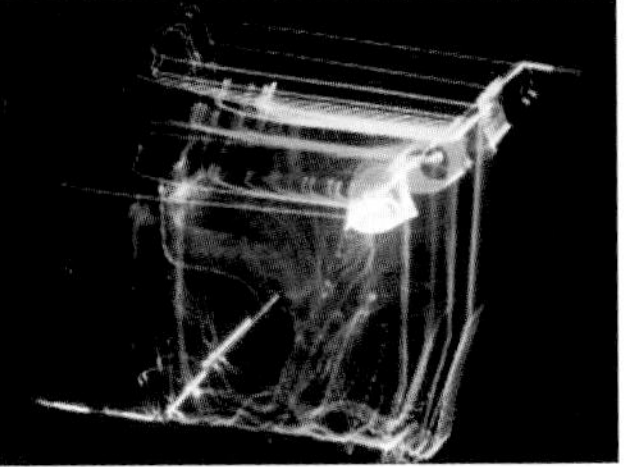

Light Machine 4 Sonic Object 6

Light Machine 4, an analog image synthesizer, used numerous dials, switches, and patch connections to create 3D animated "sonic objects." This sonic object image was created with a lot of knob twiddling and patch editing using Light Machine 4 and a vector graphic display.

TVRFX2 v1.0 by Objet d'Art Computer Service, 1994
72010.2615@compuserve.com
SMEAR
Enable YES NO
Amount - 90 +
YIQ Y IQ
JITTER
Enable YES NO
Width - 75 +
Line Frame
HORZ HOLD
Enable YES NO
At Top - 10 +
At Bottom - 0 +
Frequency - 15 +
Variation - 30 +
VERT HOLD
Enable YES NO
Start Frame 0
End Frame 30
Rolls - 44 +
Offset - 19 +
POWER ON
Enable YES NO
Start Frame 0
End Frame 30
Fwd Rev
Red - 100 +
Green - 50 +
Blue - 61 +
Random Seed 12345
Support: NW Tech (206)641-3282 71621.606@compuserve.com
OK Cancel

IPAS plug-ins such as Television Reception Effects provide dialog boxes consisting of sliders and radio buttons, giving you 3D graphics and animation at the touch of a button.

IPAS plug-ins offer artists and animators outstanding flexibility, quality and variety. For all the complexity that must always accompany such sophistication, IPAS plug-ins are, for the most part, easy to understand and apply. Imagine being able to apply rich animated and optical effects as directly as you might a particular brush or palette knife, and you begin to understand the power of IPAS plug-ins.

However, IPAS plug-ins are more than just a group of effects and utilities; they comprise a unique philosophy of CGI (computer-generated imagery) media design as well. 3D Studio/IPAS is the first 3D computer graphic program to successfully share the process of media development with the artists themselves—you can create your own plug-ins from scratch. Such extensibility offers artists the means to shape their medium on their own terms while maintaining professional quality standards. This has made the notion of 3D plug-ins universal and, in a sense, larger than 3D Studio, the program that spawned them.

Original image

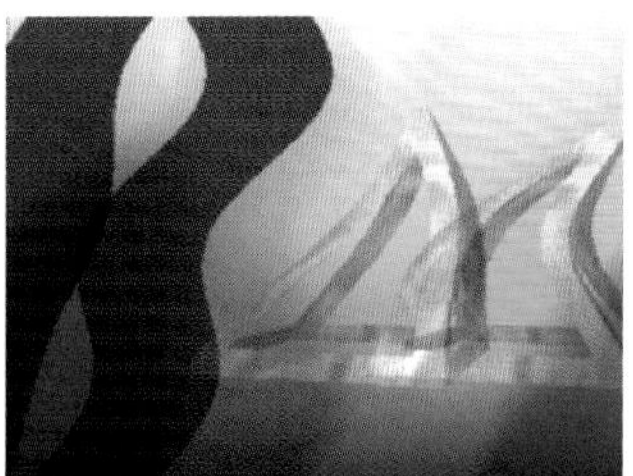

Horizontal hold TVR effect

Most IPAS plug-ins, such as Television Reception Effects, make it simple to create numerous professional-quality special effects.

Numbering 250 as of this writing, IPAS plug-ins have taken the idea of image synthesis infinitely further than light machines ever did and, happily, without the maze of tangled patch cords and instability of analog electronics. They combine to form a virtual image synthesizer that is accessible, sophisticated, predictable, and great fun to work with.

IPAS Foundations

Getting started with IPAS plug-ins begins with a little background. IPAS applications, as they were originally called, first emerged with 3D Studio Release 2. IPAS is a unique programming environment that enables C language programmers to create external processes, which can be called from within 3D Studio to perform various diverse tasks. IPAS is an acronym composed from the first letter of each of the original four IPAS applications: IXP (Image Processing External Process), PXP (Procedural Modeling External Process), AXP (Animated Stand-In External Process), and SXP (Solid Pattern External Process). With Release 3 came two additional categories, KXP (Keyframer External Process) and BXP (Bitmap External Process).

IXP plug-ins enable you to image process a Keyframer scene or series of rendered frames to produce image distortions and effects that resemble lens flares, or to make an animated sequence look as though it were drawn or painted. IXP plug-ins act something like photographic filters that can selectively color, soften, or sharpen your images. There are 78 IXPs that work singly or together using the Keyframer's Video Post dialog box.

The 68 PXP plug-ins enable you to edit the geometry of your 3D models to produce warped, rippled, or twisted geometry. As their name states, they are procedural modeling processes; this means that they work using a set of predefined steps to create new geometry from an original or to modify existing geometry. You can even create a 3D model directly from a 2D image. Furthermore, some PXPs create geometry such as detailed trees or fractal landscapes procedurally from scratch. Many PXP plug-ins can be used to create morph objects for animated geometric distortions. The PXP plug-ins are applied from the 3D Editor.

The more than 30 AXP plug-ins produce animated effects such as smoke, fire, explosions, snow, rain, and more. Many AXPs consist of particle systems, which are flocks of variable objects with some very unique properties. They can be made to change their behavior over time, for instance, making them great for simulating intricate natural phenomena. AXP plug-ins can be applied and edited in either the 3D Editor or the Keyframer using the Object Attributes dialog box.

The 32 SXP plug-ins provide an almost limitless variety of 3D solid textures and patterns, many of which can be animated. These offer numerous advantages over conventional texture mapping, such as resolution independence. SXP plug-ins can be used alone or in combination as texture, opacity, bump, specular, shininess, and self-illumination maps or masks in the Materials Editor.

KXP plug-ins are animation control programs that automatically create or modify keyframes. You can create skeletal animations or work with inverse kinematics. Skeletal animation, the process of keyframing a 3D mesh object based on a simple skeletal armature, is particularly useful for creating character animation. Inverse kinematics enables you to easily manipulate complex groups of hierarchically linked objects. The secret to the elegance of the process lies in the fact that you can define joint parameters for roll, pitch, and yaw for the joints between selected elements in the hierarchy.

BXP plug-ins are used in conjunction with other plug-ins that need to load or save proprietary bitmap file formats not directly supported by 3D Studio. For instance, the EPS File Output and Gradient Designer PXP plug-ins require BXPs to produce PostScript output and enable 3D Studio to work with a specific range of special effects. Because they do not provide the user either control or access, they are not covered in a stand-alone BXP chapter. Instead, they are mentioned along with the plug-ins that they support.

Note: *If you intend to net-render using any plug-in, either install a copy on each machine or make the plug-in's executable file read-only. The simplest way to accomplish this is through the 3DS.SET file variable SET-IPAS-RDONLY=YES. This automatically marks the plug-in executable file as read-only each time it is accessed.*

Why an IPAS Plug-Ins Reference?

So why would anyone in his right mind want to analyze 250 programs and attempt to shoehorn that data into a single book and CD reference? Part of the answer lies in the fact that we professional graphikers live in pretty damned slackless territory. I am referring to dreadlines and production schedules from hell—Federal Express meets art and animation production.

So much of what effective 3D CGI is about is the time to examine, muse upon, and live with your work as it evolves from the napkin to the screening room, boardroom, or living room. This book is about giving you back some of that time.

The notion behind the 3D Studio IPAS Plug-In Reference is this: You are dealing with demanding clients along with competition from every garage and art factory on the planet and you need an effect shot. NOW. You are certain that you have heard about the effect your client described as one that can be done quickly and inexpensively using 3D Studio and one or more IPAS plug-ins. This book and CD is designed to make the process of locating and using the plug-ins you need as painless as possible, whether you are a new or advanced 3D Studio/IPAS plug-in user.

How This Book Is Organized

The book's structure is simple. It is divided into the separate IPAS plug-in families, each with their own introduction that discusses salient issues for that family. Each chapter is further subdivided with an illustrated entry for every functioning IPAS plug-in we could locate, with alphabetical listings for all the AXPs, IXPs, PXPs, and SXPs.

The operative word here is functioning, as in it does something, however eccentric or perhaps marginally useful. I am referring to those rare plug-ins that work as specified but leave you staring blankly at the screen, wondering why anyone would want that function. Or, for that matter, why anyone would take the time required to write it. No effort was made to second-guess what future IPAS plug-in users might be looking for; however, every effort was made to be as complete as possible and to work exhaustively with each plug-in to verify its function. Therefore, some plug-ins for which we were unable to locate the author or vendor, or which simply did not function, were cut. Fortunately the vast majority of plug-ins included are obviously very useful, and many are outstanding.

Each plug-in entry contains a summary of the plug-in's essential characteristics and use along with a description of the key parameters that control it. There is also a complete list of the plug-in parameters and any parameter options, along with concise definitions for each. Every effort was made to make the parameter definitions comprehensive while keeping them as brief as possible so that you can get the information you need ASAP.

Most parameters have a value range; however, you will see that some parameters that obviously support a range of input do not show a specific value range. This is because the parameter supports any useful or practical range of adjustment—15–200 degrees, for example. The specific ranges that are included were chosen because they were associated with a specific, limited, or, at times, eccentric range of adjustment.

The parameter abbreviations were initially included to make possible labeling each associated sample image with the parameters used to create it. Due to space requirements, it would otherwise have been impossible to include them. They are also provided as a convenience for use as you record your own experiments and want to pass them on to other users. Please note that parameters that are not directly related to graphics or animation production do not have associated abbreviations.

The plug-in illustrations include the associated dialog box or dialog boxes and one or more sample images for each. The exceptions to this were the extremely rare cases for which there simply were no dialog boxes and/or no way to illustrate the plug-in's effect, as in the case of a couple of utility plug-ins. The sample illustrations were designed and produced to give you as clear a picture as possible of each plug-in's essential attributes. Although the IPAS Plug-In Reference consists of numerous images, this collection was not intended to be taken as all the permutations possible. Such a book would be difficult for most of us to lift and likely cost more than 3D Studio and the sum of 250 plug-ins.

Our main objective is to provide a reference that will quickly help you discover which plug-ins are most appropriate to your specific project or practice and to provide visual guidelines for the application of each effect.

This book is not a replacement for the manuals that accompany these plug-ins. It is a starting point designed to make you aware of the over 230 IPAS plug-ins available and to give you a visual and theoretical basis for their successful use in your 3D illustrations and animations.

IPAS plug-ins provide open and direct access to some of the most sophisticated CGI available. Along with this, they seem to provide push-button artistic facility, insight, and sensibility. This is not the case. Remember that in spite of all the fantastic effects and image processing power, IPAS plug-ins and 3D Studio form the raw materials—a starting point from which powerful, expressive, and effective artistic works can emerge. This medium needs an artist's soul and passion to drive it. It is your exhaustive experimentation, creativity, and fresh ideas that will make this happen.

Using the CD-ROM

The CD-ROM contains demonstration versions of a number of IPAS plug-ins, selected sample images from the book, FLIC animations for selected plug-ins, and with numerous 3D Studio project files and Video Post files.

The CD file structure is as follows:

All sample images, FLIC animations, project files (.PRJ) and Video Post files (.VP) that pertain to specific plug-ins are located in their associated plug-in directories. Each plug-in CD-ROM directory is shown at the center of the horizontal color bar below the plug-in name. To find any example files that were created using Yost Group's Displacement Map Modeler, for instance, look in the \DISPLACE directory.

All the plug-in demonstration programs are sorted by vendor name or a vendor name abbreviation. The subsequent file structures will vary depending upon the installation requirements for each plug-in.

Please be sure to check PLUG_IN.TXT for any last-second information and tips that might have escaped the book's production deadline.

Thanks

We produced this book in record time, something under three months in actual production for all the color illustrations and copy—can you say "slackless," boys and girls? <G>—with many months before that doing research and design and something over a month after that in print and CD-ROM production.

Five of us worked on the project (see Acknowledgments), testing, rendering, hacking some of the more arcane applications, and overall having a wonderful time fooling around with image synthesis and effects on a scale I could not have imagined even a few years ago; much less when I was designing light machines. I hope you enjoy the *3D Studio IPAS Plug-In Reference* and IPAS plug-ins as much as we have working with and documenting them.

Thanks for the ear.

bubble_i.axp
bubd_i.axp
clatch_i.axp
comt_i.axp
disint_i.axp
dust_i.axp
explod_i.axp
expvol_i.axp
firewk_i.axp
flame_i.axp
flock_i.axp
hand_i.axp
lghtng_i.axp
magic_i.axp
mapbox_i.axp
mapmov_i.axp
mshres_i.axp
pcloud_i.axp
plasma_i.axp
rain_i.axp
rings_i.axp
skin_i.axp
snow_i.axp
spurt_i.axp
stbrst_i.axp
tornad_i.axp
tuber_i.axp
vapor_i.axp
vortex_i.axp
aurora_i.axp
bubble_i.axp
bubd_i.axp
clatch_i.axp

Complex Systems Animation

Animated Stand-In External Processes (AXP) plug-ins produce a variety of animated effects based on complex systems composed of numerous 3D objects or particles. You can produce snow, rain, and animated dust, and you can explode and disintegrate any 3D mesh object. AXPs also provide dynamic image mapping and animated spline surfaces. These simplify complex effects such as refraction mapping and enable you to create smooth animated geometry from simple mesh control elements.

The majority of AXP plug-ins consist of particle systems. Particle systems are collections of unique entities with the capability to change their behavior with time; for instance, particles can vary their size, position, shape, color, or texture at any point in an animation. The fact that these changes take place en masse, on large groups of swirling entities, enables particle systems to produce startlingly naturalistic and intricate animated special effects.

AXP particle effects include bubbles, smoke, fire, fireworks, rain, and comets. Most particle effects share two essential characteristics: a bounding box or object, and a single emitter or multiple emitter array. The bounding object can be any 3D mesh object and provides information such as form, scale, orientation, and image mapping coordinates. This makes it possible to encase a particle system within any 3D object, such as dimensional typography.

Emitter elements form the origin point or points from which particles are projected into 3D space. These can be procedurally generated or created from any 3D mesh object. In the case of procedurally generated emitters, such as Axpbox, the emitter element is a cluster of vertices, each with the capability to propel particles at a specified rate depending on several interdependent variables. Whereas the emitter is a 3D model, each object vertex becomes an emitter. This is one way that an object can appear to be on fire or covered with shimmering sparks.

Particle control variables are as unique as the particles themselves, and include parameters such as nucleation points, Brownian variation, life span, rise time, and various particle shapes. Because individual particles tend to consist of simple planar or volumetric geometry such as interlocking squares, pyramids, or polyhedra, particles appear spherical, such as those in Comet. However, particles can be any shape, including the elongated particle shape used by Flame.

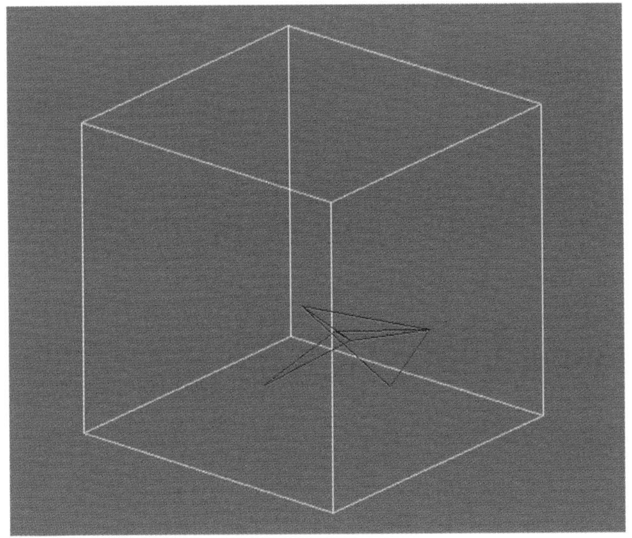

Axpbox and emitter

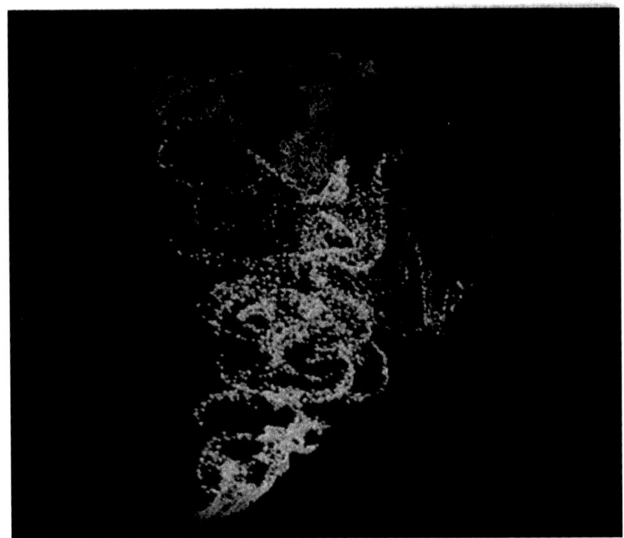

Vapor

AXP plug-ins use a a 3D object to provide scaling, orientation, and mapping information as well as an emitter array or source for particle emission. Some AXP plug-ins use the same 3D mesh as both the bounding object and emitter object.

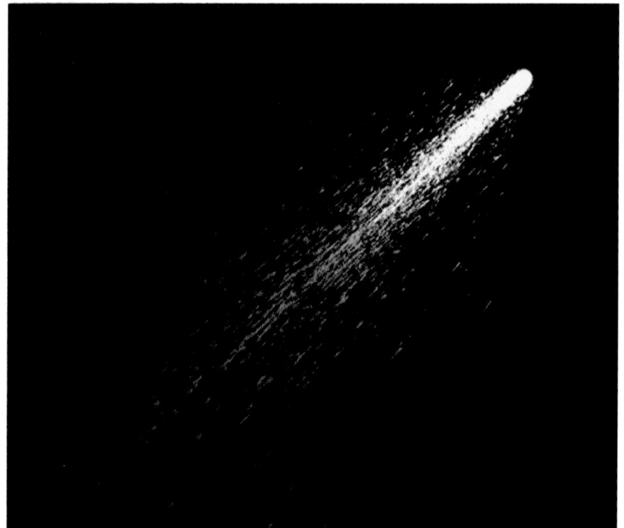
Comet

LenZFX Flare

Although most particle systems use a spherical particle, others, such as LenZFX Flare, use elongated, curvilinear-shaped particles.

Particle systems also provide control over the number, size, and emission speed of the particles, as well as a range of control over the particle path: typically one or more methods of perturbing the particles' path. This is accomplished by applying waves, dynamic functions, or chaos to the particle system. Examples of these functions include turbulence, wind speed, chaos level, and gravity. These parameters are extremely useful and can lend realism and character to particle effects.

You can add another level of refinement to AXP particle systems by applying image-mapped materials to them. This can make otherwise mundane geometric shapes become convincing steam, smoke, or fire. Materials are assigned to AXP particles by selecting Surface/Material/Assign/Object and clicking on the particle system's Axpbox or bounding object. Material texture coordinates are applied automatically either at a particle level or globally to all particles, depending upon the AXP plug-in. Remember that the use of transparency and opacity mapping can have a dramatic on render times, particularly as particles overlap.

If there is a downside to the use of particle AXP plug-ins and mapped materials with particle AXPs, it is the extended render times you will almost certainly encounter. This is no surprise when you consider that these programs must, at times, deal with tens of thousands of individual entities, each of which must be positioned in 3D space based on complex calculations such as chaotic turbulence. Add materials with texture and opacity, and it's no wonder these plug-ins can bring even the most powerful hardware to its knees.

The obvious answer to extended render times is that if you intend to do a lot of animation that must simulate natural particle-based phenomena or intricate effects that require m ultiple particle systems, you will want Warp9 PLUS for a microprocessor and a minimum of 32–64 MB of RAM. This notion carried into a small render farm consisting of just a few such machines will go a long way to widening this potential bottleneck.

Other obvious answers center around intelligent application of the complex array of AXP particle system parameters. Many times simple common sense applies, particularly with issues such as total number of particles or particle geometry—clearly, fewer and simpler is faster. Remember that fewer and simpler particles do not necessarily mean less effective or dramatic results. For those times when you must have maximum particle density, consider dividing your animation into several separately rendered segments that can be composited together in a final step.

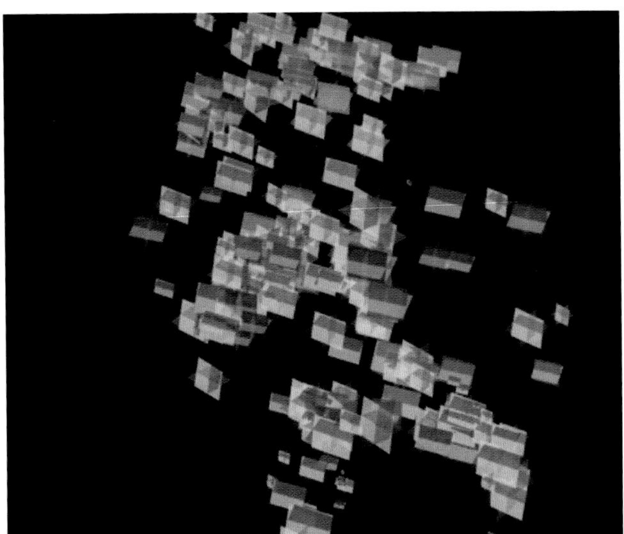

Basic particles

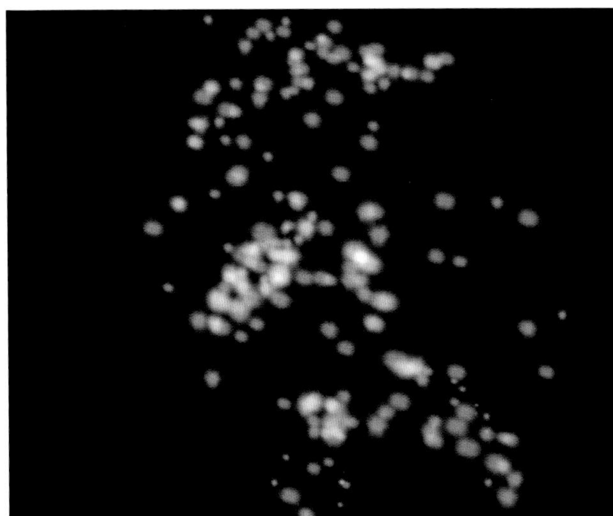
Mapped particles

Texture and opacity mapping are used to turn simple geometry into a steam effect.

For the more complex variables, study the effect of each separately, before you set each of several variables to its maximum setting. Keep in mind that many particle variables are interdependent and that thoughtlessly maximizing one or all of them will likely cause your computer to grind away for hours with no apparent benefit over a lower and faster setting. Above all, be sure to perform numerous test renders at key points in your animation to determine which parameters are most essential to your desired effect.

Using AXP Plug-Ins

Before you use an AXP plug-in, be sure that it is properly installed using its installation program or instructions. Furthermore, be sure to read and follow any accompanying instructions exactly. Attempting to shortcut this process, particularly with complex plug-ins, is a mistake. At the least you will likely receive regular error messages as the plug-in attempts to find its resource files, or the plug-in could either cause a crash or simply fail to run.

For those times when there is no installation program or documentation, copy the plug-in—*XXXXXX*_I.AXP—into your 3D Studio \Process directory.

AXP plug-ins can be applied and adjusted from either the 3D Editor or Keyframer using the Modify/Object/Attributes command and clicking on the Axpbox or object. This displays the Object Attributes dialog box. From here, click on the Name box under External Process to display the AXP Selector. Scroll through your installed AXP plug-ins and click on the name of the AXP you want to use. Click on OK and you will be returned to the Object Attributes dialog box.

Note: *Some AXP plug-ins, such as Refraction Mapping, Flame, and Vapor, require the application of PXP plug-ins for them to work properly.*

To adjust an AXP plug-in, click on the Settings button in the Object Attributes dialog box to display the selected plug-in's dialog box. With all your plug-in parameters set, exit the AXP dialog box by clicking on OK, then click on OK in the Object Attributes dialog box to return you to the 3D Editor or Keyframer. To see the results of your AXP edits, choose the render method you want from the command column and the view you want to render. Then set up the render parameters using the Render Still Image or Render Animation dialog box and click on Render.

AXP plug-ins are accessed from the AXP Selector in the Object Attributes dialog box.

The AXP Reference

The AXP plug-ins are listed alphabetically with the product name in bold type that appears at the top of each plug-in's section. The color bar below the plug-in name lists the plug-in file name, such as PLASMA_I.AXP. In addition, the 3D Studio IPAS Plug-In Reference CD-ROM path name and the vendor are shown. The CD-ROM subdirectory contains any sample files along with demonstration versions of the plug-ins where possible.

The text is divided into two areas: a summary and a parameter listing. The summary provides a look at the plug-in's characteristics and capabilities. The parameter listing displays the name of each parameter in bold type along with its corresponding abbreviation in brackets. For example:

Horiz Edge Effect [He] p,s (plain, striated) (0–100%) —
Specifies a sharp or ragged edge for the transition. The sliders control the width of the striated edge.

The bracketed abbreviations may be followed by any parameter modifiers along with their abbreviations. Where applicable, there is an adjustment range in parentheses, followed by a description of each parameter function.

Each plug-in is illustrated with a screen capture of its dialog box or boxes and one or more sample images.

Many of the project files used to create the sample images are available on the CD-ROM in the directory specified in the information bar at the beginning of each plug-in entry.

Each figure has the parameter abbreviations along with the essential values used to create that effect. The specific effect variations shown were chosen to represent as broad a range of variation as space permitted. They were also chosen on the basis of providing AXP plug-in users shortcuts and starting points for creating unique, interesting, and useful effects.

Selected AXP sample images are provided in their final rendered form. These files are located on the CD-ROM in the directory specified in the information bar at the beginning of each plug-in or in the \AXP directory.

ANIMATED DUST

Summary

Animated Dust is part of the Imagine Fractal Bouquet package. It is a particle system that simulates a spinning cloud of dust. It uses a bounding object to establish its volume and orientation. Particles appear inside the bounding object's bounding box.

The particles spin around a rotation axis that you can orient along the X,Y, or Z axis. Particles have a user-selectable chaos in their position and motion. You can separately enable or disable the chaos along X,Y, or Z. Particles are octahedrons that use the material of the bounding object.

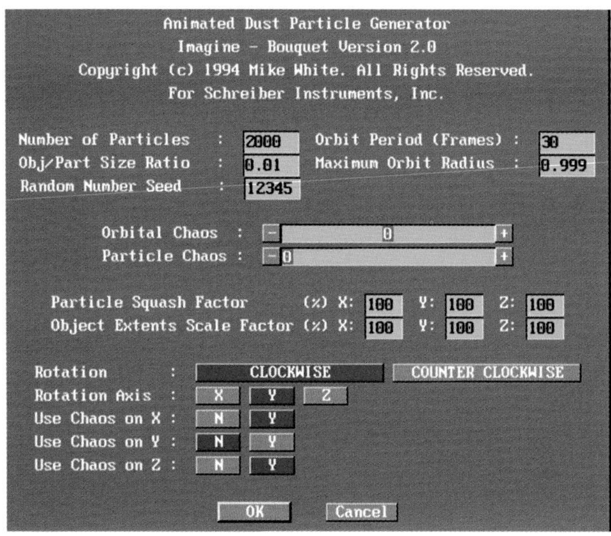

The Animated Dust dialog box.

Animated Dust Parameters

Number of Particles [N] (1–9,999) — The number of particles generated.

Obj/Part Size Ratio [S] (0.0001–0.5) — Size of the particles relative to the bounding object.

Random Number Seed [R] — Random number that controls the particles' location and motion.

Orbit Period [O] — The number of frames for a 360-degree rotation of the particles.

Maximum Orbit Radius [Mo] (0.05–0.9999) — Maximum distance that a particle can be from the center of rotation. This is expressed as a fraction of the size of the bounding object.

Orbital Chaos [Oc] (–50–50) — Amount of variation in orbital speed of the particles in frames.

Particle Chaos [Pc] (0–100) — Amount of variation in the position of particles and in the location of their centers of rotation.

Particle Squash Factor X, Y, Z [Sx] [Sy] [Sz] (0–999%) — Particle scale factor in each dimension. This enables you to change the shape of the particles

Object Extents Scale Factor X, Y, Z [Ex] [Ey] [Ez] (100–999%) — Particle path scale factor in each dimension. This enables you to change the shape of the particle cloud.

Rotation [Ro] cw, ccw (clockwise, counterclockwise) — Direction of rotation.

Rotation Axis [Ra] (x,y,z) — Sets the axis for particle rotation.

Use Chaos on X, Y, Z [Cx] [Cy] [Cz] n,y (no, yes) — Determines whether Particle Chaos effects the particle paths in each direction.

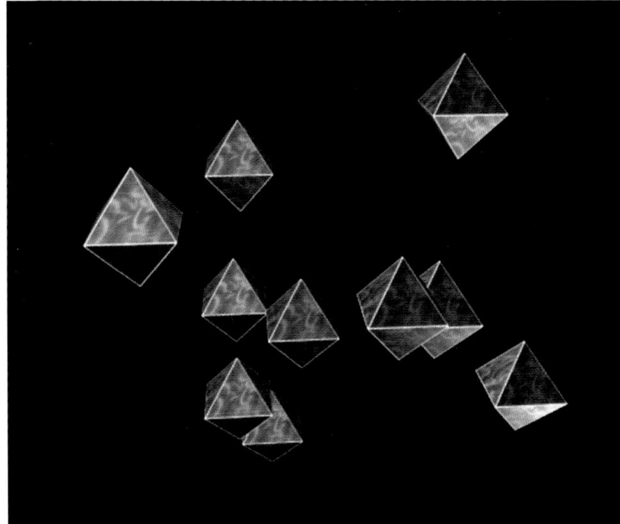

[N]10 [S]0.25 [Oc]10 [Pc]44

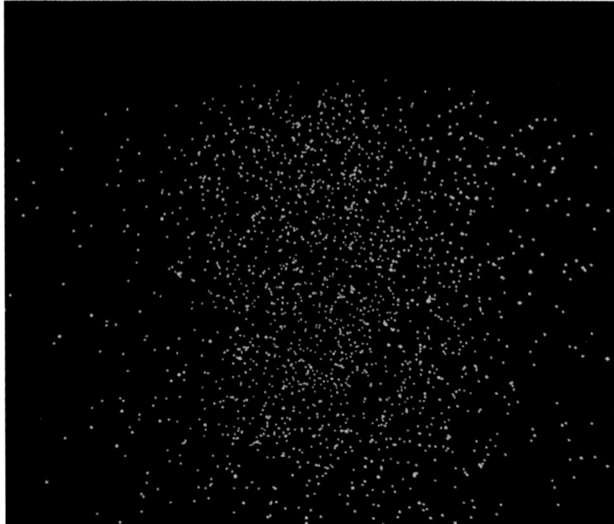

[N]2000 [S]0.01 [Oc]8 [Pc]30

Particle detail and particle cloud.

AURORAL MAPPING

AURORA_I.AXP **\aurora** **Video International**

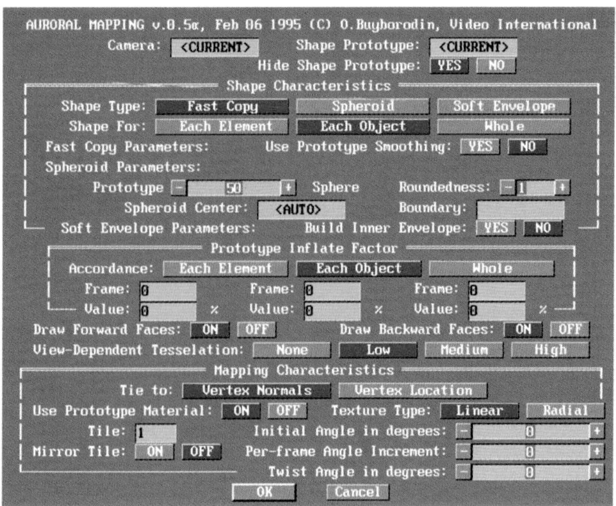

The Auroral Mapping dialog box.

Summary

Auroral Mapping adds an auroral glow around an object. It creates a transparent copy of a source object by offsetting the source object's surface as though it were being inflated. It comes with a material using self-illumination, opacity maps, and rainbow texture maps to produce an auroral glow.

Auroral Mapping uses one of three methods to produce the enlarged offset object. Fast Copy copies each face based in its surface normal. This is fast, but for planar objects the glow might look too planar. Spheroid wraps a spherical envelope around the source object. Soft Envelope generates a rounded surface that follows the contours of the source object. You can animate size of the glow by setting offset values at three different frames. The orientation of the glow can be animated by specifying a rotation per frame.

This summary was based on a prerelease version of the software.

Auroral Mapping Parameters

Camera [Ca] — Name of the camera to use. This orients the auroral mapping.

Shape Prototype [Sp] — Name of the source object for the aurora envelope.

Hide Shape Prototype [Hs] y, n (yes, no) — Determines whether the prototype object is hidden during rendering.

Shape Type [St] f, s, se (Fast Copy, Spheroid, Soft Envelope) — Selects the method used to generate the offset surface.

Shape For [Sf] e, o, w (Each Element, Each Object, Whole) — Determines the scope for generating offset meshes.

Use Prototype Smoothing [Us] y, n (yes, no) — Determines whether the offset mesh uses the smoothing groups from the prototype object.

Prototype/Sphere [Ps] (0–100) — Sets the balance between a sphere and prototype object for mesh generation using the Spheroid shape type.

Roundedness [R] (1–5) — The degree of rounding for mesh generation using the Spheroid shape type.

Spheroid Center [Sc] — Determines the location of the center of the Spheroid shape type.

Boundary [B] — Determines the boundary of the Spheroid shape type.

Build Inner Envelope [Bi] y, n (yes, no) — Determines whether an inner envelope mesh will be generated using the Soft Envelope shape type.

Accordance [Ac] e, o, w (Each Element, Each Object, Whole) — Determines how the offset (inflated) surface is calculated.

Frame 1, 2, 3 [F1] [F2] [F3] — Sets the frame points at which different offset values occur. Auroral Mapping calculates intermediate values for frames between these set points.

Value 1, 2, 3 [V1] [V2] [V3] — Sets the offset values at each specified frame.

Draw Forward Faces [Df] (on, off) — Determines whether those faces with normals facing toward the camera will be drawn.

Draw Backward Faces [Db] (on, off) — Determines whether face with normals facing away from the camera will be drawn.

View-Dependent Tessellation [Vd] n, l, m, h (None, Low, Medium, High) — Sets the level of view-dependent tessellation. When this is enabled the offset meshes will be generated with more faces the closer they are to the camera.

Tie to [T] n, l (Vertex Normals, Vertex Location) — Selects the method used to generate mapping coordinates.

Use Prototype Material [Pm] (on, off) — Determines whether the prototype object's material will be used for the aurora mesh.

Tile [Ti] — Sets the tiling for the aurora texture map.

Mirror Tile [Mt] (on, off) — Determines whether the aurora material will be tiled or scaled to fit the mesh.

Texture Type [Tt] l, r (Linear, Radial) — Selects the mapping type for the aurora material. Linear maps the texture around the edge of the source object. Radial maps the texture around the offset mesh.

Initial Angle [Ia] (–180–180) — The starting angle for the aurora mapping.

Per-frame Angle Increment [Pa] (–180–180) — The change in angle from frame to frame for animating the orientation of the aurora mapping.

Twist Angle [Ta] (–360–360) — Shifts the aurora mapping clockwise or counterclockwise.

AURORAL MAPPING cont

Video International \aurora **AURORA_I.AXP**

[St]f [V1]30 [Hs]n

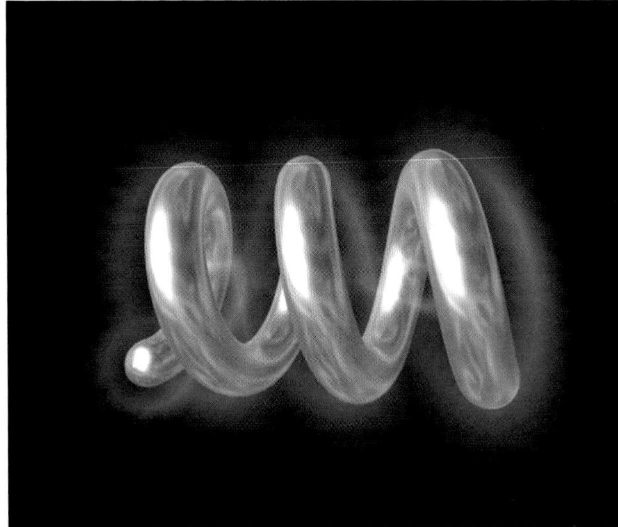

[St]f [V1]10 [Hs]y

Auroral glows using Fast Copy for a planar object and a spherical object.

BUBBLE GENERATOR

Digimation \bubbles **BUBD_I.AXP**

Summary

Bubble Generator is a particle system that uses octahedron- and icosahedron-shaped particles to produce animated bubble effects. The number of bubbles and their size, detail level, movement path, and speed can be set to simulate effects from small floating soap bubbles to air bubbles in underwater environments and simulated carbonation in liquids. The total number of bubbles can be set up to 1,500, which generally fills the entire bounding object. Additional bounding objects that use a different random number seed can be placed over the initial object if more bubbles are desired. Size range is set by specifying the minimum and maximum bubble size as a percentage of the bounding object. Speed is set in number of frames to travel from the bottom to the top of the bounding object, and exact start and stop frames can be specified. Bubbles can travel in either straight or spiral paths. By using shaped bounding volumes, bubbles can be restricted to defined shapes or travel along a user-specified path in an animation. Shaped bounding volumes are constructed by creating a shape in the 2D Shaper and attaching it to the AXP box in the 3D Editor.

Bubble Generator Parameters

# of Bubbles [#] — Sets the total number of bubbles up to 1,500.

Random # Seed [R] — Sets the bubble's start point with an arbitrary number. Each number produces a unique pattern.

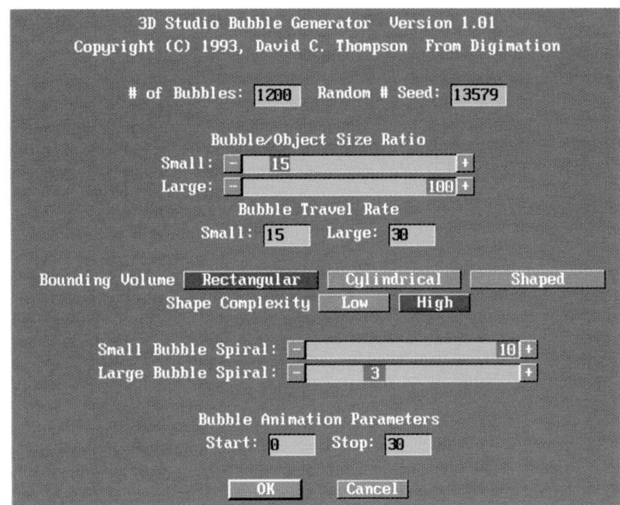

The Bubble Generator dialog box.

Bubble/Object Size Ratio [S] (Small, Large, 1–100) — Sets the minimum and maximum bubble size as a percentage of the bounding object. Numbers represent 1/10 of 1 percent.

Bubble Travel Rate [T] (Small, Large) — Sets the number of frames for a bubble to travel from the bottom to the top of the bounding object

BUBBLE GENERATOR cont

BUBD_I.AXP | \bubbles | Digimation

Frame 5

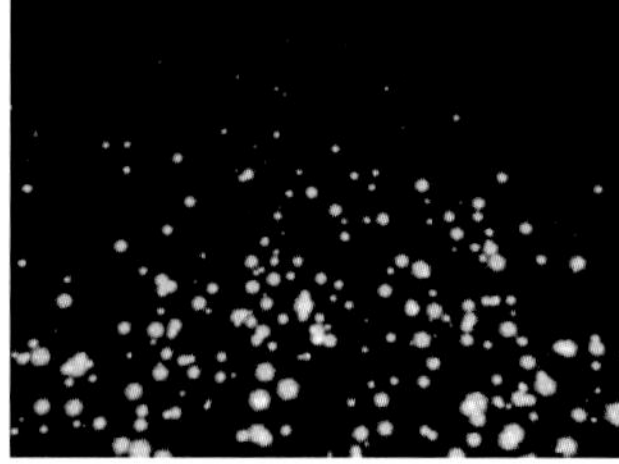

Frame 10

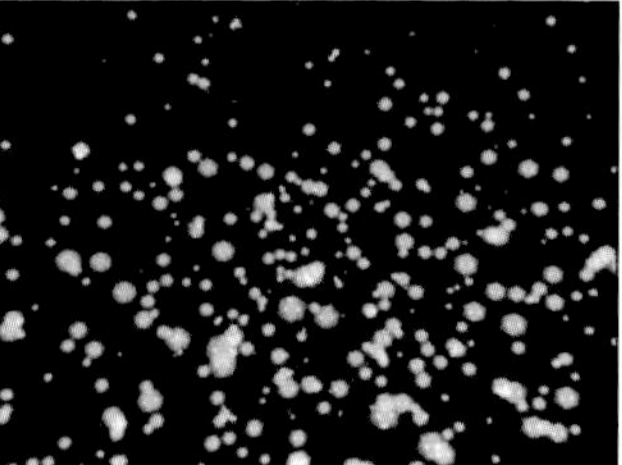

Frame 15

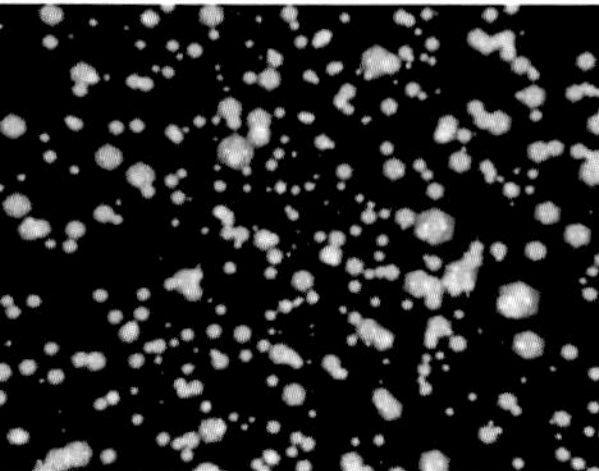

Frame 20

Bubble Generator is a particle system that simulates effects from small floating soap bubbles to air bubbles in underwater environments and simulated carbonation in liquids.

Bounding Volume [B] (Rectangular, Cylinder, Shaped) — Sets the type of bounding box shape constraint.

Shape Complexity [C] (Low, High) — Sets the bubble detail level. Low uses 8-sided bubbles, High uses 20-sided bubbles.

Bubble Spiral [SP] (Small, Large) (0–10) — Sets the amount of spiral in the bubbles' path. Larger numbers produce more spiral.

Bubble Animation Parameters [A] (Start, Stop) — Sets the start and stop frames for the bubbles. If both are set to 0, bubbles flow throughout the animation.

BUBBLE3D

BUBBLE_I.AXP | \bubbl3d | Schreiber Instruments

The Bubble3D dialog box.

Summary

Bubble3D is a particle system that produces animated bubble effects from carbonation to soap bubbles. Because Bubble3D uses an ASC file (a 3D Studio ASCII-format mesh file) to specify the bubble mesh, particles can be virtually any shape and are limited only by 3D Studio's 64,000 maximum face count. The number of faces in the bubble mesh determines the number of times it can be reproduced. Bubble3D enables you to control the path, shape, speed, start position, and size of the bubbles; the number of bubbles; and the shape and placement of the bubble emitter.

Bubble3D Parameters

Number of bubbles [#] (1–8,000) — Sets the total number of bubbles.

Size ratio [S] (.001–.5) — Sets the size of the bubbles in relation to the AXP object.

Start X,Z [XZ] (Point, Line, Circle, Ring, Square, Sphere) — Sets the particle emitter shape.

Start Diameter % [D] (1–200) — Sets the particle emitter size as a percentage of the AXP object.

Bubbles Start Y [Sy] (Bottom, Random, Burst) — Sets the bubble start point in relation to the Y axis to either the bottom of the AXP object, a random distribution based on the AXP volume, or near the top of the AXP object.

Bubble Path [P] (Helix, Random, Power) — Sets the bubble path to either a helical path, a random path changed by uniform disturbances, or a path changed by fractal-law disturbances.

Frequency [F] (0–25) — Sets the number of oscillations when using a helical path.

Initial Distribution [Id] (Random, Power) — Sets the ordering of the bubble start position.

Nucleation Points [N] (Fixed, Random) — Sets the bubble restart point when it reaches the top of the AXP object.

Mapping Characteristics [M] (Normal, Sticky) — Sets the mapping coordinates to either the AXP object or the bubble mesh object.

BUBBLE3D cont

Schreiber Instruments | **\bubbl3d** | **BUBBLE_I.AXP**

Bubbles All Same Size [Sz] (Yes, No) — Sets the bubbles to either a random or fixed size.

Bubbles Move Same Speed [Sp] (Yes, No) — Sets the bubbles to either a random or fixed speed.

Radial Expand/Contract [R] (–10–10) — Sets a linear expansion or contraction of the bubbles.

Y speed [Ys] (1–500) — Sets the speed of bubble flow in relation to the Y axis.

Amplitude [A] (0–1,000) — Sets the amplitude of the bubble path for each path setting. When using helical paths, Amplitude controls the helix radius; when used with random, Amplitude controls the amount of random disturbance or jiggle. When using power paths, Amplitude controls the amount of path divergence.

Delta Time [DT] (1–100) — Sets the arbitrary time length between frames. Larger values produce bubbles that move more rapidly.

Bubble Start Frame [Sf] — Sets the frame the bubbles will start on. Negative numbers allow the bubbles to begin their move cycle before rendering begins.

SEED [Sd] — Sets the bubbles' start point with an arbitrary number. Each number produces a unique pattern.

Calculation Mode [Cm] (Normal, Net, Cont.) — Sets the sequential rendering method used to either render the bubbles using one machine, render using a network, or to continue rendering a previous animation where it left off.

Continue Rendering on Frame [C] — Sets the frame on which to continue rendering when using the cont. rendering mode. Also specifies the frame on which to begin rendering when using a negative start frame.

Bubble Mesh Filename [Mf] (ASC format) — Sets the ASC file to use as the source geometry for each particle. The geometry must be saved in the process directory.

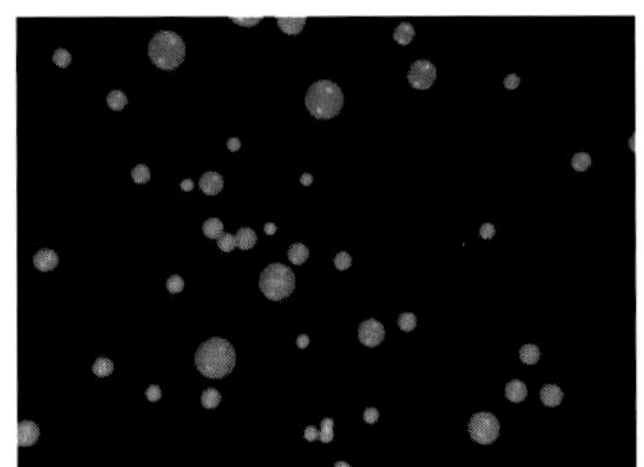

Spherical particles

Spherical particles

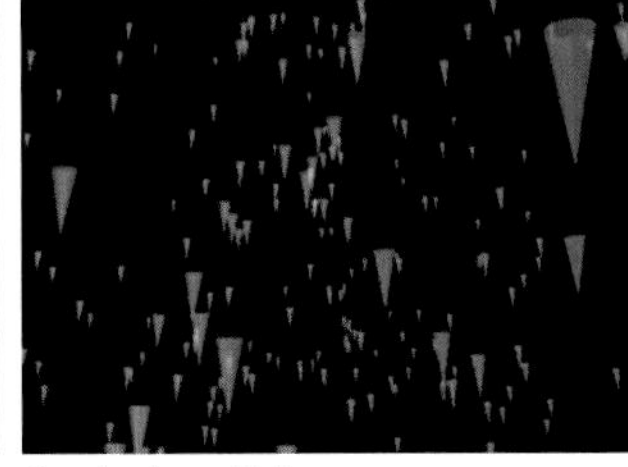

Conical particles

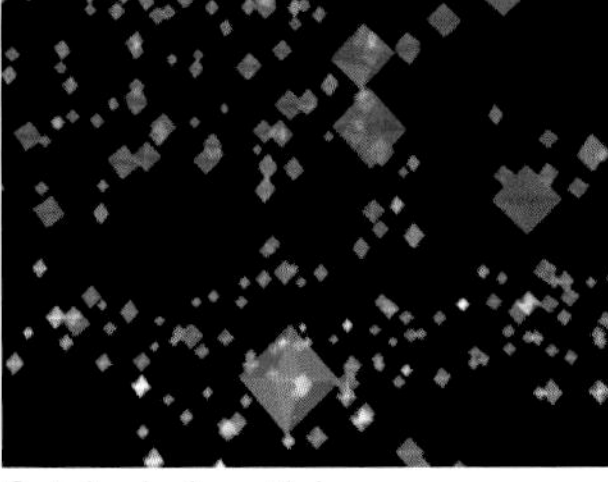

Octahedral particles

Because Bubble3D uses an ASC file to specify the bubble mesh, particles can be virtually any shape.

CARTOON HAND GENERATOR

Autodesk | **\hand** | **HAND_I.AXP**

Summary

Included with 3D Studio Release 4, Cartoon Hand Generator (Hand) generates smoothly skinned, four-fingered cartoon hands. Each hand is generated using a palm element—a flattened sphere for example—and four finger elements consisting of any number of four-sided geospheres. The geospheres define the fingers' joint objects. Animated bending and twisting is generated by linking and pivoting each finger's series of joint objects. Specifying different starting and ending diameters enables tapered spline objects to be produced.

Hand Parameters

Finger start/end diameter [Sd] [Ed] (.001–99,999) — Sets the starting and ending diameter for the spline object.

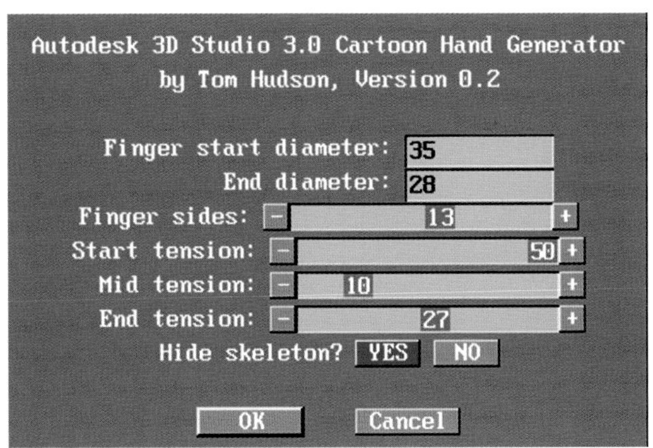

The Hand dialog box.

CARTOON HAND GENERATOR cont

HAND_I.AXP | **\hand** | **Autodesk**

Finger sides [Fs] (3–20) — Sets the number of sides around the circumference of the tube.

Start/Mid/End tension [St] [Mt] [Et] (0–50) — Sets the tension of the spline object relative to the source skeleton.

Hide skeleton (yes, no) — Hides the skeleton objects at rendering time.

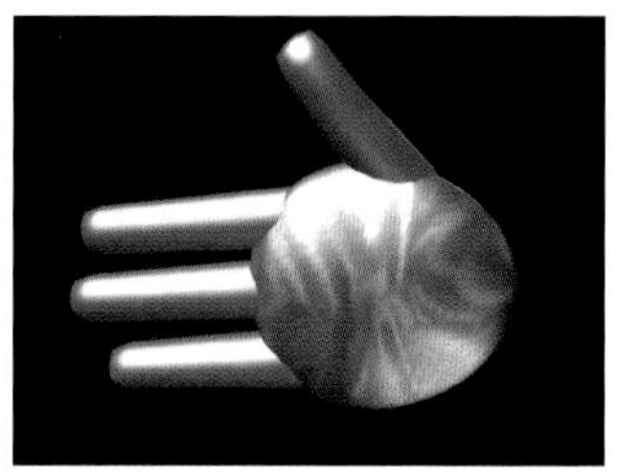
Frame 0

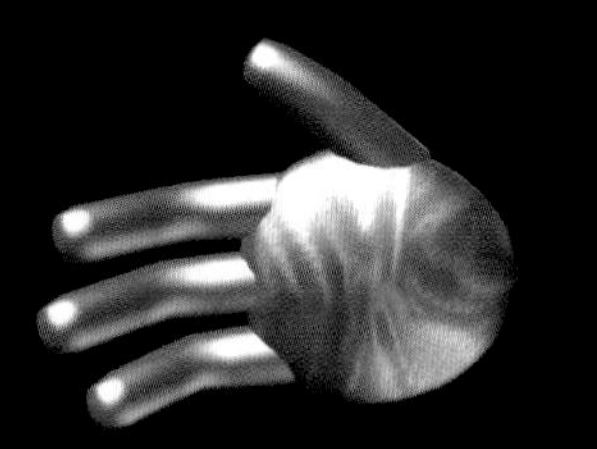
Frame 10

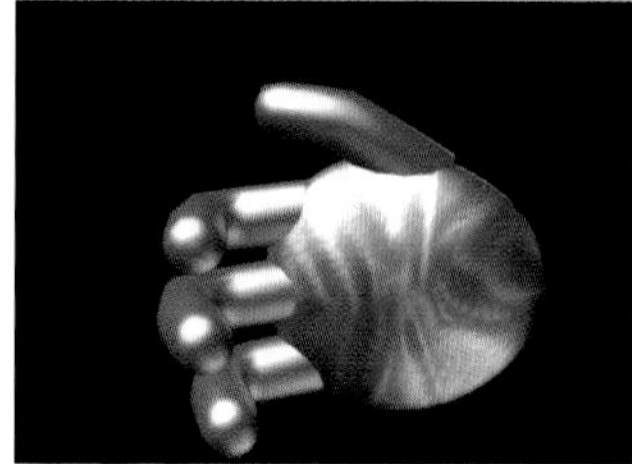
Frame 20

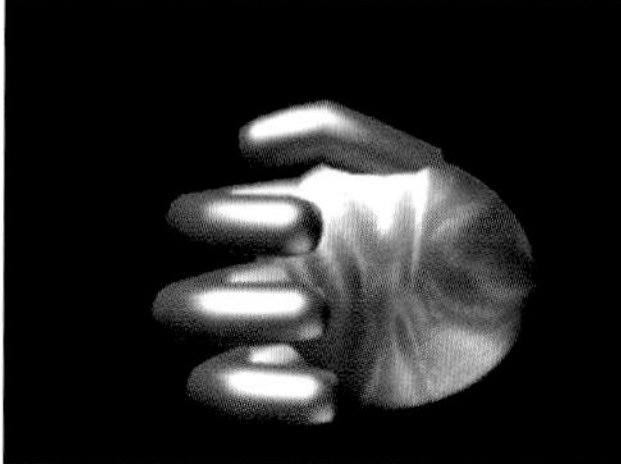
Frame 30

Hand generates smoothly bending four-fingered hands that use a control skeleton for deformation.

CLATCH

CLATCH_I.AXP | **\clatch** | **Enthed Animation**

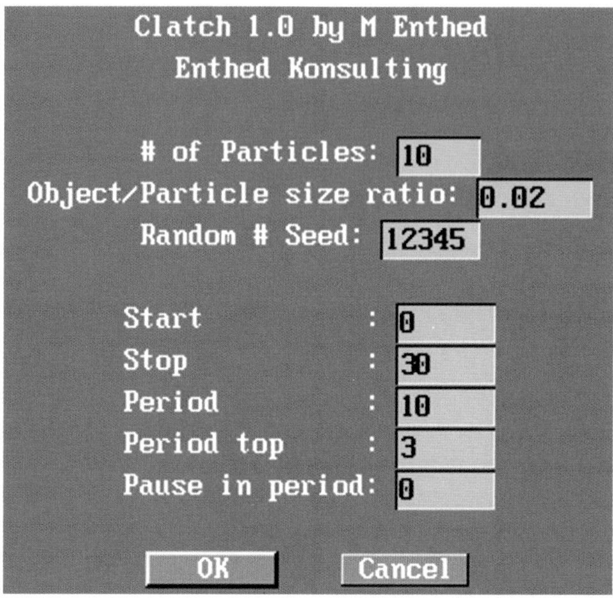

The Clatch dialog box.

Summary

Clatch is part of the Ent Tools package. It generates a cyclic explosion of particles within a bounding box object. The explosion is directed upward from a central point. The particles shoot upward, spreading out as they go. They reach the top of their travel, fall, and begin the next cycle. You can set the start and end frames for the entire sequence and the repeat cycle length in frames. You can set the point in the cycle at which the particles reach their highest point and how long they remain at the top before falling. The particles take their material from the bounding box, but do not have mapping coordinates. You can use a color-only material or an image-mapper material, such as one that uses SXPs, which does not require mapping coordinates.

Clatch Parameters

# of Particles [P] (1–8,192) — The number of particles in the explosion

Object/Particle size ratio [Op] (0.001–0.5) — Sets the size of the particles relative to the bounding box.

Random # Seed [R] — Sets a random number seed for particle generation.
Start [St] — Start frame for the explosion.
Stop [Sp] — Ending frame for the explosion.
Period [Pe] — Number of frames in one explosion cycle.
Period top [Pt] — Frame in the cycle at which the particles reach their highest point.
Pause in period [Pp] — Time in frames that the particles remain at their highest point (hang time).

Frame 0

Frame 4

Frame 10

Frame 20

One cycle of an explosion textured with an SXP.

COMET

Schreiber Instruments \comet COMT_I.AXP

Summary

Comet is a particle system that is a part of the Imagine FX package. It generates animated comets with controls for size of the comet head, length, width of tail, and particle speed. You also can select whether the tail ends abruptly or tapers off. The particles inherit the material of the bounding box, but have their own texture mapping from head to tail. If you apply a gradient or banded texture map, it is applied along the length of the comet to produce temperature and flame-like effects.

Comet Parameters

Center Radius [Cr] (1–100%) — The size of the head of the comet as a percentage of the bounding box.
Number of Particles [N] (1–21,000) — The number of particles in the comet.
Particle Size [S] (1–100) — The size of the particles relative to the bounding box.
Particle Stretch [Ps] (on, off) — Controls whether particles are stretched in the direction of motion.
Tail Type [Tt] s, t (Square, Taper) — Selects a square or tapered tail for the comet.

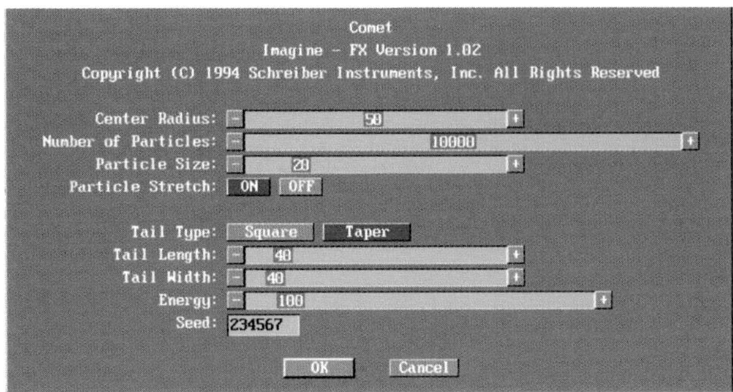

The Comet dialog box.

Tail Length [Tl] (–20–500) — Length of the comet tail relative to the bounding box.
Tail Width [Tw] (–50–1,000) — Maximum width of the comet tail relative to the Center Radius setting.
Energy [E] (1–1,000) — The amount of energy in the particles. Higher numbers produce faster particles.
Seed [Rs] — Random number seed for particle chaos.

COMET cont

COMT_I.AXP **\comet** **Schreiber Instruments**

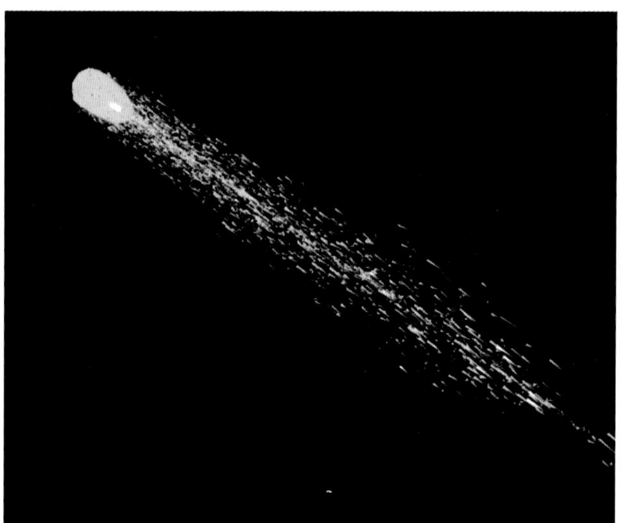

[Cr]100 [N]10000 [S]20 [Tt]t [Tl]35 [Tw]40

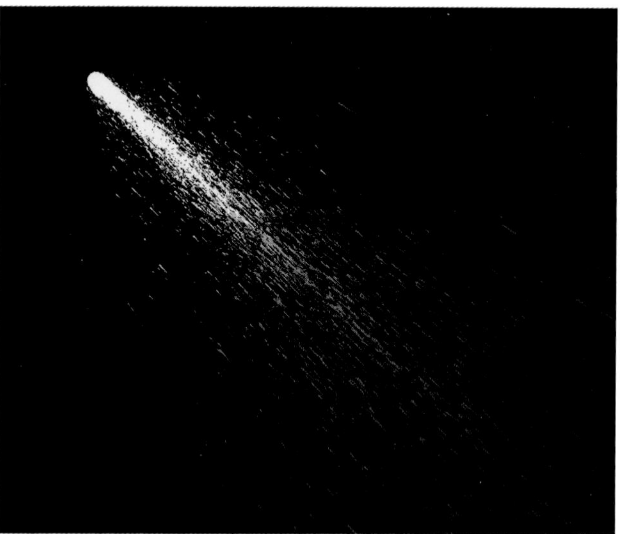

[Cr]50 [N]15000 [S]20 [Tt]s [Tl]60 [Tw]1000

Thin comet and wide comet with gradient texture map.

DISINTEGRATE

DISINT_I.AXP **\disint** **Yost Group**

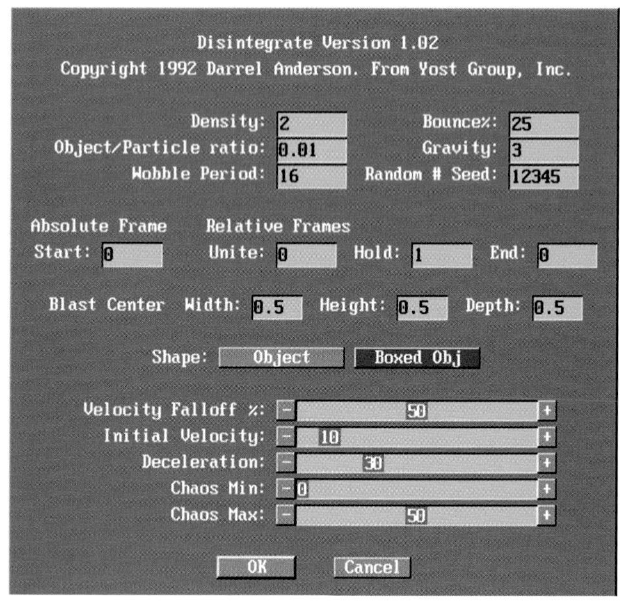

The Disintegrate dialog box.

Summary

Disintegrate is part of the Particle Systems package. It covers a selected object with particles, then explodes and scatters them outward where they bounce and finally disappear. The particles can optionally fly in and build the source object's form.

Start, Unite, Hold, and End are used to create the Disintegrate timing. The entire effect interval is referred to as the time envelope. Time envelopes resemble a graph with the X axis representing time in frames and the Y axis representing the effect strength. Start and Unite work together to set the beginning transition or the time required for the effect to reach its maximum. Unite and Hold work together to set how long the explosion sustains the maximum level. Hold and End set the ending transition or fade-out. These parameters enable you to time the number of frames over which the particles coalesce, remain together, and then fly apart.

You also can specify that the particles remain at the end of the effect. Particles are affected by gravity and friction, and they can bounce off the lower surface of a bounding box. Particles take on the material and mapping coordinates of the intact source object. The particles do not change color during the effect.

Disintegrate Parameters

Density [De] (0,1,2) — Selects the number of particles generated per face of the source object. A value of 0 produces one particle per vertex. A value of 1 produces one particle per vertex and one in the middle of each face. A value of 2 produces one particle per vertex and four scattered across each face.

Object/Particle ratio [Op] (0.0001–0.5) — The size of the particles relative to the object.

Wobble Period [W] — Sets the frequency of particle wobble during the time when the particles are coalesced (the Hold period).

Bounce% [B] (–1–100) — Sets the amount of rebound when particles hit the floor of the bounding box. A value of –1 means that instead of bouncing, particles continue falling. A value of 0 means that instead of bouncing, particles remain lying on the floor. Any value greater than 0 sets the percentage of velocity that each particle retains after a bounce. There is a maximum of four bounces per particle.

Gravity [G] (0–1,000) — Sets the strength of gravity.

Random # Seed [R] — Sets a seed value for the random numbers that provide chaos to the particles.

Start frame [Sf] — The frame number at which the process begins.

Unite frames [Uf] — The point (in frames) after the start frame at which the particles are united within the source object.

Hold frames [Hf] — The duration in frames for which the particles are united within the source object.

End frame [Ef] — The duration in frames over which the particles fade out. This takes place after the end of the hold frames.

Blast Center Width, Height, Depth [Cw] [Ch] [Cd] (0–1.0) — The location of the center of the "blast" that disintegrates the object. This is relative to the bounding object or source object.

Shape [S] o, b (Object, Boxed Obj) — Determines whether Disintegrate acts on the entire object (Object) or only on a source element of a boxed object (Boxed Obj).

Velocity Falloff% [Vf] (0–100) — Sets the initial velocity of the particles by their distance from the blast center.

Initial Velocity [V] (0–100) — Sets the speed of the particles relative to the source object.

Deceleration [D] (0–100) — Sets the amount of velocity that particles loose per frame.

Chaos Min [Cn] (0–100) — Sets the amount of chaos in particle position and movement during the hold period when the particles are together within the source object.

Chaos Max [Cx] (0–100) — Sets the amount of chaos in particle movement during the time that particle are moving.

Frame 0

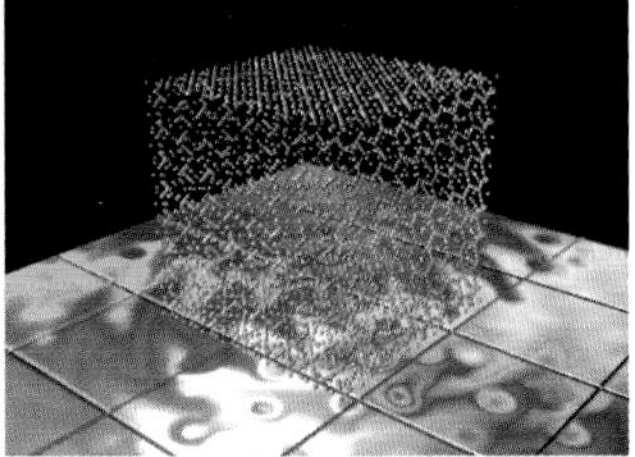
Frame 1

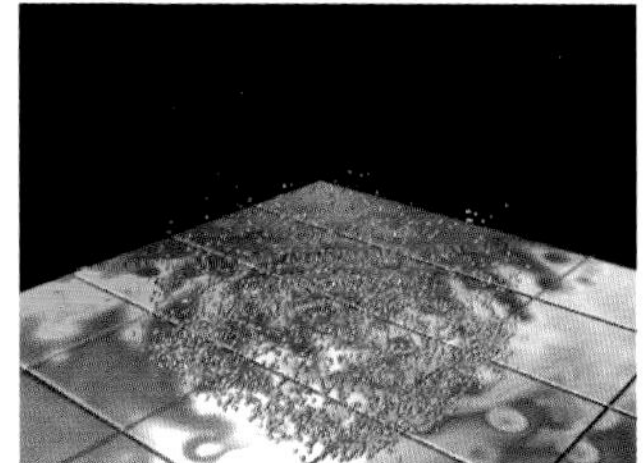
Frame 20

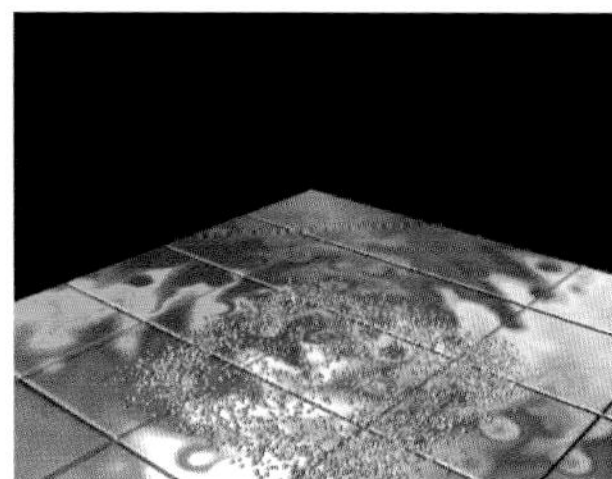
Frame 30

An animated disintegration for which the source object is hidden after the first frame.

EXPLODE

EXPLOD_I.AXP **\explode** **Yost Group**

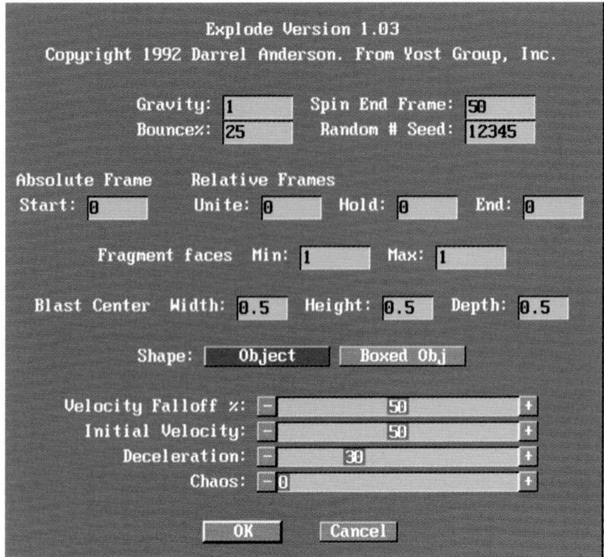

The Explode dialog box.

Summary

Explode is part Yost Group Particle Systems Disk 4 package. Explode demolishes a three-dimensional object's surface according to a variable set of physical properties.

Explode can be applied either directly to the effect object or using a bounding box or Boxed Object element. Explode gets its scale, proportion, blast center, and floor reference information from either the object you want to explode or the Boxed Object. Boxed Objects are special-purpose elements that are created specifically for providing an alternative reference for the effect. This enables you to, for example, set the floor for falling and bouncing particles to a lower plane than the bounding area of the object you want to explode.

Start, Unite, Hold, and End are used to create the explosion timing. The entire blast interval is referred to as the time envelope. Time envelopes resemble a graph with the X axis representing time in frames and the Y axis representing the effect strength. Start and Unite work together to set the beginning transition or the time required for the explosion to reach its maximum. Unite and Hold work together to set how long the explosion sustains the maximum level. Hold and End set the ending transition or fade-out. These parameters enable you to time the explosion to, for instance, start abruptly, sustain for a few frames, and slowly die out.

You can specify whether a particle is generated for each face or collections of faces, which preserves the original object's form. The Velocity Falloff, Initial Velocity, Deceleration, and Chaos sliders enable you to fine-tune and shape the blast pattern.

You can opt to use texture mapping with Explode, which takes its mapping coordinates from the original object. A given particle's color and texture is determined by each particle's position relative to the image map on the original and intact object. The particle color and texture remains consistent throughout the effect.

Explode Parameters

Gravity [G] (0–10,000) — Sets the particle acceleration down toward the floor or bounce plane.

Bounce percentage [Bp] (–1–100) — Sets the bouncing characteristics, with a –1 value specifying no bounce with sustained movement beyond the specified floor or bounce plane. A 0 value also produces no bounce with the particles stopping at the bounce plane. Any setting greater than 0 causes the particles to bounce up to four times.

Spin End Frame [Sf] — Specifies the frame at which the fragments stop spinning.

Random # Seed [R] (0—99,999) — Sets the algorithm's start point. Each arbitrary number produces a unique effect.

Absolute Frame Start [Afs] — Sets the starting frame for the explosion.

Relative Frames Unite, Hold, and End [Ru] [Rh] [Re] (Unite, Hold, End) — Work with Absolute Frame Start to control the time envelope of the effect, which specifies the rate, pattern, and timing of the blast.

Fragment faces [F] mi, ma (minimum, maximum) (1–32,000) — Controls the size of the fragments generated in the effect. Maximum values greater than 1 create random fragments or collections of faces.

Blast Center [B] w, h, d (Width, Height, Depth) (0.1–1.0) — Sets the location of the explosion within the object or boxed object.

Shape [S] o, bo (object, boxed object) — Controls whether the effect is applied to the object itself or using a Boxed Object. Boxed Objects provide increased flexibility over the location of the blast center and bounce plane.

Velocity Falloff [V] (0–100) — Sets a deceleration factor that varies the speed of the fragments as they move away from the blast center.

Initial Velocity [I] (0–100) — Sets the starting speed of the blast fragments.

Deceleration [D] (0–100) — Sets the overall rate of fragment deceleration.

Chaos [Ch] (1–100) — Specifies the amount of random variation in the spinning blast fragments along with the Initial Velocity and Gravity parameters, which affect them.

EXPLODE cont

Yost Group \explode **EXPLOD_I.AXP**

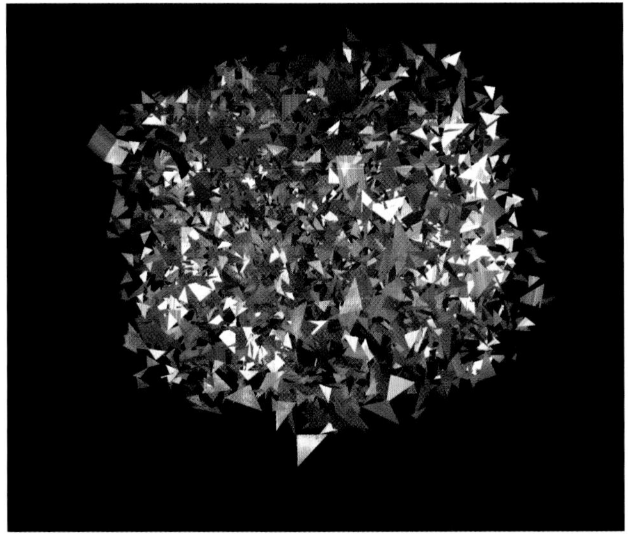

2 frames after hold

9 frames after hold

The object in the examples has a velocity falloff of 0, an initial velocity of 80, and a maximum of 3,200 faces.

EXPLODE VOLUME

Schreiber Instruments \expvolum **EXPVOL_I.AXP**

Summary

Explode Volume is part of the Imagine FX package. It is a particle explosion system with cubic boundaries, friction, and gravity. Explode Volume fills an object with tetrahedral particles that explode outward until they strike a bounding plane and then rebound. You can set the distance from the object to each of the six bounding planes. By setting the rebound energy you can control the rebound damping. Controls for gravity and friction, when combined with initial speed, can shorten or prolong the time that the particles continue to move. You can set the beginning and ending of the explosion sequence and determine whether the particles are visible before and after the explosion. The particles use the material of the bounding object, but their mapping coordinates are randomly distributed.

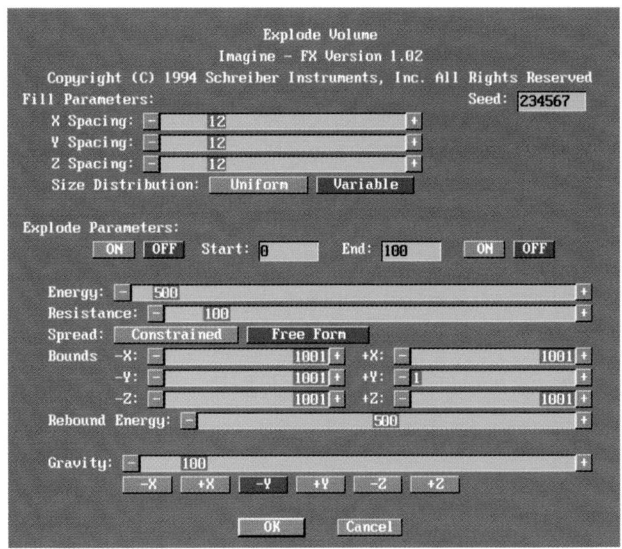

The Explode Volume dialog box.

Explode Volume Parameters

Spacing X, Y, Z [Sx] [Sy] [Sz] (2–50) — Sets the number of particles created along each axis.

Size Distribution [Sd] u, v (Uniform, Variable) — Selects the distribution of particle sizes. With Uniform, all particles are the same size. With Variable, they vary randomly.

Start frame [Sf] — Sets the starting frame for the explosion.

Start on/off [So] (on, off) — Determines whether the particles are visible before the starting frame.

End frame [Ef] — Sets the ending frame for the explosion.

End on/off [Eo] (on, off) — Determines whether the particles are visible after the ending frame.

Energy [E] (0–1,000) — Sets the starting speed of the particles.

Resistance [R] (0–10,000) — Sets the friction for particle movement.

Spread [Sp] c, f (Constrained, Free Form) — Determines whether particle movement is constrained by bounds or is free to travel until friction stops them.

EXPLODE VOLUME cont

EXPVOL_I.AXP | **\expvolum** | **Schreiber Instruments**

Bounds -X, -Y, -Z, +X,+ Y,+ Z [-X] [-Y] [-Z] [+X] [+Y] [+Z] (0–1,001) — Sets the distance in units to the bounding planes. Particles will rebound off of bounding planes. A setting of 0 means that no particle's initial motion is in that direction. A setting of 1,001 turns off a bounding plane.

Rebound Energy [Re] (0–1,000) — Sets the elasticity of rebounds. The number represents a particle's remaining energy after a collision in tenths of a percent.

Gravity [G] (0–1,000) — Sets the strength of gravity.

Gravity direction [Gd] (-x,+x,-y,+y,-z,+z) — Selects which direction gravity pulls the particles.

Seed [S] — Random number seed to control particle creation and motion.

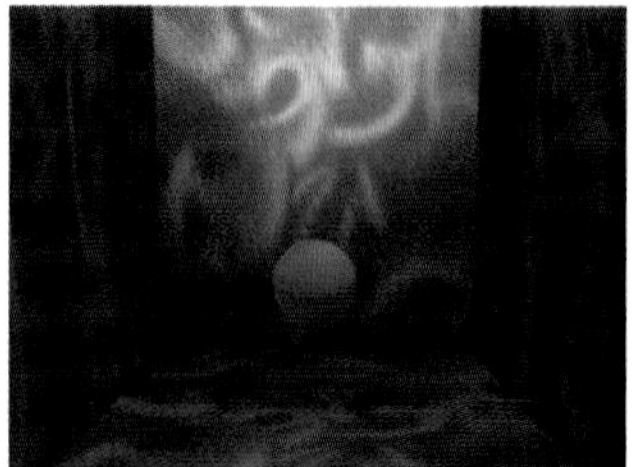
Frame 0

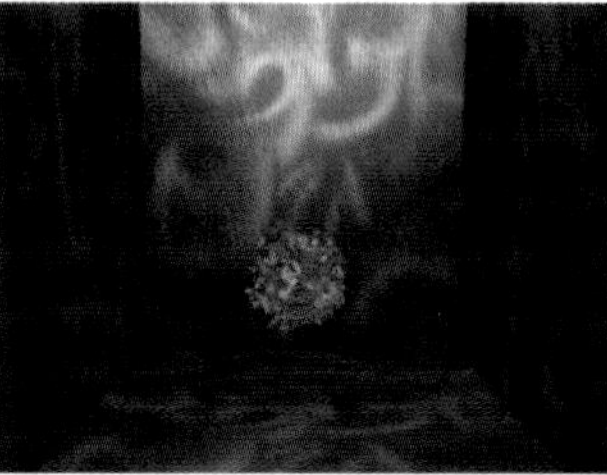
Frame 21

Frame 50

Fame 250

An explosion with particles bouncing off walls.

FIREWORKS

FIREWK_I.AXP | **\firework** | **Yost Group**

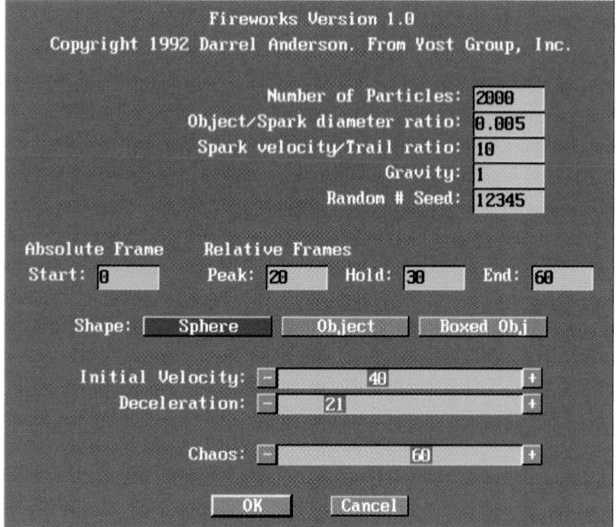

The Fireworks dialog box.

Summary

Fireworks is part of the Yost Group Particle Systems Disk #4 package. Fireworks is a particle system that simulates various fireworks effects from small spherical blasts to complex-shaped explosions. Fireworks can use the bounding shape to create colored particle blasts in any desired shape. Gravity can be used to pull the particles to the ground as the initial blast velocity falls off.

Start, Peak, Hold, and End are used to create the Fireworks effect timing. The entire effect interval is referred to as the time envelope. Time envelopes resemble a graph with the X axis representing time in frames and the Y axis representing the effect strength. Start and Peak work together to set the beginning transition or the time required for the pattern to reach its maximum. Unite and Hold work together to set how long the effect sustains the maximum level. Hold and End set the ending transition or fade-out. These parameters enable you to time the Fireworks effect to, for instance, start abruptly, sustain for a few frames, and slowly die out.

Fireworks particles use UV mapping to determine the particles' color and trail color for each frame. Particle body and tail color are determined by samples taken from the image map pixel-by-pixel for each animation frame. Body color samples are taken horizontally from left to right, across the bitmap image. Tail color samples are taken vertically from top to bottom over the bitmap. Image maps samples are uniformly spaced on the bitmap image to correspond to the total number of frames in the animation. A Chaos slider inserts random noise into the sampling process to produce more natural color effects.

Fireworks Parameters

Number of Particles [#] (1–8,190) — Sets the maximum number of particles.

FIREWORKS cont

Yost Group | **\firework** | **FIREWK_I.AXP**

Object/Spark diameter ratio [D] (0.0001–0.5) — Sets the size of the particles relative to the bounding object.

Spark velocity/Trail ratio [V] (1–100) — Sets the length of the particle's trail relative to the distance the particle moves per frame.

Gravity [G] (1–10,000) — Sets the speed the particles fall in the direction of the gravity vector.

Random # Seed [R] (0–99,999) — Sets the algorithm's start point. Each arbitrary number produces a unique initial state.

Absolute Frame, Relative Frames [Af] [Rf] s, p, h, e (Start, Peak, Hold, End) — Controls the frame envelope, intensity, and duration of the effect.

Shape [S] s, o, b (Sphere, Object, Boxed Obj) — Sets the fireworks' burst shape. Spherical sets the pattern to a sphere. Object uses the source object and Boxed Object uses a Boxed Object to determine the shape, proportion, center, and gravity direction. Boxed Objects are special-purpose elements created to provide an alternative reference for the effect.

Initial Velocity [Iv] (0–100) — Sets the initial speed of the particles as they leave the blast center.

Deceleration [D] (0–100) — Sets the rate of particle deceleration.

Chaos [C] (0–100) — Sets the amount of variance in initial velocity, spark distribution, and gravity.

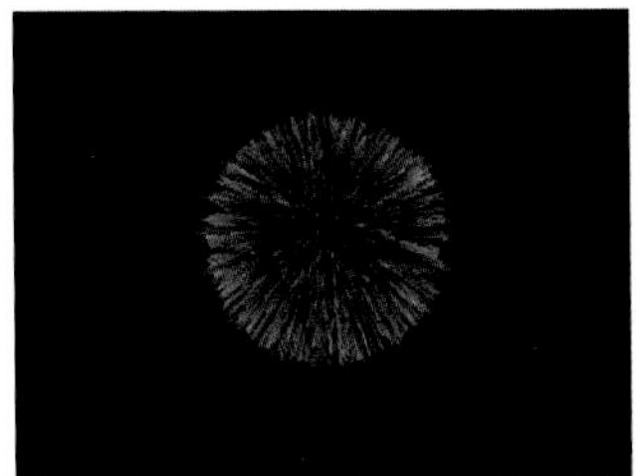

Frame 10

Frame 20

Frame 30

Frame 30

Fireworks is a particle system that simulates effects from small spherical blasts to complex-shaped explosions. Particles in fireworks use UV mapping to determine the particles' color and trail color each frame.

FLAME

Yost Group | **\flame** | **FLAME_I.AXP**

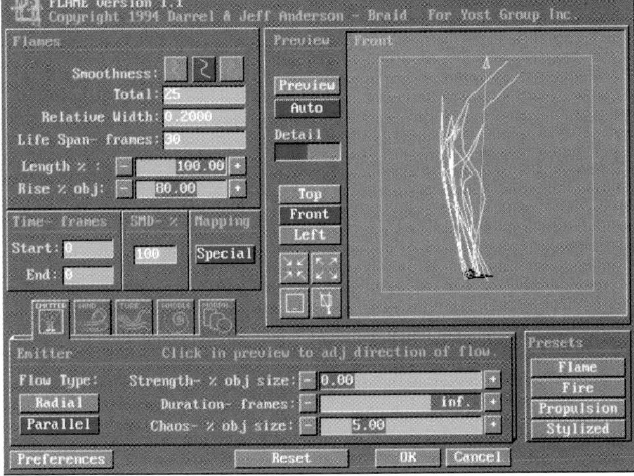

The Flame dialog box with the Emitter Index Card, Emitter preview, and adjustment icon.

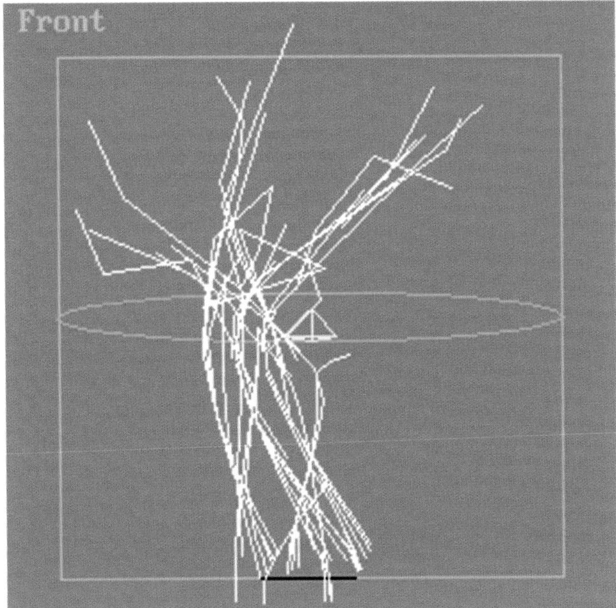

The Wind preview and adjustment icon.

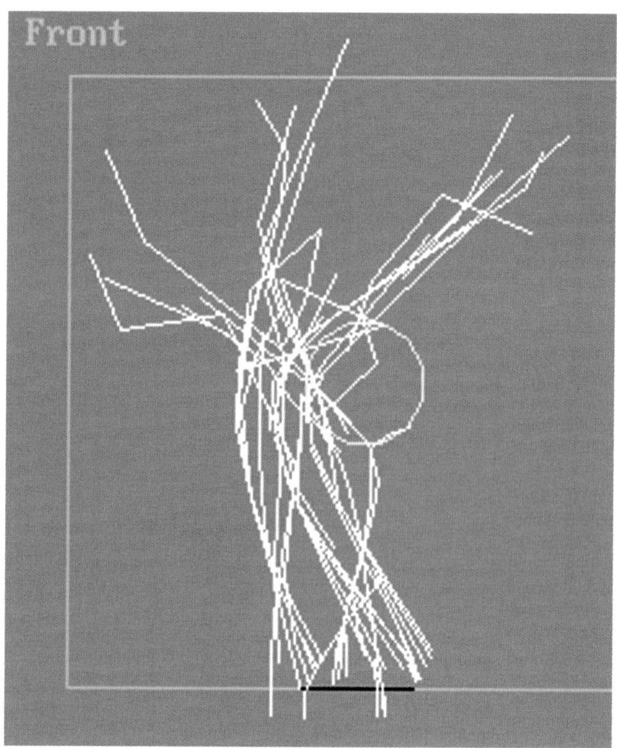

The Whorls preview and adjustment icon.

Summary

Flame is part of Yost Group's IPAS disk 6 from Schreiber Instruments. Flame is a particle system that produces animated fire and flame effects. This plug-in is very similar to Yost Group's Vapor, but with the essential difference that whereas Vapor uses a spherical particle, Flame uses elongated tendril-like particles. This gives Flame effects a unique swirling organic character that is well adapted to fire effects as well as a number of unique animated patterns.

Flame produces its effects based on its associated AXPBOX PXP, which creates a specified number of particle emitters and places them inside a bounding box of any dimension. The emitter element consists of a series of vertices, each of which is capable of sending out streams of particles. The bounding box element provides scaling information for the particle system.

Flame is controlled by a number of parameters that set the smoothness, number, width, rise, and length of the particles. You can specify the life span for each particle along with the time interval in frames for the effect.

Flame also provides five Index Cards or submenus that enable you to control the particle flow from the emitters and apply wind, turbulence, and whorls, as well as the ability to morph between multiple particle systems. This enables you to animate the location of the particles.

Much of Flame's work is accomplished interactively in a preview window. With the Emitter index card selected, for instance, you can choose either Radial or Parallel flow types and move a vector icon consisting of one or more green arrows that indicate the direction of particle flow. As the icon is clicked and dragged around the preview area, a series of white lines indicating the particle cloud are dynamically updated. This is useful for conveying a general idea of the final particle system. The Preview area is similarly updated for most of Flame's parameters.

Flame works with image map materials and includes a custom materials library, special-purpose bitmaps, a FLIC animation of an oil fire, and FLAMEO_I.SXP, which was designed to work as an opacity map. To use mapping with any particle smoothness, you highlight the Special button and assign a material to the AXP box.

Flame also provides a series of presets for quickly producing various effects including candle flames, bonfires, torches, and jet or rocket engines.

Flame Parameters

Smoothness buttons [Sm] l, m, h (low complexity, medium complexity, high complexity) — Specifies the smoothness of the individual flame tendrils. The leftmost button, low, produces angular flames with 32 faces per tendril, medium produces smooth flames with 300 faces per tendril, and high produces the smoothest flames with 600 faces per tendril. Higher face counts result in longer render times.

Total [To] — Specifies the total number of particles. The maximum number depends on the type of particle smoothness. Low can have up to 1,000 flames per object, medium can have 200 flames per object, and high can have 100 flames per object.

Relative Width [Rw] — Sets the particle width relative to the maximum dimension of the bounding cube or object.

Life Span frames [Ls] — Sets the particle's life span from emission to fade-out. Shorter life spans produce a more realistic effect.

Length [Le] (25–100%) — Sets the length of the longest flame particle relative to the height of the overall particle system rather than the bounding cube or object.

Time Start and End [Ts] [Te] — Sets the frame range for the effect. If both Start and End are set to 0, the particles stay on for the duration of the animation.

SMD % [Sm] (1–100%) — Specifies the percentage of secondary motion data used to key the effect.

Mapping Special [Ms] — Switches the option of using a special material from the DISK6.MLI that is included with Flame. Special is available for any particle Smoothness setting.

Preview and Auto — Updates the Preview particle cloud to reflect edits to Flame's parameters. Auto dynamically updates the display. The particles displayed here are useful as a preview only and do not reflect the exact character or particle count of the rendered particle system.

Detail — Sets the number of particles used to create the preview particle cloud, displayed in the Preview window. You can click and drag the red bar to the right or left to increase or decrease the number of particles.

View control (Top, Front, Left, Zoom In, Zoom Out, Zoom Bounding Cube Extents, Zoom Emitter Arrow Extents) — Specifies and switches the view. Top, Front, and Left switch between orthogonal views, and Zoom In (arrows in button) and Out (arrows out button) zoom incrementally with each mouse click. Zoom Bounding Cube Extents (located below the Zoom In button) and Zoom Emitter Arrow Extents (located below the Zoom Out button) zoom to either the bounding cube and emitter arrow extents or to just the emitter arrow extents, respectively.

Flame Presets [Fl] q, t (Quiet Candle, Turbulent Candle) — Automatically configures Flame's parameters to produce candle flame effects.

Fire Presets [Fi] b, c, f, t (Bonfire, Campfire, Fireplace, Torch) — Automatically configures Flame's parameters to produce several fiery effects.

Propulsion Presets [Pr] j, r (Jet, Rocket) — Automatically configures Flame's parameters to produce either jet or rocket engine flare effects.

Stylized Presets [St] t, th, c (Thick, Thin, Curly) — Automatically configures Flame's parameters to produce several Flame variations.

Note: *All presets are available through the Flame, Fire Propulsion, and Stylized dialog boxes, which are accessed by clicking on the buttons provided.*

Preferences — Enables a message that alerts you if you neglect to update the secondary motion data. The Preferences dialog box also enables you to select a custom interface color palette and to edit the random seed number used to calculate the particles.

Emitter Parameters

Flow Type [Ft] r, s (Radial, Parallel) — Sets the particle emission characteristics and timing for the effect. Radial enables you to adjust the particle emission by adjusting a Preview icon consisting of several vector arrows that radiate away from the emitter. Parallel enables you to adjust the particles to flow in parallel lines away from the emitter.

Strength [St] (0–200) — Specifies the distance that a particle travels as a percentage of the bounding cube or object. Strength is influenced by Rise along with the Flow Type and its associated vector arrows.

Duration [D] (1–100/inf.) — Sets the total time in frames that the Strength value affects particle momentum. Infinity (inf.) is a special case for which Strength is applied to the particle during its entire life.

Chaos [Ce] (0–20) — Scatters the particles by specifying a random offset for the particle as it is released from an emitter vertex.

The Wind Index Card.

Wind Parameter

Speed [Sp] (0–200) — Specifies the wind speed as a percentage of the size of the bounding cube or object. Wind is a directional force that runs parallel to the Top Viewport. Wind direction is adjusted in the Preview window by rotating a yellow triangle to any angle around a green circle.

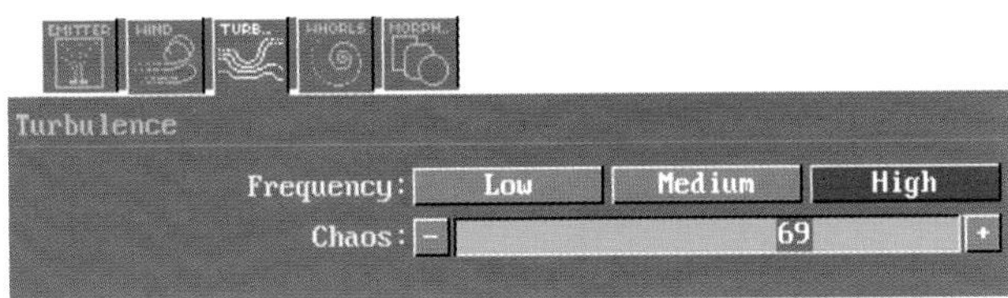

The Turbulence Index Card.

Turbulence Parameters

Frequency [Fr] l, m, h (Low, Medium, High) — Sets the Low, Medium, and High frequency of an invisible complex 3D wavy pattern that perturbs the particles.

Chaos [Ct] (0–100) — Sets the amplitude of the wavy pattern.

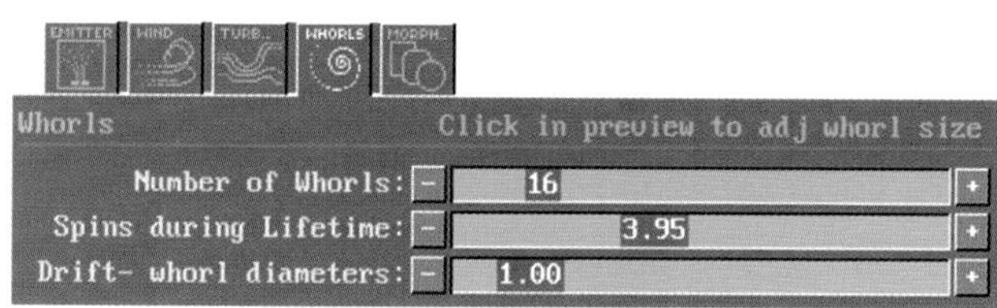

The Whorls Index Card.

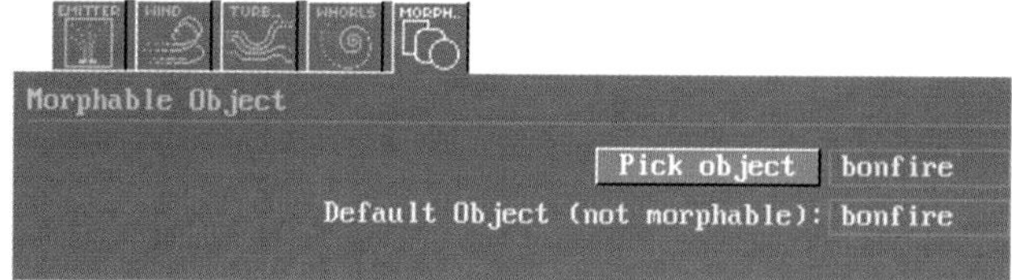

The Morphable Object Index Card.

Whorls Parameters

Number of Whorls [N] (0–100) — Sets the number of randomly spinning invisible spheres that move along the same overall path as the particles and perturb the particles. Whorls exist for approximately the same lifetime as do particles.

Spins during Lifetime [Spn] (0.00–10.00) — Sets the speed of whorl rotation, with higher speeds scattering the particles.

Drift [Dr] (0.00–10.00) — Sets the whorls to drift in a perpendicular path with respect to the particle's path. The drift value specifies a distance factor for the drift, with a setting of 3 producing a whorl distance that is three times that of the whorl diameter. The whorl diameter is set in the Preview window by resizing a yellow circle. Greater whorl diameters and drift values scatter the particles.

Morphable Object Parameter

Pick object — Specifies an emitter cube as a morph target. This enables you to, for instance, animate the location of your particle emitter.

Bonfire preset

Candle preset

Flame produces intricate swirling flame-like patterns using elongated particles, custom materials, and maps.

Summary

Flock3D is a nonlinear particle system that simulates the behavior of various flocking animals. This particle system can be used for effects ranging from schools of fish and clouds of insects to flocks of birds taking off. Individual particles, or birds, are attracted over a set distance and repelled at closer distances, which creates the flocking behavior. Because Flock3D uses an ASC file to specify the bird mesh object, particles can be virtually any shape. Birds are drawn to the center of the AXP object, the roost, and forces can be set to repel the birds from the top and bottom of the bounding object. Additionally, random noise can be added to the equation to create more natural effects. No collision avoidance is provided, so birds can pass through one another, and can only pivot around two axes.

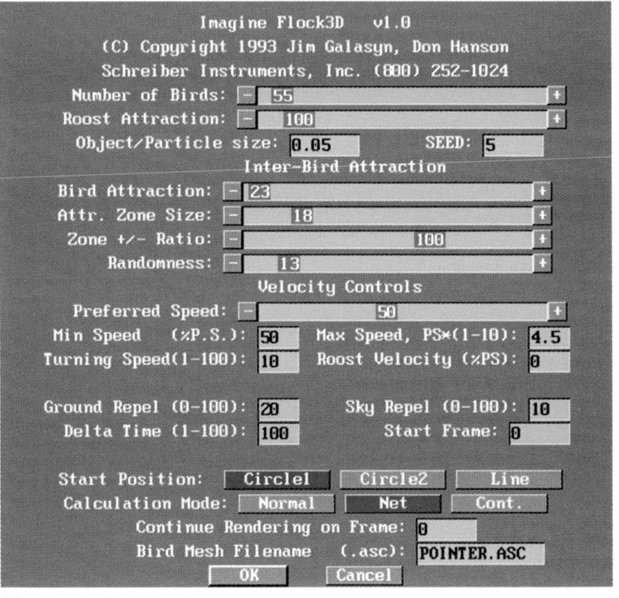

The Flock3D dialog box.

Flock3D Parameters

Number of Birds [#] (1–1,000) — Sets the total number of particles.

Roost Attraction [Ra] (1–1,000) — Sets the level of roost or center attraction.

Object/Particle size [S] (.001–.5) — Sets the size of the particles in relation to the AXP object.

SEED [Sd] — Sets the particle's start point with an arbitrary number. Each number produces a unique pattern.

Bird Attraction [Ba] (1–1,000) — Sets the amount of attraction or repulsion between individual birds.

Attr. Zone Size [Az] (1–1,000) — Sets the area of nonlinear coupling force attraction between individual birds.

Zone +/– Ratio [Zr] (–300–300) — Sets the ratio of nonlinear coupling force attraction to repulsion between individual birds.

Randomness [R] (0–100) — Sets the amount of random noise in the flight path and start positions.

Preferred Speed [Ps] (10–100) — Sets the target speed each bird will attempt to reach given no other intervening forces.

Min Speed [Ms] (0–100) — Sets the slowest speed a bird can travel as a percentage of the preferred speed.

Max Speed [Xs] (1–10) — Sets the fastest speed a bird can travel as a function of the preferred speed.

Turning Speed [Ts] (1–100) — Sets the birds' maximum angular speed and turning radius.

Roost Velocity [Rv] (0–100) — Sets the roost or object center speed as a percentage of the preferred speed to move the entire flock in the positive X direction.

Ground Repel [Gr] (0–100) — Sets the repel rate for the bottom of the AXP object.

Sky Repel [Sr] (0–100) — Sets the repel rate for the top of the AXP object.

Delta Time [Dt] (1–100) — Sets the arbitrary time length between frames. Larger values produce particles that move more rapidly.

Start Frame [Sf] — Sets the frame at which the particles will start. Negative numbers allow the birds to begin their move cycle before rendering begins.

Start Position [Sp] (Circle, Circle2, Line) — Sets the particle emitter shape as seen from the top viewport.

Calculation Mode [Cm] (Normal, Net, Cont.) — Sets the sequential rendering method used to either render the flock using one machine, rendering using a network, or to continue rendering a previous animation where it left off.

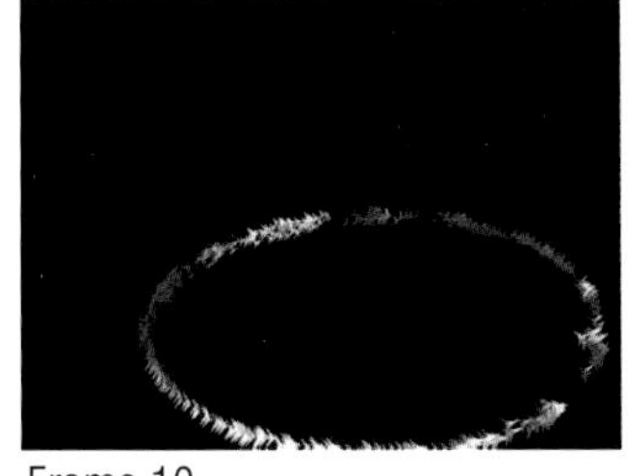
Frame 10

Frame 20

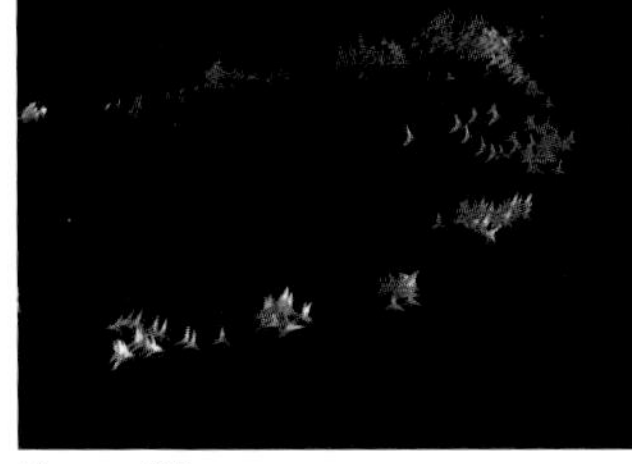
Frame 30

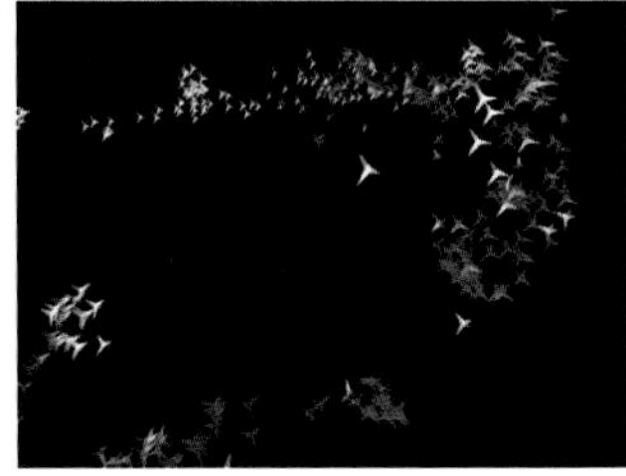
Frame 40

Flock3D uses a nonlinear particle system to simulate the grouping behavior of various flocking animals, such as schools of fish and clouds of insects.

FLOCK3D cont

FLOCK_I.AXP | **\flock3d** | **Schreiber Instruments**

Continue Rendering on Frame [C] — Sets the frame at which to continue rendering when using the Cont. rendering mode. Also specifies the frame at which to begin rendering when using a negative start frame.

Bird Mesh Filename [Mf] (ASC format) — Sets the ASC file to use as the source geometry for each bird. The geometry must be saved in the process directory, and total face count for the entire particle system is limited by 3D Studio's 64,000 maximum face count.

LIGHTNING

LGHTNG_I.AXP | **\lightnin** | **Schreiber Instruments**

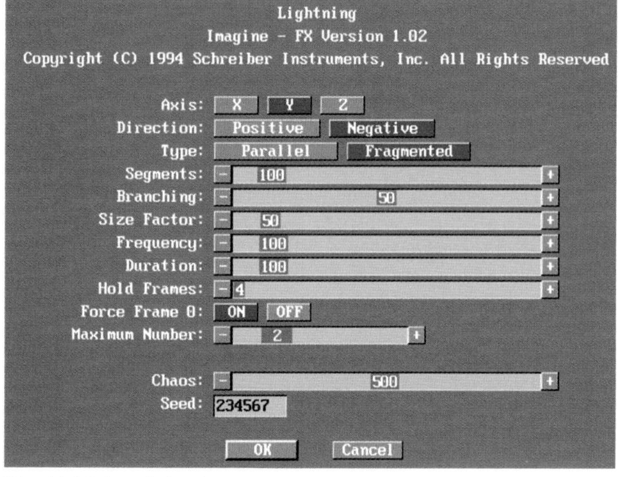

The Lightning dialog box.

Summary

Lightning is part of the Imagine FX package. It generates animated lightning and electrical discharges using randomly generated geometry within a bounding box object. You have control over the direction of the discharge, the number of strokes, and the degree of chaos in the growth of each stroke. You can choose from two branching models, and you can set the detail of the geometry and the degree of branching. Each stroke has mapping coordinates applied from beginning to end, enabling you to use texture maps to create special effects.

Lightning Parameters

Axis [Ax] (X,Y,Z) — Selects the axis along which the lightning travels.

Direction [D] p, n (Positive, Negative) — Selects the direction along the axis that the lightning travels.

Type [T] p, f (Parallel, Fragmented) — Selects a branching model. In fragmented branching, branches diverge from the main stroke. In parallel branching, strokes and branches are nearly parallel.

Segments [Se] (10–1,000) — Total number of straight segments for each stroke or branch.

Branching [B] (0–100) — Determines how much branching occurs in each stroke.

Size Factor [Sf] (1–500) — The width of each lightning stroke.

Frequency [F] (1–1,000) — Determines how often a lightning strike occurs.

Duration [D] (1–1,000) — Sets the time that it takes a typical stroke to travel across the bounding box in tenths of a frame. The duration for each stroke varies randomly around this value.

Hold Frames [H] (1–500) — The time in frames that each stroke remains on the screen after finishing its growth.

Force Frame 0 [Ff] (on, off) — Forces all strokes to occur in frame 0. This allows still images to be rendered.

Maximum Number [N] (1–6) — The number of lightning strokes.

Chaos [C] (1–1,000) — Amount of variation in placement of strokes and their branching.

Seed [S] — Random number seed for branching Chaos.

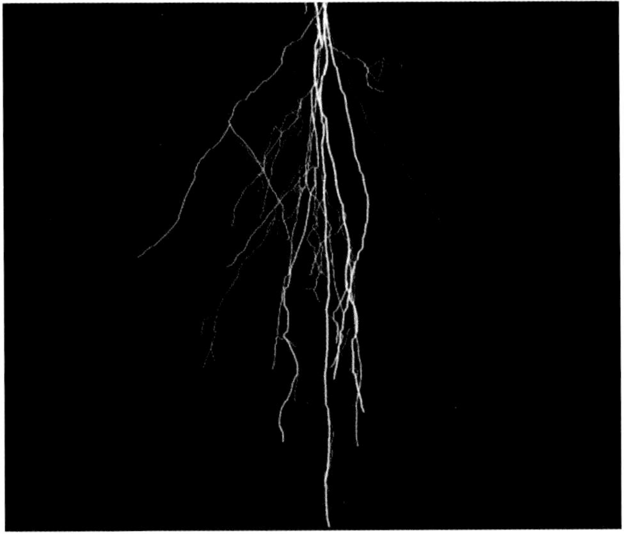

[T]f [S]100 [B]100 [C]98 [S]272727

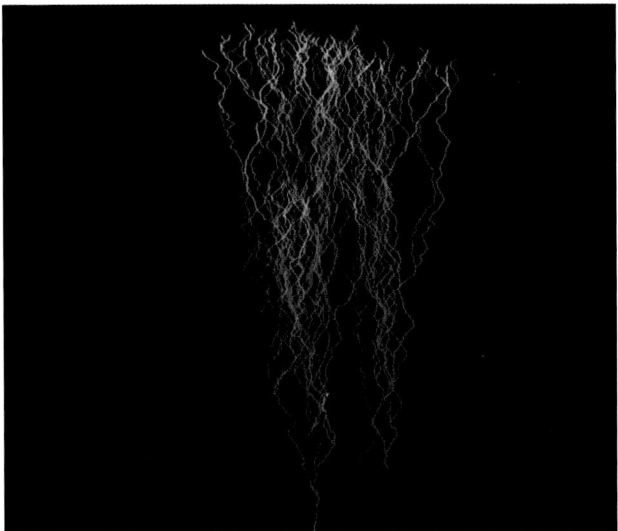

[T]p [S]200 [B]50 [C]1000 [S]272723

Branching lightning and texture-mapped parallel lightning.

MAGIC

Digimation \magic MAGIC_I.AXP

Summary

Magic is a particle system that can be used to produce effects ranging from comet trails to colored sparklers and pixie dust. Particles are not constrained to the AXP box, and the box can be moved over time to create particle trails. Magic uses the bitmap color that is applied to the box as an animated color map by sampling across the bitmap according to the number of frames. The particles begin as the color at the far left of the bitmap and end as the color at the far right of the map. If the life span of the particles in frames is smaller or larger than the number of pixels across the map, Magic will evenly divide the image to fit the required number of frames. Self-illuminated and transparent materials add to the effect, and one-sided and two-sided materials can be used to vary the effect from solid to sparkling. Additional post processing glows and highlights can enhance the effects produced by magic. See Glow, Hilite, and Lenzfx in the IXP chapter for more information.

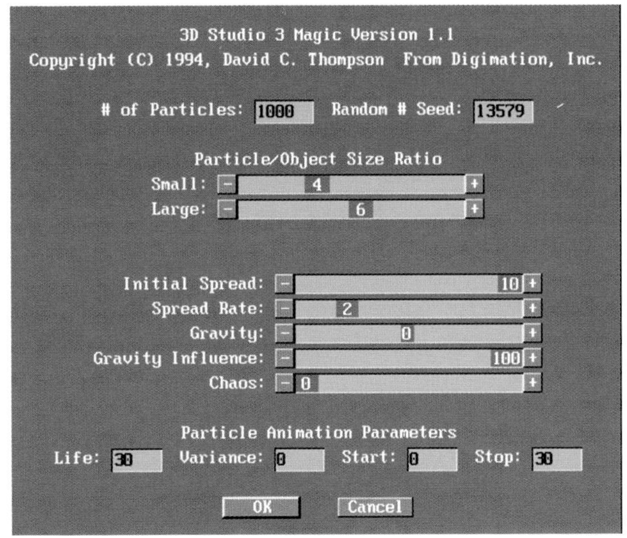

The Magic dialog box.

Magic Parameters

# of Particles [#] (1–21,845) — Sets the number of particles produced by the emitter.

Random # Seed [R] — Sets the particle's start point with an arbitrary number. Each number produces a unique pattern.

Particle/Object Size Ratio [S] (Small, Large) (1–10) — Sets the size of the smallest and largest particles in relation to the bounding box.

Initial Spread [Is] (0–10) — Sets the size of the initial emitter sphere.

Spread Rate [Sr] (0–10) — Sets the amount particles spread out after release.

Gravity [G] (–10–10) — Sets the amount the particles are pulled up or down after release.

MAGIC cont

MAGIC_I.AXP | **\magic** | **Digimation**

Gravity Influence [Gi] (0–100) — Sets the amount of influence that gravity has on the particles as a percentage.

Chaos [C] (0–10) — Sets the amount of variance in tumble rate, gravity, and spread rate.

Magic Animation Parameters

Life [L] — Sets the number of frames for which particles will be visible.

Variance [V] — Sets the amount of variance in particle life span.

Start and Stop [St] [Sp] — Sets the starting and ending frames for the particle effect.

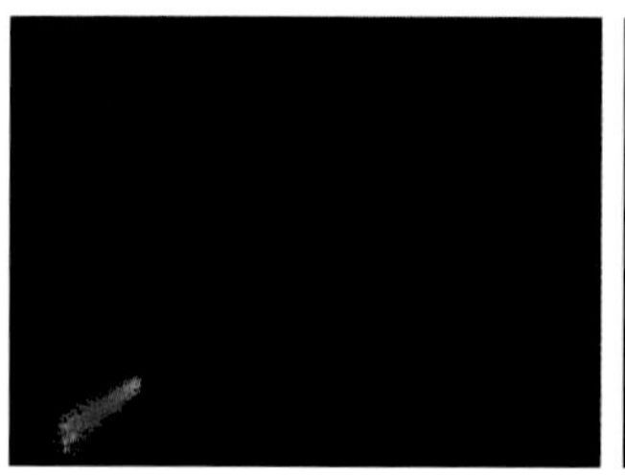
Frame 10

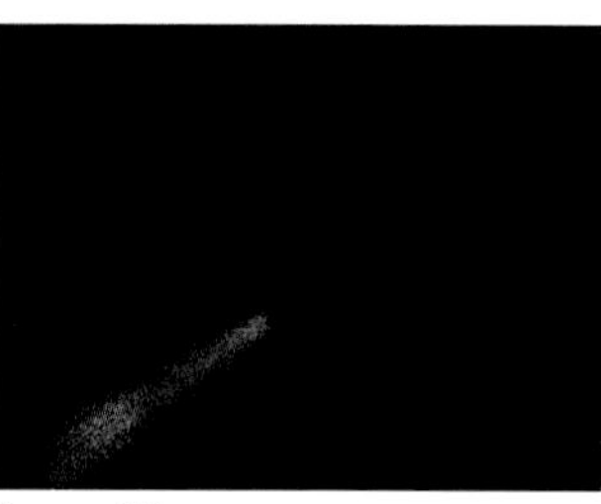
Frame 20

Frame 25

Frame 30

Magic produces particle effects that can be used to simulate animated effects such as bomb fuses, fireworks, and comet trails.

MAPMOVE

MAPMOV_I.AXP | **\mapmov** | **Enthed Animation**

MapMove 1.0 by M Enthed
Enthed Konsulting

Map movment (%):
Up/Down : 25
Left/Right: 25

Start : 0
Stop : 3000
Period : 30

OK Cancel

The MapMove dialog box.

Summary

MapMove is part of the Ent Tools package. It enables you to move a texture map across an object in an animation. You can set a starting frame and an ending frame, as well as a repeat period in frames that controls how often the movement repeats. You specify the shift up and down and the shift left to right as percentages of the bitmap. The shift is distributed across the repeat period, after which the texture returns to its original position and the movement repeats.

MapMove Parameters

Up/Down [Ud] (–9,999–9,999%) — The amount of shift of the texture map in the up/down direction.

Left/Right [Lr] (–9,999–9,999%) — The amount of shift of the texture map in the left/right direction.

Start [S] — Starting frame of the effect.

Stop [E] — Ending frame of the effect. There will be no movement after this point.

Period [P] — Length of the repeat period in frames.

Frame 0

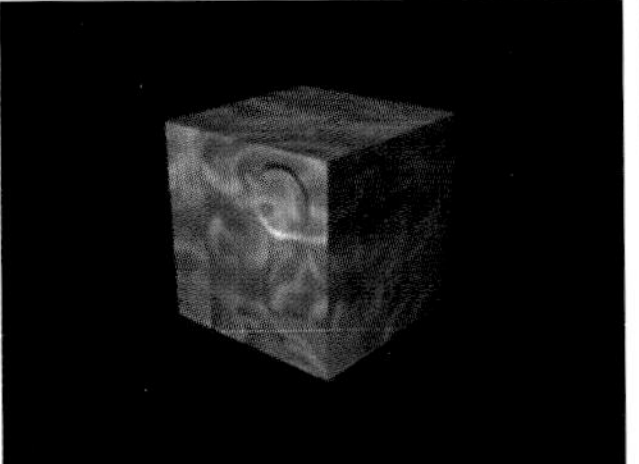
Frame 15

Frame 29

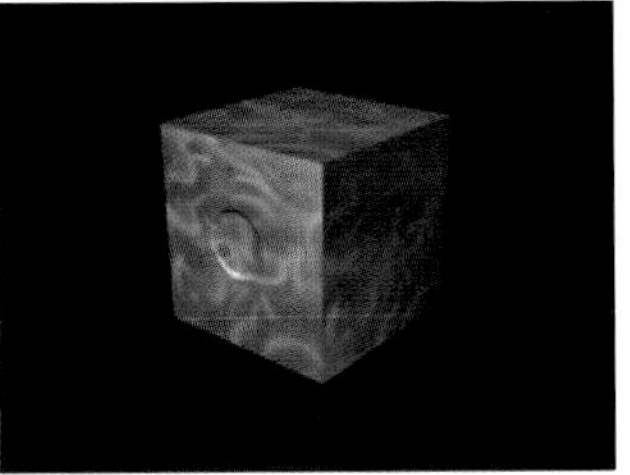
Frame 30

One complete period of map movement.

MAPPED BOX GENERATOR

Yost Group \mapbox MAPBOX_I.AXP

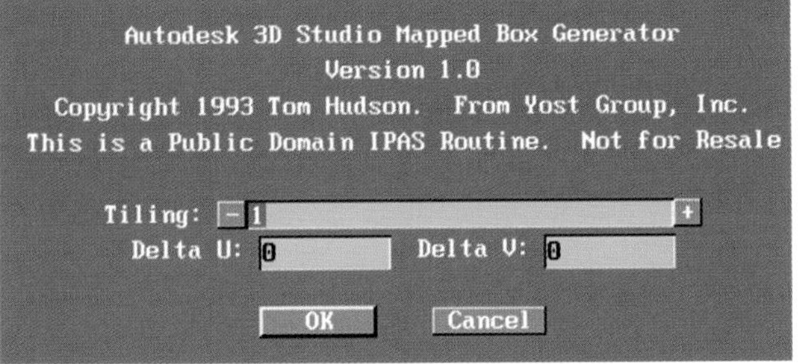

The Mapped Box Generator dialog box.

Summary

Mapped Box Generator (Mapbox) is a public-domain AXP from Yost Group, Inc. Mapbox tiles a planar projection of a texture and/or opacity map on the six sides of a box. The plug-in enables the user to select the number of tiles and to animate the tiles by sliding them across the surfaces of the box in an animation.

Mapbox Parameters

Tiling [T] (1–100) — Sets the number of tiles along each edge.

Delta U, Delta V [Du] [Dv] (–1–1) — Sets the animated change in the texture map's x-direction (Delta u) and y-direction (Delta v) over time.

[T]2 [Du].75 [Dv].75

Mapbox tiles and animates a box's slides. The sample above is a few frames into the animation.

OBJECT-SPLINE DEMO

TUBER_I.AXP **\tuber** **Autodesk**

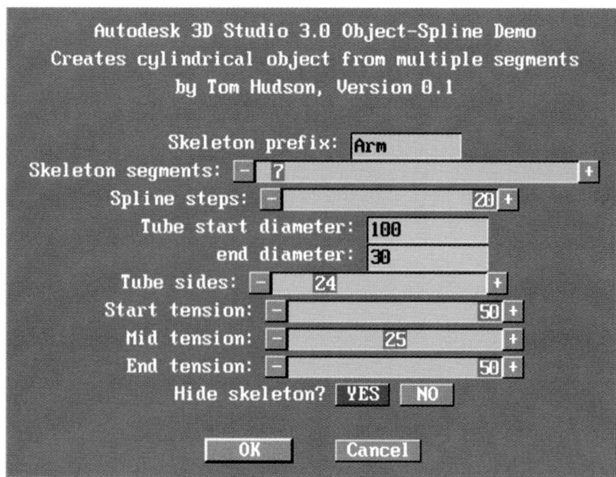

The Object-Spline Demo dialog box.

Summary

Object-Spline Demo (Tuber) is included with 3D Studio Release 4. Tuber generates smoothly skinned, tube-like spline objects from up to 99 sequentially linked joint objects with the same four-letter prefix. Animated bending and twisting can be generated by linking and pivoting objects in the series. The joint objects are generated using four-sided geospheres. You can specify independent starting and ending diameters, which enables Tuber to produce tapered or uniform tubes.

Tuber Parameters

Skeleton prefix [P] — Sets the root name of sequentially linked skeletal objects.

Skeleton segments [S] (2–99) — Sets the number of skeletal objects.

Spline steps [Ss] (1–20) — Sets the relative smoothness of the outside skin spline path. Higher numbers result in smoother paths.

Tube start/end diameter [Sd] [Ed] (.001–99,999) — Sets the starting and ending diameter for the spline object.

Tube sides [Ts] (3–100) — Sets the number of sides around the circumference of the tube.

Start/Mid/End tension [St] [Mt] [Et] (0–50) — Sets the tension of the spline object relative to the source skeleton.

Hide skeleton [H] (yes, no) — Hides the skeleton objects at rendering time.

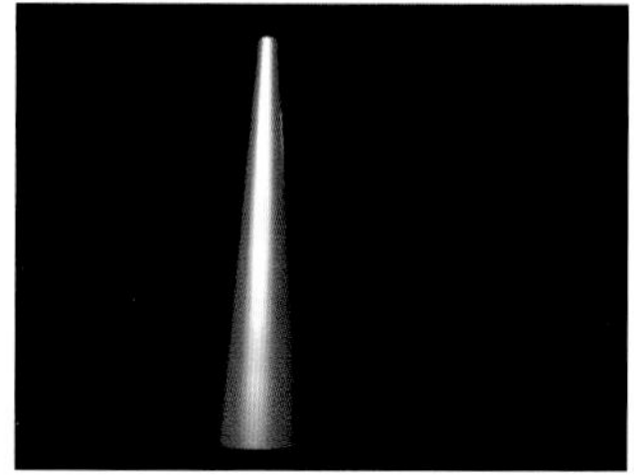

Frame 0

Frame 10

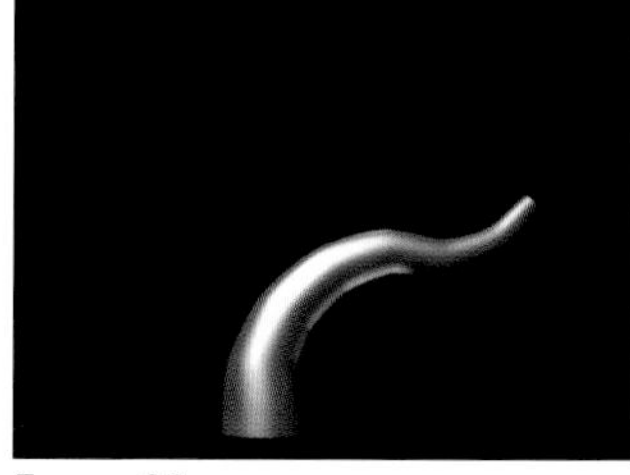

Frame 20

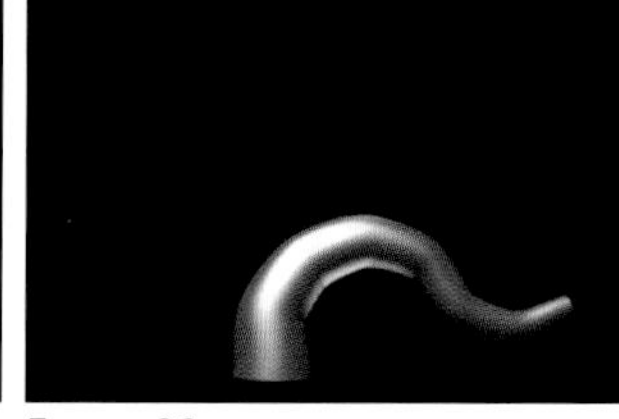

Frame 30

Tuber generates smoothly bending tube and cone-like objects that use a control skeleton for deformation.

PARTICLE CLOUD

Summary

Particle Cloud is part of the Imagine FX package. It is a particle system that generates animated clouds. Each cloud is divided into subareas that have random motion within the cloud. Each subarea is composed of particles that have their own random motion within the subarea. By varying the size and frequency of the subareas you can produce effects ranging from uniform clouds to separate clumps of particles hovering around each other. Each particle is a simple triangle and takes its material from the bounding box object. Using a material with a multi-colored texture map produces particles with varied colors because each particle's mapping coordinates vary randomly across the texture map. You can produce a softer cloud by using a face-mapped opacity map on the particles.

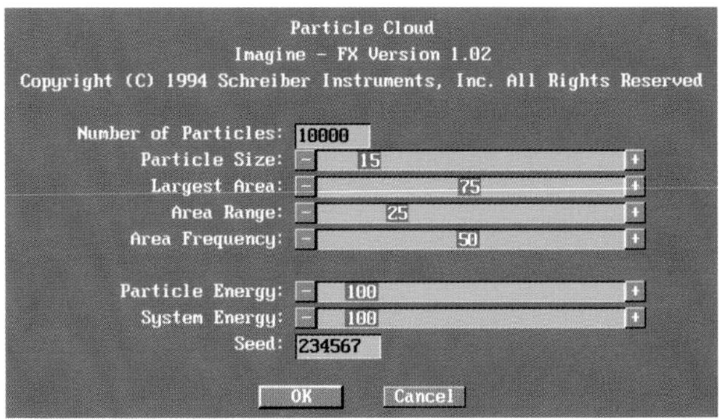

The Particle Cloud dialog box.

Particle Cloud Parameters

Number of Particles [N] (1–21,800) — The number of particles in the cloud.

Particle Size [Ps] (1–100) — Size of the particles relative to the bounding box.

Largest Area [La] (1–150) — Size of the largest subarea of the cloud relative to the bounding box. The bounding box is divided into randomly sized subareas.

Area Range [Ar] (1–100) — Sets the degree of variation in subarea size. Smaller numbers produce a more uniform cloud.

Area Frequency [Af] (1–100) — Sets the number of subareas in the cloud.

Particle Energy [Pe] (0–1,000) — Sets the speed of particle motion.

System Energy [Se] (0–1,000) — Sets the speed of subarea motion.

Seed [S] — Random number seed that controls the distribution of subareas and particles.

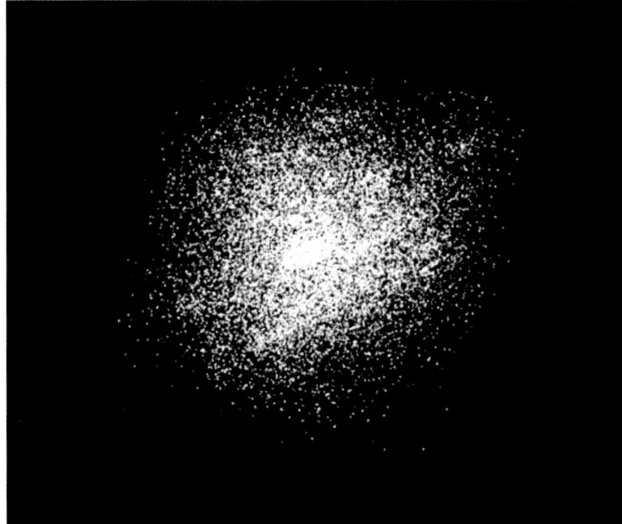

[N]20000 [Ps]20 [La]100 [Ar]10 [Af]50

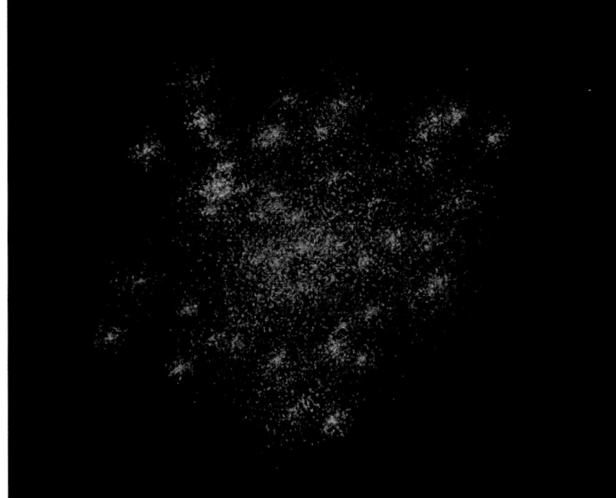

[N]20000 [Ps]30 [La]75 [Ar]50 [Af]50

A uniform cloud and an opacity/texture-mapped cloud with clumping.

RAIN MAKER

RAIN_I.AXP | **\rain** | **Yost Group**

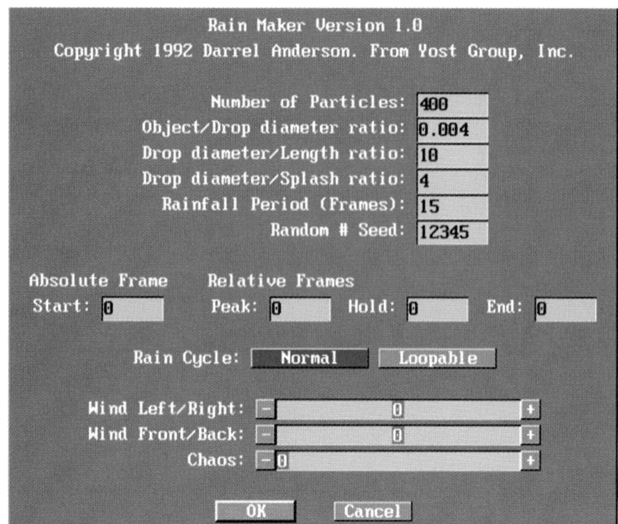

The Rain Maker dialog box.

Summary

Rain Maker is part of the Yost Group Particle Systems Disk #4 package. Rain Maker uses a particle system to simulate effects from light drizzles to heavy downpours. The process is assigned to a bounding box, and the effect's gravity vector is determined by the viewport in which the box is created (a box created in the top viewport makes the particles fall downward).

Parameters such as Drop diameter/Splash ratio, Number of Particles, and animated Wind make Rain useful for many different special effects.

Rain Maker Parameters

Number of Particles [N] (1–16,383) — Sets the maximum number of particles.

Object/Drop diameter ratio [Or] (0.001–0.5) — Sets the size of the particles relative to the bounding object.

Drop diameter/Length ratio [Dl] (0.1–100,000) — Sets the length of the particles relative to the drop diameter.

Drop diameter/Splash ratio [Ds] (1–100) — Sets the puddle size relative to the drop diameter.

Rainfall Period [R] — Controls the number of frames required for one drop to travel from the top to the bottom of the bounding box.

Random # Seed [Rs] (0–99,999) — Sets the algorithm's start point. Each arbitrary number produces a unique initial state.

Absolute Frame, Relative Frames [Af] [Rf] s, p, h, e (Start, Peak, Hold, End) — Controls the frame envelope, intensity, and duration of the effect.

Rain Cycle [Rc] n, l (Normal, Loopable) — Provides an option for a smooth, continuously looping effect.

Wind [Wlr] [Wfb] l, r, f, b (left, right, front, back) (–45–45) — A wind simulator that sets the rainfall at an angle relative to the bounding box.

Chaos [C] (0–100) — Varies the angle of rainfall randomly.

[N]1000 [Wlr]–45 [C]95

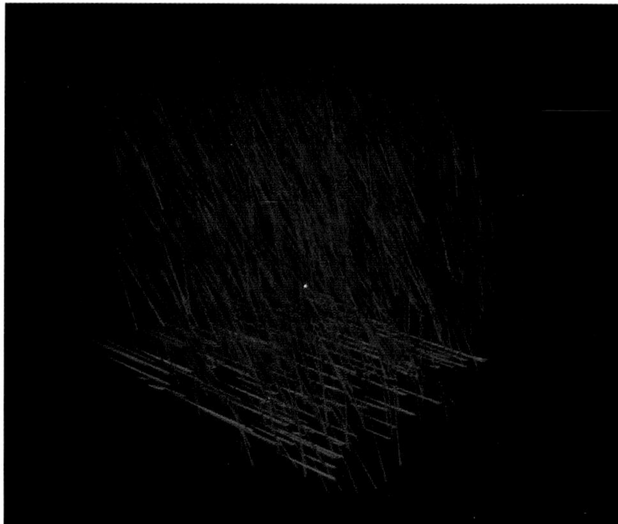

[N]1000 [Dl]50 [Wlr]–45 [C]95

Rain Maker uses a particle system to simulate effects from light drizzles to heavy downpours.

Summary

Render Time Mesh Extractor (Meshres) is part of the Yost Group Disk #7 package. It works in conjunction with Optimize to enable you to work in wireframe with a low-detail version of an object that is rendered using a high-detail mesh. Optimize lets you embed more-detailed copies of a mesh inside the optimized one. Meshres can be set to switch to the higher detail mesh for rendering. This gives you speed in wireframe views and full detail for renders. You also can set Meshres to render using a low-detail version of the mesh for quick test renders, and then switch to the high-detail version for final renders.

You must first embed one or more versions of the mesh (complete with material and mapping) inside a low-detail version using Optimize. Then you attach Meshres to the mesh. Your renders will use the low-detail mesh until you active Meshres and select one of the embedded meshes. After that, Meshres will give the embedded mesh to the renderer.

You should avoid operations that change the vertices of a mesh with an embedded mesh; this can disturb the alignment of the two meshes. Moves, rotations, and scaling are no problem, but bending, mirroring, and tapering will cause problems. For this reason you cannot use Morph on a Meshres object.

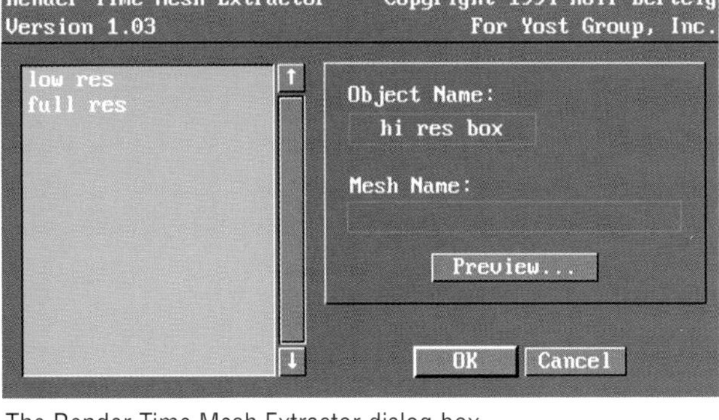

The Render Time Mesh Extractor dialog box.

Meshres Parameters

Preview [Pr] — Displays a wireframe or shaded view of the selected mesh.

Object list — Selects the embedded mesh that will be used at render time.

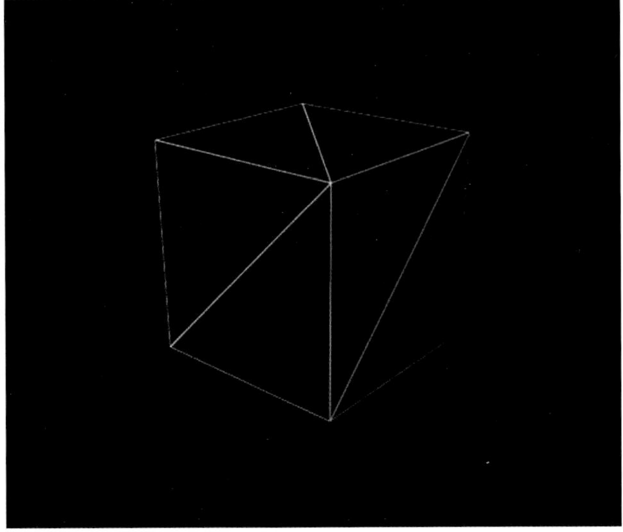

Low-resolution proxy

Imagine Detailer produces a range of fences and walls.

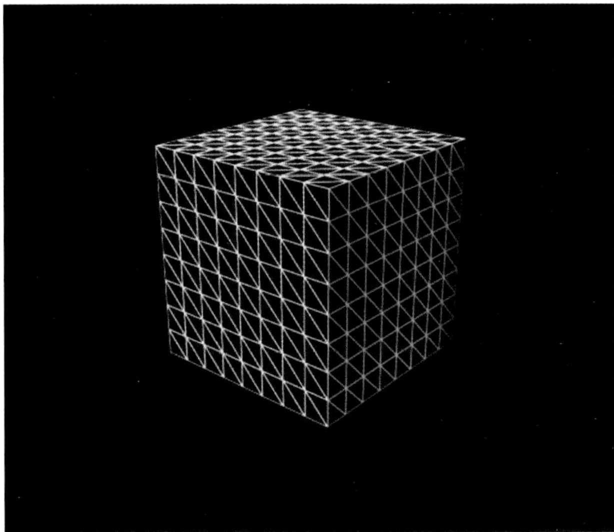

Full-resolution final

RINGS

RINGS_I.AXP \rings Schreiber Instruments

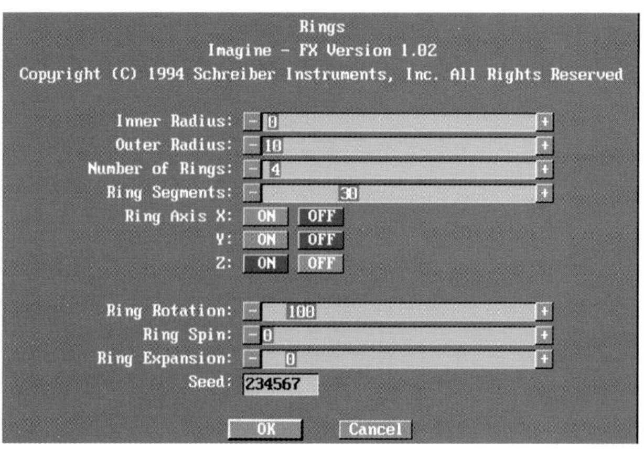

The Rings dialog box.

Summary

Rings is part of the Imagine FX package. It generates up to three separate expanding rings. These rings can tumble on one or two axes. The rings do not spin in the way that a record does. You can specify the inner and final outer radius of the ring and its growth rate. The ring has mapping coordinates built into it that wrap a texture map completely around the ring. This works for very smooth texture maps, but produces mapping errors with patterned texture maps.

Rings Parameters

Inner Radius [Ir] (–10–500) — Size of the inner radius of the rings.

Outer Radius [Or] (1–5,000) — Size of the outer radius of the rings.

Number of Rings [N] (1–100) — Number of concentric sub-rings that are generated in each ring.

Ring Segments [Rs] (4–90) — The number of line segments generated around the ring. This sets the smoothness of the ring edge.

Ring Axis X, Y, Z [Rx] [Ry] [Rz] (on, off) — Enables separate rings around each axis. This is the creation axis. The ring rotation and spin axis are at 90 degrees to this and to each other.

Ring Rotation [Rr] (0–1,000) — Speed of primary ring tumble.

Ring Spin [Rs] (0–1,000) — Speed of secondary ring tumble.

Ring Expansion [Re] (–100–1,000) — Rate of ring expansion or contraction from frame to frame.

Seed [S] — Random number seed.

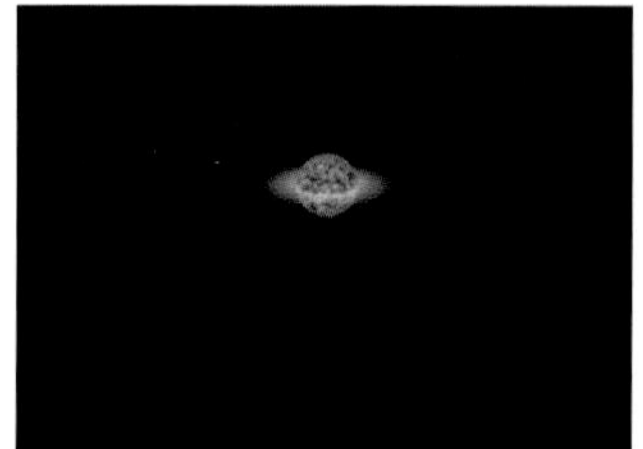

Frame 0

Frame 10

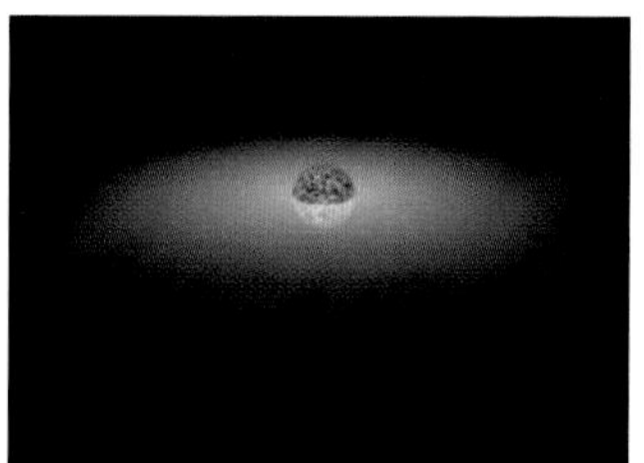

Frame 15

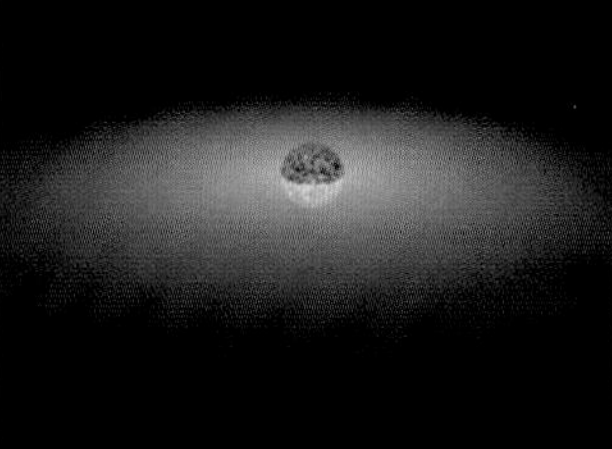

Frame 30

A single expanding ring with opacity mapping.

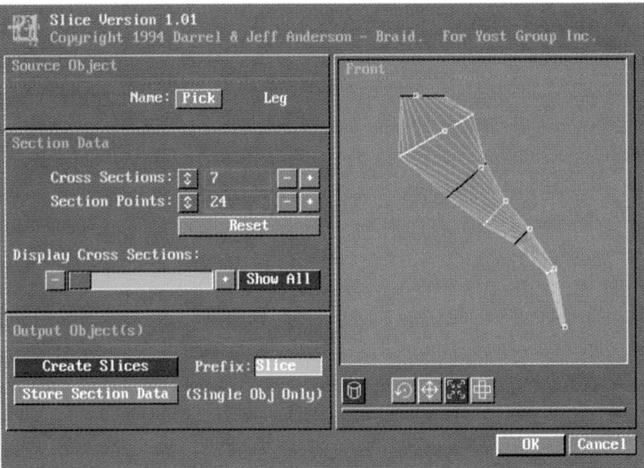

The Slice dialog box.

Summary

Skin is part of the Yost Group Disk #6 package. It generates Bézier spline surfaces at render time using low-resolution meshes as control points. The control meshes are called template objects and must consist of an ordered series of vertices organized into a series of sections. The best way to make this kind of mesh is to use the lofter. The vertices must be created in a specific order, and most other modeling methods will not produce the proper vertex order. Because of this structure, the forms produced by Skin are based on either a plane or a cylinder. A single skin object cannot branch, but if you align and overlap two control meshes, they can give the impression of one branching form.

After the control mesh is created, you can move vertices around to change the resulting spline surface. Each vertex acts as a control point, affecting the shape of the spline surface. You can select from surfaces generated by Catmull splines or the smoother B-splines, use controls to set the spline surface tension and smoothness, elect to cap one or both ends of the form, and apply a texture-mapped material to a skinned object. Skin generates its own mapping coordinates that wrap the texture once around the perimeter and once along the length of each skin object.

You can animate skinned object in one of two ways: you can morph a series of control meshes, or you can slice the control mesh into cross-section objects and animate the objects. Morphing a skinned object is just like any other morph except that you must assign the Skin AXP to a pointer object and then direct Skin to use your morph object. A pointer object can be any object that has the AXP assigned. It will not be displayed at render time. Its only use is to get around a restriction in the use of morphs with AXP plug-ins.

The second animation method of slicing the control mesh into cross-sections requires the use of a PXP plug-in called Slice. Slice separates the cross-sections into separate objects. You can then animate the cross-sections, and Skin will connect them with a spline surface.

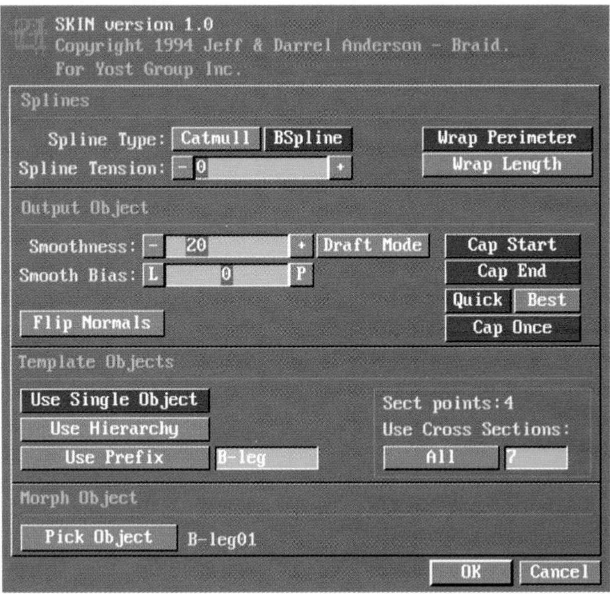

The Skin dialog box.

Skin Parameters

Spline Type [Ty] c, b (Catmull, BSpline) — Selects the type of spline used. Catmull splines pass through each control point. B-splines are smoother but less predictable.

Spline Tension [Te] (0–100) — Sets the spline tension for the surface. Larger tension values produce tighter, flatter surfaces. Smaller tension values produce smoother, more rounded surfaces.

Wrap Perimeter [Wp] (on, off) — Determines whether the skinned object is smoothly closed around its circumference.

Wrap Length [Wl] (on, off) — Determines whether the skin wraps along the length of the object. This produces a skin surface on both the outside and inside of the control mesh.

Smoothness [S] (0–100) — Determines the number of faces generated at render time by Skin. Higher numbers produce smoother surfaces.

Draft Mode [Dm] (on, off) — Forces Smoothness to a setting of 10 for draft mode rendering.

Smooth Bias [Sb] (L –100–100 P) — Controls the proportion of faces along the length of the skin (L) versus the number of faces around the perimeter (P).

Flip Normals [F] (on, off) — Determines whether the surface's face normals are flipped, turning it inside out.

Cap Start [Cs] (on, off) — Determines whether the form is capped at its starting end.

Cap End [Ce] (on, off) — Determines whether the form is capped at its end.

SKIN cont

SKIN_I.AXP \skin **Yost Group**

Quick/Best [Q] [B] — Selects one of two end-capping methods, selecting between speed and quality.

Cap Once [Co] (on, off) — Determines whether capping information is calculated for each rendering or stored in the mesh and reused.

Template Objects [To] s, h, p (single object, hierarchy, prefix) — Selects the method used to group Skin template control meshes. Single object uses a single object as the control mesh. Hierarchy uses a keyframer hierarchy to select the sections of a multiple object-control mesh. Prefix uses a name prefix to select multiple objects for a control mesh.

Use Cross Sections [Uc] (all, number of sections) — Selects the number of cross-sections from a control mesh that will be used.

Morph Object — Select the morph base object when using a morph series.

Slice Parameters

Name [N] — Selects the object to be sliced.

Cross Sections [Cs] — Sets the number of cross-sections in a control mesh.

Section Points [Sp] — Sets the number of vertices in each cross-section.

Reset [Re] — Resets Cross Sections and Section Points to the default values taken from the mesh.

Display Cross Sections [Dc] — Selects the cross-section to highlight. You also can highlight all cross-sections.

Output Objects [Oo] c, s (Create Slices, Store Section Data) — Selects whether Slice creates section objects or simply stores the section data in the original control mesh.

Prefix [Pr] — Sets the name prefix to use for the sliced sections.

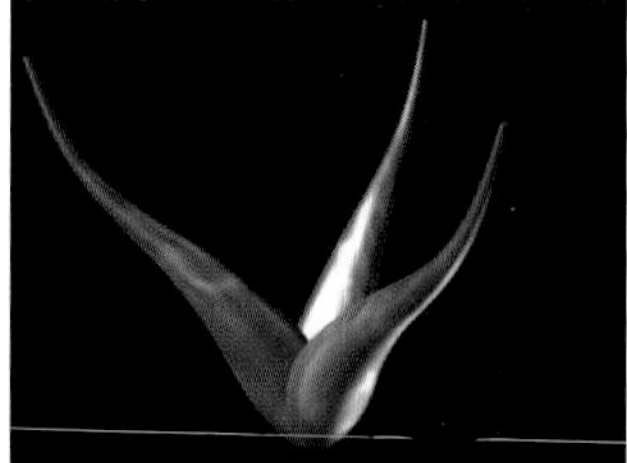
Frame 0

Frame 10

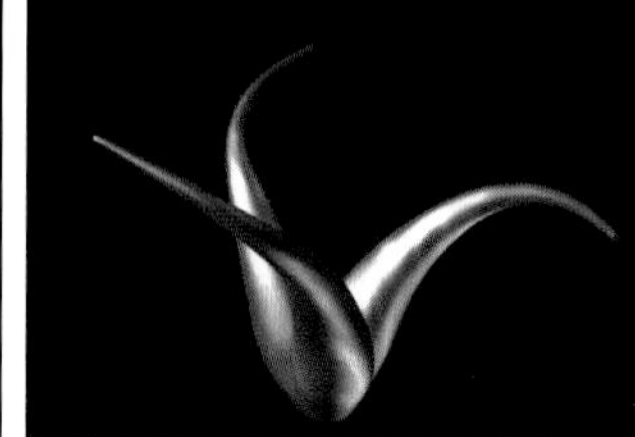
Frame 20

Frame 30

Three objects animated using Skin.

SNOWFALL

SNOW_I.AXP \snow **Yost Group**

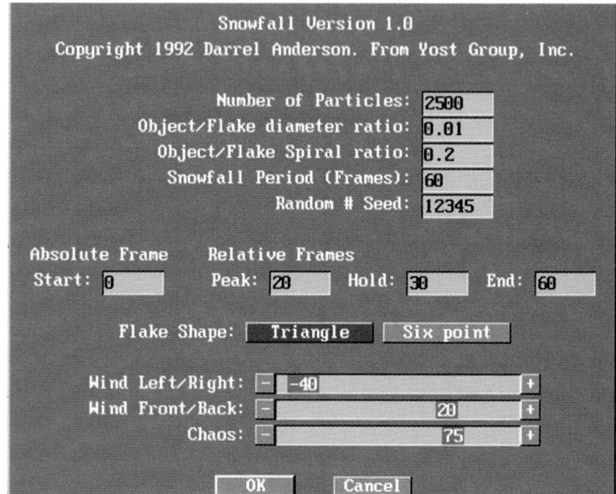

The Snowfall dialog box.

Summary

Part of the Yost Group Particle Systems Disk #4 package, Snowfall is a particle system that simulates effects from light flurries to blizzards. Snowfall uses triangular or six-pointed flat flakes that are animated using a gravity force. The flakes can be blown left and right or front and back by wind forces. A chaos slider inserts random noise to produce more natural effects.

Snowfall Parameters

Number of Particles [#] (1–21,840) — Sets the maximum number of particles.

Object/Flake diameter ratio [D] (0.0001–0.5) — Sets the size of the particles relative to the bounding object.

Object/Flake Spiral ratio [S] (0–.5) — Sets the diameter of the spiral path relative to the bounding object.

Snowfall Period [P] — Controls the number of frames required for one flake to travel from the top to the bottom of the bounding box.

Random # Seed [R] (0–99,999) — Sets the algorithm's start point. Each arbitrary number produces a unique pattern.

Absolute Frame, Relative Frames [Af] [Rf] s, p, h, e (Start, Peak, Hold, End) — Controls the frame envelope, intensity, and duration of the effect.

Flake Shape [F] t, s (Triangle, Six point) — Sets the flake to a single triangular face or two overlapping faces.

Wind [Wlr] [Wfb] l, r, f, b (left, right, front, back) (–45–45) — A wind simulator that sets the snow at an angle relative to the bounding box.

Chaos [C] (0–100) — Sets the amount of variance in angle, period, spiral diameter, and flake tumbling.

[#]500,[F]s

[#]500,[F]t

Snow is a particle system that uses triangular or six-pointed flat flakes to simulate effects from light flurries to blizzards.

SPHERE GENERATOR

Yost Group \plasma PLASMA_I.AXP

Summary

Sphere Generator is part of the Yost Group disk 2 Special Effects package. This plug-in produces plasma ball effects similar to lightning in a glass sphere. Sphere Generator simulates lightning using a radial particle system in conjunction with a self-illuminated wireframe material. Number of arcs, arc progression, size of the inner sphere generator, and arc movement in degrees control the type of effect generated. Sphere Generator does not automatically produce a glass shell or internal generator core or rod. Adding a post effect glow to plasma can enhance the lightning effect.

Sphere Generator Parameters

# of Arcs [#] (1–100) — Sets the number of arcs generated.

Inner size ratio [I] (0.001–.99) — Sets the size of the inner generator sphere as a percentage of the AXP object.

Brownian variation [B] (0.001–.99) — Sets the amount each arc varies from other arcs.

Arc progression [P] (Random, Walk) — Sets the arcs to move around the outside perimeter in an ordered or random pattern.

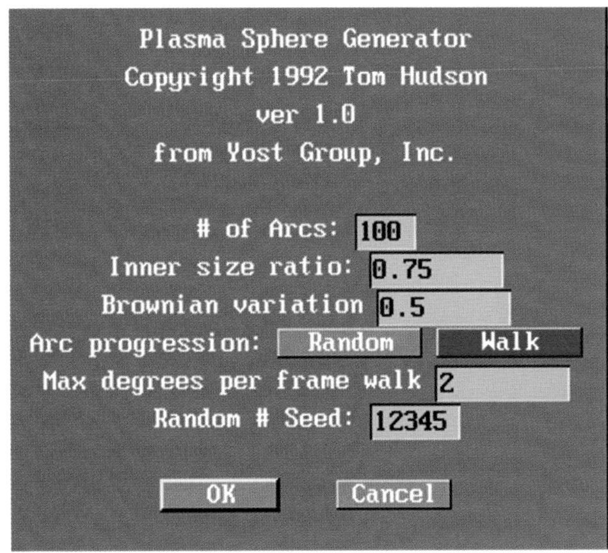

The Sphere Generator dialog box.

SPHERE GENERATOR cont

PLASMA_I.AXP \plasma **Yost Group**

Max degrees per frame walk [W] (.001–180) — Sets the amount in degrees each arc can move around the perimeter each frame.

Random # Seed [R] — Sets the arc's initial start point with an arbitrary number. Each number produces a unique pattern.

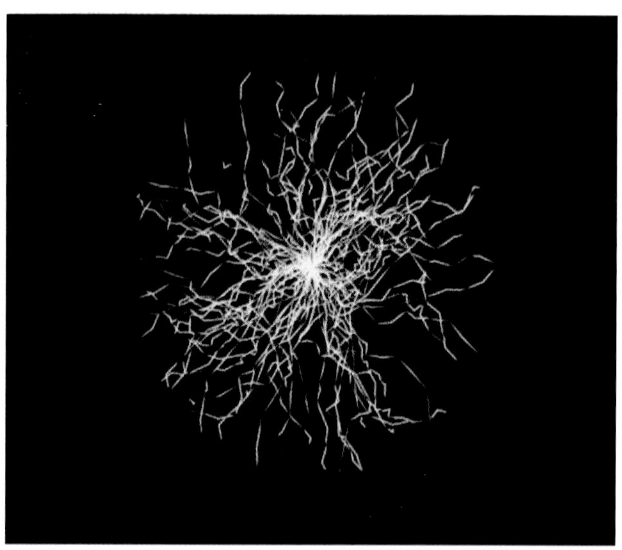

[#]1,[I].001

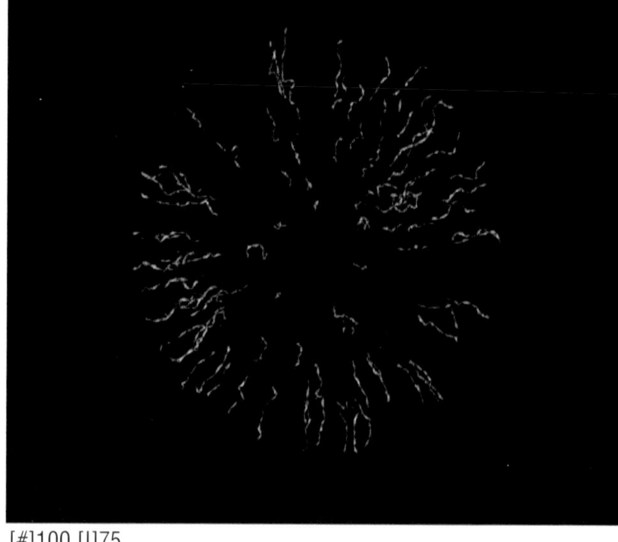

[#]100,[I]75

Sphere Generator simulates lightning using a radial particle system in conjunction with a self-illuminated wireframe material.

SPURT

SPURT_I.AXP \spurt **Yost Group**

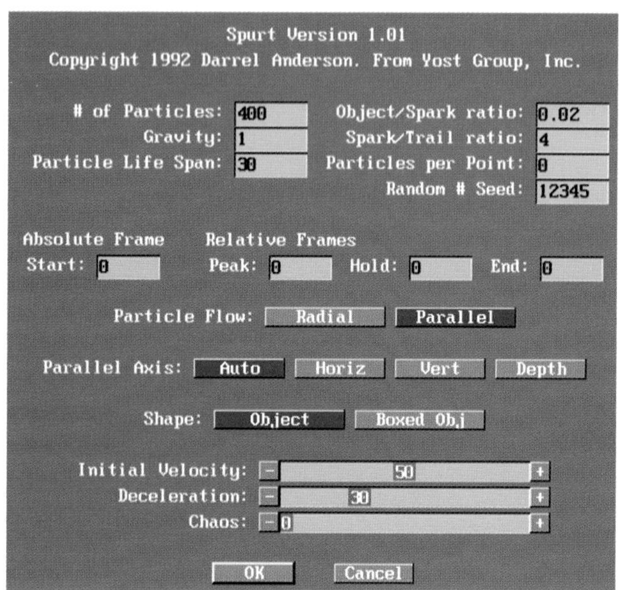

The Spurt dialog box.

Summary

Spurt is part of the Yost Group Particle Systems Disk #4 package. Spurt is a particle system that simulates jet exhaust, sparklers, water hoses, and sprinklers. The effect can use either a boxed object or the object itself, although the boxed object option offers more control over the parameters and particle emission's shape.

Start, Peak, Hold, and End are used to create Spurt's effect timing. The entire effect interval is referred to as the time envelope. Time envelopes resemble a graph with the X axis representing time in frames and the Y axis representing the effect strength. Start and Peak work together to set the beginning transition or the time required for the pattern to reach its maximum. Unite and Hold work together to set how long the effect sustains the maximum level. Hold and End set the ending transition or fade-out. These parameters enable you to time the Spurt effect to, for instance, start abruptly, sustain for a few frames, and slowly die out.

Spurt particles use UV mapping to determine the particles' color and trail color for each frame. Particle body color and tail color are determined by samples taken from the image map pixel-by-pixel for each animation frame. Body color samples are taken horizontally from left to right, across the bitmap image. Tail color samples are taken vertically from top to bottom, over the bitmap. Image maps samples are uniformly spaced on the bitmap image to correspond to the total number of frames in the animation.

Spurt Parameters

# of Particles [#] (1–8,190) — Sets the maximum number of particles.
Object/Spark ratio [Os] (0.0001–0.5) — Sets the size of the particles relative to the bounding object.
Gravity [G] (1–10,000) — Sets the speed that the particles fall in the direction of the gravity vector.
Spark/Trail ratio [St] (1–10,000) — Sets the length of the particle's trail relative to the distance the particle moves per frame.
Particle Life Span [L] (1–32,000) — Sets the length of time, in frames, between emission and fade-out of the particles.
Particles per Point [P] (0–10,000) — Sets the number of particles released at each vertex before moving on to the next.
Random # Seed [R] (0–99,999) — Sets the algorithm's start point. Each arbitrary number produces a unique initial state.
Absolute Frame, Relative Frames [Af] [Rf] s, p, h, e (Start, Peak, Hold, End) — Controls the frame envelope, intensity, and duration of the effect.
Particle Flow [Pf] r, p (Radial, Parallel) — Controls the location and shape of the particle emission pattern.
Parallel Axis [Pa] a, h, v, d (auto, horizontal, vertical, depth) — Determines the axis of the particle flow direction when Particle Flow Parallel is chosen.
Shape [S] o, b (Object, Boxed Obj) — Controls whether the effect's parameters are applied to the object itself or to the object's bounding box.
Initial Velocity [Iv] (0–100) — Sets the initial speed of the particles as they leave the blast center.
Deceleration [D] (0–100) — Sets the rate of particle deceleration.
Chaos [C] (0–100) — Controls the amount of variance in initial velocity, deceleration, particle size, and gravity.

[St]30 [Pf]r [Iv]60

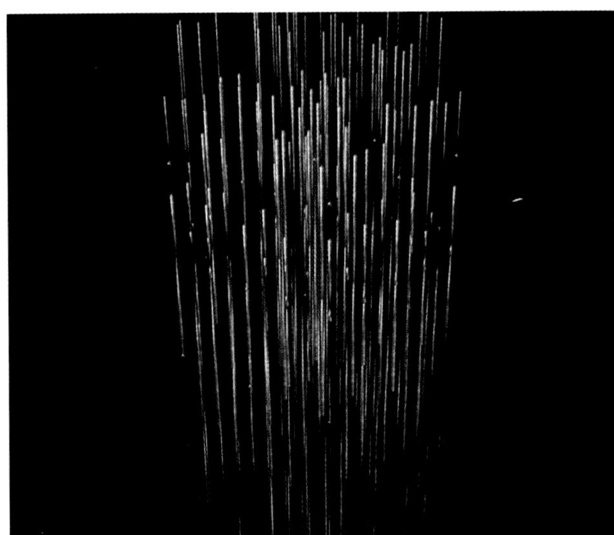
[St]20 [Pa]v [Iv]60

Spurt is a particle system that simulates jet exhaust, sprinklers, and spurting hoses. Spurt particles use UV mapping to determine the particles' water color and trail color each frame.

STARBURST

Starburst
Imagine - FX Version 1.02
Copyright (C) 1994 Schreiber Instruments, Inc. All Rights Reserved

Center Radius: 10
Number of Rays: 1000
Ray Thickness: 3
Energy: 100
Seed: 234567

OK Cancel

The Starburst dialog box.

Summary

Starburst is part of the Imagine FX package. It produces an animated starburst object consisting of a central sphere with numerous rays randomly rotating around the central sphere. You can set the size of the central sphere and the width of the rays.

The central sphere is a low-resolution sphere that is used to fill in the center. The rays have mapping coordinates running from base to tip, enabling you to add texture maps for special effects.

Starburst Parameters

Center Radius [Cr] (1–100) — Sets the radius of the central sphere.

Number of Rays [N] (0–20,000) — The number of rays generated.

Ray Thickness [T] (1–20) — Thickness of the base of each ray relative to the size of the bounding box.

Energy [E] (1–1,000) — Sets the speed of ray motion around the central sphere.

Seed [S] — Random number seed that controls the distribution of rays around the center.

[Cr]1 [N]1000 [T]2

Starburst with opacity mapping and starburst with wide rays.

[Cr]10 [N]1000 [T]20

Summary

Included with 3D Studio Release 4, Tornado generates rotating con- and cylindrical-shaped particle systems. The shape and size of the particle effect can be controlled using number of particles, particle size, inner and outer orbits, and chaos. Each particle uses the material assigned to the AXP stand-in object.

Tornado Parameters

# of Particles [#] (1–8,100) — Sets the number of particles. Very high numbers can slow rendering substantially.

Object/Particle size ratio [S] (.001–.5) — Sets the particle size as a percentage of the AXP object.

Random # Seed [Rs] — Sets the particle's initial start point with an arbitrary number. Each number produces a unique pattern.

Inner and Outer Orbit Period [I] [O] — Sets the amount of time in frames for particles on the inside or perimeter of the tornado to make one revolution.

Chaos slider [C] (0–100) — Sets the amount of irregularity in the particle system. As the value is raised, the cloud becomes more cylindrical.

Rotation [R] (clockwise, counterclockwise) — Sets the direction of particle rotation.

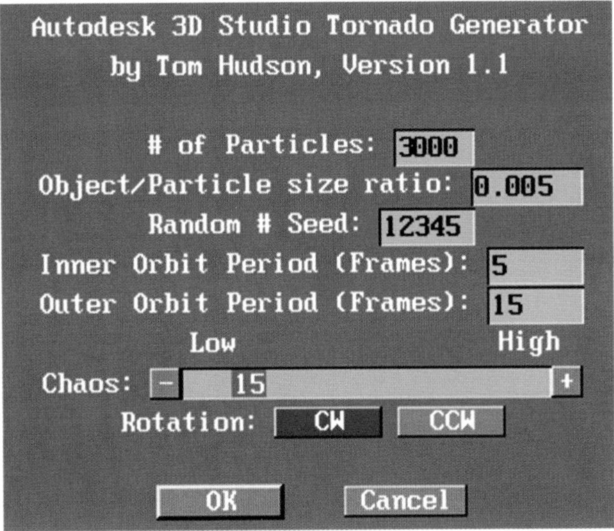

The Tornado dialog box.

[#]3000,[S].005,[C]15

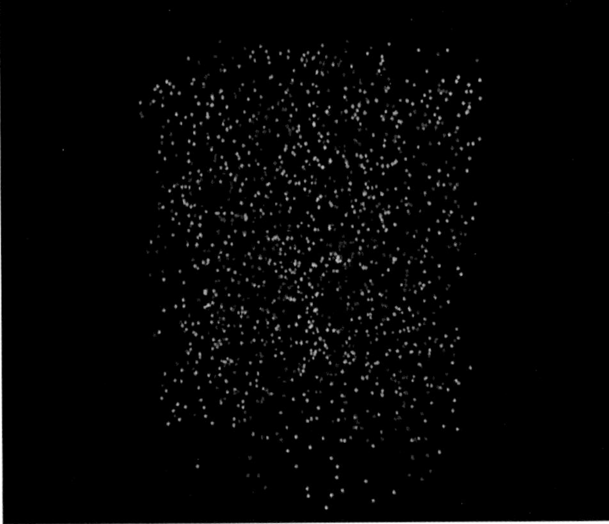

[#]1500,[S].01,[C]75

Tornado generates rotating cone- and cylindrical-shaped particle systems. Each particle uses the material assigned to the AXP stand-in object.

VAPOR

VAPOR_I.AXP **\vapor** **Yost Group**

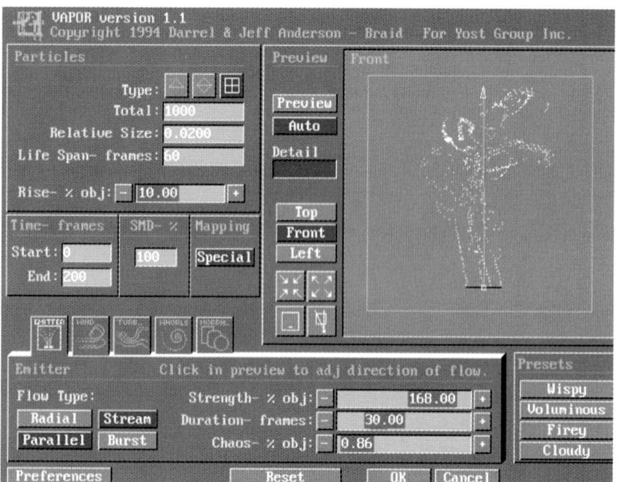

The Vapor dialog box with the Emitter Index Card, Emitter preview, and adjustment icon.

Summary

Vapor is part of Yost Group's IPAS disk 6 from Schreiber Instruments. Vapor is a particle system that produces animated smoke, steam, spark, and bubble effects. This plug-in is similar to Yost Group's Flame, but with the essential difference that whereas Flame uses a long, tendril-shaped particle, Vapor uses a more spherical-shaped particle. This makes Vapor useful for creating numerous swirling bubble and paint spatter effects.

Vapor produces its effects based on its associated AXPBOX PXP, which creates a specified number of particle emitters and places them inside a bounding box of any dimension. The emitter element consists of a series of vertices, each of which is capable of sending out streams of particles. The bounding box element provides scaling information for the particle system.

Vapor is controlled by a number of parameters that set the type, number, size, and rise of the particles. You can specify the life span for each particle along with the time interval in frames for the effect. Furthermore, you can set the particle emission timing to either Stream, which emits particles as it cycles between each emitter vertex, or Burst, which emits particles from emitter vertices en masse.

Vapor also provides five index cards or submenus that enable you to control the particle flow from the emitters, apply wind, turbulence, and whorls as well as the ability to morph between multiple particle systems. This enables you to animate the location of the particles.

Much of Vapor's work is accomplished interactively in a preview window. With the emitter index card selected, for instance, you can choose either Radial or Parallel flow types and move a

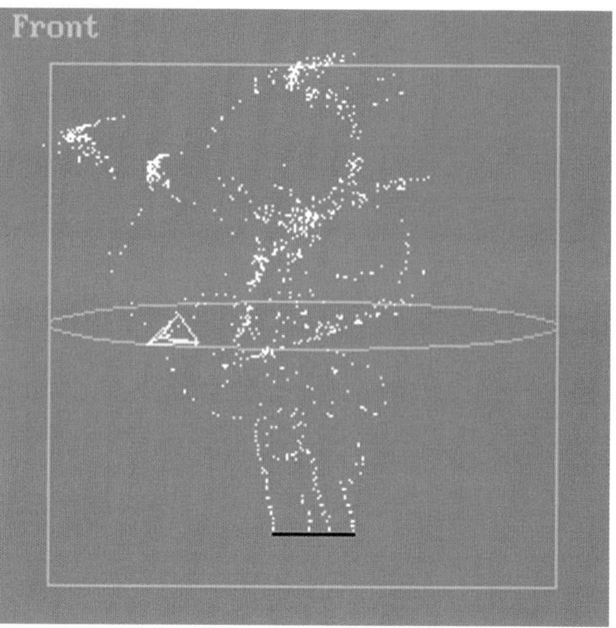

The Wind preview and adjustment icon.

vector icon consisting of one or more green arrows that indicate the direction of particle flow. As the icon is clicked and dragged around the preview area, a series of white lines indicating the particle cloud are dynamically updated. This is useful for conveying a general idea of the final particle system. The Preview area is similarly updated for most of Vapor's parameters.

Vapor also works with image map materials and includes a custom materials library and several special-purpose bitmaps. Vapor supports material mapping only with the Square particle type. To apply any material you first highlight the Special button and then assign the material to the AXP box from the 3D Editor.

Vapor also provides a series of presets for quickly producing various effects including cigarette smoke, a column of smoke, soft clouds, ground fog, and fire clouds.

Vapor Parameters

Type buttons [T] t,p,s (Triangle, Polyhedron, Square) — Specifies the type of mesh object that Vapor will use for each particle. Triangle is the simplest particle, consisting of a pyramid of four faces and four vertices. Polyhedron generates a six-sided polyhedron-shaped particle consisting of six faces and five vertices. Square creates the most complex particle, consisting of three intersecting squares.

Total [To] — Specifies the total number of particles. The maximum number depends on the type of particle. Triangle can have up to 16,380 particles per object, Polyhedron can have 10,290 particles per object, and Square can have 5,460 particles per object.

Relative Size [Rs] — Sets the particle size relative to the maximum dimension of the bounding cube or object.

Life Span frames [Ls] — Sets the particle's life span from emission to fade-out.

Rise [Ri] (0–200%) — Specifies the maximum amount of particle rise as a percentage of the height of the bounding cube or object. If the bounding area is not a cube, the height value is calculated as the average of the bounding object's width, height, and depth.

Time Start and End [Ts] [Te] — Sets the frame range for the effect. If both Start and End are set to 0, the particles stay on for the duration of the animation.

SMD % [Sm] (1–100%) — Specifies the percentage of secondary motion data used to key the effect.

Mapping Special [Ms] — Enables the option of using a special mapped material from the DISK6.MLI, which is included with Vapor. This option is available only with the Square particle type.

Preview and Auto — Updates the Preview particle cloud to reflect edits to Vapor's parameters. Auto dynamically updates the display. The particles displayed here are useful as a preview only and do not reflect the exact character or particle count of the rendered particle system.

Detail — Sets the number of particles used to create the preview particle cloud that is displayed in the Preview window. You can click and drag the red bar to the right or left to increase or decrease the number of particles.

View control (Top, Front, Left, Zoom In, Zoom Out, Zoom Bounding Cube Extents, Zoom Emitter Arrow Extents) — Specifies and switches the view. Top, Front, and Left switch between orthogonal views, and Zoom In (arrows in button) and Out (arrows out button) zoom incrementally with each mouse click. Zoom Bounding Cube Extents (located below the Zoom In button) and Zoom Emitter Arrow Extents (located below the Zoom Out button) zoom to either the bounding cube and emitter arrow extents or to just the emitter arrow extents, respectively.

Wispy Presets [Wi] c, t, co (Cigarette, Trails, Column) — Automatically configures Vapor's parameters to produce a series of intricate, curvilinear smoke trails or bubble patterns. Wispy is based on many small particles and the use of both the Triangle and Polyhedron particle types.

Voluminous Presets [Vo] s, st (Smoke Column, Steam Column) — Automatically configures Vapor's parameters to produce a soft smoky or steamy effect. Voluminous is based on a few large particles the use of the Square particle type, and the use of Mapping Special in conjunction with a special material map that must be applied to the particles.

Firey Presets [Fi] f, ss, sr (Fire Cloud, Spark Swirl, Spark Rise) — Automatically configures Vapor's parameters to produce a series of fiery effects. Firey is based on the use of a mix of many small many particles and a few large particles. It also uses a mix of Square and Polyhedron particle types with special materials used for the Square particles.

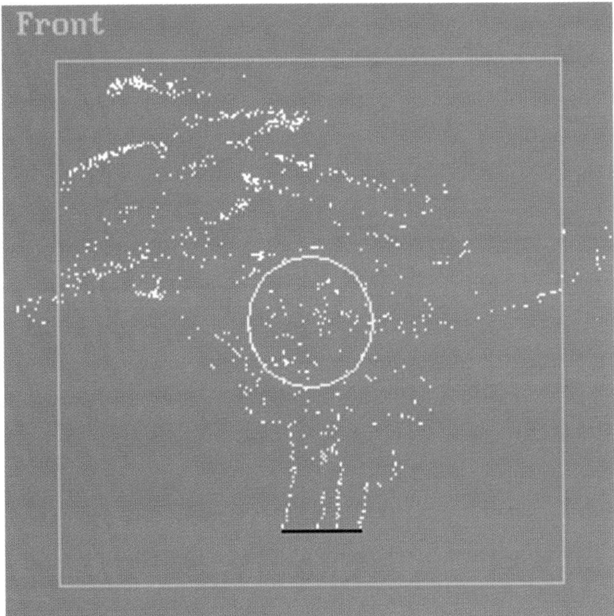

The Whorls preview and adjustment icon.

Cloudy Presets [Cl] s, g (Soft Cloud, Ground Fog) — Automatically configures Vapor's parameters to produce a soft smoky or steamy effect. Cloudy is based on a few large particles, the use of the Square particle type, and the use of Mapping Special in conjunction with a special material map that must be applied to the particles.

Note: *All preset options are accessed through the Wispy, Voluminous, Firey, and Cloudy dialog boxes, which are accessed by clicking on their associated buttons.*

Preferences — Enables a message that alerts you if you neglect to update the secondary motion data. The Preferences dialog box also enables you to select a custom interface color palette and edit the random seed number used to calculate the particles.

Emitter Parameters

Flow Type [Ft] r, p, s, b (Radial, Parallel, Stream, Burst) — Sets the particle emission characteristics and timing for the effect. Radial enables you to adjust the particle emission by adjusting a Preview icon consisting of several vector arrows that radiate away from the emitter. Parallel allows you to adjust the particles to flow in parallel lines away from the emitter. Stream and Burst determine the order that particles flow from the emitter vertices. Stream releases particles sequentially from each vertex, and Burst releases particles from all emitter vertices simultaneously.

Strength [St] (0–200) — Specifies the distance that a particle travels as a percentage of the bounding cube or object. Strength is influenced by Rise along with the Flow Type and its associated vector arrows.

Duration [D] (1–100/inf.) — Sets the total time in frames that the Strength value effects particle momentum. Infinity (inf.) is a special case in which Strength is applied to the particle during its entire life.

Chaos [Ce] (0–20) – Scatters the particles by specifying a random offset for the particle as it is released from an emitter vertex.

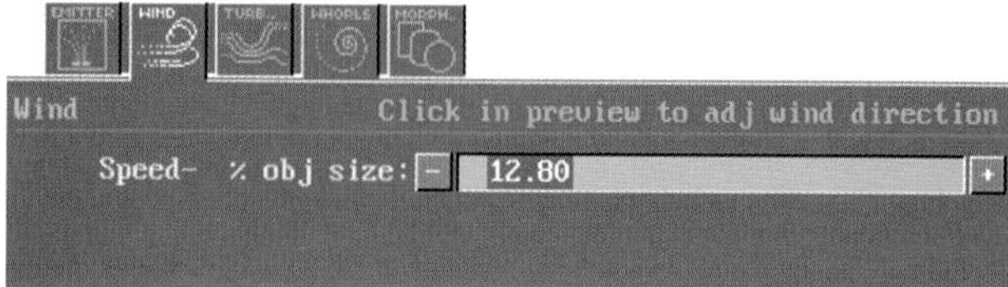

The Wind Index Card.

Wind Parameter

Speed [Sp] (0–200) — Specifies the wind speed as a percentage of the size of the bounding cube or object. Wind is a directional force that runs parallel to the Top Viewport. Wind direction is adjusted in the Preview window by rotating a yellow triangle to any angle around a green circle.

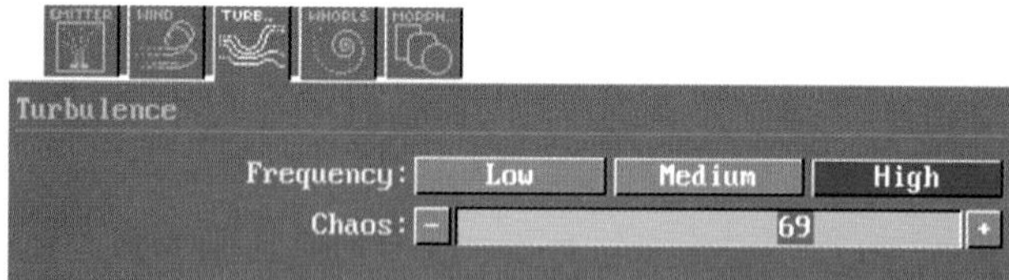

The Turbulence Index Card.

Turbulence Parameters

Frequency [Fr] l, m, h (Low, Medium, High) — Sets the Low, Medium, and High frequencies of an invisible complex 3D wavy pattern that perturbs the particles.

Chaos [Ct] (0–100) — Sets the amplitude of the wavy pattern.

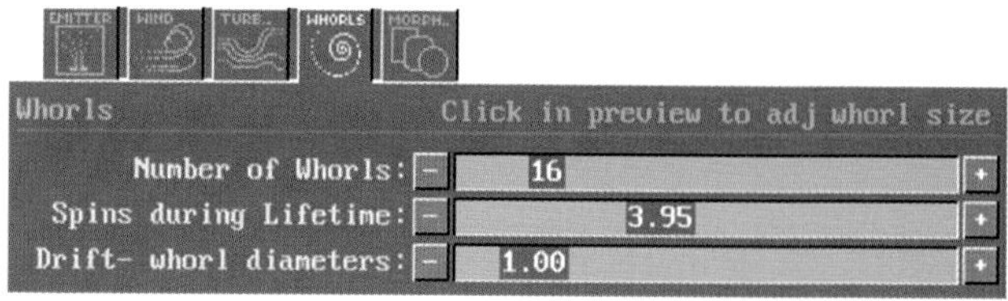

The Whorls Index Card.

Whorls Parameters

Number of Whorls [N] (0–100) — Sets the number of randomly spinning invisible spheres that move along the same overall path as the particles and perturb the particles. Whorls exist for approximately the same lifetime as do particles.

Spins during Lifetime [Spn] (0.00–10.00) — Sets the speed of whorl rotation, with higher speeds scattering the particles.

Drift [Dr] (0.00–10.00) — Sets the whorls to drift in a perpendicular path with respect to the particle's path. The drift value specifies a distance factor for the drift, with a setting of 3 producing a whorl distance that is three times that of the whorl diameter. The whorl diameter is set in the Preview window by resizing a yellow circle. Greater whorl diameters and drift values scatter the particles.

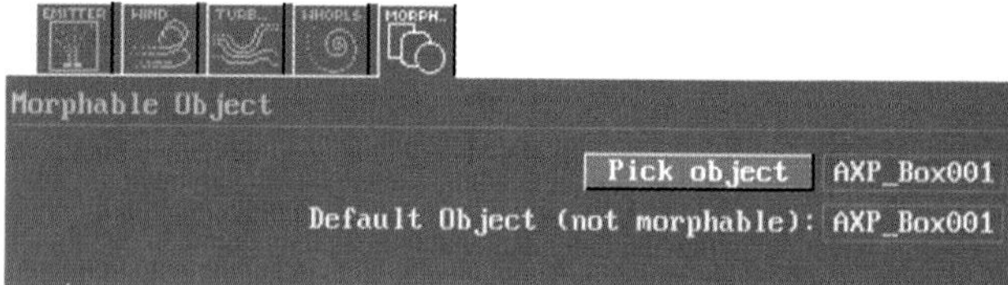

The Morphable Object Index Card.

Morphable Object Parameter

Pick object — Specifies an emitter cube as a morph target. This enables you to, for instance, animate the location of your particle emitter.

VAPOR cont

Yost Group | **\vapor** | **VAPOR_I.AXP**

Cloudy preset

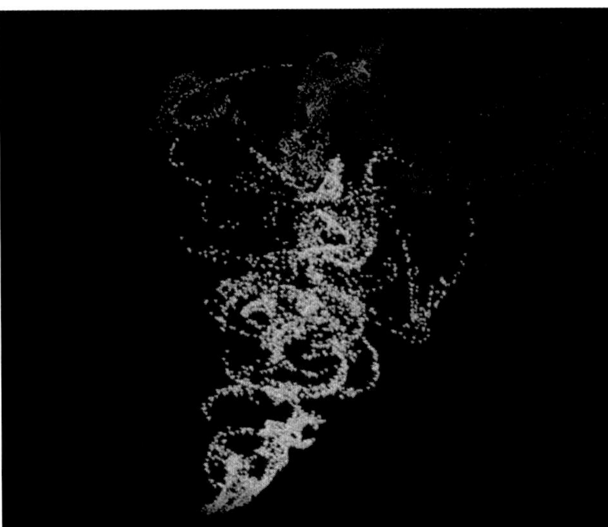

Cigar smoke preset

Vapor produces numerous animated soft smoke effects and clouds along with sharp curvilinear effects.

VORTEX3D

Schreiber Instruments | **\vortex3d** | **VORTEX_I.AXP**

Summary

Vortex3D is a particle system that can be used to simulate effects ranging from objects spiraling into a black hole to dust tornadoes and bubbles being sucked down a drain. Vortex3D uses a flow field to move objects along a spiral path toward the vortex center. By setting flow direction to Up, particles can be forced away from the vortex center and sent spiraling outward. Because Vortex3D uses an ASC file to specify the particle mesh, particles can be virtually any shape. Controls are provided to specify the amount of particle rotation in the vortex, the size of the vortex origin, and the speed of the particles. When the particle reaches the edge of the AXP object, it is returned to its origin point or a random point along the vortex where it begins a new vortex cycle.

Vortex3D Parameters

Number of particles [#] (1–8,000) — Sets the total number of particles.

Object/Particle size ratio [S] (.001–.5) — Sets the size of the particles in relation to the AXP object.

Start X,Z [Sxz] (Circle, Ring) — Sets the particle emitter shape for the X and Z axes.

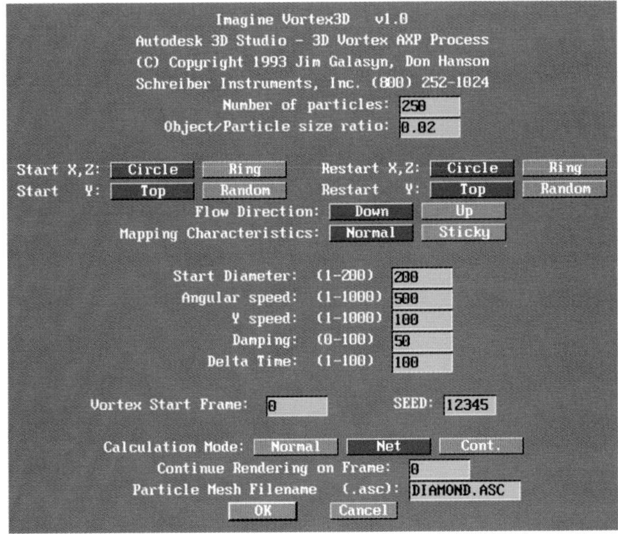

The Vortex3D dialog box.

Restart X,Z [Rxz] (Circle, Ring) — Sets the particle return point for the X and Z axes when the particle reaches the edge of the AXP object.

Start Y [Sy] (Top, Random) — Sets the particle emitter shape for the Y axis.

Restart Y [Ry] (Top, Random) — Sets the particle return point for the Y axis when the particle reaches the edge of the AXP object.

Flow Direction [F] (Down, Up) — Sets the direction of the particle flow.

Mapping Characteristics [M] (Normal, Sticky) — Sets the mapping coordinates to either the AXP object or the particle mesh object.

Start Diameter % [D] (1–200) — Sets the particle emitter size as a percentage of the AXP object.

Angular speed [As] (1–1,000) — Sets the amount and rate of particle rotation around the vortex.

Y speed [Ys] (1–1,000) — Sets the speed of particle flow in relation to the Y axis.

Damping [D] (0–100) — Sets the rate at which particles travel to the vortex center. Lower numbers produce a more cylindrical vortex, whereas higher numbers produce a more funnel-like vortex.

Delta Time [Dt] (1–100) — Sets the arbitrary time length between frames. Larger values produce particles that move more rapidly.

Vortex Start Frame [Sf] — Sets the frame on which the particles will start. Negative numbers allow the particles to begin their move cycle before rendering begins.

SEED [Sd] — Sets the particle's start point with an arbitrary number. Each number produces a unique pattern.

Calculation Mode [Cm] (Normal, Net, Cont.) — Sets the sequential rendering method used to either render the vortex using one machine, render using a network, or to continue rendering a previous animation where it left off.

Continue Rendering on Frame [C] — Sets the frame on which to continue rendering when using the Cont. rendering mode. Also specifies the frame on which to begin rendering when using a negative start frame.

Particle Mesh Filename [Mf] (ASC format) — Sets the ASC file to use as the source geometry for each particle. The geometry must be saved in the process directory, and total face count for the entire particle system is limited by 3D Studio's 64,000 maximum face count.

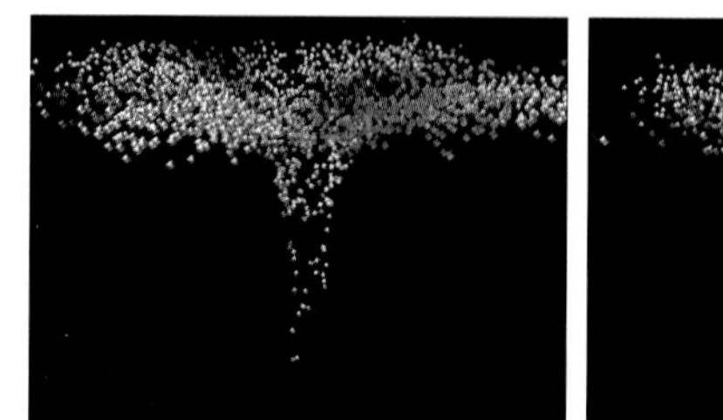

Frame 10 Frame 20

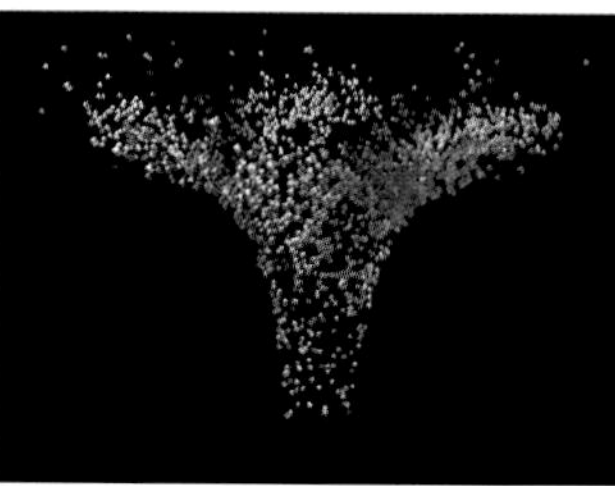

Frame 30

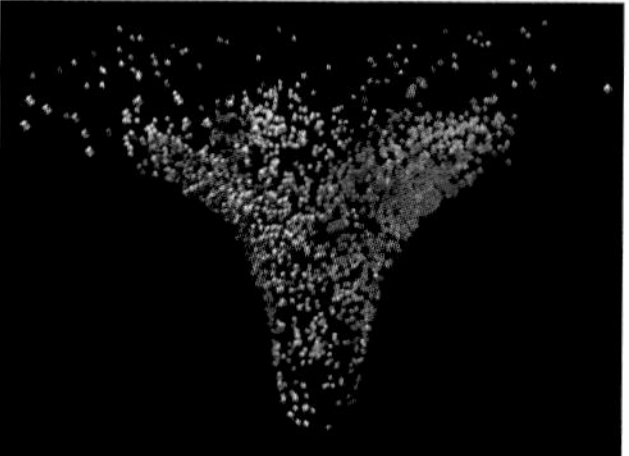

Frame 40

Vortex3D is a particle system that uses a flow field to move objects along a spiral path toward the vortex center.

afchk_i.ixp
afdiv_i.ixp
afdiv4_i.ixp
afstar_i.ixp
alpha_i.ixp
beep_i.ixp
blur_i.ixp
brick_i.ixp
brtcon_i.ixp
ckey_i.ixp
clamp_i.ixp
count_i.ixp
crack_i.ixp
crop_i.ixp
defld_i.ixp
dfilt_i.ixp
drip_i.ixp
ffaver_i.ixp
ffbw_i.ixp
ffex_i.ixp
ffmani_i.ixp
ffmat_i.ixp
ffneg_i.ixp
film_i.ixp
flare_i.ixp
flip_i.ixp
glow_i.ixp
hblur_i.ixp
hili_i.ixp
jpeg_i.ixp
legal_i.ixp
lenz_i.ixp
line_i.ixp

Two-Dimensional Special Effects

Image Processing External Processes (IXP) plug-ins create static and animated two-dimensional effects that modify or enhance rendered scenes or still images. IXP plug-ins offer a fantastic selection of effects including animated lens flares, color correction, ripples, waves, paint effects, fire, clouds, and explosions, just to name a few.

Some IXP effects simulate those found in many video editing suites such as those which spin, flip, rotate or create arrays of images or animations. You can select from transition effects that wipe between images using various patterns and geometric shapes, or key effects that enable you to key out foreground or background elements based on hue, luminance, or masks such as the alpha channel.

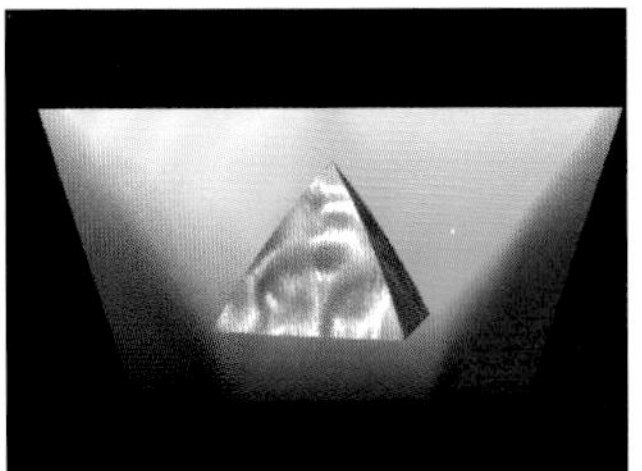

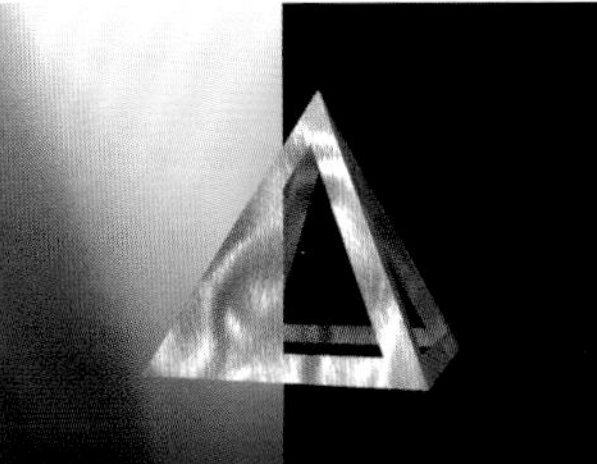

Page Flip Tranzition

IXP plug-ins Page Flip and Tranzition duplicate many of the effects found in video editing suites, including page flips and wipes.

Other IXP plug-ins simulate paint and optical phenomena. Included here are blurs, color filters, and animated paint strokes based on any conceivable size and shape. You can define dazzling lens flares not only for the flare color or size but also for the shape color and position of numerous secondary optical flares. You can work with multicolor glows or place sheets of shimmering stars over any scene object.

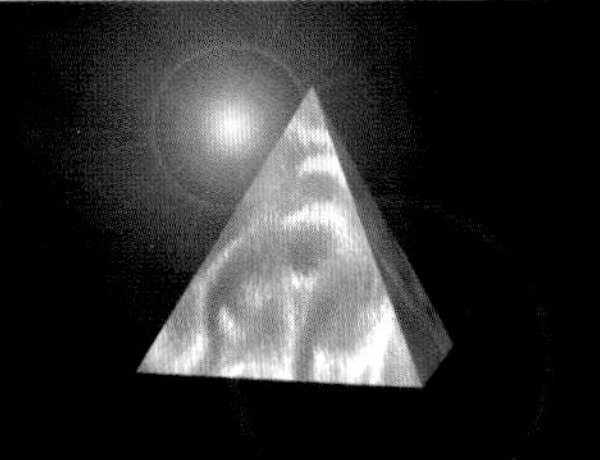

Pennello LenZFX

IXPs such as Pennello and LenZFX are capable of an enormous range of paint and optical effects that can give any image a painted look or add realistic lens flares and glows to any image or animation.

Some IXPs create effects that effectively mimic the real world. You can, for example, create realistic waves, rain drop effects, fiery explosions, and wispy clouds. Some effects even simulate television malfunctions, including ghosting, video tracking error, and signal loss.

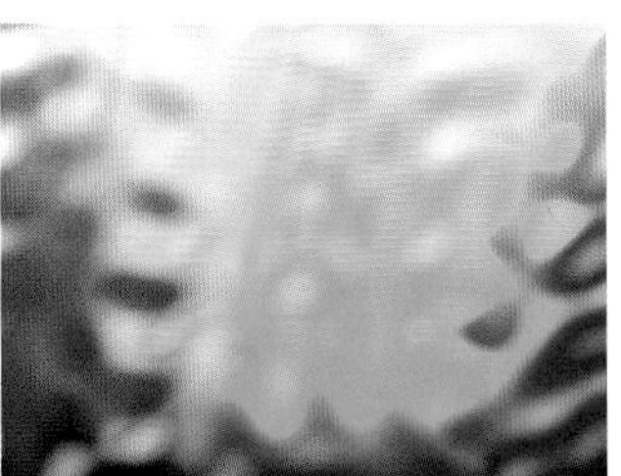

Mirage TV Reception Effects

IXPs such as Mirage and TV Reception Effects do an effective job of mimicking the real world by creating realistic wave effects or television signal loss.

Many IXP plug-ins enable you to apply their effects to specific areas of an image by using alpha channel masks. This makes it possible to limit a ripple distortion or animated glow to specific scene objects or object areas rather than the entire frame.

As with many IPAS plug-ins, IXPs are generally at their best when used in multiples, using either several passes through the same plug-in or several IXPs in combination. Often, the average effects produced by several single plug-ins are world-shaking when combined effectively.

Using IXP Plug-Ins

Before you use an IXP plug-in, be sure that it is properly installed using its installation program or instructions. Furthermore, be sure to read and follow any accompanying instructions exactly. Attempting to shortcut this process, particularly with complex plug-ins, is a mistake. At the least you will likely receive regular error messages as the plug-in attempts to find its resource files, or the plug-in could either cause a crash or simply fail to run.

For those times when no installation program or documentation is available, copy the plug-in—*XXXXXX*_I.IXP—into your 3D Studio \Process directory.

IXP plug-ins are set up in the Keyframer using the Video Post dialog box, which is accessed using the Render/VideoPost command and clicking in the camera view you want to render. Video Post is 3D Studio's compositing module, which is used for a range of tasks from layering multiple animations to applying traveling mattes. The Video Post dialog box is divided into three essential areas: the Queue window at left, the frames grid at right and the control buttons at the bottom.

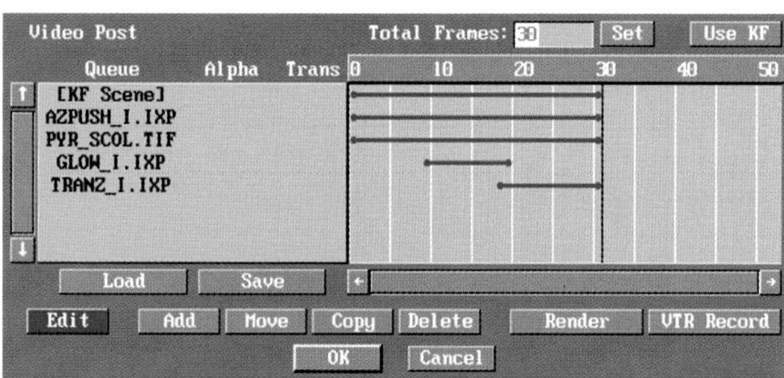

IXP plug-ins are applied via the Video Post dialog box. The Queue column sequences the current Keyframer animation with images, animations, and IXP plug-ins.

The Queue window consists of a list of all entries that are included in the current Video Post sequence. This includes Keyframer scenes, images, animated sequences, and effects along with their associated alpha masks and transitions.

Queue entries are added by highlighting the Add button and clicking in the Queue column. By default, this adds a `[KF Scene]` entry. You then click on the Edit button to bring up the Queue Entry Dialog box. You then highlight the Process button and click on the button to its right. This displays the IXP Selector, which enables you to scroll through your installed IXP plug-ins and click on the name of the IXP you want to use. Click on OK and the plug-in name appears in the button to the right of the Process button.

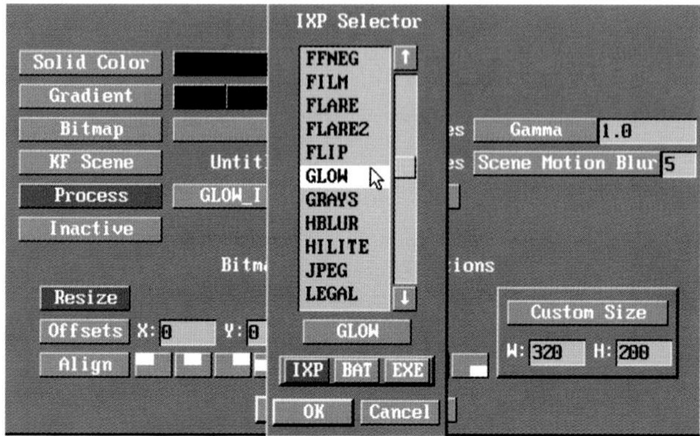

From the Queue Entry dialog box, a click on the button to the right of the highlighted Process button brings up the IXP Selector, from which you can select any installed IXP plug-in.

To adjust any IXP plug-in, click on the Setup button to the right of the IXP name to display the IXP's dialog box. These dialog boxes range from very basic, offering no parameters at all, to those that spawn numerous dialog boxes, each jammed with pull-down menus, sliders, numeric fields, and preview windows.

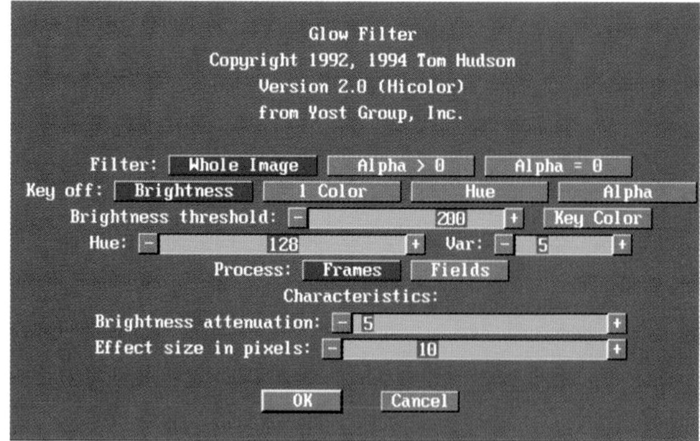

A typical IXP dialog box consists of sliders, buttons, and numeric fields along with color selection buttons that access the 3D Studio color picker. The current IXP dialog is accessed by clicking on the setup button to the right of the IXP name.

With all your plug-in parameters set, exit the IXP dialog box by clicking on its OK button, and click on OK in the Queue Entry dialog box. This returns you to the Video Post dialog box. To see the results of your IXP edits, click on the Render button and, via the Render Video Post Animation dialog box, you can render a single frame, segment, range, or all as desired.

Note: *If you plan to use alpha channel masking with IXP plug-ins, be sure to set Render/Setup /Options Render Alpha to Yes. Also be sure that Alpha has been added to the Video Post queue via the alpha control column.*

The IXP Reference

The IXP plug-ins are listed alphabetically, with the product name in bold type at the top of each page. The color bar below the plug-in name lists the plug-in file name, such as GLOW_I.IXP. The *3D Studio IPAS Plug-In Reference* CD-ROM path name and vendor are shown as well. The CD-ROM subdirectory contains any sample files along with demonstration versions of the plug-ins where possible.

The text is divided into two areas: an overview and a parameter listing. The overview provides a summary look at the plug-in's characteristics and capabilities. The parameter listing displays the name of each parameter in bold type along with its corresponding abbreviation in brackets. The following is an example parameter listing:

Horiz Edge Effect [He] p,s, (plain, striated) (0–100%) — Specifies a sharp or ragged edge for the transition. The sliders control the width of the striated edge.

The bracketed abbreviations may be followed by any parameter modifiers along with their abbreviations. Where applicable there is an adjustment range in parentheses followed by a description of each parameter function.

Each plug-in is illustrated with a screen capture of its dialog box or boxes and multiple sample images. The IXP plug-ins were applied to one of several test images based on a stainless steel pyramid set on a triangular color gradient. Variations on this include a wireframe pyramid and several background variations including the color gradient alone.

Solid pyramid

Wire pyramid

Two of the variations on a pyramid that were used as base images for the IXP effects.

The project files used to create the sample images, along with the Video Post files, are on the CD-ROM in the \IXP directory.

Each figure has the parameter abbreviations and the values used to create that effect. The specific effect variations shown were chosen to represent as broad a range of variation as space permitted. They also were chosen on the basis of providing IXP plug-in users shortcuts and starting points for creating unique, interesting, and useful effects.

The IXP sample images are provided in their final rendered form at 498x366x24 bits. These images are located on the CD-ROM in the directory specified in the information bar at the beginning of each plug-in.

ADD STAMP

TFSTMP_I.IXP **\addstamp** **Schreiber Instruments**

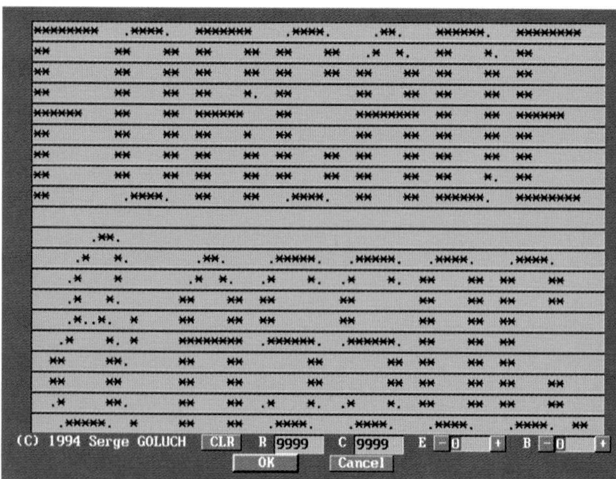

The Add Stamp dialog box.

Yellow logo lower right

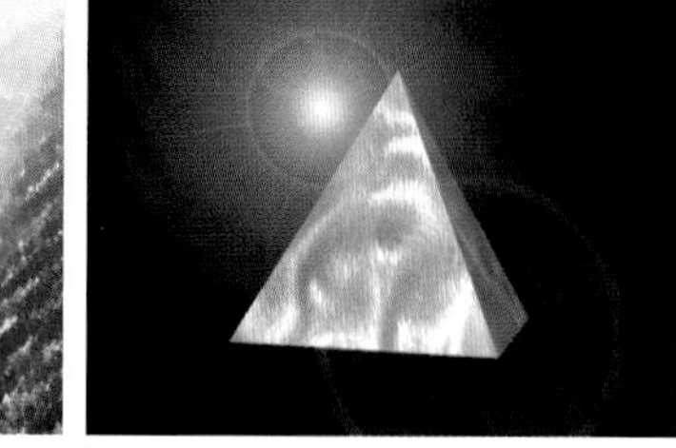

Black logo upper left

Add Stamp enables you to place a custom bitmap on the image.

Summary

Add Stamp is part of the Imagine Tool Factory package. It overlays a small bitmap on the image. You define the bitmap within the Add Stamp program using asterisk, period, and space characters. These characters represent pixels in the bitmap and are stamped onto your image at the specified location. An asterisk represents a pixel, a period represents a partially transparent pixel, and a space represents a fully transparent pixel. This gives you on, off, and in between (for anti-aliasing). You can set the color used and the location for the bitmap. There are a set of 16 animated special-effect treatments that include negation, inversion, transparency, scrolling, and animated background. The main use for Add Stamp is to add labels, logos, and copyright statements to a batch of images.

Add Stamp Parameters

Stamp design [S] — Twenty rows of 70 characters for designing your bitmap.
CLR [C1] — Color for the bitmap.
Row [R] — Location in pixels of the bitmap.
Column [C] — Location in pixels of the bitmap.
Effect type [E] — Select 1 of 16 special effects.
Border type [B] — Select 1 of 5 borders.

ALPHA

ALPHA_I.IXP **\alpha** **Yost Group**

Autodesk 3D Studio Alpha Channel Viewer
Version 1.0
Copyright 1993 Tom Hudson. From Yost Group, Inc.
This is a Public Domain IPAS Routine. Not for Resale
OK Cancel

The Alpha dialog box.

Original image

Alpha channel

Alpha displays the alpha channel from an image.

Summary

Alpha is a plug-in that extracts the alpha channel from any image. You can optionally output the alpha channel to your screen or to a file. This enables you to view the alpha channel as an aid when troubleshooting alpha masking or for customizing the alpha channel for use in the Materials Editor. There are no parameters for the plug-in.

Summary

Animated Matrix A is part of the Imagine Math Factory package. It is an animated convolution filter whereby numbers in a 3-by-3 matrix are used to process pixel values; interestingly, the matrix numbers themselves change from frame to frame. The matrix represents the current pixel and its neighbors. Numbers in the matrix indicate shifts of the pixel values. Typically, the values for those pixels are added together and then divided or multiplied by another number (the scalar). The resulting color value is placed in the current pixel and the filter moves on to the next pixel. This filter enables you to select from division, multiplication, average, minimum, and maximum operations to apply to the matrix. You can set the scalar number and a bias number that shifts the final color value up or down.

When doing animations, you place values in a second 3-by-3 matrix. These values indicate the change per frame of each position in the matrix. As the frames are processed, these values are added to the previous matrix values, thereby animating the structure of the effect. You also can animate the strength of the effect by setting a step value for the amount. The scalar and bias values also have step amounts and can be animated. The alpha channel can be used as a mask for this filter, although it uses the alpha channel only as an on/off mask.

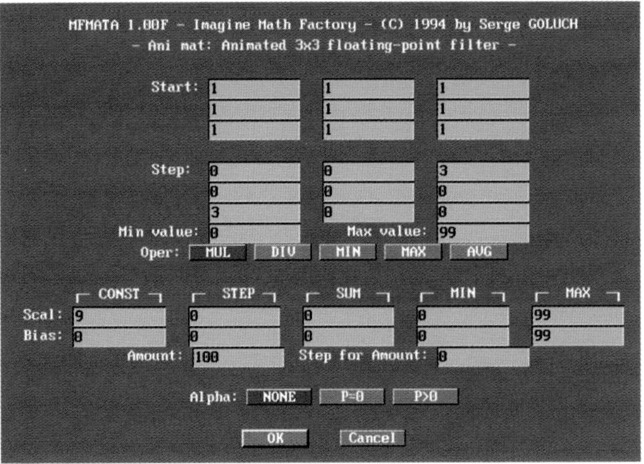

The Animated Matrix A dialog box.

Animated Matrix A Parameters

Filter design [F] — A 3-by-3 matrix of numbers that control the importance of different pixels in the calculations. Different settings here produce most of the variations in patterns.

Filter Step [Fs] — A 3-by-3 matrix of numbers that changes the values in the filter design matrix from frame to frame.

Min value and Max value [Mi] [Mx] — Clamps the matrix values to a specific range.

Operator [O] m, d, m, ma, a (mul, div, min, max, avg) — The operation to be done on the matrix of values.

Scalar [S] — The number that is used with the operator on the matrix.

Scalar step [Ss] — Change in the scalar value for each frame.

Scalar min and max [Sm] — Minimum and maximum values for scalar. Values beyond these limits are clipped.

Bias [B] — Shifts the final color value after the calculations.

Bias step [Bs] — Change in the bias value for each frame.

Bias min and max [Bn] [Bx] — Minimum and maximum values for bias. Values beyond these limits are clipped.

Amount [A] (0–100%) — Strength of the effect.

Step for Amount [P] — Change in the amount from frame to frame.

Alpha [Al] n, =0, >0 (none, =0, >0) — None applies the effect to the entire image, =0 applies the effect outside the alpha channel, and >0 applies the effect inside the alpha channel.

Frame 0

Frame 2

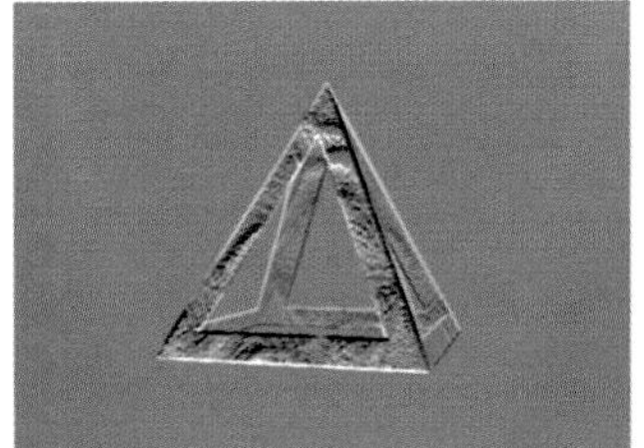

Frame 4

Frame 6

Animated effect from a normal image to an edge-detected image.

ANIMATED MATRIX B

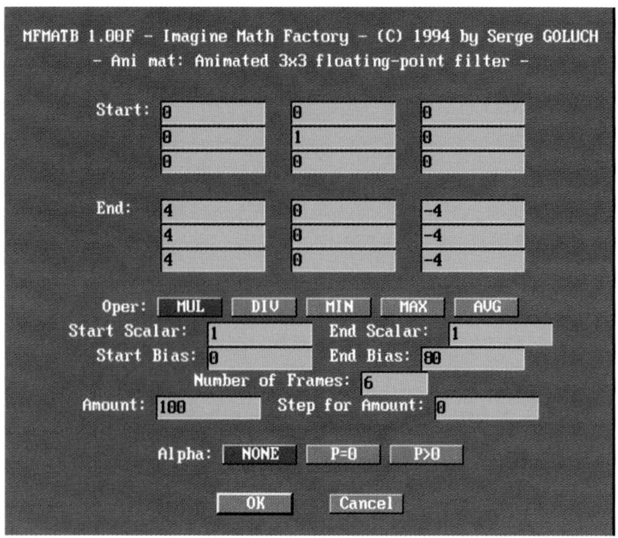

The Animated Matrix B dialog box.

Summary

Animated Matrix B is part of the Imagine Math Factory package. It is similar to Animated Matrix A, but is much simpler to use. It is a animated convolution filter whereby numbers in a 3-by-3 matrix are used to process pixel values, and the numbers themselves change from frame to frame. The matrix represents the current pixel and its neighbors. Numbers in the matrix indicate shifts of the pixel values. Typically, the values for those pixels are added together and then divided or multiplied by another number (the scalar). The resulting color value is placed in the current pixel and the filter moves on to the next pixel. This filter enables you to select from division, multiplication, average, minimum, and maximum operations to apply to the matrix. You can set the scalar number and a bias number that shifts the final color value up or down.

When doing animations, you place values in a second 3-by-3 matrix. These values indicate the final values for each position in the matrix. As the frames are processed, the original matrix's values are adjusted toward the final matrix's values, thereby animating the structure of the effect. You also can animate the strength of the effect by setting a step value for the amount. The scalar and bias values have beginning and ending values and can be animated. The alpha channel can be used as a mask for this filter, although it uses the alpha channel only as an on/off mask.

Animated Matrix B Parameters

Filter Start [S] — A 3-by-3 matrix of numbers that control the initial importance of different pixels in the calculations. Different settings here produce most of the variations in patterns.

Filter End [E] — A 3-by-3 matrix of numbers that set the final matrix in the animation. Filter Start settings are changed frame by frame to match these settings.

Operator [O] (mul, div, min, max, avg) — The operation to be performed on the matrix of values.

Start Scalar [Ss] — The initial number that is used with the operator on the matrix.

End Scalar [Es] — Ending value for an animated scalar.

Start Bias [Sb] — Starting value that shifts the color value after the calculations.

End Bias [Eb] — Ending value for animated bias.

Number of Frames [F] — Number of frames in the animation.

Amount [A] (0–100%) — Strength of the effect.

Step for Amount [P] — Change in the amount from frame to frame.

Alpha [Al] n,=0,>0 (none,=0,>0) — None applies the effect to the entire image, =0 applies the effect outside the alpha channel, and >0 applies the effect inside the alpha channel.

Frame 0

Frame 2

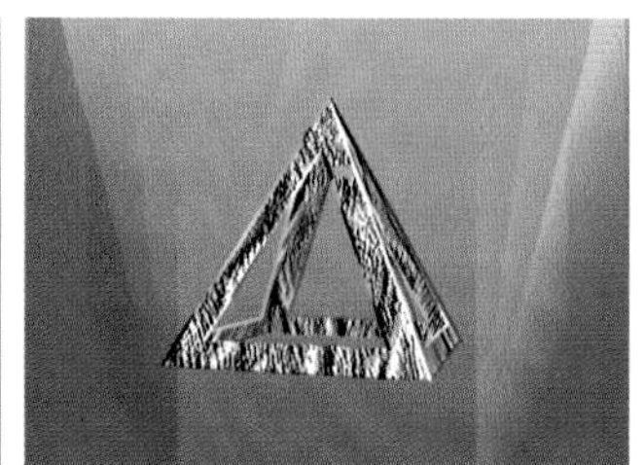

Frame 4

Frame 6

Animated effect from normal image to vertical edge detection.

ANIMATED TRANSFORMATION

Schreiber Instruments \anitrans **FFBW_I.IXP**

[C1]white

[R]0 [B]0 [C1]cyan

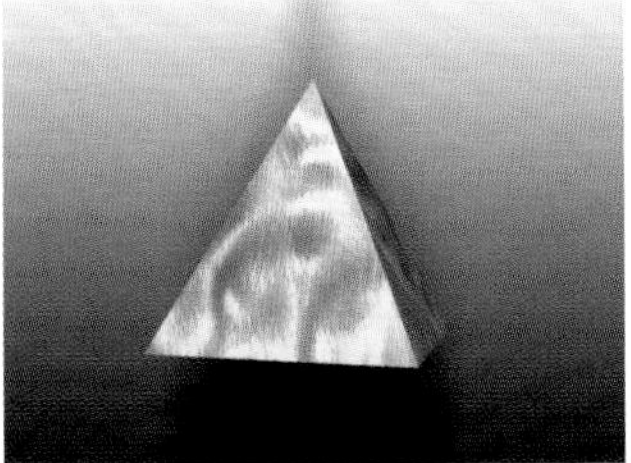
[G]0 [C1]yellow

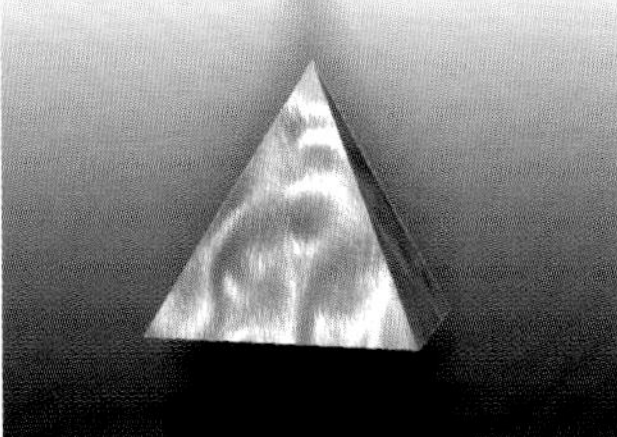
[A]=0

Grayscale and tinting effects.

Summary

Animated Transformation is part of the Imagine Filter Factory package. This is a grayscale and color tinting filter. You can convert a color image to grayscale or to a grayscale tinted with a color. You also can animate a change in tint from one color to another. If your tinting color is black, it will darken the image to black. You can use the input weight controls to subtract out a percentage of one or more color channels before processing t he image. This enables you to shift the effect of the tinting. You can use the alpha channel to mask the effect. This plug-in uses the alpha channel only as an on/off mask.

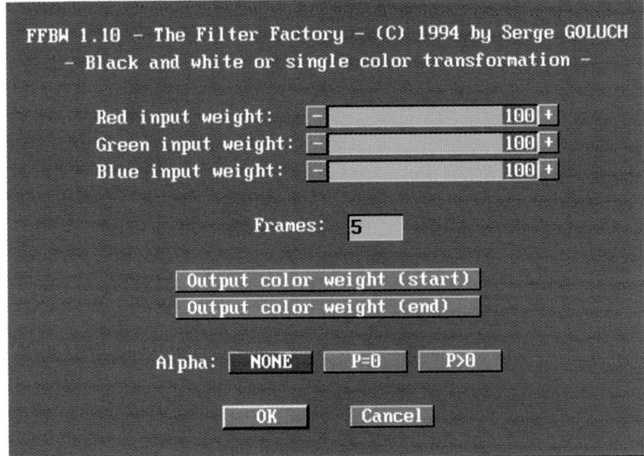

The Animated Transformation dialog box.

Animated Transformation Parameters

Red input weight [R] (0–100%) — Color shift the source image using the red channel.
Green input weight [G] (0–100%) — Color shift the source image using the green channel.
Blue input weight [B] (0–100%) — Color shift the source image using the blue channel.
Frames [F] (3–999) — Spreads the effect over this number of frames.
Output color weight start [C1] — Tinting color for the first frame. Use white for grayscale. Darker colors darken the output.
Output color weight end [C2] — Tinting color for the last frame.
Alpha [A] n,=0,>0 (none,=0,>0) — None applies the effect to the entire image, =0 applies the effect outside the alpha channel, and >0 applies the effect inside the alpha channel.

BEEP

Animation & Grafik \beep **BEEP_I.IXP**

Summary

This is a utility for video post-processing that generates an audible indicator at the end of a render. It has two controls: one determines whether it beeps between every frame or only after the last frame has been rendered, and the other control sets the number of beeps. If you really want to keep track of your processing, you can place multiple copies at different places in your queue and get beeps after each process finishes. Beep has no graphic output.

Beep Parameters

Beeps [B] (0–50) — Sets the number of beeps.
Mode [M] (Every frame, last frame) — Specifies when a beep is issued.

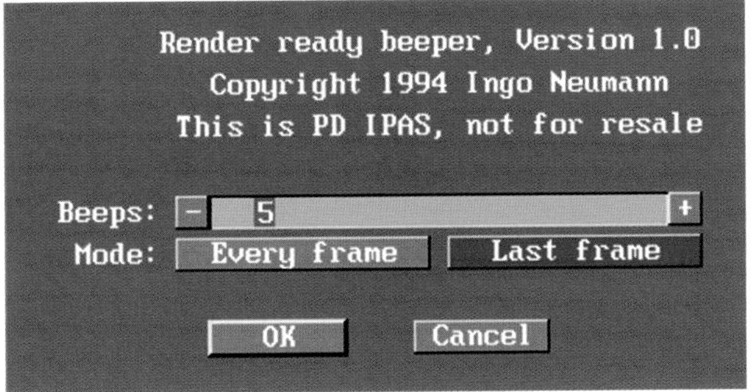

The Beep dialog box.

BLUR

BLUR_I.IXP **\blur** **Yost Group**

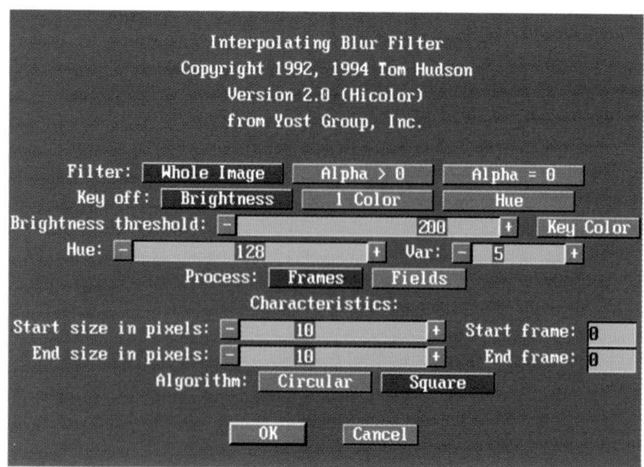

The Blur dialog box.

Summary

Blur is packaged with the Yost Group's Disk #1 Image Processing filters. The Blur filter can be used to defocus all or selected parts of an image to simulate depth of field. Blurring can be animated over a series of frames to simulate active focusing of a camera. The area of effect can be constrained based on brightness, color, or hue, or by using the alpha channel.

Blur Parameters

Filter: [F] i,=0,>0 (Whole Image, Alpha > 0, Alpha = 0) — Sets the general area of the image to be affected. If the alpha channel is used, the image must contain an alpha channel that is turned on in the Video Post queue. Blur uses the alpha channel only as an on/off mask. Whole applies the effect to the entire image, =0 applies the effect outside the alpha channel, and >0 applies the effect inside the alpha channel.

Key off: [Ko] (Brightness, 1 Color, Hue) — Specifies which pixels are blurred. Uses the brightness threshold, a key color, or a hue, with a variance range.

Brightness threshold [T] (0–255) — Sets the pixels to be filtered based on brightness.

Key Color [Kc] — Specifies the color of pixels to blur when keying off 1 Color.

Hue [H] (0–255) — Sets the hue of pixels to blur when keying off hue.

Var [V] (0–10) — Sets the amount of variance in hue allowed when keying off hue.

Process [P] f, fi (Frames, Fields) — Sets the effect to render to either frames or video fields.

Start and End size in pixels [Ss] [Es] (0–30) — Sets the amount of blur on the beginning and ending frames of an animated blur. Frames after the end frame are blurred according to the End size setting.

Start and End frame [Sf] [Ef] — Sets the beginning and ending frames of an animated blur effect.

Algorithm [A] c, s (Circular, Square) — Sets the blur quality.

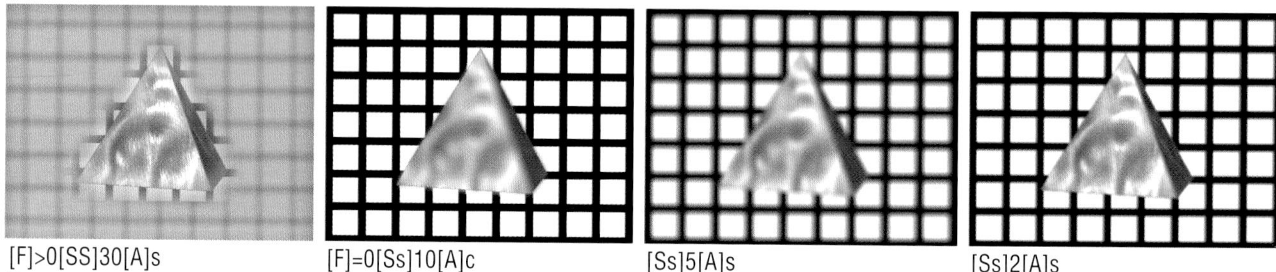

[F]>0[SS]30[A]s [F]=0[Ss]10[A]c [Ss]5[A]s [Ss]2[A]s

Though it produces superior results, the circular algorithm can significantly lengthen rendering time and is best used for smaller areas.

BRICK

Pyros Partnership **\brick** **BRICK_I.IXP**

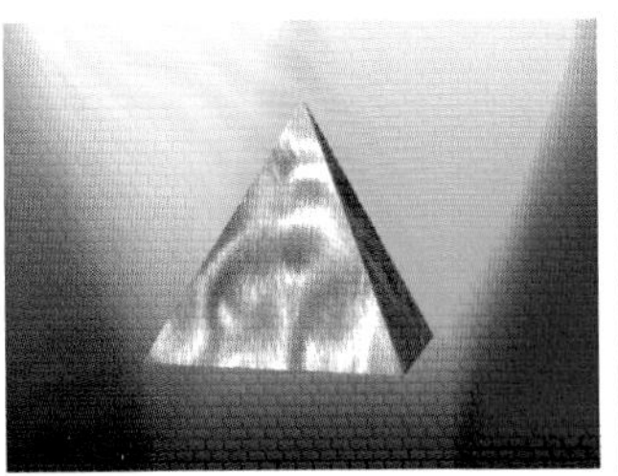

[G]8

[G]64

Brick produces a semitransparent pattern of bricks in an image. No control is given for size of the pattern or alpha masking.

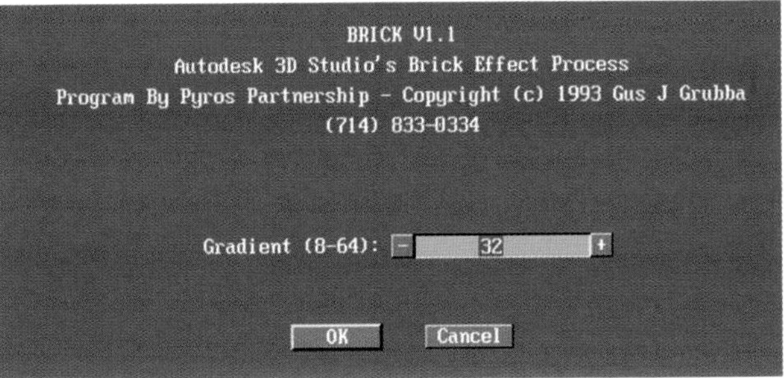

The Brick dialog box.

Summary

Brick is bundled with Pyros Partnership's Effects Library. Brick places a semitransparent brick pattern into an image or animation to simulate projection of the rendering on a brick wall.

Brick Parameters

Gradient [G] (8–64) — Sets opacity with which the pattern is applied.

BRTCON

Pyros Partnership **\brtcon** **BRTCON_I.IXP**

Summary

Brtcon is part of Pyro Partnership's Utilities package. It is a brightness and contrast control filter. You have independent control of brightness and contrast. Contrast changes can be calculated using two different methods: the absolute method does a linear contrast change, whereas the derivative method is less linear and will generally produce a smoother effect on gradients. You can mask Brtcon's effect with the alpha channel. This plug-in uses the alpha channel only as an on/off mask. Brtcon has a test mode that affects only the top half of the image, enabling you to see both the processed image and the original image at the same time.

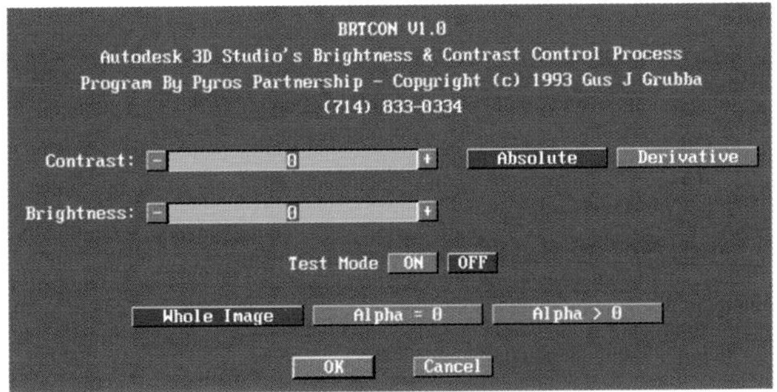

The Brtcon dialog box.

Brtcon Parameters

Contrast [C] (–128–127) — Contrast shift.
Brightness [B] (–128–127) — Brightness shift.
Contrast method [M] a, d (Absolute, Derivative) — Method of calculating contrast changes.
Alpha [A] w,=0,>0 (Whole Image,=0,>0) — Whole applies the effect to the entire image, =0 applies the effect outside the alpha channel, and >0 applies the effect inside the alpha channel.

[C]90 [M]a

[C]90 [M]d

[C]50 [B]-90 [A]>0

[C]87 [B]90

Absolute and derivative methods, alpha masking, and brightness adjustment.

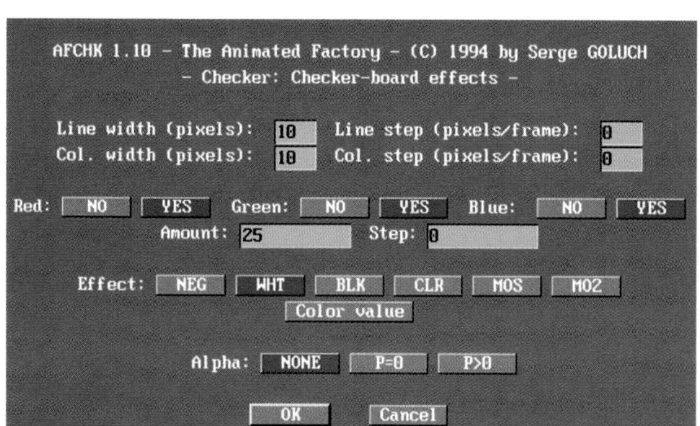

The Checker dialog box.

Summary

Checker is part of the Imagine Animated Factory. It overlays a checkerboard pattern on your image. You can specify the size of the checkers in pixels and restrict the effect to one or more color channels. The checkers can be white, black, negative, or any solid color. They also can be one of two random mosaic patterns. The pattern is blended into your image at any density from 0 to 100 percent. Both density and checker size are animatable. This filter uses the alpha channel only as an on/off mask.

Checker Parameters

Line width [Lw] (1–999) — Sets the height of the checkers in pixels.

Line step [Ls] (–99–99) — Sets size change per frame for lines.

Col. width [Cw] (1–999) — Sets the width of the checkers in pixels.

Col. step [Cs] (–99–99) — Sets size change per frame for columns.

Red, Green, Blue [R] [G] [B] (yes or no) — Applies the filter to the given color channel.

Amount [A] (0–100) — Sets the intensity percent of the effect.

Step [S] (–50–99) — Specifies size change per frame for both line and column.

Effect [E] — Color values for checker pattern.

Alpha [A] n,=0,>0 (none,=0,>0) — None applies the effect to the entire image, =0 applies the effect outside the alpha channel, and >0 applies the effect inside the alpha channel.

Frame0 Frame10

Frame20

Frame30

Animated fade in. [L]68 [C]84 [A]25 [S]25 [E]wht

Summary

Chromakey generates an alpha channel mask by keying on a specific hue and luminance in an image—for instance, a blue or green screen background. With Chromakey, video images can be combined with computer-generated 3D objects and scenes.

Chromakey provides deviation controls so that a range of values on either side of the masked values can be used to compensate for lighting or background variations. Chromakey also allows two key colors to be specified so that multiple items can be keyed-out in the same alpha mask. A blur variable can be set to smooth the transition at the edges of the original and chromakey images.

To use Chromakey as a single step in Video Post, the queue should be set up as follows: the image you want to chromakey, the Chromakey filter, the image to combine with the original, and the original image with Chromakey file selected as an alpha mask.

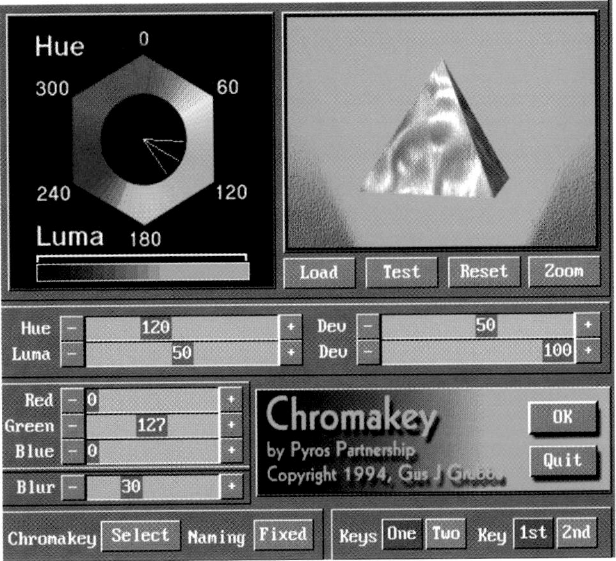

The Chromakey dialog box.

Chromakey Parameters

Hue [H] (0–360) — Sets the specific color hue to key on.
Luma [L] (1–100) — Sets the luminance of the specific color to key on.
Deviation [Hd] [Ld] (0–100) — Sets the variation in hue and luminance that is allowed in the key color.
Blur [B] (0–100) — Sets the blur at the edges of the alpha mask.
Chromakey [C] (Select) — Sets the name that the mask will be saved as.
Naming [N] f, i (Fixed, Inc) — Sets the naming type and numbering for creating mask files. Fixed uses the name you typed in [C] and Inc uses the 3D Studio XXXX0000 numbering convention for incremental frames.
Keys [K] 1, 2 (One, Two) — Sets the number of colors to key on.
Key [K#] 1, 2 (1st, 2nd) — Sets the active key when two keys are used.

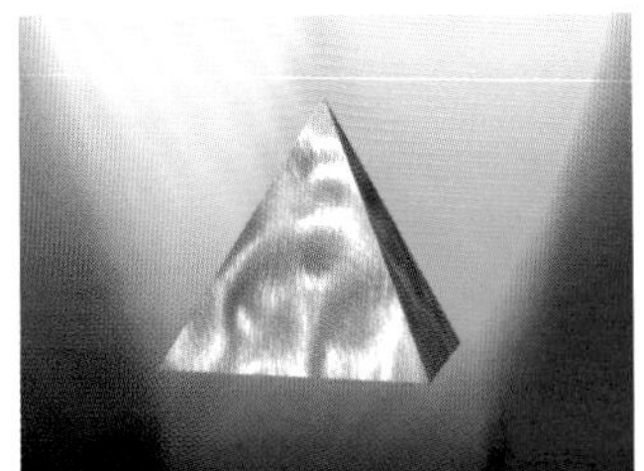
Original image

Chromakeyed image

Original image

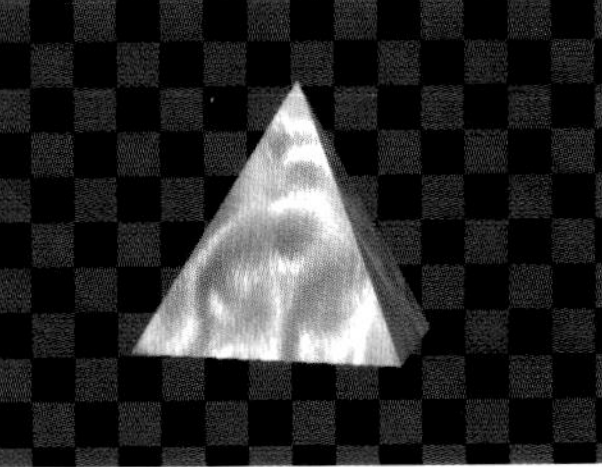
Chromakeyed image

The first pair of images shows two-color chromakeying. The second pair of images shows how deviance can be used to overcome inconsistencies in the key color.

CLAMP

CLAMP_I.IXP \clamp Yost Group

Image Luminance Clamp Process
Copyright 1992, 1993 Tom Hudson
Version 2.0 (Hicolor)
from Yost Group, Inc.

Upper limit [-] 20 [+]
Lower limit [-] 230 [+]
Clamp saturation to luminance? YES NO

OK Cancel

The Clamp dialog box.

Summary

Clamp is included with Yost Group's Special Effects Disk #2. It clamps image luminance to within an upper and lower limit. Inverting the limit settings produces a negative image.

Clamp Parameters

Upper limit [U] (0–255) — Sets the maximum luminance or upper luminance cutoff value.

Lower limit [L] (0–255) — Sets the minimum luminance or lower luminance cutoff value.

Clamp saturation to luminance [S] y,n (yes, no) — Applies the luminance clamp settings to saturation.

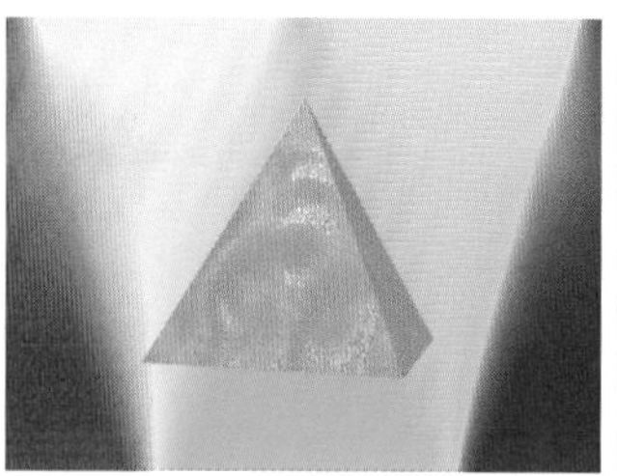

[U]160 [L]100 [S]n

[U]120 [L]100 [S]y

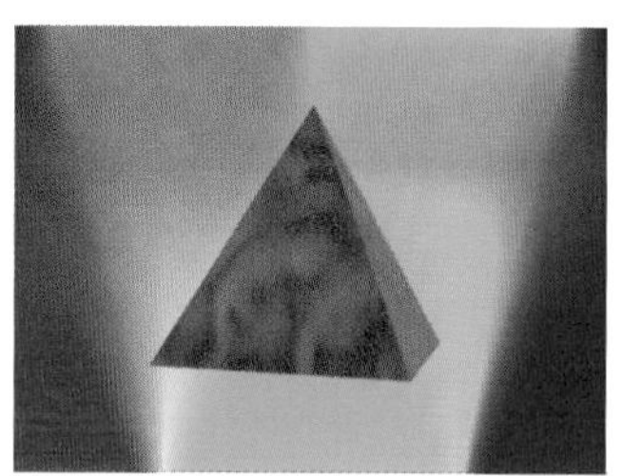

[U]40 [L]100 [S]y

[U]23 [L]230 [S]y

Clamp enables you to clip or effect specific ranges of luminance or saturation.

COLOR EXCHANGE

FFEX_I.IXP \colorxch Schreiber Instruments

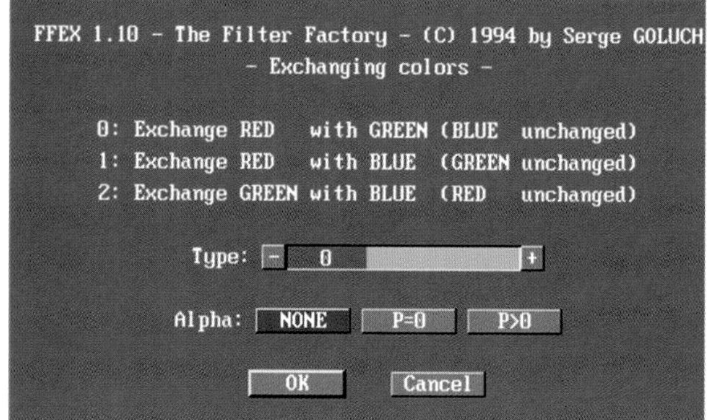

The Color Exchange dialog box.

Summary

Color Exchange is part of the Imagine Filter Factory package. It swaps one color channel for another. Color Exchange can swap the red channel for the green or the green for the blue. You can swap only two channels at a time. You can use the alpha channel to mask the effect. This filter uses the alpha channel only as an on/off mask.

Color Exchange Parameters

Type [T] (0,1,2) — Selects a pair of channels to swap: Red with Green, Red with Blue, or Green with Blue.

Alpha [A] n,=0,>0 (none,=0,>0) — None applies the effect to the entire image, =0 applies the effect outside the alpha channel, and >0 applies the effect inside the alpha channel.

COLOR EXCHANGE cont

Schreiber Instruments \colorxch FFEX_I.IXP

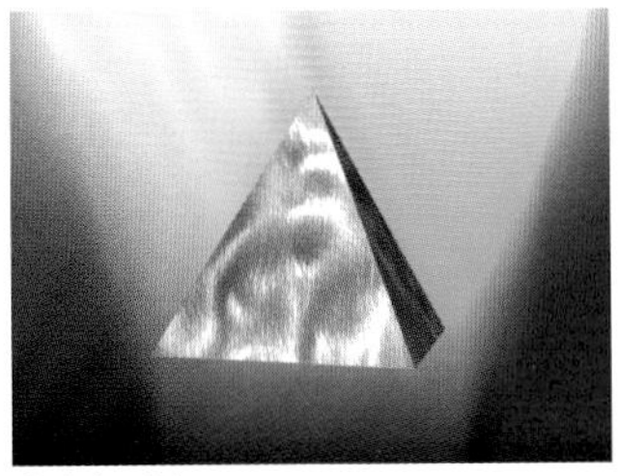

Original image [T]1

The original image and a Red with Blue swap.

COLOR STATISTICS

Schreiber Instruments \colrstat TFSTAT_I.IXP

Summary

Color Statistics is part of the Imagine Tool Factory package. It is intended as a tool for analyzing your images. It displays a histogram on top of your image showing the color distribution in that image. You can sort the histogram by hue, saturation, luminance, and frequency of occurrence. It also prints the frame number, resolution, and selected color statistics on the image.

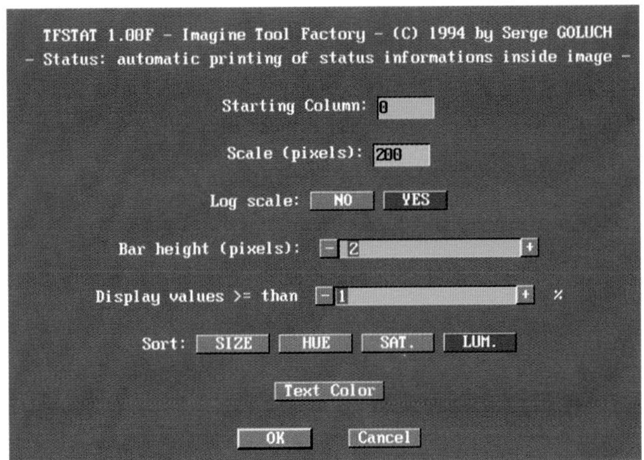

The Color Statistics dialog box.

Color Statistics Parameters

Starting Column [C] (0–99,999) — Distance from left edge to display histogram.
Scale [S] (10–99,999) — Length of the longest histogram bar.
Log scale [L] (yes, no) — Specifies a compressed logarithmic scale or linear scale.
Bar height [B] (1–20) — Height in pixels of individual bars.
Display values >= than [D] (1–100%) — Restricts values to the upper range.
Sort [So] sz, hu, sa, lm (size, hue, sat., lum.) — Quality used to sort histogram.
Text Color [C1] — Color of text printed on image.

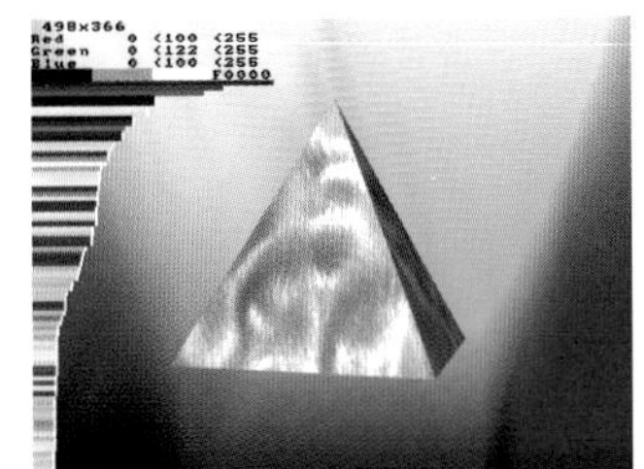
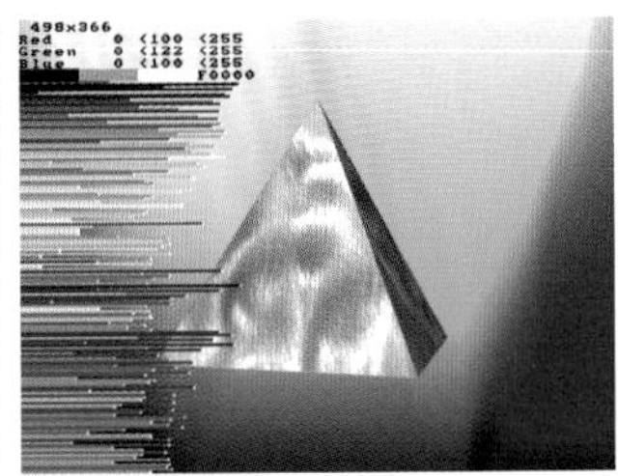

[B]4 [So]sz [L]n [B]2 [So]lm [L]y

Color statistics sorted by occurrence and by luminance.

COUNT

COUNT_I.IXP — \count — Navarro

The Count dialog box.

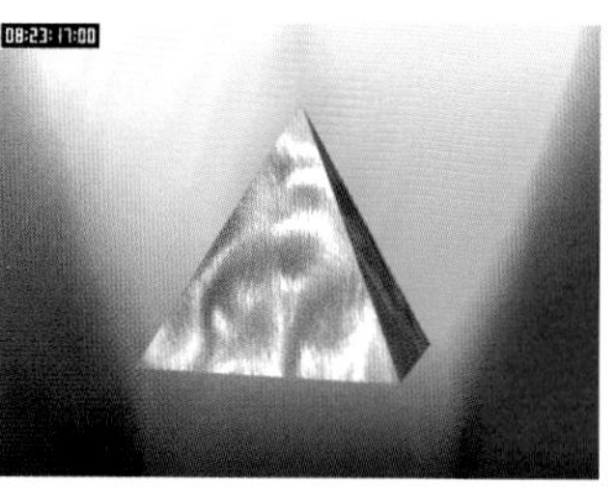
[S]6 [X]0 [Y]0

[S]5 [X]250 [Y]350

You can set the size and location of the counter.

Summary

Count is a digital time and frame counter that overlays time and frame information on your animation. You can set the starting time, specify one of three frame rates (24fps, 25fps, 30fps), choose from three sizes, and set the location and color of the counter. This program is useful in forensic animations and in tests for which you need to identify specific frames.

Count Parameters

Initial value [I] — Starting time in hours:minutes:seconds.
Frames per second [F] (24, 25, 30) — Sets Count's frame increment for the animation.
Counter size [S] 3, 5, 6 (3x5, 5x7, 6x12) — Size of the characters in pixels.
Position [P] — Location of the counter in pixels.
Background color [C1] — Background color of the counter.
Border color [C2] — Border color of the counter.
Text color [C3] — Text color of the counter.

CRACK

CRACK_I.IXP — \crack — Pyros Partnership

CRACK V1.1
Autodesk 3D Studio's Cracking Effect Process
Program By Pyros Partnership - Copyright (c) 1993 Gus J Grubba
(714) 833-0334
Crack Size (1-64): 24
Gradient (8-64): 24
Highlight: ON OFF
Whole Image | Alpha = 0 | Alpha > 0
Random | Pattern
OK | Cancel

The Crack dialog box.

Summary

Crack is bundled with Pyros Partnership's Effects Library. Crack places a semitransparent cracking and peeling pattern into an image or animation to simulate projection on an old plaster wall. This effect can be used to add noise to a rendering for which a computer-generated look is undesirable.

Crack Parameters

Crack Size [S] (1–64) — Sets the pattern density.
Gradient [G] (8–64) — Sets the pattern opacity.
Highlight [H] (on, off) — Switches highlighting of the pattern on or off.
Whole Image, Alpha=0, or Alpha >0 [I] [=0] [>0] — Whole applies the effect to the entire image, =0 applies the effect outside the alpha channel, and >0 applies the effect inside the alpha channel.

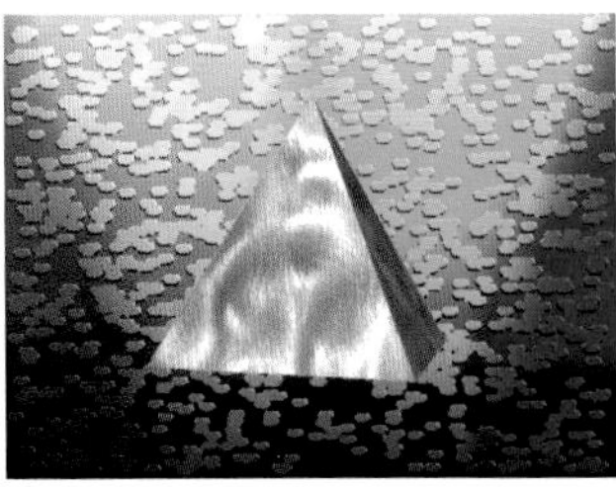

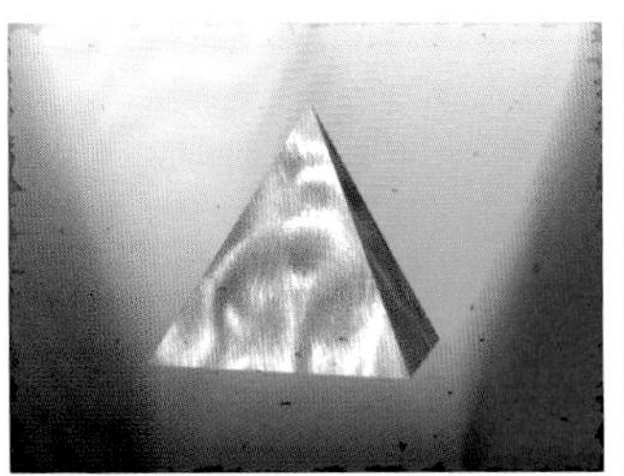
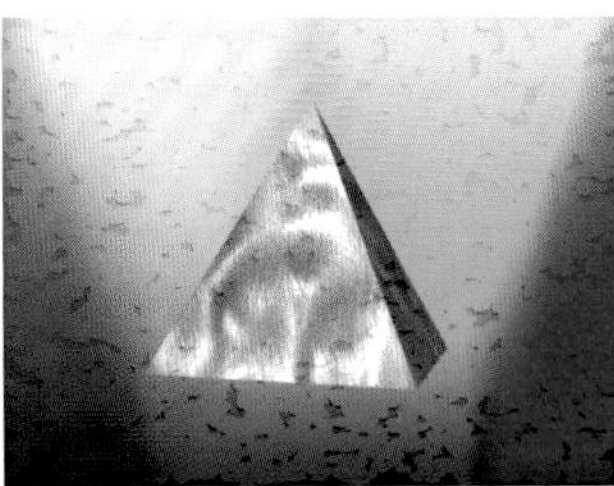

[S]1[G]64[H]on[=0] [S]64[G]64[H]on[=0] [S]50[G]45[H]off [S]20[G]25[H]off

Crack applies rips, tears, and cracks to an image to simulate aging. This effect can be useful when a computer-generated look is undesirable.

CROP

Grubba \crop CROP_I.IXP

Summary

Crop is a utility for limiting maximum brightness values for each color channel (RGB). You can set the upper cutoff point for each channel, and you can mask the effect using the alpha channel. The main uses for this are to limit illegal color for broadcast video and for CMYK separations. You also can use Crop to color shift the image and to darken the background of an object using alpha masking. This filter uses the alpha channel only as an on/off mask.

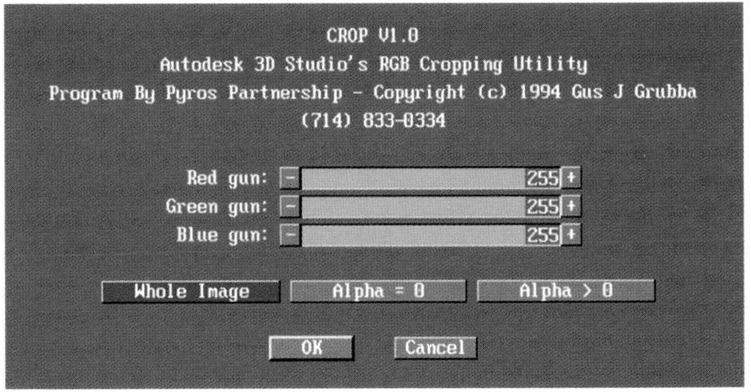

The Crop dialog box.

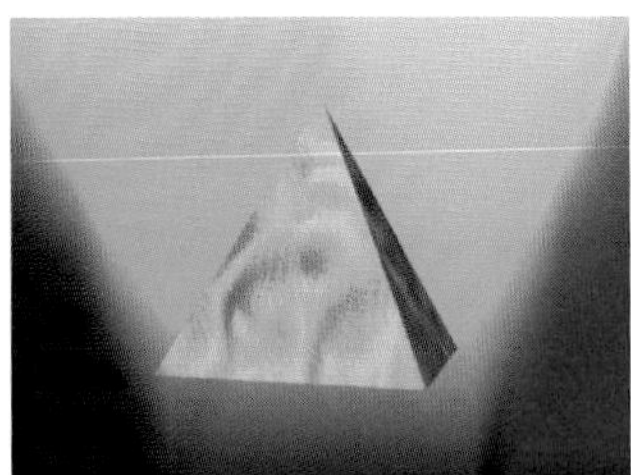
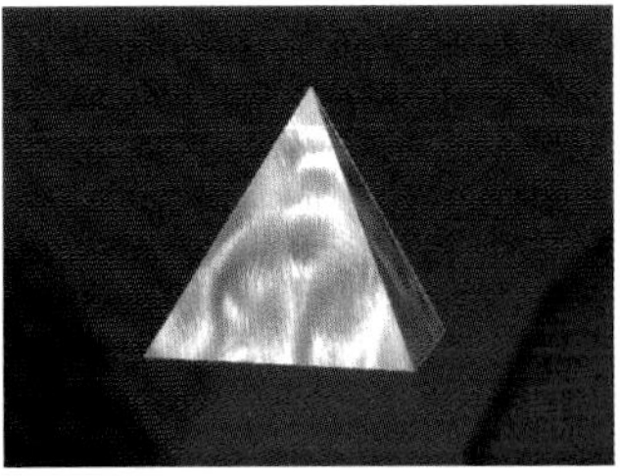

[R]25 [G]255 [B]255 [R]25 [G]25 [B]25 [A]=0

Color shifting and darkened background with alpha mask.

Crop Parameters

Red gun [R] (0–255) — Red channel limit.
Green gun [G] (0–255) — Green channel limit.
Blue gun [B] (0–255) — Blue channel limit.
Alpha [A] w,=0,>0 (whole,=0,>0) — Whole applies the effect to the entire image, =0 applies the effect outside the alpha channel, and >0 applies the effect inside the alpha channel.

CROSSHAIR GENERATOR

XHAIR_I.IXP | **\xhair** | **Yost Group**

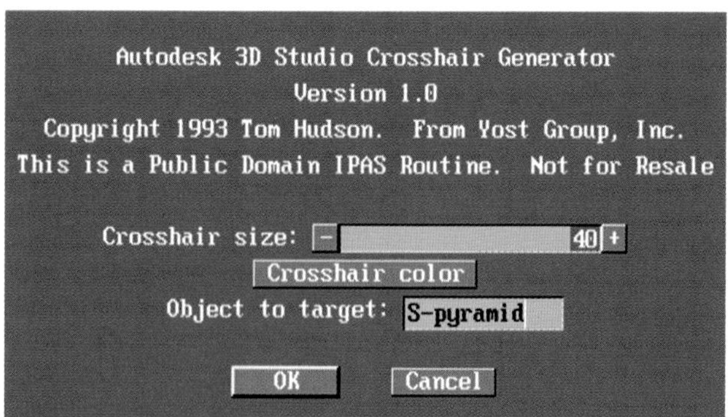

The Crosshair Generator dialog box.

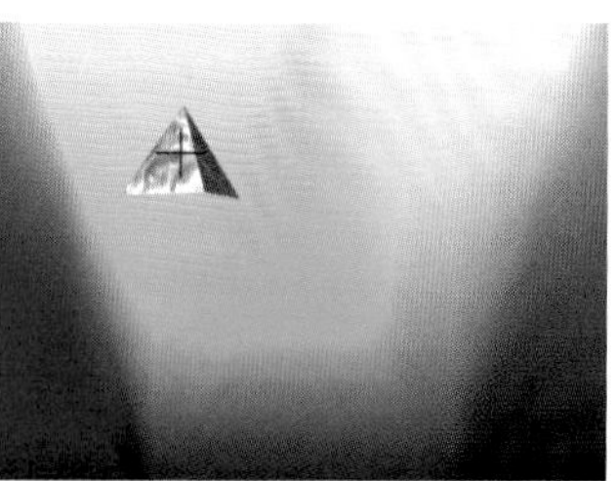

Frame 10 [S]40

Frame 25 [S]40

A crosshair following a moving object.

Summary

Crosshair Generator generates a simple plus sign or cross shape that automatically follows an object around in an animation. You can specify the size in pixels of the crosshair and its color. You must enter an object name. Because Crosshair works with object names, you cannot use a bitmap as a source image—you must render from the Keyframer scene.

Crosshair Generator Parameters

Crosshair size [S] (3–40) — Size of the crosshair in pixels.
Crosshair color [C1] — Color of the crosshair.
Object to target [O] — Object name to follow with crosshair.

DEFIELD

DEFLD_I.IXP | **\defield** | **Pyros Partnership**

DEFIELD V1.0
Autodesk 3D Studio's Field to Frame Process
Program By Pyros Partnership - Copyright (c) 1993 Gus J Grubba
(714) 833-0334
Blend? YES NO Field Order 0 1
OK Cancel

The Defield dialog box.

Summary

Defield is part of Pyros Partnership's Utilities package. It converts an interlaced by removing one
of the images of fields. Defield does this by deleting alternate scanlines (deinterlacing) and replacing them with either duplicates of the preceding line or by blending together the preceding line with the following line. Blending produces a better image at a slight cost in processing time. You must specify the field order as even or odd to tell the program which set of scanlines to keep.

Principal Defield Parameters

Blend? [B] (yes, no) — Blend the surrounding scanlines or duplicate the previous one.
Field Order [O] (0, 1) — Even or odd scanline ordering.

Interlaced original

Defielded result

Deinterlacing a video image to frames.

Summary

Dfilter is a 3x3 convolution matrix filter with both predefined and user-defined effects. The predefined effects are edge detection, blur, edge enhancement, orthogonal edging, and diagonal edging. You can create your own user-defined filter by entering numbers in the convolution matrix. It takes quit a bit of trial and error to achieve a specific effect.

The 3-by-3 convolution matrix used by these effects limits the strength of the effect. This is especially apparent in the blurs, which were too subtle to reproduce here. All the effects can be restricted to one, two, or all three color channels. This product does not use the alpha channel.

Dfilter Parameters

Filter matrix [R1] [R2] [R3] — The user-defined filter matrix rows.

Threshold to black [T] (0–750) — If the sum of a pixel's RGB values falls below this point, it is turned to black. This suppresses the scattering of dark pixels that often fill dark areas of the image.

Filter Line [F] (1–5) — Selects user-defined or one of the predefined filters.

Red, Green, and Blue Channel Active [R] [G] [B] (yes or no) — Applies the filter to the given channel.

Ramp Filter Effect? (no, in, out) — Static effect or fade the effect in or out.

Start and End Frame — Sets the beginning and ending frames for animated effect.

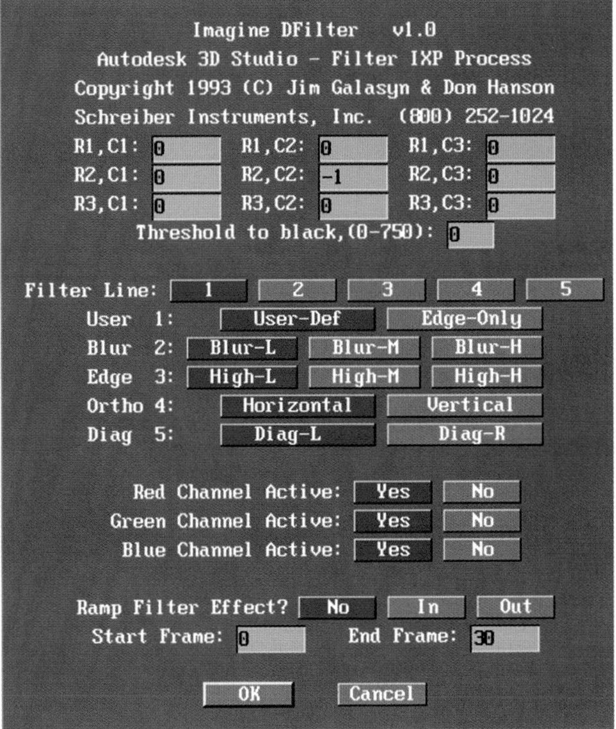

The Dfilter dialog box.

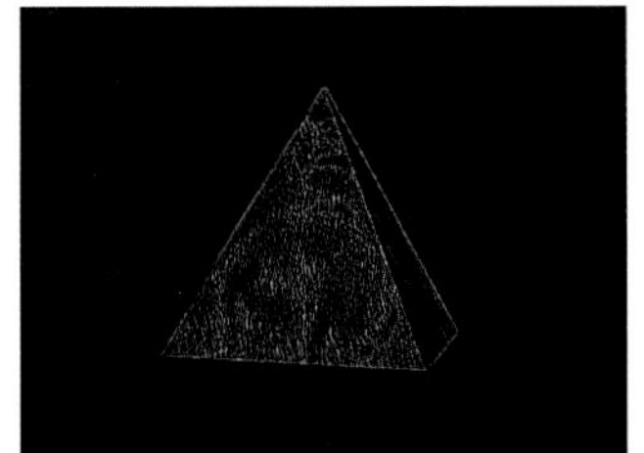

[F]1-edgeonly

[F]5-diagonal

Two predefined edge filters and two user-defined filters.

[F]1-userdef [R1]-1,-2,-1 [R2]0,0,0 [R3]1,2,1 [R]Y [G]Y [B]Y

[F]1-userdef [R1]-1,-2,-1 [R2]0,0,0 [R3]1,2,1 [R]Y [G]Y [B]Y

DIVIDE BY 4

AFDIV4_I.IXP | **\divid4** | **Schreiber Instruments**

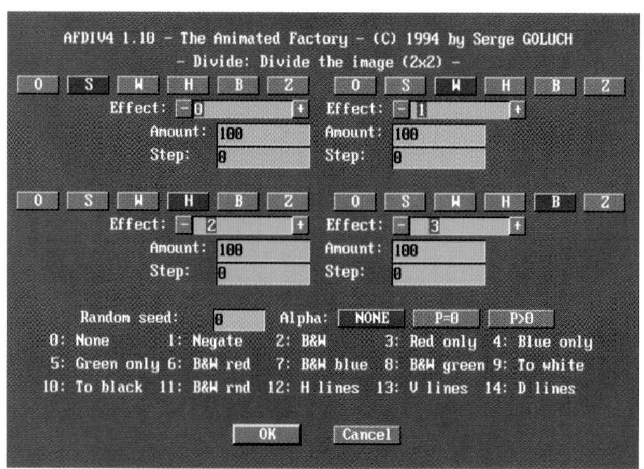

The Divide by 4 dialog box.

Summary

Divide by 4 is part of the Imagine Animated Factory. It divides the image into quadrants and applies a different effect to each. Each quadrant can contain a section of the original image or a complete, scaled-down version of the original. Quadrant effects include flipping, color tinting, color channel stripping, color overlays, random colors, and line pattern overlays. You can set and animate the strength of the effects. This filter uses the alpha channel only as an on/off mask.

Divide by 4 Parameters

Type [T] o, s, w, h, b, z — Sets the size and flipping settings for each quadrant.

Effect [E] (0–14) — Selects a predefined image effect for each quadrant.

Amount [Am] (0.0–100.0) — Sets the strength of the effects as a percentage.

Step [S] (–100–100) — Varies the amount of effect per frame.

Random seed [R] — Sets the seed number that controls the random color effect.

Alpha [A] w, =0, >0 (whole, =0, >0) — Whole applies the effect to the entire image, =0 applies the effect outside the alpha channel, and >0 applies the effect inside the alpha channel.

[T]0,0,0,0 [E]0,2,4,1

[E]0,1,1,1 [Am]100,25,50,100

[A]=0

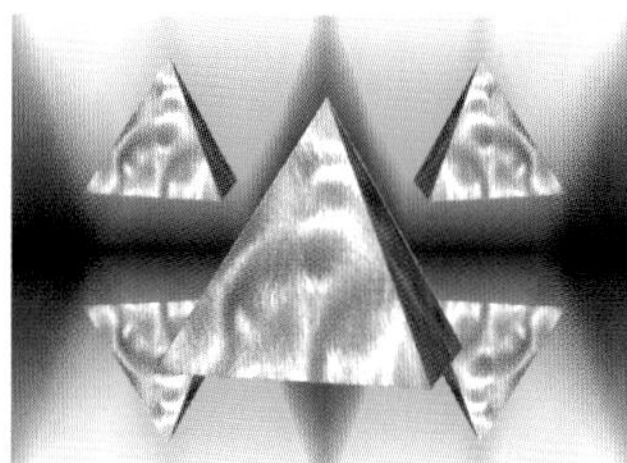
[T]S,W,H,B [A]=0

Quadrant effects, color negation, alpha masking, mirror small images with alpha masking.

DIVIDE BY ANY

AFDIV_I.IXP | **\dividany** | **Schreiber Instruments**

Summary

Divide by Any is part of the Imagine Animated Factory. It divides the image into a matrix of between 4 and 400 subimages and applies a different effect to each. Each subimage can contain a section of the original image or a complete, scaled-down version of the original. Effects include flipping, color tinting, color channel stripping, color overlays, random colors, and line pattern overlays. You also can set and animate the strength of the effects.

You apply image effects using a grid of 12 effects controls. These 12 controls are applied to the subimages in order. If your image includes more than 12 subimages, the settings cycle. You can select from 5 different repeat patterns: horizontal, vertical, diagonal, serial wrapping, and random placement. This plug-in uses the alpha channel only as an on/off mask.

Divide by Any Parameters

Transformation [T] o, s, w, h, b — Sets the size and flipping settings for each subimage.

DIVIDE BY ANY

Schreiber Instruments | **\dividany** | **AFDIV_I.IXP**

Effect [E] (0–14) — Selects a predefined image effect for each subimage.
Amount [A] (0.0–100.0) — Sets the strength of the effects as a percentage.
Step [S] (–100–100) — Varies the amount of effect per frame.
Div [D] (2–20) — Sets the number of images in the matrix. A value of 4 would mean 16 images (4x4).
Sequence type [St] h, v, d, s, r — Controls the sequence that effects cycling uses. Options are Horizontal, Vertical, Diagonal, Serial, and Random.
Random seed [R] — Sets the random number that controls the random color effect and the random sequence control.
Alpha [Al] w, =0, >0 (whole, =0, >0) — Whole applies the effect to the entire image, =0 applies the effect outside the alpha channel, and >0 applies the effect inside the alpha channel.

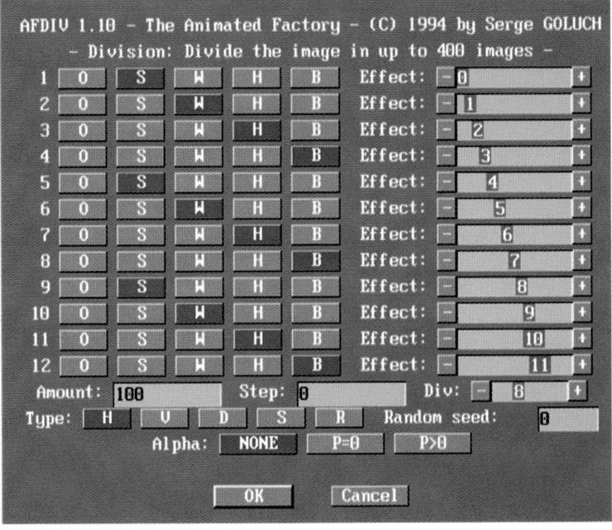

The Divide by Any dialog box.

[T]S [E]0 [D]4 [A]100

[E]11 [St]R

[E]3,4,5 [St]D [Al]=0

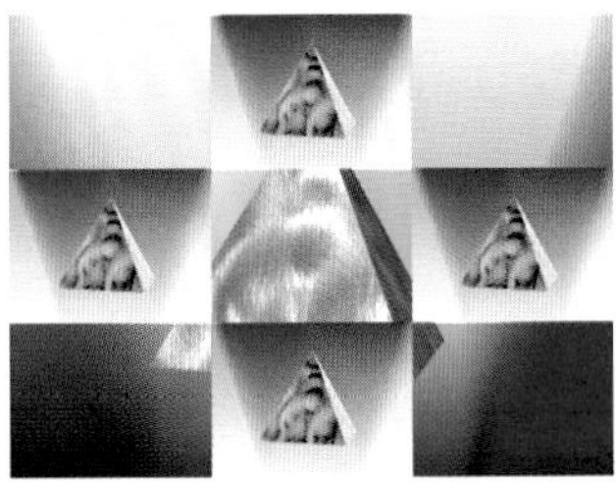

[E]11 [Al]=0

64 subimages, random tinting, diagonal sequence with alpha mask, random tinting with alpha mask.

DOTS

Autodesk | **\dots** | **4DOTS_I.IXP**

Summary

Dots is included with 3D Studio Release 4 and is available as a shareware plug-in from Yost Group. It generates a range of random animated patterns consisting of five layers of colored dots. The dot layers are built one atop the next, with layer 1 at the back and layer 5 at the front.

Dots Parameters

Color 1, 2, 3, 4, 5 [C] 1,2,3,4,5 — Specifies the dot color for each layer via the 3D Studio color picker.
Size 1, 2, 3, 4, 5 [S] 1,2,3,4,5 (1–40) — Sets the size of the dots for each layer, with larger dots requiring more time to generate.
Percent 1, 2, 3, 4, 5 [P] 1,2,3,4,5 (0–100) — Specifies the percentage of dot coverage for that layer.
Note: *It is possible to hide the dots on a given layer depending on a combination of its position, front to back, and the dot size.*

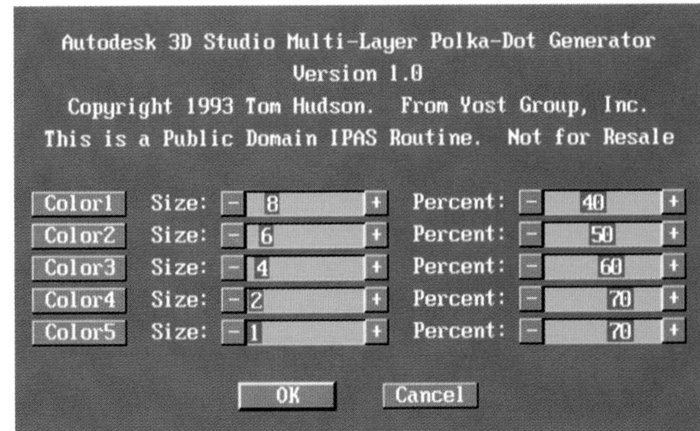

The Dots dialog box.

DOTS cont

4DOTS_I.IXP | **\dots** | **Autodesk**

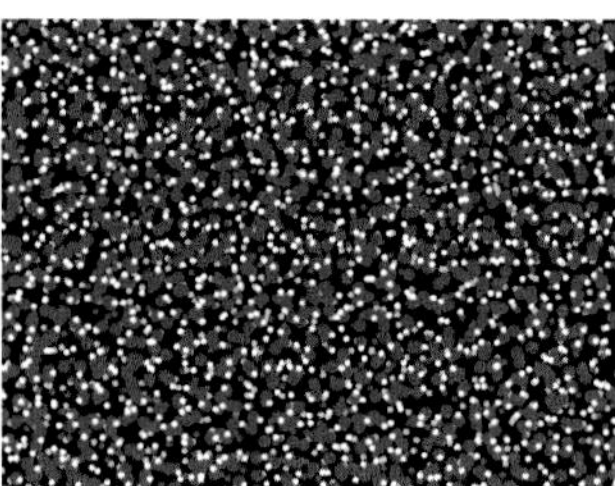
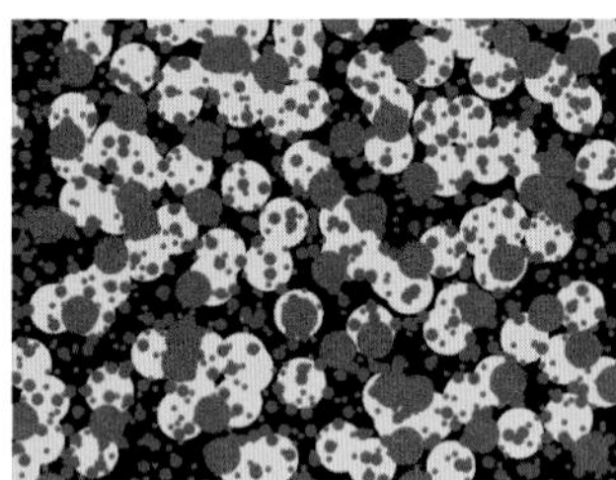
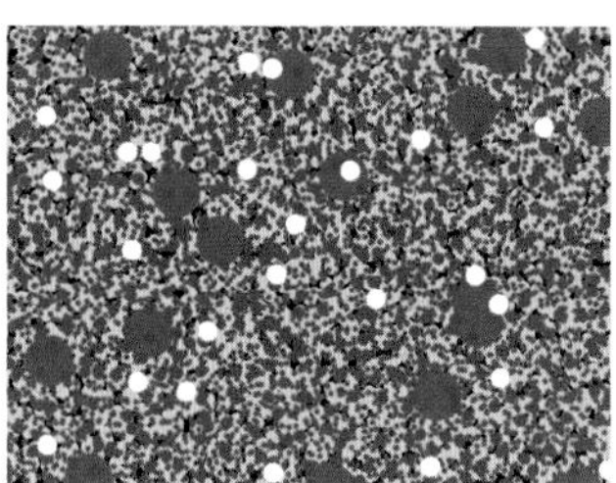

[S]5,10,5,10,5 [P]10,20,10,20,10 [S]40,30,5,10,1 [P]70,20,10,20,10 [S]10,5,40,10,16 [P]100,50,10,20,3 [S]40,3,15,10,2 [P]100,68,40,40,30

Dots produces a range of random swirling, multicolored dots. The samples were produced from the same palette of five colors.

DRIP

DRIP_I.IXP | **\drip** | **Pyros Partnership**

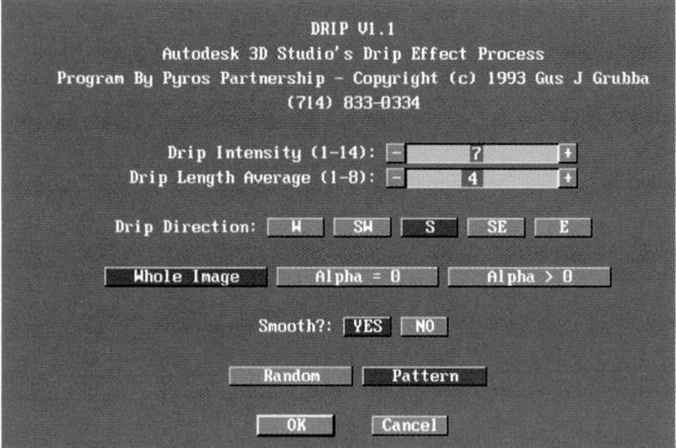

The Drip dialog box.

Summary

Drip is bundled with Pyros Partnership's Effects Library. Drip moves individual pixels in a user-specified direction and amount. This process can be used to produce a spiky, wind-blown, or dripping effect in an image or animation.

Drip Parameters

Drip intensity [I] (1–14) — Sets the strength or opacity of the effect.

Drip Length Average [L] (1–8) — Sets the average length pixels will be moved.

Drip Direction [D] w, sw, s, se, e (west, southwest, south, southeast, east) — Sets the direction the effect will move the pixels. South is considered down when looking at the screen, and pixels are not allowed to move up. No controls are given for moving the drip over time, and animated sequences appear to shimmer because the pattern is randomly applied to each frame.

Whole Image, Alpha=0, or Alpha >0 [I] [=0] [>0] — Whole applies the effect to the entire image, =0 applies the effect outside the alpha channel, and >0 applies the effect inside the alpha channel.

Smooth [S] (on, off) — Sets the displaced pixels to be smoothed or unsmoothed by the effect.

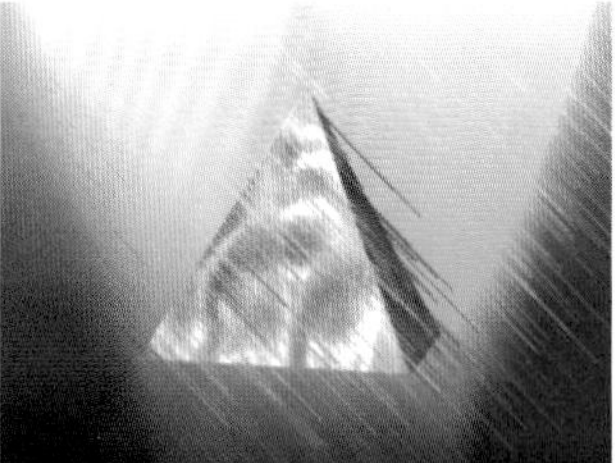

[I]14[L]1[D]S[S]yes [I]12[L]4[D]W[S]yes [I]7[L]7[D]sw[S]no [I]4[L]8[D]se[S]no

Drip can produce useful wind effects, but extreme drip settings can take considerable time to render. Animated sequences appear to shimmer because the pattern is randomly applied each frame.

FACTORY BASICS

Summary

Factory Basics is part of the Imagine Math Factory package. It is a completely programmable filter factory that uses a subset of BASIC to manipulate pixels in a image. It has a fairly complete set of functions including math function, conditionals, and a random number generator. Its main weakness is that there are only two user-defined variables and three user constants, which can make some operations more difficult than if there were more flexibility in variables.

Programs are written in text lines in the dialog box. There are four lines of text for each color channel (R,G,B), one for an overall conditional that determines whether the current pixel is processed, and two for the user-defined variables (X and Y). At run time the interpreter checks the conditional, evaluates the user variables, and then calculates each color channel's value. These values are then placed in the current pixel. The interpreter then moves on to the next pixel.

There are three value boxes for the user constants (I, J, K). Factory Basics has buttons for selecting alpha channel masking, but they don't seem to have any effect. You can, however, build alpha masking into your program by checking the alpha value of any pixel. You can write your program to an external program file, and you can tell the interpreter to run an external program file (extension IFB); however, there is no provision to load an external program file into the editor. You can instead edit the files in a text editor; given the limitations of the built-in editor, this might be the best way to work.

The BASIC interpreter understands most of the basic arithmetic operators along with integer division, logical and, and logical or. It has numerous built-in functions including trigonometry, logarithms, exponents, absolute value, radian/degree conversion, and a random number generator. The conditional functions are if, if not, if positive, and if negative. Factory Basics has several special functions for returning the color and luminance values of a pixel using either relative or absolute offsets from the current pixel. Intrinsic constants return values for pi, current frame, current row, current column, maximum row, and maximum column.

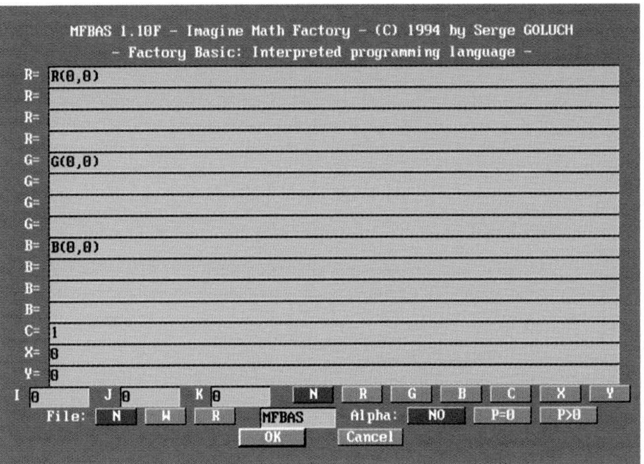

The Factory Basics dialog box.

This is a very powerful filter that enables you to create some really unusual effects that would be hard to achieve by other means. It might also try your ingenuity in the process.

Factory Basics Parameters

Color channel operations [Cc] — Four lines per channel for code to generate a color value.

Conditional operation [C] — One line that contains a condition that must be true for the program to change a pixel.

Variable operations [X] [Y] — Two lines that calculate the value of the user variables.

Global parameters [I] [J] [K] — Three user-defined global constants.

Test modes [T] (N, R, G, B, C, X, Y) — Displays the value of one of six built-in variables as the program runs. This did not seem to update for each frame.

File [F] (N, W, R) — Use the code in the dialog box (N), write the code to a file (W), or run the code in a file (R).

File name [N] — This is where you enter the name of the IFB file that you want to save to or run from.

Alpha [A] n, =0, >0 (none, =0, >0) — No applies the effect to the entire image, =0 applies the effect outside the alpha channel, and >0 applies the effect inside the alpha channel. It seemed to have no effect in this program. Instead, you must write alpha checking into your program.

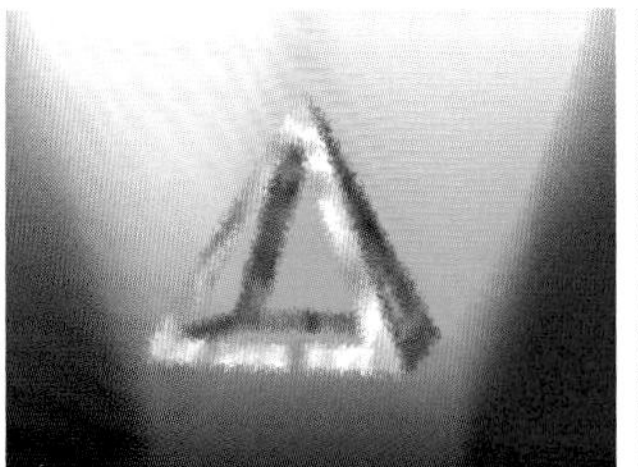

jitter.ifb

alpharnd.ifb

shift.ifb

rflip.ifb

Effects produced by Factory Basics custom programs.

FALLING STARS

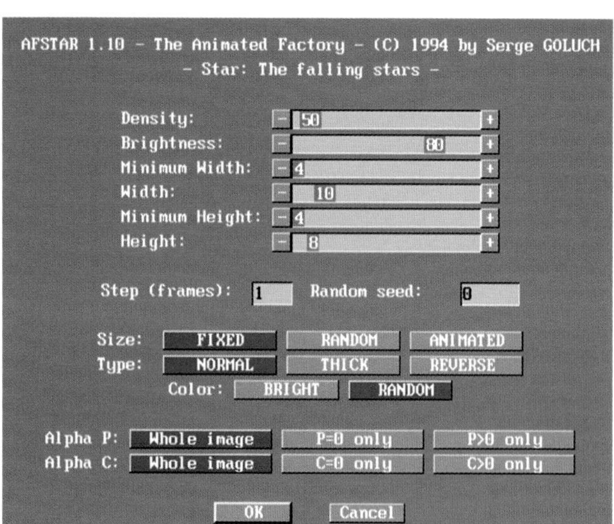

The Falling Stars dialog box.

Summary

Falling Stars is part of the Imagine Animated Factory. It applies a random scattering of four pointed stars that fall down the image in an animation. You can control the density of the stars and the length of their points. You also can control whether the points taper from or to their center points.

Stars can be either white or random colors. Besides animated falling, you can animate the size of the stars' points, making the stars appear to grow or shrink over time. Separate alpha channel controls determine where stars are placed and where the stars' points overlay the image. This plug-in uses the alpha channel only as an on/off mask.

Falling Stars Parameters

Density [D] (1–1000) — Sets the number of stars in the image.

Brightness [B] (1–100) — The brightness of the stars.

Minimum Width [Mw] (4–50) — The minimum width in pixels of star points.

Width [W] (4–50) — The average width in pixels of star points.

Minimum Height [Mh] (4–50) — Sets the minimum height in pixels of star points.

Height [H] (4–50) — The average height in pixels of star points.

Step (frames) [S] (1–999) — Number of frames required for a star to complete a fall.

Random seed [R] — Sets the random number that controls star distribution.

Size control [Sc] f, r, a (fixed, random, animated) — Selects how star sizes are generated. Fixed uses fixed sizes, random creates stars with random sizes, and animated is random with individual stars growing and shrinking.

Type [T] n, t, r (normal, thick, reverse) — Controls how the star points taper.

Color [Tc] (bright, random) — White stars or randomly colored stars.

Alpha P [Ap] i, =0, >0 (whole image, P=0, P>0) — Alpha P controls masking based on the alpha channel value at the current pixel. Whole applies the effect to the entire image, P=0 applies the effect outside the alpha channel, and P>0 applies the effect inside the alpha channel.

Alpha C [Ac] i, =0, >0 (whole image, C=0, C>0) — Alpha C controls masking based on the alpha channel value at the effect center. Whole applies the effect to the entire image, C=0 applies the effect outside the alpha channel, and C>0 applies the effect inside the alpha channel.

[D]76 [C]random

[D]817 [C]white

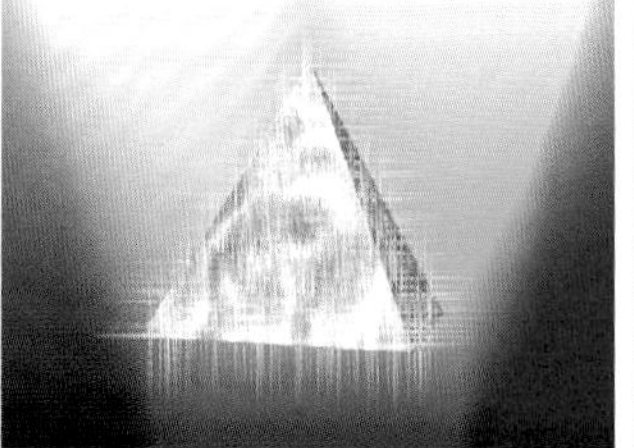
[Ap]whole [Ac]>0

[W]4 [H]50

Stars with random color, high-density stars, stars in the alpha channel, stars as linear streaks.

FAST AVERAGE

Schreiber Instruments **\fastavg** **FFAVER_I.IXP**

Original image [S]7

The original image and a 7x7 average blur.

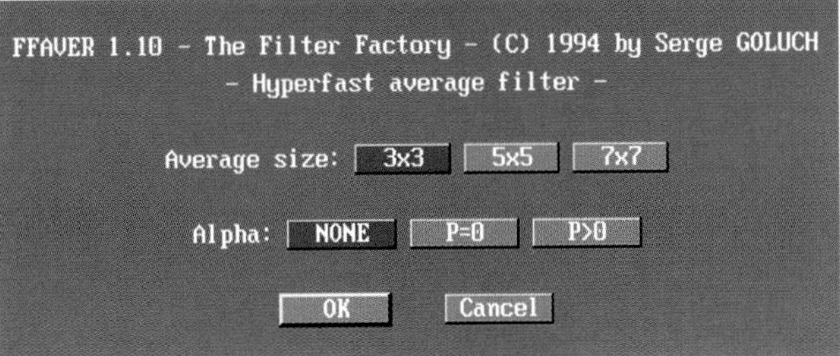

The Fast Average dialog box.

Summary

Fast Average is part of the Imagine Filter Factory package.This is a blur built for speed. In our tests, it was more than twice as fast as the generic blurs from the Matrix Filter and the Animated Filter.You can select one of three matrix sizes (3,5,7) to get three degrees of blurring.You can use the alpha channel to mask the effect.This filter uses the alpha channel only as an on/off mask.

Fast Average Parameters

Average size [S] 3,5,7 (3x3,5x5,7x7) — Selects the matrix size and strength of the blur effect.

Alpha [A] n,=0,>0 (none,=0,>0) — None applies the effect to the entire image,=0 applies the effect outside the alpha channel, and >0 applies the effect inside the alpha channel.

FILM

Pyros Partnership **\film** **FILM_I.IXP**

Summary

Film adds noise to an image to simulate film grain.The alpha channel can be used to mask part of the image, but is used only as an on/off mask.The test option enables the effect to be compared to the original image by processing only half of the image. To work properly, film must be placed before the image to process in the video post.

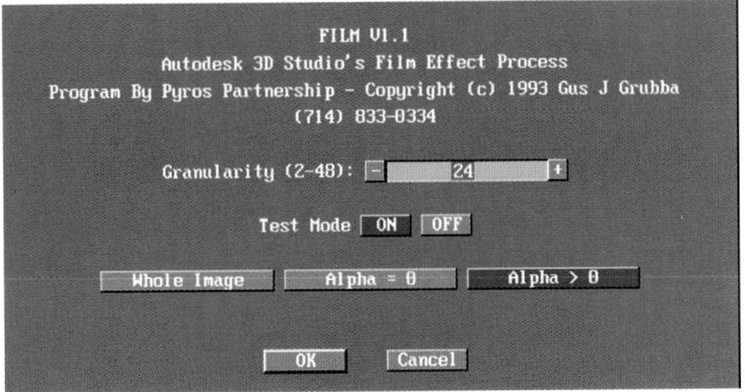

The Film dialog box.

Film Parameters

Granularity [G] (2–48) — Sets the size of the film grain noise.

Filter [F] w,=0,>0 (Whole Image,=0,>0) — Whole applies the effect to the entire image,=0 applies the effect outside the alpha channel, and >0 applies the effect inside the alpha channel.

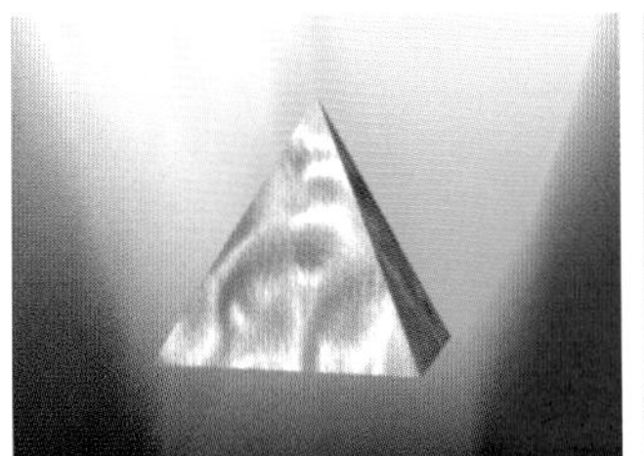

[G]24,[F]>0 [G]48,[F]>0

Film adds a variable amount of noise to an image to simulate film grain.

FLARE

FLARE_I.IXP \lensflar Yost Group

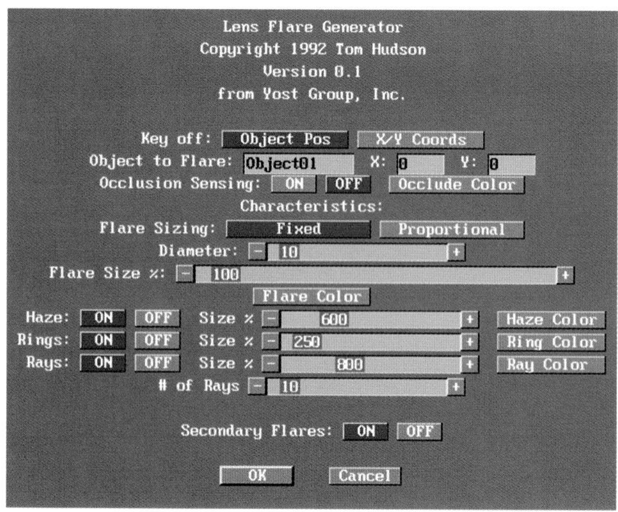

The Flare dialog box.

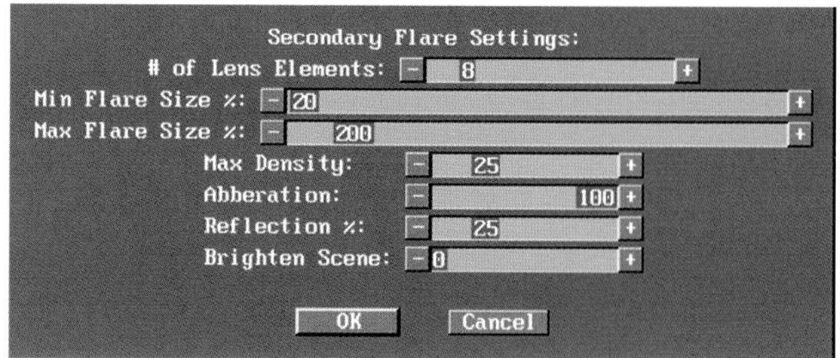

The Secondary Flare dialog box.

Summary

Flare is packaged with the Yost Group's Disk #1 Image Processing filters. The Flare filter simulates refraction effects, or lens flare, that occur inside an optical lens assembly. Lens flare can be used to increase the dramatic effect of bright spotlights or the sun in an animation or still image.

Flare Parameters

Key off [KO] p, c (Object Pos, X/Y Coords) — Sets the position based on either a scene object or X and Y coordinates.

Object to Flare [O] n, x, y (object name, X, Y) — Sets the object name or X and Y coordinates for flare location. Using a wild card in the object name text box enables you to specify multiple flare objects. Keyframer instance objects do not work with flare.

Occlusion Sensing [Os] (on, off) — Causes the flare to diminish or disappear as the flare object becomes obscured by other objects. When using occlusion, the key object should be a sphere so that the shape will be identical when viewed from any angle.

Occlude Color [Oc] — Sets the key color that Flare looks for to determine occlusion. This color must match exactly a self-illuminated material assigned to the flare object.

Flare Sizing [Fs] f, p (Fixed, Proportional) — Sets the flare size using the diameter setting or the size of the flare object. Proportional flaring will not work when using X and Y coordinates.

Diameter [D] (3–100) — Sets the size in pixels of the core of the flare when using Fixed size.

Flare Size % [F%] (1–2000) — Sets the size of the core of the flare as a percentage of the flare object when using Proportional size.

Flare Color [Fc] — Sets the flare color via the 3D Studio color picker.

Haze (Ha) o, of, s, c (on, off, size 100–2000, color) — Sets the size and color of the fuzzy aura around the flare.

Rings [Ri] o, of, s, c (on, off, size 100–2000, color) — Sets the size and color of the diffraction ring around the core of the flare.

Rays [RA] (on, off, size range 100–2000, color) — Sets the size and color of the rays emanating from the flare.

# of Rays [R#] (2–100) — Sets the number of rays.

Secondary Flares [Sf] (on, off) — Sets the flare to include or exclude smaller element flares.

Secondary Flare Parameters

# of Lens Elements [E#] (1–50) — Sets the number of optical elements simulated in the flare.

Min/Max Flare Size % [Mn] [Mx] (1–2000) — Sets the size of the secondary flares as a percentage of the primary flare.

Max Density — (0–100) — Sets the intensity of the secondary flares using this value as a limit.

Aberration [A] (0–100) — Sets the difference in hue between secondary flares that simulate chromatic aberration.

Reflection % [RF] (0–100) — Sets the reflection intensity of the primary flare in the secondary flare.

Brighten Scene [Bs] (yes, no) — Sets the amount by which the flare will brighten or wash out the scene.

FLARE cont

Yost Group | \lensflar | FLARE_I.IXP

Frame 6

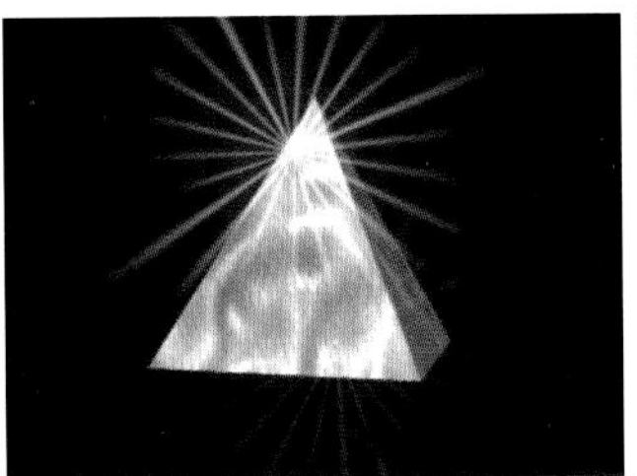

Frame16

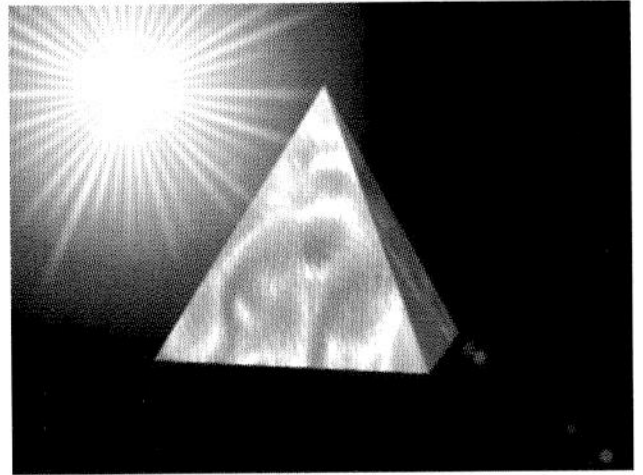

Frame 6

Frame 16

In the first segment, the flare is set to [FS]fix[D]40[HA]500[RI]250[RA]1000[R#]45. In the second series, the flare is set to [FS]prop[S%]150[HA]850[RI]180[RA]750[R#]90. The second frame in each segment shows the effect of occlusion.

FLIP

Yost Group | \flip | FLIP_I.IXP

Summary

Flip is included with Yost Group's Special Effects Disk #2. It flips an image horizontally, vertically, or both.

Flip Parameters

Flip Horizontally [H] y, n (yes, no) — Specifies horizontal flip.
Flip Vertically [V] y, n (yes, no) — Specifies vertical flip.

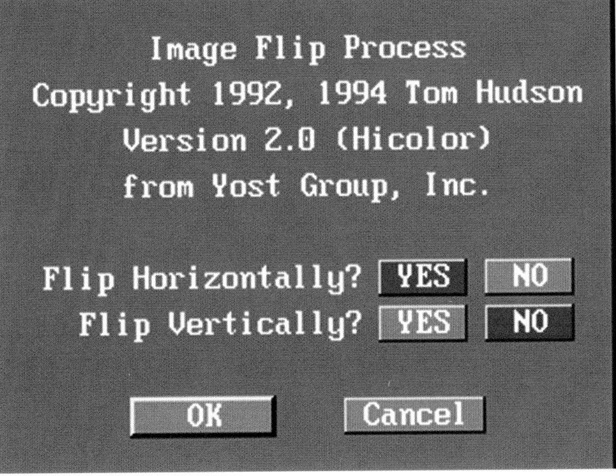

The Flip dialog box.

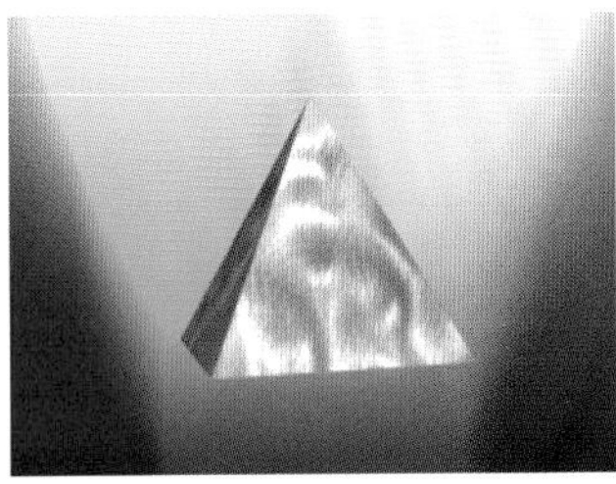

[H]y [V]n

[H]y [V]y

Flip performs horizontal or vertical image flips.

GLOW

Yost Group | \glow | GLOW_I.IXP

Summary

Glow is packaged with the Yost Group's Disk #1 Image Processing filters. The Glow filter produces a white glow or halo effect around an object. This effect works well for very bright light sources, which cause the image to appear overexposed. The area of effect can be constrained based on brightness, color, or hue, or by using the alpha channel.

GLOW cont

GLOW_I.IXP \glow **Yost Group**

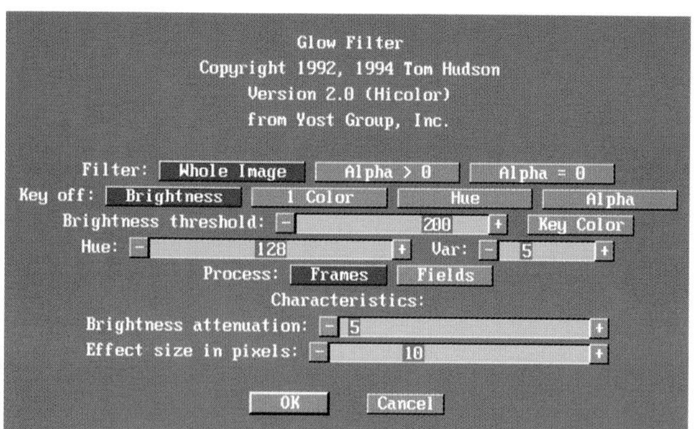

The Glow dialog box.

Glow Parameters

Filter: [F] (Whole Image, > 0, = 0) — Sets the general area of the image to be affected. If the alpha channel is used, the image must contain an alpha channel that is turned on in the Video Post queue. Glow uses the alpha channel only as an on/off mask. Whole applies the effect to the entire image, =0 applies the effect outside the alpha channel, and >0 applies the effect inside the alpha channel.

Key off: [KO] b, 1, h, a (Brightness, 1 Color, Hue, Alpha) — Sets the specific pixels to affect using the brightness threshold, key color, hue, and variance parameters.

Brightness threshold [T] (0–255) — Sets the pixels to be filtered based on brightness.

Key Color [Kc] — Specifies the color of pixels to glow when keying off 1 Color.

Hue [H] (0–255) [md] Sets the hue of pixels to glow when keying off hue.

Var [V] (0–10) — Sets the amount of variance in hue allowed when keying off hue.

Process: [P] (Frames, Fields) — Sets the effect to render to either frames or video fields.

Brightness attenuation [Ba] (0–30) — Sets the brightness falloff.

Effect size in pixels [S] (0–30) — Sets the amount of glow applied to the edge of the glow object.

[Ba]50[S]15

[Ba]5[S]5

[Ba]50[S]15

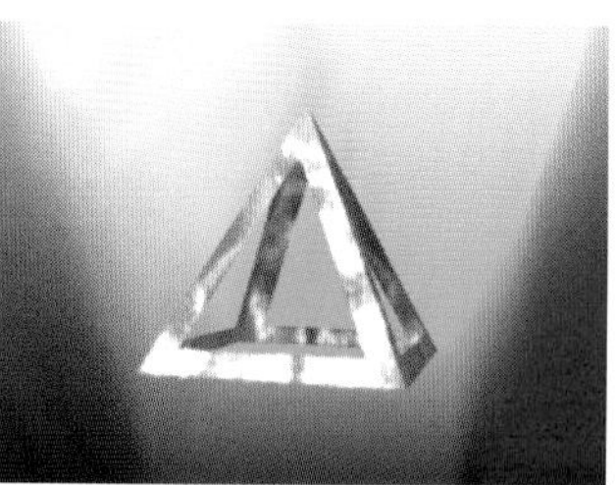

[W][H][Ba]15[S]5

Glow provides a versatile soft white halo effect, but falloff can be too sharp for some effects. Large glow areas can significantly slow render times.

HBLUR

HBLUR_I.IXP \hblur **Pyros Partnership**

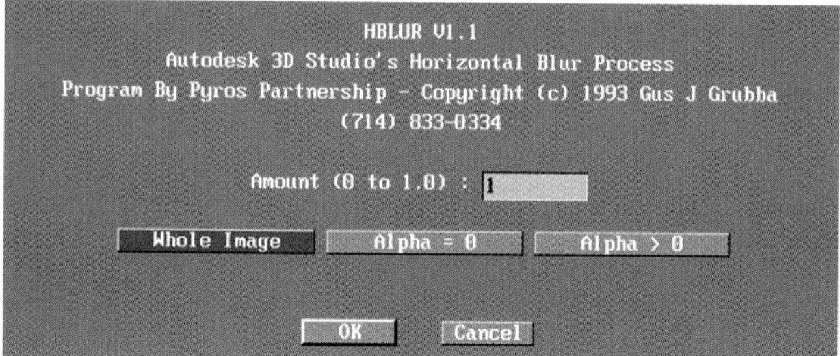

The Hblur dialog box.

Summary

Hblur is a basic horizontal blur filter. You can set the blur amount ranging from 0 to 1.0 and you can mask the effect with the alpha channel. The blur range is suitable for subtle blurs. It will not allow for strong blurs, although you can run an image through the filter multiple times to increase the effect.

Hblur Parameters

Amount [A] (0–1.0) — Strength of the blur effect.

Alpha [Al] w, =0, >0 (Whole Image, =0, >0) — Whole applies the effect to the entire image, =0 applies the effect outside the alpha channel, and >0 applies the effect inside the alpha channel.

HBLUR cont

Pyros Partnership | **\hblur** | **HBLUR_I.IXP**

[A]1.0
Maximum blur.

HILIGHT

Yost Group | **\hilight** | **HILI_I.IXP**

Summary

Hilight is packaged with the Yost Group's Disk #1 Image Processing filters. The Highlight filter applies star-shaped highlights to selected image areas, simulating a photographer's star-cross filter. The number of star points is user-defined, and the stars can be rotated over a series of frames for an animated effect. The area of effect can be constrained based on brightness, color, or hue, or by using the alpha channel.

Hilight Parameters

Filter [F] (Whole Image, > 0, = 0) — Sets the general area of the image to be affected. If the alpha channel is used, the image must contain an alpha channel that is turned on in the Video Post queue. Hilight uses the alpha channel only as an on/off mask. Whole applies the effect to the entire image, =0 applies the effect outside the alpha channel, and >0 applies the effect inside the alpha channel.

Key off [Ko] b, 1, h (Brightness, 1 Color, Hue) — Sets the specific pixels to affect using the brightness threshold, key color, hue, and variance parameters.

Brightness threshold [T] (0–255)— Sets the pixels to be filtered based on brightness.

Key Color [KC] — Specifies the color of pixels to highlight when keying off 1 Color.

Hue [H] (0–255) — Sets the hue of pixels to highlight when keying off hue.

Var [V] (0–10) — Sets the amount of variance in hue allowed when keying off hue.

Process [P] f, fi (Frames, Fields) — Sets the effect to render to either frames or video fields.

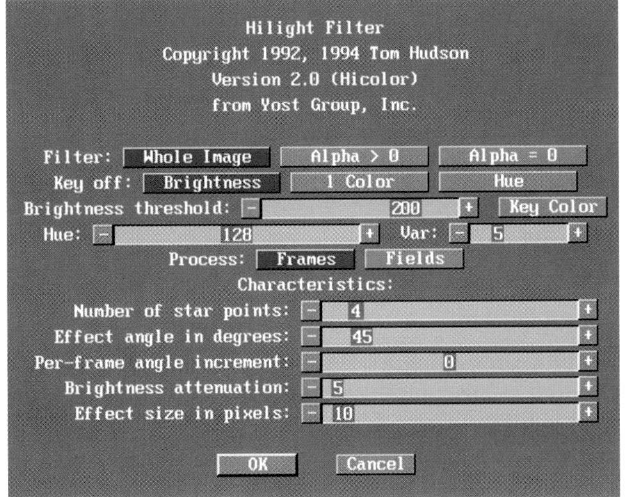

The Hilight dialog box.

Number of star points [P#] (0–30) — Sets the number of points for each highlight.

Effect angle in degrees [A] (0–360) — Sets the rotation for each highlight star.

Per-frame angle increment [Fa] — Sets the amount each star is rotated each frame.

Brightness attenuation [Ba] (0–100) — Sets the brightness falloff.

Effect size in pixels [S] (0–1000) — Sets the size in pixels of the highlight that will be applied.

[Ba]5[S]1000

[Ba]5[S]50

[F]>0[Ko]bri

[Ba]5[S]20

Using Hilight to place star highlights on specular areas can add that extra sparkle to your images. By processing the entire alpha channel, the effect can produce a spiky glow on an object.

JPEG

JPEG_I.IXP **\jpeg** **Pyros Partnership**

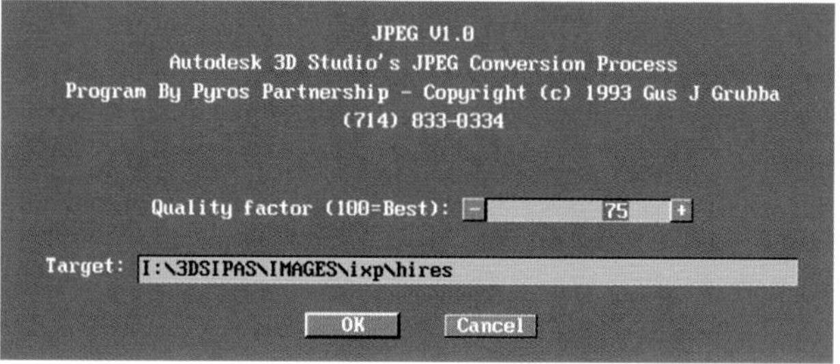

The Jpeg dialog box.

Summary

Jpeg is part of Pyros Partnership's Utilities package. It writes a lossy JPEG compressed file as part of a video post process. You place Jpeg as the last process in a video post queue and render the queue. You do not need to specify that 3D Studio render to disk—Jpeg does this on its own. You can set the output quality factor and the output file name. This filter has been largely superseded by recent releases of 3D Studio that can read and write JPEG files directly. The output of Jpeg does not go through 3D Studio's gamma correction process, and so the output differs from 3D Studio's.

Jpeg [Q]75

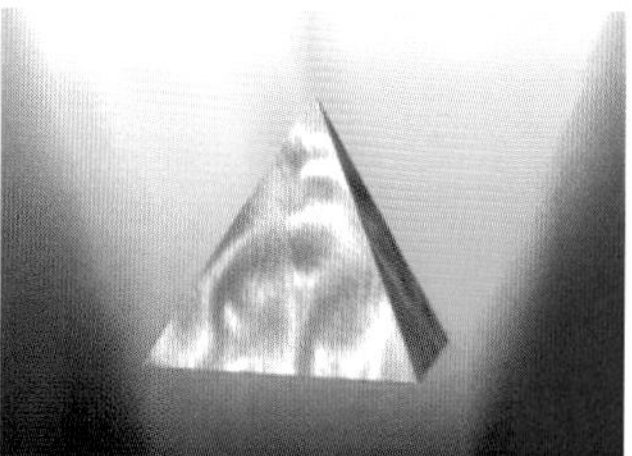
3D Studio [Q]75

Jpeg output is not gamma corrected.

Jpeg Parameters

Quality factor [Q] (0–100) — Image quality desired. Smaller numbers reduce the file size by removing image detail.
Target [T] — The path and name of the output file.

LEGAL

LEGAL_I.IXP **\legal** **Pyros Partnership**

Summary

Legal is part of Pyros Partnership's Utilities package. It checks and corrects the limits of images intended for video output. You set limits on the strength of the chroma and luminance components of a video signal. Legal will either correct those pixels that exceed your limits or render them as black to mark them in test renders. You can instruct Legal to reduce either color saturation or luminance to correct illegal pixels. You can select either NTSC or PAL type video, set gamma, and set black pedestal. 3D Studio will also do video color checking and flagging enabled by editing the 3DS.SET file; however, Legal adds more controls for fine-tuning the settings. Color correction can cause some banding.

LEGAL cont

Pyros Partnership — \legal — **LEGAL_I.IXP**

Legal Parameters

Chroma Limit [Cl] (0–180) — Maximum chroma levels allowed.
Composite Amplitude Limit [Ca] (0–180) — Maximum luminance levels allowed.
Reduction [R] s, l (Saturation, Luminance) — Method to use to correct colors.
System [S] n, p (NTSC, PAL) — Destination video system.
Mark illegal colors? [M] (yes, no) — Correct pixels or mark them by rendering as black.

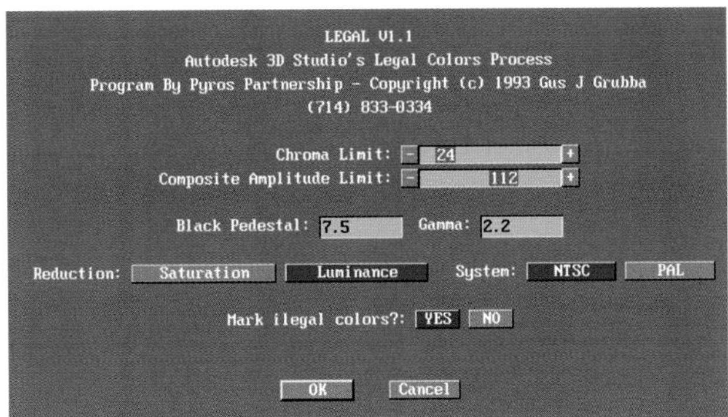

The Legal dialog box.

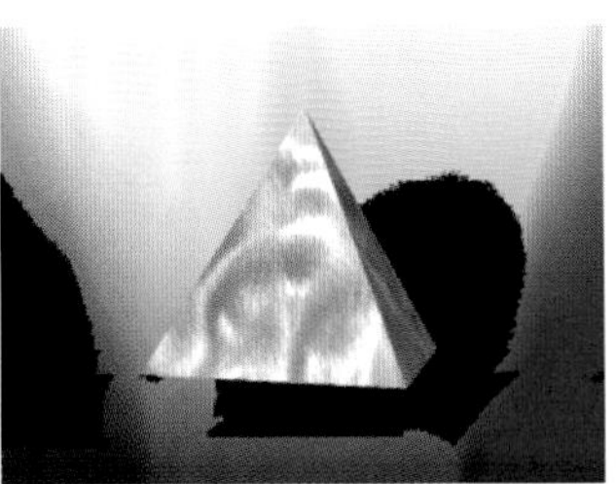

[Cr]24 [M]yes [Cr]24 [M]no
Marking and correcting illegal video colors.

LENZFX

Digimation — \lenzfx — **LENZ_I.IXP**

Summary

LenZFX consists of four basic effects: Aura, Flare, Starlight, and ZFocus. Aura places a glow around selected object, objects, or specific areas of the screen. Flare simulates lens flares with as many 15 secondary flares each with individual control. Starlight creates a single or multiple star bursts, and ZFocus simulates variable focus or simulated depth-of-field based on the camera-to-subject distance. LenZFX comes with numerous preset effects and gradient files useful for each of its effect types.

Flare, LenZFX's most complex module, uses one or more 3D Studio scene lights as sources to produce synthetic lens flares. Flare simulates the effect produced in a real-world camera when a light source such as the sun shines directly in the lens. Flare enables you to precisely tailor lens element by lens element the structure, optical properties, and interaction between a virtual camera lens and each scene light. Not only can you control the size, intensity, and color of the glow that forms around the light source, you also can specify the number, size, rotation angle, and thickness of light rays that extend from its center. Furthermore, you can set up to 15 secondary flares, any of which can be adjusted for their position along the optical axis between the lens and the light source, and for their shape, size, and color.

You also can animate many of the flare's properties, including ray number, ray rotation, glow size, and overall intensity. This is accomplished using an Envelope dialog box, which displays curved or linear splines on a graph with the x axis representing animation frames and the y axis representing the current LenZFX parameter. You can create, move, and delete keys as well as scale or shift groups of keys. You also can save and load envelopes, which is great when you want to synchronize multiple animated effects. This adds fidelity and variation to the flares or any LenZFX effect.

Additional effect options such as Move in Scene and Fade behind objects lend further realism to Flares (or Auras) by enabling them to interact with scene objects.

Turbulence, available for both Flare and Aura, dramatically extends LenZFX capabilities by enabling you to create a range of startlingly real turbulent effects, from fiery, multilayered plasma blasts to moonlit clouds and steam. The turbulence pattern is controlled by a number of interdependent variables that specify pattern detail, motion, density, and overall quality.

As each effect parameter is edited, a full-color preview is updated to reflect the change. You also can opt to see a sample animation of the current effect. Although this does not include the scene animation, the sample animation is useful to get an idea of how the effect will work.

Aura enables you to place a glow in a 3D Studio scene using a bitmap or alpha channel mask, or with one or more objects. You can glow only the edges of an object, across the object, or by brightness, hue, or single color. Auras can consist of any color combination, as well as numerous concentric and asymmetric patterns.

Starlight is a cross-star and star burst generator. It is applied using the same methods as Aura and is capable of some fascinating effects. For instance, you can key the effect to an object by hue so that as an object moves or spins, variations in color across it also produce waves of stars.

The key to much of the variation possible with these effects is their use of linear and radial gradients for control of color, size, and transparency. *Gradients* are color bands that ramp from one color or value to another. If the ramp is applied as a linear gradient, the color or value attribute will vary from the center to the edge, producing a concentric variation. If the ramp is applied as radial gradient, the attribute will vary clockwise, starting at the 12 o'clock position and continuing 360 degrees around the effect.

A gradient extends from 0–99 and can be divided into up to 99 flags, each with its own number, color, and value. Right-clicking with the mouse on any existing flag brings up an RGB/HLS color dialog box for editing the current color, or you can right-click anywhere along the flag area to set a new color. After a color flag is edited, the gradient is updated with the new color smoothly blended in. You also can use bitmap images for any gradient. This enables you to add either static texture or animated texture to light and to glow patterns. This is useful for creating shimmering and explosive effects. Also, any gradient can be saved for use in any of LenZFX modules.

ZFocus blurs a specific range of the image, simulating the effect of a camera lens's limited focusing range. You can select manual or auto focus based on the camera-to-subject distance along with a focal range, which establishes the area around the focal point that will be in focus. You also can animate the focal distance, focal range, background blur, or scene blur.

Flare Global Parameters

Size [S] (0–500%) — Sets the overall size of the entire flare effect. The L button enables you to animate size.
Intensity [I] (0–500%) — Sets the overall brightness and opacity of the entire flare effect. The L button uses the brightness of the flare light instead of the intensity setting.
Rotation [Ro] (0–360°) — Sets the Flare's rotation angle. The S button turns rotation on or off for the secondary flares.
Vanish Pt [Vp] (0–2000) — Sets the point at which the flare disappears as it moves away from the camera.
Move in Scene Box [Ms] — Sets flare to disappear behind scene objects.
Fade Behind Objects Box [Fbo] — Sets flare to fade as it passes behind scene objects.
Affect Alpha Box [Aa] — Places flare on alpha channel to enable compositing.
Affect Zbuffer Box [Az] — Saves flare information to the Abuffer during rendering.
Turbulence Box [T] — Accesses the Turbulence dialog box.
Lights Button — Specifies which camera and lights will be used for the Flare effect.
Glow Button [G] — Accesses the Glow dialog box.
Rays Button [R] — Accesses the Rays dialog box.
Secondary Flares Button [Sf] — Accesses the Secondary Flares dialog box.
Note: *E buttons indicate animation option via an Envelope dialog box.*

Flare Glow Parameters

Size [S] (0–500%) — Sets the size of the glow as a percentage of screen size.
Glow Linear Color [LC] Sets the circular glow color beginning at the center and extending to the edge.
Glow Radial Color [RC] Sets the circular glow color beginning at 12 o'clock and continuing clockwise for 360 degrees.
Glow Linear Transparency [LT] Sets the circular transparency beginning at the center and extending to the edge.
Glow Radial Transparency [RT] Sets the circular transparency beginning at 12 o'clock and continuing clockwise for 360 degrees.
Glow Radial Size [RS] Sets the circular glow scale beginning at 12 o'clock and continuing clockwise for 360 degrees.
Note: *The Gradient buttons allows adjustment of the gradient using RGB and HLS color models. The UV Map buttons load a bitmap as a source for the gradient.*

Flare Ray Parameters

Size [S] (0–500%) — Sets the size of the rays as a percentage of screen size.
Points [Po] (0–250) — Sets the number of rays.
Thickness [Th] (0–100) — Sets thickness of the rays.
Rotation [Ro] (0–180°) — Sets the rotation angle of the rays.
Note: *All gradients are the same as Glow Parameters.*

Flare Secondary Flare Parameters

Secondary Flare Number [Sf] (1–15) —Accesses the parameters and gradients for each secondary flare.
On and Off buttons — Switches each secondary flare on or off.
Secondary flare shape [Sfs] (circle, octagon, hexagon, or ellipse) — Specifies the shape for each secondary flare.
Secondary Flare Size [Sfsi] (0–200) — Sets the size of each secondary flare.

Lens Plane [Lp] (–50–100) — Sets the spatial position relative to the light source of each secondary flare. Negative values place the secondary flare behind the light.

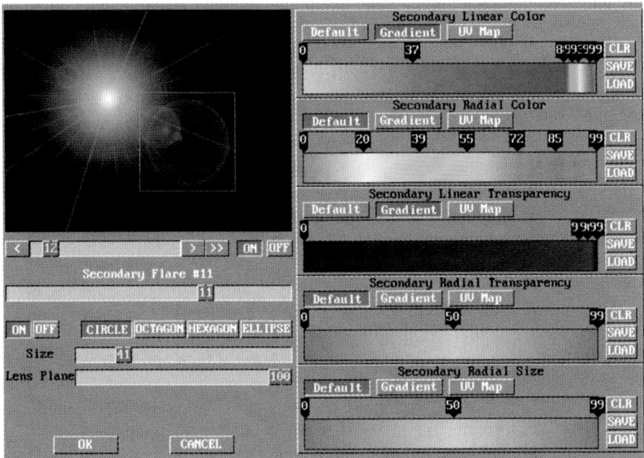

The Secondary Flares dialog box controls the shape, size, and position of multiple flares that simulate real-world lens elements. Similar dialog boxes are provided for control of the Flare Glow and Rays, which are the multiple light rays emanating from each light source.

Note: *All gradients are identical to Glow Parameters.*

Aura Parameters

Effect Area [Ea] w, n, i, o, a, ia (Whole Image, Normal Mask, Inverted Mask, By Object, Alpha Channel, Inverted Alpha) — Specifies where the glow will be applied. Whole Image glows the entire image. Normal Mask uses a bitmap mask with a cutoff value from 0–255. Inverted Mask inverts the luminance values of a bitmap. By Object glows any number of scene objects. Alpha Channel uses an alpha channel as a mask for the glow. Non Alpha uses an inverted alpha channel.

Effect By [Eb] ap, e, b, h, s (All Pixels, Edge, Brightness, Hue, Single Color) — Specifies how the glow will be applied. All Pixels glows all pixels in the effect area. Edge glows all pixels at the edge of an object or mask. Brightness glows every pixel within a specific luminance value as set in a dialog box. Hue glows every pixel within a specific range of color as set in a dialog box. Single Color glows only a specific RGB color.

Size [S] (0–100%) — Sets the size of the glow as a percentage of screen size.

Fall Off [Fo] (0–100) — Specifies how quickly the glow dims beginning at the center and extending to the edge.

Vanish Pt. [Vp] (0–2000) — Sets the point at which the glow disappears as it moves away from the camera. A numeric input box is provided for distances up to 9,999,999,999 units.

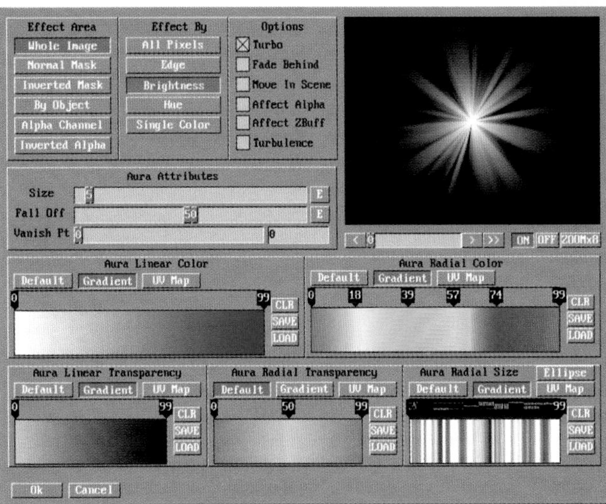

The Aura dialog box is used to place shaped or uniform multicolored glows along the edges or across the surfaces of selected objects.

Note: *All other parameters, options, and gradients are identical to Glow Parameters.*

Starlight Parameters

Star Points [Sp] (1–200) — Sets the number of star points.

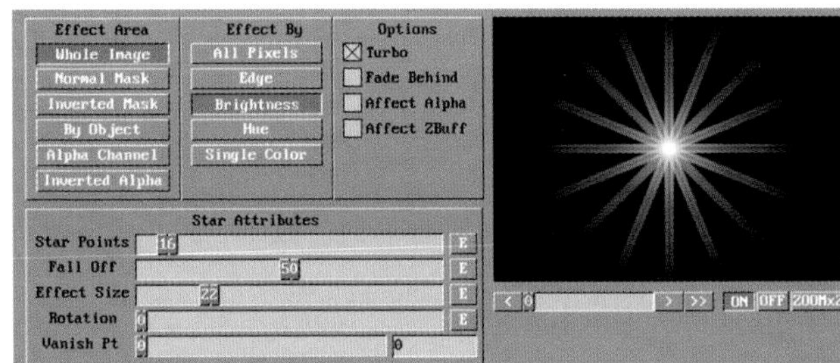

The Starlight dialog box controls the number of and size of stars that can be keyed to an object or any screen area. The lower portion of the dialog box (not shown) offers the same parameters as Aura.

Note: *All other parameters, options, and gradients are identical to Glow Parameters.*

ZFocus Parameters

Focus Type [Ft] (Dispersion, Proximity) — Specifies the method used for calculating the blur. Dispersion is more accurate and Proximity is faster.

Scene Blur [Bl] (0–30) — Applies a uniform blur to the entire scene.

LENZFX cont

LENZ_I.IXP \lenzfx Digimation

Manual Focus [Mf] (0–2000) — Sets focus at a specific distance from the camera. A numeric input box is provided for values up to 9,999,999 units.

Auto Focus [Af] — Uses the camera target to determine focus.

Track Object [To] — Specifies an object to keep in focus throughout an animation.

Focal Radius [Fr] (0–200) — Sets the scene's focal range. A numeric input box is provided for values up to 9,999,999 units.

Background Blur [Bb] (0–30) — Applies a uniform blur to a background image.

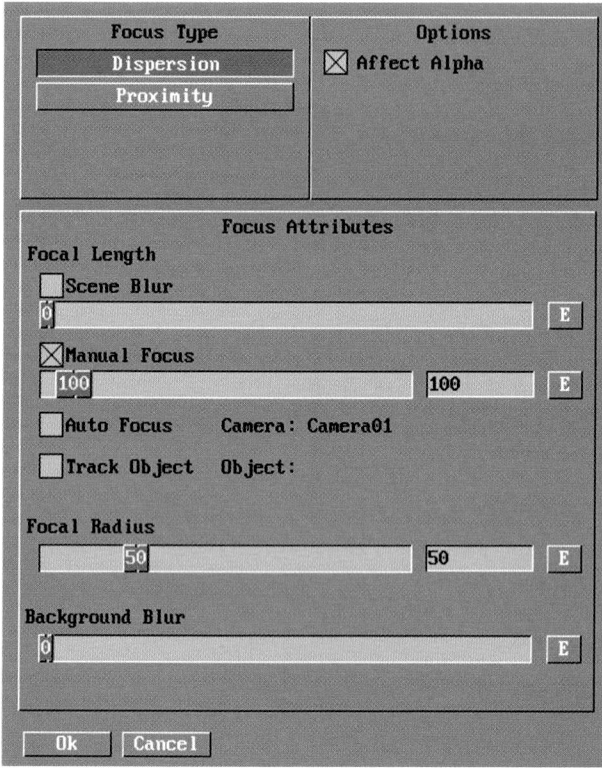

The ZFocus dialog box is used to blur specific ranges of a 3D scene based on the distance from the camera and an f-stop or focus range setting.

Note: *E buttons indicate animation option via an Envelope dialog box.*

Turbulence Parameters

Movement [Tm] — Specifies the direction of movement for the turbulence. Speed increases as the arrow is moved away from center. A right-click returns motion to center.

Seed [Tse] — Specifies the number that is used as a random seed for turbulence calculation.

Linear or B-Spline [Tli] [Tbs] Specifies that turbulence be calculated based on either linear or b-spline functions. B-spline takes longer and produces softer effects.

Color [Tc] (0–100) — Sets the amount of color variation in turbulent areas with higher values producing dramatic color shifts.

Trans [Tt] (0–100) — Varies proportionally the contrast of the turbulence with respect to the glow or flare.

Brght [Tbr] (0–100) — Varies the overall brightness in the turbulent areas.

Affect Control — Accesses the Affect Control Envelope dialog box, which uses a spline function to control the pattern distribution from center to edge.

Density Control — Accesses the Density Control Envelope dialog box, which uses a spline function to control the pattern density from center to edge.

Size [Ts] (0–500) — Sets the size and detail level for the pattern of turbulence. Smaller settings create finer patterns.

Speed [Tsp] (0–500) — Works with Movement to set motion speed for the turbulence.

Clamp 1 and 2 [Tc1] [Tc2] (0–255) Sets upper and lower limits of the value range that displays the turbulence.

Favor [Tf] (0–500) — Varies the pattern based on Clamp 1 and 2 settings, with 250 favoring neither.

Edge [Te] (0–500) — Sets the overall pattern contrast.

Qlty [Tq] (0–100) — Sets the number of times the turbulence is calculated, with higher values resulting in more realistic and detailed effects.

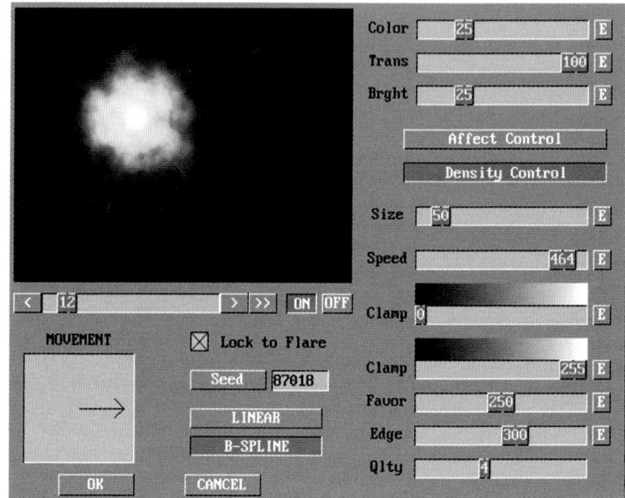

Both Aura and Flare provide a Turbulence dialog box that simulates a range of effects from steam to plasma blasts.

Envelope Parameters

Clear Envelope — Restores the envelope the last saved settings.
Add Key — Adds a key via mouse input.
Create Key — Adds a key via X and Y values.
Move Key — Rescales the key and moves it along the spline.
Shift Keys — Translates a range of keys along the timeline.
Scale Keys — Scales a range of keys relative to the timeline.
Linear and Curved — Switches between linear or curved splines.

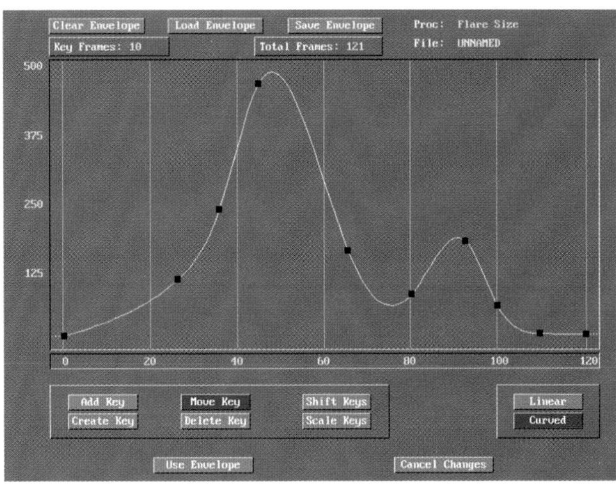

The Envelope dialog box is used to animate—via a spline curve and graph—those parameters with an E button.

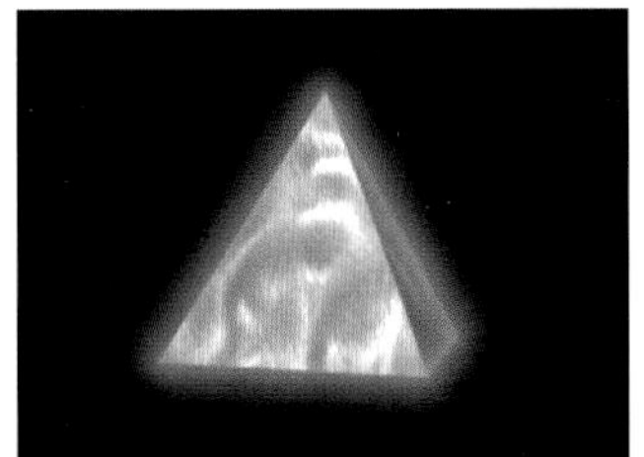
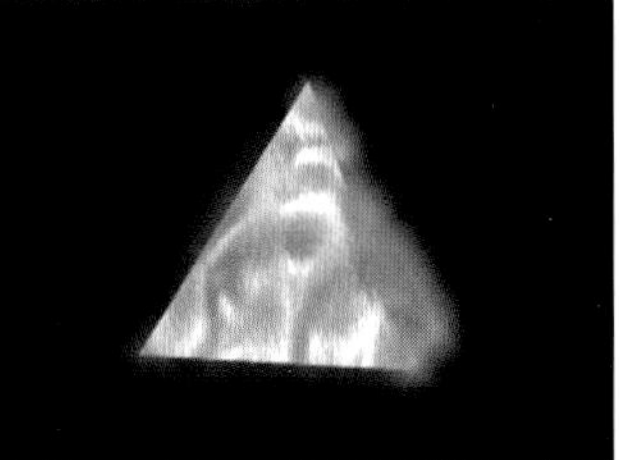
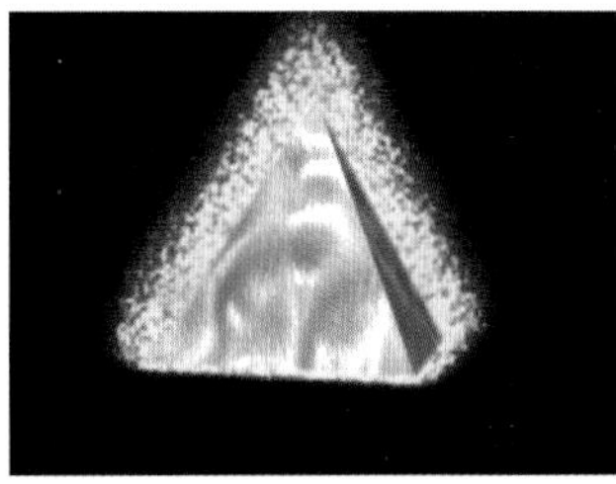

Aura [Ea]o[Eb]ap Aura [Ea]o[Eb]e Aura [Ea]o[Eb]b Aura [Ea]o[Eb]e [T]

Aura produces a range of multicolored glows that can placed over the entire object, its edges only, or selected objects' areas by brightness, hue, mask, or alpha channel. The turbulence option creates a range of moving patterned glows.

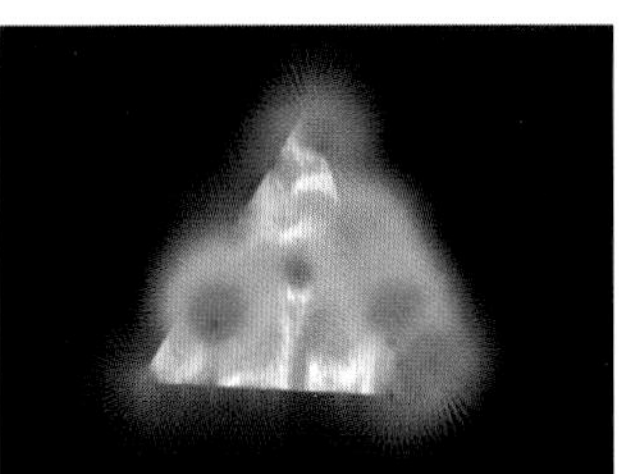

Starlight [Sp]8 [Ea]o [Eb]245 Starlight [Sp]5 Starlight [Ea]o Starlight [Sp]50 [Ea]o [Eb]65

Starlight distributes stars over the surface or edge of an object by brightness, hue, or alpha channel. Asymmetric star patterns can be produced using StarRadial Size with UV maps such as random3.gra which is included with the plug-in.

LENZFX cont

LENZ_I.IXP \lenzfx Digimation

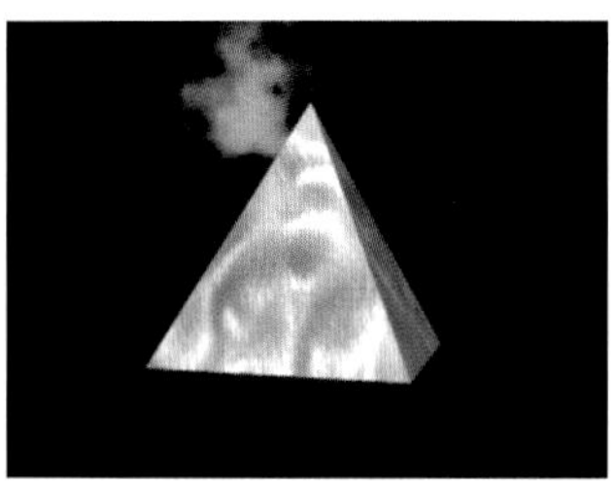
Flare [T]

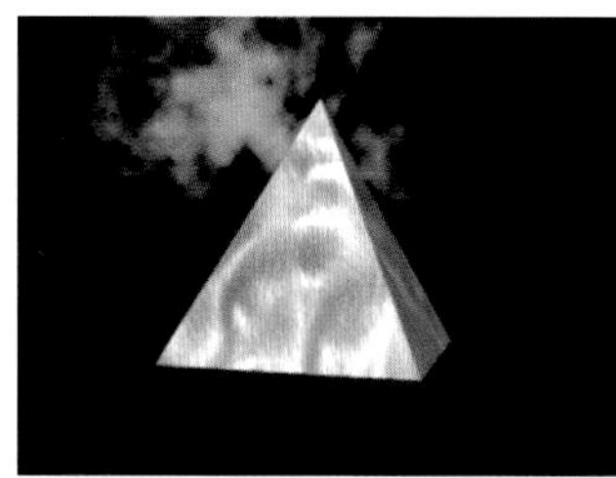
Flare [T]

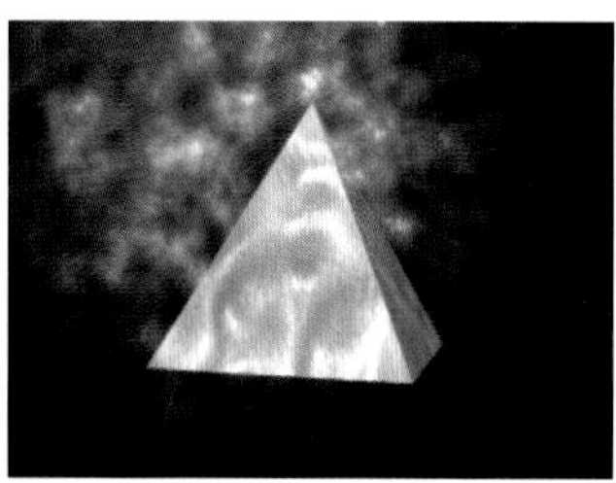
Flare [T][R]

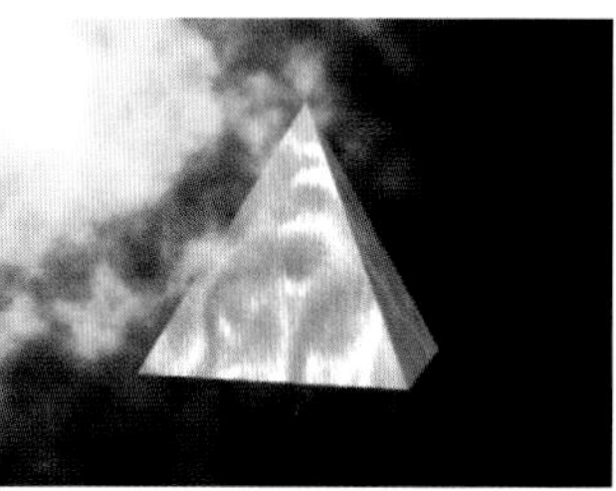
Flare [T]

Turbulence with Flare offers a range of effects from steam to clouds as well as numerous animated explosive effects. Adding rays and secondary flares adds realism to the flare effect.

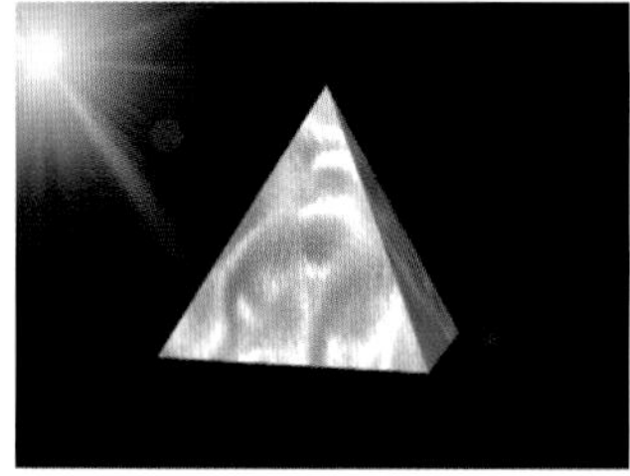
Flare Colorsun

Flare Default

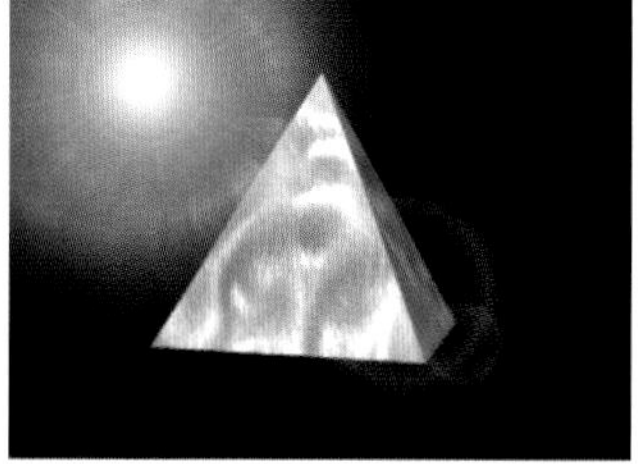
Flare Brtlight

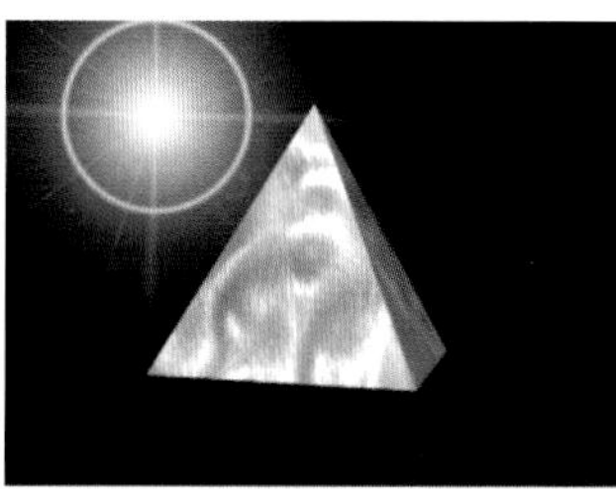
Flare Aliensun

Both symmetrical and asymmetrical effects are possible using Flare. Rings, segmented rings, rays, and soft star textures can be easily produced. This allows for rich complex effects without the need to layer or composite.

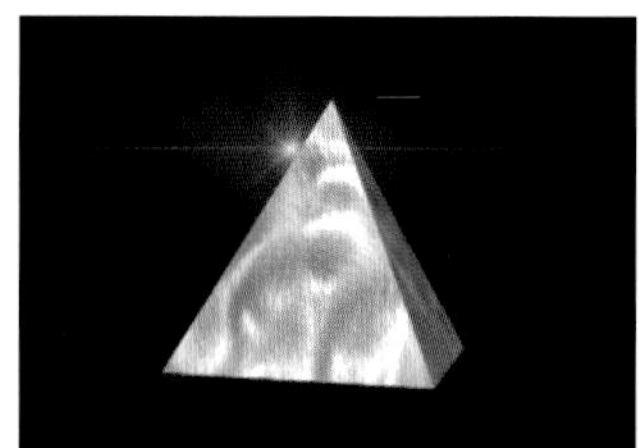
Flare LW2LF

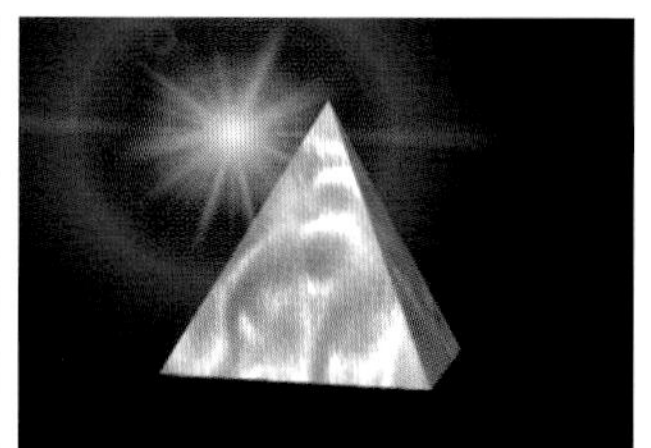
Flare LF2

ZFocus [Ft]d [Mf]

ZFocus [Ft]d [Mf]

Flares (images based on flare example LZR files) can be built from single as well as multiple star patterns and rings. ZFocus was used with Manual Focus set and the distance varied to produce variable softness that simulates depth of field.

Summary

Line is bundled with Pyros Partnership's Effects Library. Line performs an edge detection on all or part of an image or animation, and provides controls for varying line color and background color. Line also enables the background image to randomly show through in various patches of the processed image.

Line Parameters

Cutoff [C] (4–64) — Sets the threshold of the edge detection process.

Background Color [C1] — Sets the background color using the standard RGB/HLS sliders.

Line Color [C2] — Sets the line color using the standard RGB/HLS sliders when line is set to use line color.

Lines [L] o,l (Original, Use Line Color) — Sets line color to the color from the original underlying image or the solid color specified in line color.

Background [B] r,p (Random, Plain) — Sets the effect to randomly enable the background image to show through holes in the autotraced image.

Filter [F] (Whole Image, > 0, = 0) — Sets the general area of the image to be affected. If the alpha channel is used, the image must contain an alpha channel that is turned on in the Video Post queue. Whole applies the effect to the entire image, =0 applies the effect outside the alpha channel, and >0 applies the effect inside the alpha channel.

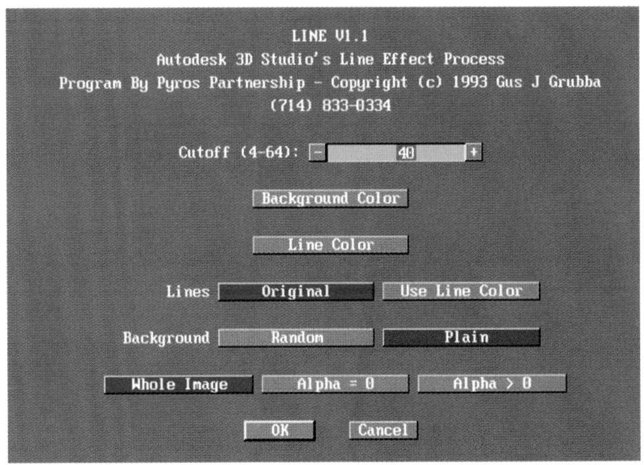

The Line dialog box.

[C]64[L]l[B]p[F]>0

[C]4[L]l[B]p

[C]34[L]l[B]r

[C]15[L]o[B]r[F]>0

Complex cracked patterns result when line is applied to background gradients. This effect can be useful when used with an alpha channel masking scene objects.

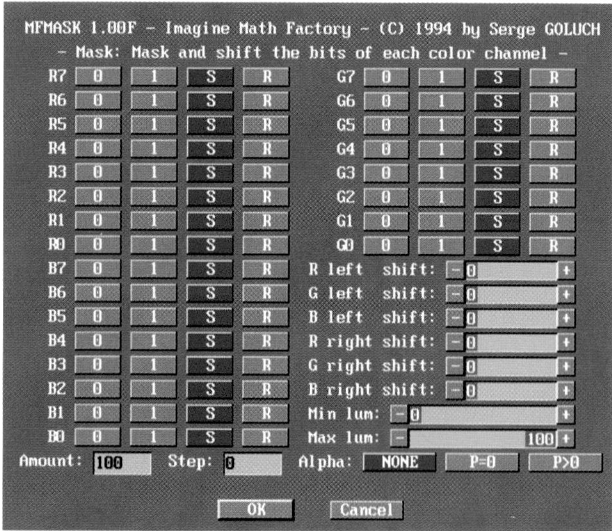

The Mask dialog box.

Summary

Mask is part of the Imagine Math Factory package. It enables you to alter an image's red, blue, or green color channels using simple binary arithmetic.

Mask uses an array of highlighted buttons to maintain, reset, or shift individual bits, which creates various color shifts, tints, and banded patterns. Furthermore, Mask provides control over the percentage with which the filter is blended into the original image along with a step value that varies the effects frame by frame.

Essential to working with Mask is a basic understanding of the way 24-bit color is specified. In a true color (24-bit) image, each color channel consists of eight binary digits, or bits, which are numbered from 7 to 0. For instance, Red is represented by bits R7–R0, with R7 being the most significant bit and R0 the least significant bit.

Thus, for a given color the red channel might consist of an eight-bit byte such as 01101101. The integer 1, at right, is the byte's least significant bit (R0) and the integer 0, at extreme left, is the byte's most significant bit (R7).

The most pronounced Mask effects are produced by varying the bit range toward the most significant bit. Changing the R7 bit from the default same setting to a value of 1, for example, produces a dramatic result. Mask effects decrease successively as you change each lower order bit (R6, R5, R4, and so on) until the given effect becomes imperceptible.

Mask Parameters

R7 to R0 [R7] to [R0] 0, 1, s, r (zero, one, same, reversed) — Sets each bit for the red color channel. 1 always sets a given bit value to 1, 0 always sets it to zero, a same setting leaves the bit unchanged, and reversed flips the bit value.

G7 to G0 [G7] to [G0] 0, 1, s, r (0, 1, same, reversed) — Sets each bit for the green color channel. 1 always sets a given bit value to 1, 0 always sets it to zero, a same setting leaves the bit unchanged, and reversed flips the bit value.

B7 to B0 [B7] to [B0] 0, 1, s, r (0, 1, same, reversed) — Sets each bit for the blue color channel. 1 always sets a given bit value to 1, 0 always sets it to zero, a same setting leaves the bit unchanged, and reversed flips the bit value.

Left shift [Ls] r, g, b (red, green, blue) (0–8) — Shifts the red, green, or blue channel bits to the left by the number set on the shift slider.

Right shift [Rs] r, g, b (red, green, blue) (0–8) — Shifts the red, green, or blue channel bits to the right by the number set on the shift slider.

Min lum and Max lum [Mn] [Mx] (0–100) — Applies the effect only in the luminance range set on the maximum and minimum sliders.

Amount [Am] (0.0–100.0) — Sets the effect amount as a percentage, with 0 having no effect and 100 applying the full effect.

Step [S] (–50.0–50.0) — Works with Amount to vary the effect frame by frame.

Alpha [A] n, =0, >0 (none, =0, >0) — None applies the effect to the entire image, =0 applies the effect outside the alpha channel, and >0 applies the effect inside the alpha channel.

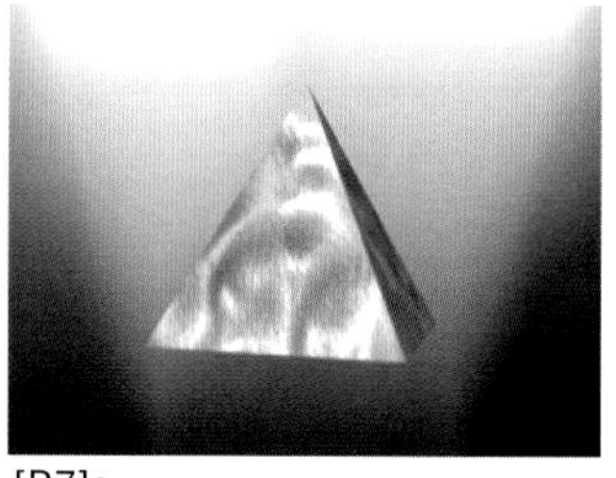
[R7]s

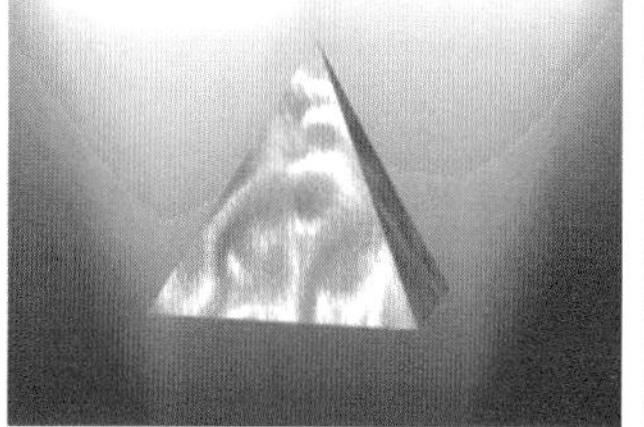
[R7]1

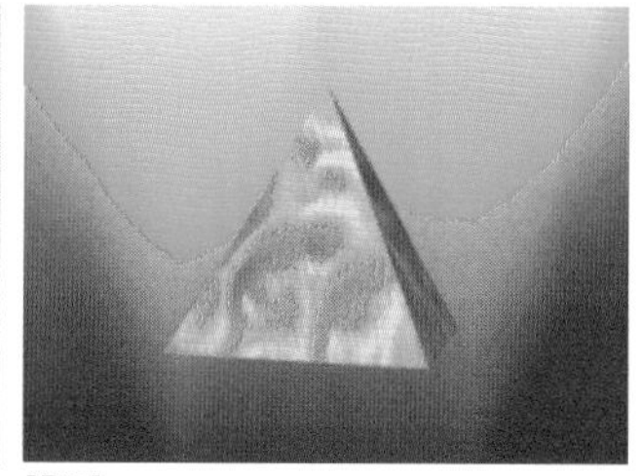
[R7]r

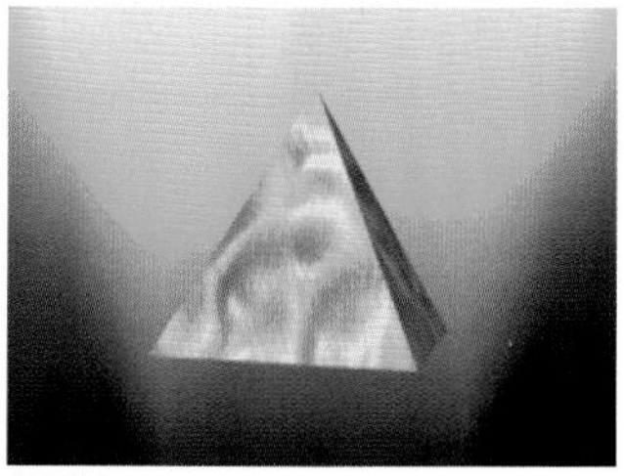
[R7]0

Changing the most significant bit in the red channel produces a pronounced color shift. A same setting produces a pass-through of the original image.

Schreiber Instruments \mask MASK_I.IXP

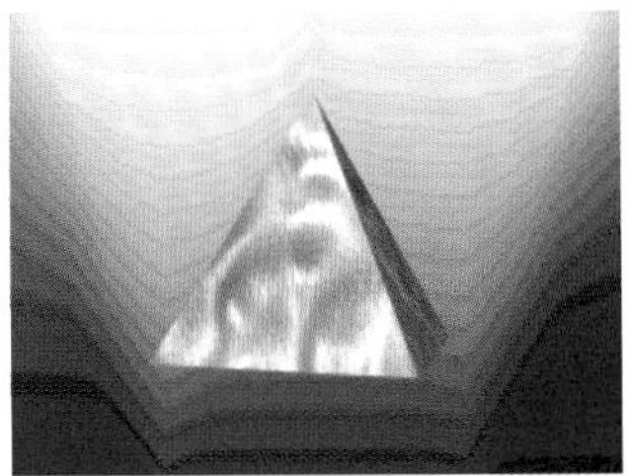

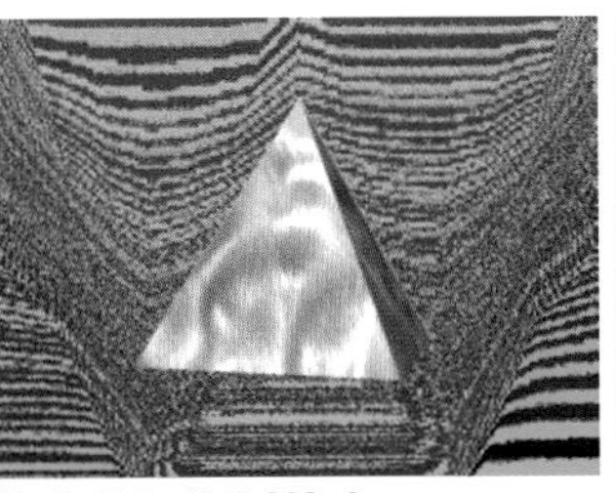

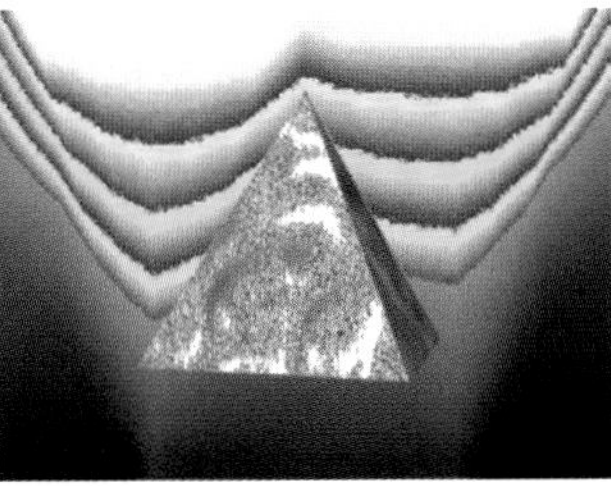

[Ls]b4 [A]n [Ls]b8 [A]n [Ls]g7 [Ls]b2 [A]=0 [Ls]g3 [Ls]b1 [A]n [Mn]40

Bit shift produces a range of banded and solid tints. Any effect can be applied either through an alpha mask or a luminance range.

MATRIX 3

Schreiber Instruments \matrix_3 MFMAT3_I.IXP

Summary

Matrix 3 is part of the Imagine Math Factory package. It is a convolution filter whereby numbers in a 3-by-3 matrix are used to process pixel values. The matrix represents the current pixel and its neighbors. Numbers in the matrix indicate shifts of the pixel values. Typically, the values for those pixels are added together and then divided or multiplied by another number (the scalar). The resulting color value is placed in the current pixel and the filter moves on to the next pixel. Matrix 3 enables you to select from division, multiplication, average, minimum, and maximum operations to apply to the matrix. You can set the scalar number and a bias number that shifts the final color value up or down. There are sliders that enable you to constrain the effect to a certain area based on luminance levels. When doing animations, you can set the starting strength of the effect and increment or decrement it from frame to frame. The alpha channel can be used as a mask. This filter uses the alpha channel only as an on/off mask.

Matrix 3 Parameters

Filter design [F] — A 3-by-3 matrix of numbers that controls the importance of different pixels in the calculations. Different settings here produce most of the variations in patterns.

Operator [O] m, d, mi, ma, a (mul, div, min, max, avg) — The operation to be performed on the matrix of values.

Scalar [S] (–9,999,999–100,000,000) — The number that is used with the operator on the matrix.

Bias [B] (–999,999–100,000,000) — Shifts the final color value after the calculations.

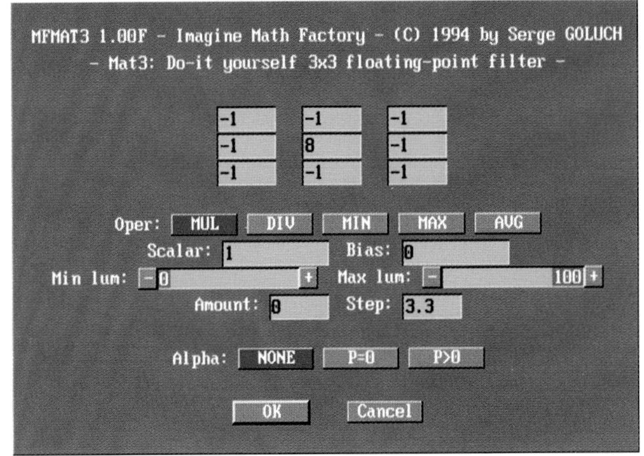

The Matrix 3 dialog box.

Min lum [Mn] (0–100%) — Lower luminance cutoff point of the effect.

Max lum [Mx] (0–100%) — Upper luminance cutoff point of the effect.

Amount [A] (0–100%) — Strength of the effect.

Step [P] (–50–50) — Change in the amount from frame to frame.

Alpha [Al] n, =0, >0 (none, =0, >0) — None applies the effect to the entire image, =0 applies the effect outside the alpha channel, and >0 applies the effect inside the alpha channel.

MATRIX 3 cont

MFMAT3_I.IXP \matrix_3 **Schreiber Instruments**

Frame 7

Frame 14

Frame 21

Frame 28

Animating the amount of the effect from 23 percent to 92 percent.

MATRIX 5

MFMAT5_I.IXP \matrix_5 **Schreiber Instruments**

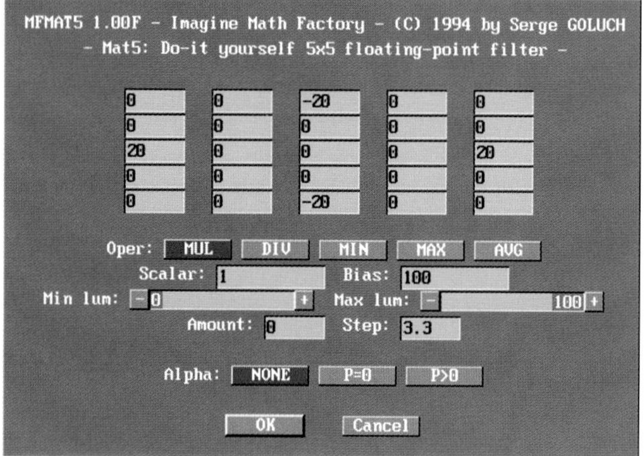

The Matrix 5 dialog box.

Summary

Matrix 5 is part of the Imagine Math Factory package. It is a convolution filter whereby numbers in a 5-by-5 matrix are used to process pixel values. The matrix represents the current pixel and its neighbors. Numbers in the matrix indicate shifts of the pixel values. Typically, the values for those pixels are added together and then divided or multiplied by another number (the scalar). The resulting color value is placed in the current pixel and the filter moves on to the next pixel. Matrix 5 enables you to select from division, multiplication, average, minimum, and maximum operations to apply to the matrix. You can set the scalar number and a bias number that shifts the final color value up or down. Sliders enable you to constrain the effect to a certain area based on luminance levels. When doing animations, you can set the starting strength of the effect and increment or decrement it from frame to frame. The alpha channel can be used only as an on/off mask.

Matrix 5 Parameters

Filter design [F] — A 5-by-5 matrix of numbers that controls the importance of different pixels in the calculations. Different settings here produce most of the variations in patterns.

Operator [O] (mul, div, min, max, avg) — The operation to be performed on the matrix of values.

Scalar [S] (–9,999,999–100,000,000) — The number that is used with the operator on the matrix.

Bias [B] (–9,999,999–100,000,000) — Shifts the final color value after the calculations.

Min lum [Mn] (0–100%) — Lower luminance cutoff point of the effect.

Max lum [Mx] (0–100%) — Upper luminance cutoff point of the effect.

Amount [A] (0–100%) — Strength of the effect.

Step [P] (–50–50) — Change in the amount from frame to frame.

Alpha [Al] n,=0,>0 (none,=0,>0) — None applies the effect to the entire image, =0 applies the effect outside the alpha channel, and >0 applies the effect inside the alpha channel.

MATRIX 5 cont

Schreiber Instruments | **\matrix_5** | **MFMAT5_I.IXP**

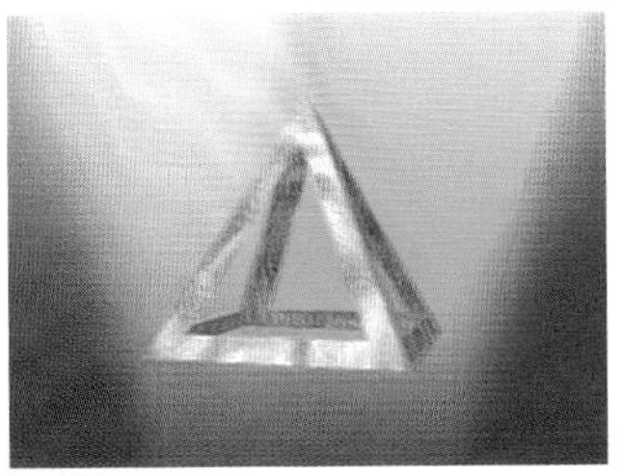
Frame 7

Frame 14

Frame 21

Frame 28

Animating the amount of the effect from 23 percent to 92 percent.

MATRIX BY COLOR

Schreiber Instruments | **\matrix_c** | **MFMATT_I.IXP**

Summary

Matrix by Color is part of the Imagine Math Factory package. It is a convolution filter whereby numbers in a 3-by-3 matrix are used to process pixel values for each of the three color channels. There is a red matrix, a green matrix, and a blue matrix. The matrix represents the current pixel and its neighbors. Numbers in the matrix indicate shifts of the pixel values. Typically, the values for those pixels are added together and then divided or multiplied by another number (the scalar). The resulting color value is placed in the current pixel and the filter moves on to the next pixel. This filter enables you to select either division or multiplication operations to apply to the matrix. You can set the scalar number and a bias number that shifts the final color value up or down. Scalar and bias are separate for each color channel.

When doing animations, you can set the starting strength of the effect and increment or decrement it from frame to frame. The alpha channel can be used only as an on/off mask.

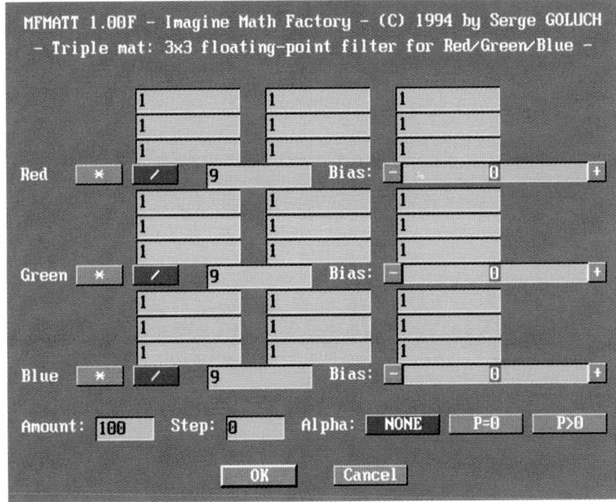

The Matrix by Color dialog box.

Matrix by Color Parameters

Filter design [F] — A 3-by-3 matrix of numbers that control the weighting of different pixels in the calculations for each color channel.

Operator [O] (mul, div) — The operation to be done on the matrix of values for each color channel.

Scalar [S] — The number that is used with the operator on the matrix.

Bias [B] (–255–255) — Shifts the final color value after the calculations.

Note: *Filter design, Operator, Scalar, and Bias are duplicated for each of the three color channels (red, green, and blue).*

Amount [A] (0–100%) — Strength of the effect.

Step [St] (–50–50) — Change in the amount from frame to frame.

Alpha [Al] n,=0,>0 (none,=0,>0) — None applies the effect to the entire image, =0 applies the effect outside the alpha channel, and >0 applies the effect inside the alpha channel.

MATRIX BY COLOR cont

MFMATT_I.IXP **\matrix_c** **Schreiber Instruments**

Blur and brighten red

Edge detect grn

Edge detect red & grn

Alpha mask

Different filter effects on different color channels.

MATRIX FILTER and ANIMATED FILTER

FMAT_I.IXP, FFMANI_I.IXP **\matrix** **Schreiber Instruments**

FFMAT 1.10 - The Filter Factory - (C) 1994 by Serge GOLUCH
- High speed filtering -

Filter: \IFF\FILTERS\3BLUR

OK Cancel

The Matrix Filter dialog box.

FFMANI 1.10 - The Filter Factory - (C) 1994 by Serge GOLUCH
- Animated use of .MAT filters -

Filter: \IFF\FILTERS\3BLUR

Start amount: 0
Middle amount: 50 Frames: 10
End amount: 100 Frames: 10

Alpha: NONE P=0 P>0

OK Cancel

The Animated Filter dialog box.

Summary

Matrix filter and Animated filter are part of the Imagine Filter Factory package. The Matrix filter calls and runs external filter effects that are applied at full strength across the entire image. The Animated filter differs from Matrix in that it has several controls to adjust the strength of the effect from frame to frame. It also enables you to use the alpha channel for masking. Both use the same predefined matrix filter files for their effects.

These effects are based on matrix pixel calculations and tend to produce mostly blurs or sharpening effects. The sharpening effects include several types of edge-enhancing filters. The blurs range from basic blurs to edge erosion filters. There are 3x3 matrix versions that have a small effect on your image, 5x5 versions that have a larger effect, and 7x7 versions that have the most pronounced effect.

The product comes with 102 predefined filters, and you can create your own filter files from scratch. A *filter file* is a text file with a specific format that is documented in the user guide. Your best bet is to edit copies of the existing filters using any text editor. There also is a test program called TGMAT.EXE, which runs from the DOS command line, to test custom filters. TGAMAT also is useful as a batch processing utility that does not require 3D Studio.

The Animated filter uses the alpha channel only as an on/off mask. The Matrix filter doesn't use the alpha channel at all.

Matrix Filter and Animated Filter Parameters

Filter [F] — The path and name of the predefined filter.

Start amount [S] (0–100%) — Strength of the effect in the first frame of an animated filter.

Middle amount [M] (0–100%) — Strength of the effect in the middle frame of an animated filter.

End amount [E] (0–100%) — Strength of the effect in the last frame of an animated filter.

Frames [Fm] (3–999) — Number of frames from start to middle of an animated filter.

Frames [Fe] (3–999) — Number of frames from middle to end of an animated filter.

Alpha [A] n,=0,>0 (none,=0,>0) — None applies the effect to the entire image, =0 applies the effect outside the alpha channel, and >0 applies the effect inside the alpha channel.

MATRIX FILTER and ANIMATED FILTER cont

Schreiber Instruments \matrix **FMAT_I.IXP, FFMANI_I.IXP**

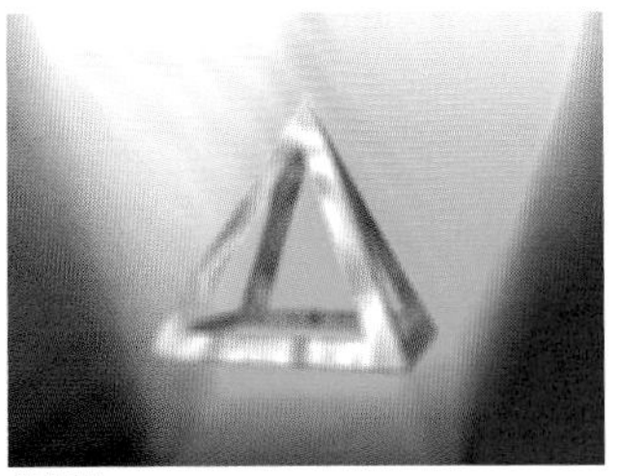
[F]7focus
Predefined matrix filters.

[F]7laplace

[F]7parch

[F]7proj_dr

[F]7erode
More predefined filters.

[F]7stran_h

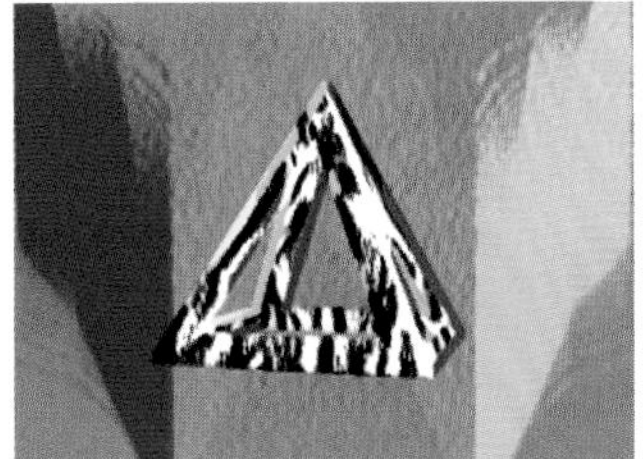
[F]7stran_v

[F]3xenon

MIRAGE

Digimation \mirage **MIRAGE_I.IXP**

Summary

Mirage produces a wide range of animated linear waves, concentric ripples, color distortions, and color cycling effects. Mirage is useful for producing numerous effects, transitions, and wipes both subtle and garish, from decloaking spaceships to vibrant psychedelic typography and backgrounds. You also can simulate natural phenomena including atmospheric heat distortions, raindrops on water, sparks, and shimmers.

Mirage's masking is a particularly powerful feature because it enables you to constrain any Mirage effect to a grayscale image, alpha channel, or animated mask, and thus to affect a specific area of the screen. The program is accessible via Process/Setup from Video Post, and although it works in 8-bit color mode, it works best in 24-bit true color.

Mirage consists of four dialog boxes: Mr. Wizard, Waves, Ripples, and Color Control. Mr. Wizard provides a selection of preset effects and enables you to select, save, or edit any effect as well as to create and maintain your own library of effects. The currently selected effect appears in an animated preview window.

The Waves, Ripples, and Color Control dialog boxes are used to edit existing effects and to create your own effects from scratch. The Waves dialog box is used to specify and apply up to 100 animated linear waves that move across your animation. It provides multiple sliders and numeric input boxes that control parame-

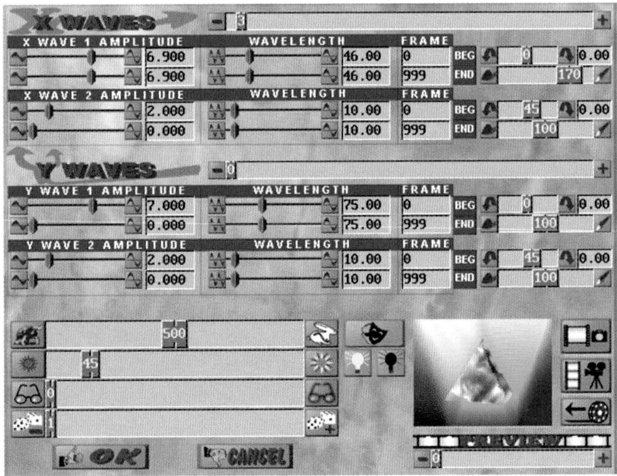

The Mirage Waves dialog box.

ters such as the number of waves, wave amplitude, wave length, and frame beginning and ending. You also have independent control over the rotation, rotation rate, and speed of travel for any of four wave sets, two in the X axis and two in the Y axis. Additional variables add both brightness and darkness to the image anywhere a wave rises or falls. The Wave dialog box provides a Preview Box and Preview Frame Slider, which enables you to view specific still frames or the entire animation.

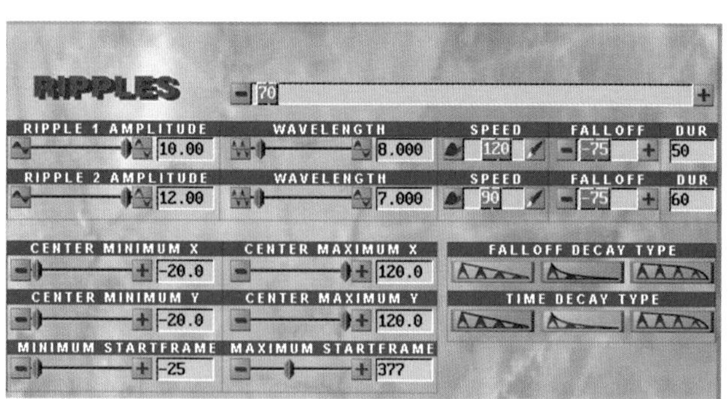

The Mirage Ripple dialog box—detail. All global features are the same as the Wave dialog box.

The Ripples dialog box enables you to apply up to 5,000 concentric ripples to still images or animation. Like Wave, Ripple provides an array of parameters that control amplitude, wavelength, speed, and duration. Its Falloff and Time Decay controls enable you to tweak the look and behavior of the ripples as they move away from their origin. Also like Wave, Ripple provides Scene Speed, Brightness, Light ON and Off, Blur, Random Seed, Masking, and a Preview window.

The Color Control dialog box consists of two sliders, a preview window, and preview controls identical to Wave and Ripple. The first slider controls the color cycling speed, and the second controls the range of color cycling from 0 to 255 or the full true-color palette.

Wave Parameters

Number of waves X and Y [Wx] [Wy] (0–100) — Sets the number of X and Y waves.

1 and 2 Begin and End Amplitude X and Y [Wba] X-Y, 1-2 [Wea] X-Y, 1-2 (–1,000–10,000) — Sets the rise and fall of the waves as a percentage of screen size.

1 and 2 Begin and End Wavelength X and Y [Wbl] X-Y, 1-2 [Wel] X-Y, 1-2 (–1,000–10,000) — Sets the distance between or frequency of the waves.

1 and 2 Begin Frame and End Frame [Fb1-2] [Fe1-2] (0–99,999) — Specifies when the distortion will start and end.

Rotation and delta rotation [Rw] [Rd] (Rotation –180–180) (Delta rotation –999–9,999) — Sets the start angle and rate of rotational change for the wave set.

Speed [Ws] x1-2 and y1-2 (0–199) — Sets the speed of travel for individual wave sets.

Scene speed [Ss] (0–999) — Sets the global speed for all Wave and Ripple distortions.

Brightness [B] (0–300) — Sets global lightness and darkness across both Wave and Ripple distortions.

Light on and off [Lon] [Lof] (yes, no) — Brightens or darkens the image where Waves or Ripples rise out of or recede into the image.

Blur [B] (0–100) — Applies a range of blur to the image.

Random Seed [Rs] — Randomizes distortion effects.

Ripple Parameters

Number of ripples [Rn] (0–5000) — Sets the number of ripples.

1 and 2 Amplitude and Wavelength [R1a] [R2a] [R1w] [R2w] — Same as Wave.

Speed 1 and 2 [Rs] 1-2 — Same as Wave Speed.

Falloff 1 and 2 [Rf] 1-2 (–100–100) — Defines how ripples act as they move out from center.

Duration 1 and 2 [Rd] 1-2 (0–99,999) — Sets the time it takes for the ripple to disappear.

Falloff Decay Type [Rfd] — Defines the Ripple amplitude as it disappears. Provides linear, exponential, and logarithmic profiles.

Time Decay Type [Rtd] — Defines the Ripple amplitude rate as it disappears. Provides linear, exponential, and logarithmic profiles.

Centering Values Minimum and Maximum [CmiX] [CmiY] [CmaX] [CmaY] — Sets the screen position for the ripple effect.

Start Frame Minimum and Maximum [Sfmi] [Sfma] — Sets the start and end frames for the effect.

Note: *Additional ripple parameters are identical to Wave parameters. Ripple also provides identical preview functions.*

Color Control Parameters

Color Change Speed [Cs] (0–199) Sets the color cycling speed.

Color Change Amount [Ca] (0–255) Sets the color cycling palette.

Frame 0

Frame 10

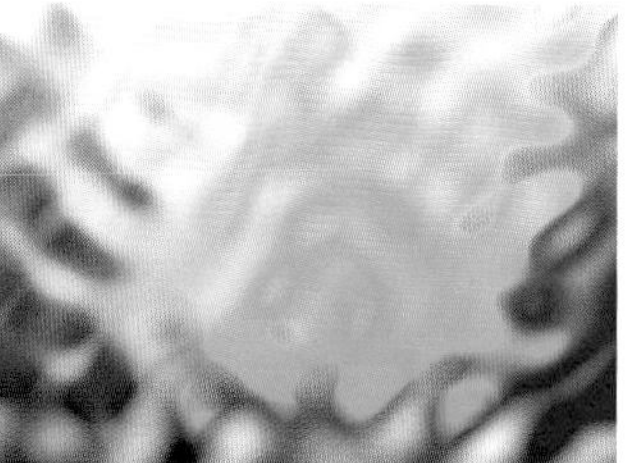
Frame 15

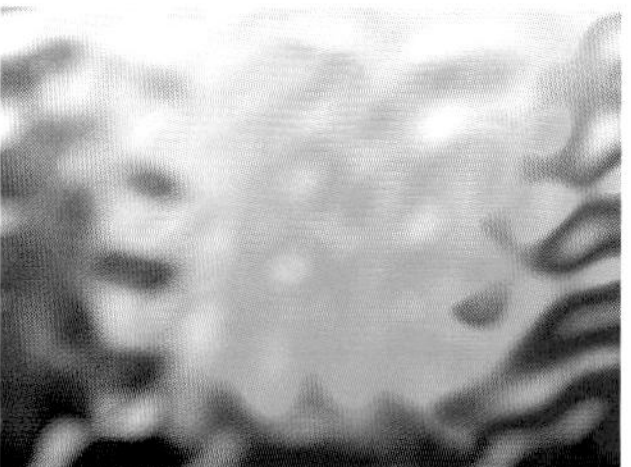
Frame 30

Linear wave sets can be applied independently for X and Y. This sequence used—[Wx]9, [Wy]3, [WbaX1]8, [WblX1]14, [WbaX2]2, [WblX2]10, [WbaY1]10, [WblY1]100, [WbaY2]0, [WblY2]0, [Ws]70, [Ss]500, [B]27, [Lon]yes, [Lof]yes.

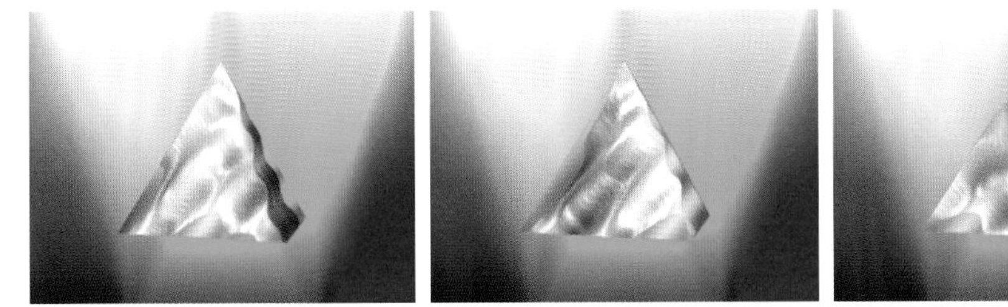

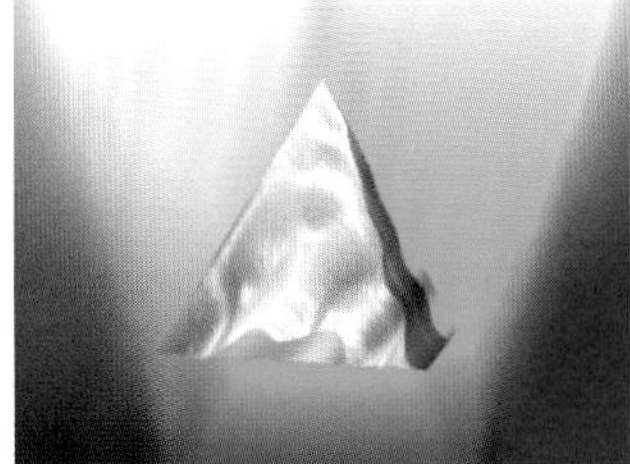

Frame 0 Frame 10 Frame 20 Frame 30

Alpha channel masks can be used to affect a specific screen area. The following parameters are common to these frames: [Wx]3, [Wy]0, [WbaX1]7, [WblX1]46, [WbaX2]2, [WblX2]10, [Ws]170, [Ss]500, [B]45, [Lon]yes, [Loff]yes.

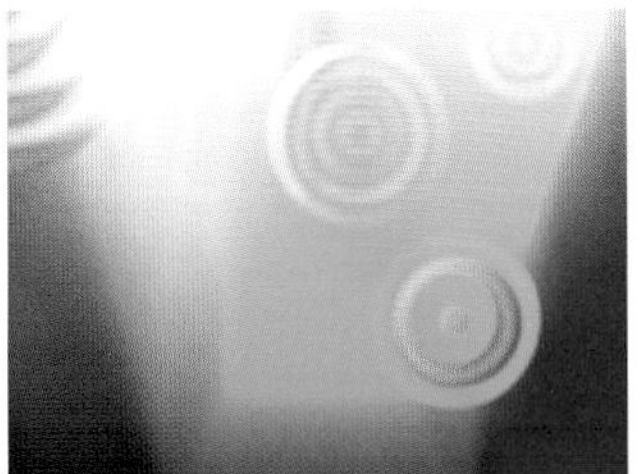

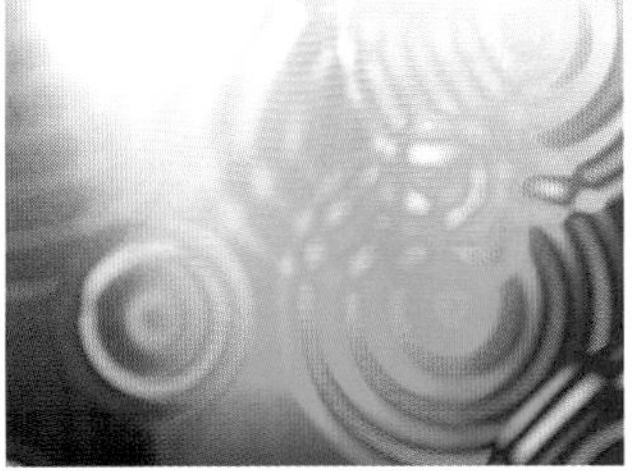

Frame 0 Frame10 Frame20 Frame30

Ripples are applied as concentric waves. Here, the following parameters were set: [Rn]70, [R1a]10, [R1w]8, [R2a]12, [R2l]7, [Rs1]120, [Rs2]90, [Rf1]75, [Rf2]75, [Rd1]50, [Rd2]60.

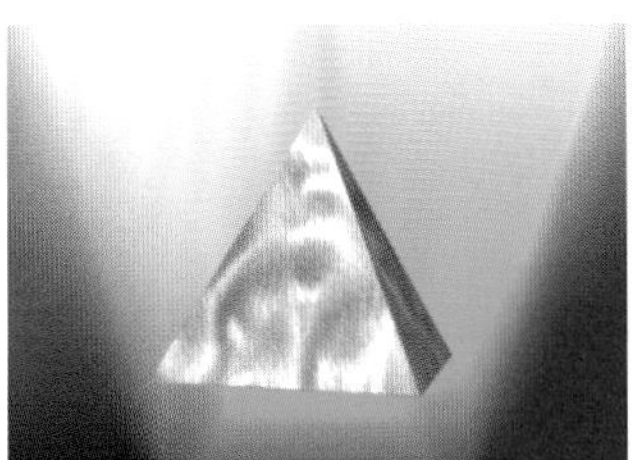
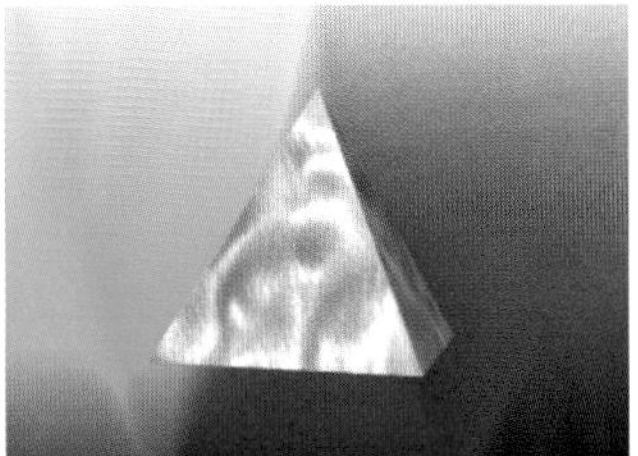
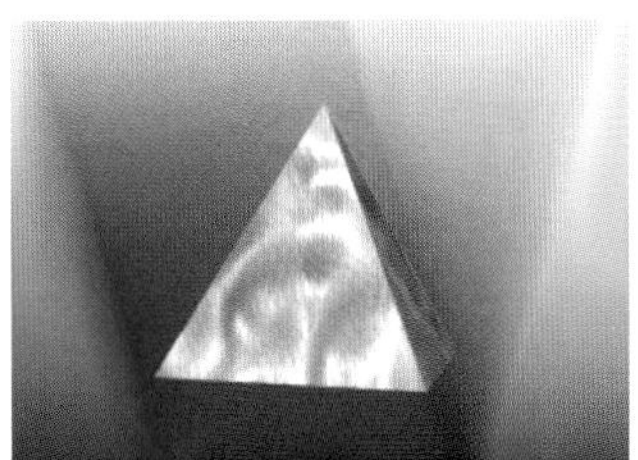
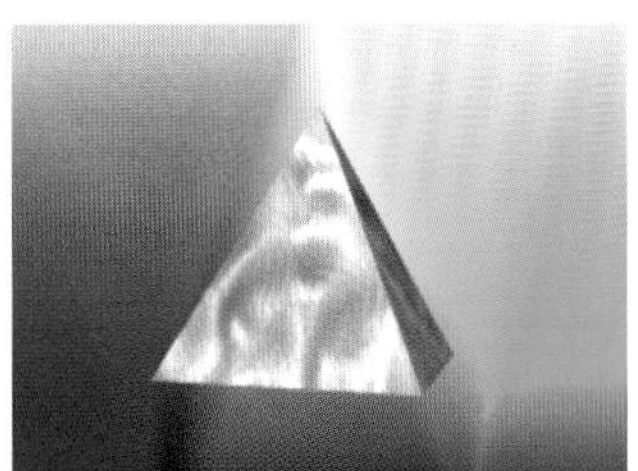

Frame 0 Frame 10 Frame 20 Frame 30

Color cycling provides control of cycling speed and color range. Color Change Amount was set to 255 and Color Speed to 300.

MONOCHROME

MONO_I.IXP **\mono** **Yost Group**

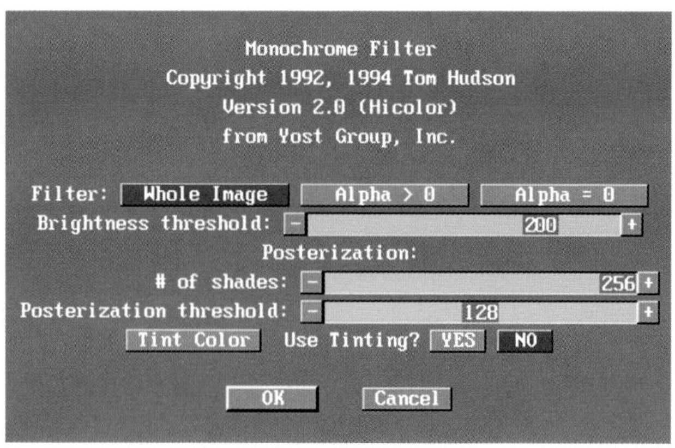

The Monochrome dialog box.

Summary

Monochrome is packaged with the Yost Group's Disk #1 Image Processing filters. The Monochrome filter converts color images into various grayscale bit depths. The filter also can be used to posterize or color tint an image. The area of effect can be constrained based on brightness, color, or hue, or by using the alpha channel.

Monochrome Parameters

Filter [F] (Whole Image, > 0, = 0) — Sets the general area of the image to be affected. If the alpha channel is used, the image must contain an alpha channel that is turned on in the Video Post queue. Monochrome uses the alpha channel only as an on/off mask. Whole applies the effect to the entire image, =0 applies the effect outside the alpha channel, and >0 applies the effect inside the alpha channel.

Brightness threshold [T] (0–255) — Sets the pixels to be filtered based on brightness.

# of shades [S] (2–256) — Sets the number of shades of gray used in the filtered image.

Posterization threshold [P] (0–359) — Determines the division between two shades when the number of shades is set to 2.

Tint Color [Tc] — Sets the color to tint the image with.

Use Tinting [Ut] (yes, no) — Specifies if the color specified in Tint Color will be used to tint the image.

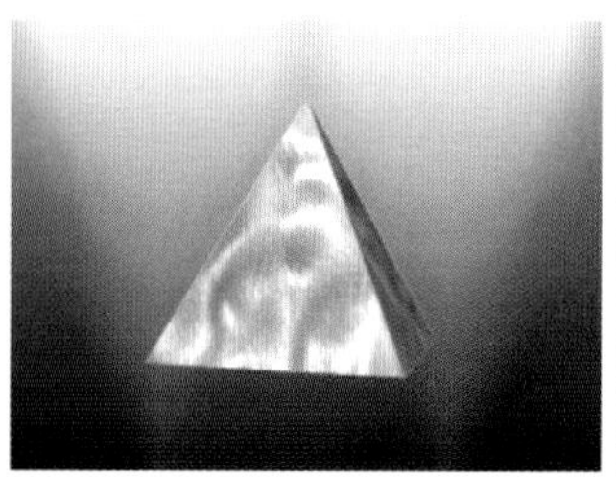

[S]256[Ut]yes

[S]2[P]150[Ut]no

[S]120[Ut]yes

[S]36[Ut]no

Monochrome is useful for posterization and tinting effects as well as grayscale conversion.

NEGATE

Schreiber Instruments — **\negate** — **FFNEG_I.IXP**

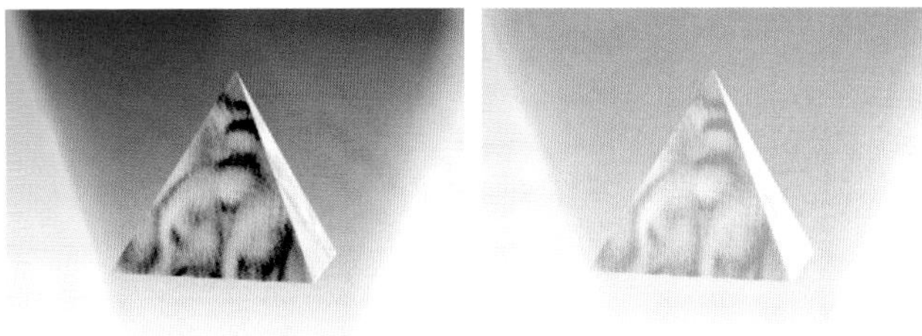

[Sc]100 [Sc]180
Negation with normal brightness and with increased brightness.

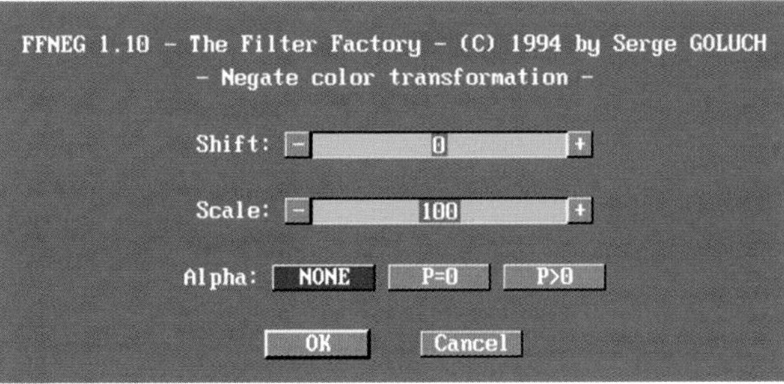

The Negate dialog box.

Summary

Negate is part of the Imagine Filter Factory package. It produces a color negative of the image. You can adjust the brightness of the image both before and after processing it. Making adjustments at both stages enables you to shift the value range for the image and change the image's contrast as well as its brightness. You can use the alpha channel to mask the effect. This filter uses the alpha channel only as an on/off mask.

Negate Parameters

Shift [Sh] (–255–255) — Brightness adjustment applied to the image before processing it.

Scale [Sc] (1–200%) — Brightness adjustment applied to the image after processing it.

Alpha [A] n,=0,>0 (none,=0,>0) — None applies the effect to the entire image, =0 applies the effect outside the alpha channel, and >0 applies the effect inside the alpha channel.

NEGATIVE

Pyros Partnership — **\negative** — **NEGAT_I.IXP**

Summary

Negative is part of the Pyros Partnership's Medias Library package. Negative inverts the colors in an image to produce the effect of a film negative. The alpha channel can be used to mask part of the image, but is used only as an on/off mask. The render alpha option must be on to use alpha masking.

Negative Parameter

Filter [F] w,=0,>0 (Whole Image,=0,>0) — Whole applies the effect to the entire image, =0 applies the effect outside the alpha channel, and >0 applies the effect inside the alpha channel.

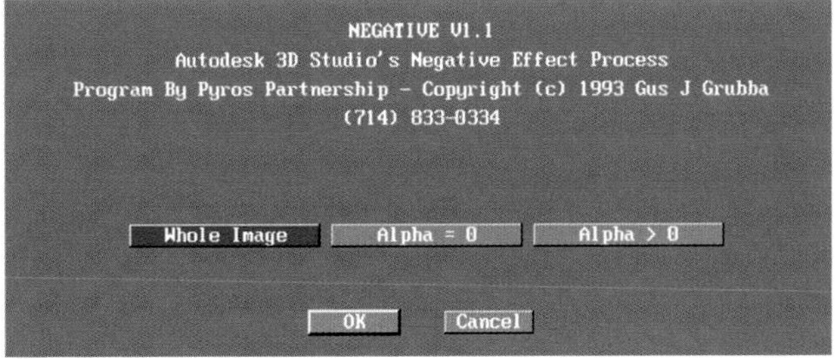

The Negative dialog box.

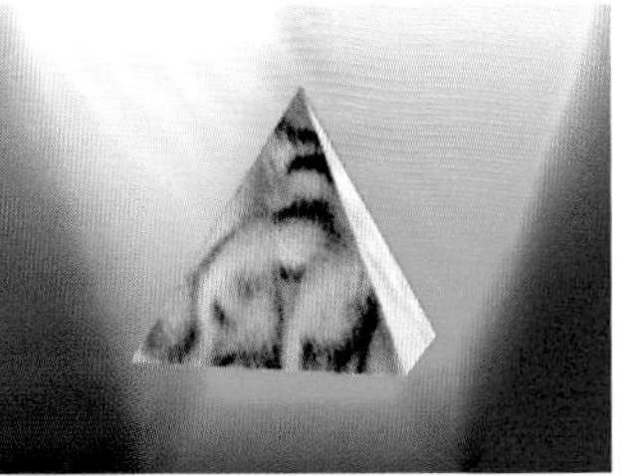

[F]w [F]>0
Negative inverts the colors in an image to produce the effect of a film negative.

NO ALPHA

NOALPH_I.IXP | **\noalpha** | **Yost Group**

The No Alpha dialog box.

Summary

No Alpha removes the alpha channel from an image in the video post queue. This eliminates alpha masking in complex queues with multiple images that have conflicting alpha channels. This program has no parameters and simply returns the image with the alpha channel removed.

OIL

OIL_I.IXP | **\oil** | **Pyros Partnership**

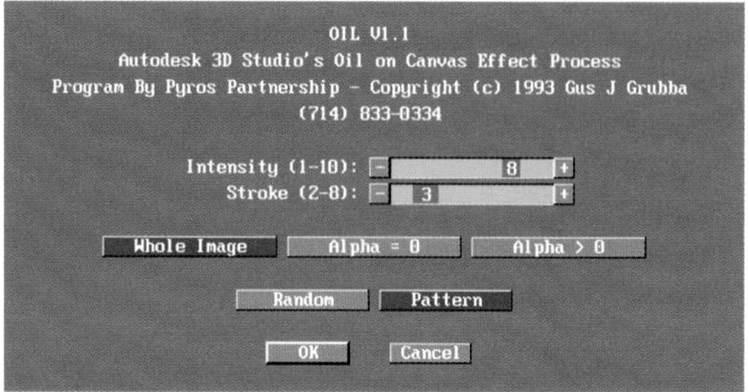

The Line dialog box.

Summary

Oil is part of the Pyros Partnership Paints Package. It produces a pattern of brush strokes across the entire image or a portion defined via the alpha channel.

Oil Parameters

Intensity [I] (1–10) — Defines the intensity of the effect.
Stroke [S] (2–8) — Varies the aggressiveness of the effect.
Alpha [A] w,=0,>0 (Whole Image,=0,>0) — Whole applies the effect to the entire image, =0 applies the effect outside the alpha channel, and >0 applies the effect inside the alpha channel.

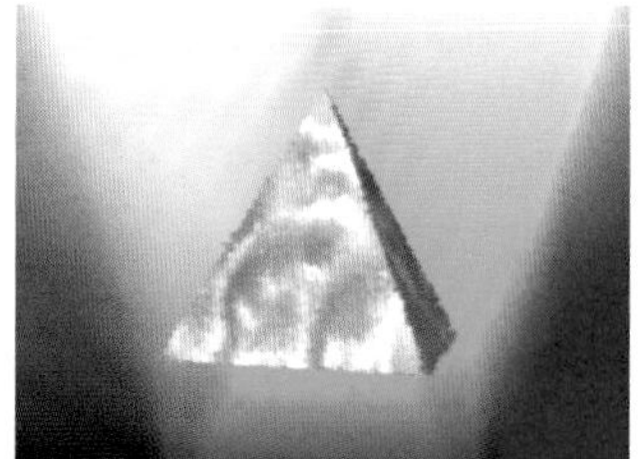

[I]10 [S]2 [W] | [I]8 [S]8 [A]=0 | [I]8 [S]8 [A]>0 | [I]10 [S]8 [W]

Oil produces a pattern of brush strokes over an image.

OLD MOVIE

Pyros Partnership \oldmovie OLDMV_I.IXP

Summary

Old Movie is part of the Medias Library package. Old Movie adds dust and scratches and fades the color of an image to simulate an old movie. Vertical scratches move across the image, and dust and fungus are applied randomly to each frame to appear animated. Old Movie also wobbles an animation by moving each frame slightly horizontally and vertically.

Old Movie Parameters

Vertical Scratch [Vs] (0–20) — Sets the number of vertical scratches or lines that will run through the sequence.

Dust Particles, Fungus [D] [F] (0–10) — Sets the amount of white and black single pixel noise that is added to the image.

Color Loss [Cl] (0–100%) — Sets the amount the image will fade from color to grayscale.

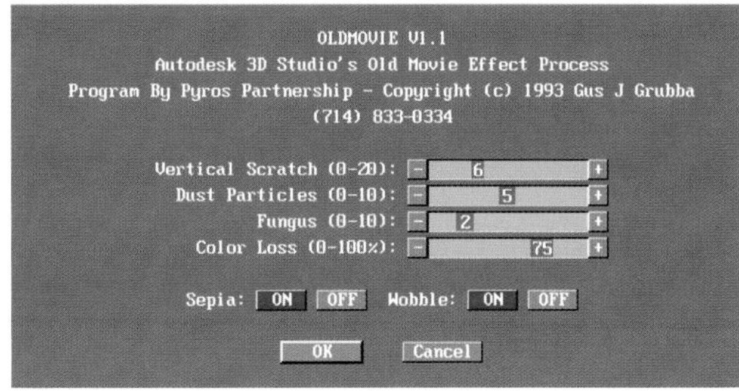

The Old Movie dialog box.

Sepia [S] (on, off) — Converts the image to a sepia-tinted monochrome.

Wobble [W] (on, off) — Sets the animation to shift both horizontally and vertically to simulate projector wobble.

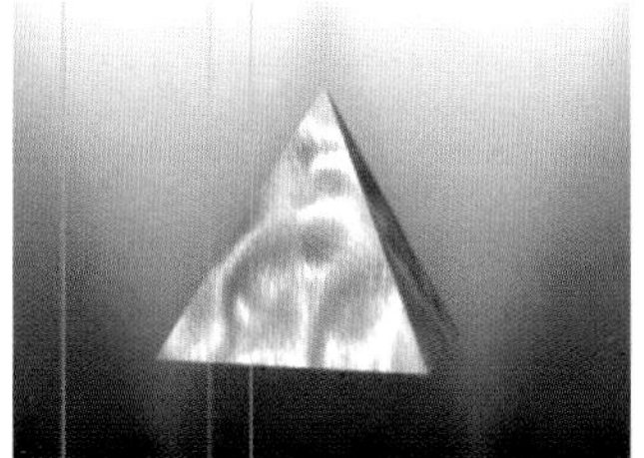

[Vs]3 [D]3 [F]2 [Cl]100%

[Vs]16 [D]10 [F]10 [Cl]60%

[Vs]5 [D]2 [F]10 [Cl]80% [S]on

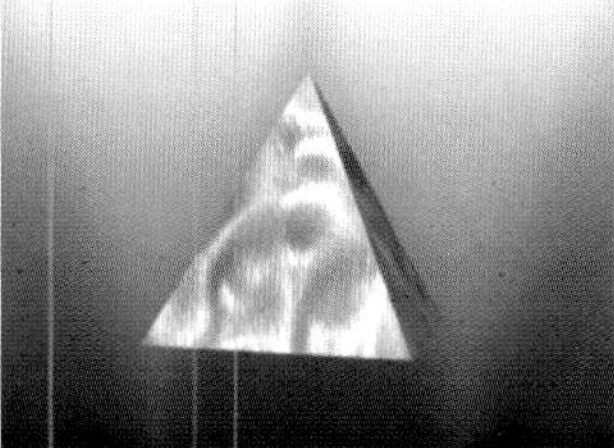

[Vs]3 [D]10 [F]1 [Cl]100%[S]on

Old Movie adds wobble, dust, and scratches and fades color to simulate an old movie.

PAGE FLIP

Pyros Partnership \pageflip PGFLIP_I.IXP

Summary

Page Flip is part of the Pyros Partnership's Transitions Library package. It produces a page flip that optionally rotates either the top or bottom of the frame toward camera.

Page Flip Parameters

Depth [D] (0–100) — Sets the degree of perspective or distortion and with that the frame scale for the transition.

Flip and Flop [Fli] [Flo] — Sets the flip direction, with flip rotating the bottom of the frame away from camera and flop rotating the top of the frame toward camera

Background Color [C] — Specifies a background color using RGB or HLS color space.

Number of Frames [F] — Sets the frame range for the flip or flop.

Starting Frame [F] — Sets the start frame for the transition.

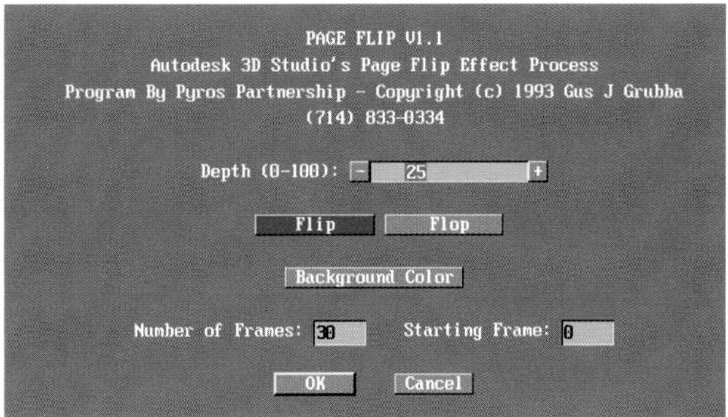

The Page Flip dialog box.

PAGE FLIP cont

PGFLIP_I.IXP | **\pageflip** | **Pyros Partnership**

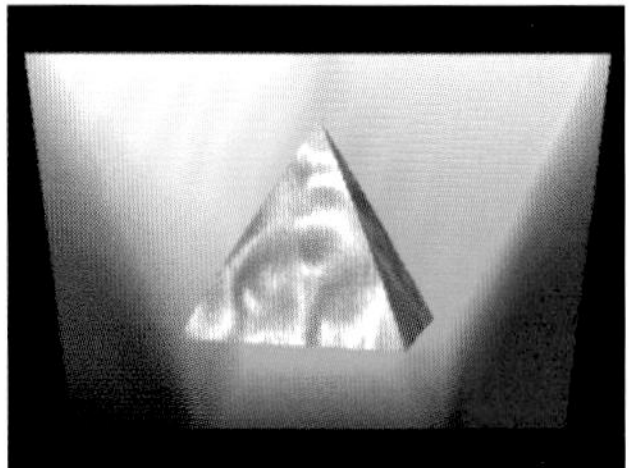

[D]25 Frame 6

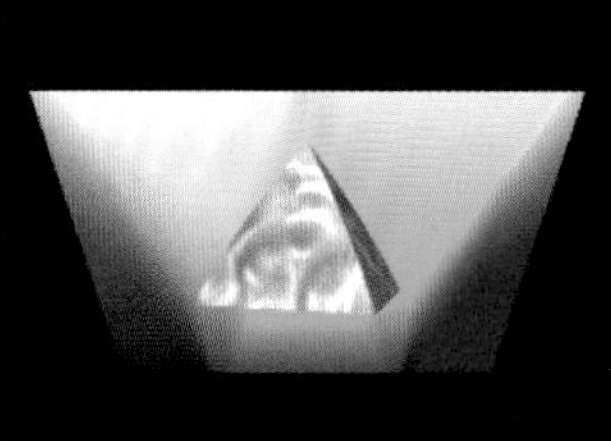

[D]25 Frame 12

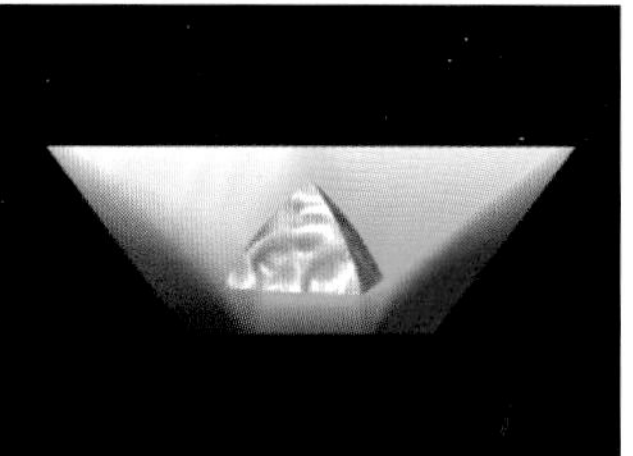

[D]25 Frame 18

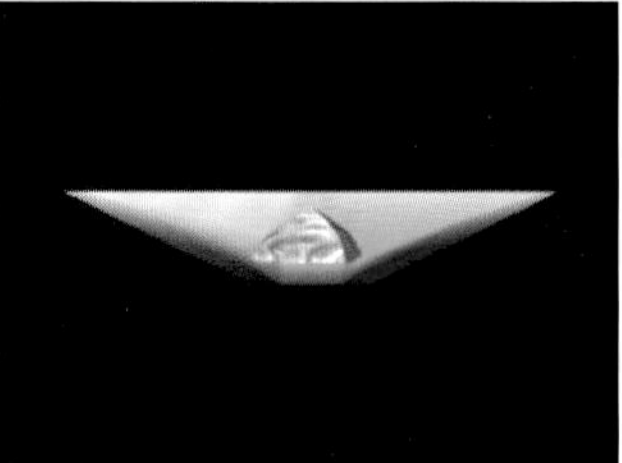

[D]25 Frame 24

Flip, shown in the sequence, begins with a full-frame image, and Flop ends with a full frame.

PAROUT

PAROUT_I.IXP | **\parout** | **Pyros Partners**

The Parout dialog box.

Summary

Parout is a plug-in that writes the images from a video post queue to a PAR board. The PAR (Personal Animation Recorder, from Digital Processing Systems, Inc.) is an adapter card with a dedicated hard disk that enables your computer to play back full-screen animations to a tape deck in real time. You place Parout as the last process in a video post queue and render the frames to your hard disk using a net render queue. Any number of machines on the network can render frames from the animation. You then place the machine that hosts the PAR board in slave mode, and it collects the frames in proper order and transfers them to the PAR while the animation is being rendered.

Parout Parameters

PAR Directory [P] — This is the directory on the PAR drive that holds your finished animation. Do not enter a drive letter here or Parout will not work.

Delete Images [D] y, n (yes, no) — Tells Parout to delete the original frame files as they are written to the PAR.

PENNELLO

PNLO_I.IXP | **\xaos** | **Xaos**

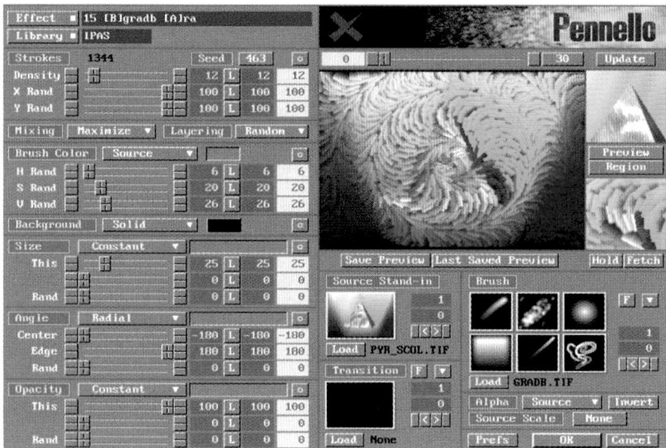

The Pennello main dialog box. The preview window and region windows are located at the right.

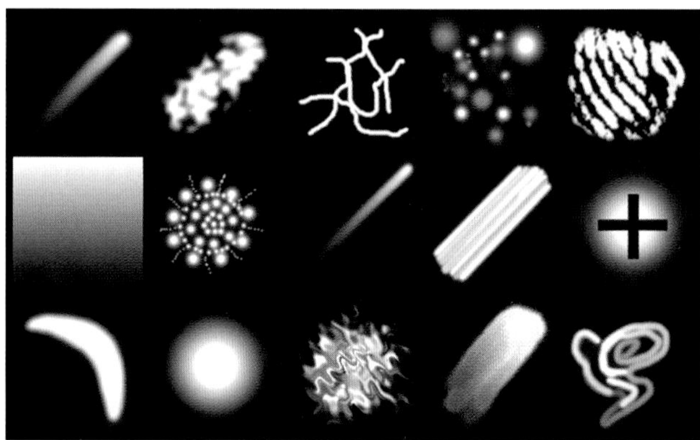

A sample of the 75 Pennello brushes: brush, char, cracks, dotsi, fngpr, grad, jelly, line, markf, plus, ripple, sphere, squiggly, stroke, and vasili.

Summary

Pennello is a special-effects engine that applies grayscale brushes to 3D illustrations or animation frames to create unique textures, backgrounds, patterns, and special effects. The range of still and animated effects possible with Pennello is vast, to say the least. You can easily make a 3D scene look painted, drawn, spotted, cracked, scumbled, stippled, spattered, or otherwise modified by any number of painterly manis

Essential to Pennello effects are its various brushes, which consist of any grayscale image file supported by 3D Studio. Pennello is supplied with 76 brushes. Brushes can be any resolution and are loaded into the Brush Panel for display in windows that are 48 pixels square. In spite of this the original brush size is maintained at render time, making it essential to consider brush size as it relates to image size.

Brushes can be varied for the density or number of times they are applied to the image (strokes). The stroke density range is dependent upon the resolution of a stand-in image that is used to preview each effect. This, along with random values for x and y position of the strokes, is adjusted via sliders.

Each parameter slider can be used to set a single value or can be independently moved to set starting and ending frame values. This is accomplished by Alt-clicking on the sliders and moving them to the desired values.

Brushes can be further varied for brush color, background color, size, angle, and opacity. Brush and background colors can be determined from several options, including a solid color, the source image, and a transition image.

Brush size, angle, and opacity can be set as constant, or can vary using, for instance, random, radial, horizontal, or vertical ranges, each of which can be further randomized using a Rand slider. Along with this fantastic range of variables, Pennello adds stroke, brush color, size, angle, and opacity options that allow you numerous temporal tweaks that smooth each effect.

Pennello provides three view areas that are used to preview each effect. The largest of these is the preview window, which renders the current effect when the Preview button is clicked on. The smaller windows to the right of the preview window display the selected region and a render of that region. This is useful for a quick look at a section of an image or for instances wherein high stroke densities can make a full preview slow considerably.

Pennello enables you to maintain effects libraries from which you can save and load effects. A default library is provided, which contains a number of interesting effects and useful starting points for creating your own effects.

Brush Parameters

Stroke Density [Sd] (0–100) — brusheSets the number of brush strokes.

Stroke X Rand and Y Rand [Sxr] [Syr] (0–100) — Sets the amount of random horizontal or vertical brush spacing.

Mixing [M] c, m, a (Composite, Maximize, Add) — Composite maintains the color of each brush stroke with no interaction with either the background or subsequent brush strokes. Maximize enables brush strokes to be affected by each other such that the stroke with the highest alpha or opacity is applied. Add additively combines the colors of overlapping brush strokes which can quickly create a white image.

Layering [La] o, r (Ordered, Random) — Ordered layering obscures or overlaps the bottom and right sides as brush strokes are added. Random layering avoids the uniform fish-scale look of ordered layering.

Brush Color [Bc] s, so, t, bst, bts (Solid, Source, Transition, Blend S->T, Blend T->S) — Solid works from any color chosen from RGB or HLS sliders. Source works from the colors in the current source image and brushes a new image based on the source color located at the center of each brush stroke. Transition works from the colors in the current transition image and brushes a new image based on the transition color located at the center of each brush stroke. Blend works from either source image to transition image or transition image to source.

H-Rand [Hr] (0–100) — Randomizes the original color's hue whether solid or image-based.

S-Rand [Sr] (0–100) — Randomizes the original color's saturation whether solid or image-based.

V Rand [Vr] (0–100) — Randomizes the original color's value whether solid or image-based.

Background [Bg] s, so, t (Solid, Source, Transition) — Same as brush color.

Size Constant [Sc] (this 0–100) — Holds brush size to a fixed size as set by the This slider.

Size Random [Sr] (this 0–100) (that 0–100) — Varies brush size randomly between the range set by the This and That sliders.

Size Radial [Sra] (center 0–100) (edge 0–100) — Varies brush size between the settings of Center and Edge sliders based on an invisible circle that is centered on and masks the image.

Size Horizontal [Sho] (left 0–100) (right 0–100) — Varies the brush size as a function of each brush stroke's position along the horizontal axis. The range of size is set on the left and right sliders.

Size Vertical [Sv] (top 0–100) (bottom 0–100) — Varies the brush size as a function of each brush stroke's position along

PENNELLO cont

the vertical axis. The range of size is set on the top and bottom sliders.

Size by Hue [Sh] (Hue0 0–100) (Hue255 0–100) — Varies brush size as a function of the hue range set by the Hue0 and Hue255 sliders.

Size by Saturation [Ss] (Unsat. 0–100) (Satur. 0–100) — Varies brush size as a function of the saturation range set by the Unsat. and Satur. sliders.

Size by Value [Sv] (Dark 0–100) (Bright 0–100) — Varies brush size as a function of the value range set by the Dark and Bright sliders.

Rand slider [Rs] (0–100) — Adds further randomness to the value set on the This slider by randomly varying the size of the brush bitmap.

Note: *Angle and Opacity parameters are identical to Size parameters.*

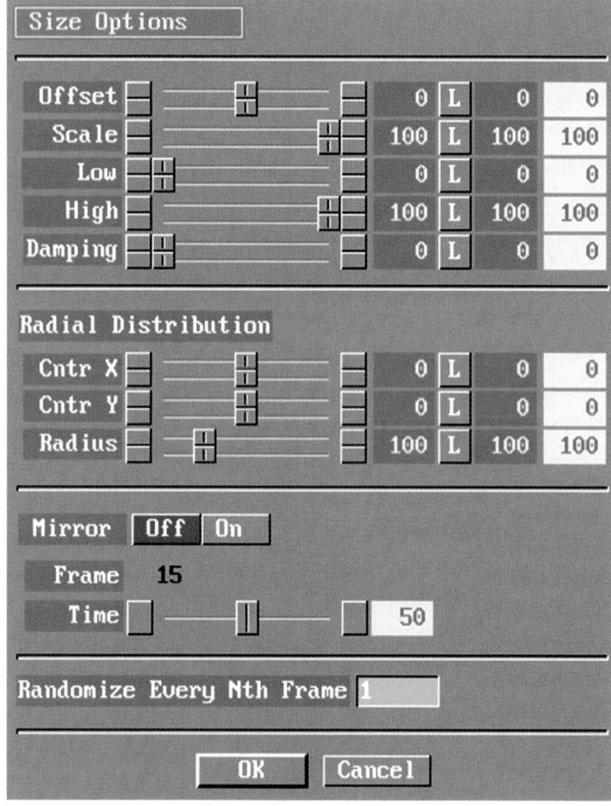

The Size Options dialog box provides a number of additional variables for smoothing animated effects. Similar dialog boxes are provided for strokes, brush color, background, angle, and opacity.

Option Parameters

Note: *These parameters are available from the options menus, which are accessed by clicking on the circle buttons.*

Damping [Ds] [Db] (stroke, brush color) — Smooths the transitions between frames for stroke size and brush color.

Randomize Every Nth Frame [Rf] (stroke, brush color, size, angle, opacity) — Sets a new seed value at the frame interval specified. An attribute Rand slider must be set to greater than 0 for the effect to work.

Use for all Attributes [Ua] (off, on) — Sets a new seed value for any attribute with a Rand slider setting greater than 0.

Mirror [M] (off, on) — Produces a reflection of the current interpolation method at the frame specified by the time slider. The parameter then reverses itself, continuing backward along a timeline.

Time [Tf] (frame number) — Sets the end frame for the chosen interpolation method to flip and reverse.

Offset size [Of] (–100–100) — Adds a positive or negative percentage of the brush bitmap to the size settings. The resulting size is clipped at 100 percent.

Scale size [Ss] (0–100) — A percentage of brush size created from both the size and offset settings.

Low and High [L] [H] (0–100) — Filters out stroke sizes set by the Low and High sliders.

Radial Distribution [Rd] (CntrX –200–200, CntrY –200–200, Radius 0–400) — Works with Size Radial [Sra] and varies the position and radius of an invisible circle that is used to mask the image.

Interpolation Parameters

Note: *These parameters are located in the interpolation menus, which are accessed by clicking on the L button.*

Linear [Il] — Applies uniform interpolation that changes consistently between frames.

Slow Trans [Ist] — Changes values gradually at the beginning and end, and rapidly during the middle frames.

Fast Trans [Ift] — Similar to Slow Trans with a steeper curve that produces a more distinct change than Slow Trans.

SF Ramp [Isf] — Changes values gradually until the middle frames, where change increases exponentially.

FS Ramp [Ifs] — The opposite of SF ramp, with rapid changes at first and gradual changes at the end.

Slow In/Out [Isio] — Changes take place rapidly at both starting and ending frames and slowly in the middle frames.

Fast Trans [Ifio] — Similar to Slow In/Out with more dramatic shifts into and out of the middle frames.

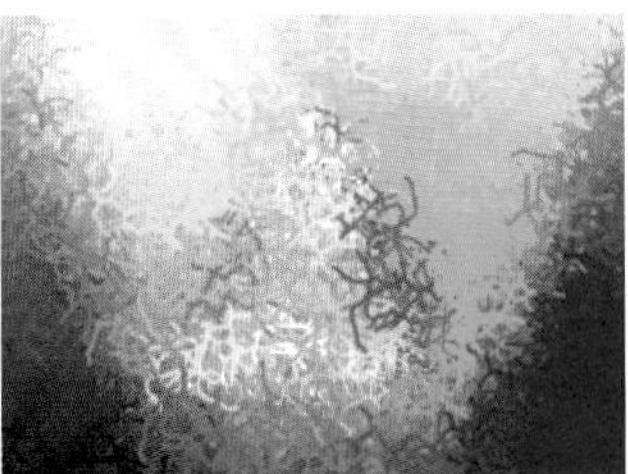
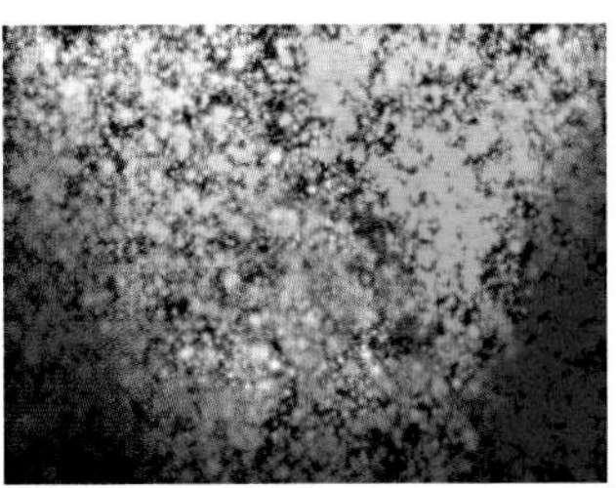
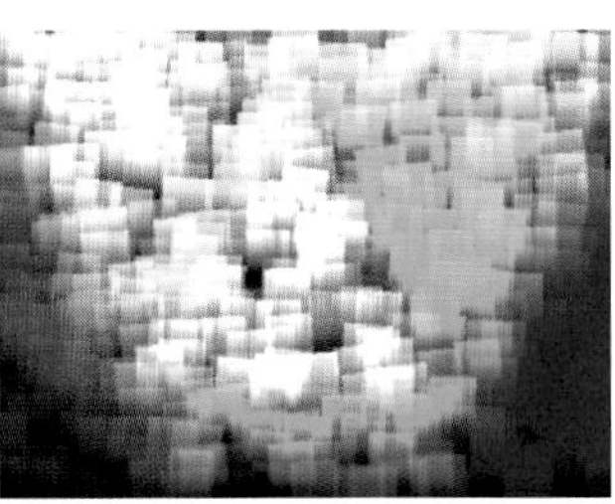

[B]char [Sd]1813 [B]cracks [Sd]1344 [B]dotsi [Sd]910 [B]grad [Sd]560

The brush type controls the type of mark used to build a new image from a source image.The images used a solid white background, the source image, and solid black backgrounds, respectively. All brushes are included with Pennello.

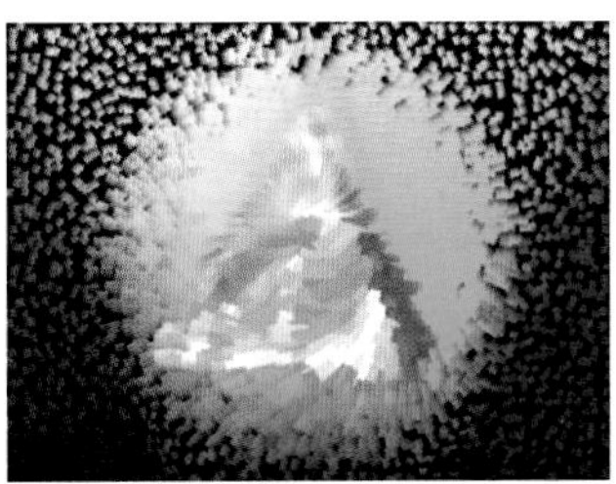

[B]line [Sd]1680 [B]stroke [Sd]1131 [B]squiggly [Sd]3072 [B]markf [Sd]1564

These images used a mix of random size, angle, and density.The vignette in image three was created with Size radial, and the effect in image four resulted from Angle radial.

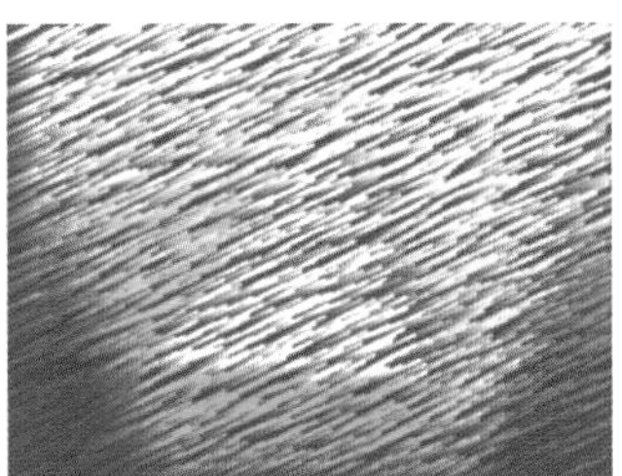
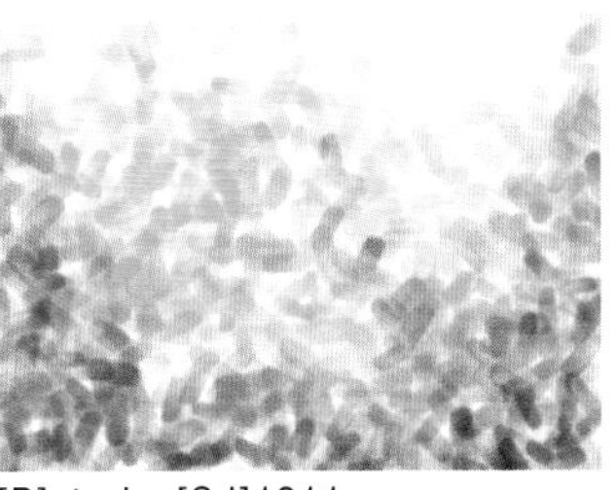
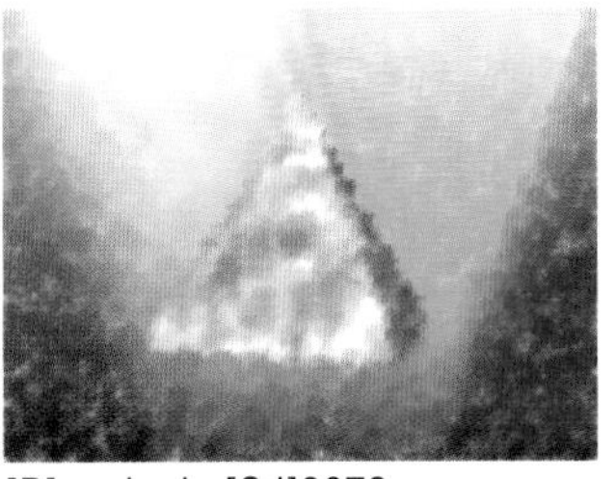

[B]line [Sd]1680 [B]stroke [Sd]1311 [B]squiggly [Sd]3072 [B]markf [Sd]1564

Image 1 used Mixing Add with Angle constant; 2 used random brush angle, wide range of random saturation and value; 3 used a narrow range of random saturation and value; and 4 used angle set to constant with size and opacity by (source image) saturation.

[B]vasili [Sd]1131

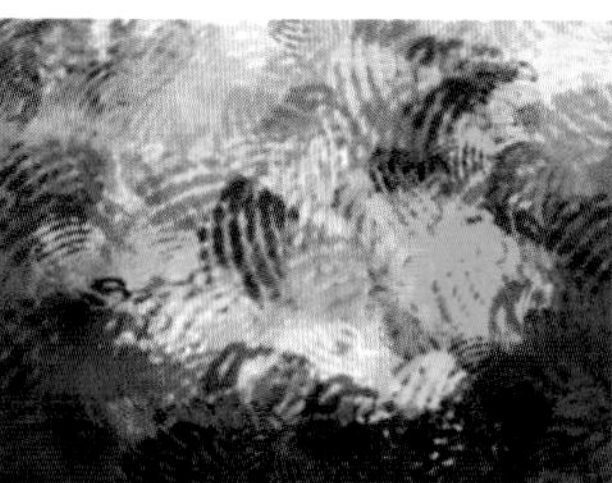
[B]fngpr [Sd]336

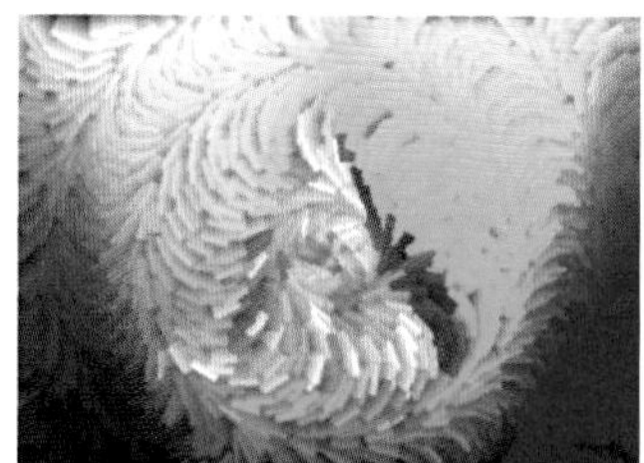
[B]gradb [Sd]1344

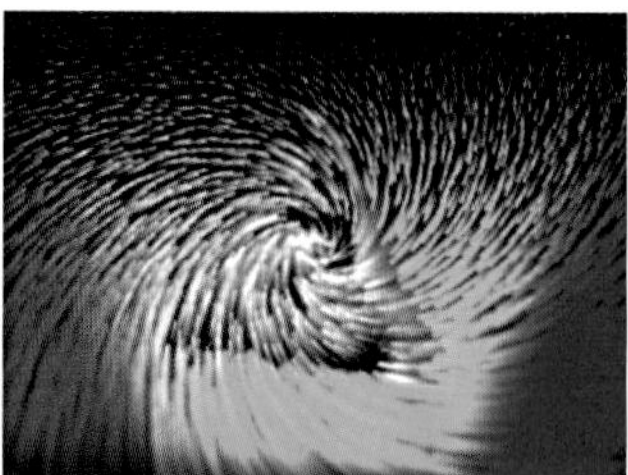
[B]brush [Sd]2352

Vasili was used with random hue, saturation, and size. Fngpr was used with maximum random hue and value. Gradb was used with Angle radial set to its max range. Brush was used with Angle radial fixed at 180, which held the rotation to a single sweep. Size by value caused the brush to fall off at the top of the image.

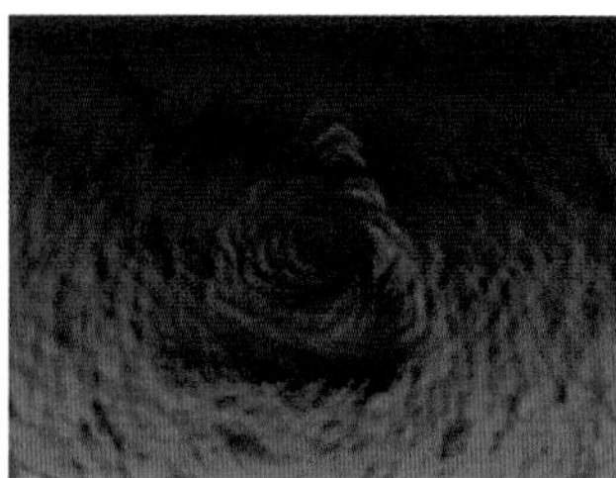
[B]ripplea [Sd]1680

[B]sphereb [Sd]1344

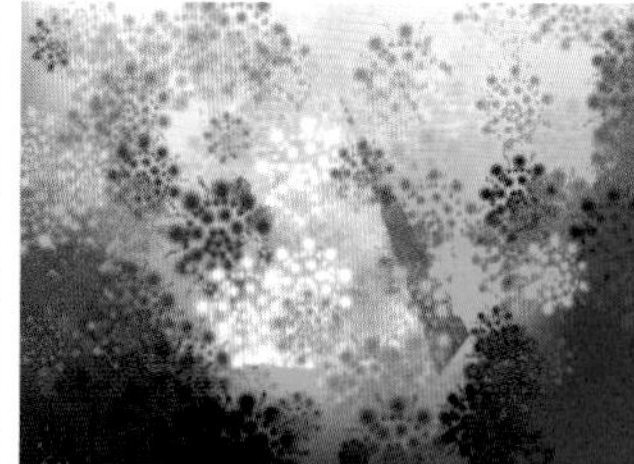
[B]jelly [Sd]108

[B]plus [Sd]221

The Ripplea was used with solid color for foreground and background, and Brush size and angle were set to radial at fixed values. Sphereb was used with no x or y random values, which created the grid look, and size by value allowed the brush to fall off at the top. Jelly was used with minimal stroke density, and Brush color with hue random was set to add color variation. Plus was used with solid colors to completely obscure the base image.

PINGPONG

Schreiber Instruments | **\pingpong** | **AFPP_I.IXP**

Summary

Pingpong is part of the Imagine Animated Factory. It takes one to four smaller copies of your image and bounces them around on the screen. They bounce off the sides of the screen and can leave fading tails as they go. You specify the number of images, their starting location, direction, and speed. You also can set the number of copies of the image that make up the tails and whether the tails fade out or chop off. The background can be either the original image or black. You can get some odd clipping effects when tails cross each other. This plug-in does not use the alpha channel.

Pingpong Parameters

Size [S] (2–20) — Sets the image size as a fraction of the original image. 2 means 1/2 of the original, 20 means 1/20.

Start line [Sl] (0–100) — The starting position as percentage of the screen.

Start col [Sc] (0–100) — The starting position as percentage of the screen.

Vert. Speed [Vs] (–50–50) — Increments the vertical speed per frame.

Hor. Speed [Hs] (–50–50) — Increments the horizontal speed per frame.

Type [T] s, w, h, b — Sets the orientation of images: s for normal, w for invert X, h for invert Y, and b for invert X and Y.

Number of pictures [P] — Specifies the number of small images to bounce around.

Number of frames [F] — Sets the frame range for the effect. The effect cycles if [F] is less than the total number of animation frames.

Tail size [Ts] (0–20) — Sets the number of copy images that form the tail.

Tail type [Tt] (hard or soft) — Tail finish effect: fade out or chop off.

Source [Sc] — Use original image or black as background.

Frame 0

Frame 8

Frame 18

Frame 26

[P]2 [S]4,6 [Vs]5,30 [Hs]5,22 [Ts]8 [Tt]Soft

PIXEL

Pyros Partnership | **\pixel** | **PIXEL_I.IXP**

Summary

Pixel is part of the Medias Library package. Pixel breaks an image into a series of blocks that reflect the color of the underlying image. The effect can be animated so that the effect changes in scale over time. The alpha channel can be used to mask part of the image, but is used only as an on/off mask.

Pixel Parameters

Starting/Ending Pixel Size [Ss] [Es] (1–200) — Sets the size of the blocks into which the image will be pixelated. The effect can be animated by setting the starting and ending pixel size so that the block size grows larger or smaller.

Number of frames [#F] — Sets the number of frames to process in an animated effect.

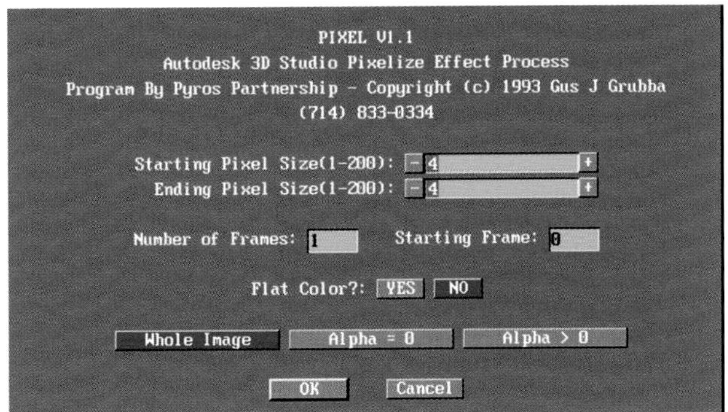

The Pixel dialog box.

PIXEL cont

PIXEL_I.IXP \pixel **Pyros Partnership**

Starting Frame [Sf] — Sets the frame on which the effect will begin.
Flat Color [Fc] (yes, no) — Flattens the color palette.
Filter [F] w,=0,>0 (Whole Image,=0,>0) — Whole applies the effect to the entire image, =0 applies the effect outside the alpha channel, and >0 applies the effect inside the alpha channel.

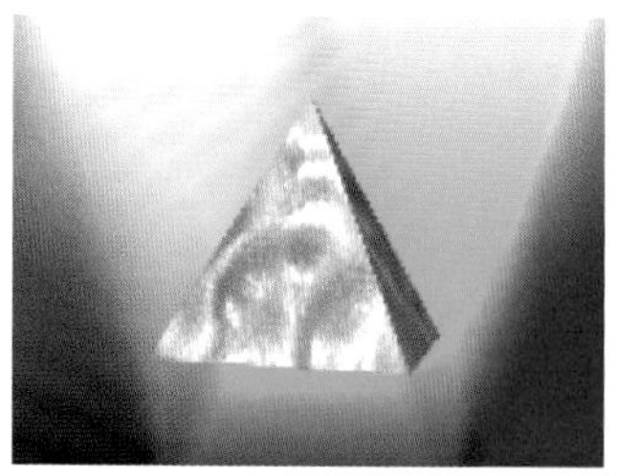
[Ss]3

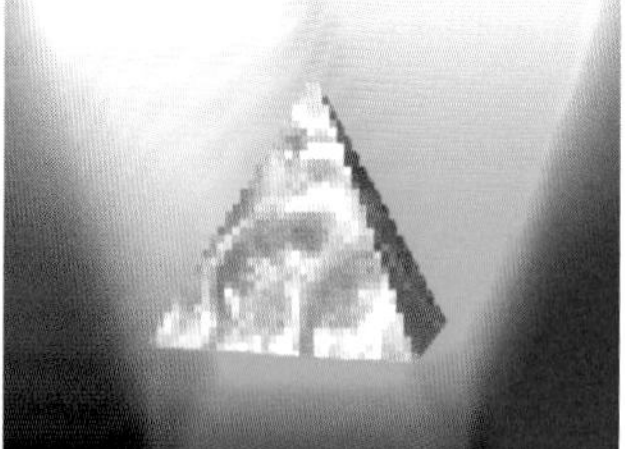
[Ss]6 [F]>0

[Ss]15 [Fc]yes [F]>0

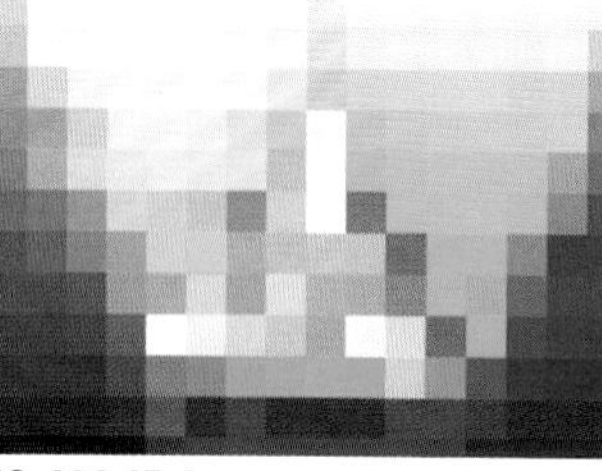
[Ss]32 [Fc]yes

Pixel breaks an image into a series of blocks that can be animated in scale.

PIXELATE

AFPIX_I.IXP \pixelate **Schreiber Instruments**

The Pixelate dialog box.

Summary

Pixelate is part of the Imagine Animated Factory. It pixelates your image to give it a low-resolution look. You can limit the effect to one or more color channels. You can specify the height and width of the pixels, and you can animate the size. You can pixelate the entire image or mask the effect with the alpha channel. This plug-in uses the alpha channel only as an on/off mask.

Pixelate Parameters

Line width [Lw] (1–999) — Sets the initial height of pixels.
Line step [Ls] (–99–99) — Increments the pixel height per frame.
Column width [Cw] (1–999) — Sets the initial width of pixels.
Column step [Cs] (–99–99) — Increments pixel width per frame.
Red, Green, Blue [R] [G] [B] (yes or no) — Pixelates the given color channel.
Alpha [Al] (none, =0, >0) — Alpha channel masking of the effect.

PIXELATE cont

Schreiber Instruments | **\pixelate** | **AFPIX_I.IXP**

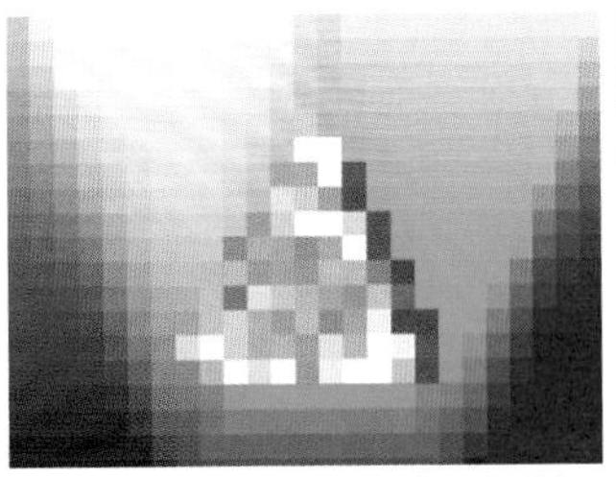

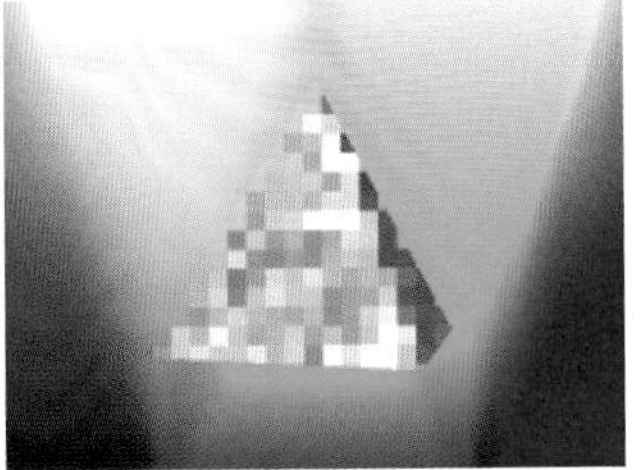

[Lw]20 [Cw]20 [R]Y [G]Y [B]Y [R]Y [G]N [B]Y [Al]>0 [Lw]38 [Cw]5

Normal pixelation, blue-channel pixelation, alpha masking, and nonsquare pixels.

PLAQUE

Pyros Partnership | **\plaque** | **PLAQUE_I.IXP**

Summary

Plaque is bundled with Pyros Partnership's Effects Library. Plaque converts the image into a dense grid of overlapping, black-bordered quadrilaterals. This effect can be animated, but no control is given to vary parameters over time. The effect is applied randomly to each frame so that the plaques appear to flicker or shimmer.

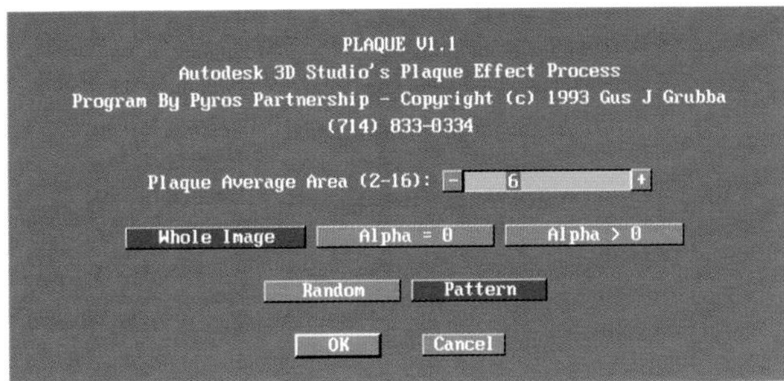

The Plaque dialog box.

Plaque Parameters

Plaque Average Area [Pa] (2–16) — Sets the average size of individual quadrilaterals.

Filter [F] (Whole Image, > 0, = 0) — Sets the general area of the image to be affected. If the alpha channel is used, the image must contain an alpha channel that is turned on in the Video Post queue. Whole applies the effect to the entire image, =0 applies the effect outside the alpha channel, and >0 applies the effect inside the alpha channel.

Pattern [P] r, p (Random, Pattern) (0–55) — Sets the patterning of the effect.

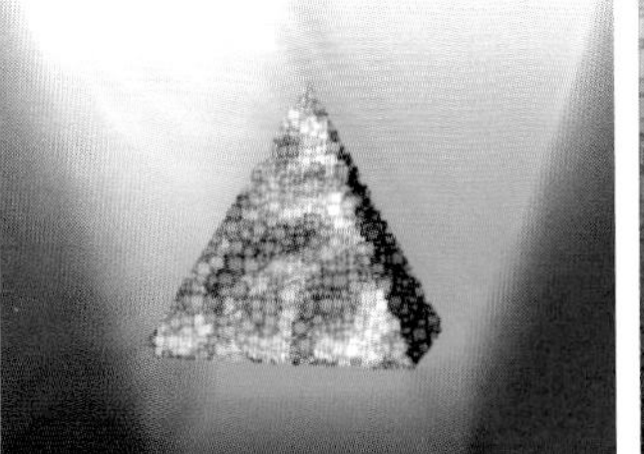

[PA]2[P]rand [PA]16[P]patt [PA]6[F]A>0[P]rand [PA]12[F]A=0[P]patt

Plaque applies a complex colored mosaic of squares and rectangles to an image that appear to flicker when animated.

PRINT ON FRAME

TFPRN_I.IXP **\printfrm** **Schreiber Instruments**

TFPRN 1.00F - Imagine Tool Factory - (C) 1994 by Serge GOLUCH
- Print: printing information inside any image -
1 Row: 20 Col: 0 Color Font: 1
Size: small font 8x8
2 Row: 40 Col: 0 Color Font: 2
Size: medium font 8x14
3 Row: 60 Col: 0 Color Font: 3
Size: large font 8x16
4 Row: 80 Col: 0 Color Font: 3
Color: red
5 Row: 100 Col: 0 Color Font: 3
Color: blue
6 Row: 325 Col: 180 Color Font: 3
Position: 325,180
7 Row: 345 Col: 200 Color Font: 3
Position: 325,200
8 Row: 160 Col: 0 Color Font: 3
OK Cancel

The Print on Frame dialog box.

Text control

Image information

Samples of the information and formatting available.

Summary

Print on Frame is part of the Imagine Tool Factory package. It is a utility for adding up to eight lines of text to your images. The lines of text can be up to 79 characters wide and can contain ASCII codes from 32 to 254. You have independent control of each line of text for position, color, and font size. There are three font sizes 8x8, 8x14, and 8x16. You can embed special codes that print information such as date, time, current frame, image size, and alpha status. You are supposed to be able to print the scene name on the image, but we could not get that to work. You can override the text color within a line of text using embedded codes.

Print on Frame Parameters

Row [R] (0-9,999) — Row on which to print the text.
Col [C] (0-9,999) — Column on which to start the text.
Color [Cl] — Text color.
Font [F] (1,2,3) — Select one of three font sizes.
Text [T] — Text to print on the image
Note: *Each of these parameters are duplicated for each of the eigth lines of text that you can print on the image.*

PUNTILINEA

PUNTI_I.IXP **\punti** **Pyros Partnership**

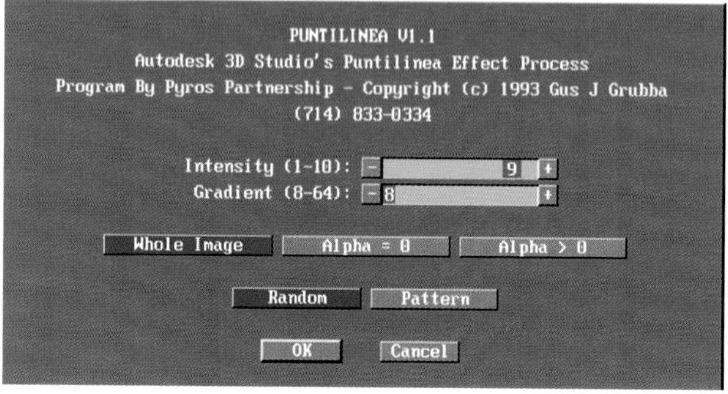

The Puntilinea dialog box.

[I]6 [G]50 [A]>0

[I]10 [G]30 [A]=0

Puntilinea produces a variable pattern of small squares.

Summary

Print on Frame is part of the is part of the Pyros Partnership's Paints Library package. It produces a pattern of small, square elements that can be varied for density and gray level as well as masked via the alpha channel.

Puntilinea Parameters

Intensity [I] (0–10) — Sets the pattern density.
Gradient [G] (8–64) — Controls the gray level within the pattern elements.
Alpha [A] w,=0,>0 (Whole Image,=0,>0) — Whole applies the effect to the entire image, =0 applies the effect outside the alpha channel, and >0 applies the effect inside the alpha channel.

QUATRO

Pyros Partnership \quatro QUATRO_I.IXP

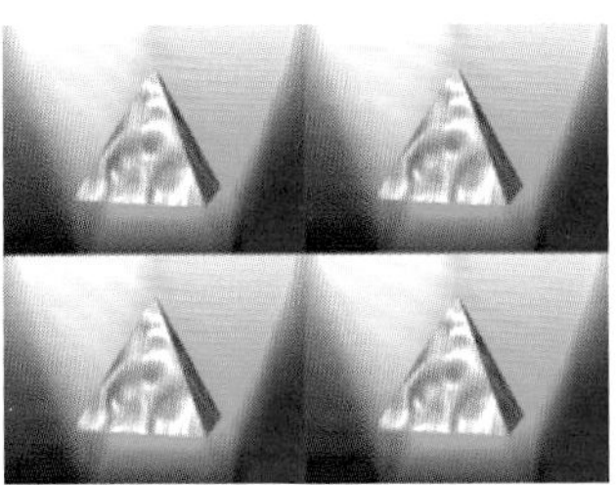

[W]2 [H]2 [W]3 [H]4

Quatro compresses or expands the image to fit the specified image grid.

Summary

Quatro is part of the Pyros Partnership's Transitions Library package. It divides the screen into an array of rectangles, each of which contain a scaled copy of an original image or animation.

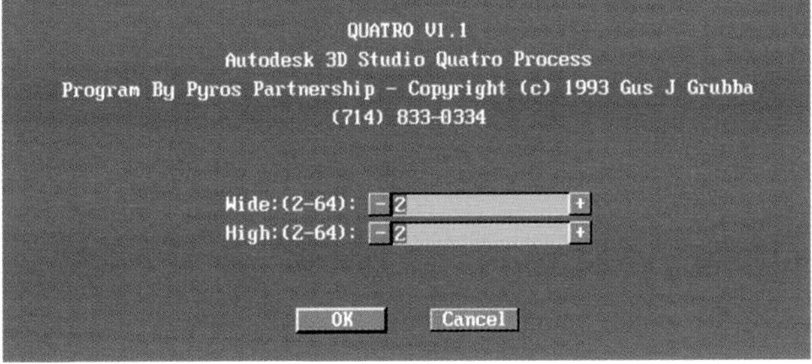

The Quatro dialog box.

Quatro Parameters

Wide [W] (2–64) — Sets the number of image columns.
High [H] (2–64) — Sets the number of image rows.

QUICKTIME MOVIE MAKER

Animetix \qtime MOVIE_I.IXP

Summary

Quicktime Movie Maker is a filter that exports an animation to a QuickTime movie file. You place this as the last item in your video post queue. When you render, it outputs each frame to a MOV file. You can select one of three compression levels and whether Movie Maker overlays frame numbers on your image. There is a setting for intended frames per second and one for quicktime keyframes. *Quicktime Keyframes* are special frames that contain an entire screen's image. Most normal frames are stored as changes from the preceding frame. Keyframes make it easier to play the movie in reverse at the cost of larger animation files.

To output the movie file, you do a video post render. You don't need to tell 3D Studio to output to disk—Movie Maker does that as each frame renders, and having 3D Studio write output files will only increase your rendering time. This program is most useful as a way to export animations to multimedia packages and to distribute cross-platform animations.

Quicktime Movie Maker Parameters

Filename [F] — The name of the output file.
Compression [C] l, m, h (Low, Medium, High) — Compression level required. Higher compression means lower image quality.
Frame numbers [N] (on, off) — Determines whether Movie Maker places frame numbers in the lower right corner.

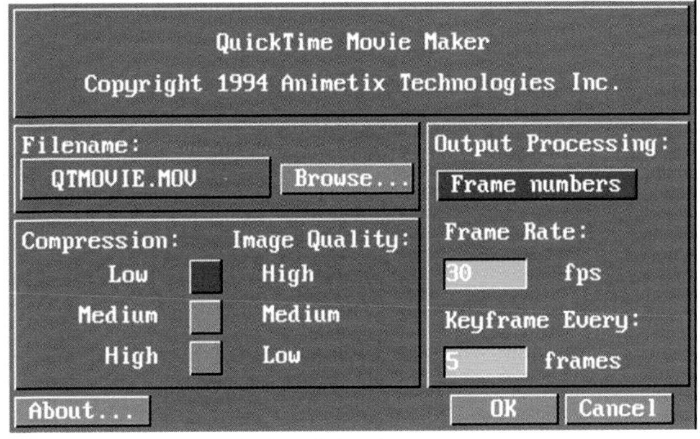

The Quicktime Movie Maker dialog box.

Frame Rate [R] — Sets the intended playback speed.
Keyframe Every [R] — Selects how often a special keyframe is written.

QUICKTIME MOVIE MAKER cont

MOVIE_I.IXP \qtime **Animetix**

Frame 12

Frame 18

Sample QuickTime frames with frame numbers.

RAINBOW

AFRNBW_I.IXP \rainbowa **Schreiber Instruments**

AFRNBW 1.10 - The Animated Factory - (C) 1994 by Serge GOLUCH
- Rainbow: Rainbow color modification -

Red Phase Shift: 0 Step: 0
Green Phase Shift: 45 Step: 0
Blue Phase Shift: 90 Step: 0

Red Scale: 1 Step: 0
Green Scale: 1 Step: 0
Blue Scale: 1 Step: 0

Amount : 50 Step: 0

Type: Vert. Hor. Diag. Circle
Circle Line: 50 Circle Col: 50

Alpha: NONE P=0 P>0

OK Cancel

The Rainbow dialog box.

Summary

Rainbow is part of the Imagine Animated Factory. It applies a chromatic interference pattern to images using overlapping sinusoidal patterns, resulting in rainbowlike color patterns. You can select linear or circular patterns and the density of the effect. You also can specify the center location for circular patterns. Independent settings control scale and phase of the red, green, and blue channels. Phase controls the overlap of the sine waves to determine color blending. Rainbow enables you to animate the overall density, scale, and phase of the pattern. You can apply the effect to the entire image or mask the effect with the alpha channel. This plug-in uses the alpha channel only as an on/off mask.

Rainbow Parameters

Red Phase Shift and Step [Rp] (0–360) — The phase shift in degrees for the red channel and step value for animations.

Green Phase Shift and Step [Gp] (0–360) — The phase shift in degrees for the green channel and step value for animations.

Blue Phase Shift and Step [Rp] (0–360) — The phase shift in degrees for the blue channel and step value for animations.

Red Scale and Step [Rs] (0.0–10000.0) — The scale factor for the red channel wave pattern and step value for animations.

Green Scale and Step [Gs] (0.0–10000.0) — The scale factor for the green channel wave pattern and step value for animations.

Blue Scale and Step [Bs] (0.0–10000.0) — The scale factor for the blue channel wave pattern and step value for animations.

Amount [M] (0–100) — Sets the density of the effect.

Amount Step [As] — Increments the density percent per frame.

Type [T] (Vert., Hor., Diag., Circle) — Specifies the wave pattern orientation.

Circle Line [Cl] — Y coordinate of the circle center.

Circle Col. [Cc] — X coordinate of the circle center.

Alpha [A] n,=0,>0 (none,=0,>0) — None applies the effect to the entire image, =0 applies the effect outside the alpha channel, and >0 applies the effect inside the alpha channel.

RAINBOW cont

Schreiber Instruments \rainbowa **AFRNBW_I.IXP**

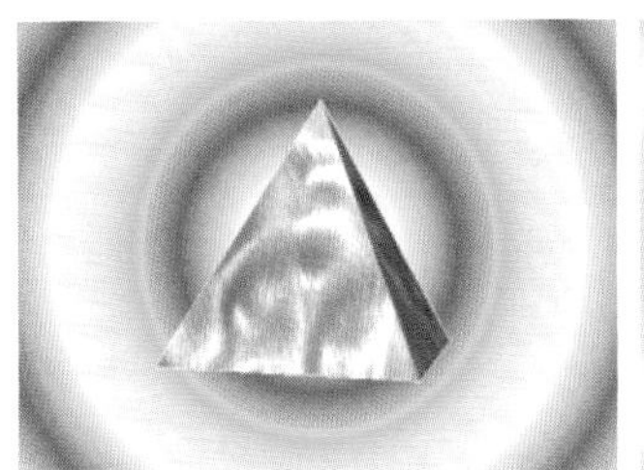
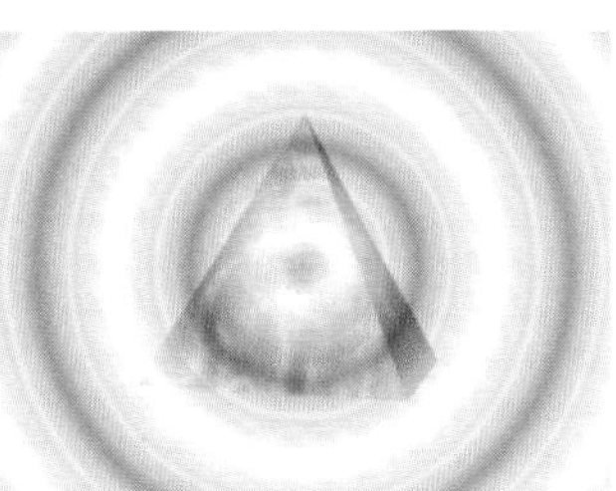

[Rp]0 [Gp]30 [Bp]60 [T]D   [Rs]0.05 [Gs]0.05 [Bs]0.05 [T]V [A]>0   [Rp]0 [Gp]45 [Bp]90 [T]C [A]=0   [Rs]0.1 [Gs]0.2 [Bs]0.05

Diagonal bars, short waves with alpha masking, phase-shifted waves, and phase-shifted with harmonic scaling.

RGB ADJUST

Schreiber Instruments \rgbadj **FFCLR_I.IXP**

Summary

RGB Adjust is part of the Imagine Filter Factory package. It is a color correction filter. With this you can adjust brightness and contrast independently for each color channel. RGB Adjust has Shift and Scale controls for each channel. Shift is a fairly straightforward brightness control—you can shift the brightness up or down. Shifting the brightness of one channel increases or decreases the prevalence of that color in the image.

The Scale control changes the contrast of the image. Its effects on the image are harder to predict. A Scale value of 100% uses all the existing brightness value range for that channel, causing no change in the image. A low Scale percentage reduces the number of brightness values and increases the contrast of the color channel. A high Scale percentage expands the middle gray values into the highlight areas, which reduces the contrast for that color channel. Changing the contrast of color channels can be used to produce both subtle and extreme color shifts in the image. You can use the alpha channel to mask the effect. This filter uses the alpha channel only as an on/off mask.

RGB Adjust Parameters

Red shift [Rs] (–255–255) — Brightness adjustment for the red channel.

Green shift [Gs] (–255–255) — Brightness adjustment for the green channel.

Blue shift [Bs] (–255–255) — Brightness adjustment for the blue channel.

Red scale [Rc] (1–200%) — Contrast adjustment for the red channel.

Green scale [Gc] (1–200%) — Contrast adjustment for the green channel.

Blue scale [Bc] (1–200%) — Contrast adjustment for the blue channel.

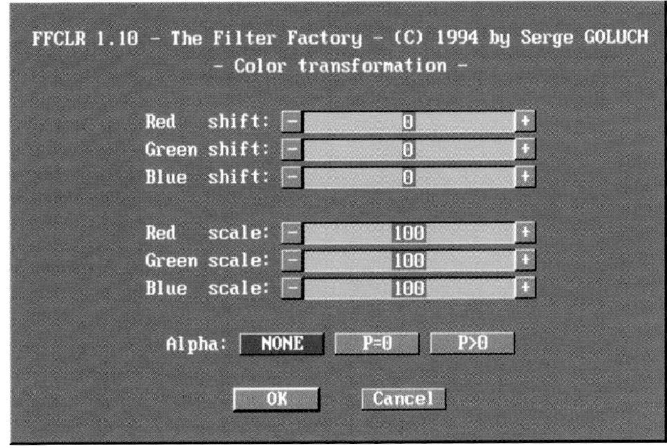

The RGB Adjust dialog box.

Alpha [A] n,=0,>0 (none,=0,>0) — None applies the effect to the entire image, =0 applies the effect outside the alpha channel, and >0 applies the effect inside the alpha channel.

Note: *This program crashes and drops you out to DOS if you set any of the Scale values to 0%. The usable range is 1–200%.*

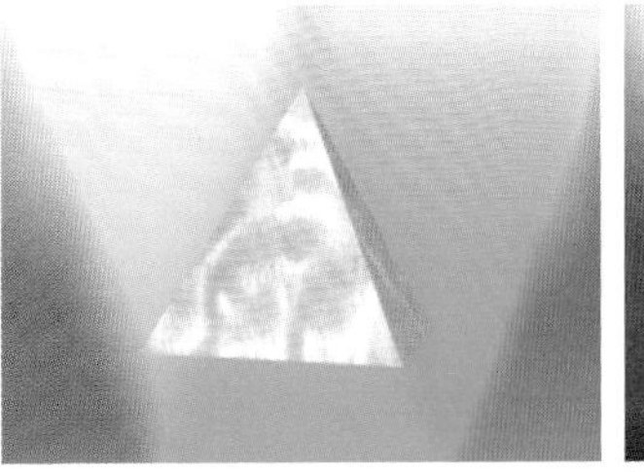

[Gs]60   [Rc]40

Increased green brightness, increased red contrast.

ROTATE

ROTATE_I.IXP | **\rotate** | **Pyros Partnership**

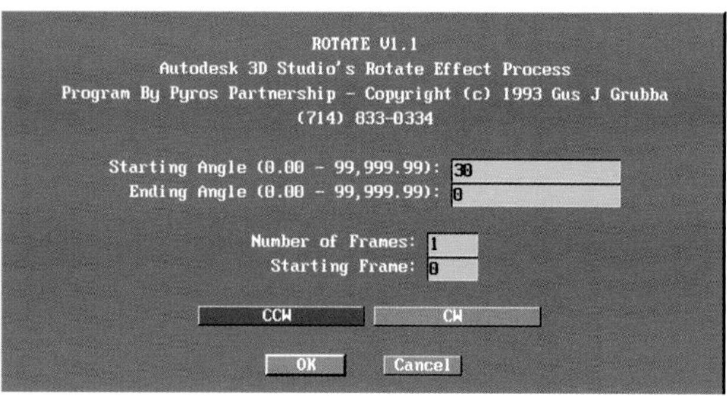

The Rotate dialog box.

Summary

Rotate is part of the Pyros Partnership's Transitions Library package. It rotates an image or animation through a specific range and for a specific number of frames. The effect can be set for either clockwise or counterclockwise rotation.

Rotate Parameters

Starting Angle [S] (0–99,999.99) — Sets the starting angle for the rotation.
Ending Angle [E] (0–99,999.99) — Sets the ending angle for the rotation.
Number of Frames [F] — Sets the number of frames for the rotation.
Starting Frame [S] — Sets the starting point for the rotation.
CCW or CW [CCW] [CW] — Sets the direction of rotation.

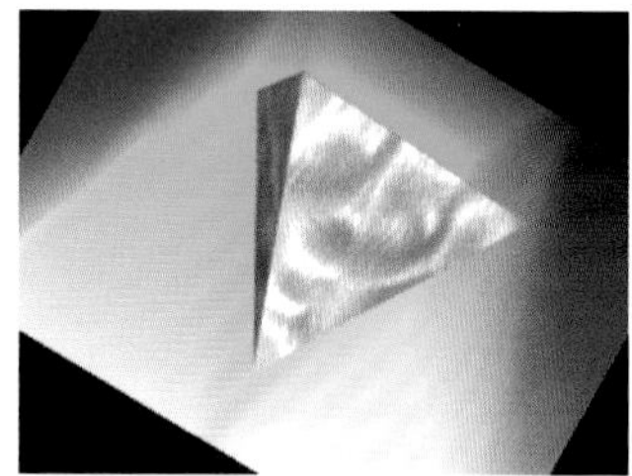
Frame 6

Frame 12

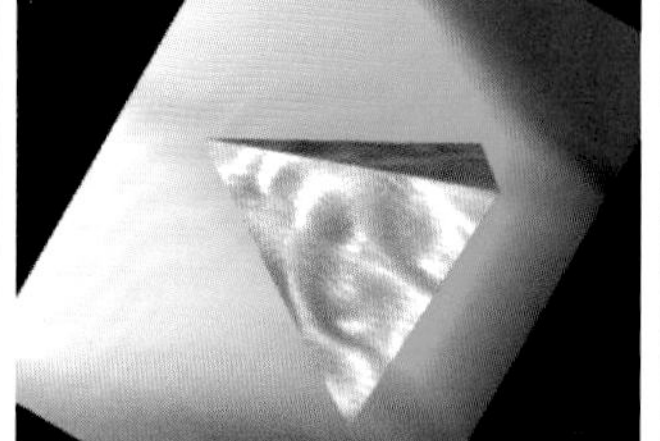
Frame 21

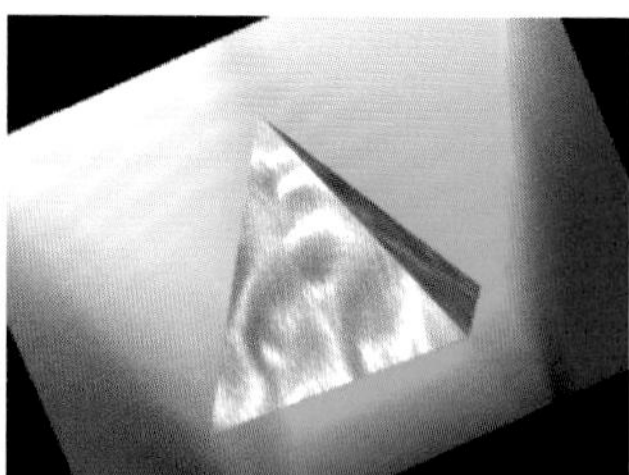
Frame 27

The sequence was set as a 180-degree, counterclockwise rotation.

ROUGH

ROUGH_I.IXP | **\rough** | **Pyros Partnership**

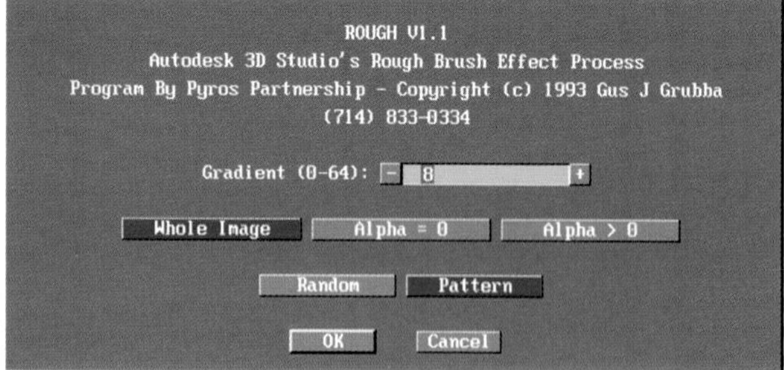

The Rough dialog box.

Summary

Rough is part of the Pyros Partnership's Library package. It produces a gritty, stucco-like pattern that can be varied for its contrast and masked to affect specific image areas via the alpha channel.

Rough Parameters

Gradient [G] (8–64) — Controls the gray level within the pattern elements.
Alpha [A] w,=0,>0 (Whole Image,=0,>0) — Whole applies the effect to the entire image, =0 applies the effect outside the alpha channel, and >0 applies the effect inside the alpha channel.

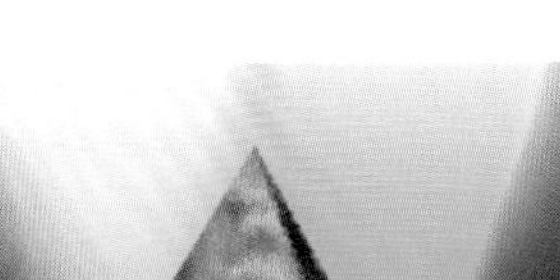

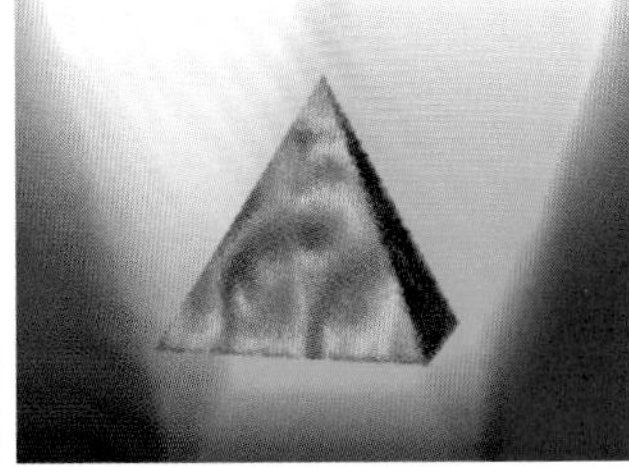

[G]50 [A]>0 [G]30 [A]=0

Rough produces a variable gritty pattern that can be masked using the alpha channel.

SEEZ

Yost Group \seez SEEZ_I.IXP

Summary

SeeZ is a filter that displays the Z buffer generated when you render a scene. The Z buffer is a grayscale image that IPAS programs can use to determine depth in a scene. Brighter areas are closer, darker areas are farther back. This filter enables you to see the Z buffer so that you can troubleshoot IPAS problems. You also can use this program to output the Z buffer to a separate file.

There are no parameters for this program. You place it after the Keyframer scene in your video post queue. When you render to the screen, SeeZ displays the Z buffer rather than the normal image. When you render to disk, it outputs the Z buffer rather than the normal image. Programs that generate SIRDS (single-image random-dot stereograms) images need Z buffer information to generate a 3D image. SIRDS images are those strange images often called "Magic Eye" images that enable you to see a 3D image as long as you can cross your eyes in just the right way.

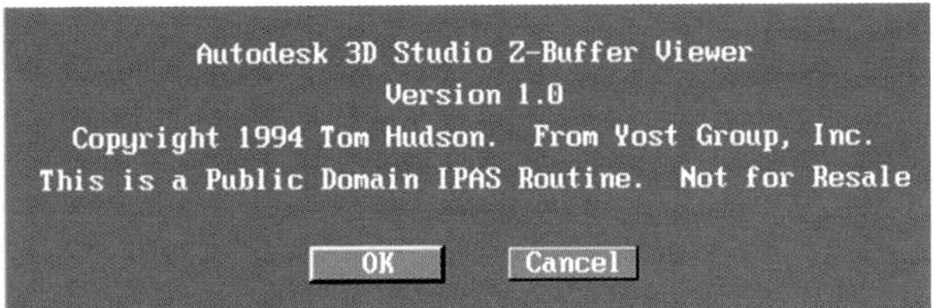

Autodesk 3D Studio Z-Buffer Viewer
Version 1.0
Copyright 1994 Tom Hudson. From Yost Group, Inc.
This is a Public Domain IPAS Routine. Not for Resale

OK Cancel

The SeeZ dialog box.

original image Z buffer

SeeZ displays the Z buffer generated by a scene.

SHIFT AND GHOST

AFSHFT_I.IXP \shiftgh Schreiber Instruments

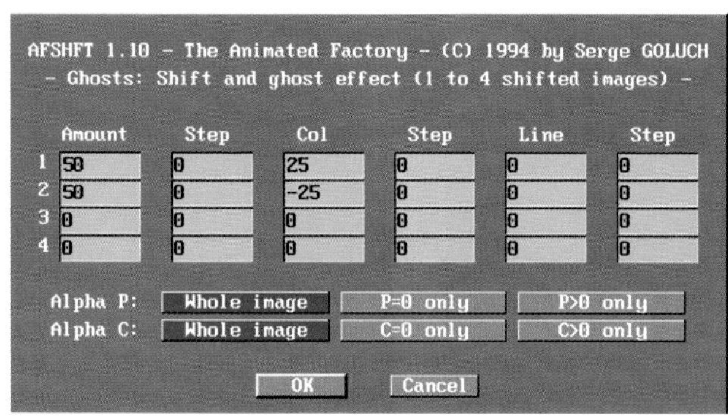

The Shift & Ghost dialog box.

Summary

Shift and Ghost is part of the Imagine Animated Factory. It composites one to four copies of the original image. The copies can be shifted individually in X and Y. You can set the transparency of each copy. The source for each copy can be either the entire image or a section masked by the alpha channel. You can apply the effect to the entire image or mask it with the alpha channel. This plug-in uses the alpha channel only as an on/off mask.

Shift and Ghost Parameters

Amount [A] 1,2,3,4 (0–100) — Sets the intensity of the effect.

Amount Step [As] 1,2,3,4 — Sets the increment amount per frame.

Column [C] 1,2,3,4 (–100–100) — Specifies the percentage of horizontal image shift.

Column Step [Cs] 1,2,3,4 — Increments the horizontal shift per frame.

Line [L] 1,2,3,4 (–100–100) — Specifies the percentage of vertical image shift.

Line Step [Ls] 1,2,3,4 — Increments the vertical shift per frame.

Alpha P [Ap] i,=0,>0 (whole image, P=0, P>0) — Alpha P controls masking based on the alpha channel value at the current pixel. Whole applies the effect to the entire image, P=0 applies the effect outside the alpha channel, and P>0 applies the effect inside the alpha channel.

Alpha C [Ac] i,=0,>0 (whole image, C=0, C>0) — Alpha C controls masking based on the alpha channel value at the effect center. Whole applies the effect to the entire image, C=0 applies the effect outside the alpha channel, and C>0 applies the effect inside the alpha channel.

[Cs]20 [Ls]-15

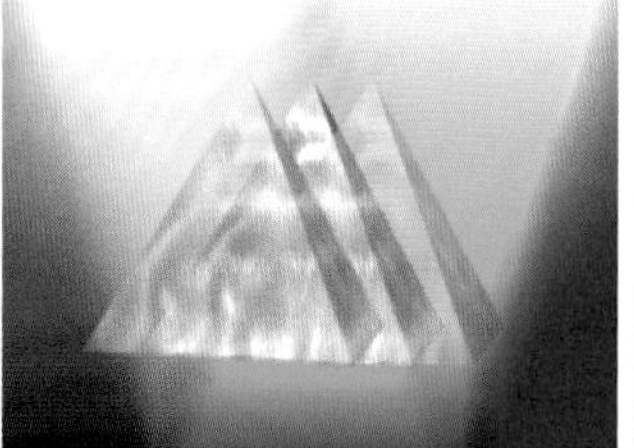

[Cs]10,-10 [Ls]0,0 [Ap]whole [Ac]>0

[Cs]10,-10,0,0 [Ls]0,0,10,-10 [Ap]whole [Ac]>0

[Cs]10,-10,0,0 [Ls]0,0,10,-10 [Ap]=0 [Ac]>0

Various shifted images and subimages with and without alpha masking.

SINEWAVE

Summary

Sinewave is part of the Imagine Animated Factory. It applies a sine wave pattern of lightened and darkened areas to images. You can control amplitude and wavelength along with brightness and darkness. You can set and animate the width of each wave line. Orientation can be either vertical or horizontal. You also can apply the effect to the entire image or mask the effect with the alpha channel. This plug-in uses the alpha channel only as an on/off mask.

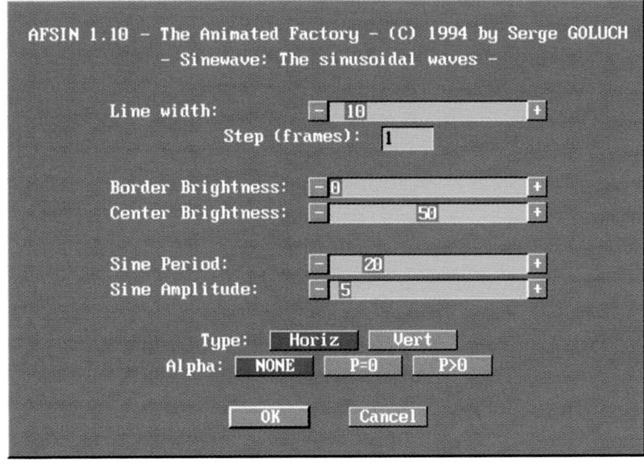

The Sinewave dialog box.

Sinewave Parameters

Line width [L] (1–100) — Sets the width of the wave lines as percentage of image size.

Step (frames) [F] (1–999) — The number of frames over which wave action repeats.

Border Brightness [Bb] (0–100) — Image brightness between wave lines.

Center Brightness [Cb] (0–100) — Image brightness along wave lines.

Sine Period [S] (0–100) — Sets the wavelength of the waves as a percentage of image size.

Sine Amplitude [As] (0–100) — Sets the height of the waves as a percentage of image size.

Type [T] (Horiz/Vert) — Wave pattern orientation.

Alpha [A] n,=0,>0 (none,=0,>0) — None applies the effect to the entire image, =0 applies the effect outside the alpha channel, and >0 applies the effect inside the alpha channel.

[L]10 [S]20 [As]5

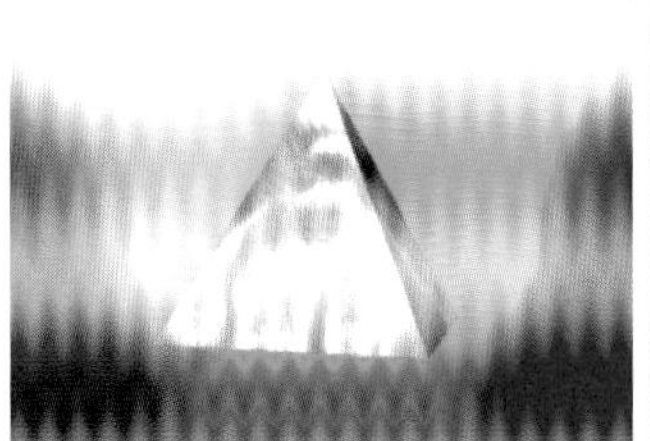

[L]48 [S]5 [As]5

[L]5 [S]1 [As]5

[Bb]0 [Cb]50 [A]>0

Sine wave pattern, large smooth waves, high-frequency waves, and waves masked by alpha channel.

SMUDGE

SMUDGE_I.IXP \smudge Pyros Partnership

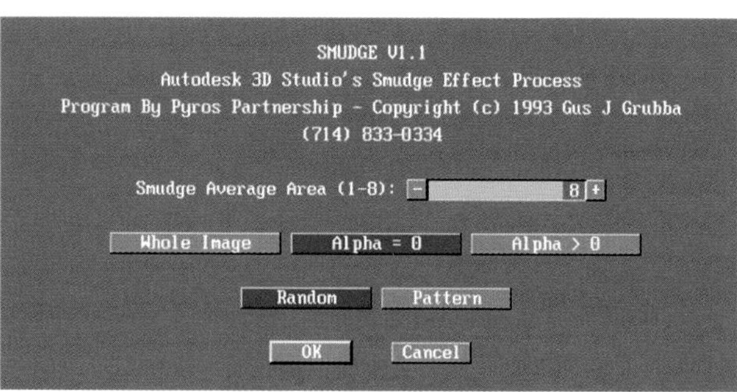

The Smudge dialog box.

[S]3 [A]w

[S]8 [A]=0

Smudge produces a blur pattern that can be masked using the alpha channel.

Summary

Smudge is part of the Pyros Partnership's Paints Library package. It produces a blur pattern that can be masked using the alpha channel.

Smudge Parameters

Smudge Average Area [S] (1–8) — Controls the gray level within the pattern elements.

Alpha [A] w,=0,>0 (Whole Image,=0,>0) — Whole applies the effect to the entire image, =0 applies the effect outside the alpha channel, and >0 applies the effect inside the alpha channel.

SQUASH

SQUASH_I.IXP \squash Pyros Partnership

SQUASH V1.1
Autodesk 3D Studio's Squash Effect Process
Program By Pyros Partnership - Copyright (c) 1993 Gus J Grubba
(714) 833-0334
Horizontal Start % (0-100): 0
End % (0-100): 100
Vertical Start % (0-100): 0
End % (0-100): 0
Background Color
Number of Frames: 30 Starting Frame: 0
OK Cancel

The Squash dialog box.

Summary

Squash is part of the Pyros Partnership's Transitions Library package. It squashes an image or animation horizontally or vertically for a specific frame range.

Squash Parameters

Horizontal Start [Hs] (0–100%) — Sets the starting amount of horizontal squash.

Horizontal End [He] (0–100%) — Sets the ending amount of horizontal squash.

Vertical Start [Vs] (0–100%) — Sets the starting amount of vertical squash.

Vertical End [Ve] (0–100%) — Sets the ending amount of vertical squash.

Background Color [C] — Sets the background color.

Number of Frames [F] — Sets the number of frames for the squash.

Starting Frame [S] — Sets the starting point for the squash.

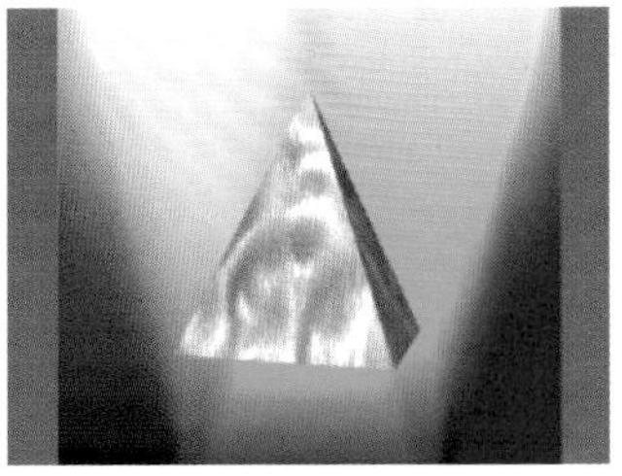
Frame5

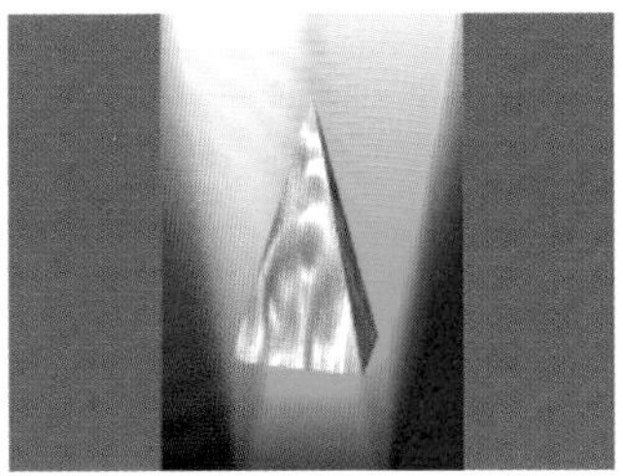
Frame15

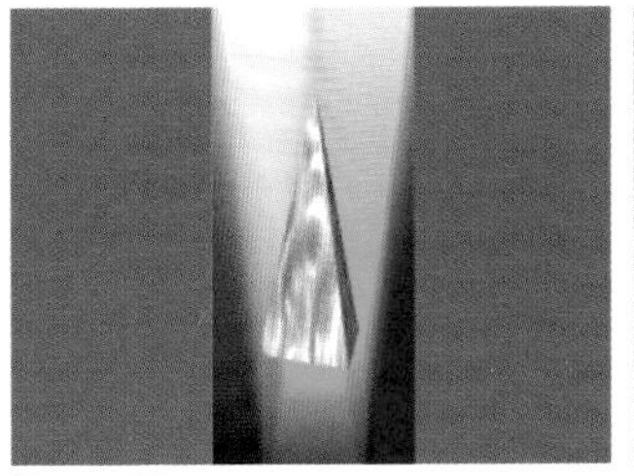
Frame20

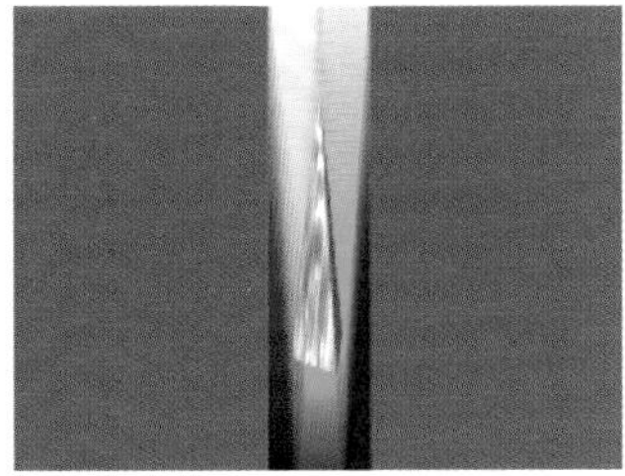
Frame25

The sequence was set as a 100 percent horizontal squash over 30 frames. The background color was set to a warm gray.

STARS

Yost Group \yost\discl STAR_I.IXP

Summary

Stars is included with 3D Studio Release 4 and also is available as part of the disc 1 image processing filters from Yost Group. Stars functions as a 3D star environment that renders a background image or sequence of background images. Its effect varies depending upon where it is placed in Video Post's queue. If it is placed at the top of the queue, for instance, it works as a starfield background for all subsequent queue entries. If placed later in the queue, and used in conjunction with a transparency method such as an alpha channel, it functions as a starfield foreground.

Stars also provides variable Motion blur based on camera position and motion.

Star requires a star database from which it creates each new starfield, and includes a utility for creating new star databases. This is accomplished from the DOS prompt by typing **STARMAKE**, a file name to which to save the star data, and the number of stars you want.

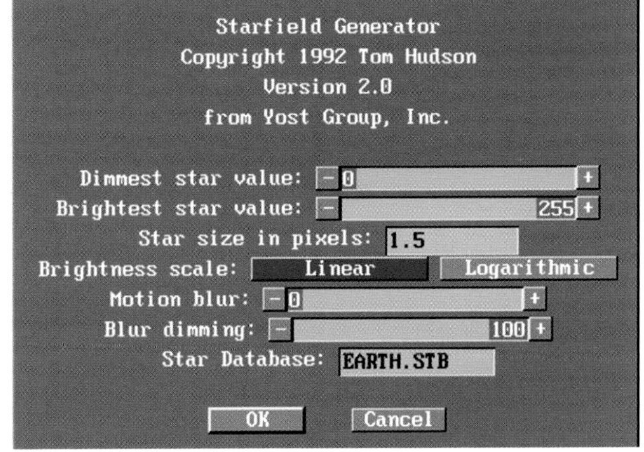

The Stars dialog box.

Stars Parameters

Dimmest/ Brightest star value [Ds] [Bs] (0–255) — Sets the luminance value for the brightest and dimmest stars. Determines the range of values of the starfield. The default values are 0 and 255, respectively.

Star size in pixels [S] (0.1–999) — Sets the size in pixels of individual stars.

Brightness scale [B] l, lo (Linear, Logarithmic) — Sets the star brightness to logarithmic or linear. Logarithmic is a more subtle and realistic effect.

Motion blur [Mb] (0–100) — Sets the percentage amount of motion blur based on the amount of movement since the previous frame. Motion blur must be rendered over at least two frames to show its effect.

Blur dimming [Bd] (0–100) — Sets the percentage value that the trail of each star will be dimmed when using motion blur.

Procedural Seed [Ps] (0–999999) — Sets the algorithm's start point with an arbitrary number. Each number produces a unique pattern.

# of Stars [#S] — Specifies the number of stars to include in the current starfield.

Star Database [SD] (file name) — Specifies the star database.

STARS cont

STAR_I.IXP | **\yost\discl** | **Yost Group**

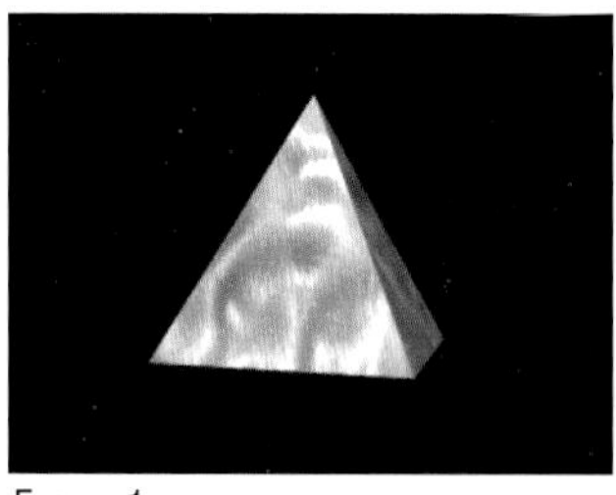
Frame1

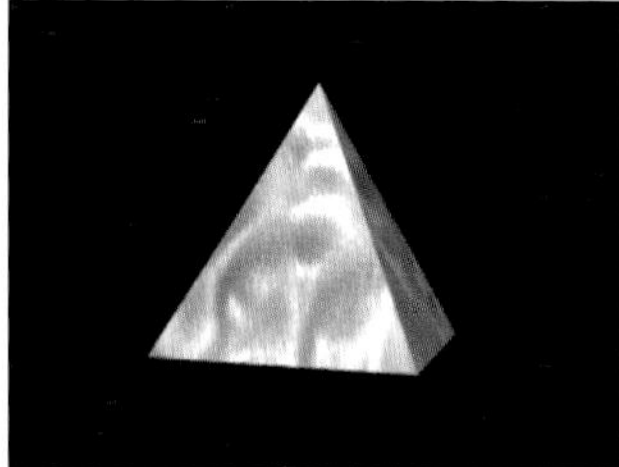
Frame2

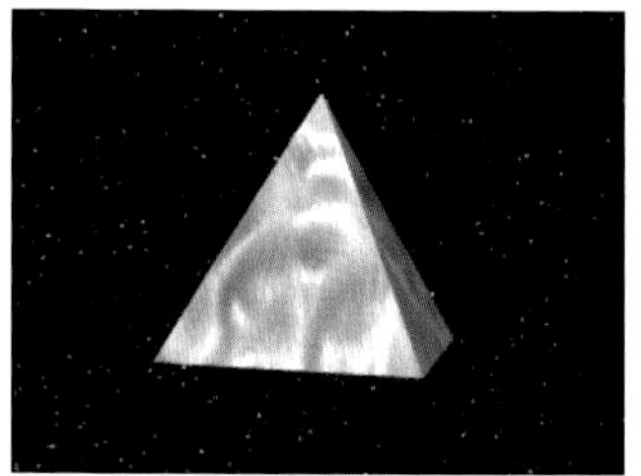
Frame1

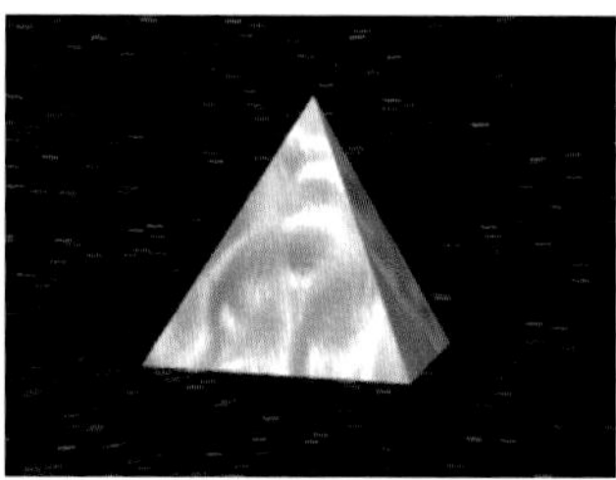
Frame2

Stars was used to generate the background stars in these images. The first set uses the default database of 5,000 stars with star size set at 3 and Motion blur and Blur dimming set at 100. The second set of images uses a star database with 50,000 stars and the same settings.

SWIRL

SWIRL_I.IXP | **\swirl** | **Pyros Partnership**

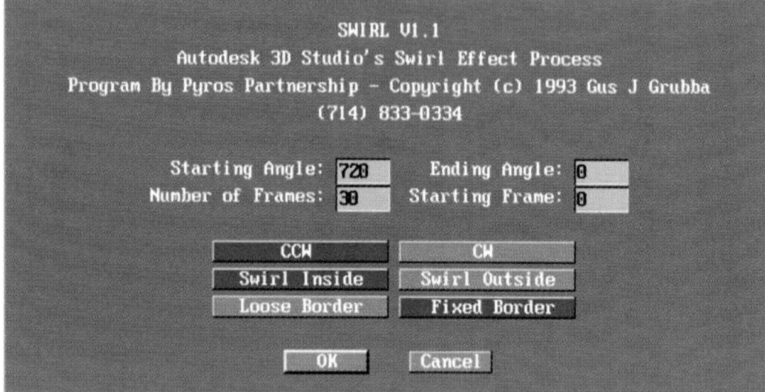

The Swirl dialog box.

Summary

Swirl is part of the Pyros Partnership's Transitions Library package. It swirls an image or animation, producing a whirlpool effect. The image border can be fixed or can tear away from the frame edges, thus revealing a black background.

Swirl Parameters

Starting Angle [Sa] (0–9,999) — Sets the starting swirl angle.
Ending Angle [Ea] (0–9,999) — Sets the ending swirl angle.
Number of Frames [F] — Sets the total number of frames for the swirl.
Starting Frame [S] — Sets the swirl starting point.
CCW or CW [CCW] [CW] — Specifies clockwise or counter-clockwise rotation.
Swirl Inside or Swirl Outside [Si] [So] — Inside centers the swirl on the image center, and Outside swirls the image edges.
Loose Border or Fixed Border [Lb] [Fb] — Enables the border to tear away or remain fixed on the frame edges.

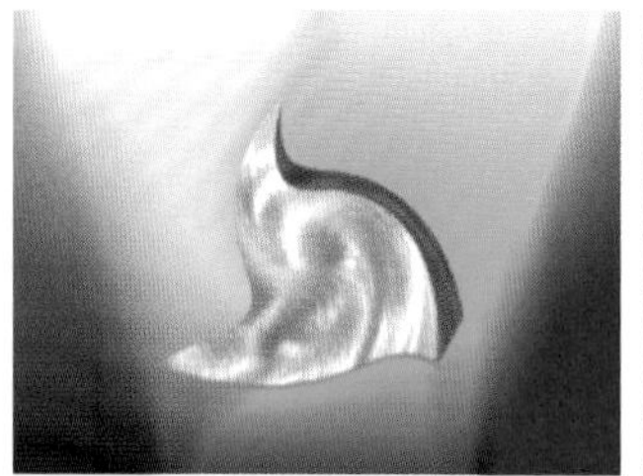
Frame0

Frame10

Frame20

Frame25

The sequence was set for an inside swirl. [Sa]0 [Ea]720 [CCW] [Fb].

SWIRL cont

Pyros Partnership \swirl **SWIRL_I.IXP**

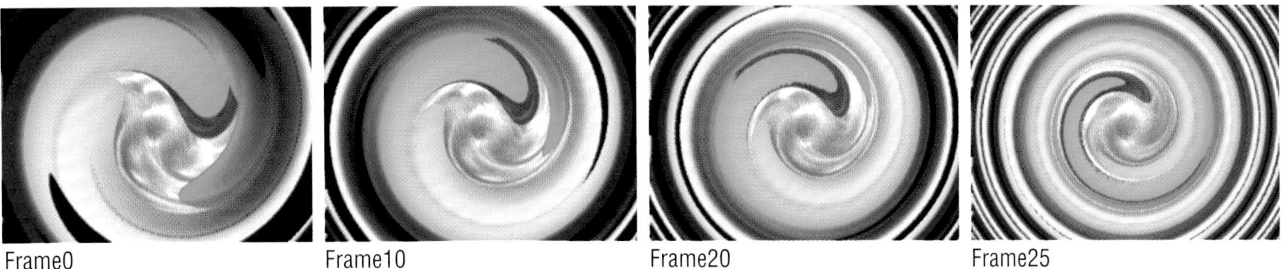

Frame0 Frame10 Frame20 Frame25

The sequence was set for an outside swirl. [Sa]0 [Ea]720 [CCW] [Fb].

TELEVISION RECEPTION EFFECTS 1

Schreiber Instruments \tvfx1 **TVRFX1_I.IXP**

Summary

Television Reception Effects 1 is part of the Television Reception Effects package, which is a series of effects that simulate a number of television and videotape player aberrations such as poor television reception, signal interference, and tracking error.

Television Reception Effects 1 provides signal loss, snow, tracking error, ghost, and interference effects. Some of the TVE1 effects animate, and they can be used singly or in any combination via the individual enable switches provided.

Signal loss simulates the picture break-up and distortion that happens when a television signal is poor. The lost picture areas can either be replaced with black or, using Freeze, pixels from the previous line. A density control is provided that specifies percentage of screen coverage for the effect.

Snow produces a white pattern of small dots that can be varied for both density and opacity.

Tracking error simulates the picture drop-outs or noise that occurs when a videotape player is not tracking properly. Tracking error can be adjusted for vertical screen position and density.

As the name suggests, Ghost produces a ghosted image that is offset horizontally from the original. The ghost image can be set to either add or subtract its colors from the original image. Furthermore, you can vary the amount of ghost color from 0 to 100 percent.

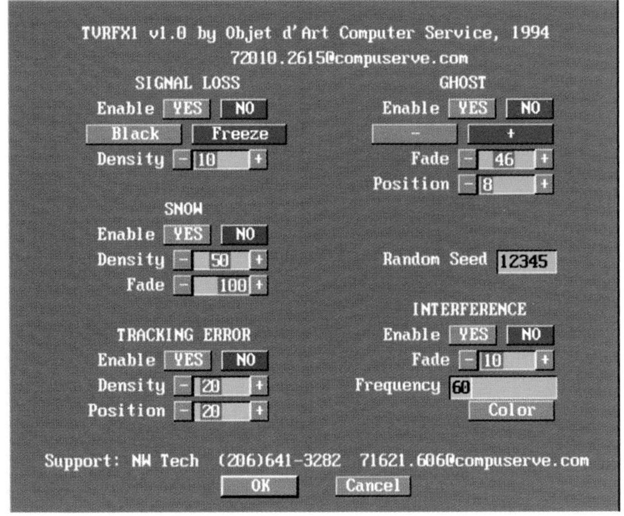

The Television Reception Effects 1 dialog box.

Interference adds a variable interference pattern to the original. This pattern can range from several soft horizontal bands to numerous diagonal and moiré patterns.

Signal Loss Parameters

Enable [Sle] y, n (yes, no) — Turns signal loss on or off.

Black or Freeze [Bl] [Fr] — Specifies what happens when the signal is lost. Black inserts black and Freeze inserts the previous scanline.

Density [De] (0–100) — Specifies how often the signal will be lost, with higher numbers making the effect more pronounced. This controls the percentage of the image that will be affected.

Snow Parameters

Enable [Sn] y, n (yes, no) — Turns snow on or off.
Density [De] (1–100) — Controls the snow density.
Fade [Fa] (1–100) — Sets the opacity of the snow, with higher numbers producing more opaque snow.

Tracking Error Parameters

Enable [Te] y, n (yes, no) — Turns tracking error on or off.
Density [De] (1–100) — Controls the tracking error density.
Position [Po] (1–100) — Controls the vertical position of the effect.

Ghost Parameters

Enable [Ge] y, n (yes, no) — Turns ghost on or off.
- or + [-] [+] — Specifies whether the ghost effect adds or subtracts color from the image.
Fade [Fa] (1–100) — Sets how much of the ghost image color is combined with the original. Colors are summed using YIQ color space.
Position [De] (1–100) — Positions the ghost image horizontally.

Interference Parameters

Enable [Ie] y, n (yes, no) — Turns interference on or off.
Fade [Fa] (1–100%) — Sets the amount of interference that is added to the image.
Frequency [Fr] (30–3,000,000) — Sets the frequency of the waveform that is used to calculate the interference pattern.
Color [Co] — Sets the interference pattern color.
Random Seed [Rs] — Sets the seed number used to calculate each effect.

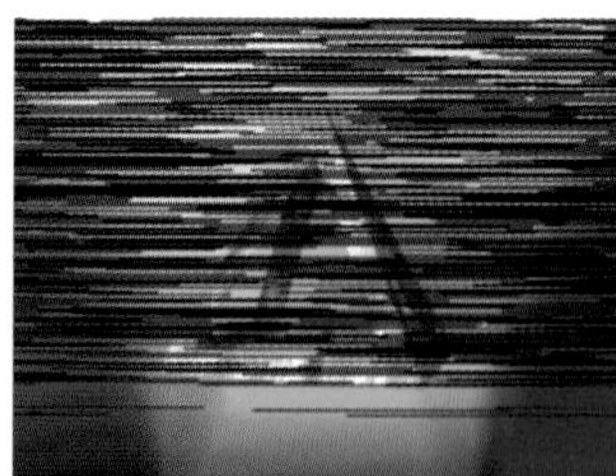
[Sle] [Bl]80 [De]38

[Sle] [Fr] [De]90

[Sn] [De]100 [Fa]50

[Te] [De]90 [Po]85

Signal loss produces either a series of black horizontal drop-outs or blurred distortions. Snow and tracking errors simulate their real-world counterparts.

[Ge] [+] [Fa]100 [Po]15

[Ge] [-] [Fa]100 [Po]15

[Ie] [Fa]59 [Fr]360

[Ie] [Fa]100 [Fr]1748

Ghosting can be set to either add or subtract color from the original, and interference can be set to a range of moiré-like patterns.

Summary

Television Reception Effects 2 is part of the Television Reception Effects package, which is a series of effects that simulate a number of television and videotape player aberrations such as poor television reception, signal interference, and tracking error.

Television Reception Effects 2 provides smear, jitter, horizontal hold, vertical hold, and a power-on effect. Some of the TVE2 effects produce animation, and they can be used singly or in any combination via the individual enable switches provided.

Smear produces a horizontal smear or blur. The degree of smear is controlled by a slider, and ranges from subtle to very soft. Additional controls specify how the blur is applied. You can apply the blur to luminance only, hue only, or both.

Jitter produces horizontal tearing over a specified distance. You can select from either line mode, which randomly displaces each horizontal line, or frame mode, which randomly displaces chunks of the image followed by a small line displacement.

Horizontal Hold produces the effect of a television with a misadjusted horizontal hold control. In this case, the image is distorted by a series of wave patterns that move through the frame. The pattern is produced by first displacing the image along the top and/or bottom of the frame. A sine wave also is applied, which further distorts the image and produces a wave motion.

Vertical Hold creates the flipping or rolling-frame effect of a TV's misadjusted vertical hold control. Vertical Hold provides a frame range for the effect, along with the number of rolls or speed and the vertical offset.

Power On simulates the color and value shift that happens when a real-world color TV tube warms up. The effect can be compared to a fade in or fade out with separate control over the red, green, and blue color channels.

Smear Parameters

Enable [Se] y, n (yes, no) — Turns smear on or off.

Amount [A] (1–100) — Controls the amount of horizontal blur.

YIQ, Y, or IQ [Yi] [Y] [Iq] — Specifies how the blur is applied. YIQ applies blur to both the luminance and hue, Y applies blur to luminance only, and IQ applies it to hue only.

Jitter Parameters

Enable [Je] y, n (yes, no) — Turns jitter on or off.

Width [W] (1–100) — Controls the amount of horizontal image or frame displacement from 0 to 1/5 of the frame resolution.

Line or Frame [L] [F] — Line displaces each horizontal line independently. Frame first displaces groups of horizontal lines followed by a small displacement on each line.

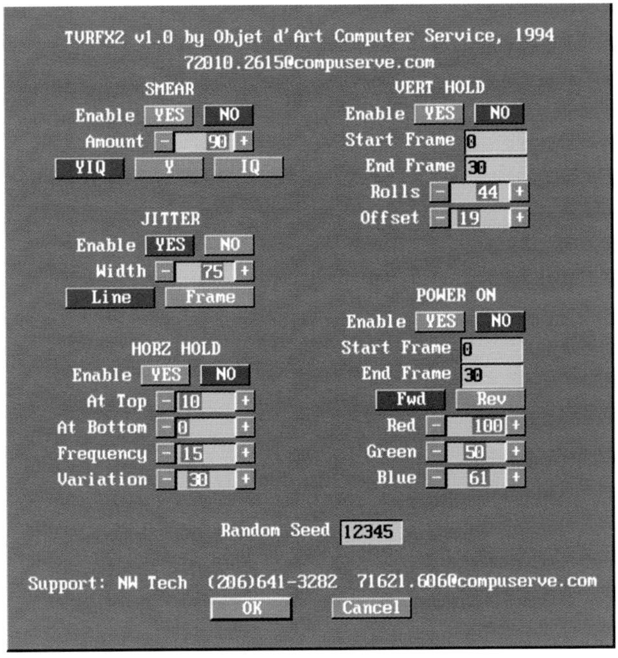

The Television Reception Effects 2 dialog box.

Horizontal Hold Parameters

Enable [He] y, n (yes, no) — Turns horizontal hold on or off.

At Top [T] (0–100) — Controls the amount of horizontal image displacement at the top of the screen. The image can be displaced from 0 to 5 times the screen width.

At Bottom [B] (0–100) — Controls the amount of horizontal image displacement at the bottom of the screen. The image can be displaced from 0 to 5 times the screen width.

Frequency [Fr] (1–100) — Sets the frequency of the sine wave that is used to distort and produce wave motion in the image.

Variation [V] (0–100) — Varies the sine wave amplitude from 0 to 1/2 of the displacement set by the At Top and At Bottom controls.

Vertical Hold Parameters

Enable [Ve] y, n (yes, no) — Turns horizontal hold on or off.

Start Frame and End Frame [Sf] [Ef] — Sets the starting and ending frames for the effect.

Rolls [Ro] (–100–100) — Specifies the number of rolls for the range set using Start Frame and End Frame.

Offset [Of] y, n (0–100) — Sets a vertical image offset or starting point for the effect.

Power On Parameters

Enable [He] y, n (yes, no) — Turns horizontal hold on or off.

Start Frame and End Frame [Sf] [Ef] — Sets the starting and ending frames for the effect.

Fwd or Rev [Fw] [Re] — Sets Power On to fade-in or fade-out.

Red, Green, and Blue [R] [G] [B] (1–100) — Sets the speed with which the color fades in or out. Lower numbers provide a faster effect.

Random Seed [Rs] — Sets the seed number used to calculate each effect.

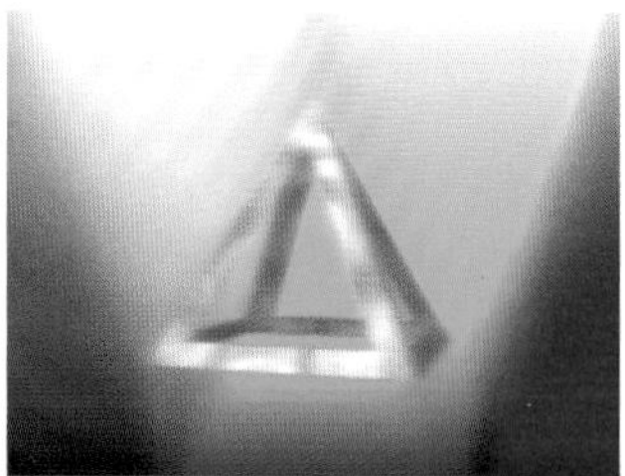

[Se] [A]80 [Yi]

[Se] [A]97 [Yi]

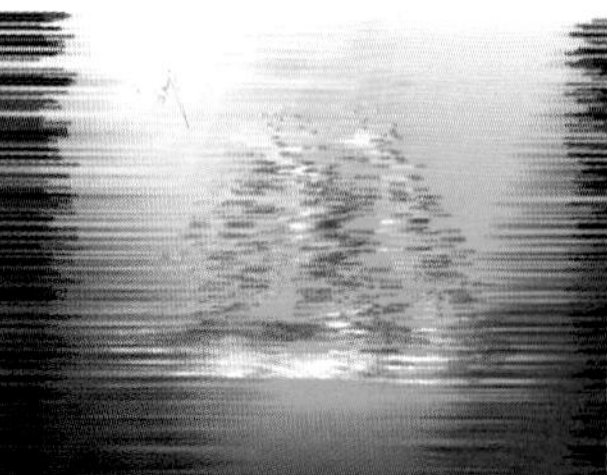

[Je]y [W]75 [L]

[Je] [W]75 [F]

Smear provides a subtle to extremely soft horizontal blur, and Jitter randomly affects each line or line groups.

[He]y [T]10 [B]0 [Fr]15

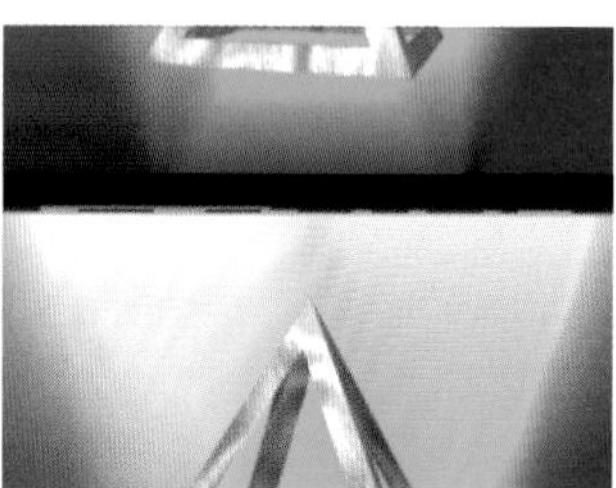

Vert Hold [Of]30

[He]y [T]90 [B]10 [Fr]30 [Ve]y [Of]79

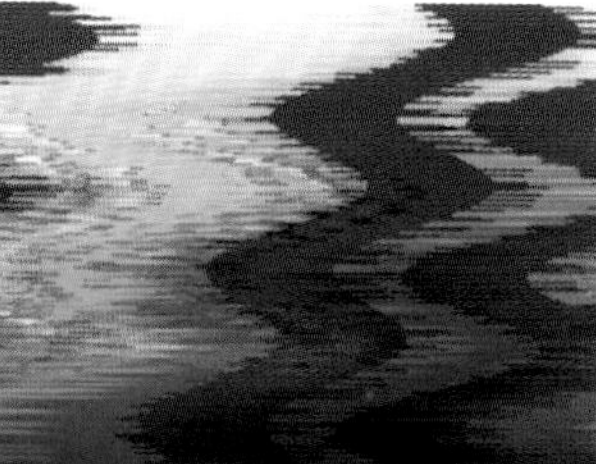

[Je]y [W]50 [L] [He] [T]25 [B]10 [Fr]30

Horizontal and vertical hold simulate their real-world counterparts. Television Reception effects can be used in any combination.

THERMO

Pyros Partnership | **\thermo** | **THERMO_I.IXP**

[T]c [P]50 [T]w [P]100

Color temperature adjustment: cooler and warmer.

Summary

Thermo is part of Pyros Partnership's Utilities package. It enables you to adjust the "temperature" of your images. You can specify that you want to make your image cooler or warmer and set a percentage of change. You can mask the effect using the alpha channel.

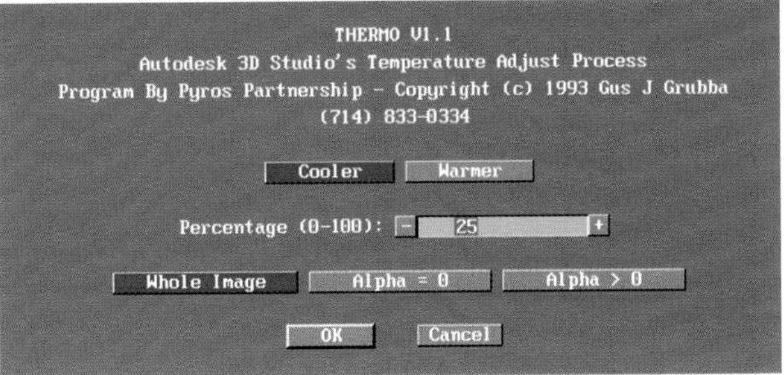

The Thermo dialog box.

Thermo Parameters

Temperature [T] c, w (Cooler, Warmer) — The direction of color shift.

Percentage [P] (0–100) — The amount of color shift.

Alpha [A] w, =0, >0 (Whole Image, =0, >0) — Whole applies the effect to the entire image, =0 applies the effect outside the alpha channel, and >0 applies the effect inside the alpha channel.

TRANZITION

AZ Technology | **\tranzitn** | **TRANZ_I.IXP**

Summary

Tranzition produces a variety of horizontal, vertical, and special-effect transitions between current scene frames and a selected image, color, or noise effect. You also can produce transitions between two images or rendered sequences.

Wipes can move right to left, left to right, top to bottom, or bottom to top. Furthermore, they can expand from or contract to the sequence's center. These can be combined using Tranzition's Boolean operators, And, Or, Xor, and Special, to create additional shaped wipes including multiple diamonds and circles.

An expanding box wipe, for example, is accomplished by setting center transitions for both horizontal and vertical components with Invert set to no for both. The manual provides a chart for each Boolean operation, which makes creating, locating, and applying the desired wipe simple.

Tranzition provides several edge treatments: sharp-edged (plain), with a color border, ragged (striated), or consisting of randomly placed pixels (dusty).

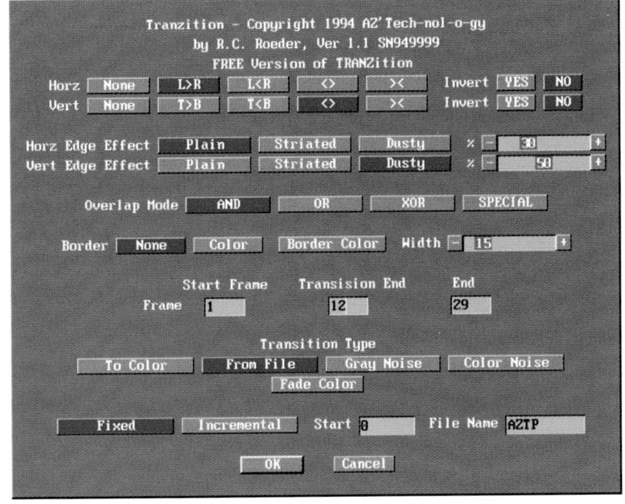

The Tranzition dialog box.

Tranzition also includes AZPOP_I.IXP and AZPUSH_I.IXP, which are used to read and write the results of Tranzition's effects to and from the Video Post queue. Of these, AZPUSH_I.IXP is most essential as it must follow any scene frame or bitmap that is used in a transition.

Tranzition Parameters

Horz or Vert [H] [V] n, lr, rl, tb, bt e, c (none, left to right, right to left, top to bottom, bottom to top, expand, contract) — Sets the horizontal or vertical component of the wipe. None turns the horizontal or vertical component off. Left to right moves the wipe from left to right, and right to left produces the opposite effect. Expand enlarges the wipe and contract collapses it.

Invert [I] y, n (yes, no) — Changes the processing order for the transition. A normal setting wipes from the current rendered frame to a color, image, or noise. Setting invert to yes reverses this order.

Horiz or Vert Edge Effect [He] [Ve] p, s, d (Plain, Striated, Dusty, 0–100%) — Specifies a sharp, ragged, or dithered edge for the transition. The sliders control the width of the striated or dusty edge.

Overlap Mode [O] a, o, xo, s (and, or, exclusive or, special) — These are Boolean operations that control the shape and direction of the transition.

Border and Border Width [B] n, c (0–100%) — Sets the thickness in percentage of screen size of the color border. The color border can be used with plain, striated, or dusty edge effects.

Border Color [Bc] — Sets the border color using RGB or HLS color models.

Start Frame and End [Sf] [Ef] — Specifies the current sequence and must match Video Post's range bar start and end settings.

Transition End [Te] — Sets the end frame for the transition.

Transition Type [Tt] c, f, gn, cn (To Color, From File, Gray Noise, Color Noise) — Specifies the transition type, with To Color being a solid color, From File being any bitmap, and Gray Noise or Color Noise being TV snow.

Fade Color [Fc] — Sets the fade color using RGB or HLS color models.

Fixed and Incremental [F] [I] — Enables individual or sequences of image files to be used for creating compound transition effects. Fixed writes a single AZF image file for the transition sequence, and Incremental writes a series of images for the transition.

Start [Si] — Sets the start frame for the incremental images.

[H]lr [Tt]f [He]p

[V]tb [Tt]f [He]p [B]9

[H]e [Tt]f [He]s

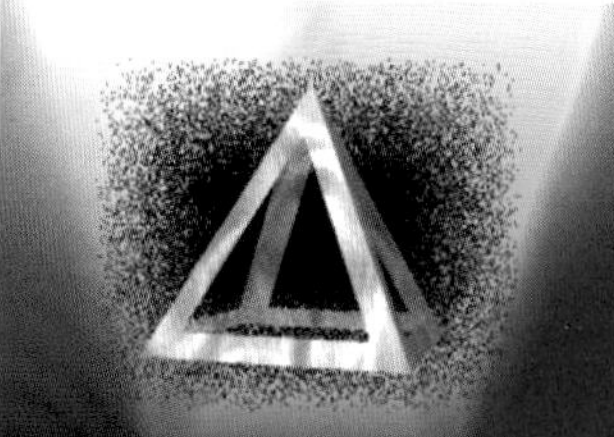
[H]e [V]e [Tt]f [He]d

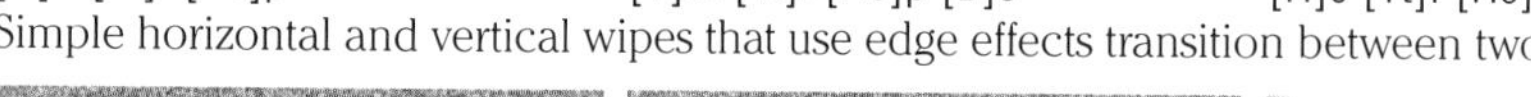
Simple horizontal and vertical wipes that use edge effects transition between two images.

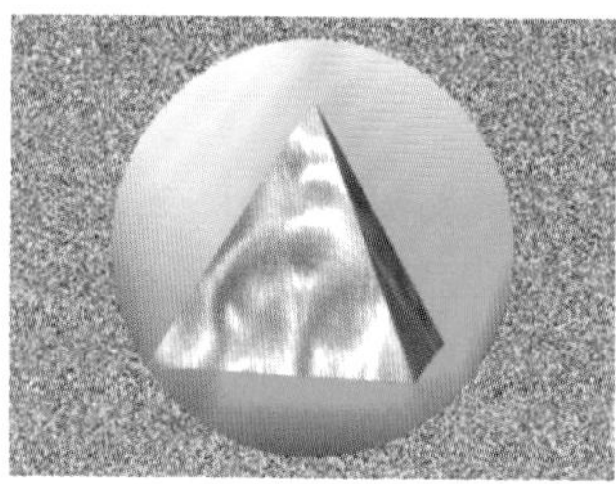
[H]lr [V]tb [Tt]gn [O]s

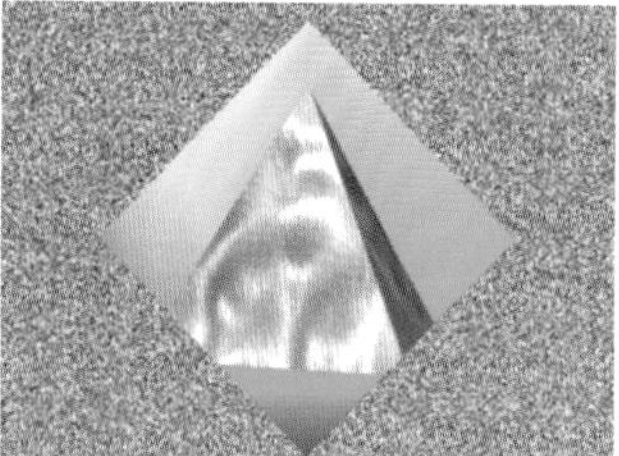
[H]e [V]tb [Tt]gn [O]s

[H]lr [Tt]cn [O]s

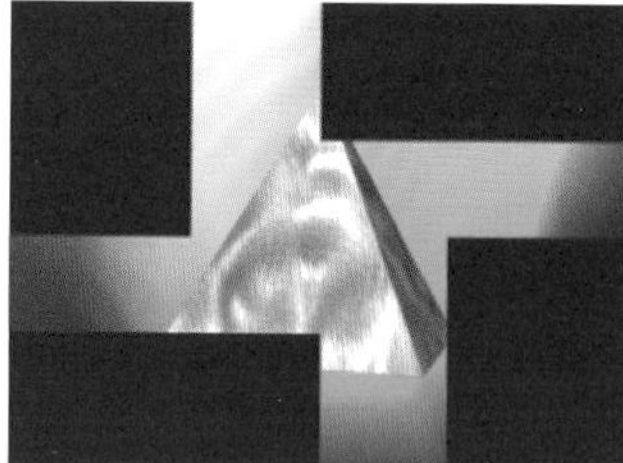
[V]e [Tt]c [O]s

Special overlap mode provides circle, diamond, diagonals, and multiple element wipes. In addition to using scene frames and bitmaps, you can opt for gray noise, color noise, or solid color transitions.

TRANZITION cont

AZ Technology | **\tranzitn** | **TRANZ_I.IXP**

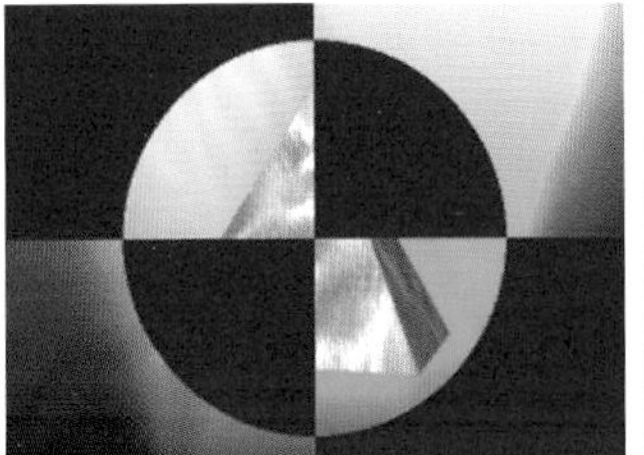
[H]rl [V]tb [Tt]c [O]s

[H]lr [V]tb [Tt]c [He]d [O]s

[H]lr [V]c [Tt]f [O]s

[H]lr [V]c [Tt]f [O]s

Numerous patterned wipes are possible using various combinations of horizontal and vertical components in special overlap mode.

VAN GOGH

Pyros Partnerships | **\vangogh** | **VANGO_I.IXP**

Summary

Van Gogh is part of the Pyros Partnerships' Paints Library package. It uses a variable series of semitransparent black and white rectangles to produce a range of patterns from scattered squares to randomly hatched or woven textures. The patterns can blend with or completely obscure the original image or frame.

Van Gogh Parameters

Intensity [I] (1–12) — Sets the pattern density.
Gradient [G] (8–64) — Sets the pattern opacity.
Stroke [S] (2–12) — Sets the size of pattern elements.
Alpha [A] w,=0,>0 (Whole Image,=0,>0) — Whole applies the effect to the entire image, =0 applies the effect outside the alpha channel, and >0 applies the effect inside the alpha channel.

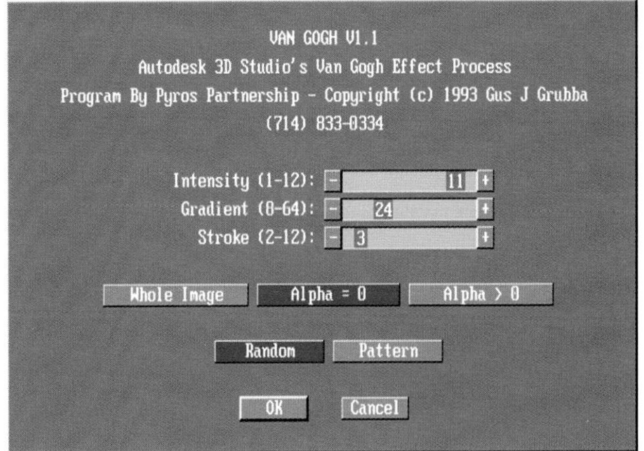

The Van Gogh dialog box.

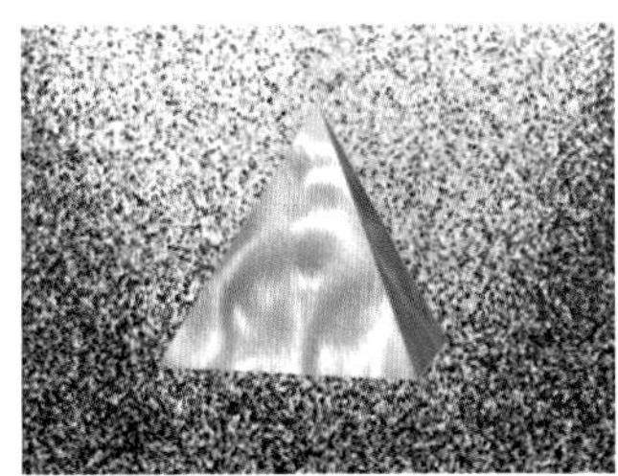
[I]11 [G]24 [S]3 [A]=0

[I]8 [G]32 [S]5 [A]=0

[I]9 [G]8 [S]9 [A]=0

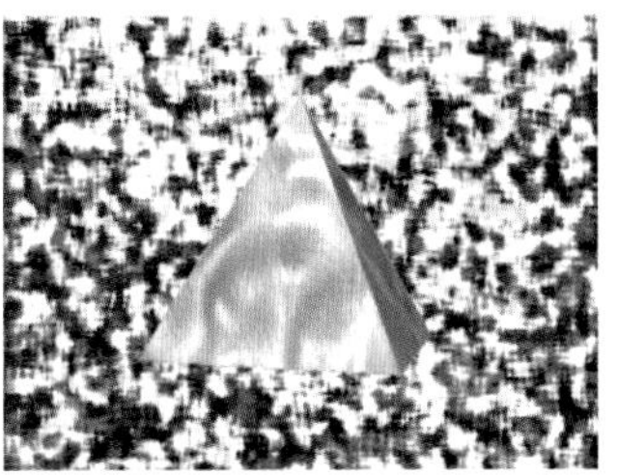
[I]12 [G]8 [S]12 [A]=0

Varying intensity, gradient, and stroke produces a range of spotted and hatched patterns, any of which can be masked via the alpha channel.

VERTICAL BLUR

VBLUR_I.IXP **\vblur** **Autodesk**

The Blur dialog box.

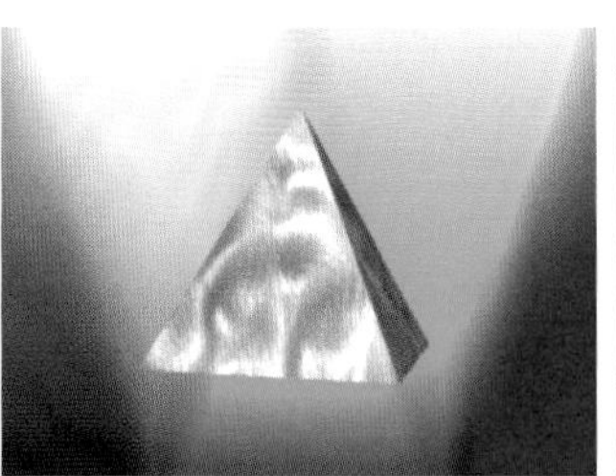

[A]0

[X]1

The image at left has no blur applied and the one at right has maximum blur.

Summary

Vertical blur is included with 3D Studio Release 4. It is designed to reduce NTSC or PAL flicker by performing a weighted blur on groups of three scan lines. It produces a subtle blur on non-video-captured images.

Vertical Blur Parameter

Amount [A] (0–1) — Sets the degree of blurring.

WARP

AFWARP_I.IXP **\warp** **Schreiber Instruments**

AFWARP 1.10 - The Animated Factory - (C) 1994 by Serge GOLUCH
- Warp: Warp this image ! -

Density (1-1000): 100
Amount (1-100): 80
Start length (pixels): 50
Step (pixels/frame): 0
Start shift (pixels): 0
Step (pixels/frame): 0

Direction: RIGHT DOWN LEFT UP
Amount variation: DECR. INCR. NONE
Random seed: 0 Copy source: NO YES

Alpha P: Whole image P=0 only P>0 only
Alpha C: Whole image C=0 only C>0 only

OK Cancel

The Warp dialog box.

Summary

Warp is part of the Imagine Animated Factory. It is designed to give the impression of an image smearing across the screen as it moves out of view. You can transition either to black or back to the original image. This program could be improved with the option to transition to a specific image. You can use the alpha channel to select a section of the image to move, and you also can use the alpha channel to mask the smearing effect. This plug-in uses the alpha channel only as an on/off mask.

Warp Parameters

Density [D] (0–1000) — Sets the density of the streaks in the effect.

Amount [A] (0–100) — Sets the percentage of transparency of the effect.

Start length [Sl] (0–200) — Sets the initial length of streaks.

Length Step [Ls] (–50–50) — Increments the streak length per frame.

Start shift [Ss] (1–200) — The initial shift of the image.

Shift Step [St] (–50–50) — Increments the step per frame.

Direction [Dr] (right, left, up, down) — Specifies the direction of shift.

Amount variation [Av] — Increments the effect transparency per frame.

Random seed [R] — Varies the random streaks.

Copy source [C] (yes or no) — Uses the original image or black as background.

Alpha P [Ap] i,=0,>0 (whole image, P=0, P>0) — Alpha P controls masking based on the alpha channel value at the current pixel. Whole applies the effect to the entire image, P=0 applies the effect outside the alpha channel, and P>0 applies the effect inside the alpha channel.

Alpha C [Ac] i,=0,>0 (whole image, C=0, C>0) — Alpha C controls masking based on the alpha channel value at the effect center. Whole applies the effect to the entire image, C=0 applies the effect outside the alpha channel, and C>0 applies the effect inside the alpha channel.

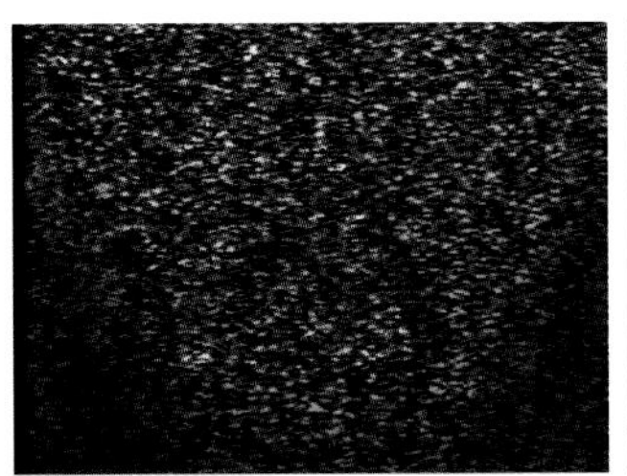
Frame 1

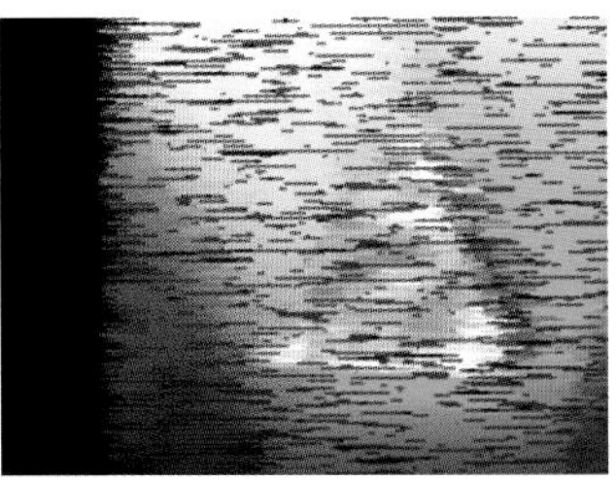
Frame 8

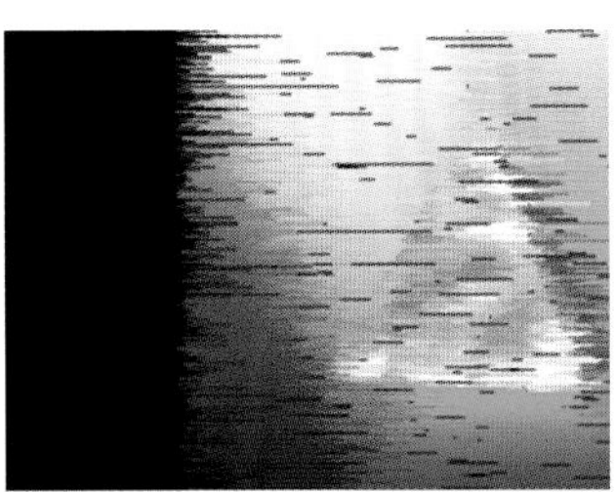
Frame 14

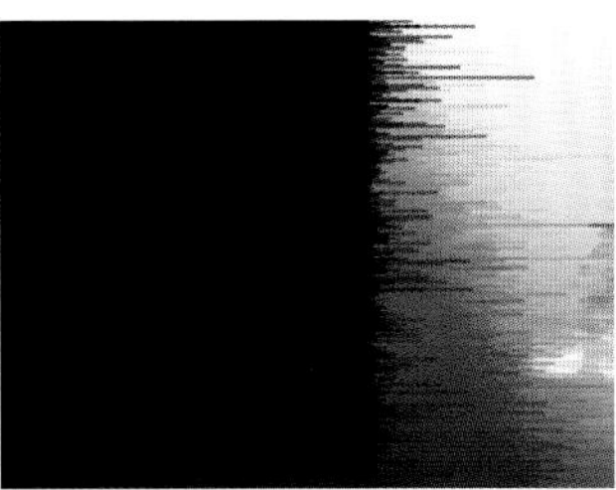
Frane 30

An animated warp to the right with a black background.

4jumb_i.pxp
addvert_i.pxp
adfnce_i.pxp
array_i.pxp
attrib_i.pxp
axpbox_i.pxp
b_i.pxp
blob_i.pxp
box_i.pxp
browse_i.pxp
chked_i.pxp
clnobj_i.pxp
colch_i.pxp
cvldet_i.pxp
deform_i.pxp
delvert_i.pxp
dsplac_i.pxp
eps_i.pxp
eyebrow_i.pxp
ffd_i.pxp
fract_i.pxp
fracun_i.pxp
fusion_i.pxp
gears_i.pxp
grades_i.pxp
grids_i.pxp
guided_i.pxp
hedra2_i.pxp
kbtdrf_i.pxp
light_i.pxp

Magic Rocks

Procedural Modeling External Processes (PXP) plug-ins produce or modify 3D mesh objects from within the 3D Editor. Using PXP plug-ins, you can create unique geometry from scratch while minimizing or bypassing manual modeling entirely. PXP plug-ins are suggestive of Magic Rocks—a curiosity consisting of multicolored pebbles that when dropped in a water-filled aquarium grow intricate underwater terrains—but with enormously more flexibility and control.

Using PXP plug-ins you can create entire forests or gardens consisting of intricately textured and colored 3D trees, shrubs, and flowers. You can select from variables that specify the age, season, and species of a deciduous tree; the blossom color and detail level of a rose; or the size, density, and mix of trees for a forest.

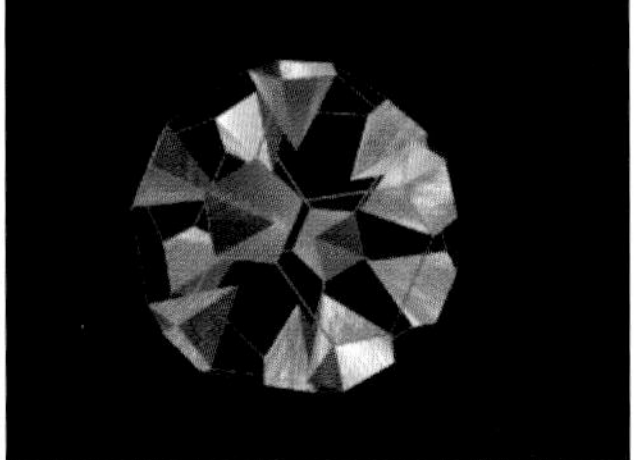

Silicon Garden Hedra2
PXP plug-ins generate a range of detailed geometry from forests to polyhedra.

You also can select from geometry generators that enable you to interactively create fascinating symmetric geometry based on numerous polyhedra such as icosahedrons, tetrahedrons, and star polyhedra. You can generate chain-link fences, concrete walls, precast highway barriers, and spans of telephone poles and railroad tracks complete with textures for wire, wood ties, and rails.

PXP plug-ins offer fractal terrain generators that produce topographic 3D models from predefined geological survey data or using an internal random terrain generator. These can be used along with various image maps to produce mountains, rolling meadows, streams, gravel roads, and asphalt parking lots.

One of the most compelling PXP processes is displacement mapping, which creates intricate geometry by using the luminance values of an image map to displace the vertices of a mesh object. This opens up enormous possibilities for creating unique 3D geometry directly from a 2D paint image.

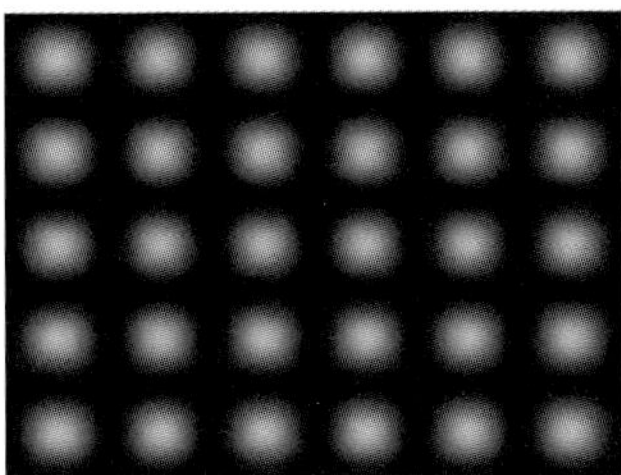
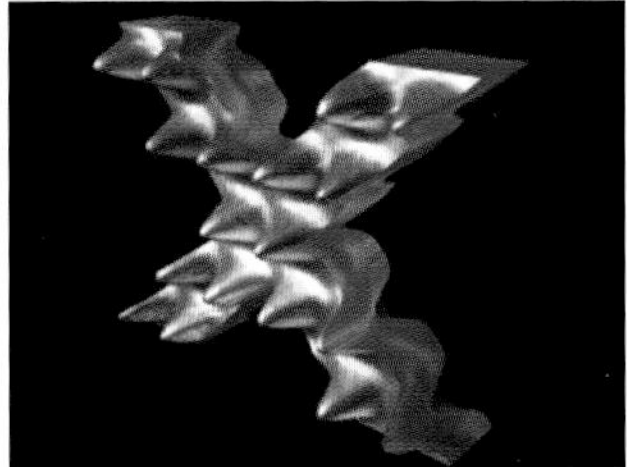

GRID4.TIF Displace
The grid image at left was used to displace and create a smooth rippling surface in the 3D X mesh.

PXP plug-ins also provide a selection of modelers that enable you to produce and edit NURBS (non-uniform rational b-spline) surfaces and work with metaball elements. NURBS create complex curved surfaces using nonlinear mathematics to produce a model. A lattice consisting of multiple control points or nodes is used to smoothly deform each NURBS patch. Metaball modelers use multiple spherical reference objects, each with variable attraction or repulsion, which blend into uniform surfaces. Metaball modeling can produce complex objects quickly and with relatively few elements. Both modeler types are useful for creating geometry that requires smooth, naturalistic form that can be difficult or impossible to create using 3D Lofter or 3D Editor techniques.

Along with their capability to create new geometry, PXPs also enable you to deform, optimize, and tessellate any 3D model. Furthermore, you can create 3D arrays of mesh objects that are scaled, rotated, and distributed over the surface of a selected object. Optimization and tessellation enable you to increase or decrease the geometry in your models based on individual project requirements. Interestingly, you also can use the results of many of these operations as morph targets for animating smoothly varying warps, bends, and twists in selected areas of a mesh or its entirety.

Deformation processes are often carried out using a template object that consists of a series of control points or control elements. These control points are then moved, rotated, or scaled, and used to smoothly interpolate and create a new version of the original 3D mesh object.

A number of PXP plug-ins expand on the IXP plug-ins by enabling you to produce startling animated color effects and compositing. You can even paint a 3D object interactively in virtual space.

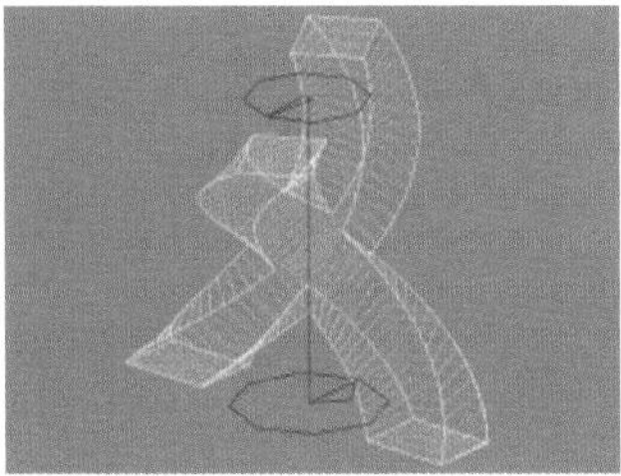

Twist wireframe and template Twisted object

PXP plug-ins often use template objects (at left in red) to reshape or distort 3D objects.

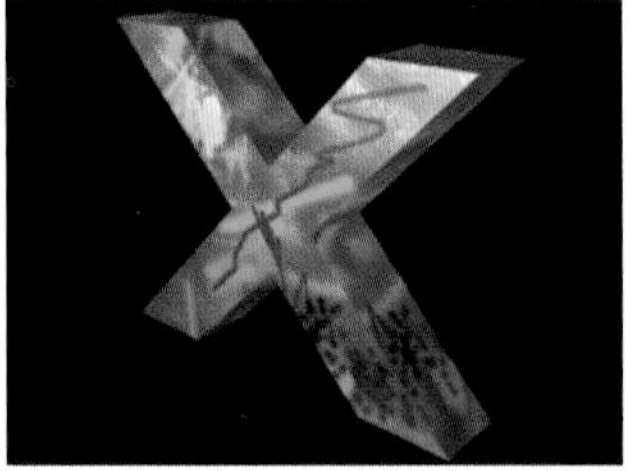

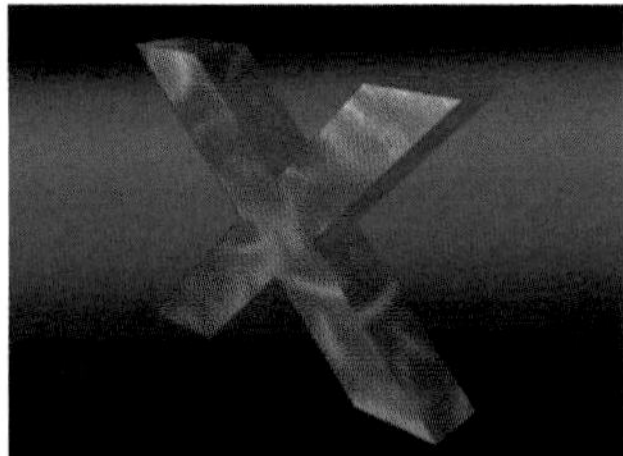

MeshPaint 3D Gradient Designer

PXP plug-ins enable you to paint directly on a 3D object or produce multilayered compositing.

PXP plug-ins work particularly well either using multiple passes of the same plug-in or in combination. Their collective attributes not only make many impossible processes possible, they also speed and smooth the production process as well.

Using PXP Plug-Ins

Before you use a PXP plug-in, be sure that it is properly installed using its installation program or instructions. Furthermore, be sure to read and follow any accompanying instructions exactly. Attempting to shortcut this process, particularly with complex plug-ins, is a mistake. At the least you will likely receive regular error messages as the plug-in attempts to find its resource files, or the plug-in could either cause a crash or simply fail to run.

For those times where there is no installation program or documentation, copy the plug-in—*XXXXXX*_I.PXP—into your 3D Studio \Process directory.

PXP plug-ins are used in the 3D Editor and accessed through the PXP Selector, displayed through the Program menu or by pressing f12. The PXP Selector enables you to scroll through your installed PXP plug-ins and choose the one you want to use. Selecting a plug-in and clicking on OK displays the plug-in's dialog box. PXP dialog boxes range from the very basic, offering no parameters at all, to those that spawn additional dialog boxes, each with supplementary pull-down menus, sliders, numeric fields, and preview windows. Some plug-ins, however, have no dialog box; in such cases, a message appears in the 3D Editor Prompt line, informing you about subsequent steps.

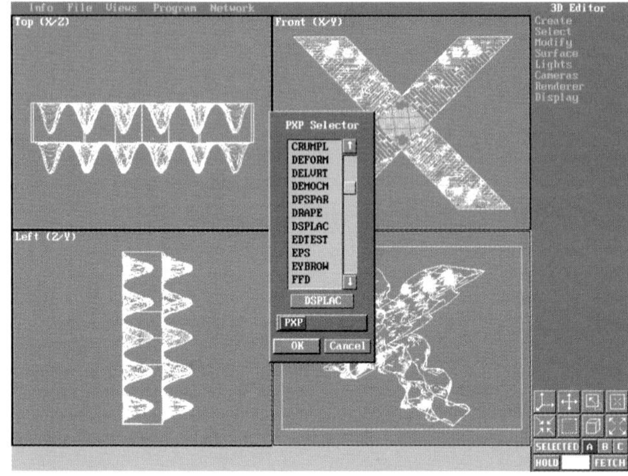

PXP plug-ins are accessed from the PXP Selector in the 3D Editor.

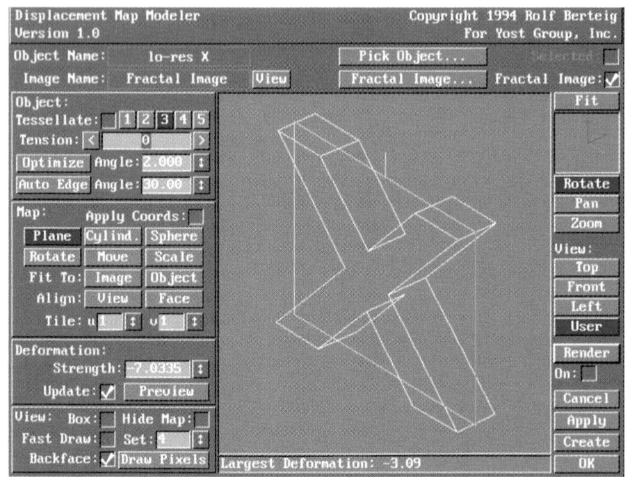

PXP dialog boxes typically consist of multiple buttons, sliders, and numeric fields that control and specify each parameter.

After setting the parameters, click on OK to exit the plug-in's dialog box and return to the 3D Editor. To see the results of your PXP edits, choose the render method you want from the command column to display the Render Still Images dialog box, then set up the render parameters and click on Render.

Note: *For many PXP plug-ins to function properly, they must have an adequate number of evenly distributed faces from which to work. Many often require that you tessellate the original object several times. Create/Object/Tessellate/Edge with edge tension set to 0 works well to accomplish this.*

The PXP Reference

The PXP plug-ins are listed alphabetically with the product name in bold type which appears at the top of each plug-in's section. The color bar below the plug-in name lists the plug-in's file name, such as DEFORM_I.PXP. As well, the CD-ROM path name and vendor are shown. The CD-ROM subdirectory contains any sample files along with demonstration versions of the plug-ins where possible.

The text is divided into two sections: a summary and a parameter listing. The summary provides a look at the plug-in's characteristics and capabilities. The parameter listing displays the name of each parameter in bold type along with its corresponding abbreviation in brackets. For example:

Horiz Edge Effect [He] p,s (plain, striated) (0–100%) — Specifies a sharp or ragged edge for the transition. Thesliders control the width of the striated edge.

When applicable, the bracketed abbreviations are followed by parameter modifiers and their abbreviations, and an adjustment range. A description of the parameter's function follows this information.

The plug-ins are illustrated with their dialog boxes and one or more sample images. Many of the PXP plug-ins were applied to a test image consisting of a stainless steel *X*.

Note: *Many of the project files used to create the sample images are available on the CD-ROM in the directory specified in the information bar at the beginning of each entry.*

Each figure has the parameter abbreviations along with the essential values used to create that effect. The specific effect variations shown were chosen to represent as broad a range of variation as space permitted, and on the basis of providing PXP plug-in users shortcuts and starting points for creating unique, interesting, and useful effects.

Selected PXP sample images are provided in their final rendered form. These files are located on the CD-ROM in the directory specified in the information bar at the beginning of each plug-in or in the \PXP directory.

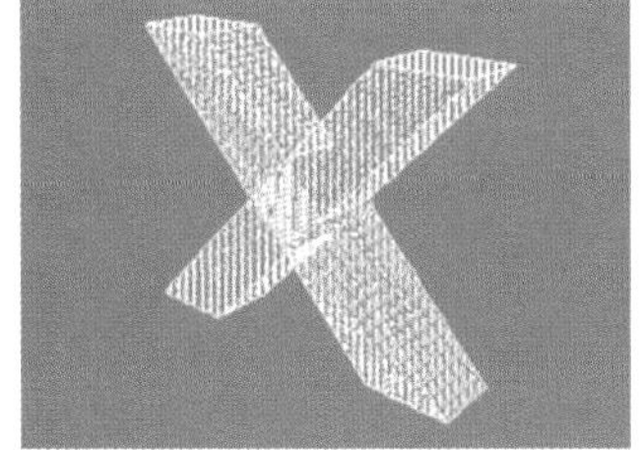

Wireframe X

Rendered X

Many of the PXP plug-ins were applied to a stainless steel *X*.

3D SURF

3DSURF_I.PXP \3dsurf **Schreiber Instruments**

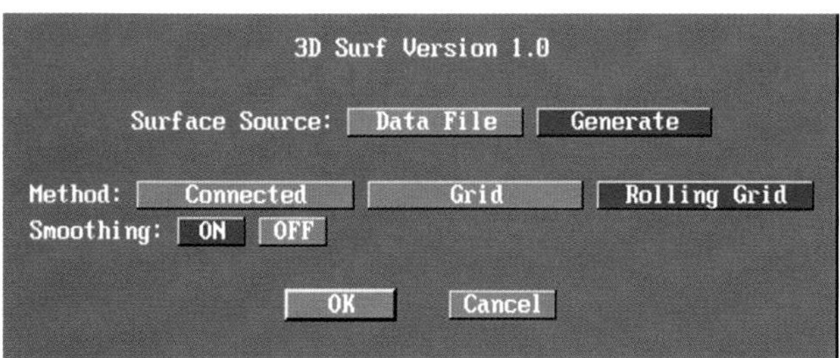

The 3D Surf dialog box.

Summary

3D Surf is part of the Imagine series from Schreiber Instruments. It generates a terrain surface from a predefined data file of points or from an internal random terrain generator.You can choose to produce a mesh composed of either an irregular network of points that exactly match the points in the data file,or a regular rectangular grid of points that are mapped to the surface defined by the points in the data file.A data file is a simple text file listing the X,Y,Z coordinates of each point on the terrain surface.Many surveying programs produce this kind of data.

3D Surf includes an AutoLISP program for AutoCAD that converts object points into coordinate data for a 3D Surf data file.It also includes a materials library with predefined materials for many terrain surfaces such as meadow,stream,snow,gravel, and asphalt.

3D Surf Parameters

Surface Source [S] d,g (Data File,Generate) — Data source for the surface mesh.Data File reads an external data file. Generate produces a surface from an internal random terrain generator.

Method [M] c,g,r (Connected,Grid,Rolling Grid) —The method 3D Surf uses to generate a mesh from the data points.Connected uses the data points as vertices in the mesh and connects them with an irregular triangular network.Grid maps a rectangular grid mesh to the data points. Rolling Grid maps a rectangular grid to the data points while damping irregularities in the surface curves.

Smoothing [Sm] (on,off) — Determines whether 3D Studio smoothing groups are assigned.

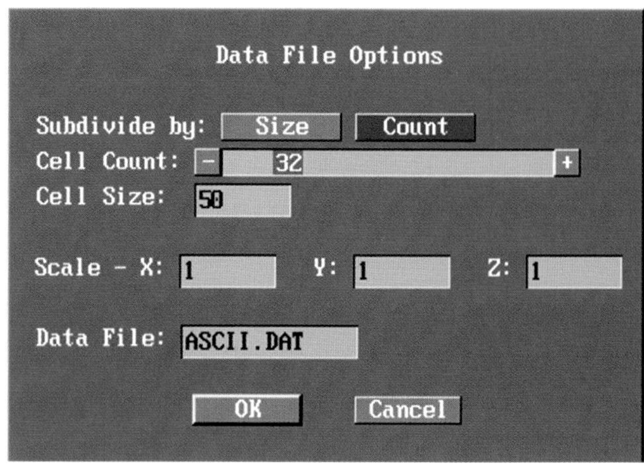

The Data File Options dialog box.

Data File Parameters

Subdivide by [Sd] s,c (Size,Count) — Specifies the level of mesh detail using either size or number of cells (divisions) in the overall mesh surface.This determines whether the Cell Count or the Cell Size parameter is used.

Cell Count [Cc] (2–180) — Number of divisions along each side of the mesh surface.A cell count of 10 would give a total of 100 mesh cells.

Cell Size [Cs] (0.000001–99,999) —The size of an individual mesh cell in 3D Studio units.

Scale X, Y, Z [Sx] [Sy] [Sz] (–99,999–99,999) — Controls the scaling of the mesh surface in the X,Y,and Z dimensions.

Data File [D] — Specifies the name of the data file that will be used to generate the mesh surface.This file must be in the current directory (usually the 3D Studio home directory).

Terrain Generator Parameters

Surface Chaos [Sc] (1–40) — Determines the amount of deviation from a flat surface in a generated terrain.A larger number produces a more irregular surface.

Surface Size [Ss] (0.000001–99,999) —The overall size of the surface mesh in 3D Studio units.

Subdivide by [Sd] s,c (Size,Count) — Specifies the level of mesh detail using either size or number of divisions in the overall mesh surface.This determines whether the Cell Count or the Cell Size parameter is used.

Cell Count [Cc] (2–180) — Number of divisions along each side of the mesh surface.A cell count of 10 would give a total of 100 mesh cells.

Cell Size [Cs] (0.000001–99,999) —The size of an individual mesh cell in 3D Studio units.

[S]g [M]r [Sc]4 [Ss]2500 [Sd]c [Cc]32 [D]mountain.dat

Terrains generated by 3D Surf from the random generator and from a data file.

Terrain Options

Surface Chaos: - 20 +

Surface Size: 500

Subdivide by: Size Count

Cell Count: - 32 +

Cell Size: 50

OK Cancel

The Terrain Options dialog box.

ADDVERTS

Schreiber Instruments \addverts ADDVERT_I.PXP

Summary

AddVerts is part of the Imagine 3DTurbo package. It is used to add vertices to existing meshes. You can add vertices to an object by using any one of three options. Match Object enables you to pick an existing object and match the number of vertices in it. Number enables you to enter a specific number of vertices to add. Percent increases the number of vertices by a specified percent.

AddVerts Parameters

Select Object(s) [S] n, p (By Name, Pick Single) — You can pick a single object from the screen or select multiple objects by name.

Statistics [St] — Choosing this button displays a scrollable list of the selected objects with their face and vertex counts.

Match Object [M] — Enables you to select a object to match vertex count.

Number [N] (0–65,535) — Sets a number of vertices to add.

Percent [P] (0–100%) — Sets the percentage of increase in the vertex count.

CleanObject First [C] — Option to invoke the CleanObject duplicate removal function. Setup selects the CleanObject operations.

QuickDraw Last [Q] — Option to invoke the QuickDraw edge hiding function. Setup selects the QuickDraw angle.

Object creation [O] m, c (Modify Existing, Create New) — Selects whether the program will modify the existing mesh or create a copy.

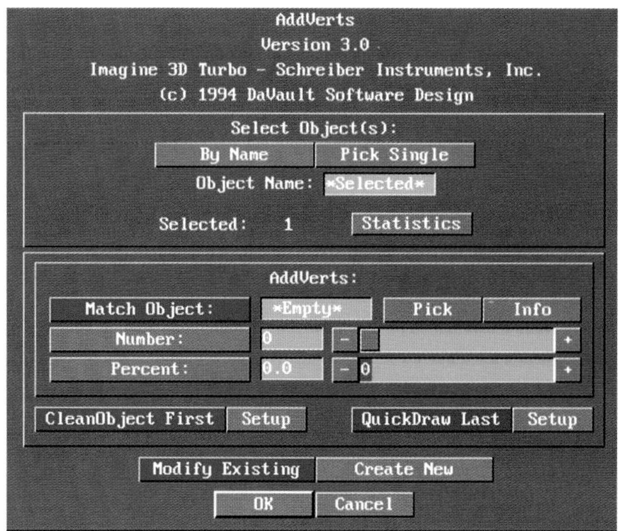

The AddVerts dialog box.

ARRAY

ARRAY_I.PXP \array **Enthed Animation**

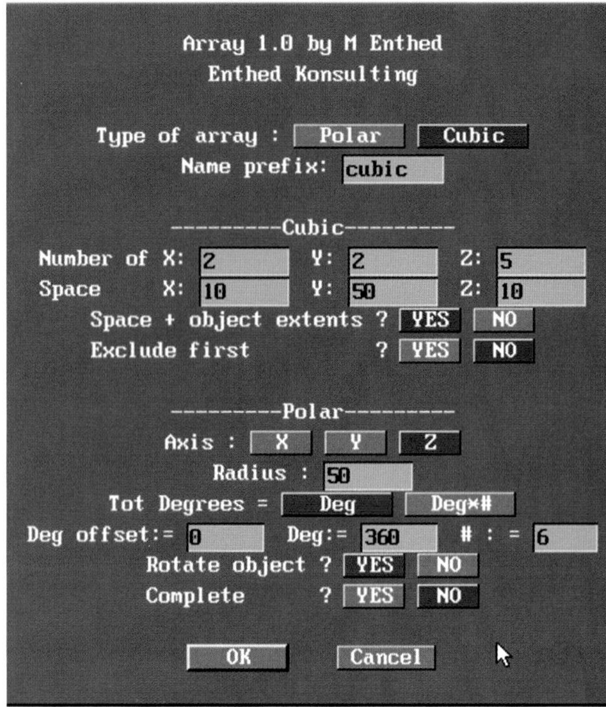

The Array dialog box.

Summary

Array is part of the Ent Tools package. It makes arrayed copies of an object. Arrays can be either cubic along X, Y, or Z or polar around X, Y, or Z. You specify the name prefix and Array makes a series of new objects.

Array Parameters

Type of array [T] p, c (Polar, Cubic) — Selects the type of array. Polar is radial around an axis. Cubic makes copies along each axis.

Name prefix [P] — Enter the prefix name of the objects in the array.

Cubic array

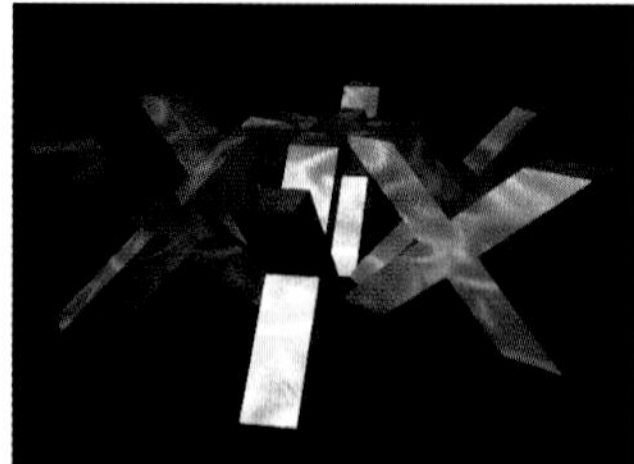

Polar array

A 2x2x3 Cubic array and a six-object Polar array.

Number of X, Y, Z [Nx] [Ny] [Nz] — The number of copies in each axis of a cubic array.

Space X, Y, Z [Sx] [Sy] [Sz] — Spacing between each object in each axis of a cubic array.

Space + object extents [S] y, n (yes, no) — Determines whether the spacing is calculated as the distance between objects (yes) or the distance from object to object (no).

Exclude first [E] y, n (yes, no) — No creates a copy of the original object; yes does not.

Axis [Ax] x, y, z — Selects the axis that the array is aligned with.

Radius [R] — Radius of the polar array.

Tot Degrees [Td] d, d# (Deg, Deg*#) — Determines whether the total degrees in the array are set by the Degrees value or whether that value is considered the degrees per object in the array.

Deg offset [O] — Shifts the starting point of the array around the axis.

Deg [D] — Number of degrees in the array. This can be either total degrees or degrees per object.

[#] — Number of objects in the array.

Rotate object [Ro] y, n (yes, no) — Rotates the objects as they are copied around the axis.

Complete [C] y, n (yes, no) — Changes how the copy count is calculated. If Complete is selected (yes), then the last copy is at the same point as the first. Three copies arrayed in 360 degrees would produce copies at 0, 180, and 360 degrees. If Complete is not selected, then three copies in 360 degrees would produce copies at 0, 120, and 240 degrees.

Summary

Attrib enables you to change the object attribute settings for multiple objects at once. You can turn on or off settings for Matte Object, Casts Shadows, Receives Shadows, Frozen, Fastdraw, and Hidden. These changes can be applied to all objects or to only the currently selected objects.

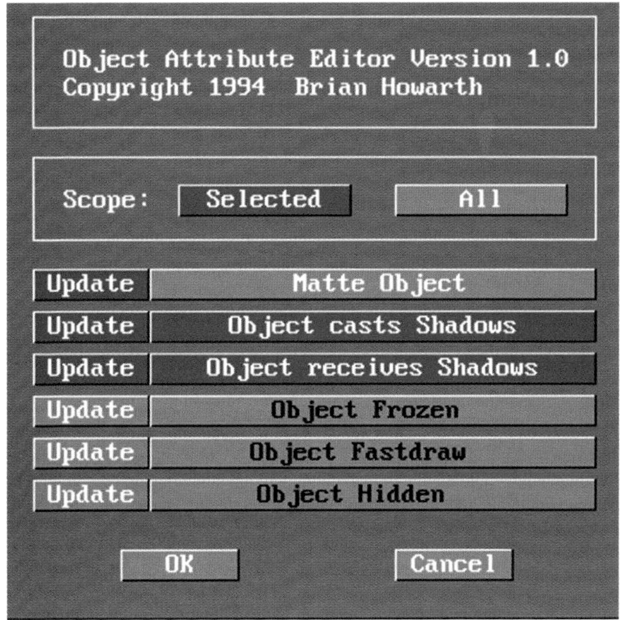

The Attrib dialog box.

Attrib Parameters

Scope [S] s, a (Selected, All) — Controls which objects are changed.

Matte Object [M] y, n (yes, no) — Determines whether an object is a matte object.

Object casts Shadows [C] y, n (yes, no) — Determines whether an object casts shadows onto other objects.

Object receives Shadows [R] y, n (yes, no) — Determines whether an object receives shadows cast by other objects.

Object Frozen [F] y, n (yes, no) — Determines whether an object is frozen.

Object Fastdraw [Fd] y, n (yes, no) — Determines whether an object is drawn in fastdraw mode.

Object Hidden [H] y, n (yes, no) — Determines whether an object is hidden.

Update 1–6 [U1]–[U6] y, n (yes, no) — Associated with each of the six setting buttons. Determines whether the object's setting is changed or left unchanged.

AXPBOX

Yost Group \axpbox AXPBOX_I.PXP

Summary

Axpbox is part of Yost Group's IPAS3 disk #6. It is used in conjunction with the AXP particle effects Flame and Vapor, also from Yost Group. Axpbox produces a single special-purpose object called an emitter cube. Emitter cubes, as the name suggests, perform the dual function of being both a bounding cube and emitter for the given effect, with the former defining the effect area and the latter acting as a source that discharges the particles.

You can specify the number of emitter points, the size of the emitter relative to the size of the bounding box, and the axpbox size in 3D Studio units. You also can opt for a default cube or any object as an emitter, which is useful for flaming objects, for instance.

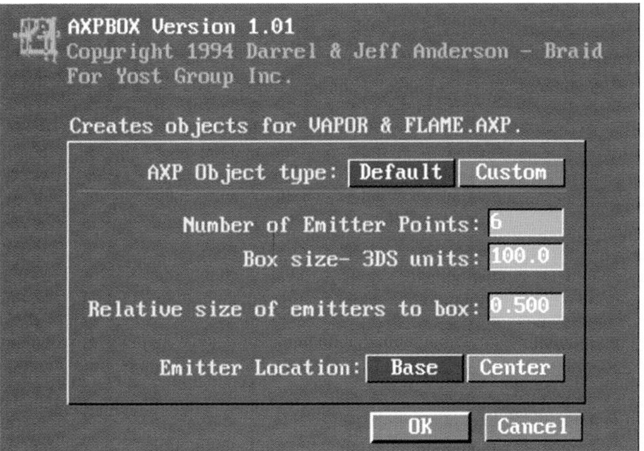

The Axpbox dialog box.

AXPBOX cont

AXPBOX_I.PXP — **\axpbox** — **Yost Group**

Axpbox Parameters

AXP Object Type [T] d, c (Default, Custom) — Specifies the use of a default cube or any 3D object as the particle emitter.
Number of Emitter Points [P] — Specifies the number of vertices that will be created for the particle emitter element.
Box size [B] — Sets the axpbox size in 3D Studio units.
Relative size of emitters to box [Rs] — Sets the size of the cube relative to the emitter.
Emitter Location [E] b, c (Base, Center) — Sets the emitter location within the bounding cube and affects both default and custom emitters.

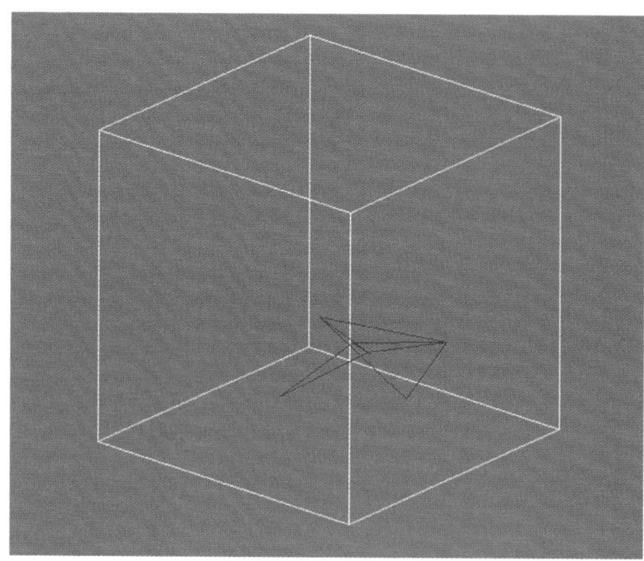

[T]d [P]6 [Rs].5
Axpbox produces an emitter box consisting of a bounding cube and three or more emitters (shown in red).

BLOB SCULPTOR

B_I.PXP — **\blobsc** — **The Blob Team**

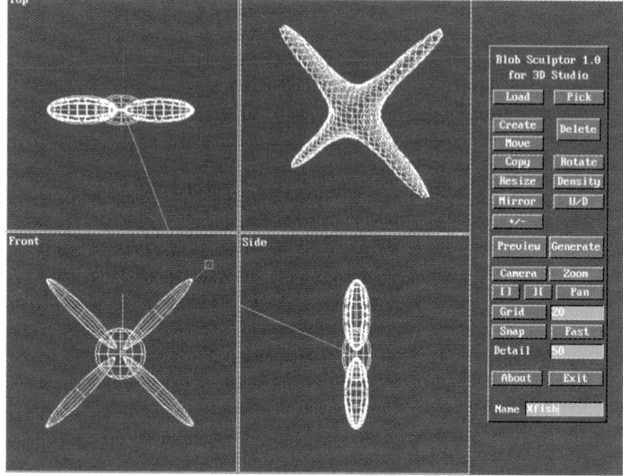

The Blob Sculptor dialog box.

Summary

Blob Sculptor is a blob (or metaball) modeler. With it you can model objects using spherical elements that flow and smooth into each other. This is especially useful for modeling rounded organic objects. The modeling process consists of arranging several spherical components and adjusting the size and degree of smoothing between each. You can choose to make a component either negative or positive. Negative components have a subtractive effect and are used to create concave areas or holes. Positive components are additive and build smooth transitions between blob elements.

Interestingly, Blob Sculptor's spherical elements can be scaled independently in X, Y, or Z, which is useful for modeling nonuniform objects. A detail setting determines the mesh resolution that is generated in 3D Studio. There is no provision for seeing your 3D Studio scene or its objects in Blob Sculptor. This plug-in is intended as a modeler only; there are no built-in provisions for animation.

The interface consists of four viewports with standard views showing a wireframe representation of the blob components. The Iso view is actually a perspective view, and from here you can see a wireframe preview of the current blob object by clicking on the Preview button. When you have finished building your object, click on the Generate button to create a 3D mesh object equivalent in 3D Studio. Blob Sculptor embeds its blob component information in the 3D mesh. This enables you to further modify the original blob object after you have generated a 3D mesh.

This summary is based on a prerelease version of the software.

Blob Sculptor Parameters

Load [L] l, s, m, n (load, save, merge, new) — Blob file operations. You can load, save, or merge a proprietary BLB file format. New clears the current model and starts a new one.

Pick [Pi] — Pick a previously created blob object from the current 3D Studio scene by name.

Create [Cr] — Creates a new blob component.

Delete [De] — Deletes a blob component.

Move [M] — Moves a blob component.

Copy [C] — Copies a blob component.

Rotate [R] — Rotates a blob component.

Resize [Xy] — Resizes a blob component. When you choose a component, sizing handles appear, which you can drag to resize the component. You can resize in only one axis at a time.

Density [D] — Enables you to adjust the falloff of the blob component's surface influence. A larger difference between the component's size and its maximum density (shown in blue) produces smoother surfaces. This is a lot like the falloff of spotlights.

Mirror [Mr] — Mirrors a blob component according to the direction of the Mirror direction toggle. Objects are mirrored across the axis indicator.

Mirror direction — u, l (u/d, l/r) — Specifies up/down mirroring or left/right mirroring.

+/- [Pn] — Switches a blob component between positive and negative strength value.

Preview [Pr] — Produces a smoothed mesh preview in the Iso window.

Generate [Ge] — Creates the mesh object in 3D Studio using the name specified.

Camera [Ca] — Enables you to move the camera and its target point to change the Iso viewpoint.

Zoom [Z] — The left mouse button zooms in on a view, the right button zooms out.

[] [Zw] — Enables you to draw a zoom window.

][[Zp] — Zooms to the previous level.

Pan [P] — Pans the view by picking in the new center of the view.

Grid [G] — Turns the grid off and on and enables you to enter a grid spacing value.

Snap [S] — Turns snap to grid on and off.

Preview speed [Ps] f, s (fast, slow) — Selects fast or slow preview mode.

Detail [Dt] — Determines the detail level of the mesh in preview and when the object is generated.

Name [N] — Enter a name for the new object.

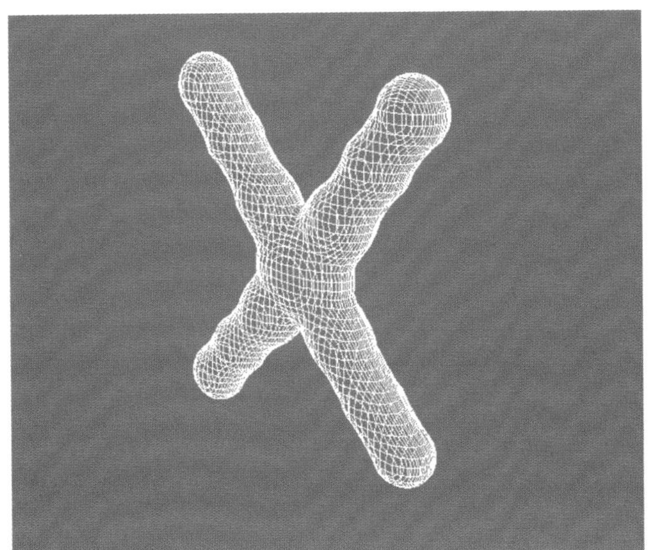

Wireframe view
Blob modeling produces rounded organic forms.

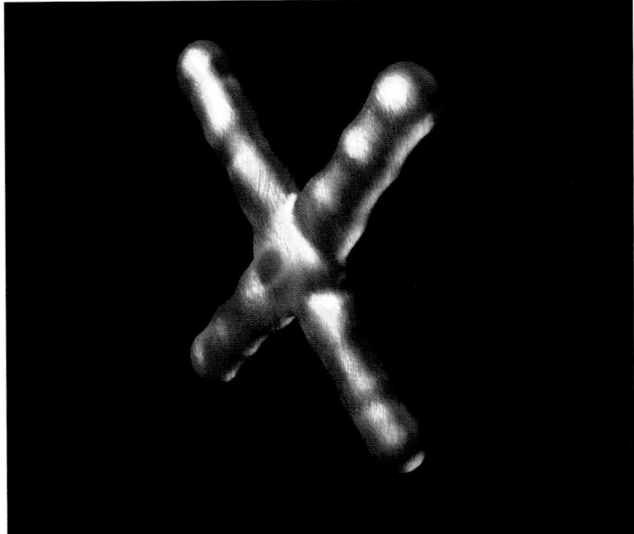

Rendered blob object

CAMERA MAPPING

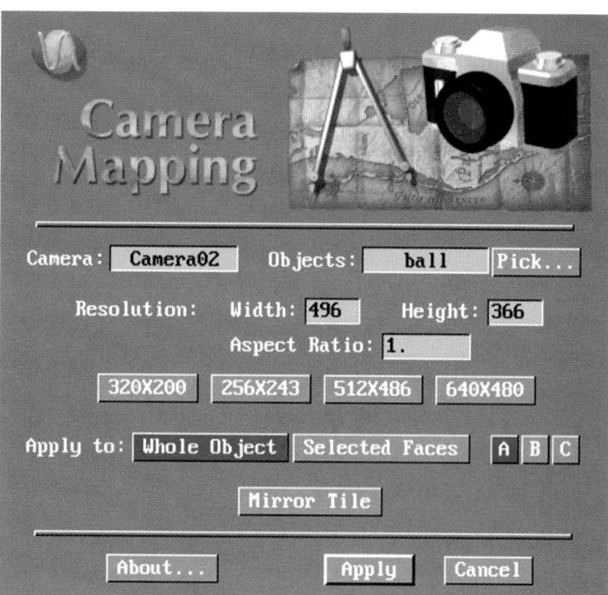

The Camera Mapping dialog box.

Summary

Camera Mapping is a camouflage plug-in. You can use it to hide objects by blending them into their surroundings, or you can reveal objects by unblending them. Camera Mapping does this by mapping an image of the scene onto an object using a modified planar projection from the camera's point of view. You must first render the scene without the object to be camera mapped, then assign that bitmap to a texture-mapped material and apply it to the object. You then use Camera Mapping to apply the new mapping coordinates. Now when you render the scene, the object seems to disappear.

You can use a combination of Camera Mapping and texture morphing to produce objects that move into position and then fade into the surroundings. The reverse effect gives you objects that fade in from nowhere. You will normally want to use self-illuminated, non-shiny materials because they enhance the chameleon effect, but a little shininess or shading from lights can produce an object that is on the edge of visibility.

Camera Mapping Parameters

Camera [C] — The name of the current camera. You can select this field and choose a camera from a scrolling list.

Objects [O] — The name of the object to be mapped. Choosing Pick enables you to choose an object from your scene.

Resolution Width, Height [W] [H] — The width and height of the image to be rendered. This tells the plug-in the proportion of the image. Some standard resolutions are provided.

Aspect Ratio [Ar] —The pixel aspect ratio of the image to be rendered.

Apply to [Ap] w,s (Whole Object, Selected Faces) — Determines whether the mapping is applied to the entire object or to preselected faces.

Selection set [Ss] A, B, C — Selects faces from one of the three standard selection sets.

Mirror Tile [M] e, d (enabled, disabled) — If Mirror Tile is enabled, the texture will be tiled to fill the background size. If it is disabled, the texture will be scaled to match the background size. In most cases the sizes will be the same and you will disable mirror tile.

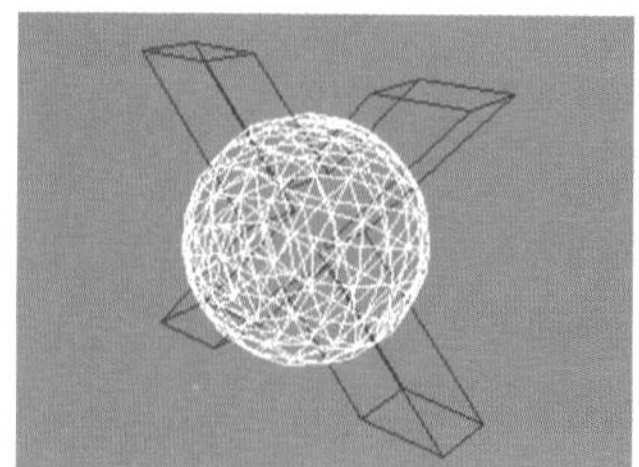
Wireframe scene

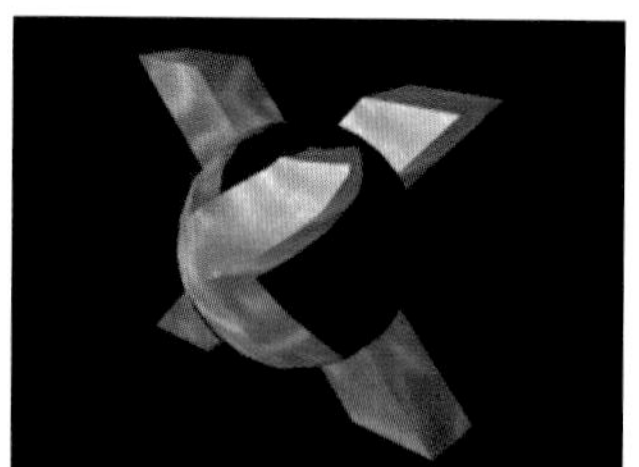
Spherical mapped ball

Camera-mapped ball

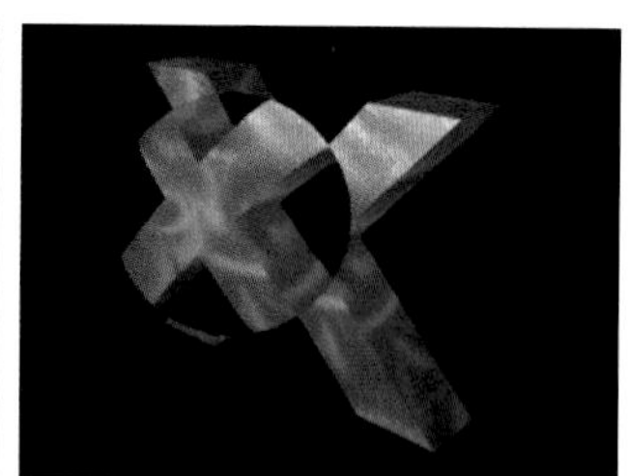
Camera-mapped ball moved

Camouflage using camera mapping.

Summary

Included with 3D Studio Release 4, Checked is a manual pattern generator that enables you to create multiple patterns based on a four-color palette and four granularity settings that govern the pattern size. The palette colors are defined by clicking on their define buttons, which brings up the 3D Studio color picker. The pattern can be edited by clicking on the desired color, then clicking on the grid squares you want to edit.

Checked uses CHK_I.BXP to load and save patterns in CHK format for use as backgrounds, image maps, or projection spotlights.

Note: *Checked will lock up if 3D Studio is running in 24-bit mode.*

Checked Parameters

Define — Sets the color displayed in the adjacent color swatch.
Size [S] 32, 64, 128, 256 — Controls the size of the pattern.
See Grid — Switches a gray grid of 2x2 blocks.

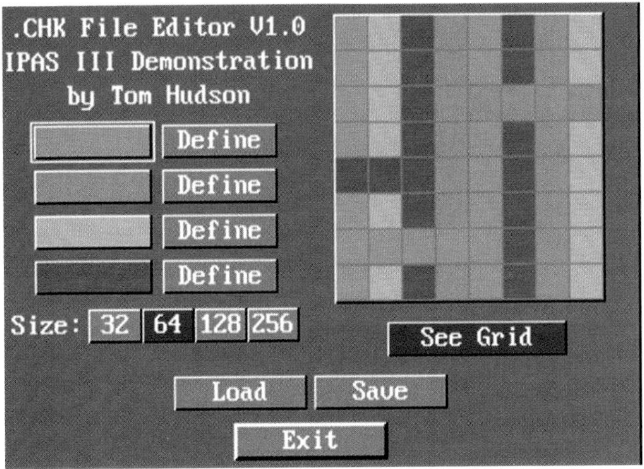

The Checked dialog box.

[S]64
Checked enables you to create patterns based on a palette of four colors.

CHRISTMAS LIGHT GENERATOR

XMAS_I.PXP \xmas **Yost Group**

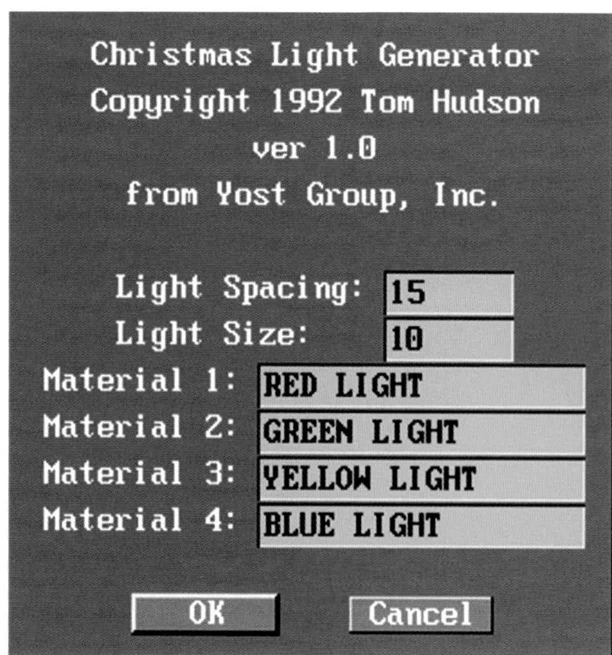

The Christmas Light Generator dialog box.

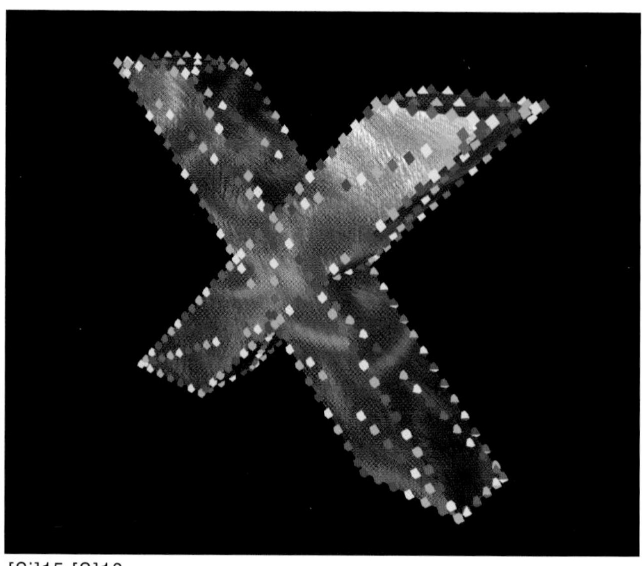
[Si]15 [S]10
Christmas Light Generator distributes multiple octahedrons along the visible edges of any 3D object.

Summary

The Christmas Light Generator is part of Yost Group's Special Effects disk #2. It creates an object consisting of a series of octahedrons and distributes them along the visible edges of any 3D object.

Four materials are automatically assigned to the strings of octahedrons, which simulate strings of Christmas lights. For the materials assignment to work properly, the material names shown in the dialog box must match exactly corresponding materials within the current 3D Studio materials library.

Christmas Light Generator Parameters

Light Spacing [Si] (.01–9,999) — Sets the distance between lights.
Light Size [S] (.01–9,999) — Sets the size of each light.
Material 1, 2, 3, 4 [M1] [M2] [M3] [M4] — Sets the materials for each of the four light groups.

CIVIL DETAILOR

CVLDET_I.PXP \cibvildet **Schreiber Instruments**

Summary

Civil Detailor is part of the Imagine Civil Detailor package. The civil detailor package consists of six plug-ins that create various 3D objects commonly seen in architectural and civil engineering drawings. The plug-in creates numerous barriers such as curbs, fences, and guard rails and objects including railroad tracks and telephone poles. It uses Lofter (LFT) files to determine the path for each object.

Civil Detailor includes a materials library along with the image maps required for rendering each object.

Sound Walls, Barriers & Posts Parameters

Barrier Type [B] (1–19) — Selects the barrier type by number. There are 19 types of barriers to choose from: 1–3 are standard fences, 4–7 are sound walls, 8–10 are barrels, and 11–19 are a range of wood and steel posts.
Facing [F] l, r (Left, Right) — When asymmetrical barriers are created, this specifies whether the finished side faces to the right or left. These buttons have no effect if the fence is symmetrical.
Barrier Path (.LFT) [Bp] — Civil Detailor requires that the user create and save a 3D lofter path (LFT) file.

Height [H] (.01–99,999) — Sets the height in feet above the path. If posts are created, they extend approximately twice their diameter below the path to accommodate minor ground plane fluctuations. The scaling defaults to 1 foot equals 1 3D Studio unit. The height option is not displayed if the fence has a fixed height.

Spacing [S] (.01–99,999) — Sets the maximum spacing between posts or barrels.

Note: *The Height and Spacing parameters are in a separate dialog box that is accessed only when these options are available. This is consistent throughout the plug-in.*

The Sound Walls, Barriers & Posts dialog box.

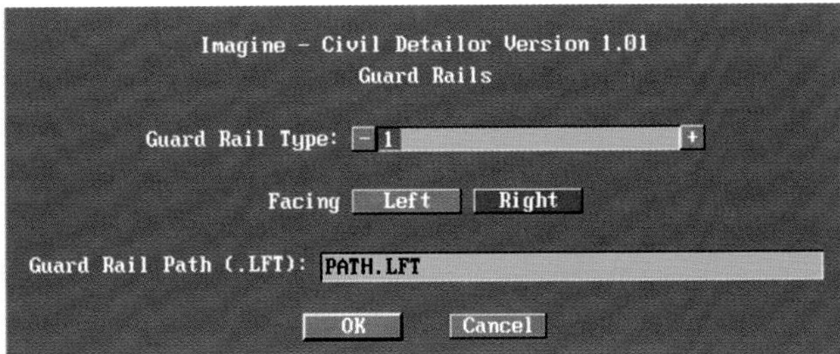

The Guard Rails dialog box.

Guard Rails Parameters

Guard Rail Type [G] (1–15) — Sets the type of guardrail to be created. 1–9 gives the user a range of W-beams with wood, steel, or concrete posts; 10–13 provides a range of steel tubes with wood or steel posts; and 14–15 are steel or wood beams with matching posts.

Note: *All other parameters are the same as Sound Walls, Barriers & Posts.*

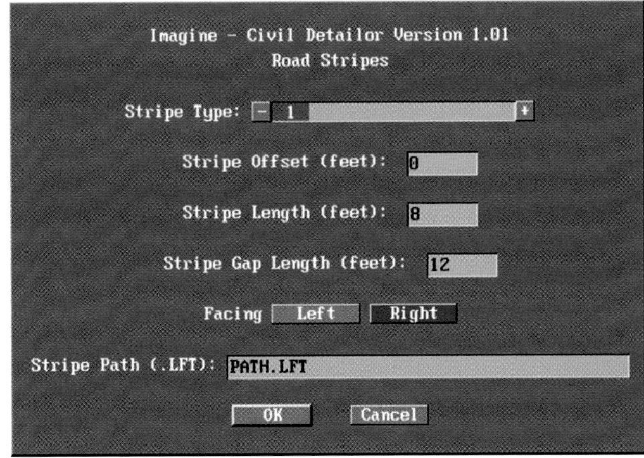

The Road Stripes dialog box.

Road Stripes Parameters

Stripe Type [St] (1–7) — Sets the type of stripe to be created. 1 is a solid white stripe, 2 is a solid yellow stripe, 3 is a dashed white stripe, 4 is a dashed yellow stripe, 5 is double solid yellow stripes, 6 is double solid/dashed yellow stripes, and 7 is a solid wide white stripe. All the stripes are 4 inches wide, except 7, which is 12 inches wide and is to be used as a stop line.

Stripe Offset [So] (–99,999–99,999) — Sets the distance in feet that the selected stripe is offset from the path line. A positive value offsets the line to the right, and a negative value offsets the line to the left.

Stripe Length [Sl] (0–99,999) — Sets the length in feet of the stripes when a dashed stripe type is selected.

Stripe Gap Length [Sg] (0–99,999) — Sets the distance in feet between the dashed stripes.

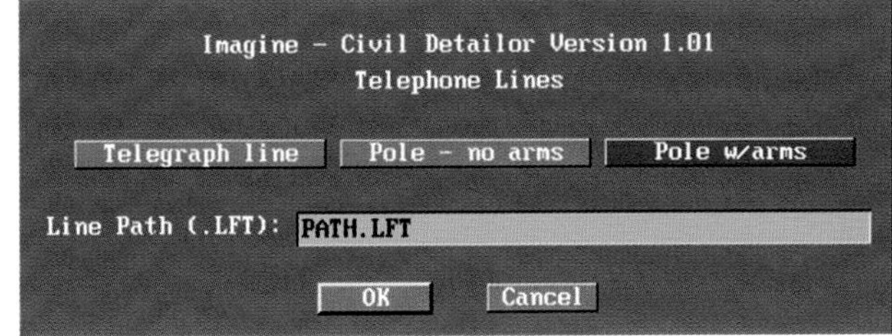

The Telephone Lines dialog box.

Telephone Lines Parameters

Pole type [Pt] t, p, pa (Telegraph line, Pole - no arms, Pole w/arms) — Radio buttons that specify the type of pole to be created.

Number of Lines [Nl] (0–9) — Sets the number of lines to be created. Choosing 0 omits all lines, elements, and arms, creating just the poles.

CIVIL DETAILOR cont

Line Elements and No Line Elements [Le] [Ln] — Controls whether the lines are created with faces. They must be created with faces in order to be seen when rendered.

Line Segments [Ls] 1, 2, 4, 8 — Controls the number of wire segments between poles. 8 produces a fairly smooth draping wire, and 1 produces a straight line.

Note: *The Number of Lines, Line Elements, and Line Segments parameters are available in the Construction Options dialog box.*

Imagine - Civil Detailor Version 1.01
Mass Transit Lines

Transit Line Type: - 1 +

Line Path (.LFT): PATH.LFT

OK Cancel

The Mass Transit Lines dialog box.

Mass Transit Lines Parameter

Transit Line Type [Tl] (1–6) — Selects the type of mass transit line (track) by number. 1–5 produce standard train tracks with materials options such as concrete or wooden ties. 6 produces a monorail and is the only one of these that accesses a Construction Options dialog box.

The Concrete Barriers dialog box.

Concrete Barriers Parameter

Barrier Type [Bt] (1–6) — Selects the type of barrier by number. 1 produces a curb, 2–3 produce sound walls, and 4–6 produce concrete highway barriers. Barrier height and spacing parameters are accessed in the Construction Options dialog box.

Pennello

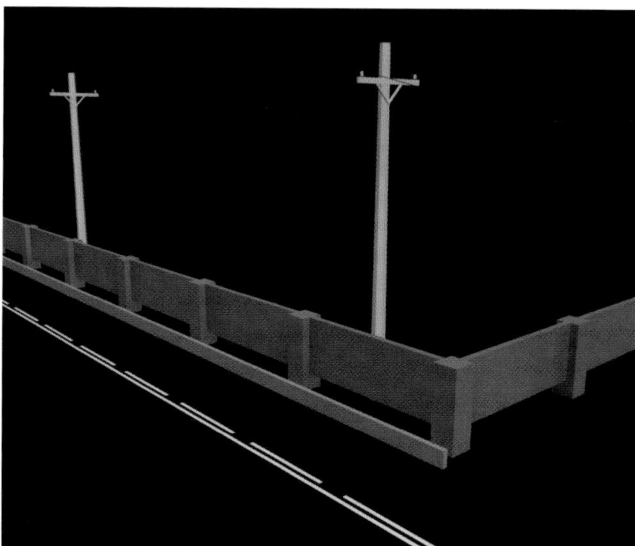

LenZFX

These figures used concrete barriers, road stripes, telephone lines, and mass transit lines.
Civil Detailor produces a range of walls, train tracks, fences, road stripes, barriers, and telephone lines.

Summary

CleanObject is part of the Imagine 3DTurbo package. It removes duplicate vertices, duplicate faces, and unreferenced vertices. These extra structures arise from some mesh-editing processes and some IPAS programs, and are common when importing meshes from DXF. This removal of duplicates is not the same as the more extensive mesh optimization done by the Turbo module in this package. You have the option of calling the QuickDraw plug-in from this package as part of the processing.

CleanObject Parameters

Select Object(s) [S] n, p (By Name, Pick Single) — You can pick a single object from the screen or select multiple objects by name.

Statistics [St] — Choosing this button displays a scrollable list of the selected objects with their face and vertex counts.

Clean Object by removing [C] dv, uv, df, vf (Duplicate Vertices, Unreferenced Vertices, Duplicate Faces, Duplicate Verts in Face) — Enables specific cleanup operation. Duplicate Vertices performs the same function as 3D Studio's vertex weld. The weld threshold is fixed at 0.00001. Duplicate faces are faces that share all three points. Unreferenced vertices are vertices that are not attached to any faces. Duplicate Verts in Face finds faces that have two or three of the same vertices.

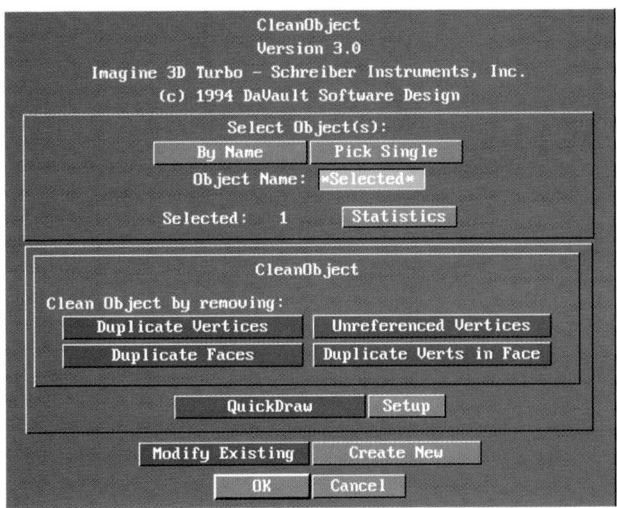

The CleanObject dialog box.

QuickDraw [Q] — Option to invoke the QuickDraw edge hiding function. Setup selects the QuickDraw angle.

Object creation [O] m, c (Modify Existing, Create New) — Selects whether the program will modify the existing mesh or create a copy.

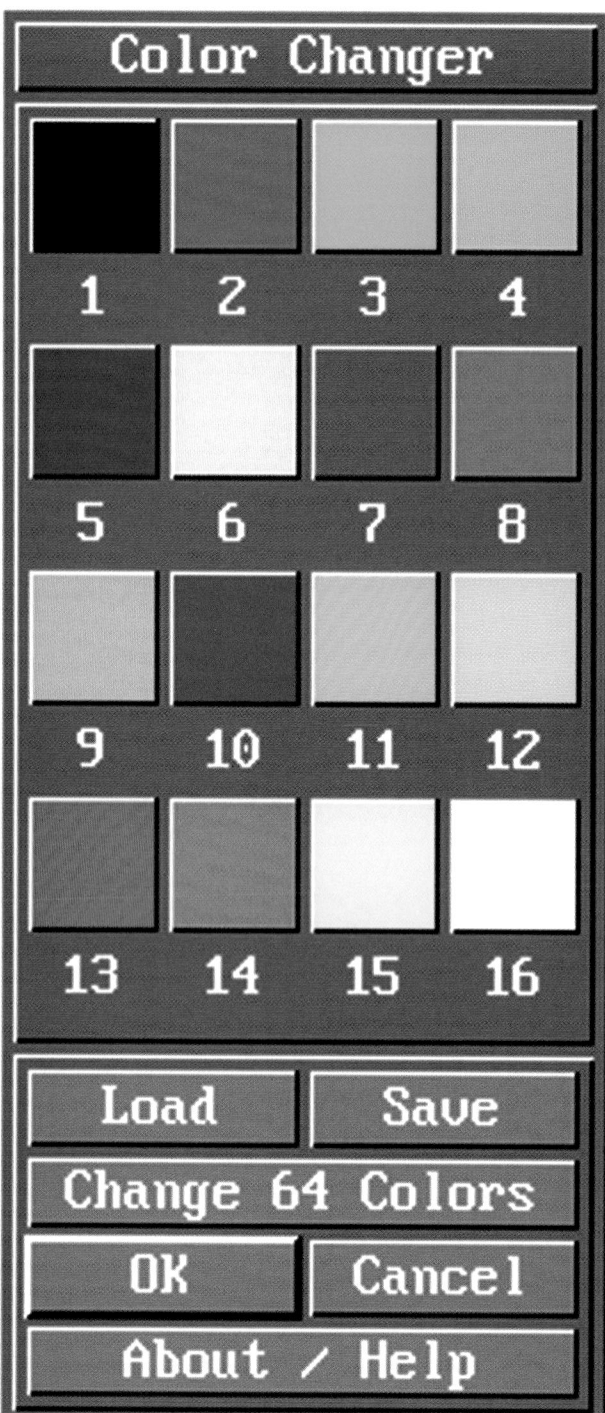

The Color Changer dialog box.

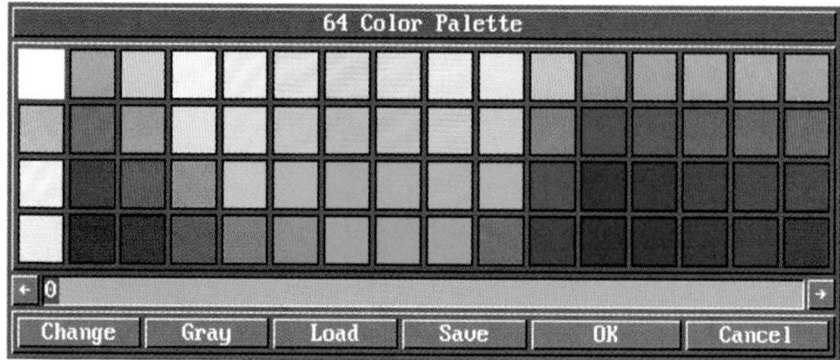

The wireframe color dialog box.

Summary

Color Changer the screen colors in 3D Studio.You can change the 16 interface colors that affect such items as the screen background, menu background, and text, and you can change the 64 colors that can be assigned to the wireframe of an object. When you change a color, Color Changer displays a standard 3D Studio color picker dialog box, enabling you to change the color using RGB and HLS controls. After you have created a group of custom colors, you can save them as a palette file that you can load whenever you want to change colors.

The main limitation of this product is that your color changes are volatile. If 3D Studio has to switch video modes, such as when switching to the Materials Editor or viewing a rendered image, it resets the screen colors to their default settings. This limits Color Changer to use as a method of testing or previewing new interface colors. You must then write down the RGB values and edit the corresponding RGB color values in the Color Register Parameters section of the 3DS.SET file. This will make screen color changes permanent.

Color Changer Parameters

Interface color 1–16 [C1]–[C16] — Color samples of the 16 user interface colors. Select a color to change it.
Load [L] — Loads a predefined palette file.
Save [S] — Saves a palette file.
Change 64 Colors [Cc] — Displays a dialog box to change the 64 wireframe colors.

Wireframe Color Palette Parameters

Wireframe color 1–64 [C1]–[C64] — Color samples of the 64 wireframe colors. Use the scroll bar to select a color, then click on the Change button.
Change [C] — Changes the value of the selected wireframe color.
Gray [G] — Changes the wireframe color palette to a range of grays.

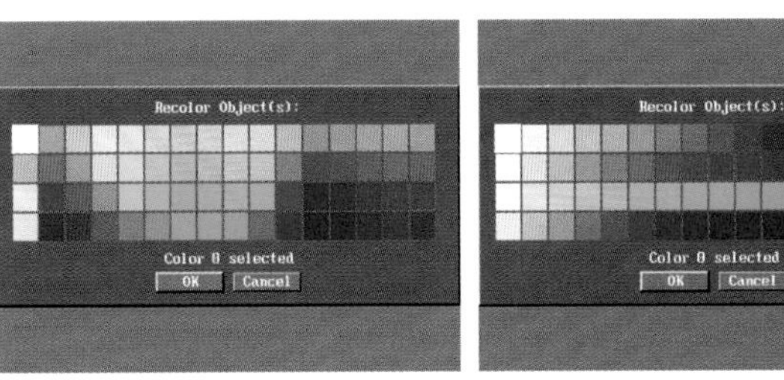

Original palette   Custom palette

Custom wireframe colors.

DEFORM

Yost Group \deform DEFORM_I.PXP

Summary

Deform is part of Yost Group's IPAS3 disk #6. Deform enables you to smoothly deform a mesh object using a 3D template. The plug-in is applied in two steps: creating the template and applying the deformation based on the Deform parameter settings. The template consists of a 3x3x3 or 4x4x4 lattice of points that surround the object. It can be adjusted using any combination of modify vertex or modify object functions. This results in a new object that is reshaped and rescaled to fit edits to the template.

Alternatively you can use dual templates, which adds flexibility by enabling you to deform only a specific object region. You also can apply deformation to groups of objects.

If you opt to produce more than a single object, the deformation is distributed incrementally along the object series. Because the resulting objects have the same vertex count as the original, they can be used as morph targets for animated effects.

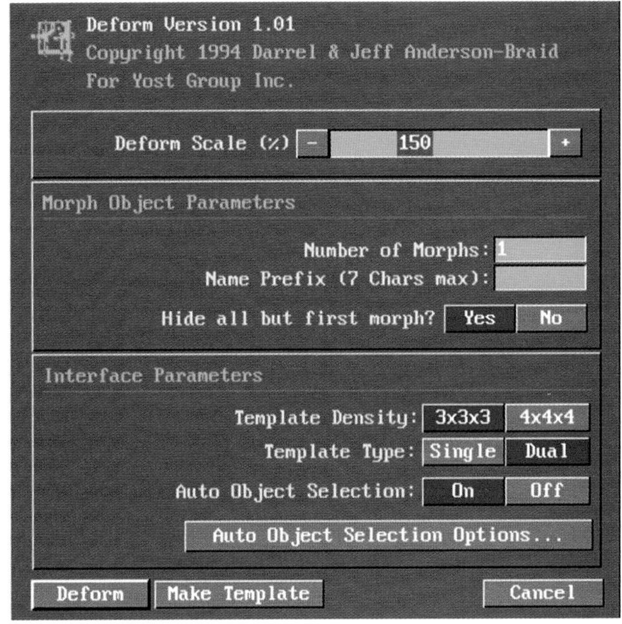

The Deform dialog box.

Deform Parameters

Deform Scale % [Ds] (1–400) — Sets the deform scale between the original object and the edited template. Values less than 100 deform the object within the template, and values greater than 100 deform the object beyond the template.

Number of Morphs [M] — Specifies the number of morph objects or Stretch objects that will be created. This enables you to apply the deformation in stepped increments.

Name Prefix — Sets the name prefix for the morph objects produced by Deform.

Hide all but first morph? (yes, no) — Specifies whether to hide all but the first morph object.

Template Density [Td] 3, 4 (3x3x3, 4x4x4) — Sets the density of the deformation lattice.

Template Type [Tt] s, d (Single, Dual) — Single uses one template to deform all the vertices in a 3D mesh, and Dual enables you to use two templates to deform an object region.

Auto Object Selection and Options — Sets which object is deformed after selecting the edited template. Options enables you to specify the name of your source template and the mesh selection method.

Deform — Enables you to select the template and object you want to deform.

Make Template — Creates a template for the selected object.

DEFORM cont

DEFORM_I.PXP \deform **Yost Group**

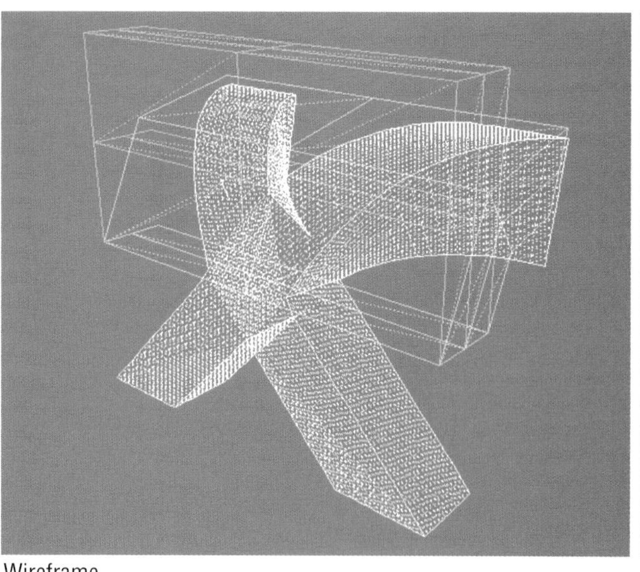

Wireframe [Ds]150 [Tt]d

Deform uses a 3D lattice (shown in yellow) to reshape a 3D mesh object, an object region, or a group of objects.

DELETEVERTS

DELVERT_I.PXP \delverts **Schreiber Instruments**

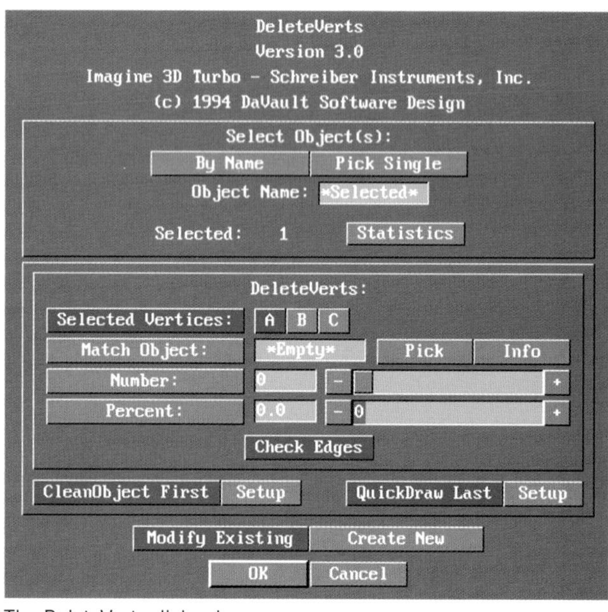

The DeleteVerts dialog box.

Summary

DeleteVerts is part of the Imagine 3DTurbo package. It is used to remove vertices from existing meshes. You can remove vertices from an object using any one of four options. Selected Vertices deletes the vertices that have been previously selected in any combination of 3D Studio's A, B, or C selection sets. Match Object enables you to pick an existing object and match the number of vertices in it. Number enables you to enter a specific number of vertices to remove. Percent decreases the number of vertices by a specified percent.

DeleteVerts Parameters

Select Object(s) [S] n, p (By Name, Pick Single) —You can pick a single object from the screen or select multiple objects by name.

Statistics [St] — Choosing this button displays a scrollable list of the selected objects with their face and vertex counts.

Selected Vertices A, B, C [Sa] [Sb] [Sc] (on, off) — Selects which selection sets of vertices to delete.

Match Object [M] — Enables you to select a object to match vertex count.

Number [N] (0–65,535) — Sets a number of vertices to add.

Percent [P] (0–100%) — Sets the percentage of increase in the vertex count.

DELETEVERTS cont

Schreiber Instrument \delverts **DELVERT_I.PXP**

Check Edges [Ce] e, d (enabled, disabled) — When Check Edges is enabled, it removes vertices from the edges of meshes. If disabled, it does not change edge vertices.

CleanObject First [C]—Option to invoke the CleanObject duplicate removal function. Setup selects the CleanObject operations.

QuickDraw Last [Q] — Option to invoke the QuickDraw edge hiding function. Setup selects the QuickDraw angle.

Object creation [O] m, c (Modify Existing, Create New) — Selects whether the program will modify the existing mesh or create a copy.

DISPLACEMENT MAP MODELER

Yost Group \displace **DSPLAC_I.PXP**

Summary

Displacement Map Modeler (Displace) is part of Yost Group's IPAS3 disk #7. It enables you to reshape or create new geometry based on the grayscale or luminance values of a bitmap image. It is similar to bump mapping, which alters an object's surface normals at render time to produce roughened surfaces. Bump mapping, however, has no effect on the actual geometry.

Displacement modeling actually uses the relative gray levels in a bitmap to displace or move a 3D mesh's vertices, with white producing the greatest displacement and black producing no displacement. Unlike bump mapping, displacement mapping is capable of dramatic changes in an object's overall form or topology.

Displace accomplishes this by enabling you to use any 3D Studio–supported bitmap format or its own fractal images to move selected vertices. You can choose from planar, cylindrical, and spherical mapping coordinates, each of which apply the bitmap to the geometry in the same way as the Material Editor's maps are applied. Each map type uses a corresponding icon that enables you to interactively deform a model simply by moving or scaling the icon. The degree or scale of displacement is set by the strength function.

You also can use Displace as a vertex editor for interactively editing geometry by applying solid colored maps to specific areas of your 3D model. For instance, because a solid white bitmap acts as a positive displacement, it also works well as means of pushing or pulling selected vertices. When used with planar mapping, the effect is similar to extrusion; when used with spherical mapping, the effect produces both subtle and dramatic curves in your geometry.

Displace also enables you to tessellate and optimize the resulting geometry. This is useful for producing geometry that is detailed enough to accurately reflect the selected bitmap while being as efficient as possible. Tesselation can be performed on any of five detail levels that incrementally increase the vertex and face count. You might opt to use either positive tension,

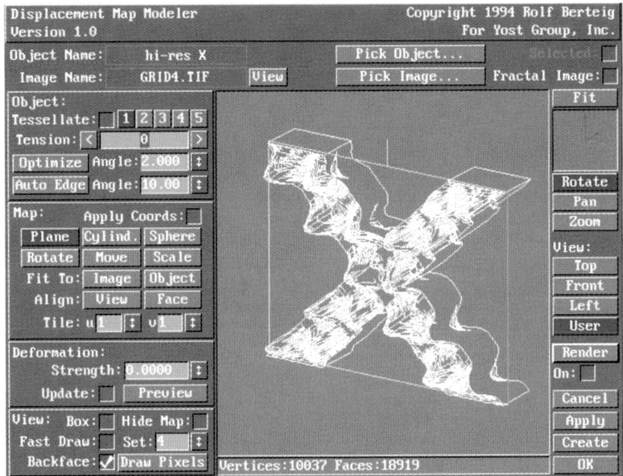

The Displacement Map Modeler dialog box.

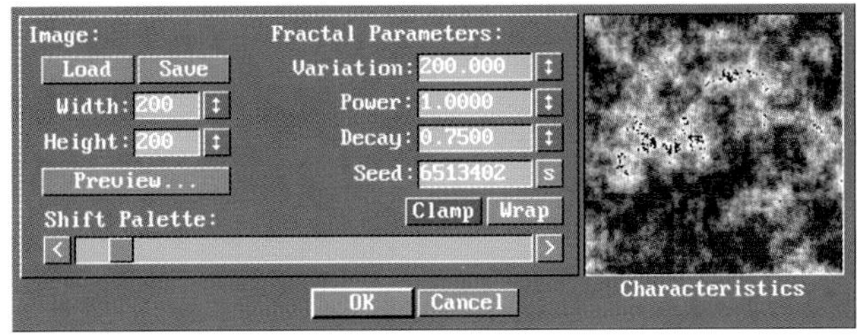

The Fractal Image dialog box.

which produces convex geometry, or negative tension, which creates a concave effect. Optimize throws away selected faces based on the angles of adjacent faces, which lets you specify the final level of mesh detail.

The results of Displace can optionally be used as morph targets by using the Create command. You can vary any of Displace's functions, and as long as you do not either tessellate or optimize the mesh, Displace will maintain the same vertex count and thus produce a useful morph object.

Displace Parameters

Pick Object — Enables you to pick any 3D mesh object from the current 3D Studio file. The chosen mesh name appears in the Object Name field.

Pick Image — Enables you to pick a bitmap image in any of 3D Studio's formats. The chosen image name appears in the Image Name field.

View — Enables you to view the selected bitmap image.

Fractal Image [Fi] — Enables you to use a fractal image rather than a bitmap image to displace the geometry. Selecting the Fractal Image option displays the Fractal Image dialog box, which enables you to load, save, preview, and specify the resolution and parameters of a fractal image.

Fractal Parameters [Fw] [Fh] [Fv] [Fp] [Fd] [Fs] [Fc] [Fwr] (Width 1–100, Height 1–1,000, Variation, Power, Decay, Seed, Clamp, Wrap) — These parameters set the various characteristics of a fractal image, which is optionally used to displace the geometry. Variation works with Power to set the grayscale used in the image. Power varies the contrast of the image. Decay produces smoothing while holding the overall pattern consistent. Seed sets the number used to generate the fractal pattern. When Clamp is set, all intensity values above 255 and below 0 are clamped at 255 and 0, respectively. When Wrap is set, the intensity values outside the range of 0–255 wrap additively, producing a new grayscale value. Shift Palette cycles the gray levels without affecting the pattern. Width and Height specify the resolution of the fractal pattern. Preview displays the fractal image at the current proportion.

Note: *The Fractal Parameters are found in the Fractal Image dialog box, which is accessed by clicking on the Fractal Image check box.*

Tessellate [T] 1, 2, 3, 4, 5 — Enables you to subdivide the 3D mesh with any of five levels of complexity, allowing you to set a mesh detail level that is appropriate to the displacement image.

Tension [Te] (–100–100) — Varies the mesh smoothing based on positive tension, which produces a rounding effect, or negative tension, which produces a concave effect.

Optimize Angle [Oa] (0–90) — Reduces the mesh complexity of selected faces based on a specified angle. The process is based on the relative angles of the mesh's surface normals. Any face with a normal angle greater than the angle setting is not removed.

Auto Edge Angle [Ae] — Specifies the mesh visibility based on the angle between the surface normals of adjacent faces.

Map [M] p, c, s, (planar, cylindrical, spherical) — Specifies the mapping coordinate method used by Displace, with each producing the same result as its counterpart in the 3D Editor. Rotate, Move, and Scale enable you to orient the map icon, which varies the displacement.

Fit To [F] i, o (Image, Object) — Image forces the map icon to the proportions of the displacement image, and Object fits the map icon to a bounding box of the current object.

Align [A] v, f (View, Face) — Aligns the image map to the current view or to a specific face.

Tile u and Tile v [Tu] [Tv] (0–99) — Sets the number of repeat images independently along the U and V axes, with U equivalent to horizontal and V equivalent to vertical.

Apply Coords [Ac] When checked, applies the same mapping coordinates used in displace to the current object.

Deformation Strength [Ds] Sets the greatest distance that any vertex will be displaced from the mapping plane. The Preview button redraws the viewport and also can be used to remove the effects of the Optimize and Auto Edge functions. Update dynamically updates the display as various functions are applied, which, depending upon computer speed, can make the deformation process interactive.

Geometry view controls (Box, Hide Map, Fast Draw 0–100, Backface, Draw Pixels) — Specifies the way geometry is displayed in the viewport. Box switches box mode on and off. Hide Map switches the mapping icon on and off. Fast Draw specifies the number of displayed faces. Backface switches backfaces on or off. Draw Pixels displays the corresponding pixel from the bitmap at each object vertex, which, given sufficient tesselation, can give a grayscale approximation of the image mapped to the mesh.

Viewport controls (Fit, Rotate, Pan, Zoom, Top, Front, Left, User) — These work as their 3D Studio counterparts to provide a view of the current object.

Render — Renders the current view in your choice of flat or Gouraud shading. This is set through a render preferences dialog box that is accessed by holding down the shift key and clicking on the Render button. The On button provides a dynamic rendered view as each variable is changed.

Apply and Create — Apply enables you to apply the displacement to the geometry without leaving the Displacement dialog box. This allows you to apply multiple displacement operations to the geometry in a single session. Create produces a new object with the current displacement properties, which enables you to create morph objects.

[Ds]60 [M]s

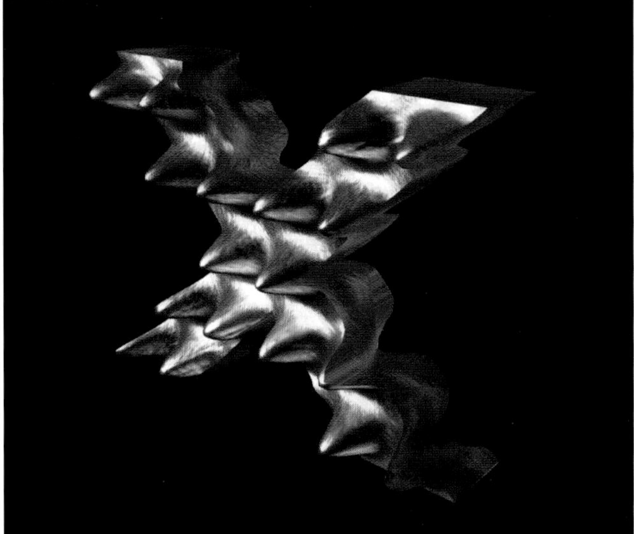

[Ds]60 [M]p

GRID4.TIF, a grid of blurry dots, was applied to the mesh using spherical and planar mapping coordinates.

EPS OUTPUT

Autodesk \epsout EPS_I.PXP

Summary

Included with 3D Studio Release 4, EPS Output produces Encapsulated PostScript (EPS) files directly from the 3D Studio renderer. EPS renders are produced as you would any render to disk with the exception that you must add .EPS to the file name. 3D Studio uses EPS_I.BXP as a means of creating the EPS format files.

EPS output can be configured for orientation, data format, page size, and resolution.

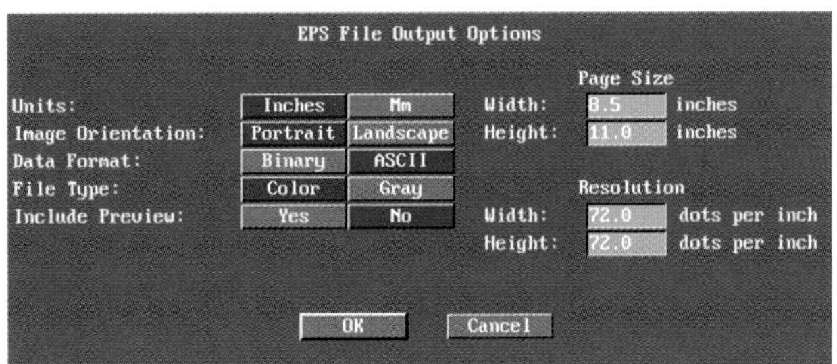

EPS File Output Options

				Page Size	
Units:	Inches	Mm	Width:	8.5	inches
Image Orientation:	Portrait	Landscape	Height:	11.0	inches
Data Format:	Binary	ASCII			
File Type:	Color	Gray		Resolution	
Include Preview:	Yes	No	Width:	72.0	dots per inch
			Height:	72.0	dots per inch

OK Cancel

The EPS Output dialog box.

EPS Output Parameters

Units [U] i, m (inches, millimeters) — Specifies inches or millimeters as EPS Output units.

Image Orientation [Io] p, l (Portrait, Landscape) — Specifies vertical or horizontal page format.

Data Format [D] b, a (Binary, ASCII) — Specifies the data format. ASCII format is approximately twice the size of binary format; however, some PostScript printers are unable to accept binary format.

File Type [Ft] c, g (Color, Gray) — Specifies either 24-bit true color or 8-bit grayscale output.

Note: *For grayscale output, remember to set the 3D Studio Dither Truecolor option to NO.*

Include Preview — Specifies whether a preview TIFF image will be included in the EPS file. This is useful for page makeup programs such as QuarkXpress or PageMaker.

Page Size [Ps] w, h (Width, Height) — Specifies the page size in inches or millimeters.

Resolution [R] w, h (Width, Height) — Specifies the EPS file resolution in dots per inch or millimeters.

EYEBROWSE

EYEBROW_I.PXP | **\eyebrows** | **Digimation**

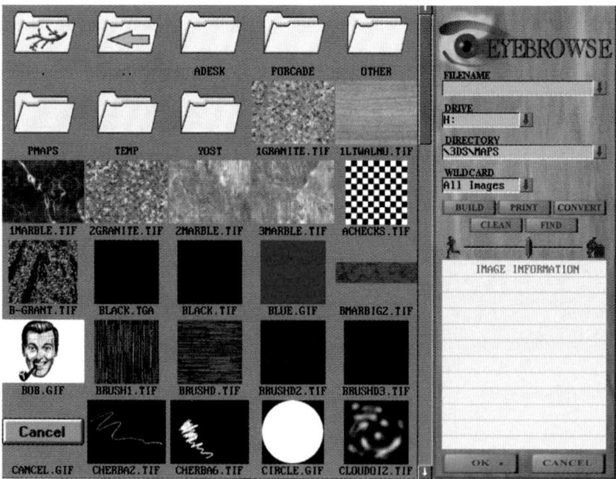

The Eyebrowse dialog box.

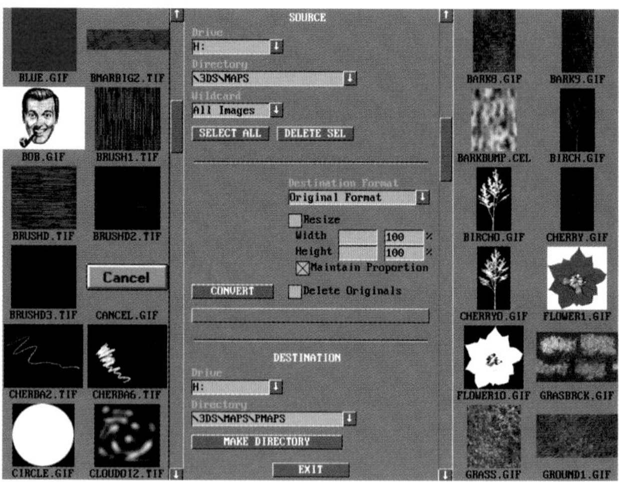

The Convert dialog box.

Summary

Eyebrowse is a utility program that scans selected drives and directories for images based on user-specific search criteria. The resulting selection set appears in the image window initially as an array of file names, from which it builds an array of 30 color icons. You then click on any image icon to display its file size, resolution, creation date and time, aspect ratio, background color, and gamma in an information window at the lower right of the screen. Clicking on the magnifying glass icon displays a full-resolution version of the selected image. You also can rename an image, delete an image, or attach a reference to an external text file.

You can search for an image or group of images by image type, or by keywords for all networked drives and subdirectories. You can print image catalogs at several detail, contrast, and brightness settings. Choosing the Convert button displays the Convert dialog box, with which you can convert any image or group of images to a new file format or resolution.

Eyebrowse Parameters

Filename — Enables you to type a file name from the current directory or select it with the mouse from the Combo box arrow icon. The Combo box is an alphabetical listing of images from all search directories.

Drive — Sets and displays the current local or network drive.

Directory — Sets and displays the current local or network directory.

Wildcard — Specifies the file extension for the current search.

Build — Builds thumbnails for the current directory and, optionally, its subdirectories.

Print — Prints an image catalog for the current directory and, optionally, its subdirectories. You can vary contrast, brightness, or resolution at 150, 300, or 600 dpi. You also can opt to create thumbnails.

Convert — Displays the Convert dialog box, in which you move images from a source to a destination directory while optionally converting the file between image formats or resizing the image. Supported formats are BMP, CEL, FLC, FLI, GIF, JPG, TGA, TIF, GRD, LZF, GRA, FRC, YUV, CHK, EPS, FUN, and TVC.

Clean — Deletes all image thumbnails from the current directory and optionally its subdirectories.

Find — Enables you to search subdirectories, all drives, and archives, and single step for specified image types. Single step enables you to step through the result of the last search.

Performance slider — Sets the trade-off between speed and space optimization. Settings to the left favor speed whereas settings to the right favor disk optimization.

FRACTAL UNIVERSE

Summary

Fractal Universe produces multicolored static and animated turbulence patterns. It enables you to create a range of turbulent effects from fiery, multilayered plasma to cloudy or steamy patterns. The turbulence pattern is controlled by a number of interdependent variables that specify pattern detail, motion, density, and overall quality. Each turbulent pattern is saved in a proprietary FUN format that can be used as a 3D Editor scene background, projection spotlight, any material map through the Materials Editor, or as the basis for numerous effects using the Video Post dialog box in the Keyframer.

You also can animate several of the turbulence properties including size, speed, favor, and edge by clicking on the associated E button for the parameter. This action brings up an Envelope dialog box that displays curved or linear splines on a graph with the X axis representing animation frames and the Y axis representing the current Fractal Universe parameter. You can create, move, and delete keys as well as scale or shift groups of keys. You also can save and load envelopes, which is great when you want to synchronize multiple animated effects.

As each effect parameter is edited, a full-color preview is updated to reflect the change. You also can opt to see a sample animation of the current effect.

Fractal Universe Parameters

Movement [M] — Specifies the direction of movement for the turbulence. Speed increases as the arrow is moved away from center. A right-click returns motion to center.

Frames [Fr] — Specifies the number or frames for the turbulence animation or cycle.

Seed [S] — Specifies the number that is used as a random seed for turbulence calculation.

Linear or B-Spline [Li] [Bs] Specifies that turbulence be calculated based on either linear or b-spline functions. B-spline takes longer and produces softer effects.

Image Size [I] Specifies the resolution for the turbulence pattern in pixels.

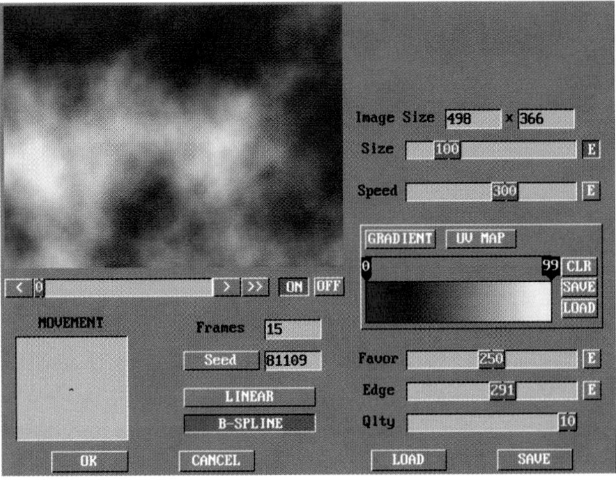

The Fractal Universe dialog box.

Size [S] (0–500) — Sets the size and detail level for the pattern of turbulence. Smaller settings create finer patterns.

Speed [Sp] (0–500) — Works with Movement to set motion speed for the turbulence.

Gradient or UV Map [Gr] [Uv] — Specifies the color palette and distribution used to create the turbulence pattern. Gradient uses a linear multicolor gradient that can be adjusted anywhere along its range using RGB or HLS color models. UV Map uses any image to create the turbulence.

Favor [F] (0–500) — Varies the turbulence pattern based on the value distribution displayed by the Gradient or UV Map. Adjusting this slider higher than 250 favors a higher luminance range, and values below 250 favor a lower luminance range.

Edge [E] (0–500) — Sets the overall pattern contrast.

Qlty [Q] (0–10) — Sets the number of times the turbulence is calculated, with higher values resulting in more realistic and detailed effects.

Note: *Fractal Universe comes with FUN.BXP, which enables 3D Studio to use its proprietary (FUN) bitmap format.*

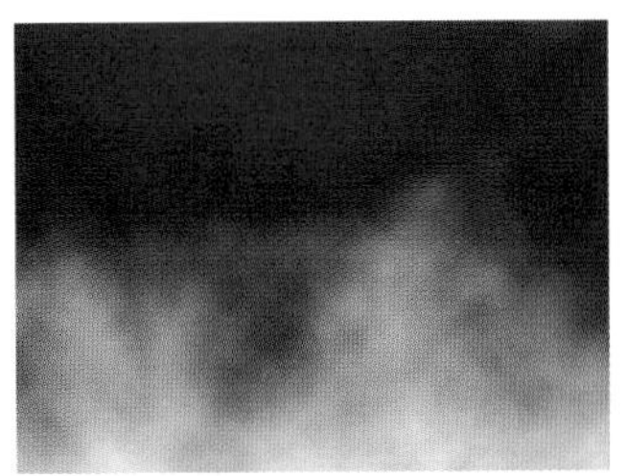

[S]500

[S]350

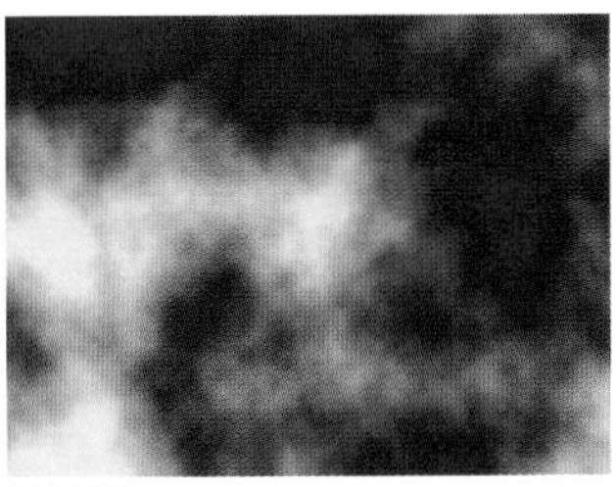

[S]200

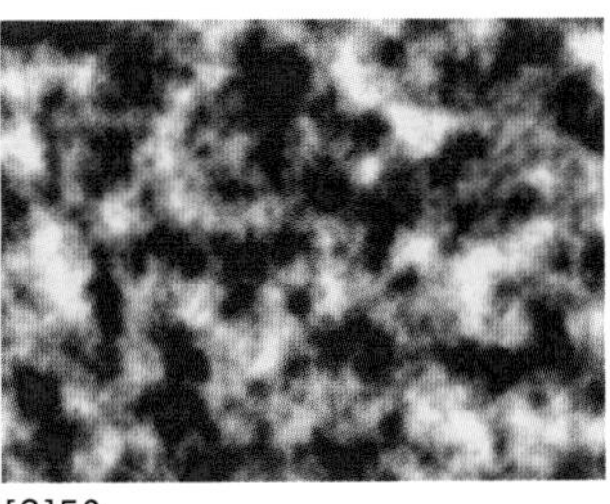

[S]50

A sequence showing the effect of varying the size. The following parameters were the same for the images: [Bs] [F]250 [E]426 [Q]5.

FRACTAL UNIVERSE cont

FRACUN_I.PXP \funivers **Digimation**

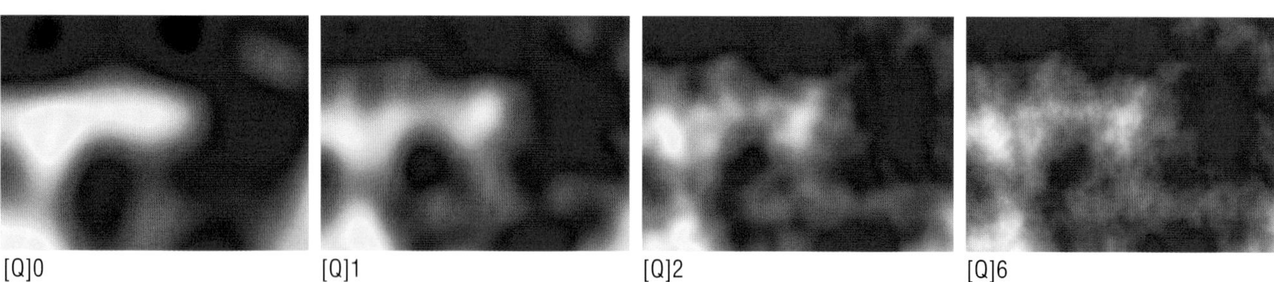

[Q]0 [Q]1 [Q]2 [Q]6

Quality produces a range of pattern extending from soft and curvilinear to sharply defined. The following parameters were the same for the images: [Bs] [S]200 [F]250 [E]250.

FRACTALIZE

FRACT_I.PXP \fractliz **Yost Group**

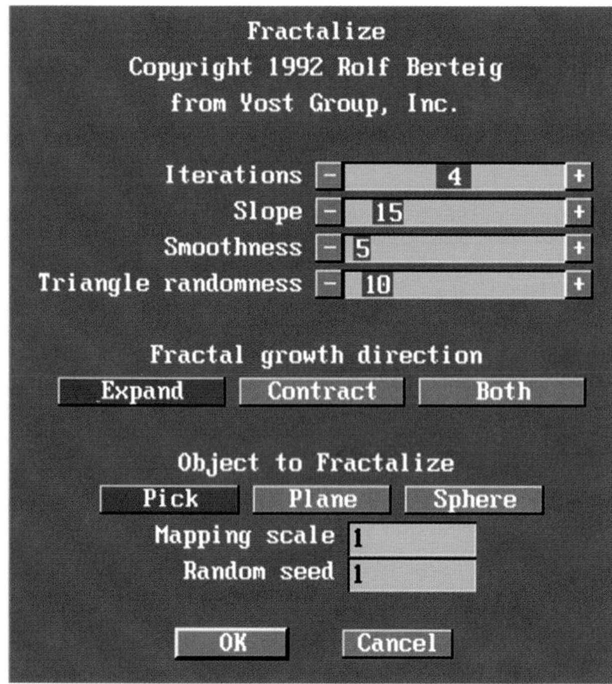

The Fractalize dialog box.

Summary

Fractalize is part of the Silicon Garden package. It randomly tessellates a copy of an object and shifts the faces randomly in or out. It also builds a planar or spherical fractalized surface from scratch. The primary use for this plug-in is to generate random terrains for Silicon Garden. You also can use it to roughen the surface of any object. It provides control over the degree of tessellation, smoothness of the surface, amount of distortion, and the degree of randomness on the new mesh. Surfaces are displaced either in, out, or both, perpendicular to the surface normals of each face.

Fractalize Parameters

Iterations [I] (1–7) — Degree of tessellation.

Slope [Sl] (0–100%) — Displacement distance as a percentage of the triangle edge length.

Smoothness [Sm] (0–100%) — Degree of smoothness of the mesh. At 100% the mesh is very smooth; at 0% it is very irregular.

Triangle randomness [T] (0–100%) — Degree of randomness in the size of triangles.

Fractal growth direction [D] e, c, b (Expand, Contract, Both) — Determines the direction in which surfaces are distorted based on the surface normal direction. Expand and Contract shift all the faces one direction or the other. Both randomly shifts faces in or out.

Object to Fractalize [O] pi, pl, s (Pick, Plane, Sphere) — Selects the object on which the fractalized mesh will be based. Sphere and Plane generate new geometry based on settings in Fractalize. Pick enables you to pick an existing object in your scene for the source object.

Mapping scale [M] — Enables you to change the number of mapping tiles in the new mesh.

Random seed [R] — A random number seed that enables you to change and re-create different random patterns.

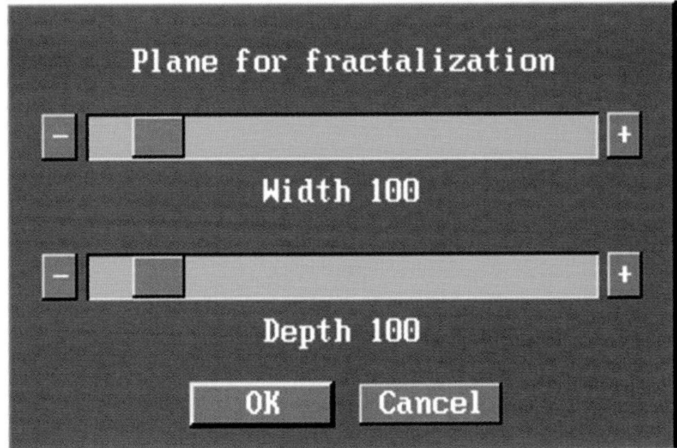

The Plane for Fractalization dialog box.

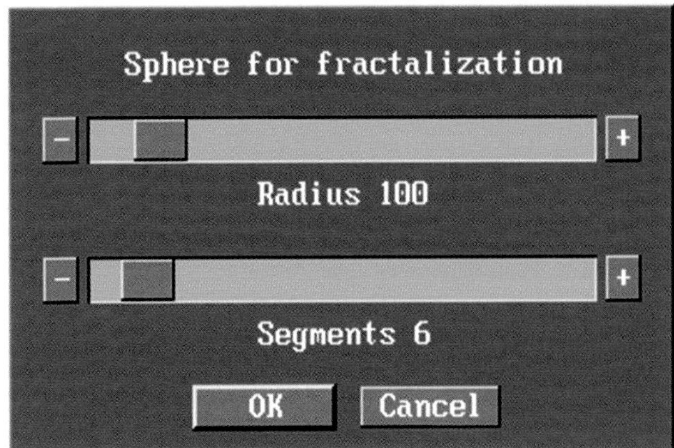

The Sphere for Fractalization dialog box.

Plane Parameters

Width [Pw] (0–1,000) — Width of the generated plane in units.

Depth [Pd] (0–1,000) — Depth of the generated plane in units.

Sphere Parameters

Radius [Sr] (0–1,000) — Radius of the generated sphere in units.

Segments [Ss] (4–32) — Number of latitude and longitude segments around the sphere.

[I]5 [Sl]15 [Sm]5 [T]10 [D]b

[I]7 [Sl]25 [Sm]5 [T]10 [D]e

A fractalized object and a randomly generated terrain.

FREE FORM DEFORMATIONS

FFD_I.PXP \ffd Korensky

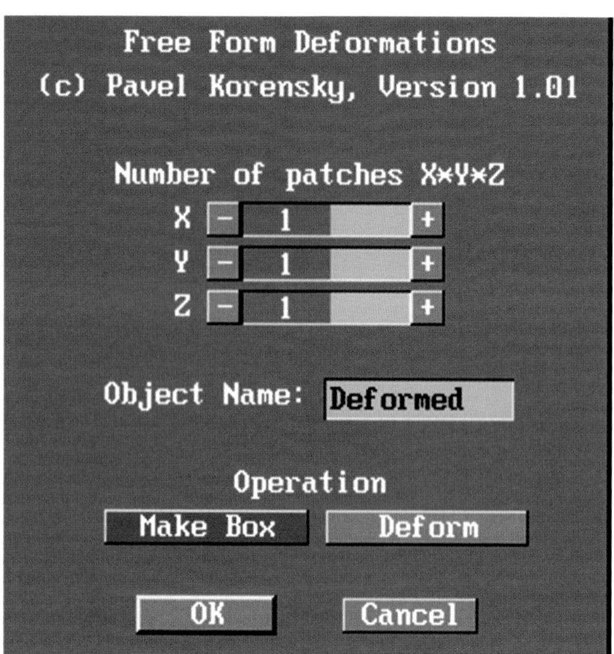

The Free Form Deformations dialog box.

Summary

Free Form Deformations is a free-form mesh deformation tool. The program is first used to place a series of control points or box around a specified object. The box consists of an array of control vertices. You must set Display/Geometry/VertTicks to on to see the control points clearly. Individual points or groups of points are then moved using any of the Modify/Vertext functions. The plug-in produces a deformed copy of the original object based on the control point edits. The resulting objects are suitable for use as morph targets.

For Free Form Deformation to function properly, it must have an adequate number of evenly distributed faces from which to work; Create/Object/Tessellate/Edge with edge tension set to 0 works well.

FFD Parameters

Number of patches X, Y, Z [X] [Y] [Z] (1–2) — The number of control patches along each side of the control grid. Each patch has four control points. Two patches together have seven control points.

Object Name [N] — The name to use for the new deformed object.

Operation [O] m, d (Make Box, Deform) — Selects whether to make a control grid box or to deform an object.

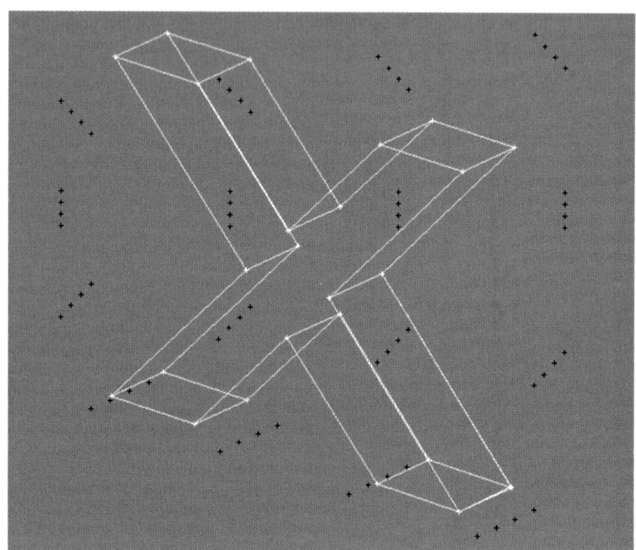

Modified control grid with original object

Deformed object

Twisting an object with free-form deformations.

GEAR TEETH GENERATOR

Autodesk \gears GEARS_I.PXP

Summary

Included with 3D Studio Release 4, Gear Teeth Generator produces a range of circular gear-like arrays consisting of multiple box and tapered box elements. You can specify the number of elements or teeth, their thickness across the gear circumference, their radius and height around the gear circumference, and their taper.

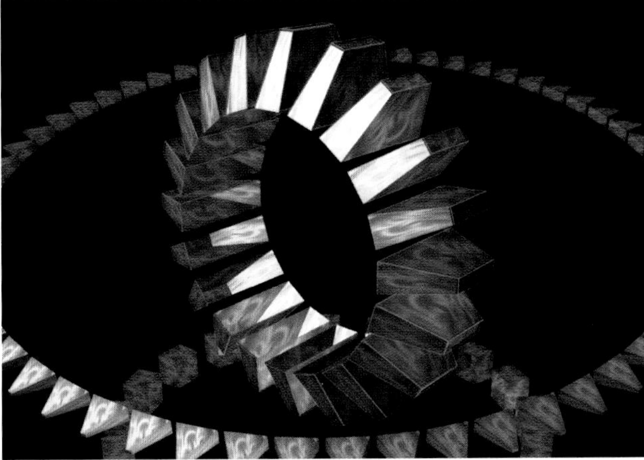

Gear Teeth Generator produces a range of gear-like arrays in any taper, thickness, or diameter.

The Gear Teeth Generator dialog box.

Gear Teeth Generator Parameters

Teeth [T] (0–1,000) — Sets the number of teeth, which will be evenly spaced around the gear's circumference.

Radius 1 — Sets the gear's inside diameter or base for the gear teeth.

Radius 2 — Sets the gear's outside diameter or top for the gear teeth.

Thickness — Sets the thickness of the teeth across the gear circumference.

Taper % — Sets the relative size of the teeth from the base radius to the top radius.

GRADIENT DESIGNER

HSC Software \gradient GRADES_I.PXP

Summary

Gradient Designer produces multicolored static and animated gradients that can be saved in its proprietary GRD format. These preset files can be used in the Materials Editor, 3D Editor, or Keyframer to create numerous effects and transitions, such as animated image maps, projection spotlights, backgrounds, traveling mattes, and transitions.

Gradient Designer's GRD files are saved and applied at user-specified resolutions that can be edited easily. The file storage requirements are resolution independent and very efficient, with simple static presets requiring around 5 KB of storage space. The number of frames in an animated GRD file has no effect on the file size.

Gradient Designer is available for use from either the 3D Editor or the Keyframer. It can produce composites working from either static images or animated sequences. For instance, when working in the 3D Editor using Options/Load Background, you

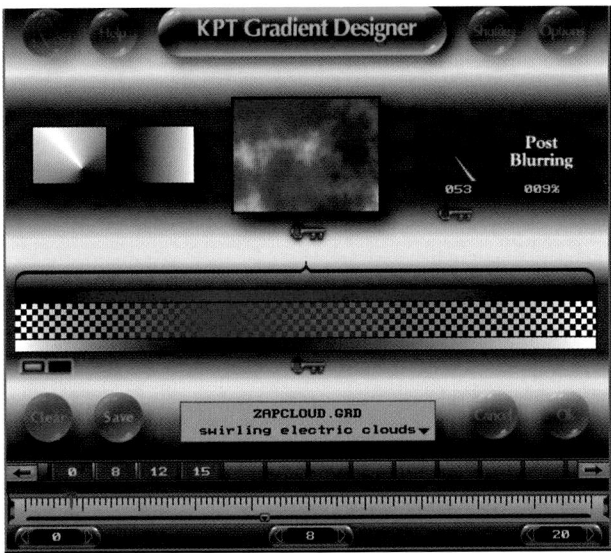

The Gradient Designer dialog box.

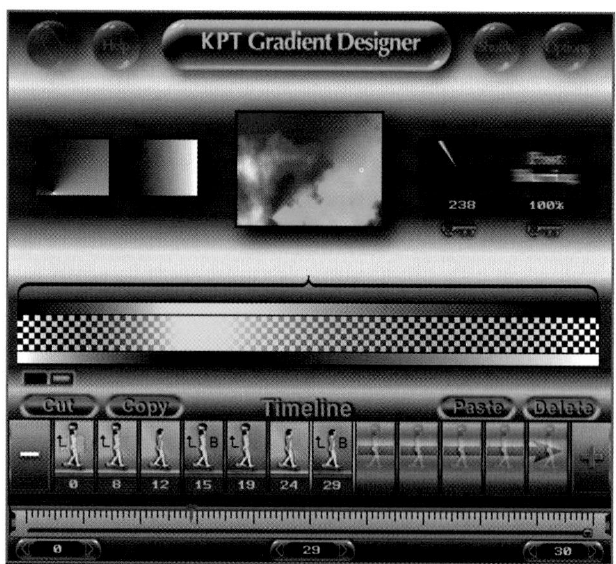

The Keyframe Editor controls pop-up below the gradient bar.

can load only a single image; however, when working in the Keyframer, Load Background enables you to work with animation sequences. This is useful for compositing animated gradient effects with 3D Studio animations or for creating layered effects with Gradient Designer alone.

Gradient Designer uses linear interpolation between keyframes to create animated effects. You can key gradient variables such as color, opacity, gradient origin, and blurring. You also can key the apply mode, such as circular sunburst or linear blend and looping control parameters; however, such keyframes will not be smoothly interpolated. Keyframes are set by moving to the frame you want to change and simply changing the parameter. The animation can be played back and viewed in the preview window.

Note: *You can switch between the main dialog box and the Keyframe Editor by clicking on the small rectangles located at the left of the interface.*

Gradient Designer Parameters

Help button — Displays a list of keyboard equivalent commands.

Shuffle Button [Sh] a, n, c, a, al, l, o, d (all parameters, none, colors, apply mode, algorithm, looping, origin, direction) — Sets the parameter or parameters that are randomized each time the Shuffle button is clicked.

Options button [O] n, p, r, l, d, a, s, m, sc, d, tu, td (normal apply, procedural blend, reverse blend, lighten only, darken only, add, subtract, multiply, screen, difference, tie me up, tie me down) — Specifies the apply mode used to blend the gradient into the background image or sequence. Normal applies the gradient based on its opacity. Procedural blend combines the gradient and background based upon additive pixel luminance, and reverse blend uses subtractive pixel luminance. Lighten and darken look at the combination of the gradient effect and the background and apply the effect only in the color channels with the lighter or darker intensity, respectively. Add multiplies the intensities of both image and background. Subtract removes the gradient color from the background using subtractive color. Multiply darkens the image using the dark effect channels. Screen is the opposite of multiply. Difference produces saturated color variations using the difference colors between effect and background. Tie me up and tie me down produce a range of vibrant color effects.

Algorithm Control [Ac] l, c, e, r, s, rb (linear blend, circular sunburst, elliptical sunburst, radial sweep, square burst, rectangular burst) — Defines the basic shape for the gradient. Linear blend produces a smooth linear gradient. Circular sunburst produces a radial gradient. Elliptical sunburst produces an elliptical gradient based on the image proportions. Radial sweep produces a circular wedge-like sweep. Square and rectangular burst are similar to circular and elliptical sunburst.

Loop Control [Lc] sa, sb, ta, tb, n, pr, pl, pi, po, r (sawtooth a>b, sawtooth b>a, triangle a>b>a, triangle b>a>b, no distortion, pinch right, pinch left, pinch inward, pinch outward, repeat) — Defines the linearity and repeat number for the gradient loop. Sawtooth produces a continuous gradient loop and triangle produces a mirrored loop. The a>b and b>a settings specify the start, middle, and endpoint for the loop. Repeat simply repeats the loop by the number indicated.

Direction Control [Dc] — Sets the angle for the directional algorithm's linear blend and radial sweep. Holding down the shift key while adjusting this control snaps the angle to the frame corners and to 45-degree increments.

Post Blurring [Pb] (0–100) Sets the amount of blur applied to the gradient.

Gradient bar [Gb] — Enables you to set the color, opacity, and color range for the gradient using an eyedropper tool that is dragged over a color spectrum or the transparency ramp. A moveable black bracket, which sits above the color spectrum, can be resized and positioned to establish the range of the currently selected color. You can select from eight color ranges in the gradient bar's spectra submenu. The gradient bar also provides access to dozens of preset gradient effects.

Note: *Gradient Designer comes with GRD_I.BXP, which enables 3D Studio to use its proprietary (GRD) bitmap format.*

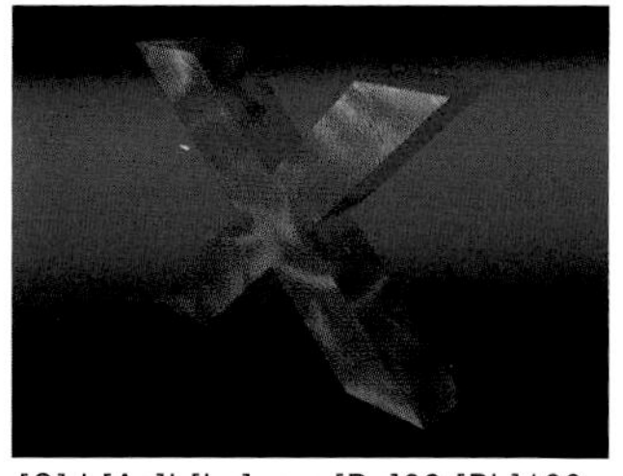
[O]d [Ac]l [Lc]sa n [Dc]88 [Pb]100

[O]p [Ac]c [Lc]tb pi [Pb]80

[O]td [Ac]c [Lc]ba po [Pb]45

[O]r [Ac]l [Lc]sa po [Dc]293 [Pb]9

Gradient Designer provides multiple gradient types and image processing options, any of which can be combined with background images and animations.

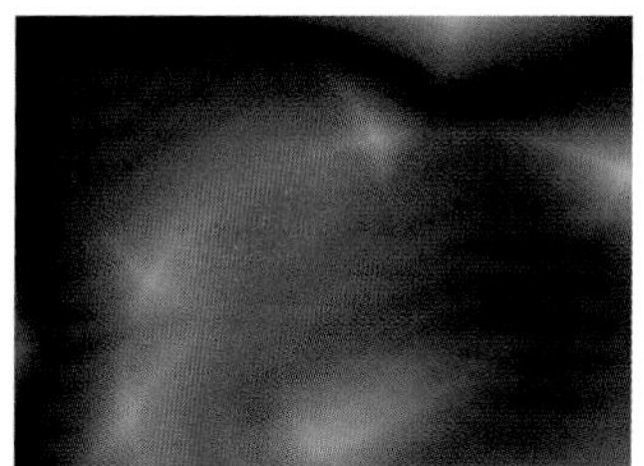
Frame 0

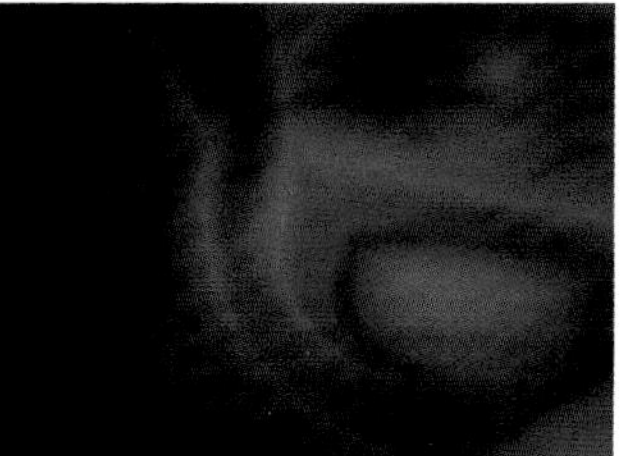
Frame 15

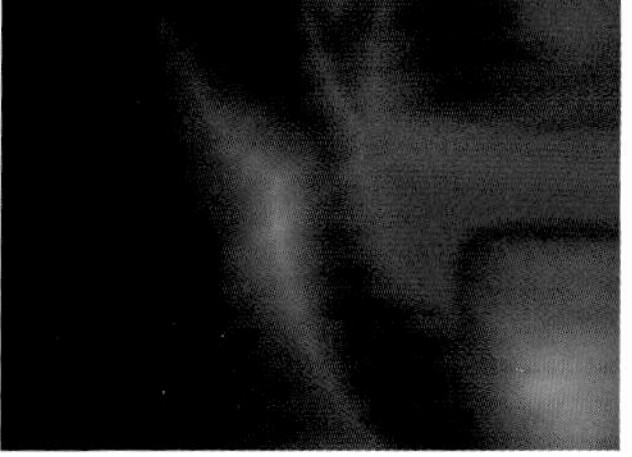
Frame 20

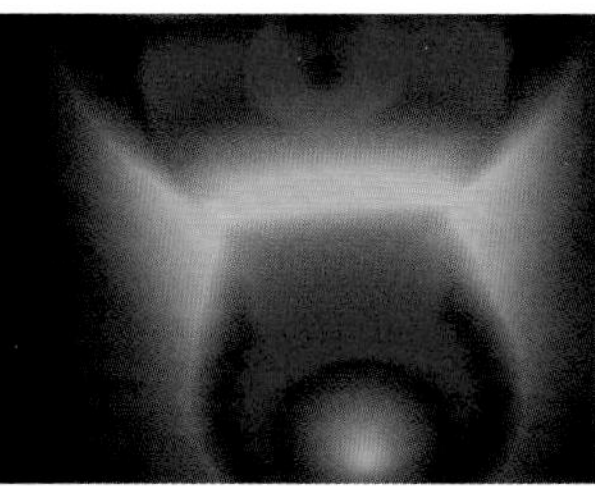
Frame 30

Gradient parameters such as color, opacity, and origin can be keyframed to produce striking effect animations. This sequence used layering and color changes along with elliptical sunbursts that move in relation to each other.

GRIDS

Autodesk \grids GRIDS_I.PXP

Summary

Included with 3D Studio Release 4, Grids produces a range of 2D and 3D grids. You can specify length, width, height, and number of divisions.

Grids Parameters

Length [L] g (Grids) — Sets the grid length in 3D Studio units, with Grids specifying the number of divisions along the length axis.

Width [W] g (Grids) — Sets the grid width in 3D Studio units, with Grids specifying the number of divisions along the width axis.

Height [H] g (grids) — Sets the grid height in 3D Studio units, with Grids specifying the number of divisions along the height axis.

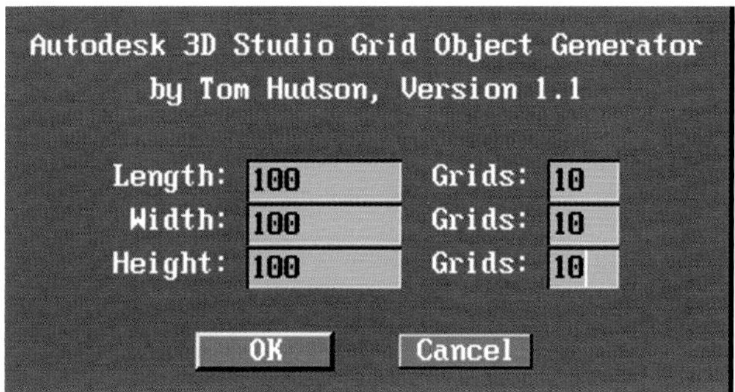

The Grids dialog box.

GRIDS cont

GRIDS_I.PXP | **\grids** | **Autodesk**

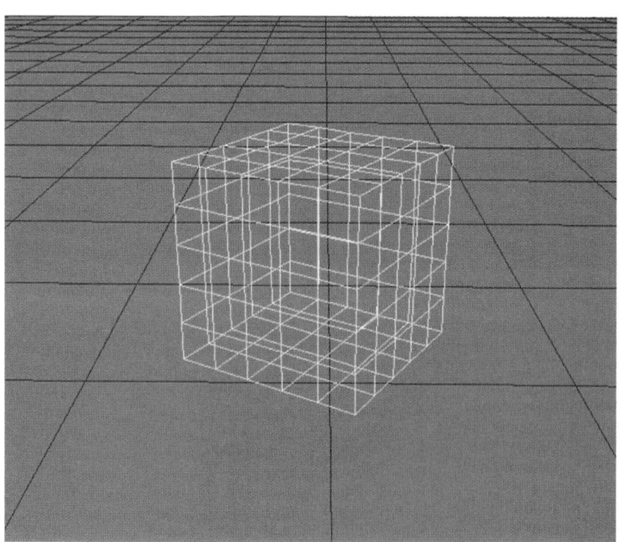

Grids produces a range of 2D and 3D grids.

GUIDED

GUIDED_I.PXP | **\guided** | **Animagic**

The Guided dialog box.

Summary

Guided is an interface toolbox for 3D Studio IPAS and Script applications that enables you to build dialog boxes by dropping interface elements onto the screen. You can move and size the interface elements using your mouse. Guided gives you a full selection of dialog elements including buttons, edit fields, check boxes, sliders, scroll bars, frames, and images; you can set attributes and add comments to each element. Several layout commands enable you to cut and paste elements and to change their stacking order. Built-in reference backgrounds for the 3D Editor, Keyframer, and Materials Editor enable you to build your dialog boxes in the context of the intended screen. When you are satisfied with the layout of your dialog box, Guided writes a file that contains the code needed to produce the dialog box in either IPAS SDK format or in Script format. You can then use the custom dialog box in your programs.

Guided Parameters

Item Types [It] (Button, Editable, U/D Box, Checkbox, Slider, Scroller, Text, (G) Text, Icon, Box, Frame, Boxchar, Image, Custom) — The elements that you can add to a dialog box. Select one to drop it on your dialog box.

Files [F] (Load, Save, Make, New) — File commands to load and save custom dialog box files, make a dialog box code file, and start a new dialog box.

Mode [M] (Move, Size, Dupe, Selection) — Changes the editing mode.

Edit [E] (Cut, Copy, Paste, Delete) — Element editing commands.

Selection [S] (Add, Remove, All, None, 1, 2, 3, 4) — Selection set commands to add and remove elements from the four selection groups.

GUIDED cont

Animagic \guided **GUIDED_I.PXP**

Levels [L] (To Front, To Back, Arrange) — Element stacking controls.
Components [C] (Definitions, Statistics, Select) — Element information.
Attributes [At] (Setup, Background, Attributes) — Element attribute settings and background setup.
System [Sy] (Config, Palette, Quit) — General configuration, color palette control, and exiting Guided.
Item Action [Ia] (Move, Size) —Editing mode.
Windows [W] (Coord Box, Info Box) — Move the coordinate and info boxes on the layout screen.
Custom Code [Cc] (Feel Func, See Func) — Custom code controls.
Misc [Mi] (About, Help) — Displays program information and accesses online help.

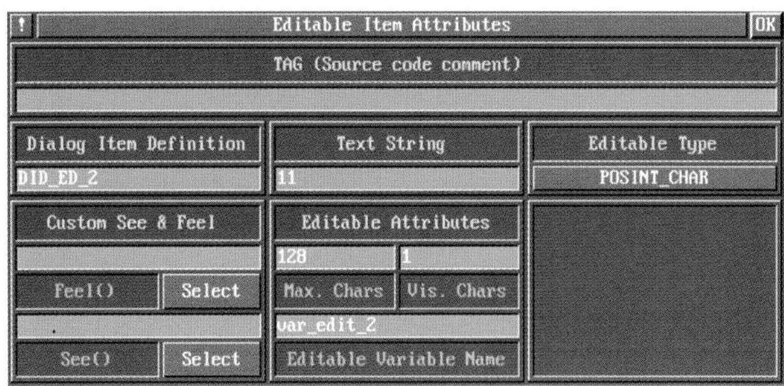

The Attribute Edit dialog box.

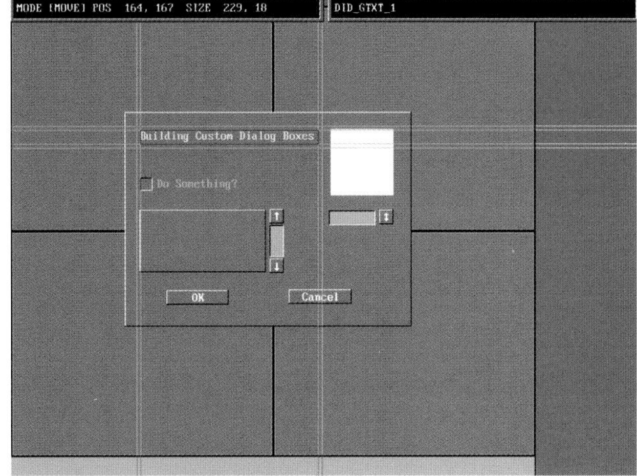

The dialog box layout screen.

HEDRA2

Yost Group \hedra2 **HEDRA2_I.PXP**

Summary

Hedra2 is part of the IPAS3 Disk #7 package. It is similar to the public domain Hedra plug-in also by the Yost Group. Both Hedra and Hedra2 are regular and quasi-regular polyhedron generators (a polyhedron is a multisided, three-dimensional object made up of polygons). Hedra2 enables you to edit the geometry in real time in either a wireframe or flat shaded preview window.

The process works by selecting from any of five Hedra2 families, such as Tetra or Star1. This places a starting polyhedron in the viewport for editing. Editing is accomplished by clicking on the various buttons and spinners that set and scale each object axis. The results of each edit can be viewed in real time in either wireframe or Gouraud rendered form.

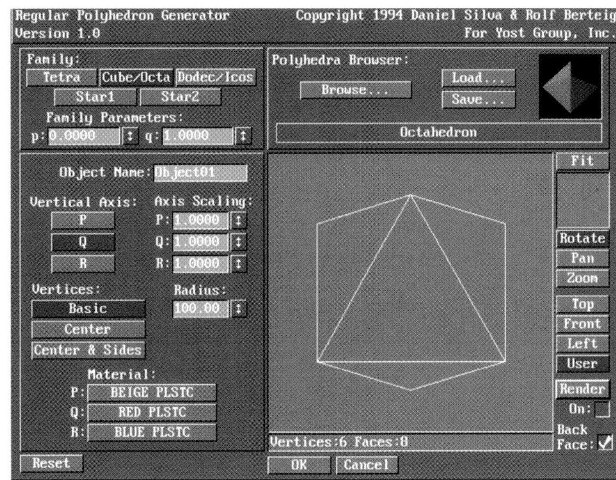

The Hedra2 dialog box.

HEDRA2 cont

HEDRA2_I.PXP **\hedra2** **Yost Group**

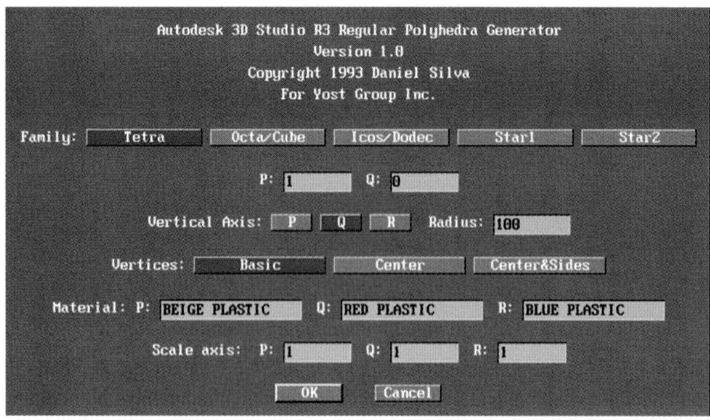

The Hedra dialog box.

The preview window provides a selection of view functions, such as zoom, pan, and fit, that work the same as their 3D Studio counterparts. Holding shift while clicking on the render button displays a solid color dialog box with RGB and HLS sliders to change the shading color. Also included is the polyhedra browser, which displays a dialog box that enables you to scroll through and choose from any of 34 preset shapes. You can save and load polyhedra in a proprietary POL format.

Hedra2 also enables you to assign up to three materials to the resulting objects.

Hedra2 Parameters

Family [F] t, c, d, S1, S2 (Tetra, Cube/Octa, Dodec/Icos, Star1, Star2) — Sets the basic type of polyhedron. Selecting Tetra creates a tetrahedron, selecting Cube/Octa produces either a cube or an octahedron. Dodec/Icos produces either a dodecahedron or an icosahedron, and Star1 and Star2 are general names representing more complex geometry such as a great dodecahedron.

Family Parameters [Fp] [Fq] — Linked values that change a polyhedron's vertices to facets (p) and facets to vertices (q). When the Tetra button is on, for example, a tetrahedron will be produced at either extreme. If, on the other hand, the Cube/Octa button is on, a cube is created at one extreme, and an octahedron is created at the other. Star2 creates a great dodecahedron at one extreme, and a small, stellated dodecahedron at the other.

Note: *To avoid confusion, remember that the family parameters labels (p) and (q) are not directly associated with the axis labels (P) and (Q).*

Axis scaling [Ap] [Aq] [Ar] — The p, q, and r represent the three possible types of facets in a Hedra2 polyhedron (a cube has one type of facet, a square, and a great rhombicuboctahedron has three types: squares, octagons, and hexagons). Changing the scale values stretches the facets inward or outward along a vector that runs from the center of the facet to the center of the polyhedron's bounding sphere.

Vertical Axis [Va] P, Q, R — Sets the P, Q, or R axis to vertical.

Vertices [V] b, c, c/s (Basic, Center, Center&Sides) — Changes the level of tesselation on the polyhedron's facets.

Radius [R] — Sets the radius of the polyhedron's bounding sphere in 3D Studio units.

Material [M] p, q, r — Assigns any material to the facets by facet type. Spherical mapping coordinates must be applied to the polyhedron in the 3D Editor before the scene can be rendered.

[F]S2 [Fp].5 [Aq]2

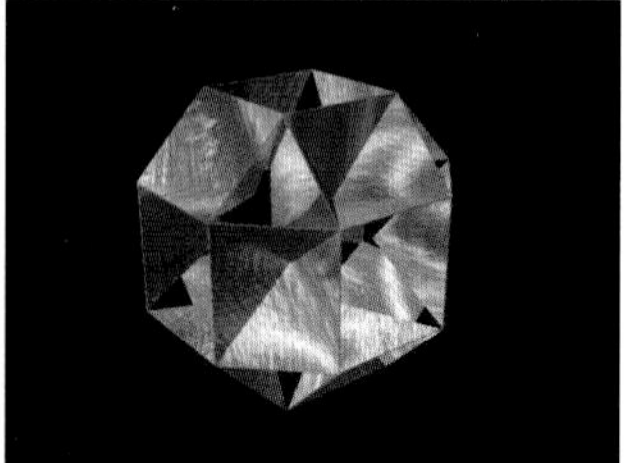

[F]c [Ar]5

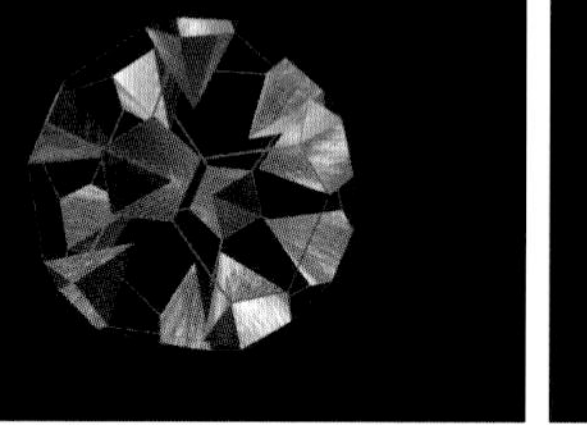

[F]d [Fp].5 [Aq].5

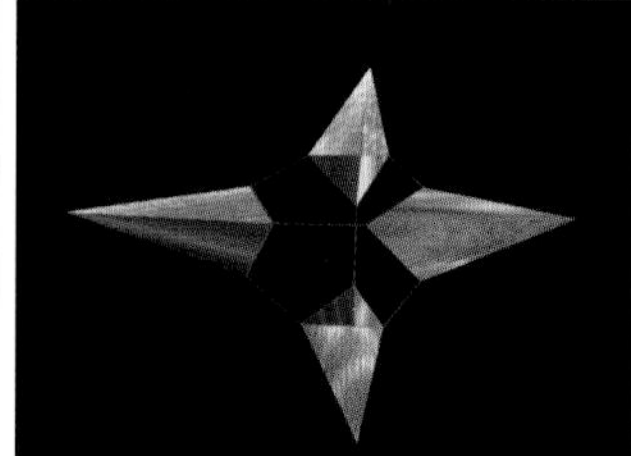

[F]t [Fp].4 [Ap]4

All samples used the basic vertices option.

Summary

Included with 3D Studio Release 4, Image Browser is a utility program that scans single or multiple disk directories for images based on user-specific search criteria. The resulting selection set is displayed in the file display window as an array of white rectangular icons and file names. The total number of files in the selection is displayed in the report window.

You can then select individual file icons for display or view a slide show of the entire selection set. As each file is selected its file size, resolution, creation date and time, aspect ratio, background color, gamma, and attached comments are displayed. You also can elect to view a report that is a complete listing of this data for all members of the selection set.

If you choose Build Index, Image Browser creates a series of proxy images that are displayed along with the file names in the file display window. The time required to build each index is proportionate to the number and resolution of the images in the specified search path.

Image Browser Parameters

3DS Map Paths or Single — Specifies the Browse search path. You can either scan the 3D Studio map paths as specified in Info/Configure/Map Paths or key in a single search path. The Browse button enables you to select the search path interactively.

Build Index — Creates an index that includes color proxy images of each image file in the specified search path.

Search For — Specifies whether to search for all files, a specific character sting or file extension, or keywords that can be imbedded in some image file formats such as TGA.

The Image Browser dialog box.

Report — Displays the 3D Studio text editor, which displays a listing of each image in the current selection set along with its file size, resolution, creation date and time, aspect ratio, background color, gamma, and any embedded comments.

Slide Show — Displays a full-resolution slide show of the entire selection set. If the image is larger than the display, it is scaled to fit. Clicking the mouse stops the slide show and returns you to the Image Browser dialog box.

View Image — Displays the currently selected image at full resolution. If the image is larger than the display, the image is scaled to fit.

Summary

Imagine Detailor consists of two plug-ins, Fence and Wall, which combine to produce more than 120 3D fences and walls. You can select from wood, wrought iron, chain link, and slat fences along with brick, stucco, and concrete walls. You also can specify post spacing and post cap types.

Imagine Detailor uses LFT files to determine the path for both fences and walls. Imagine Detailor also includes a materials library along with the image maps required for rendering each object.

The Fences dialog box.

The Fence Construction Options dialog box.

Fence Parameters

Fence Type [Ft] (1–107) — Selects the fence type by number. Fence types include variations of split rail (1–4), heavy split rail (5–6), post with pipes (7–10), barbed wire posts (11–12), wire mesh with posts (13–14), small wire mesh with posts (15–16), ski fence with metal posts (17), chain link (18–25), stockade (26–29), slat (30–31), construction with metal posts (32), picket (33–36), board (37–50), solid board (51–55), panel solid board (56–59), board on board (60–64), board and batten (65–68), louver (69–72), vertical solid panel (73–77), column solid panel (78–81), wrought iron (82–88), column with rails iron (89–97), plastic security (98–100), and posts only (101–107).

Complexity [C] f, pf, m, d (Face, Post & Face, Moderate, Detailed) — All fences are created at maximum detail. Complexity applies only when Fences is used in AutoCAD.

Fence Path (.LFT) — Specifies the 3D Lofter path used to produce the fence. This path should be saved to a local \3DS\LOFTS directory.

Post Spacing [Ps] — Sets the maximum distance between each post element.

Post Cap [Pc] (1–19) — Specifies 1 of 19 different fence post caps.

The Walls dialog box.

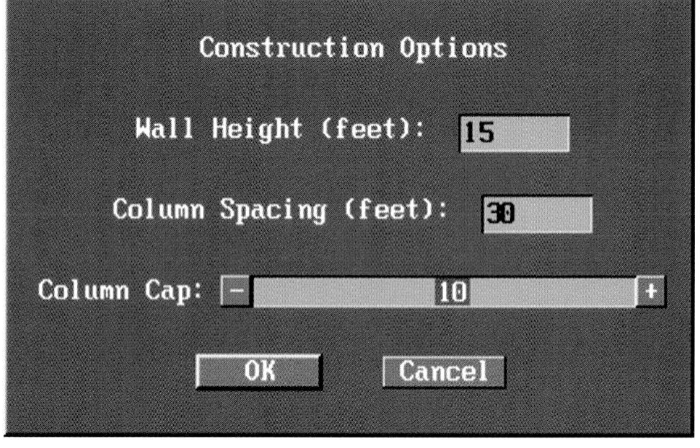

The Wall Construction Options dialog box.

Wall Parameters

Wall Type [Wt] (1–17) — Selects the wall type by number. Wall types include variations of concrete (1–2), timber tie (3), stone (4–6), brick (7–9), flair stone (10–13), castle wall (14–15), and wood poles (16–17).

Wall Path (.LFT) — Specifies the 3D Lofter path used to produce the wall. This path should be saved to a local \3DS\LOFTS directory.

Post Material [Pm] b, s, c, bl, st (brick, stone, concrete, block, stucco) — Sets the material type for some wall types.

Concrete Wall Material [Wm] c, cb, s (concrete, concrete block, stucco) — Sets the material type for some wall types.

IMAGINE DETAILOR cont

Schreiber Instruments \detailor ADFNCE_I.PXP, ADWALL_I.PXP

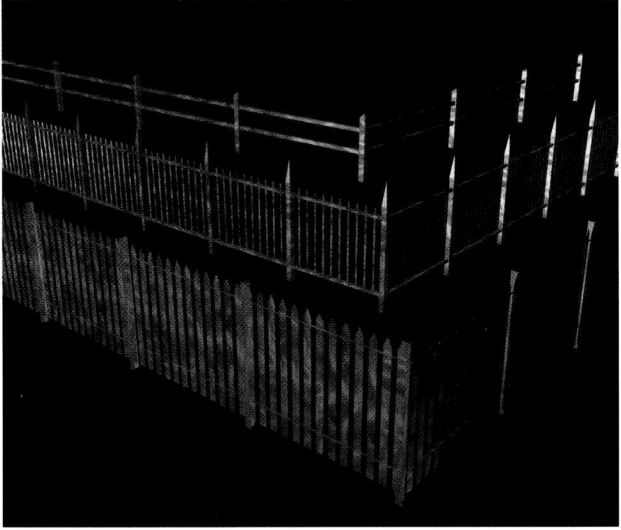

Fences [Ft] 1, 82, 32

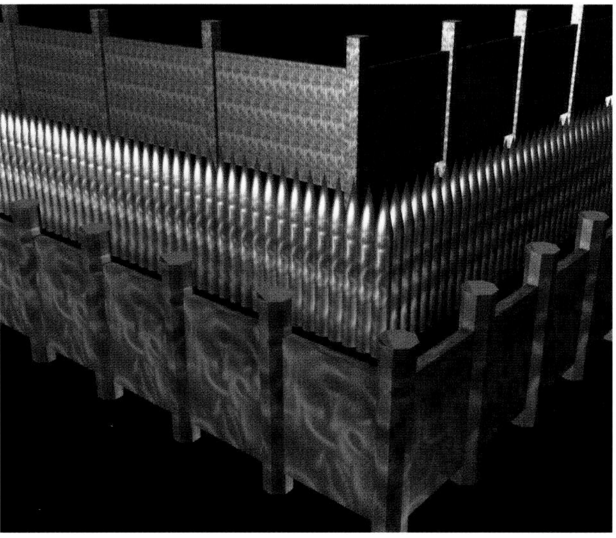

Wals [Wt] 8, 16, 6

Imagine Detailer produces a range of fences and walls.

IMAGINE LUGE

Schreiber Instruments \luge LUGE_I.PXP

Summary

Luge is part of the Imagine Morphology package. Luge animates the extrusion of lofted shapes along a path by calculating the path length and dividing it into a specified number of morph targets. A specified section of the mesh can also be animated along the loft path, and mapping can travel with the section or be taken from any section of the object. Mapping coordinates are retained in the resulting morph targets. Targets for each frame of the animated effect are necessary to produce a smooth morph, and all cross-sections of the source shape must have the same number of vertices. Therefore, lofted source objects must be extruded with endcaps and optimization turned off. Source objects created in the 3D Editor must have endcaps removed to use Luge. Luge is also available as an AXP plug-in.

Luge Parameters

Maximum length [Mx] (1–100) — Sets the percentage amount of the whole lofted path for the luge section's maximum length.

Minimum length [Mn] (1–100) — Sets the percentage amount of the maximum length for the luge section's minimum length.

Cross-section scale [S] (start, end) — Sets the beginning and ending size of the extruded shape.

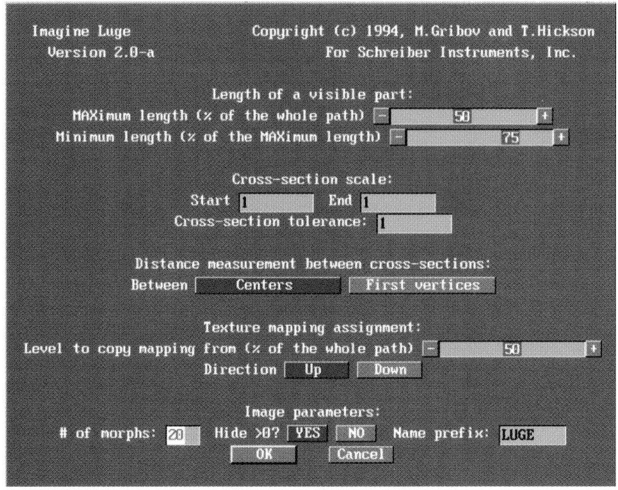

The Luge dialog box.

Cross-section tolerance [T] — Sets the variance allowed in searching for the next cross-section on the path. The tolerance must be raised to use Luge on curved paths.

Distance measurement between cross-sections [Dc] (Centers, First vertices) — Sets the type of measurement used when searching for the next cross-section.

IMAGINE LUGE cont

LUGE_I.PXP \luge **Schreiber Instruments**

Texture Parameters

Level to copy mapping from [L] — Sets the percentage amount of the whole lofted path to copy mapping from.
Direction [D] — Sets the direction the mapping section will travel.

Image Parameters

# of morphs [#] — Sets the number of morph targets. This number should correspond with the number of frames for the animated effect.
Hide > 0 [H] — Hides all but the first morph target.

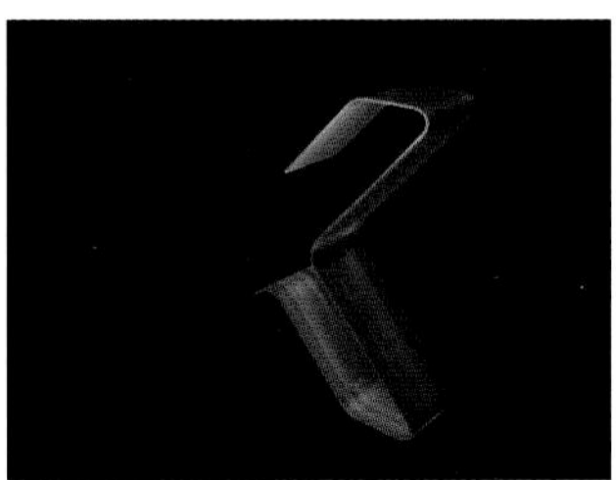

Frame 5

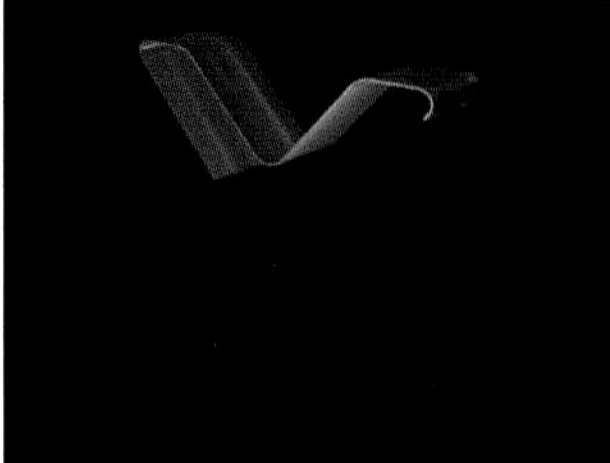

Frame 10

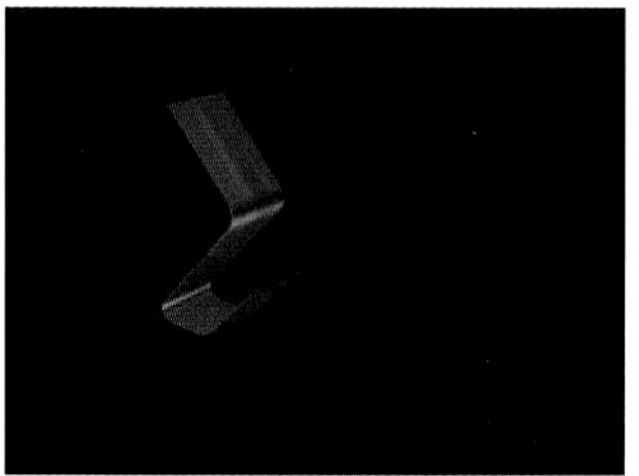

Frame 15

Frame 20

Luge animates the extrusion of a specified section of the mesh along the loft path, and mapping can travel with the section or be taken from any section of the object.

IMAGINE PYTHON

PYT203_I.PXP \python **Schreiber Instruments**

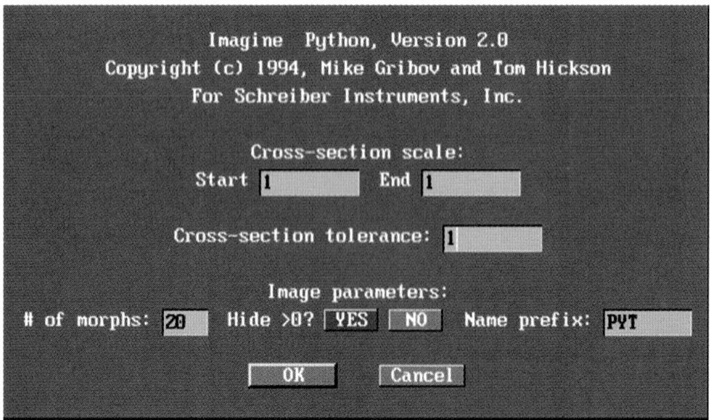

The Python dialog box.

Summary

Python is part of the Imagine morphology package. Python animates the extrusion of lofted shapes along a path by calculating the path length and dividing it into a specified number of morph targets. Mapping coordinates are removed in the resulting morph targets. Targets for each frame of the animated effect are necessary to produce a smooth morph, and all cross sections of the source shape must have the same number of vertices. Therefore, lofted source objects must be extruded with endcaps and optimization turned off.

Python Parameters

Cross-section scale [S] (Start, End) — Sets the beginning and ending size of the extruded shape.
Cross-section tolerance [T] — Sets the variance allowed in searching for the next cross section on the path. The tolerance must be raised to use Python on curved paths.
# of morphs [#] — Sets the number of morph targets. This number should correspond with the number of frames for the animated effect.
Hide >0 [H] — Hides all but the first morph target.

IMAGINE PYTHON cont

Schreiber Instruments \python **PYT203_I.PXP**

Frame 9

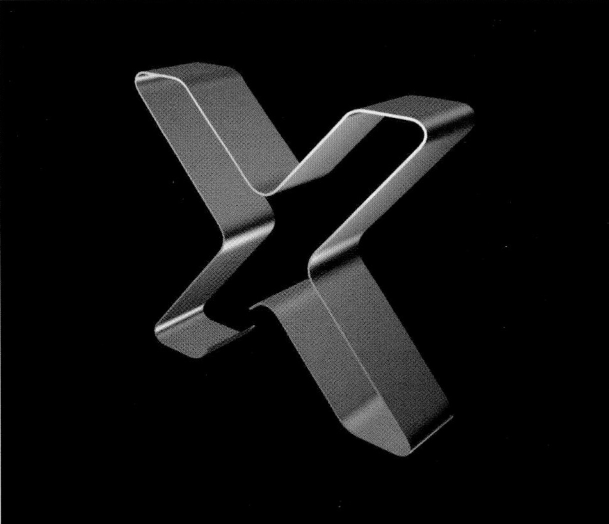

Frame 18

Python animates the extrusion of a shape along a path, a useful effect for animated writing effects.

JUMBLE

Autodesk \jumble **4JUMB_I.PXP**

Summary

Jumble is an object randomizer bundled with 3D Studio Release 4. Jumble requires an object that represents the individual unit to transform along with an array of multiple objects to jumble. After the jumble variables are set, the single representative element is picked and the grouped object to jumble is chosen. Jumble then produces the number of morph targets set in its dialog box. By morphing from the original ordered array to the jumbled object, objects appear to tumble into chaos. If the order is reversed, objects move from chaos to order.

Unique effects can be produced by jumbling single objects, which produces everything from small spines on the surface of the geometry to twisted and exploded corrugated siding. This is accomplished by specifying the same geometry for both the source and jumble objects. Boxes and spheres can be used as the single element to produce similar results. The effects of using jumble on single objects vary depending on how the mesh is constructed. Using lofted objects that have been separated into elements and rejoined produce the exploded corrugated effect. Tessellated objects take on a more ordered, spiky appearance. In both cases it is desirable to have a considerable level of geometric detail or high polygon count to produce a smoothly jumbled object.

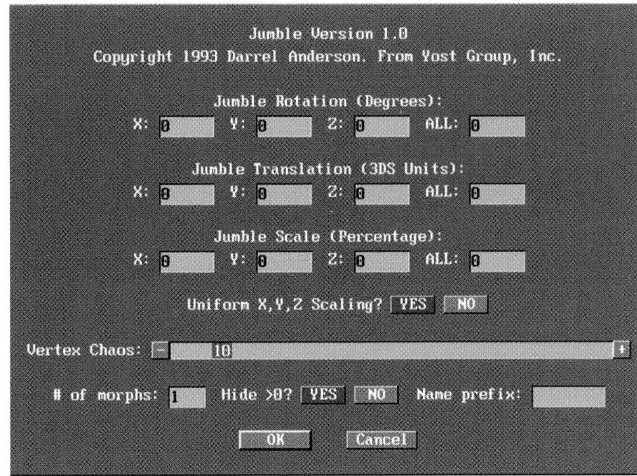

The Jumble dialog box.

Jumble Parameters

Jumble Rotation, Translation, Scale [R] [T] [S] — Sets the maximum rotation degree, maximum translation position, and scale of the jumbled object. Variables can be individually set for each axis, or a single variable can be used for all axes.

Uniform X, Y, Z Scaling [U] (yes, no) — Sets the object to maintain its original aspect ratio or to be scaled independently on each axis.

Vertex Chaos [C] (0–100) — Sets the amount of randomization for individual object vertices represented as a percentage of rotation, transformation, and scaling. A setting of zero reproduces a duplicate of the original object. Values greater than zero crumple individual objects.

# of morphs [M] — Sets the number of morph targets to produce. Higher numbers produce a wobble as the object jumbles because the random transform number in each morph target is different.

Hide >0 [H] (yes, no) — Sets all jumble objects beyond the first to be hidden or all objects to be displayed.

Name prefix — Sets the name prefix for the jumble morph targets.

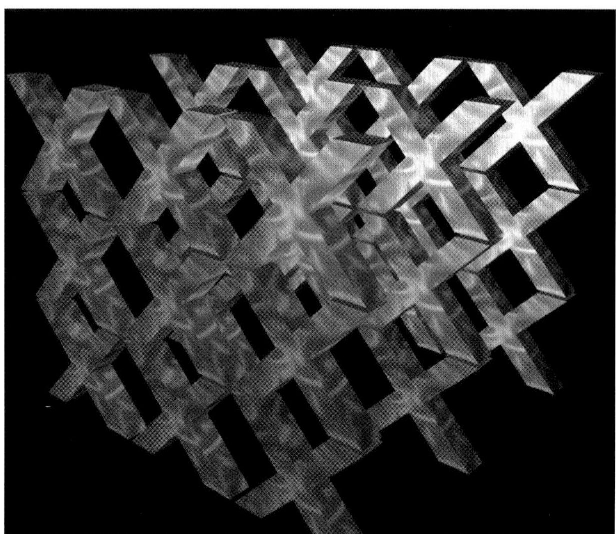

Original object

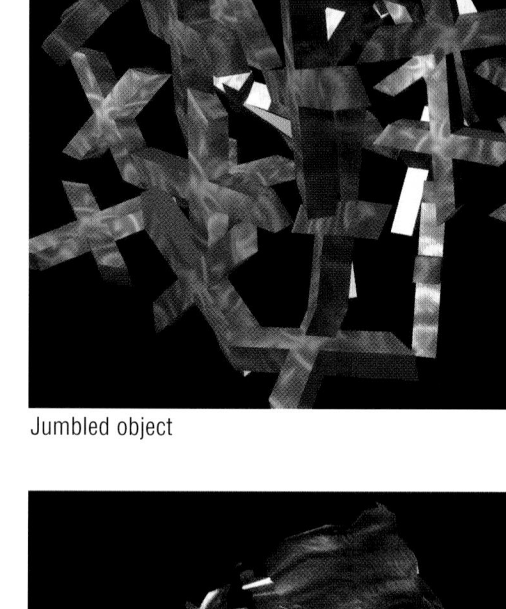

Jumbled object

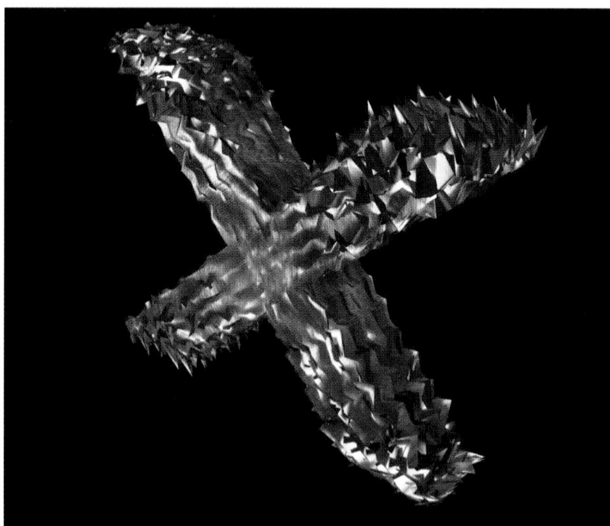

Tessellated mesh

Lofted mesh

Using jumble on individual objects rather than arrays can produce uniformly spiny objects or exploded and corrugated objects, depending on how the mesh is constructed.

Summary

Keyboard Transformations enables you to transform 3D Studio objects explicitly with the keyboard. You can translate, scale, or rotate any object in either relative or absolute modes. For translate or scale operations, this is accomplished by first highlighting the type of transformation you want, and entering the required distance or scale separately for X (width), Z (depth), and Y (height). If you are performing an absolute translation, you must enter both the source and destination coordinates. You then select the object you want to transform, and the plug-in creates a copy translated, rotated, or scaled accordingly. You can not perform multiple transformations in a single session.

You can set up any transformation using either coordinate input or selected points on the object itself. For instance, you can scale an object from a point established by its minimum width, by its center depth, or by its maximum height, or you can rotate an object around its maximum width.

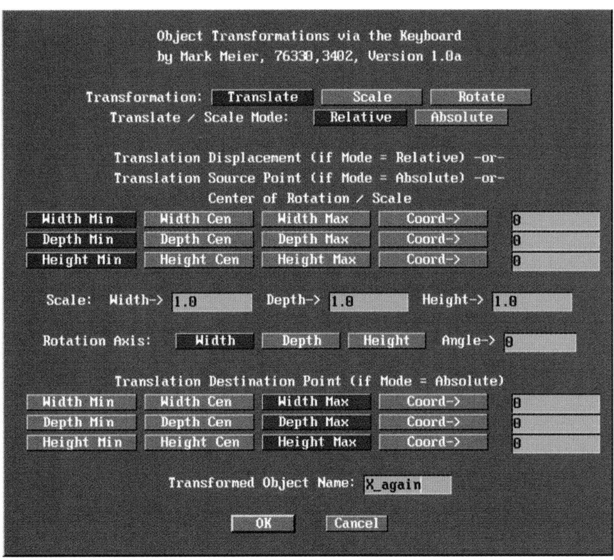

The Keyboard Transformations dialog box.

Keyboard Transformations Parameters

Transformation [T] t, s, r (Translate, Rotate, Scale) — Specifies the type of translation.

Translate/Scale Mode [Ts] r, a (Relative, Absolute) — Specifies the mode of translation, with absolute requiring two sets of coordinates or a source point and a destination point.

Source [S] wm, wc, wma, cx, dm, dc, dma, cz, hm, hc, hma, cy (width minimum, width center, width maximum, coordinate X, depth minimum, depth center, depth maximum, coordinate Z, height minimum, height center, height maximum, coordinate Y) — Sets the translation displacement if mode is relative, the translation source point if mode is absolute, or the center of rotation or scale.

Scale [Sc] w, d, h (Width, Depth, Height) — Specifies the scale factor for width, depth, and height.

Rotation Axis [Ra] w, d, h, a (Width, Depth, Height, Angle) — Specifies the center and angle of rotation.

Destination [D] wm, wc, wma, cx, dm, dc, dma, cz, hm, hc, hma, cy (width minimum, width center, width maximum, coordinate X, depth minimum, depth center, depth maximum, coordinate Z, height minimum, height center, height maximum, coordinate Y) — Sets the translation destination point if mode is absolute.

Transformed Object Name — Specifies the name for the transformed object. If the name exists, a 3D Studio dialog box enables you to rename the object prior to creating it.

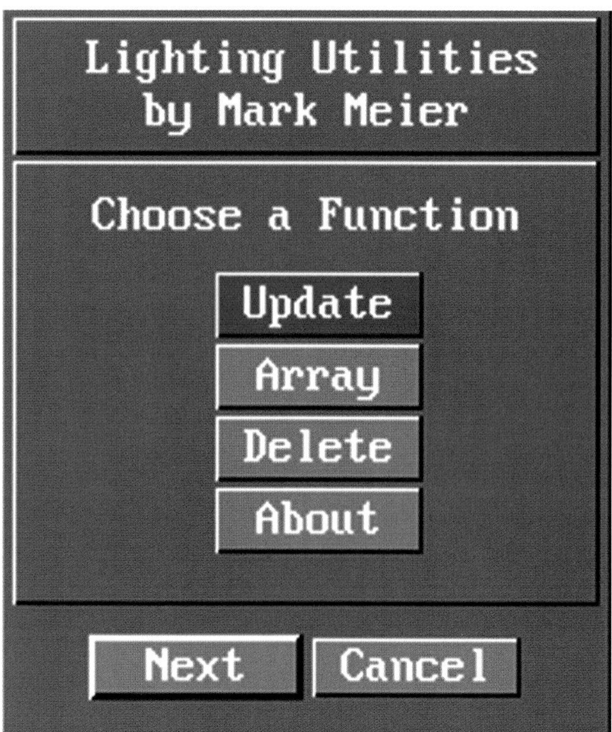

The Lighting Utilities dialog box.

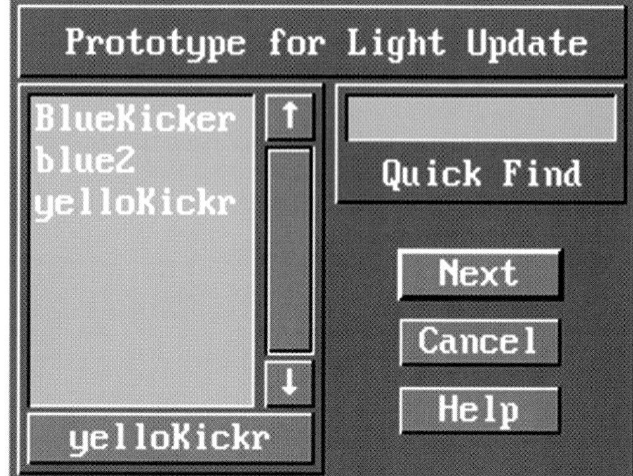

The Update dialog box.

Summary

Lighting Utilities enables you to create arrays of lights, to delete multiple lights by name, and to copy the settings from one light to other lights.

The Update function enables you to copy selected settings from one light to other lights. You begin by selecting a prototype light, then you select the lights to be updated. After they are selected you can specify which settings to copy. There are 13 possible settings, including color, on/off, shadow, exclusion lists, and location.

The Delete function enables you to select lights from a scrollable list and then delete them. You can tag and untag lights individually or using wild-card searches. A Quick Find function searches the list of lights as you type a name. After you have selected all the lights you want to delete, the plug-in will delete them all at once.

With the Array function you can create both polar and rectangular arrays of lights. For rectangular arrays you can specify both the number in the array and the spacing in all three dimensions. Polar arrays can be created using pivot axes in either top, front, or side orientations. Spotlights can be rotated or not.

Lighting Utilities Parameter

Function [F] u, d, a (Update, Array, Delete) — Select the utility function.

Update Parameters

On/Off [Oo] — Enables copying of the on/off status of the light.
Atten/Range [Ar] — Enables copying of the attenuation and range settings.
Shadow [Sh] — Enables copying of the shadow settings.
Cone/Hs/Fo [Co] — Enables copying of the cone, hot spot, and falloff settings.
Color [Cl] — Enables copying of the color settings.
Location [Lo] — Enables copying of the location of the light.
Target Pt [Tp] — Enables copying of the location of the target.
Roll/Aspect [Ra] — Enables copying of the roll and aspect settings.
Projector [Pr] — Enables copying of the projector settings.
Exclude [Ex] — Enables copying of the exclusion list.
Multiplier [Mu] — Enables copying of the multiplier setting.
Rect/Circ [Rc] — Enables copying of the shape of the light.
Overshoot [Ov] — Enables copying of the overshoot settings.
Most [M] — Activate most settings. Location and target point are not activated.
None [N] — Deactivate all settings.

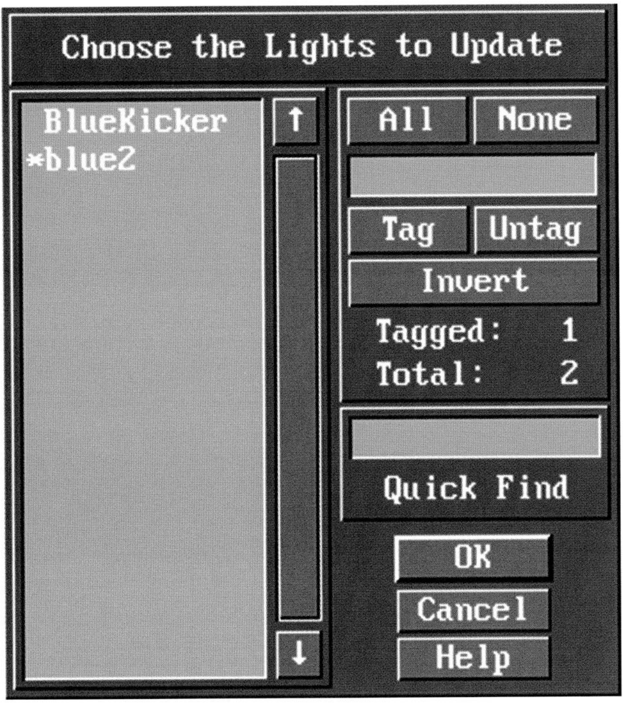

The Delete Selection dialog box.

Delete Parameters

Tagging controls [Tc] — This is a set of controls for using wild-card searches to tag and untag multiple lights. This works just like object selection in 3D Studio. These controls are present in most selection dialog boxes in this plug-in.

Quick Find [Qf] — This is a fast name locator. Begin typing a name in this box, and the scroll list will scroll to names that match what you type. This is present in all selection dialog boxes in this plug-in.

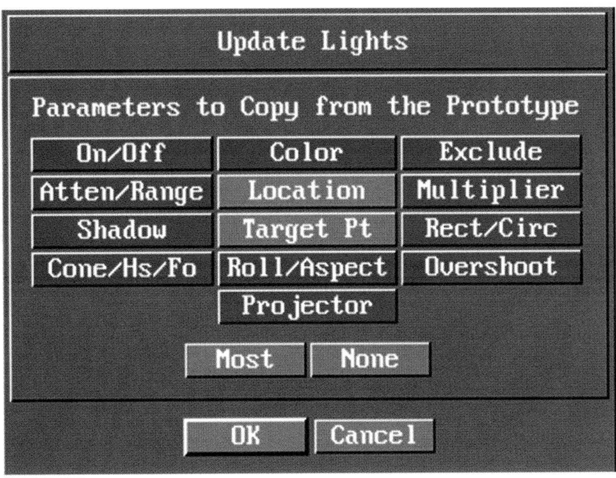

The Array dialog box.

Array Parameters

Rectangular [Re] — Switches to a rectangular array type.

Count width, depth, height [Cw] [Cd] [Ch] — The number of copies in the array in each dimension of a rectangular array. Width is X, depth is Z, and height is Y.

Spacing width, depth, height [Sw] [Sd] [Sh] — The distance between copies in each dimension of a rectangular array.

Polar [Po] — Switches to a polar array type.

Creation Plane [Cp] t, f, s (Top, Front, Side) — Orientation for the polar array pivot axis.

Count [Cn] — Number of copies in the polar array.

Radius [Rd] — Radius of the polar array.

Start Angle [Sa] — Starting angle of the polar array.

Angle to Fill [Af] — Total number of degrees in the polar array.

Rotate Spotlights [Rs] — Determines whether spotlights will be rotated as they are copied.

Name Prefix [Np] — The name prefix that will used for the new lights.

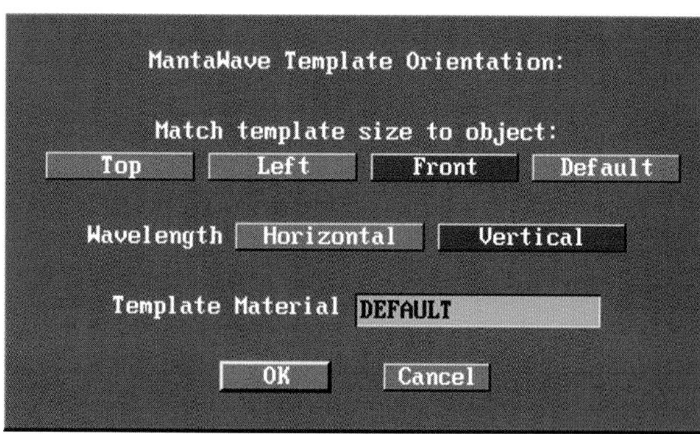

The MantaWave Template dialog box.

MantaWave Version 1.0
Copyright 1992 Darrel Anderson. From Yost Group, Inc.
Max Amplitude at: Edges Center
Min Amplitude % - 10 +
Amplitude Curve: - 50 +
Wave Period: 4 # of morphs: 4
Hide >0? YES NO Name prefix: bang
OK Cancel

The MantaWave Parameters dialog box.

Summary

MantaWave is part of Yost Group's Special Effects Procedural Modeling disk #3. MantaWave creates one or more objects that are deformed using a sine wave template. The template is produced using the MantaWave Template dialog box, which enables you to align and orient the template and thus the deformation to the mesh object.

The template is then adjusted using Modify/Vertex/Move to position the template as desired, with wave amplitude and frequency being set by the relative scale of the template. The final steps include setting the maximum amplitude position, minimum amplitude percentage, and the amplitude curve using the MantaWave Parameters dialog box. These parameters enable you to further shape and position the wave effect.

If you opt to produce more than a single object, the wave deformation is distributed incrementally along the object series based on the Wave Period. This enables you to specify the speed with which the wave deformation moves through the objects. Because the resulting objects have the same vertex count as the original, they can be used as morph objects, thus making them useful for creating smooth rippling and undulating animated effects.

For MantaWave to function properly it must have an adequate number of evenly distributed faces from which to work. Furthermore, MantaWave often requires that you tessellate the original object several times; Create/Object/Tessellate/Edge with edge tension set to 0 works well.

MantaWave Parameters

MantaWave Options (Create Template, Set Parameters) — Create Template enables you to create a template object by using the MantaWave Template dialog box. Set Parameters enables you to set MantaWave's parameters in the MantaWave parameters dialog box.

MantaWave Axis [Ma] t, l, f, d (Top, Left, Front, Default) — Positions MantaWave's effect to the 3D object. Top, Left, and Front automatically align the template and scale it to the selected object. Default produces a predefined template.

Wavelength [W] h, v (Horizontal, Vertical) — Sets the direction—horizontal or vertical—of wave motion.

Template Material [Tm] Enables you to specify a material for the template.

Max Amplitude at [A] e, c (Edges, Center) — Sets the position of maximum amplitude relative to either the object's edges or its center.

Min Amplitude % [Ma] (0–100%) [Tm] Specifies the smallest wave amplitude permitted as a percentage of the maximum amplitude set by the scale of the template.

Amplitude Curve [Ac] (–100–100) — Defines the wave contour from maximum to minimum, with 0 being linear, less than 0 producing a convex curve, and greater than 0 producing a concave curve.

Wave Period [Wp] — Sets the time period (in frames) for one cycle of wave motion.

# of morphs [M] — Specifies the number of morph objects or MantaWave objects that will be created. This enables you to apply the deformation in stepped increments.

Hide >0 (yes, no) — Specifies whether to hide all but the first morph object.

Name prefix — Sets the four-character prefix for the objects produced by MantaWave.

MANTAWAVE cont

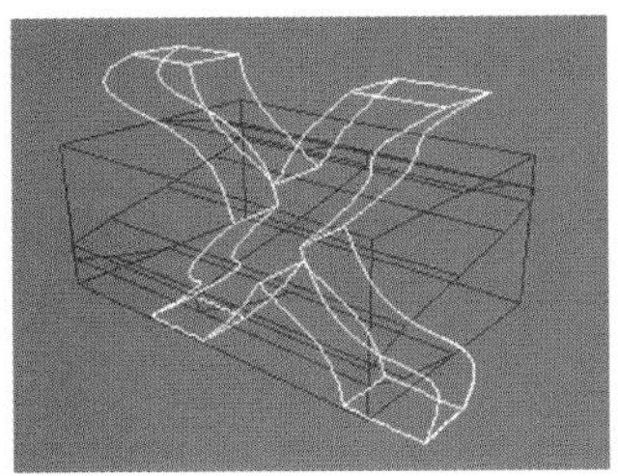
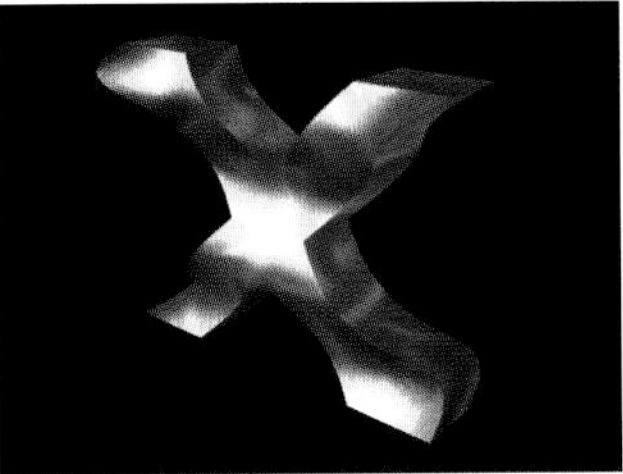
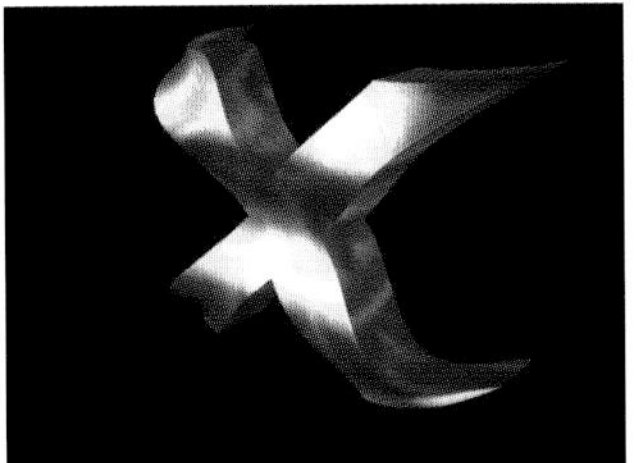

Wireframe morph 0 | Morph 0 | Morph 1 | Morph 2

MantaWave uses a sine wave template (shown in red) to deform and produce a morphable 3D mesh object or series of objects.

MATH MESHER

Schreiber Instruments \mathmesh MATH_I.PXP

Summary

This plug-in uses mathematical formulas to generate mesh objects. You can choose from a list of predefined template formulas that you can modify, or you can enter your own formulas. Math Mesher includes a rotatable preview window that you can render in wireframe, flat shaded, or Gouraud shaded modes. After entering or changing the formula, choosing Preview displays the new mesh in the preview window. If you choose Create Object, Math Mesher asks you for a new object name, to build the object, and then to exit to 3D Studio. Math Mesher will add smoothing groups to the object, but it does not add mapping coordinates.

This summary was based on prerelease software.

Math Mesher Parameters

Start x, y [Sx] [Sy] — The start angle for the X and Y functions.

End x, y [Ex] [Ey] — The end angle for the X and Y functions.

Steps x, y [Stx] [Sty] — The number of face segments along the X and Y directions.

User constants a, b, c [A] [B] [C] — User-definable floating point constants for use in the formula.

Scale [Sc] — Overall scale of the object.

Smooth [Sm] y, n (yes, no) — Determines whether smoothing groups are applied.

Formulas x, y, z [Fx] [Fy] [Fz] — Formulas for the x, y, and z functions. You have room for approximately 65 characters.

Templates [T] — This is a scrollable list of predefined template formulas. The forms include helix, mobius strip, plane, sphere, and shell.

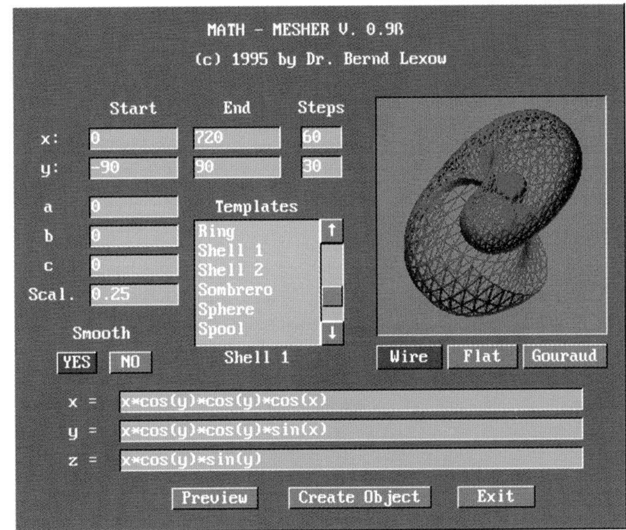

The Math Mesher dialog box.

Preview [P] — Generates an object in the preview window based on the current formula.

Create Object [C] — Creates a 3D Studio object and exits the plug-in.

Preview window [Pw] — Displays the current object. You can rotate the view using the mouse.

Shade mode [Sh] w, f, g (Wire, Flat, Gouraud) — Selects the current preview display mode. Wire is wireframe, Flat is shaded, and Gouraud is smooth shaded.

MATH MESHER cont

MATH_I.PXP \mathmesh **Schreiber Instruments**

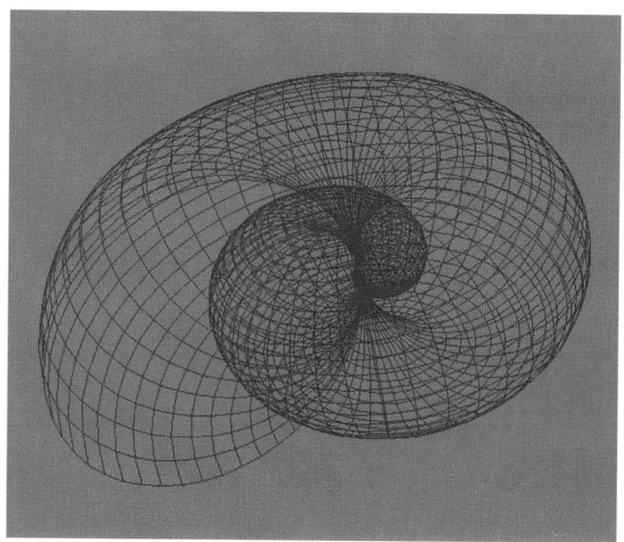

[T]shell [Ex]720 [Stx]90 [Sty]45

A mathematically defined object.

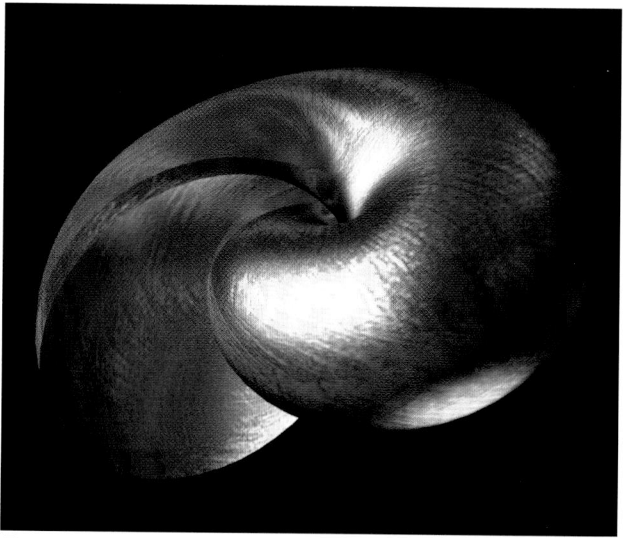

The rendered object

MELT

MELT_I.PXP \melt **Yost Group**

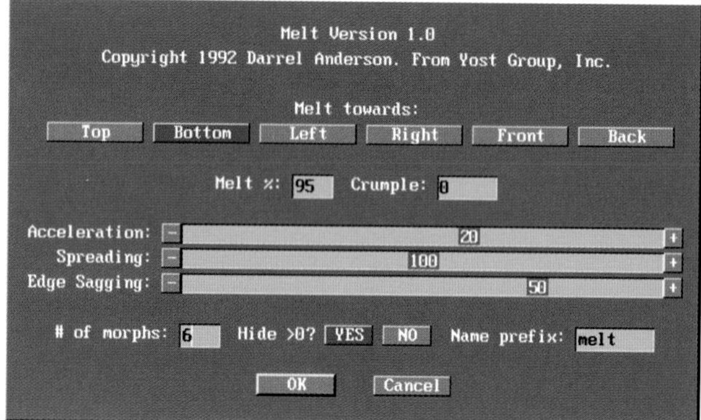

The Melt dialog box.

Summary

Melt is part of Yost Group's Special Effects Procedural Modeling disk #3. Melt collapses a 3D mesh object in any one of six directions, making it appear as though it is melting. As the object melts its edges droop and an expanding pool forms.

Melt is controlled by several parameters, including the direction in which it melts, the total melt amount, and the amount of edge spread and sag.

If you opt to produce more than a single object, the melt deformation is distributed incrementally along the object series. Because the resulting objects have the same vertex count as the original, they can be used as morph objects, thus making them useful for producing animated melting objects.

For Melt to function properly it must have an adequate number of evenly distributed faces from which to work. Furthermore, Melt often requires that you tessellate the original object several times; Create/Object/Tessellate/Edge with edge tension set to 0 works well.

Melt Parameters

Melt towards [Mt] t, b, l, r, f, b (Top, Bottom, Left, Right, Front, Back) — Sets the direction of the melt; the default is bottom.

Melt % [M] (1–100) — Sets the total amount of melt or collapse as a percentage of the original object size.

Crumple [C] — Enables you to add dents, making the object appear to crumple as well as melt.

Acceleration [A] (–100–100) — Specifies whether the melting speed changes over time. Values greater than 0 cause the melting action to start slowly and pick up speed. Values less than 0 result in deceleration, and 0 produces a linear melting action.

MELT cont

Yost Group \melt **MELT_I.PXP**

Spreading [Sp] (–100–300) — Sets how the original object volume is preserved, with numbers greater than 0 causing the object to spread as it melts and numbers less than 0 causing it to split or shear.

Edge Sagging [Es] (–100–100) — Causes parts of the object to melt at different rates, with values greater than 0 causing points farther from the object's center to collapse faster. Values less than 0 cause the object to melt from the center out.

# of morphs [M] — Specifies the number of morph objects or skline objects that will be created, enabling you to apply the deformation in stepped increments.

Hide >0 (yes, no) — Specifies whether to hide all but the first morph object.

Name prefix — Sets the four-character prefix for the objects produced by Skline.

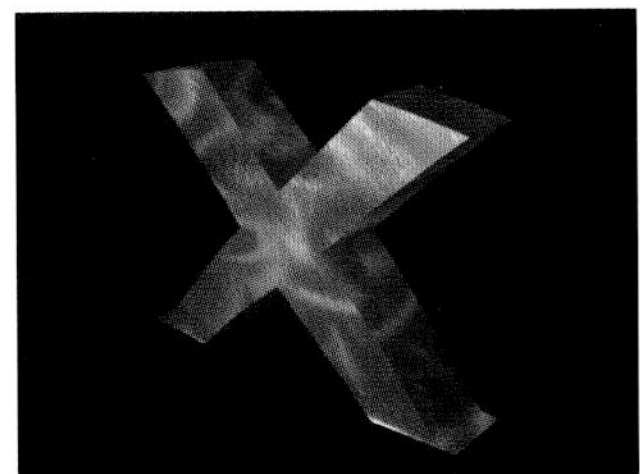

Morph 0

Morph 1

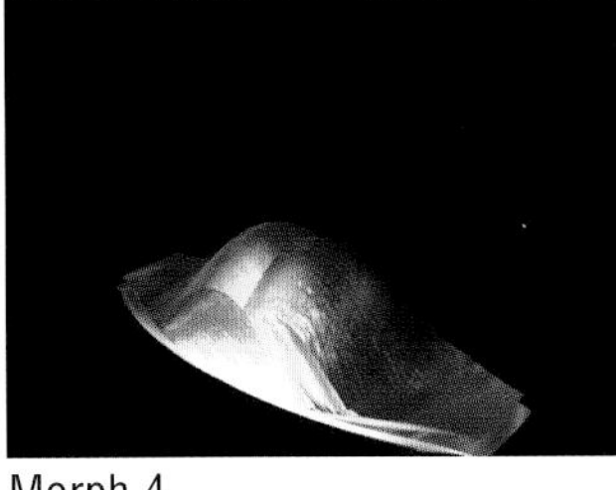

Morph 4

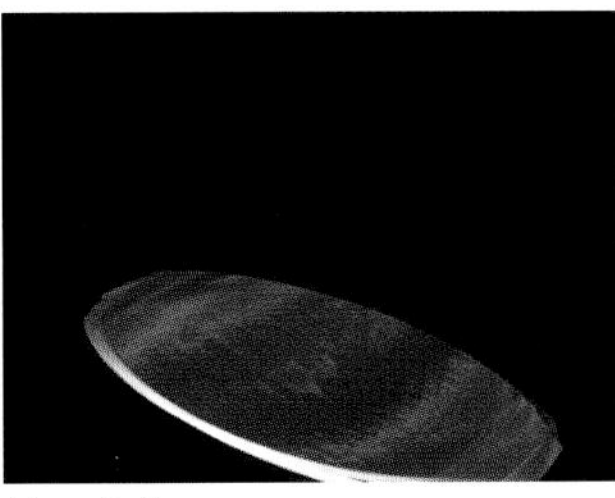

Morph 6

Melt was set to produce six morphs to melt from the original to 95 percent of the original's size. Additional parameters were [Mt]b, [A]20, [Sp]100, [Es]50.

MESHPAINT 3D

Positron Publishing \meshpnt **PAINT_I.PXP**

Summary

MeshPaint 3D is a 3D paint program that enables you to paint any 3D Studio model in real time. It functions as an interactive texture mapper that uses 3D Studio's planar, cylindrical, or spherical mapping coordinates to control how each 3D object is interactively colored or textured.

Briefly, MeshPaint 3D works like this: Load any 3D Studio mesh file or project file into 3D Studio and apply either planar, cylindrical, or spherical mapping coordinates to the model. Using the PXP plug-in selector, load MeshPaint 3D, which pops up over the 3D Studio interface. Click on MeshPaint's Pick button, and choose any object from the file lister.

This action places a wireframe version of the model in the viewport. You can then adjust the viewpoint on the wireframe using the various view control buttons provided. By clicking on the Paint button, a white Gouraud-shaded version of the object appears in the viewport, signaling that you are ready to paint using any brush in the currently loaded Brush Set. You also can opt to paint with a custom brush consisting of a 2D image, which enables you not only to color but to texture the model as well.

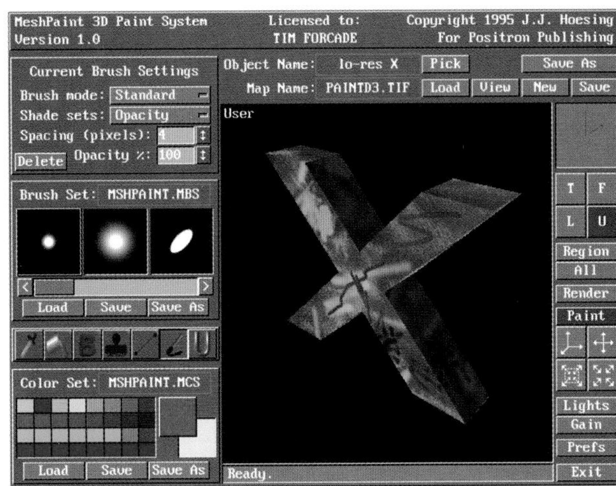

The MeshPaint 3D dialog box.

As you paint, the currently loaded 2D map image is updated and can be viewed by clicking on the View button, which provides a scrollable full-resolution look at the map. MeshPaint's speed depends upon your computer and the selected brush mode. Even with a minimal computer system, however, you can apply brush strokes spontaneously by specifying the paint performance preferences appropriate to your system.

Remember that the same laws that apply to texture mapping apply to MeshPaint's interactive texture mapping. For MeshPaint 3D to work predictably you must give close consideration to how the selected mapping coordinates will affect the model you plan to paint. Whether you choose planar, cylindrical, or spherical mapping coordinates, all of MeshPaint's brush strokes are applied perpendicular to the coordinate method.

Suppose that you will paint a cube that has planar mapping coordinates applied to it, and suppose that these coordinates are applied parallel to the front of the cube. This means that if you paint on the cube's front face, the resulting brush strokes will follow the path of your cursor and, as with any planar map, project through the cube and appear reversed on the opposite face. If, however, you paint on a face that is not perpendicular to the planar coordinates—say the side or top of the cube—your brush strokes will flow along the perpendicular specified by those same coordinates. This can produce unwanted horizontal bands of color.

The best solution for MeshPaint 3D is to break your object into subgroups, each with its own separate mapping coordinates. Each subobject should be separately loaded and a separate map interactively created and saved for it. Although this might not be as direct as some would like, it is straightforward and relatively easy to do.

MeshPaint 3D provides multiple brush shapes and modes such as Transition mode, which blends between two colors. You also can control brush opacity and the spacing between brush strokes, as well as the size, softness, aspect ratio, and rotation of the brush itself. There is one level of undo, but no redo.

MeshPaint 3D enables you to load, view, and use any 2D image as a map or starting point from which to begin painting. In fact, the speed with which it renders mapped objects makes it both useful and time saving when you want to quickly view a series of texture map options on a given model. It is also very effective when used as a means of accurately placing reference marks on image maps or masks that will be edited in paint software such as HiRes QFX or Photoshop. This can save considerable time when you want to create 3D Studio materials that will use multiple image maps.

MeshPaint 3D Parameters

Brush mode [B] s, t, f (standard, transition, fade) — Sets the method of color application. Standard applies a smooth uniform single color. Transition fades between two selected colors. Fade fades-out a single color at the end of the brush stroke.

Shade sets [Ss] o, i (opacity, intensity) — Specifies the brush effect with opacity varying the brush transparency and intensity placing a black border around the brush stroke.

Spacing [Sp] (1–255) — Specifies the distance between brush marks, which enables you to continuously vary brushing from solid to dotted or dashed.

Opacity % [O] (1–100) —Varies the brush transparency.

Brush Set [Bs] (load, save, save as) — Enables you to load and save sets of up to six brushes.

Set Brush Shape Linear or Round [Bl] [Br] s, a, r, f (size 1–64, aspect 1–100, rotation 0–179, feathering 0–100) — Sets the size, shape, and softness of the current brush. Linear produces a linear intensity falloff and round produces a spherical falloff. Size sets the overall brush size, aspect produces an elliptical shaped brush, rotation sets the angle for elliptical brushes, and feathering sets the degree of softness.

Note: *All brush shape variables are accessed by double-clicking on the brush window you want to edit.*

Icon menu [I] e, f, b, s, l, p (eyedropper, fill, blur, stamper, line tool, paint brush, undo) — This is a series of functions that are accessed from a row of seven icons. Eyedropper enables you to pick up any color from the workspace, fill produces a color fill of a preset color range, blur provides variable blur for softening image areas, stamper enables you to paint with a specified image up to 64 pixels square, line tool paints a point-to-point line, and paint brush is the standard painting mode. Undo reverses the last action.

Note: *The following fill, blur, stamper, and line settings are accessed by double-clicking on the corresponding icon.*

Fill settings [Fr] [Fg] [Fb] (0–255) — Sets the red, green, and blue ranges, which control the color fill function.

Blur settings [Bl] s, sp (size 1–64, spacing 1–255) — Blur size controls the amount of blur, and spacing sets the distance of brush travel between each application of blur.

Stamper settings [St] s, o (spacing 1–255, opacity 1–100) — Controls how 2D images are used as custom brushes or stamps. Spacing sets the distance of brush travel between each stamp application, and opacity sets the opacity of each stamp.

Line settings [Li] v, m (viewport, map) — Specifies whether the line wraps around the 3D object or is drawn straight across the object.

Color Set [Cs] (load, save, save as) — Enables you to load and save color palettes of up to 32 colors.

Pick — Enables you to pick the 3D mesh object to be painted.

Load — Loads the image map that will be applied to the 3D mesh object.

View (Brush, Stamper, Done) — Provides a scrollable window that displays the current map image. Brush enables you to specify an area up to 64 pixels square as a brush, and Stamper enables you to specify an area up to 128 pixels square as a stamp.

New (color, x, y) — Enables you to create a new image map at any resolution and any background color.

Viewport buttons (top, front, left, and user) — Sets the view shown in the viewport.

Region or All — Sets whether a region (which is set by clicking and dragging a window over the desired area) or the entire view will be rendered.

Render or Paint — Render produces a Gouraud, or flat shaded, render of the current view. Paint first renders the view and then enables you to paint.

Lights — Moves the lights used to render the object to either side of the camera.

Gain — Compresses the overall intensity of the workspace view to enable you to view darker textures.

Note: *The following preference functions are accessed by clicking on the Prefs button.*

Wireframe Detail (1–100) — Sets the level of detail in wireframe mode.

Wireframe BG — Sets the background color, in wireframe mode, from white to black.

Preview Size (16–255) — Sets the size in pixels of the region around the brush that is updated when painting. Higher values are appropriate for faster computers.

Wraparound [W] uv, u, v, n (U and V, U only, V only, None) — Specifies what happens when a brush stroke is applied to the edge of a map. U and V turns on wrap for all edges, U only turns on wrap for the right and left edges, V turns on wrap for the top and bottom, and none clips the brush stroke within the map borders.

Painting [Pa] i, p, f, s (Instant, Preview, Fast, Slower) — Sets which portion of the screen is updated as you paint. Instant updates the entire workspace, Preview updates only the region around the brush, Fast previews during painting and paints only after the brush is released, and Slower provides the most interactive preview and also paints only after the brush is released.

Shading [Sh] s, f (smooth, flat) — Switches between Gouraud and flat shading.

Save, Use, and Cancel — Enables you to save the current preferences or use them for the current session only.

3D object

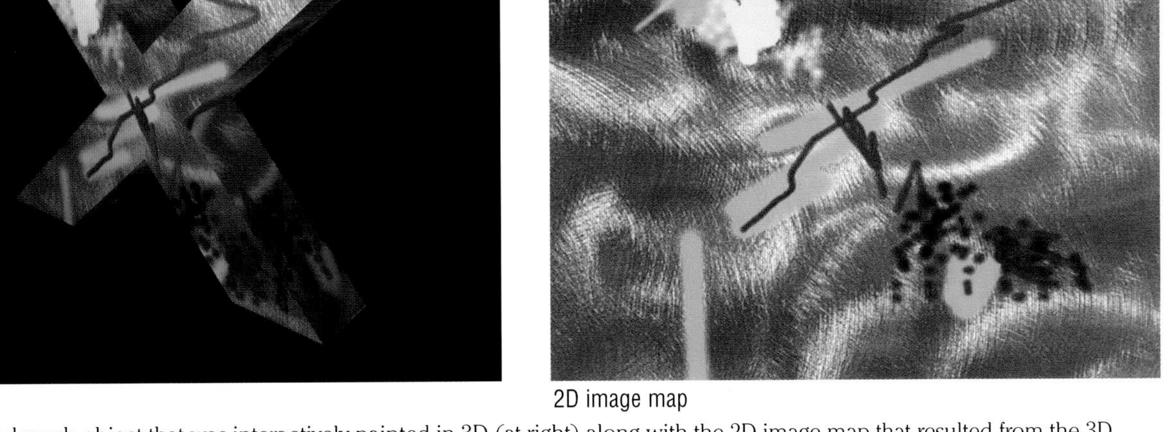

2D image map

The rendered mesh object that was interactively painted in 3D (at right) along with the 2D image map that resulted from the 3D painting process.

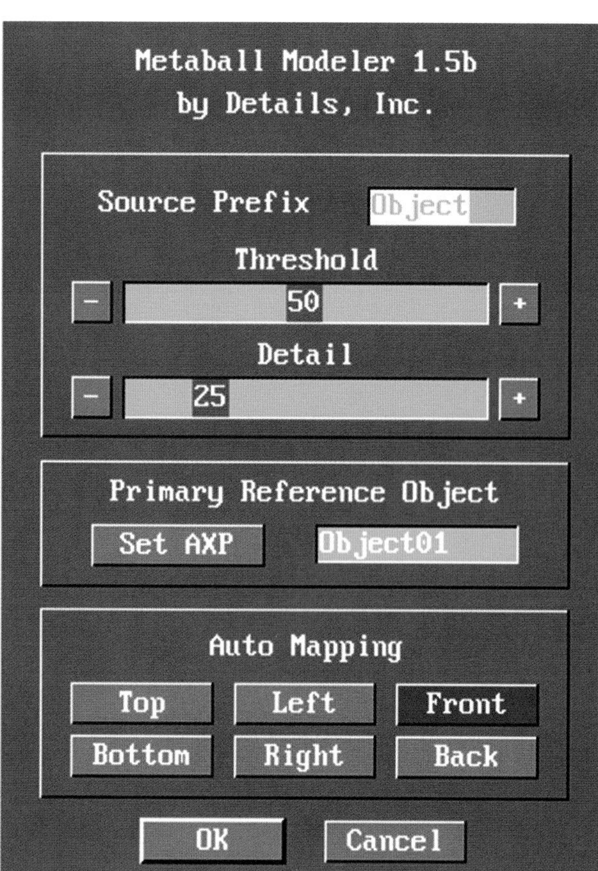

The Metaball Modeler dialog box.

Summary

With Metaball Modeler you can model objects using spherical elements that flow into each other. This modeling method is especially useful for modeling rounded organic objects. These spherical elements are called blobs, metaballs, or reference objects. Each reference object has a field strength associated with it that determines how much it merges with or repels other reference objects. A larger field strength pulls more of other surrounding reference objects toward itself and causes them to blend more completely. Metaball Modeler then creates a mesh around the merged reference objects. This is a little like shrinkwrapping a bunch of tomatoes. Reference objects can have both positive and negative field strengths. A negative field doesn't add to the final mesh. Instead, it pushes on the other reference objects, shifting their surfaces and adding dimples and even holes. Pushing a reference object with negative strength through one with positive strength produces a hole.

With Metaball modeler you begin inside the 3D Studio 3D Editor by creating reference objects using L-spheres. They are arranged and scaled to the approximate size of the desired object. Then, Metaball Modeler is used to flow a smooth mesh around the reference objects. You can specify the amount of detail (number of faces) that Metaball Modeler produces in your mesh. The strength and blobbiness of each object is determined by the color assigned to its wireframe. Colors 19, 23, 27, and 31 are positive field strengths. Colors 3, 7, 11, and 15 are negative field strengths.

Metaball Modeler is a combination of a PXP and an AXP. For modeling you use the PXP in the 3D Editor to produce a mesh object. For animations you use the AXP on a series of animated reference objects to produce an animated mesh object. The AXP has the same controls as the PXP but it adds two controls (parametric envelope strength and detail) that enable you to change the amount of detail and the field strength from frame to frame using a spline control envelope. This lets you animate a series of reference objects that start out as separate objects and then flow together as the animation progresses.

This summary is based on a prerelease version of the software.

Metaball Modeler PXP Parameters

Source Prefix [P] — This is the prefix name for the reference object series. The Modeler will use any numbered objects in this series to generate the final mesh. The final mesh object will be given this name without series numbering.

Threshold [T] (1–100) — This is the distance that the field strength of a reference object extends beyond its immediate surface. It is expressed as a percentage of the radius of the reference object A larger value extends the effect of a reference object outward.

Detail [D] (5–100) — Determines the number of faces and the detail in the final mesh object.

Set AXP [Sa] — Assigns the settings to the AXP.

Primary Reference Object [Pr] — This is the first object in the series of reference objects and the one to which you would assign the AXP.

Auto Mapping [Am] t, l, f, b, r, k (Top, Left, Front, Bottom, Right, Back) — Selects one of the six automatic mapping directions. Metaball modeler assigns planar mapping coordinates from one of these directions.

Strength Envelope Parameters

Envelope [E] — A line or curve that sets the strength or detail across a range of frames.
Object [O] — Selects the reference objects that will be changed.
Reset [Re] — Restores the original settings.
Load [L] — Loads an envelope settings file from disk.
Save [S] — Saves an envelope settings file to disk.
Add Key [A] — Adds a key via mouse input.
Create Key [C] — Adds a key via X and Y values.
Move Key [M] — Rescales the key and moves it along the spline.
Shift Keys [Sh] — Translates a range of keys along the timeline.
Scale Keys [Sc] — Scales a range of keys relative to the timeline.
Linear or Curved [Lc] l, c — Selects whether the envelope is a line or a curve.
Use Envelope [U] — This button instructs the plug-in to use the envelope you have chosen.

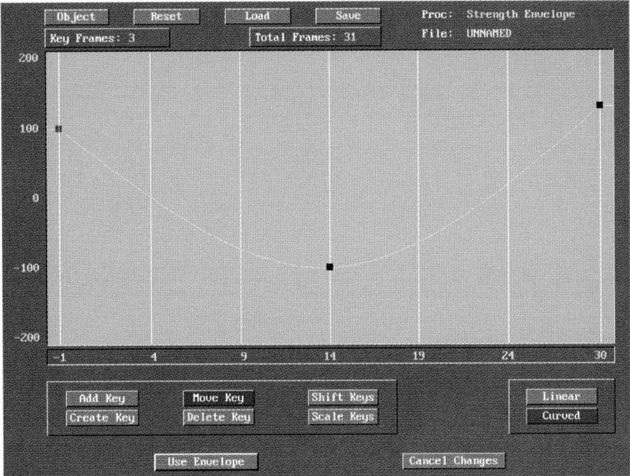

The Strength Envelope dialog box.

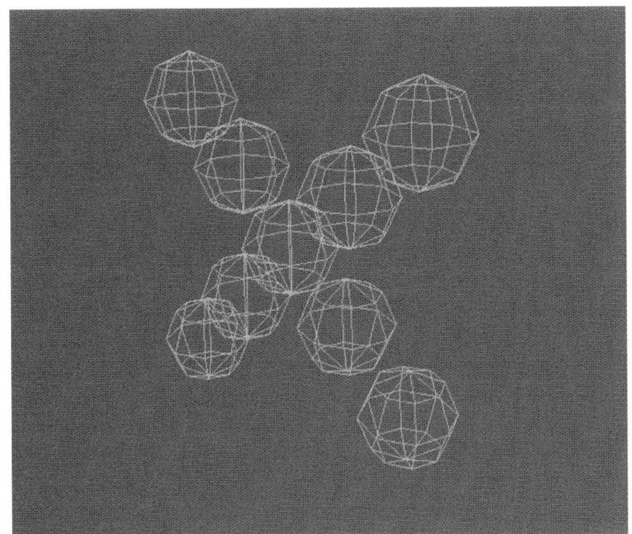
Reference objects

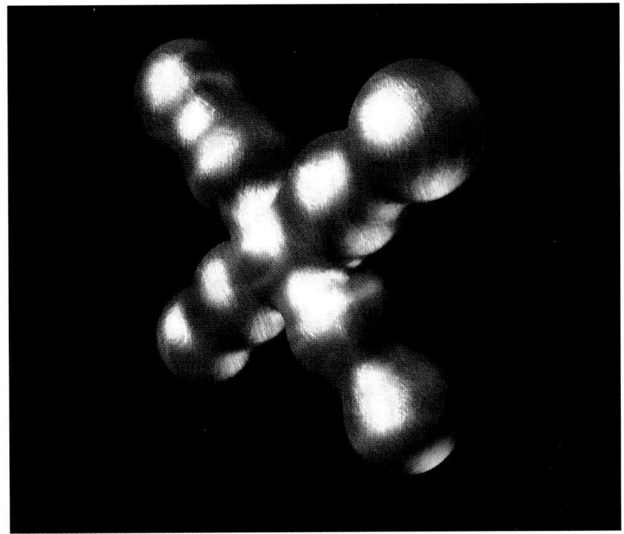
Rendered mesh

Metaballs blended into a rounded mesh.

METAREYES MODELER

FUSION_I.PXP, MASIGN2_I.PXP, METAX2_I.AXP \metareye Reyes-De Espona Infográphica

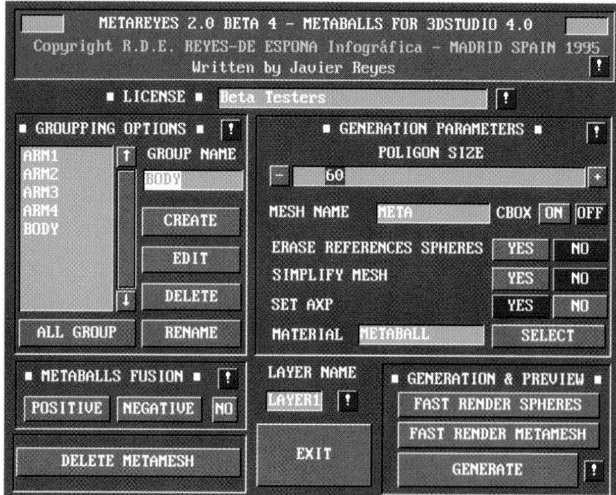

The MetaReyes Modeler dialog box.

Summary

MetaReyes Modeler is a metaball modeler. Metaball modelers use spherical metaballs (or reference objects) that are blended together to produce rounded organic forms. Metaballs have a field strength associated with them that determines how much they blend together. When the field strength is negative, it pushes on surrounding metaballs causing dimples and holes.

The MetaReyes Modeler is a combination of a PXP, an AXP, and an SXP. The PXP sets all the parameters and generates a static mesh. The AXP uses the settings from the PXP and generates a new mesh for each frame of an animation. The SXP is used in the material applied to a mesh object to help smooth the surface.

You begin a metaball model in the 3D Editor by creating and arranging L-spheres or G-spheres into an approximation of the form that you want to build. MetaReyes calls these spheres reference spheres and uses them as metaball elements. After you have the arrangement you want, you invoke the Modeler PXP. The Modeler enables you to set the field strength of each metaball using wireframe colors. Different colors indicate different strengths, some positive and others negative.

The MetaReyes Modeler has a unique option called Grouping, which enables you to specify which metaballs are smoothed into which other metaballs. Without Grouping, metaballs group together whenever any get near another. With Grouping, a metaball will blend only with another metaball from the same group. A metaball can be in more than one blending group. This is similar to how smoothing groups work in 3D Studio.

Two preview windows are available that show fast rendered views of the reference spheres and of the resulting mesh. After you have the mesh you want, you can choose Generate to build the mesh in the 3D Editor. You will need to add mapping coordinates to the mesh if you want to texture map it.

The MetaReyes AXP is attached to the first reference sphere in the scene. It uses the settings from the PXP and generates a new mesh for each frame. This enables you to animate the motion of the reference spheres to produce liquid blending and flowing effects. The mesh produced by the AXP cannot use mapping coordinates.

This summary is based on a prerelease version of the software.

MetaReyes Modeler Parameters

Group list [Gl] — A scrolling list of named groups. Select one to make that the current group.

Group Name [Gn] — The current group name. You can enter a new name here.

Create [C] — Create a new group using the name in the Group Name text box.

Edit [E] — Switches to the 3D Studio scene so that you can select the members of a group.

Delete [D] — Deletes a named group. The reference spheres are removed from the group, not deleted.

Rename [R] — Changes the name of the current group.

All Group [Ag] — Assigns all reference spheres to the current group.

Metaballs Fusion [Mf] p, n, no (Positive, Negative, No) — Enables you to change the color and fusion strength of reference spheres. Positive assigns colors representing positive fusion values, and Negative assigns colors representing negative fusion values. No changes a reference sphere's color to white, thus making it a non-metaball object.

Delete Metamesh [Dm] — Deletes the currently generated metamesh.

Poligon Size [Ps] (1–500) — Controls the size of the polygon faces used to generate the mesh. This value represents tenths of a unit.

Mesh Name [Mn] — The name assigned to the metamesh when it is generated.

Cbox [Cb] (on, off) — Enables a clipping box. This restricts the metamesh surface that is generated to an area bounded by a box object, allowing you to generate a test mesh more quickly.

Erase Reference Spheres [Er] y, n (yes, no) — Determines whether the reference spheres are deleted after the metamesh is generated.

Simplify Mesh [Sm] y, n (yes, no) — When enabled, Simply Mesh produce a mesh with fewer faces. This avoids problems of exceeding 3D Studio's face count limit.

Set AXP [Sa] y, n (yes, no) — Places the current settings in the AXP module.

Material [Ma] — Selects the material to apply to the metamesh.

Layer Name [Ln] — Enter the current layer name. Layer names define the reference spheres that will be used to generate a metamesh.

Fast Render Spheres [Fs] — Displays a dialog box showing a fast rendered view of the reference spheres with their colors.

Fast Render Metamesh [Fm] — Displays a dialog box showing a fast rendered view of the metamesh.

Generate [G] — Generates a metamesh using the current settings.

Fast Render Parameters

Shade type [St] g, f, w (Gouraud, Flat, Wire) — Selects a shade type for the preview. Wire is wireframe mode, Flat is shaded mode, and Gouraud is smooth shaded mode.

View controls [Vc] r, p, z, f (Rotate, Pan, Zoom, Fit) — Changes the current view.

View select [Vs] (t, f, r, l) — Select a standard view direction: top, front, right, or left.

Preview window [Pw] — Use your mouse in this window to rotate the model in real time.

MetaReyes AXP Parameters

Poligon Size [Ps] (1–500) — Controls the size of the polygon faces used to generate the mesh. This value represents tenths of a unit.

Simplify Mesh [Sm] y, n (yes, no) — When enabled, Simplify Mesh produces a mesh with fewer faces. This avoids problems of exceeding 3D Studio's face count limit.

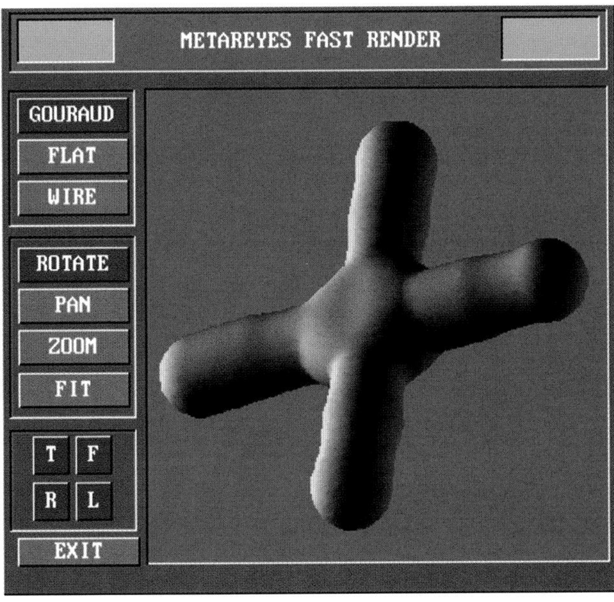

The Fast Render dialog box.

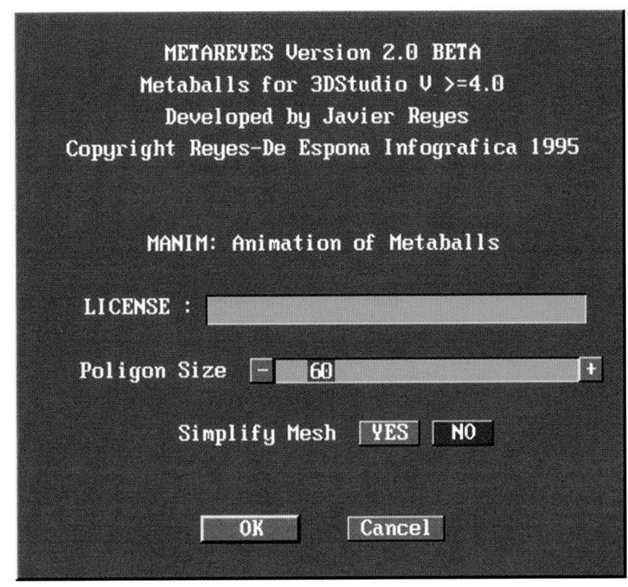

The MetaReyes AXP dialog box.

METAREYES MODELER cont

FUSION_I.PXP, MASIGN2_I.PXP, METAX2_I.AXP \metareye Reyes-De Espona Infográphica

Reference spheres

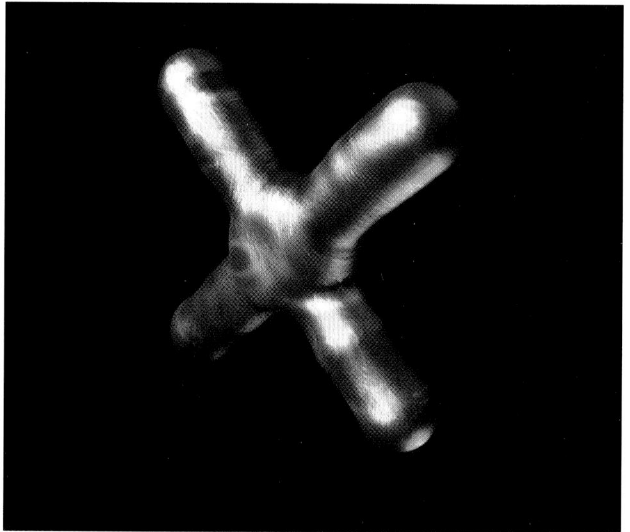

Rendered metamesh

Organic forms created with metaball modeling.

NURSERY

NURSRY_I.PXP \nursery Schreiber Instruments

The Nursery dialog box.

Summary

Nursery is part of the Imagine series from Schreiber Instruments. It generates realistic trees with user-selectable species, season, size, and density. You select a species from a list of 58. You then can specify the month of the year. Nursery uses appropriate materials to display the foliage as it would appear in that month.

Three detail settings determine the number of branches and the density of the foliage. The leaves are just simple diamond shapes with colors mapped to them for all species, but the branching patterns are based on the actual branching patterns of the selected species. You can enter the desired height of the tree and the X, Y, and Z coordinates of its base. The species, detail, and height of the tree control the overall complexity of the tree and how long it takes to generate. Generating a complex tree can take several minutes.

Nursery Parameters

Type [T] (1–58) — Selects 1 of 58 different tree types.
Month [M] (1–12) — You control the foliage by setting the month of the year.
Detail [D] l, m, h (Low, Medium, High) — Density and complexity of branching and foliage.
Height [H] (5.6–420) — Height in feet of the finished tree.
Location X, Y, Z [Lx] [Ly] [Lz] — Location of the base of the tree.

[T]32 [M]10 [D]h [H]15
Quaking Aspen and Eastern Redbud trees.

[T]35 [M]7 [D]l [H]20

OBJECT BOXER PROCESS

Autodesk \box BOX_I.PXP

Summary

Included with 3D Studio Release 4, Object Boxer Process demonstrates the basic functions of a PXP plug-in and interface. Box builds a bounding box around a selected object.

Object Boxer Process Parameter

Box Color [Bc] d, o (Default, From Object) — Specifies whether the resulting bounding box will use the 3D Studio default material or the material from the selected object.

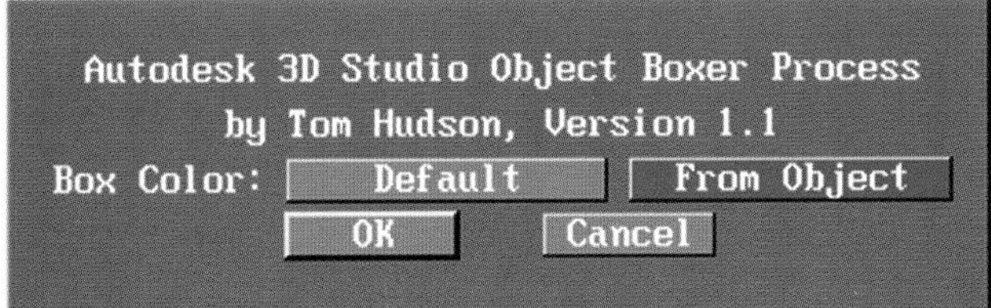

The Object Boxer Process dialog box.

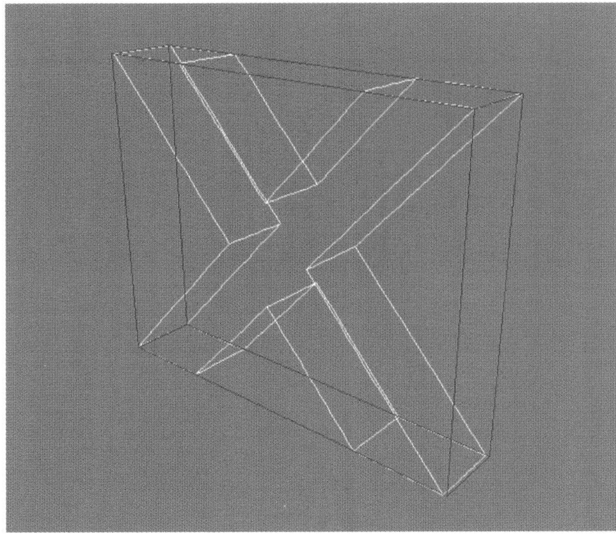

Object Boxer Process builds a bounding box (shown in red) around selected 3D mesh objects.

OBJECT CRUMPLER

CRUMPL_I.PXP \crumple Yost Group

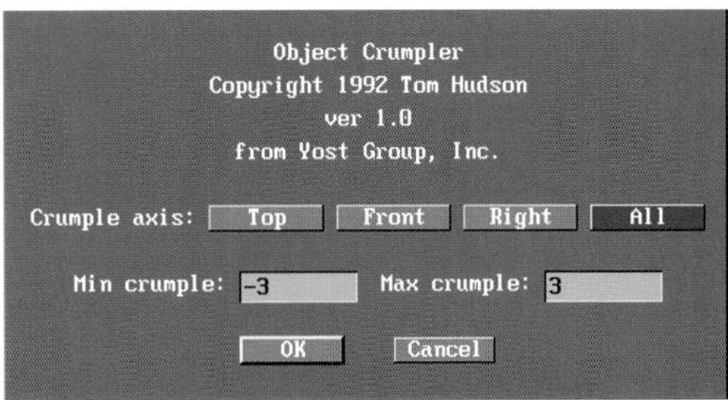

The Object Crumpler dialog box.

Summary

Object Crumpler is part of Yost Group's Special Effects disk #2. Object Crumpler randomly displaces a 3D object's vertices in one or all axes by a specified range. This produces a range of intricately textured versions of the original.

Object Crumpler Parameters

Crumple axis [Ca] t, f, r, a (top, front, right, all) — Specifies the axis or axes to which Crumple will be applied.

Min crumple [Mn] — Sets the minimum displacement value relative to the object center.

Max crumple [Mx] — Sets the maximum displacement value relative to the object center.

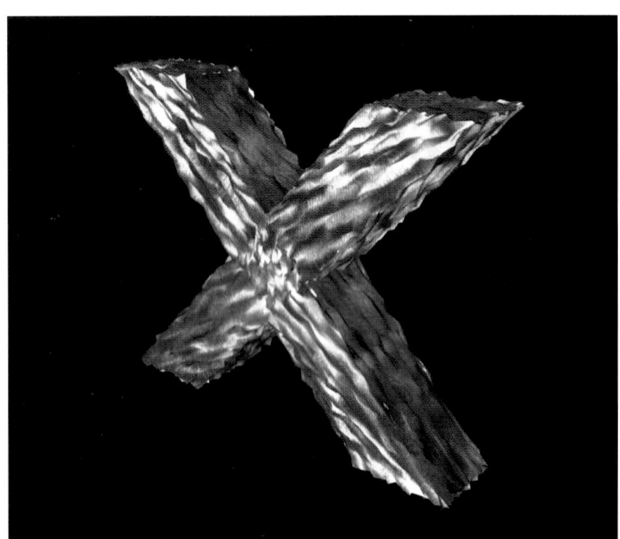

[Ca]a [Mn]–3 [Mx]3

[Ca]a [Mn]–15 [Mx]15

Crumple uses maximum and minimum settings to produce a range of intricate objects.

Summary

Optimize is part of Yost Group's IPAS3 disk #7. It enables you to increase or decrease 3D mesh complexity using tessellation or optimization, respectively. Tessellation can be performed at any of five detail levels that incrementally increase the vertex and face count. You can opt to use either positive tension, which produces convex geometry, or negative tension, which creates a concave effect. You can use Auto Edge to set the level of mesh visibility based on the angle between the surface normals of adjacent faces.

Optimize throws away selected faces based on the angles of adjacent faces and is useful for minimizing face count while maintaining the maximum level of mesh detail. Optimize also provides a bias function, which enables you to minimize generating long, thin, triangular faces. Such faces can cause problems with rendering and Boolean operations, and can make it difficult if not impossible to smoothly bend or otherwise deform a mesh.

You also can set Optimize to deal effectively with meshes that have two or more materials assigned to them. The Protect Material Boundaries function, for example, preserves the face boundaries between multiple materials.

One of Optimize's most powerful attributes is the capability to optionally embed and extract multiple versions of the mesh to the 3DS or PRJ file. This is useful for storing multiple versions with different optimization or tessellation applied. This is great when you want to imbed a complex version of an object and use it with an optimized (low resolution) version for fast screen redraws while setting up an animation. At render time you can call the complex version using MSHRES.AXP for the highest-quality render.

Optimize Parameters

Pick Object and Selected — Enables you to pick any 3D mesh object from the current 3D Studio file. The chosen mesh name appears in the Object Name field. Selected applies Optimize to only those faces selected in the 3D Editor.

Extract and Embed — Enables you to load and save multiple optimized versions to and from the 3DS or PRJ file. This can add considerably to the model's mesh storage requirements because each embedded version is roughly the size of the original.

Text Editor — Displays the 3D Studio text editor for embedding text in the current object.

Tessellate [T] 1, 2, 3, 4, 5 — Enables you to subdivide the 3D mesh with any of five levels of complexity or mesh detail.

Tension [Te] (–100–100) — Varies the mesh smoothing based on positive tension, which produces a rounding effect, or negative tension, which produces a concave effect.

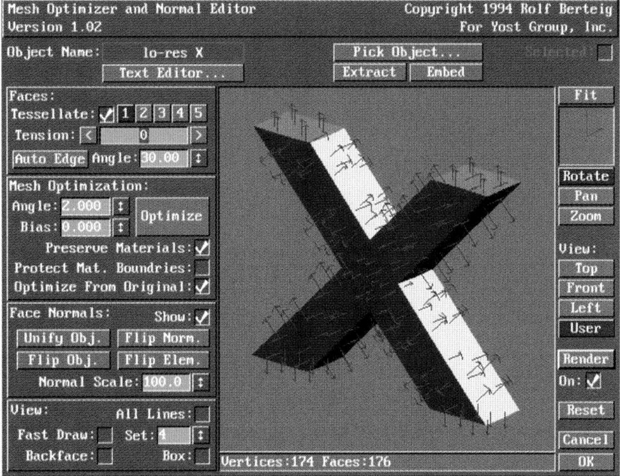

The Optimize dialog box.

Auto Edge [Ae] — Specifies the mesh visibility based on the angle between the surface normals of adjacent faces.

Optimize Angle [Oa] (0–90) — Reduces the mesh complexity of selected faces based on a specified angle. The process is based on the relative angles of the mesh's surface normals. Any face with a normal angle greater than the angle setting is not removed.

Bias [B] (0–1) — Enables you to avoid generating long, thin, triangular faces that can make deformation difficult or complicate Boolean operations. As bias is increased, thin faces are reduced.

Preserve Materials — Maintains multiple materials assignments by storing materials that might disappear during optimization.

Protect Material Boundaries — Preserves original multiple material boundaries by preventing collapsed faces, which can shift or distort the boundaries.

Optimize From Original — Bases the optimization on the original mesh rather than the one displayed in the viewport.

Face Normals [Fn] u, fn, fo, fe (unify object, flip normal, flip object, flip element, show, normal scale 0–100) — Enables you to view and manage the object's surface normals. Unify object sets the object's surface normals to the same direction, usually outward. Flip normal reverses the normals for individual faces as each blue normal vector is clicked. Flip object reverses the object's normals. Flip Element reverses the normals for all the faces of any given element. Show switches the display of blue normal vectors on and off, and normal scale sets the length of the blue normal vectors.

Geometry view controls (All Lines, Fast Draw 0–100, Backface, Box) — Specify the way geometry is displayed in the working viewport. All Lines switches the display of construction lines on and off. Fast Draw specifies the number of

OPTIMIZE cont

DSPLAC_I.PXP — **\optimize** — **Yost Group**

displayed faces. Backface switches backfaces on and off. Box switches box mode on and off. Set specifies the face detail when FastDraw is checked.

Viewport controls (Fit, Rotate, Pan, Zoom, Top, Front, Left, User) — These controls work as their 3D Studio counterparts to provide a view of the current object.

Render — Renders the current view in your choice of flat or Gouraud shading. This is set in a render preferences dialog box that is accessed by holding down the shift key and clicking on the Render button. The On button provides a dynamic rendered view as each variable is changed.

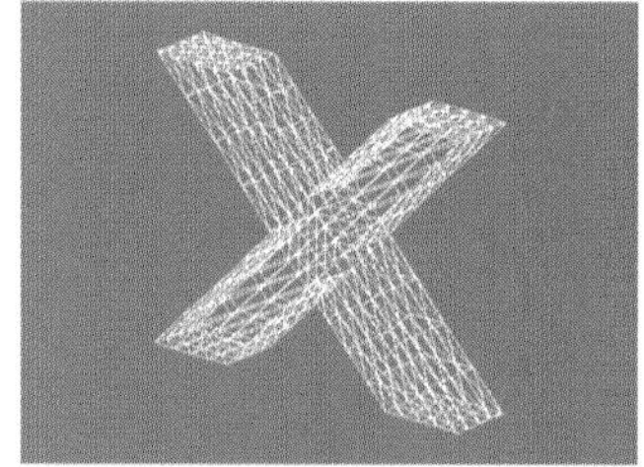

Before optimization

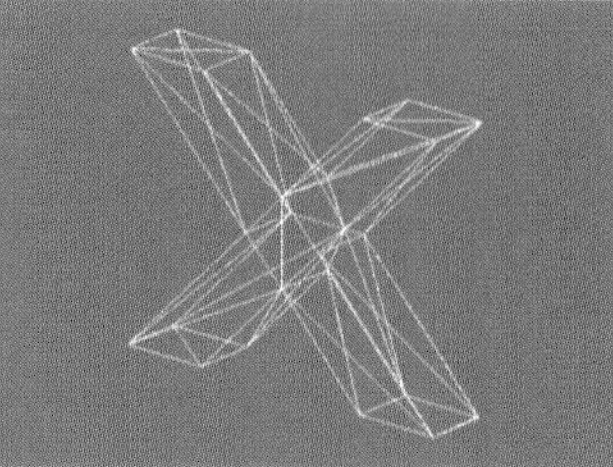

After optimization

The face count of this object was reduced from 704 to 46 with no apparent change in the mesh. Bias was set to 0. Optimize works well on complex models as well by enabling you to balance face count against object detail.

ORDER

ORDR_I.PXP — **\order** — **Schreiber Instruments**

Summary

Order is part of the Imagine Morphology package. It is a simple utility that reverses the vertex order in a mesh. This is needed for Luge (also in Morphology). Luge works by moving along a lofted object, and can only move from beginning to end. Order enables you to switch the beginning to the end of a loft by switching vertex order.

PAGE ROLL

ROLPG_I.PXP — **\pageroll** — **Schreiber Instruments**

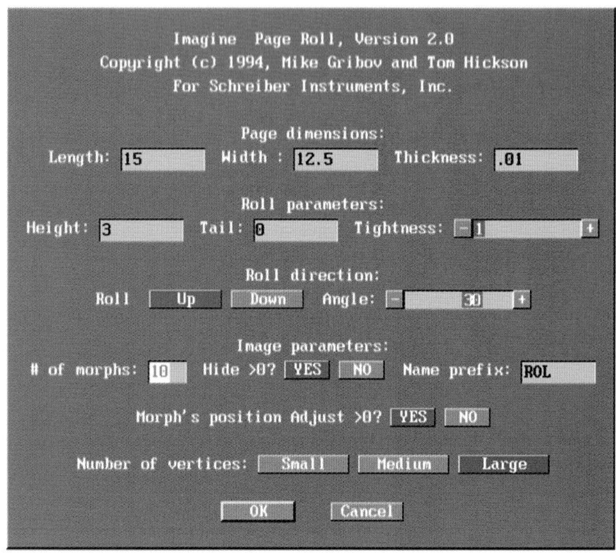

The Page Roll dialog box.

Summary

Page Roll is part of the Imagine Pages package. (Turn Page is the other plug-in in this package.) Page Roll generates a morph series to simulate a piece of paper curling from flat to a roll. You can specify the size and thickness of the sheet, the size of the roll, and which direction it rolls. The roll can be aligned with an edge or angled so that it starts at a corner.

Page Roll Parameters

Length [L] — Length of the original page.

Width [W] — Width of the original page.

Thickness [T] (.000001–.001) — Page thickness.

Roll Height [Rh] — Height of the roll.

Roll Tail [Rt] — Portion of the page that does not roll. If this is 0, the entire page will roll up.

Roll Tightness [Rti] (1–100%) — Determines how tight the gap between rolls is.

Roll direction [Rd] u, d (Up, Down) — Sets the direction of the roll.

Roll Angle [Ra] (0–45) — Shifts the roll from the edge to a corner.

# of morphs [N] (1–999) — The number of intermediate morph objects.

Hide >0 [Hd] y, n (yes, no) — Hides morph objects after the first one.

Name prefix [P] — Used to name the morph series.

Morph's position Adjust >0 [Pa] y, n (yes, no) — Adjusts the morph objects to keep their positions aligned in the keyframer.

Number of vertices [V] s, m, l (Small, Medium, Large) — Selects the level of mesh detail to control smoothness. Small produces 8 vertices along a roll, Medium produces 32 vertices, and Large produces 256 vertices.

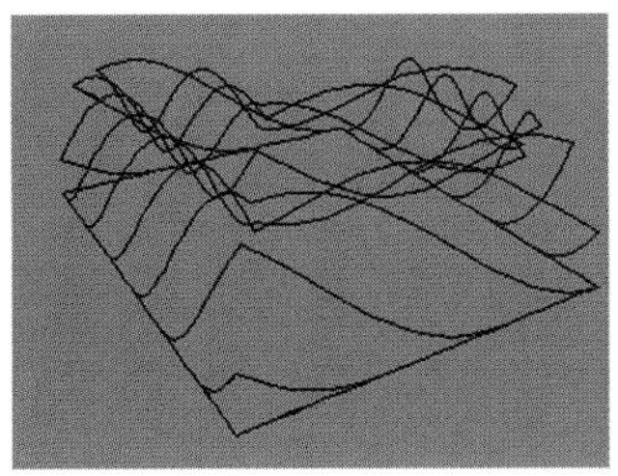
Morph wireframes

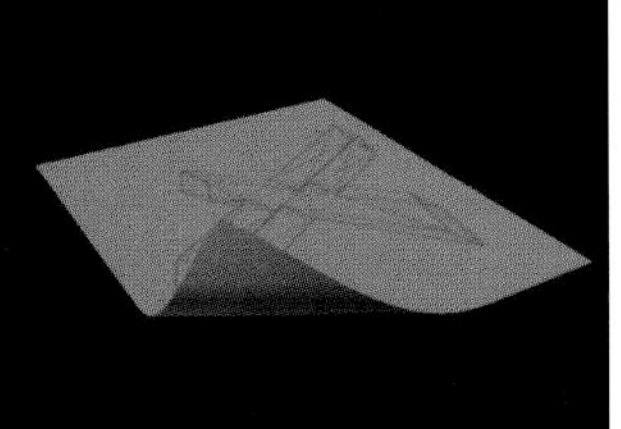
Frame 6

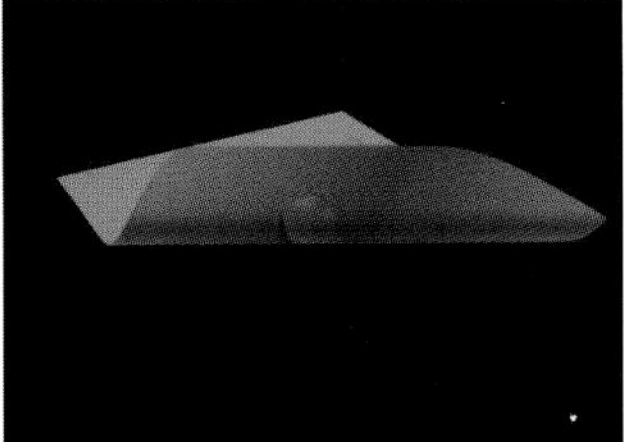
Frame 12

Frame 24

The source objects and frames from a page roll animation.

PAGE TURN

Schreiber Instruments \pageturn TRNPG_I.PXP

Summary

Page Turn is part of the Imagine Pages package. (Roll Page is the other plug-in in this package.) Page Turn generates a morph series to simulate a page from a book turning over. You can specify the size and thickness of the sheet, the size of the turn, and which direction it turns. The turn can be aligned with an edge or angled so that it starts at a corner. You can select two types of page turn: a freestanding sheet or a page from a book.

Page Turn Parameters

Length [L] — Length of the original page.

Width [W] — Width of the original page.

Thickness [T] — Page thickness.

Type [Tp] s, b (Sheet, Book) — Selects the type of page turn. Sheet turns a flat sheet, Book turns a page from a book.

Turn direction [Rd] u, d (Up, Down) — Sets the direction of the turn.

Turn Angle [Ra] (0–45) — Shifts the turn from the edge to a corner.

# of morphs [N] (1–999) — The number of intermediate morph objects.

Hide >0 [Hd] y, n (yes, no) — Hides morph objects after the first one.

Name prefix [P] — Used to name the morph series.

Morph's position adjust >0 [Pa] y, n (yes, no) — Adjusts the morph objects to keep their positions aligned in the keyframer.

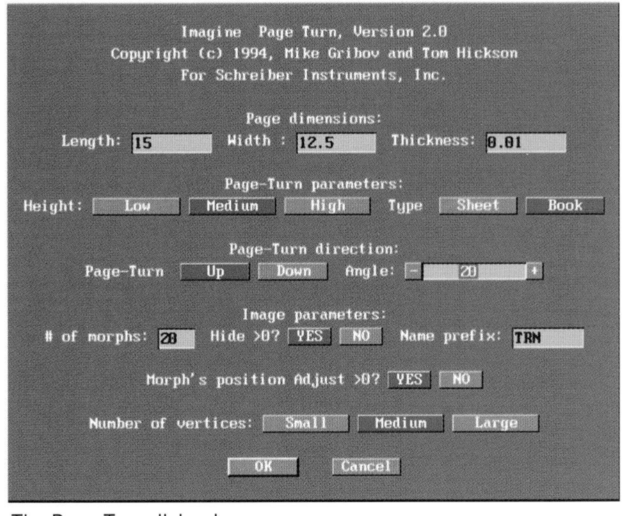

The Page Turn dialog box.

Number of vertices [V] s, m, l (Small, Medium, Large) — Selects the level of mesh detail to control smoothness. Small produces 8 vertices along a turn, Medium produces 32 vertices, Large produces 256 vertices.

PAGE TURN cont

TRNPG_I.PXP | **\pageturn** | **Schreiber Instruments**

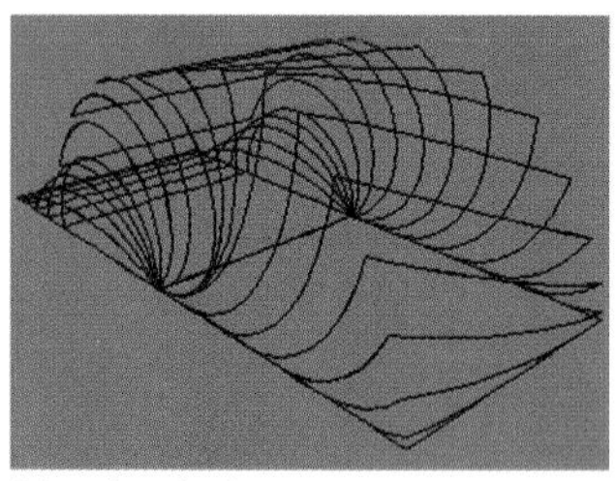
Morph wireframes

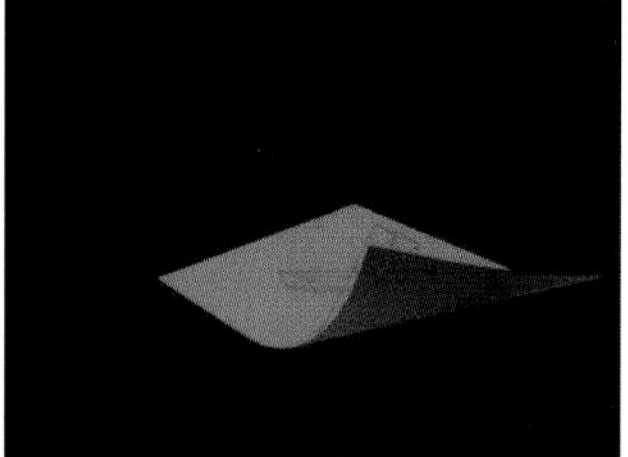
Frame 6

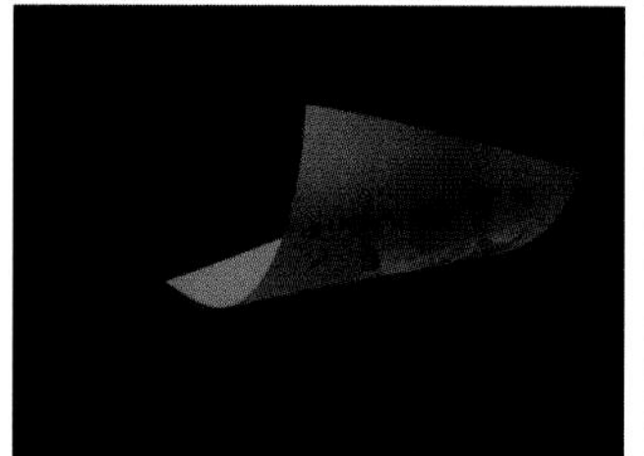
Frame 9

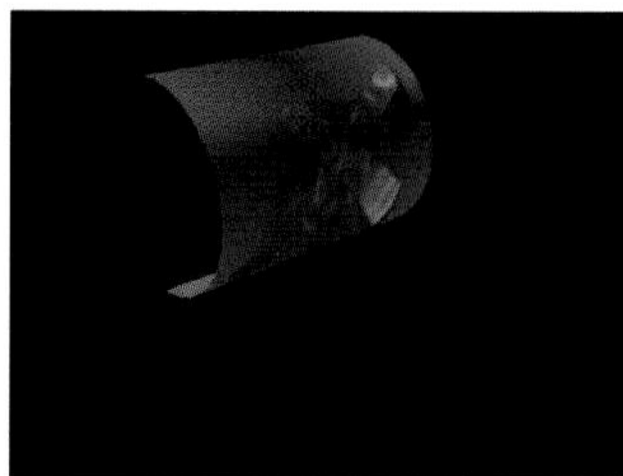
Frame 15

The source objects and frames from a page turn animation.

PAR CONTROL

PARC_I.PXP | **\parctl** | **Pyros Partnership**

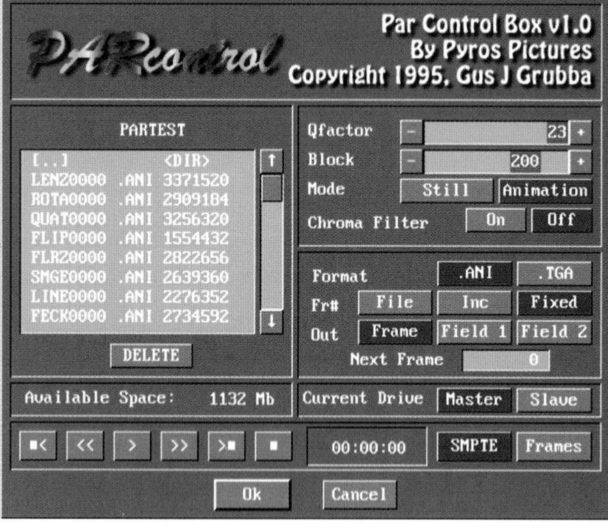

The Par Control dialog box.

Summary

Par Control enables a Personal Animation Recorder from Digital Processing Systems, Inc. to be controlled from within 3D Studio. Controls are provided to play back and delete animations stored on the PAR drive. Time can be viewed in SMPTE time code or by frames, and files from both the master and slave drives are available. Par Control also provides settings for quality and compression level for animations being output to the par from 3D Studio. Renderings saved as TGA files can be saved as still frames or animations in both frame and field mode.

Par Control Parameters

Qfactor [Q] (1–23) — Sets the amount of image compression.
Block [B] (16–255) — Sets the maximum compressed file size for each animation frame.
Mode [M] (Still, Animation) — Sets renderings to be saved as still files or animations.
Chroma Filter [C] (on, off) — Sets chroma to be limited to legal colors or saved as rendered.
Format [F] (.ANI, .TGA) — Sets PAR files to be viewed as standard PAR ANI files or TGA files. 3D Studio will not directly read ANI files.
Fr# [#] — Sets each frame to be viewed as a fixed part of an animation or each frame as a separate file. File plays back an entire ANI animation, and Fixed displays a specified frame.
Out [O] (Frame, Field 1, Field 2) — Sets whether the source animation is output in frames, field order 1, or field order 2.
Next Frame [Nf] — Sets the frame advance rate.
Current Drive [CD] (Master, Slave) — Sets the active drive to the master or slave PAR drive.

PAR IFL

Pyros Partnership | **\parifl** | **PARI_I.PXP**

Summary

Par IFL creates an image file list, or IFL, from saved on a PAR drive (Personal Animator Recorder, from Digital Processing Systems, Inc.). An IFL file is a ASCII text list of the files to be played back in sequence. This enables you to use PAR animations for animated backgrounds and materials, and with projection spotlights. The animation is chosen from the PAR directory listing window, and PAR IFL specifies a prefix as well as the number of frames in the animation. For PAR IFL to work properly, the format must be set to .TGA and the frame number must be set to File in the Par Control. The par drive and IFL file both must be set in 3D Studio map paths.

Par IFL Parameters

Name prefix [N] — Sets the four-letter prefix that each frame of the source animation begins with.

Start and End [S] [E] — Sets the beginning and ending frame of the source animation.

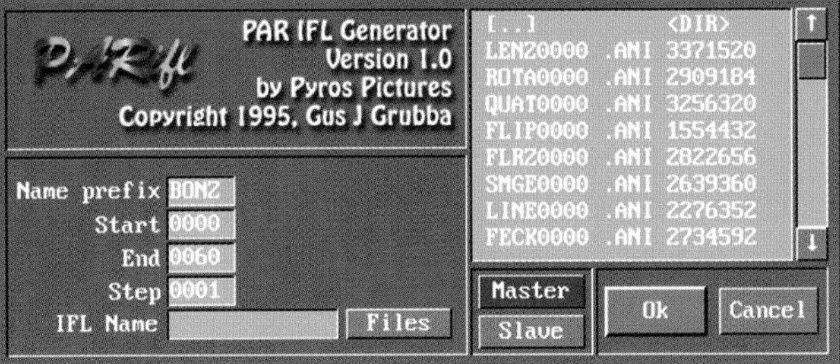

The Par IFL dialog box.

Step [ST] — Sets the frame advance rate.

IFL Name and Files [I] — Sets the IFL file name and path. The IFL file type must be added.

Master and Slave [M] [SL] — Sets whether the source animation is on the master or slave PAR drive.

PATCH MODELER

Digimation | **\bpatch** | **BPATCH_I.PXP**

Summary

Patch Modeler is a NURBS modeler that enables you to create planar and cylindrical patch objects that can be exported to 3D Studio as 3D mesh objects. Patches can be edited by adjusting the lattice of control nodes that surround each patch. You can rotate, 2D scale, 3D scale, and move individual nodes or groups of nodes, which reshape the patch. Multiple patches can be joined to form larger or more detailed objects; you cannot, however, delete a patch.

Patch Modeler provides the familiar icon panel with control over its viewports. Display and drawing aids include a display grid, grid snap, and the ability to hide the lattice while retaining view of its control nodes.

Patch objects can be exported to the 3D Editor with or without assigned smoothing groups or texture coordinates. You can import any mesh object that originated in Patch Modeler into it for further editing; however, any edits made to the geometry in the 3D Editor will be ignored by Patch Modeler. Furthermore, only one mesh object can be loaded into Patch Modeler at a time.

This summary is based on a prerelease version of Patch Modeler.

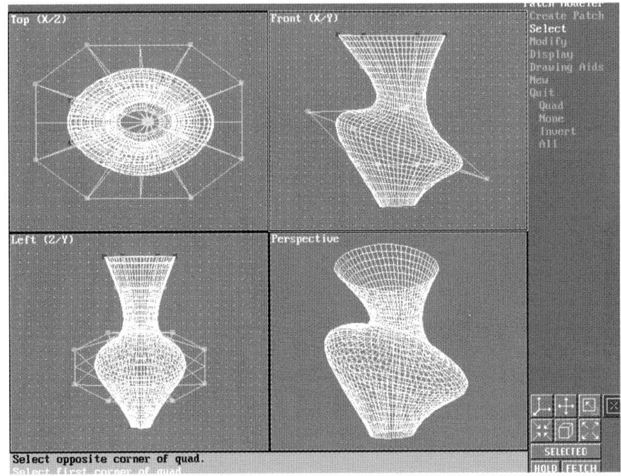

The Patch Modeler dialog box.

Patch Modeler Parameters

Create Patch (planar, cylindrical) — Creates or adds a planar or cylindrical patch and corresponding control lattice. Planar produces a planar patch and 4x4 control lattice in the XZ plane or adds a planar patch to an existing planar or cylindrical patch. Cylindrical produces a cylindrical patch and 4x8 control lattice in the XZ plane or adds a cylindrical patch to an existing cylindrical patch.

Get Mesh (Selected, By Name, Disk) — Get Mesh imports Patch Modeler geometry from the 3D Editor. The mesh object must have been created in Patch Modeler, and any edits to the geometry made in the 3d Editor are ignored. Selected imports selected objects, By Name enables you to select from a list of 3D Editor objects, and Disk loads a BEZ patch model file from disk.

Put Mesh (Scene, Disk) — Put Mesh exports Patch Modeler geometry to the 3D Editor as a 3D mesh object. Scene exports the current patch object as a 3D mesh to the current scene, and Disk saves BEZ patch model files to disk.

Select (Quad, None, Invert, All) — Enables you to create a selection set or group of lattice control nodes. Quad uses a variable window to select one or more control nodes, which are included in the current selection set. Any selected control nodes are highlighted in red. None clears the current selection set. Invert flips the selection to include all those not currently selected. All selects all control nodes in the current patch object.

Modify (Move, Rotate, 2D Scale, 3D Scale) — Enables you to edit individual control nodes or selection sets of nodes, which reshape the patch. Move translates the point anywhere in 3D space. Rotate spins two or more control nodes around their local axis or around the global axis as set by the Modify/Axis command. 2D and 3D Scale enable you to scale control nodes, relative to the local or global axes, in two or three dimensions.

Note: *You can switch between local and global axes using the Local Axis icon, located at the far right of the icon panel.*

Modify Detail (Increase, Decrease) — Incrementally sets the patch object display and mesh detail both as displayed in the Patch Modeler and as exported to the 3D Editor. Increase adds progressively more detail, and with that more geometry to the 3D mesh.

Modify Axis (Place, Show, Hide, Home) — Modify Axis enables you to position and display the global axis. Home returns the axis to the world space center: 0, 0, 0—X, Y, Z.

Display (Geometry, Lattice) — Controls the display of object vertices as either dots or ticks, and switches the control lattice on or off.

Drawing Aids (Grid, Snap, Node, Vertical Snap) — Controls the various editing aids such as grid display, snap modes, and the display size of control notes.

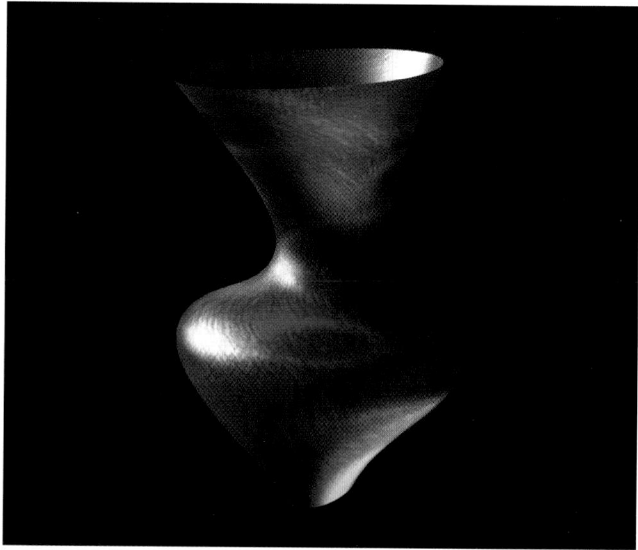

Patch Modeler enables you to create and edit NURBS geometry for export into the 3D Editor as a mesh object.

PLACE

Yost Group | **\place** | **PLACE_I.PXP**

Summary

Place is part of Yost Group's IPAS Disk #5. It places one object on the surface of another. The main use for this plug-in is to place objects such as trees on an irregular surface like a terrain. When you execute Place, it asks you to select the surface for placement, then for the object to place. After they are selected, Place copies the placed object and calculates the center of the base of the copy. It then locates this point on the surface and puts the object copy there.

Several objects on an irregular terrain
Place puts one object precisely on the surface of another.

PUPPETEER

Schreiber Instruments | **\puppeter** | **PUPPET_I.PXP**

Summary

Puppeteer is a character animation and motion control program that enables you to create, capture, or edit motion data. It works directly with Ascension Technology's Flock of Birds or from any of a number of predefined motion files. A Puppeteer puppet can represent the motion of any character or machine, from humans or dragons to dancing pickup trucks or swaying cityscapes.

Puppeteer's process is based on the use of nodes, links, joints, and joint restrictions, which form a constraints-based skeletal object called a puppet. The base object in any puppet is the node, which is a point that can move anywhere in 3D space but can never rotate. A link is a connection between two nodes. Links can change position and rotation. A joint consists of the planar or spherical motion restrictions that relate one or more links.

The Puppeteer user interface assumes the entire 3D Studio screen and duplicates the structure and several of the Keyframer's view and menu functions. It consists of a menu bar along the top, icons down the left side, a command column, an icon panel for view control, and the animation frame slider along the bottom.

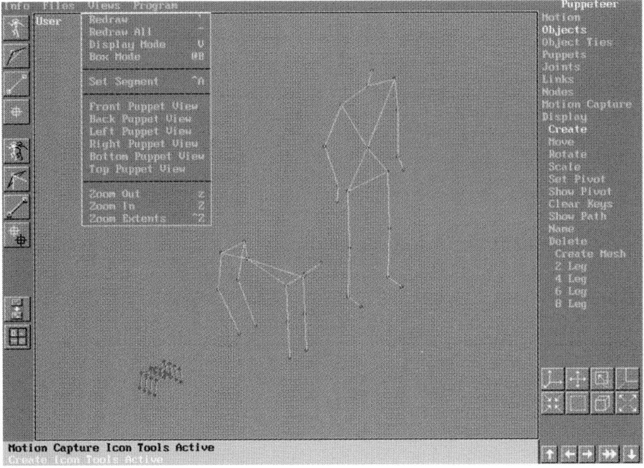

The Puppeteer dialog box.

The menu bar is divided into Info, Files, Views, and Program pull-down menus. These combine to provide essential information and access to motion and mesh files as well as view controls such as zoom and redraw.

The icons in the vertical icon column along the left side of the screen function differently depending upon whether the right or left mouse button is used to highlight them. The icons duplicate many of the more commonly used commands that are also available through the command column located at the right of the viewports. The upper eight icons can be switched through three sets of commands– create, animate, and motion capture.

Puppeteer's command column works the same as 3D Studio's command columns, and provides access to all puppet create and editing functions along with motion capture and setup.

The program also provides a number of keyboard shortcuts for speeding view control and editing functions.

Puppeteer Pull-Down Menus

Info (About Puppeteer, Configuration, Scene Info) — Sets the motion file path, object file path, and pick resolution for the current Puppeteer session. Scene provides scene information including mesh object, puppet, and joint count.

Files (New, Load, Merge, Save, Import Meshes, Export Meshes, Load Motion Data, Quit) — Enables you to reset, load, merge, and save several types of motion and mesh data files that contain Puppeteer entities and motion. Import loads 3D mesh objects and any associated keyframes. This includes parent and dummy objects for any objects with hierarchical links. Export sends a mesh object to the 3D Editor along with current position, orientation, material references, mapping, vertex, and face information. Load Motion Data loads DAT (Flock of Birds ASCII) and TRC (Motion Analysis ASCII) formats.

Views (Redraw, Redraw All, Display Mode, Box Mode, Set Segment, Zoom Out, Zoom In, Zoom Extents) — Controls display functions including the capability to switch between full draw and fast view modes as well as box mode, which displays all meshes as a bounding box. Set Segment defines the current animation segment.

Program (Text Editor) — Displays the 3D Studio text editor, which enables you to edit ASCII motion control files.

Puppeteer Command Column

Motion (Move Node, Lock Node, Unlock Node, Weighted Node, Weightless, Lock Joint, Unlock Joint, Suspend Link, Activate Link, Adjust Keys, Clr Node Keys) — These commands, many of which are available from the vertical icon column (animation icons), are used to animate a puppet. Move drags any attached nodes along with the selected node. Lock Node enables you to lock connected nodes during move operations. Weighted affects the motion of a node by adding drag as it is moved. Suspend Link enables moves to distort the distance between nodes. Adjust Keys adjusts the length of any motion sequence for removing a motion segment, creating slow motion, or repeating motion segments. Clear Node Keys removes all keyframes from the selected node or range of nodes.

Objects (Create, Move, Rotate, Scale, Set Pivot, Show Pivot, Clear Keys, Show Path, Name, Delete) — Enables you to create a mesh object by revolving it around a selected link. You can then move, rotate, scale, or edit the object's pivot point and name. Show Path switches the object's motion path.

Object Ties (Tie Mesh, Show Ties, Remove Ties, Center Pivot, Pivot At Tie, Move To Tie, Toggle Update, Hide Tied, Update Objects) — Defines the relation of mesh objects to a puppet. Tie Mesh enables you to tie a mesh to a node, link, or set of links, thus defining how the mesh moves as the puppet moves. Center Pivot centers the pivot point at the mesh center. Move To Tie translates the object to the tie pivot. Update Objects updates the rotation and position keyframes for all mesh objects based on the current ties.

Puppets (Create, Move, Rotate, Scale, Adjust, Center Pivot, Attach, Remove, Name, Create All, Delete All, Delete, Orientation, Interp Node, Copy Motion) — These commands create, define, and edit a collected group of links or a puppet. Adjust enables you to rename and change the puppet's color. Attach lets you attach additional links to a puppet. Copy motion is used to copy and scale the motion from one puppet relative to the scale of another.

Joints (Define, Lock, Unlock, Suspend, Activate, Adjust, Name, Delete) — Enables you to define and edit joint parameters. You can specify planar, spherical, or locking and define joint restrictions for each.

Links (Create, Move, Adjust, Suspend, Activate, Name, Delete) — Enables you to create and adjust the links that describe the structure of the nodes. Adjust enables you to change the color of any link. Suspend allows move and rotate edits to distort the distance between two nodes. Activate makes the link rigid.

Nodes (Create, Move, Display, Adjust, Lock, Unlock, Weighted, Weightless, Show Path, Name, Delete) — Enable you to create and define nodes that describe puppet motion. Weighted affects the motion of a node by adding drag as it is moved.

Motion Capture (Serial Setup, FOB Setup, Point Capture, Stream Capture, Reduce Data, Load Motion, Editor) — Setup for motion capture port and hardware. Serial Setup selects and sets the serial port to the proper baud rate.

Display (Hide, Unhide, Puppet Views, Geometry) — Specifies which objects and entities are displayed along with the view type. You can hide or unhide all, all objects, selected objects, all puppets, selected puppets, joints, links, and nodes. Geometry can be displayed in box mode, fast draw, or full draw.

Summary

QuickDraw is part of the Imagine 3DTurbo package. It hides the edges between the faces of a mesh based on the angle between the faces. This has the effect of reducing visual clutter on the screen and speeding up screen redraws. No geometry is changed. It only affects whether edges are visible or not. This is exactly the same function performed by the 3D Studio Release 3 and 4 command sequence Modify/Edge/AutoEdge.

QuickDraw Parameters

Select Object(s) [S] n, p (By Name, Pick Single) — You can pick a single object from the screen or select multiple objects by name.

Statistics [St] — Choosing this button displays a scrollable list of the selected objects with their face and vertex counts.

Hide operation [H] h, u (Hide Edges, Unhide All) — Selects whether to hide edges or to make all edges visible.

Percent off Co-Planar [P] (0–100) — Hides edges based on the angle between two faces. A value of 0 hides only edges between completely coplanar faces. A value of 50 hides edges between faces with angles of up to 90 degrees. You can set the value by using the slider or by typing a value.

Object creation [O] m, c (Modify Existing, Create New) — Selects whether the program will modify the existing mesh or create a copy.

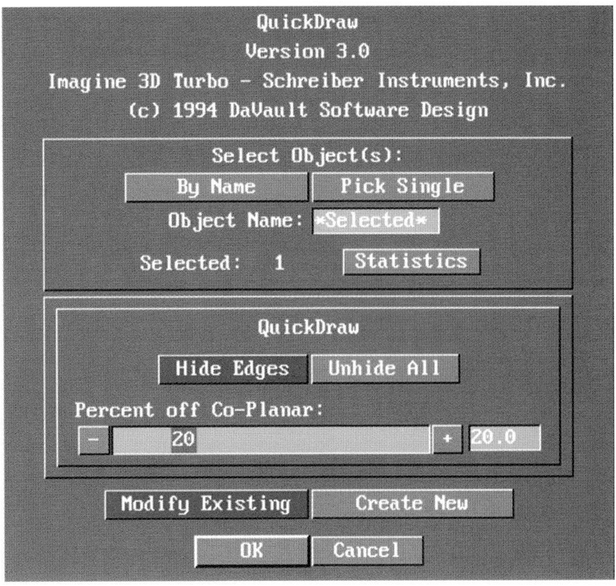

The QuickDraw dialog box.

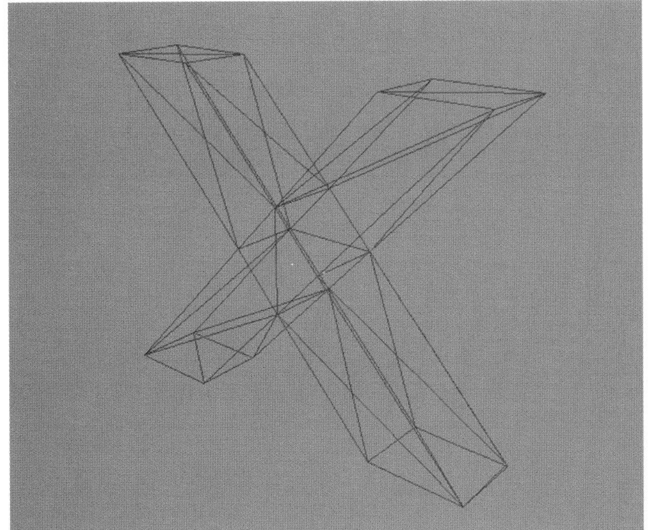

Original mesh

Cleaned mesh

Coplanar edges cleaned up with QuickDraw.

RADIAL MORPH

RADIAL_I.PXP **\morph** **Schreiber Instruments**

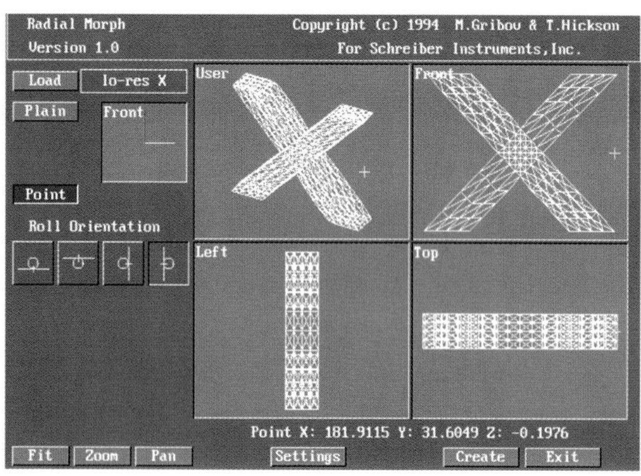

The Radial Morph dialog box.

Summary

Radial Morph is part of the Imagine Morphology package. Radial Morph rotates an object's vertices around a specified point and creates an animated bending of the object using morph targets. This point can be moved to any location in 3D space, and objects can be rotated in the user view to further control the direction of the bend. A series of buttons allow the object rotation to be specified in relation to the front view. Morph targets are then generated to animate the effect. Targets for each frame of the animated effect are necessary in order to produce a smooth morph.

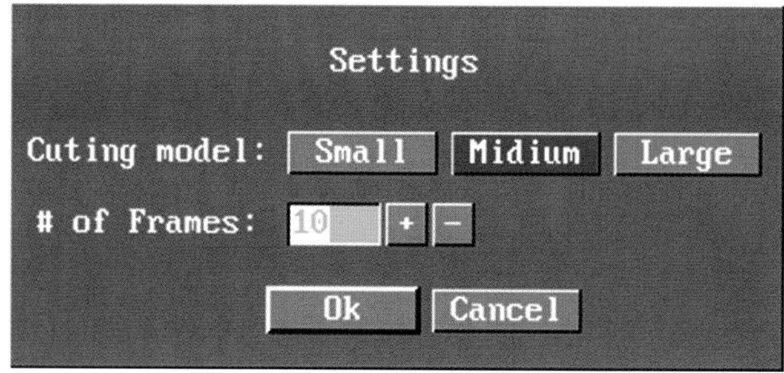

The Settings dialog box.

Radial Morph Parameters

Load [L] — Loads the source object for radial deformation.
Plain [P] — Sets the object's plane of orientation in the user view.
Point [PT] — Sets the location of the point of rotation.
Roll Orientation [R] (up, down, left, right) — Sets the direction the object will be rolled in relation to the point of rotation.

Settings Parameters

Cuting model [C] (Small, Midium, Large) — Sets the number of sections into which the object will be divided when it is cut for bending.
# of Frames [#] — Sets the number of frames and number of morph targets that will be generated.

Frame 1

Frame 4

Frame 7

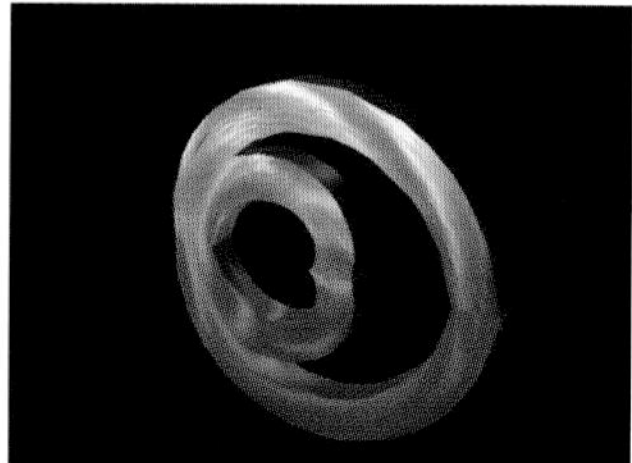

Frame 10

Radial Morph rotates an object's vertices around a specified point and creates an animated bending of the object using morph targets.

Summary

Reshape is part of Yost Group's Special Effects Procedural Modeling disk #3. Reshape uses a template consisting of a copy of a 3D mesh object as a control hull to smoothly modify the original object's form. The template is produced in a single step with no parameters and creates two copies of the original object. The first copy is aligned to the original and the second is offset 100 units in the Y axis. All edits are performed on the first template copy, with the second hidden for use as a backup.

The template can be adjusted by modifying any vertex, vertex group, or its faces. Reshape uses these adjustments to determine how the mesh will be interpolated into a smoothed object or series of objects. The final steps include setting the tension, range, influence, and magnitude parameters using the Reshape dialog box. These parameters enable you specify a range of stretching effects from those which very closely reflect the template adjustments to using the template points as magnetic effectors. This yields sharper to softer results, respectively.

If you opt to produce more than a single object, the wave deformation is distributed incrementally along the object series. Because the resulting objects have the same vertex count as the original, they can be used as morph objects, thus making them useful for creating transition effects that animate a given surface from rough to smooth, for instance.

For Reshape to function properly it must have an adequate number of evenly distributed faces from which to work. Furthermore, Reshape often requires that you tessellate the original object several times; Create/Object/Tessellate/Edge with edge tension set to 0 works well.

Reshape Parameters

Reshape Options (Create Template, Set Parameters) — Create Template produces a template object in a single step. Set Parameters enables you to set Reshape's various parameters in the Reshape Parameters dialog box.

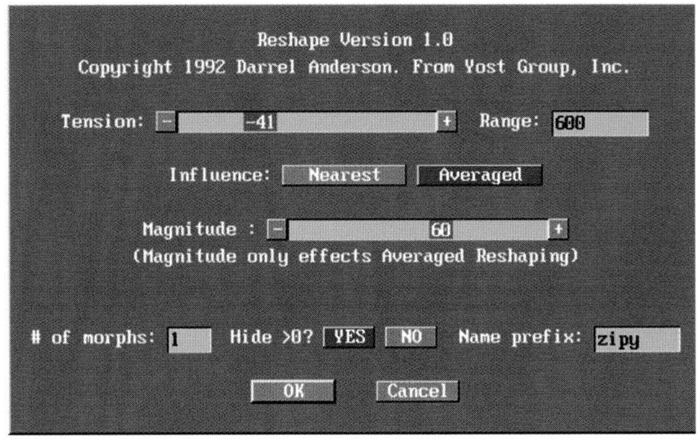

The Reshape dialog box.

Tension [T] (–100–100) — Specifies the amount of spline interpolation, with a value of 0 being linear, <0 convex, and >0 concave.

Range [R] — Specifies the size of the effect area around the moved vertices.

Influence [I] n, a (Nearest, Averaged) — Sets the type of reshaping. Nearest produces a precise result with the moved vertices maintaining their exact locations. Average uses the vertices like magnets that affect the surface more generally.

Magnitude [Ma] (0–100%) — When using averaged influence, sets the extent of the reshape.

# of morphs [M] — Specifies the number of morph objects or Reshape objects that will be created. This enables you to apply the deformation in stepped increments.

Hide >0 (yes, no) — Specifies whether to hide all but the first morph object.

Name prefix — Sets the four-character prefix for the objects produced by Reshape.

RESHAPE cont

RESHAP_I.PXP \reshape **Yost Group**

Wireframes

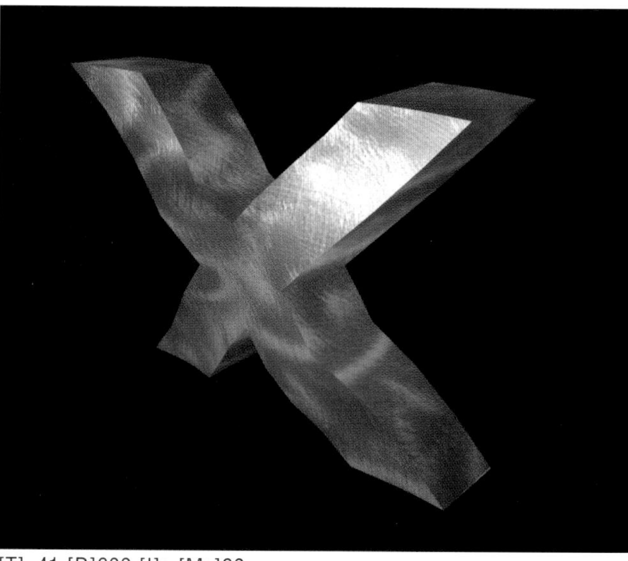

[T]–41 [R]600 [I]a [Ma]60

Reshape uses a copy of the original 3D mesh object (shown in red) as a control hull to deform and produce a morphable 3D mesh object or series of objects.

RIPPLE

RIPPLE_I.PXP \ripple **Autodesk**

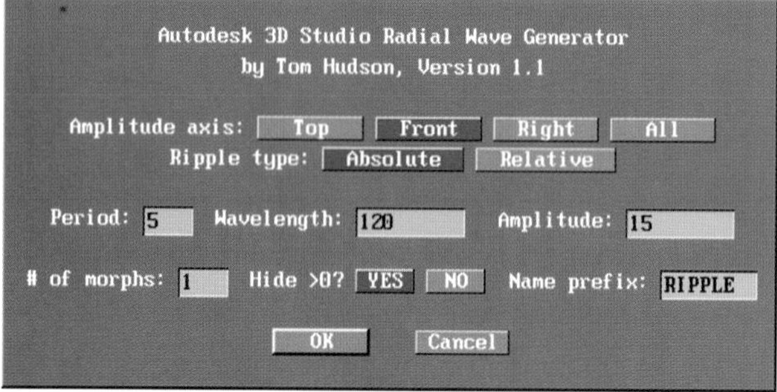

The Ripple dialog box.

Summary

Included with 3D Studio Release 4, Ripple applies a concentric or radial sine wave deformation to any 3D mesh object. You can apply the effect through any individual object axis or all axes simultaneously, and you can specify the period, wavelength, and amplitude, which combine to shape and vary the deformation. The ripple origin can be set as either the center of the mesh object you want to deform or as the center of any alternative 3D object. This enables you to place the ripple origin anywhere relative to the affected object.

Ripple also produces morph targets and can be used to produce cyclic animated ripples.

Ripple Parameters

Amplitude axis [Aa] t, f, r, a (top, front, right, all) — Specifies the axis to which the ripple will be applied. Top applies the ripple parallel to the XZ plane, front applies the ripple parallel to the XY plane, and right applies the ripple parallel to the ZY plane. All applies the ripple through X, Y, and Z combined.

Ripple type [Rt] a, r (Absolute, Relative) — Absolute applies the deformation such that the ripple amplitude moves the object vertices only in line with the selected wave axis. Relative applies the deformation such that the amplitude moves the vertices on a 3D vector away from the selected center point.

Period [P] — The time in frames for the ripple to complete one cycle. The period must be greater than one for animation.

Wavelength [W] — The radius of a single ripple for one period.

Amplitude [A] — The height of the ripple.
# of morphs [M] — Specifies the number of morph objects that will be created. This enables you to apply the deformation in stepped increments or to animate Ripple.

Hide >0 (yes, no) — Hides all but the first morph object.
Name prefix — Sets the name prefix for the morph objects produced by Ripple.

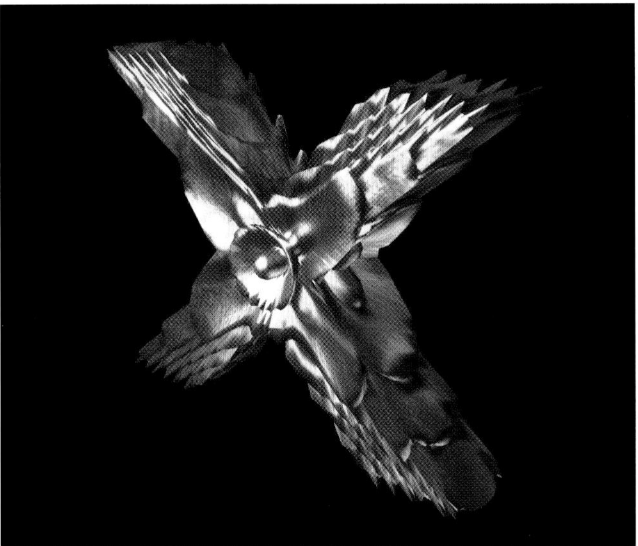

[Aa]t [Rt]r [P]10 [W]10 [A]15
Ripple applies a concentric wave function to a 3D mesh object.

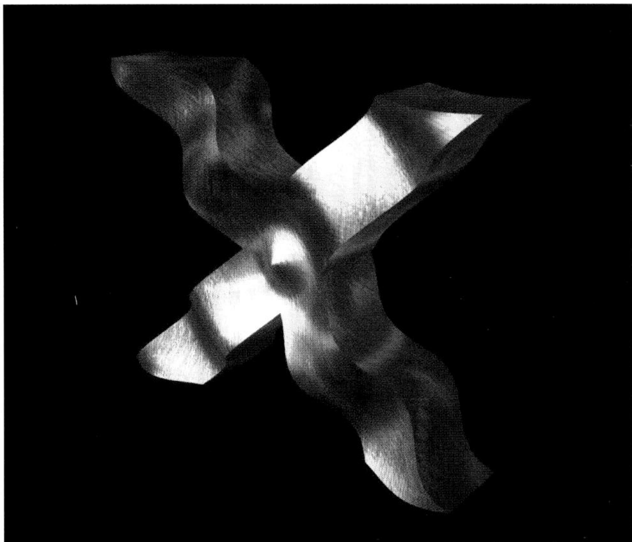

[Aa]f [Rt]a [P]5 [W]120 [A]15

SCATTER

SCATTR_I.PXP **\scatter** **Yost Group**

The Scatter dialog box.

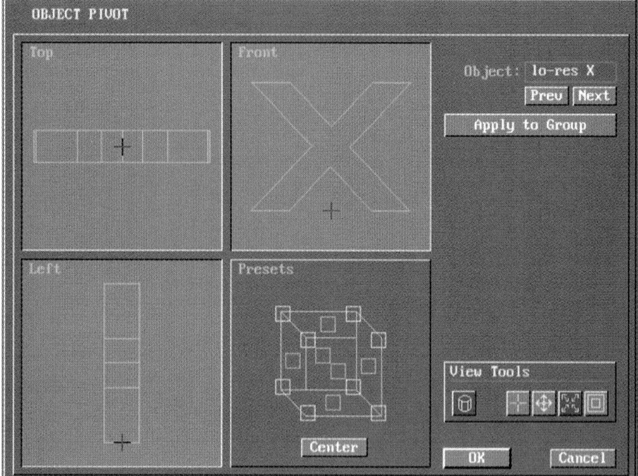

The Object Pivot dialog box.

Summary

Scatter is part of Yost Group's IPAS3 disk #6. Scatter produces a variety of arrays from single or multiple source objects. These object arrays are distributed as clusters in 3D space or positioned relative to the surface of a specified distribution object. Transformations for rotation, translation, and scaling can be applied independently in the X, Y, and Z axes. Transformations are applied randomly to produce a range of variation of size and orientation in the scattered objects. You also can apply vertex chaos, which displaces scattered object vertices for even greater variation.

Source and distribution objects are chosen from any object in the current 3D Studio mesh or project file. You also can use multiple object groups, which must be specified as sequentially named objects such as zany001, zany002, zany003. This enables you to scatter dissimilar objects while preserving the individual pivot points of each. Source objects can be spaced randomly, evenly, or by specified numbers of faces, and you also can specify that each object be rotated perpendicular to the distribution object.

If you opt to produce more than a single object, the Scatter morphs vertex chaos and transformation values only and distributes them incrementally along the specified number of objects.

Scatter Parameters

Source Object Options [So] u, n, s, vc (Use Group, Number of duplicates, Relative Scale, Vertex Chaos) — Sets the options for the object or objects that will be arrayed or scattered. Use Group specifies the use of a sequentially named group (such as zany0000, zany0001, zany0002). Number of duplicates and Relative Scale specify the number of objects that will be scattered and their scale relative to the original. Vertex Chaos produces random vertex displacement, which produces a range of variation from object to object.

Distribution Object Options [Do] sr, se, sn, p, sf (Spacing Random, Spacing Even, Spacing Nth, Perpendicular, Selected Faces) — Sets the options for the object that the source objects will be scattered on. Random, Even, and Nth spacing scatter the source object randomly, based on the total number of distribution object faces, or spaced by every nth face. When Perpendicular is on, source objects are forced to be perpendicular to their associated faces; when Perpendicular is off, source objects are placed at their original orientation. Selected Faces uses the faces selected in the 3D Editor.

Number of Morphs [M] — Specifies the number of morph objects or Stretch objects that will be created. This enables you to apply the deformation in stepped increments.

Prefix — Sets the name prefix for the morph objects produced by Scatter.

Hide Morphs — Hides all but the first morph object.

Bound Morphs — Prevents random movement of the distributed objects during a morph animation.

Object Pivot Options — Displays the Object Pivot dialog box, from which you can interactively set the object pivot point for the source object.

Rotate W, H, D, and Equal [Rw] [Rh] [Rd] (0–180°) [Re] — Sets the rotation values independently along the horizontal, vertical, and depth axes for the source objects. Equal forces the same value for each.

Translate W, H, D, and Equal [Tw] [Th] [Td] (0–180°) [Te] — Sets the translation values independently for horizontal, vertical, and depth axes of the source objects. Equal forces the same value for each.

Scale W, H, D, Equal, and Aspect [Sw] [Sh] [Sd] (0–180°) [Se] — Sets the scale values independently for horizontal, vertical, and depth for the source objects. Equal forces the same value for each, and Aspect maintains the proportions of the original.

Preferences — Specifies custom interface colors and a random seed number used to calculate random transformations.

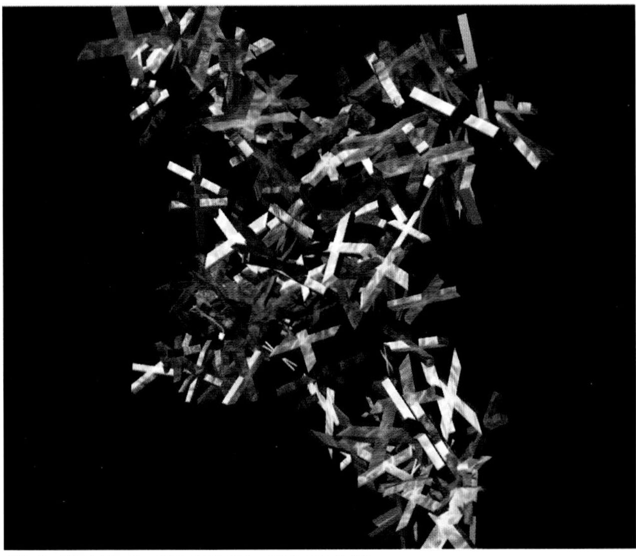

[So]n200 [Do]p [Rh]45 [Rw]90 [Rd]45

[So]n200 vc5

Scatter copies and translates a source object over a specified distribution object. Translation and Vertex chaos values can be independently varied to produce a range of effects.

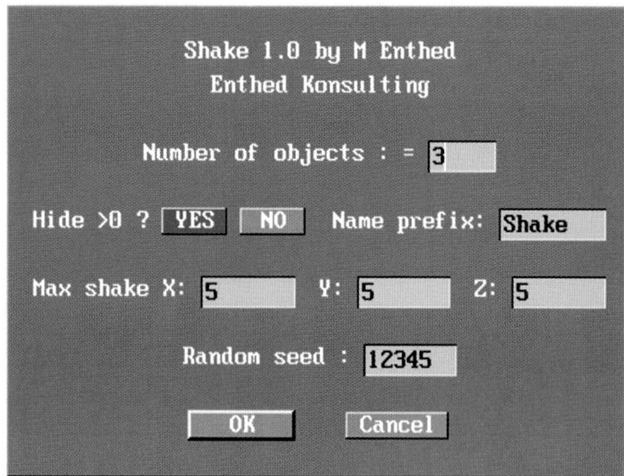

The Shake dialog box.

Summary

Shake is part of the Ent Tools package. It creates one or more copies of an object with the vertices randomly shifted. This produces effects ranging from a slight roughening of the surface to complete scrambling of the original object. You can then morph between the resulting objects, producing an animation of an object that shakes (or contorts). You can limit the vertex displacement to one or more axes.

Shake Parameters

Number of objects [N] (1–9,999) — The number of copies to make.
Hide >0 [H] y, n (yes, no) — Hides all copies after the first one.
Name prefix [P] — Specifies the first four letters of the name used for the object series.
Max shake X, Y, Z [Mx] [My] [Mz] (0–999,999) — The maximum displacement in each axis.
Random seed [R] — A random number seed that enables you to change or reproduce a given random sequence.

[X]2 [Y]2 [Z]2
Shake randomly shifts vertices.

[X]20 [Y]20 [Z]20

SHAKE cont

Enthed Animation | **\shake** | **SHAKE_I.PXP**

[X]0 [Y]10 [Z]0
Shake randomly shifts vertices.

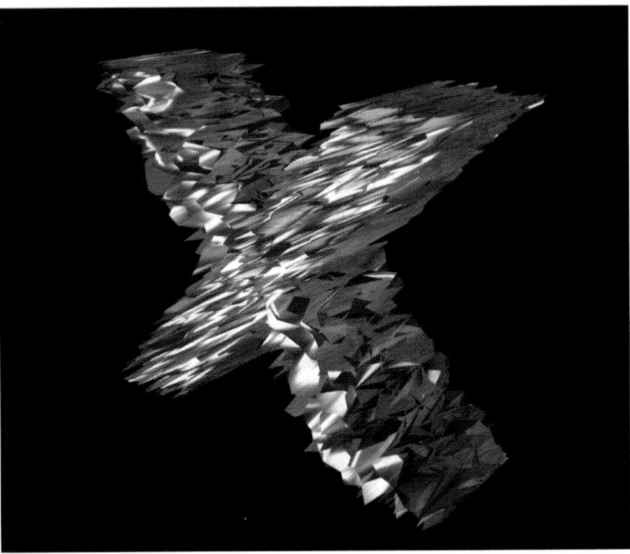

[X]0 [Y]0 [Z]80

SILICON GARDEN

Yost Group | **\garden** | **SG_I.PXP**

Summary

Silicon Garden is part of Yost Group's IPAS Disk #5. It uses adjustable patterns to grow trees, bushes, flowers, and repetitive structures. You can set options for gravity, wind strength, overall scale, and random seed number. You also can select whether geometry is optimized or whether vertex counts remain the same for different settings within a pattern type. This enables you to generate objects under different wind and gravity settings that can be morphed.

There are five types of tree patterns available. Willow, deciduous, evergreen, and tropical generate complex three-dimensional trees with detailed controls. Forest uses simple crossed planes with texture and opacity maps to generate a random forest of trees. You can set the size and density of the forest as well as whether it is composed of evergreens, deciduous, or mixed species.

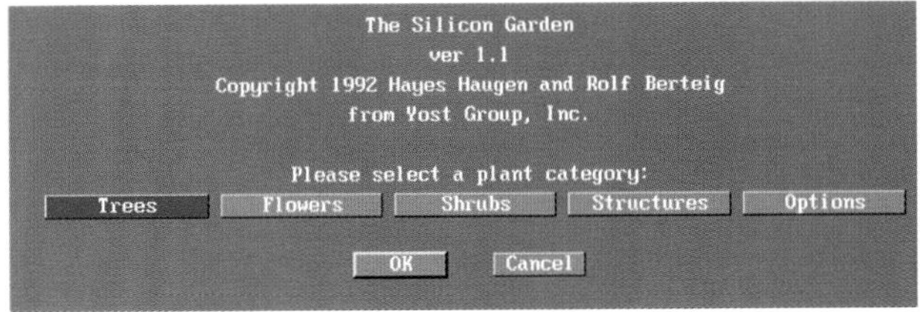

The Silicon Garden dialog box.

The five types of flower patterns—campion, mycelis, rose, sunflower, and a generic flowering bush—provide user control of size and flower color. The shrubs provide controls for size, complexity, and proportion. The shrub types are oil palm, fern, reed, rhododendron, and a generic shrub.

The structure category contains chains, chain link fence, 2D and 3D spirals, a 3D Hilbert curve, and four kinds of 2D fractal lattices.

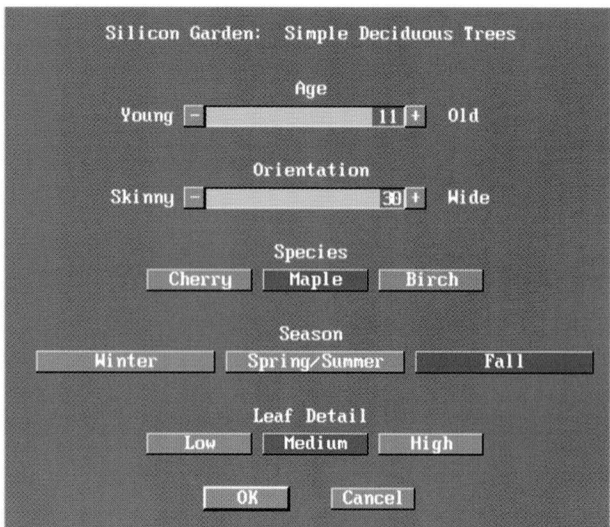

The Deciduous Tree dialog box.

Silicon Garden Parameters

Category [C] t, f, sh, st, o (Trees, Flowers, Shrubs, Structures, Options) — Selects one of the pattern families or options.

Deciduous Tree Parameters

Age [A] (5–11) — The age of the tree. This affects the size, shape, and complexity.

Orientation [O] (0–30) — Determines the proportion of width to height of the tree. A higher number makes a wider tree.

Species [S] c, m, b (Cherry, Maple, Birch) — Selects one of three species. This affects the foliage shape, bark color, and trunk thickness.

Season [Se] w, s, f (Winter, Spring/Summer, Fall) — Selects the season represented. This affects the foliage's color and presence.

Leaf detail [L] l, m, h (Low, Medium, High) — Controls the method used to generate leaves. Low produces simple leaves of a minimal diamond-shaped geometry with no texture mapping. Medium uses realistic texture maps with opacity maps on simple geometry. High uses complex geometry with texture maps.

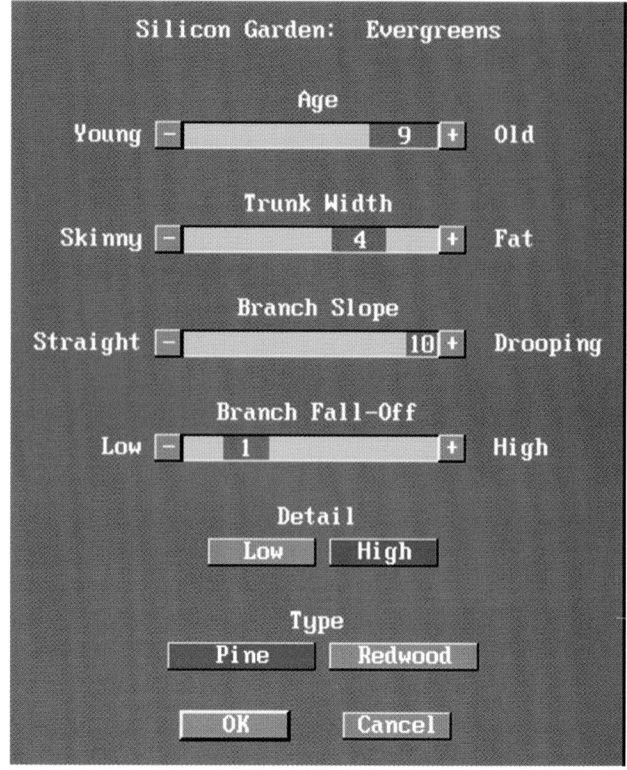

The Evergreen Tree dialog box.

Evergreen Tree Parameters

Age [A] (6–9) — The age of the tree. This affects the size, shape, and complexity.

Trunk Width [Tw] (1–5) — Determines the width of the trunk and branches.

Branch Slope [Bs] (0–10) — Causes the branches to droop by the specified amount.

Branch Fall-Off [Bf] (0–5) — Simulates the loss of lower branches on some evergreens. Larger numbers drop more branches.

Detail [D] l, h (Low, High) — Controls the detail of branches and trunks. High is needed if the branches are to curve.

Type [T] p, r (Pine, Redwood) — Selects one of two evergreen species. This affects the needle and bark texture maps.

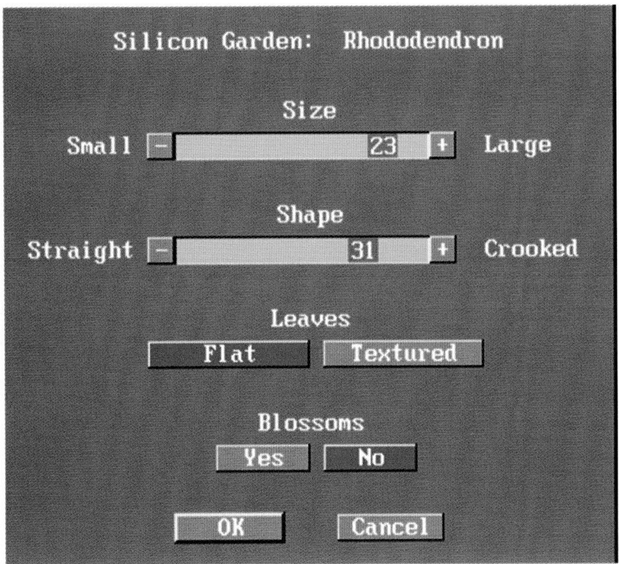

A Shrubs dialog box.

Rhododendron Shrub Parameters

Size [Sz] (10–25) — Determines the size and complexity of the bush.

Shape [Sh] (0–40) — Selects the degree of crookedness in the branching pattern. Larger numbers mean more crooked branches.

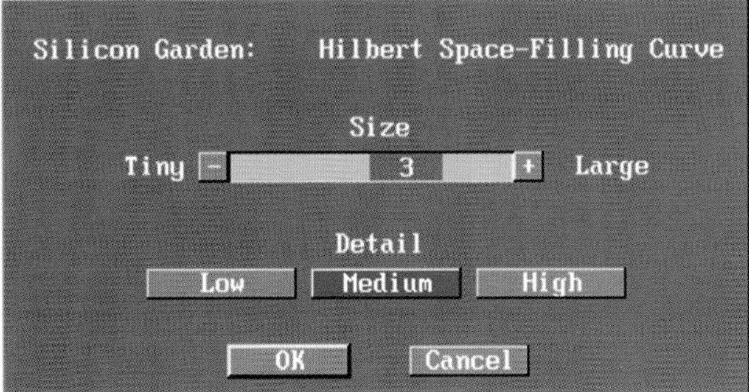

A Structures dialog box.

Leaves [L] f, t (Flat, Textured) — Selects between basic diamond-shaped leaves and simple planes with opacity-mapped realistic textures.

Blossoms [Bl] y, n (yes, no) — Controls the generation of geometry-based blossoms.

Hilbert Curve Structure Parameters

Size [Sz] (1–4) — Determines the number of iterations of the pattern and its overall size.

Detail [D] l, m, h (Low, Medium, High) — Selects one of three detail levels for the segments. Low uses three-sided tubes, Medium uses four-sided tubes, and High uses seven-sided tubes. The corners are open.

[A]11 [O]30 [S]m [Se]f [L]m

[A]9 [Tw]4 [Bs]10 [Bf]1 [D]h [T]p [Sz]23 [Sh]31

Maple and pine generated by Silicon Garden.

SILICON GARDEN cont

SG_I.PXP **\garden** **Yost Group**

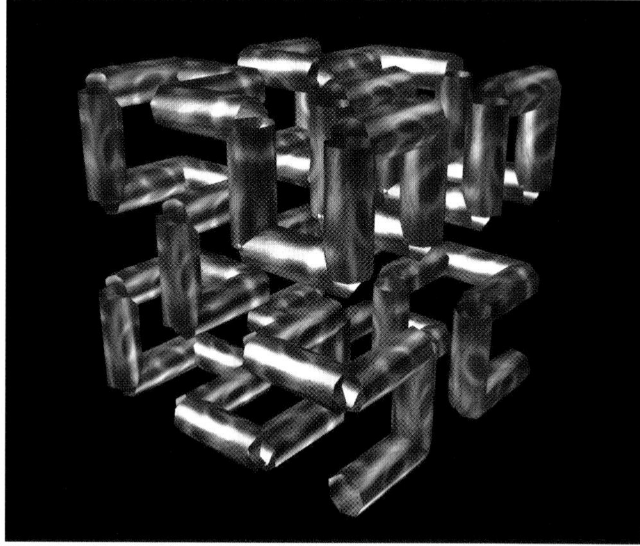

[L]t [Bl]y [Sz]1 [D]h

Rhododendron and space-filling curve generated by Silicon Garden.

SIZE

SIZE_I.PXP **\size** **Enthed Animatio**

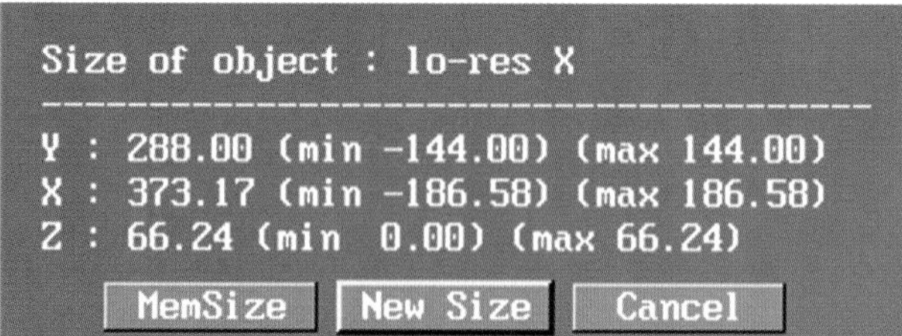

The Size dialog box.

Summary

Size is a part of the Ent Tools package. Size reports the X,Y, and Z dimensions of a selected object, along with its maximum and minimum world space dimensions. Dimensions are provided in 3D Studio units. You can display the memory required to construct and render a single object as well as the accumulated memory requirements for rendering a group of objects. Size also lists an object's total number of vertices and faces. the memory size functions do not include the memory requirements for object materials or maps.

Size Parameters

MemSize — Displays the object's memory information.

New Size — Prompts you to select a new object about which to display information.

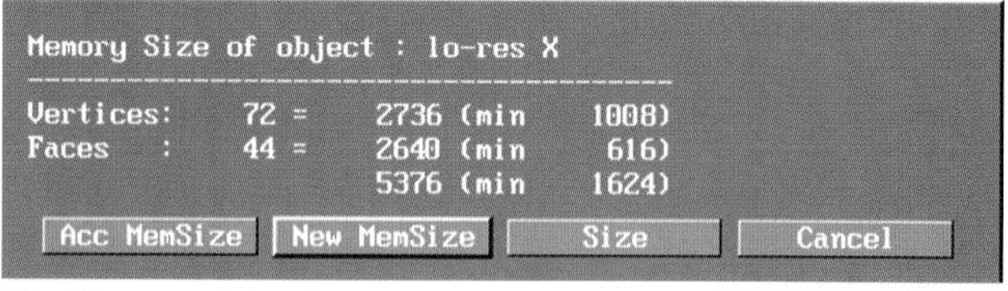

The Memory dialog box.

Memory Parameters

Acc MemSize — Displays the cumulative memory required by all objects selected this session.

New MemSize — Prompts you to select a new object about which to display information.

Size Displays the object's size information.

Accumulated Memory Parameters

Reset Acc — Resets the cumulative memory figures.
MemSize — Displays the object's memory information.
Size Displays the object's size information.

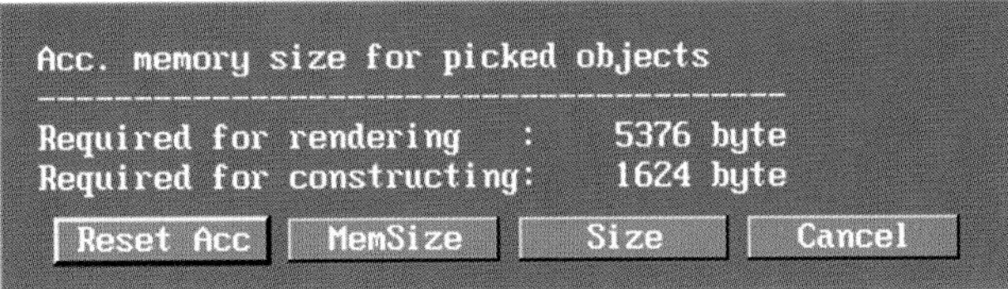

The Accumulated Memory dialog box.

SKLINE

Summary

Skline is part of Yost Group's Special Effects Procedural Modeling disk #3. Skline creates one or more objects that are deformed using an adjustable spline path called a template. The template is produced using the Skline Template dialog box, which enables you to align the template to the mesh object and specify the number of template control points.

The template is then adjusted using Modify/Vertex/Move to position the template control points as desired. The final step consists of setting the tension, number of objects, and a name prefix using the Skline Parameters dialog box and clicking on the template object and the 3D mesh object you want to deform. If you opt to produce more than a single object, the deformation is distributed incrementally along the object series. Because the resulting objects have the same vertex count as the original, they can be used as morph objects, thus making them useful for characterizing your models or producing animated wind-blown effects, for example.

For Skline to function properly it must have an adequate number of evenly distributed faces from which to work. Furthermore, Skline often requires that you tessellate the original object several times; Create/Object/Tessellate/Edge with edge tension set to 0 works well.

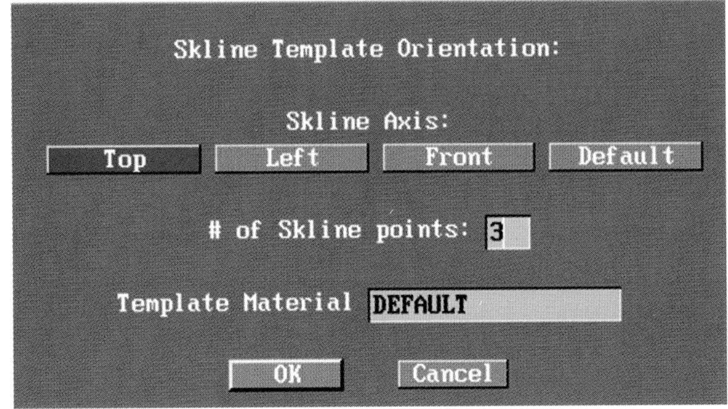

The Skline Template dialog box.

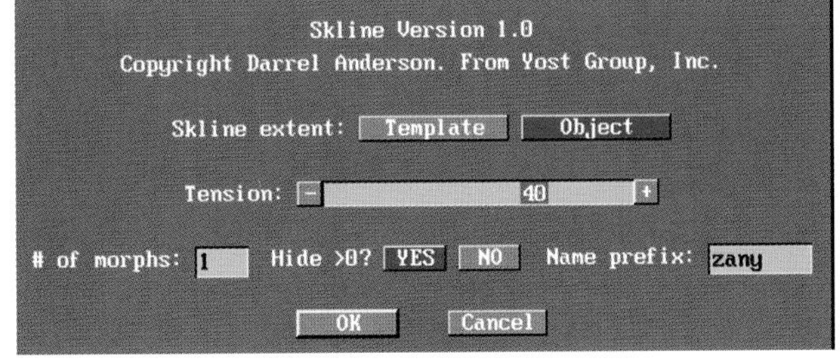

The Skline Parameters dialog box.

Skline Parameters

Skline Options (Create Template, Set Parameters) — Create Template enables you to create a template object by using the Skline Template dialog box. Set Parameters enables you to set Skline's parameters by using the Skline Parameters dialog box.

Skline Axis [Sa] t, l, f, d (Top, Left, Front, Default) — Sets the base plane for the template that orients Skline's effect to the 3d object. Top, Left, and Front automatically align the template to the selected view and scale the template to the selected object on the axis that is perpendicular to the view. Default produces a top-aligned template that is 200 units long.

# of Skline points [P] — Sets the number of control points that are used to adjust the template spline and thus the 3D object.

Template Material [Tm] — Enables you to specify a material for the template.

Skline extent [Se] t, o (Template, Object) — Switches between the height of the template or the object height as the area for the effect. Template is useful for affecting only part of an object, and Object is useful when you want the effect to be aligned to the exact object height.

Tension [T] (–100–100) — Sets the spline tension, and with that the strength of the mesh deformation.

# of morphs [M] — Specifies the number of morph objects or skline objects that will be created. This enables you to apply the deformation in stepped increments.

Hide >0 (yes, no) — Specifies whether to hide all but the first morph object.

Name prefix — Sets the four-character prefix for the objects produced by Skline.

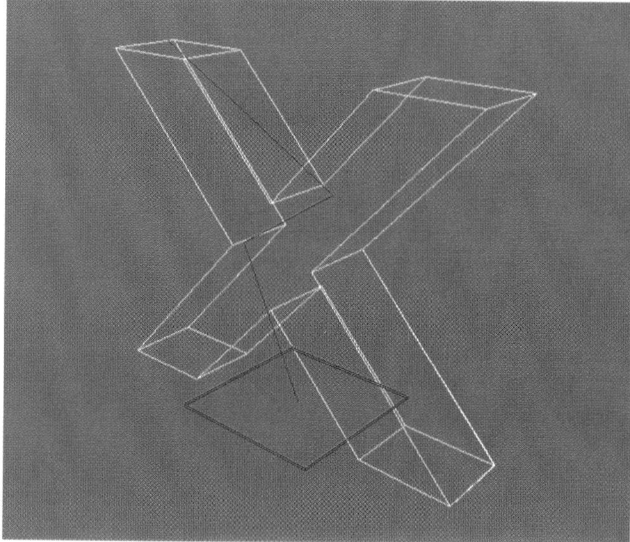

Wireframe [Sa]t [P]3

[Se]o [T]40

Skline uses a cardinal spline template (shown in red) to deform and produce a morphable 3D mesh object or series of objects.

Summary

Smooth, part of the BonesPro package, smoothes out angular geometry in a selected mesh and is intended to smooth the junction between objects joined using Boolean union. Version 1.5 includes a large window to preview smooth effects in wireframe, flat shading, or Gouraud shading. The preview window can be set to any of the standard orthographic views or the user view. Smooth can be applied multiple times within the preview window, and Undo and Reset buttons enable a previous smoothing to be undone or all smoothing to be removed. Individual points or entire objects can be smoothed or blended. The Blend option allows the smoothing of only concave areas of the model. This area of effect can be reversed to include only convex areas using inverse orientation. The effect of smoothing or blending is highly dependent on the number and length of faces in a mesh. Too few faces can cause smoothing to be choppy or faceted, and elongated faces can cause unpredictable results. Tessellating remedies these problems in most meshes. Because Smooth permanently alters the mesh once it is applied, holding or saving files before its use is recommended.

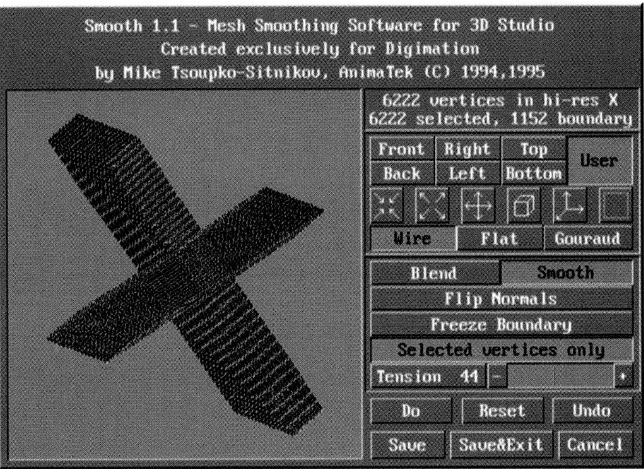

The Smooth dialog box.

Smooth Parameters

Blend [B] — Smoothes only concave areas of the selected mesh or vertices.

Smooth [S] — Smoothes all areas of the selected mesh or vertices.

Tension [T] (0–100) — Sets the number of smoothing passes on the selected mesh. Higher values produce a smoother mesh. Lower numbers can be applied numerous times for more control over degree of smoothing. Values less than 10 are sufficient to smooth most meshes.

Flip Normals [N] — Sets the normal orientation when using Blend. Flip can be used to process objects with inverted normals or to process concave areas instead of convex.

Freeze Boundary [F] — Sets the effect of Smooth on vertices at the edge of an open mesh. Smooth normally allows edge vertices to be blended, whereas Freeze leaves edge vertices unsmoothed.

Selected vertices only [V] — Sets Smooth to process only selected vertices.

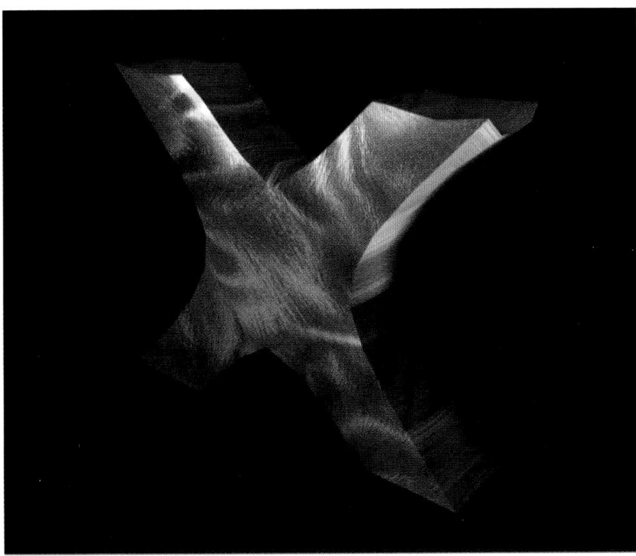

[B]5

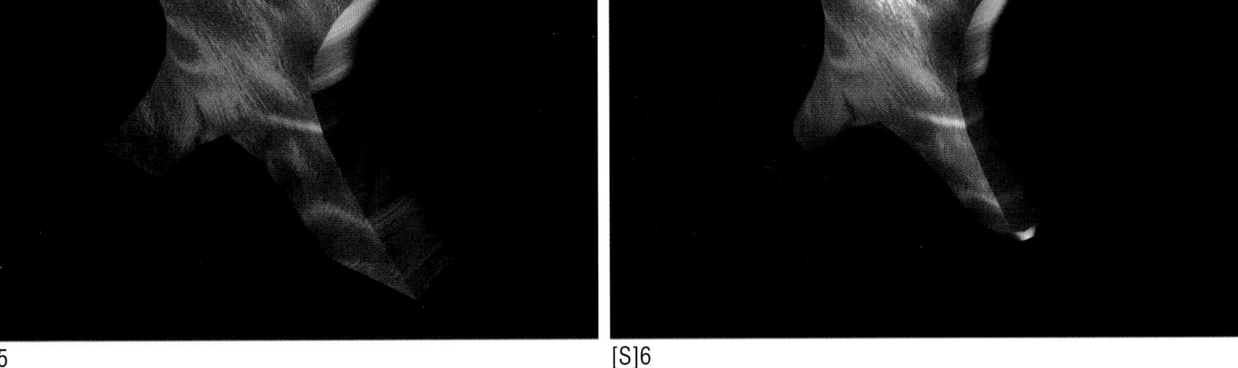

[S]6

The effect of smoothing or blending is highly dependent on the number and length of faces in a mesh. The first and second images use a uniform tessellated mesh. The following image pair uses a lofted mesh with elongated, irregular faces.

SMOOTH cont

SMOOTH_I.PXP **\smooth** **Digimatio**

[B]70

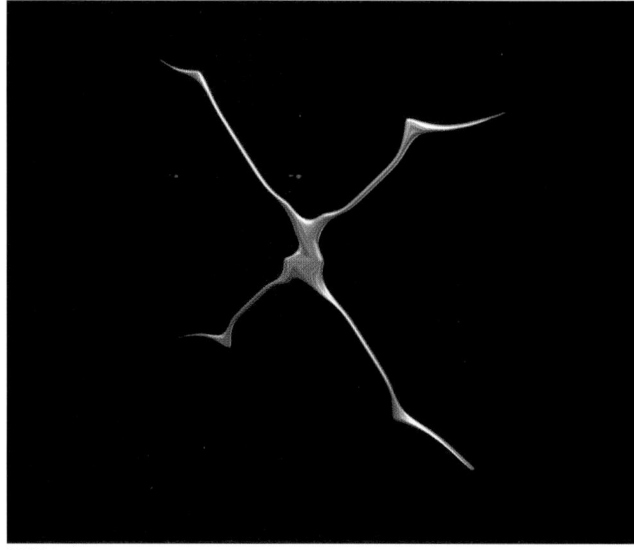

[S]50

The effect of smoothing or blending is highly dependent on the number and length of faces in a mesh. The first and second images use a uniform tessellated mesh. This image pair uses a lofted mesh with elongated, irregular faces.

SPHERIFY

SPHIFY_I.PXP **\spheriy** **Yost Group**

Object->Sphere
Copyright 1992 Tom Hudson
ver 1.0
from Yost Group, Inc.

This process repositions object vertices so that they all lie on the surface of an imaginary sphere whose diameter is equal to the length of the longest dimension of the object. Each vertex is projected outward from the center of the object's volume.

OK Cancel

The Spherify dialog box.

Summary

Spherify is part of Yost Group's Special Effects disk #2. It produces a spherical version of any 3D mesh object by taking all the vertices of the original object and scaling them into a bounding sphere. The bounding sphere's diameter is equal to the original object's longest dimension.

Spherify requires considerable vertices to work properly and often requires you to tessellate the original object several times to get a smooth object; Create/Object/Tessellate/Edge with edge tension set to 0 works well. Because the resulting object has the same vertex count as the original, the resulting object is useful for morphing from the original to a sphere. There are no parameters for this plug-in. You simply select the object you want to spherify, and the program creates the new object.

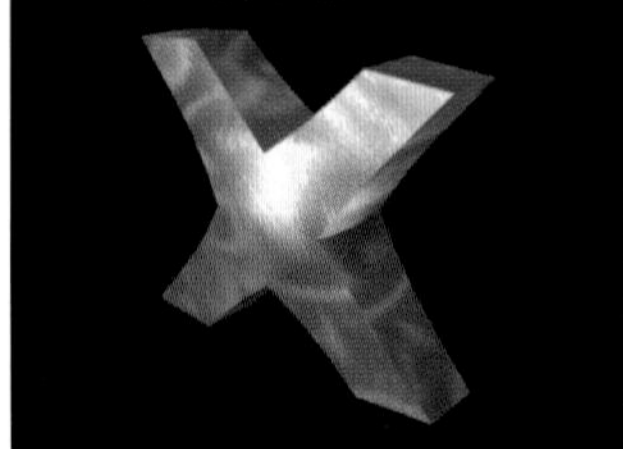

Frame 5

Frame 10

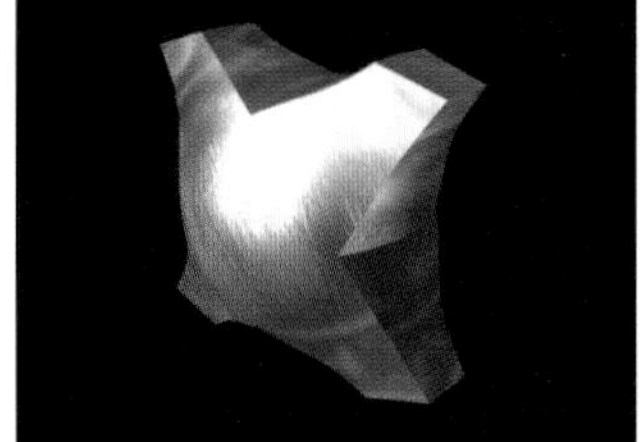

Frame 15

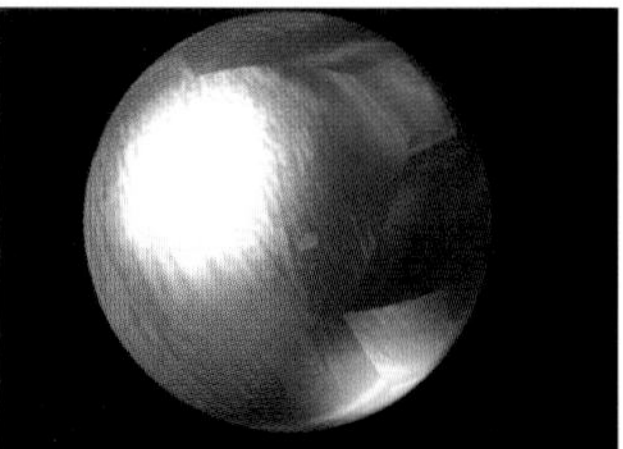

Frame 30

Spherify was used to morph from an original object into a sphere.

Summary

Stretch is part of Yost Group's Special Effects Procedural Modeling disk #3. Stretch produces weighted, nonlinear mesh deformations from any 3D mesh object based on a 3D box template. The template is produced in a single step with no parameters and is automatically aligned and scaled to the bounding area of the selected mesh. The template can then be adjusted using Modify/Object/Move and /Scale. Stretch uses these adjustments to determine how the mesh will be stretched or collapsed.

Using the Stretch Parameters dialog box, you then specify the axis to be deformed along with the anchor type and resistance value. The anchor type sets the area, in the original object, from which the points will be pulled to create the deformation. The points are adjusted either away or toward the anchor depending on the resistance value setting. If you opt to produce more than a single object, the stretch is distributed incrementally along the resulting object series. Because the resulting objects have the same vertex count as the original, they can be used as morph objects for animated effects.

For Stretch to function properly it must have an adequate number of evenly distributed faces from which to work. Furthermore, Stretch often requires that you tessellate the original object several times; Create/Object/Tessellate/Edge with edge tension set to 0 works well.

Stretch Parameters

Stretch Options (Create Template, Set Parameters) — Create Template enables you to create a template object. Set Parameters enables you to set Stretch's parameters in the Stretch Parameters dialog box.

Template Material [Tm] — Enables you to specify a material for the Stretch template.

Note: *Stretch Options and Template Material are available in the Stretch Options dialog box.*

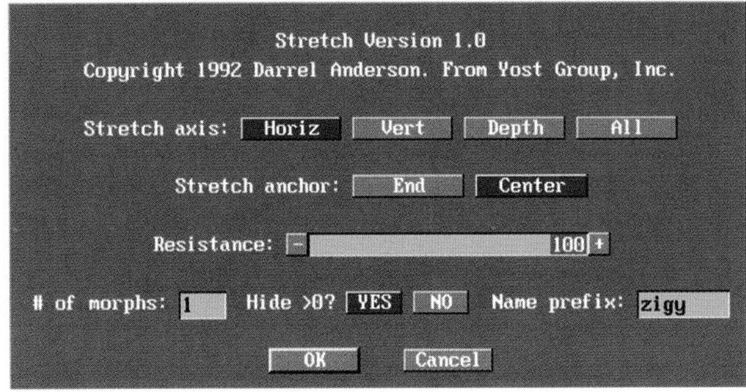

The Stretch dialog box.

Stretch axis [Sa] h, v, d, a (Horiz, Vert, Depth, All) — Specifies the axis for the deformation.

Stretch anchor [San] e, c (End, Center) — Switches the Stretch anchor area between the end and the center of the original mesh object. End fixes one end of the mesh object based on the relative distance of the object's edges to the template edges. The closer end will be fixed and the vertices will be pulled away from or toward that end. Center deforms the object based on the vertices' relative position from its center.

Resistance [R] (–100–100) — Specifies how far the vertices move relative to the Stretch Anchor. Settings greater than 0 cause vertices that are closer to the anchor to move less with resistance decreasing away from the anchor. Settings less than 0 produce the opposite effect.

# of morphs [M] — Specifies the number of morph objects or Stretch objects to be created. This enables you to apply the deformation in stepped increments.

Hide >0 (yes, no) — Specifies whether to hide all but the first morph object.

Name prefix — Sets the four-character prefix for the objects produced by Stretch.

STRETCH cont

STRECH_I.PXP | **\stretch** | **Yost Group**

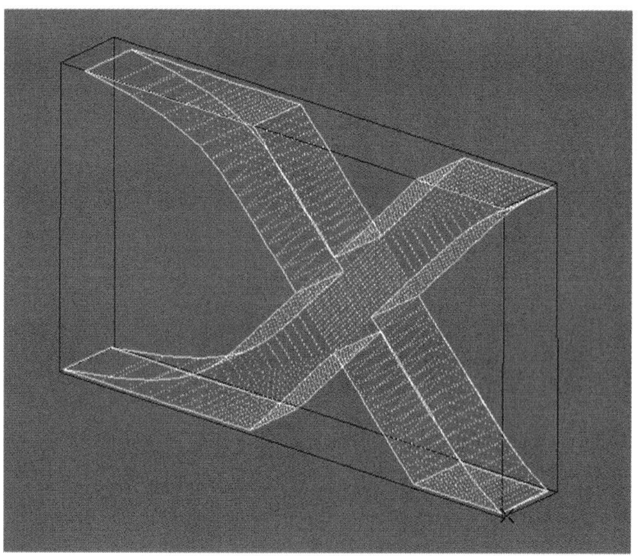

Wireframe

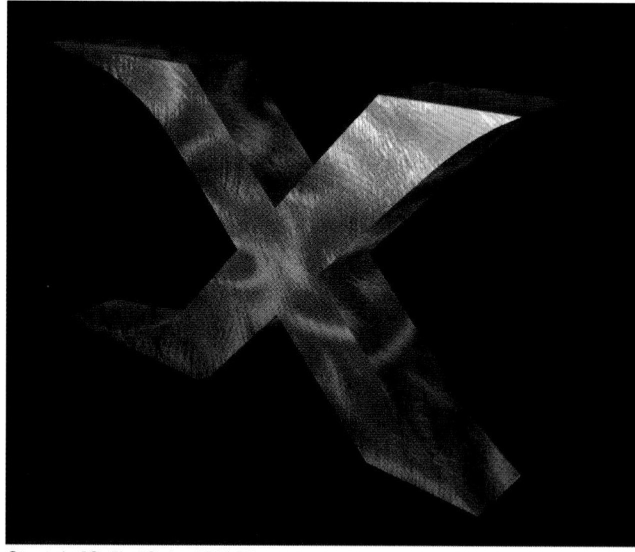

Stretch [Sa]h [Se]c [R]100

Stretch uses a template (shown in red) to produce nonlinear defomations in a single 3D object or a series of morphable 3D mesh objects.

THUMBVIEW FILE BROWSER

TVMOD_I.PXP | **\tvobj** | **Animetix**

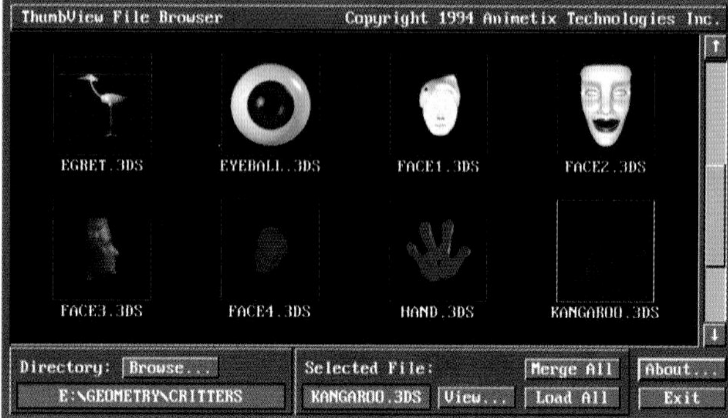

The ThumbView File Browser dialog box.

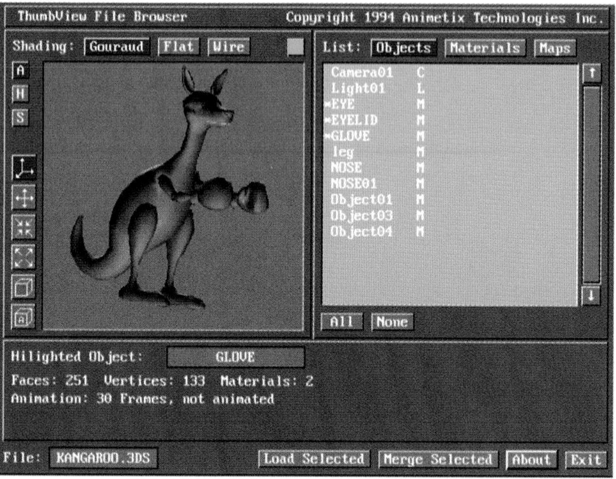

The Viewer dialog box.

Summary

ThumbView File Browser is a browser for 3D Studio mesh files. It displays the meshes within 3DS and PRJ project files.You begin by selecting a directory.The browser then displays a list of all the mesh files in that directory.If a thumbnail has been created for that file, it will be displayed; if not, an X appears instead. If the file has been changed since the thumbnail was created, the thumbnail appears with an X superimposed on it. When you find the file you want, you can either load it or merge everything in it into your current scene.You also can view the contents of the file.

When viewing a mesh file, you are given an image window, an object list window, and a status window. The image window shows a simple shaded view of all the objects in the mesh file. You can select from Gouraud shading, flat shading, and wireframe shading. There are controls for zooming, panning, and rotating around the object. You can directly control your viewpoint in the shaded window by picking inside the window with the mouse and moving the cursor. By default, all objects in the file are visible, but you can elect to display only selected objects.

The object list window shows a scrollable list of the objects, cameras, and lights in the file. You also can display a list of all the materials and bitmaps used in the file. As you highlight objects in this window, the browser displays information about that object in the status window. You can tag objects to select them and then merge the selected objects into your scene.

The ThumbView File Browser comes with a DOS program to build thumbnail views of your mesh files. It uses 3D Studio in command-line rendering mode to render small sample images of each mesh file. Processing an entire directory of files can take some time, but generating thumbnails in this way ensures that they accurately represent your files.

ThumbView File Browser Parameters

Sample images [S1]–[S8] — Sample mesh thumbnail images. You can scroll through all the mesh files in the selected directory.

Directory [D] — Selects the current source directory.

Merge All [M] — Merges all objects from the mesh file into your scene.

Load All [L] — Loads the selected mesh file into 3D Studio.

View [V] — Displays the selected mesh file in the viewer window.

Viewer Parameters

Shading [S] g, f, w (Gouraud, Flat, Wire) — Sets the shading mode. Gouraud gives a smooth shaded image. Flat gives a flat shaded image without smoothing. Wire displays the objects in wireframe, similar to 3D Studio's rendered wire mode.

Display icons [Di] a, h, s (all, highlighted, selected) — Selects which objects are displayed. All displays all objects in the file. Selected displays objects that are tagged as selected in the object list window. Highlighted displays the object currently highlighted in the object list window.

View icons [Vi] r, p, zi, zo, az, az (rotate, pan, zoom in, zoom out, zoom all, auto zoom) — Icons to control the view display. You can rotate your viewpoint, pan the window, zoom in, and zoom out. Zoom all enables you to zoom to the extents of the objects, and Auto zoom automatically zooms to fit the selected objects in the view.

List [Li] o, mt, mp (Objects, Materials, Maps) — Selects the type of information displayed in the list window. You can display objects, materials assigned to objects, and bitmap files used in the materials.

Load Selected [Ls] — Loads the selected objects into 3D Studio.

Merge Selected [Ms] — Merges the selected objects into your scene.

All [A] — Tags all objects in the file as selected. You can tag individual objects by double-clicking on their names in the object list.

None [N] — Untags all objects. You can untag individual objects by double-clicking on their names in the object list.

THUMBVIEW MATERIAL BROWSER

TVMAT_I.PXP **\tvmat** **Animetix**

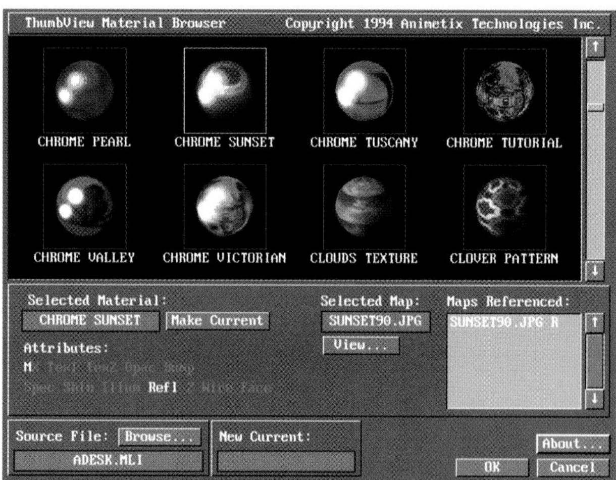

The ThumbView Material Browser dialog box.

Summary

ThumbView Material Browser is a program to browse through material libraries. You load a material library and scroll through the materials in it. If you have prebuilt thumbnail images for your materials, you will see them on-screen; if not, you will just see a given material's name under an X. If you select a material, the browser displays information about that material such as whether it has a texture map, bump map, and other such settings. If there are any associated bitmap files, the browser displays a list of them and you can select and view them. If you want to use a material, you can make it the current material. The browser loads the library and sets the selected material to be the current material.

The ThumbView Material Browser comes with a DOS program to build thumbnail views of the materials in libraries. It uses 3D Studio in command-line rendering mode to render sample images from a 3DS mesh file. This can take a while, but it enables you to apply the textures to a custom sample shape and ensures that the thumbnail image is rendered accurately.

ThumbView Material Browser Parameters

Sample images [S1]–[S8] — Sample material thumbnail images. You can scroll through the entire material library.
Source File [S] — Select the current material library file.
Maps Referenced [M] — A scrolling list of the bitmap files associated with the selected material and how they are used.
View [V] — Displays the currently selected bitmap image.

Viewing an associated bitmap file.

Summary

Turbo is part of the Imagine 3DTurbo package. It optimizes and reduces meshes by removing vertices and faces. This reduces the size of meshes, giving you smaller files and reduced rendering times. You can set an error threshold to control how much change is allowed in an object. Faces and vertices are removed if their removal would result in a flat surface that is within the error threshold setting. Smoothing groups are maintained, but mapping coordinates are often removed. You have the option of calling the QuickDraw and CleanObject plug-ins from this package as part of the processing.

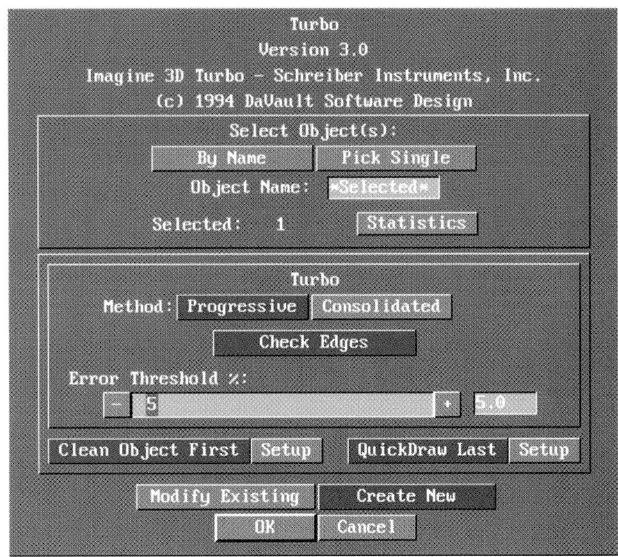

The Turbo dialog box.

Turbo Parameters

Select Object(s) [S] n, p (By Name, Pick Single) — You can pick a single object from the screen or select multiple objects by name.

Statistics [St] — Choosing this button displays a scrollable list of the selected objects with their face and vertex counts.

Method [M] p, c (Progressive, Consolidated) — Selects the method that Turbo uses to analyze the mesh. The Progressive method processes each vertex in turn. Consolidated analyzes the entire mesh and then removes vertices.

Check Edges [Ce] e, d (enabled, disabled) — When Check Edges is enabled, Turbo removes vertices from the edges of meshes. If disabled, Turbo does not change edge vertices.

Error Threshold % [E] (0–100) — Determines the allowable amount of change in the form of an object when optimizing it. A low value does not affect the shape of the object. A higher value has a greater effect on the shape of the object. You can change this value by typing a value or using the slider.

Clean Object First [C] — Option to invoke the CleanObject duplicate removal function. Setup selects the CleanObject operations.

QuickDraw Last [Q] — Option to invoke the QuickDraw edge hiding function. Setup selects the QuickDraw angle.

Object creation [O] m, c (Modify Existing, Create New) — Selects whether the program will modify the existing mesh or create a copy.

Original mesh

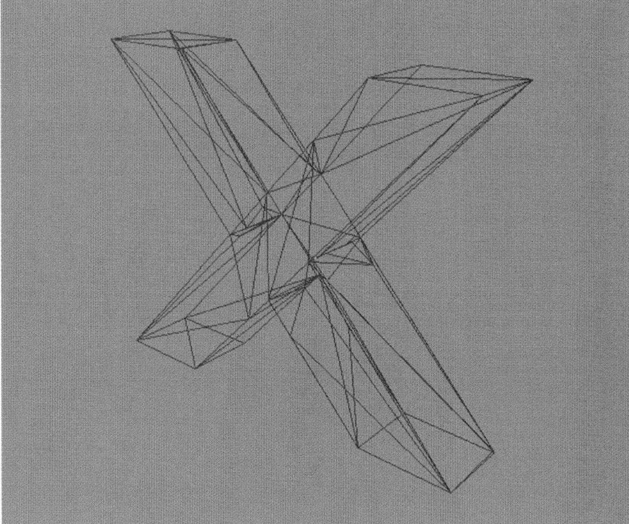

Optimized mesh

Mesh optimization using Turbo.

The Twist Template dialog box.

Twist Version 1.0
Copyright Darrel Anderson. From Yost Group, Inc.
Twist extent: Template Object
Twist Direction: Clockwise Counter Clockwise
# of full twists: 0 Bias: - 0 +
# of morphs: 6 Hide >0? YES NO Name prefix: twst
OK Cancel

The Twist Parameters dialog box.

Summary

Twist is part of Yost Group's Special Effects Procedural Modeling disk #3. Twist produces clockwise or counterclockwise twists in any 3D mesh along a specified axis that is set using a template. The template is produced using the Twist Template dialog box, which enables you to align the template to the mesh object. The template consists of a base at one end and a dial at the other. The dial is then rotated to the desired angle using Modify/Element/Rotate.

The final steps consist of setting the extent, direction, number of twists, a bias, and a name prefix using the Twist Parameters dialog box. If you opt to produce more than a single object, the twist is distributed incrementally along the object series. Because the resulting objects have the same vertex count as the original, they can be used as morph objects for animated effects.

For Twist to function properly it must have an adequate number of evenly distributed faces from which to work. Furthermore, Twist often requires that you tessellate the original object several times; Create/Object/Tessellate/Edge with edge tension set to 0 works well.

Twist Parameters

Twist Options (Create Template, Set Parameters) — Create Template enables you to create a template object by using the Twist Template dialog box. Set Parameters enables you to set Twist's parameters by using the Twist Parameters dialog box.

Template Axis [Ta] t, l, f, d (Top, Left, Front, Default) — Sets the base plane for the template that orients Twist's effect to the 3D object. Top, Left, and Front automatically align the template to the selected view and scale the template to the selected object on the axis that is perpendicular to the view. Default produces a top-aligned template that is 200 units long.

Template Material [Tm] — Enables you to specify a material for the Twist template.

Twist extent [Te] t, o (Template, Object) — Switches between the height of the template or the object height as the area for the effect. Template is useful for affecting only part of an object, and Object is useful when you want the effect to be aligned to the exact object height.

Twist Direction [Td] cw, ccw (Clockwise, Counter Clockwise) — Switches the twist direction between clockwise and counterclockwise.

# of full twists [N] — Specifies any number of full twists.

Bias [B] (–100–100) — Sets the linearity or nonlinearity of the twist. A bias of 0 produces a linear twist. Positive bias moves the twist's halfway point toward the template base, and negative bias moves it toward the end.

# of morphs [M] — Specifies the number of morph objects or Twist objects that will be created. This enables you to apply the deformation in stepped increments.

Hide >0 (yes, no) — Specifies whether to hide all but the first morph object.

Name prefix — Sets the four-character prefix for the objects produced by Twist.

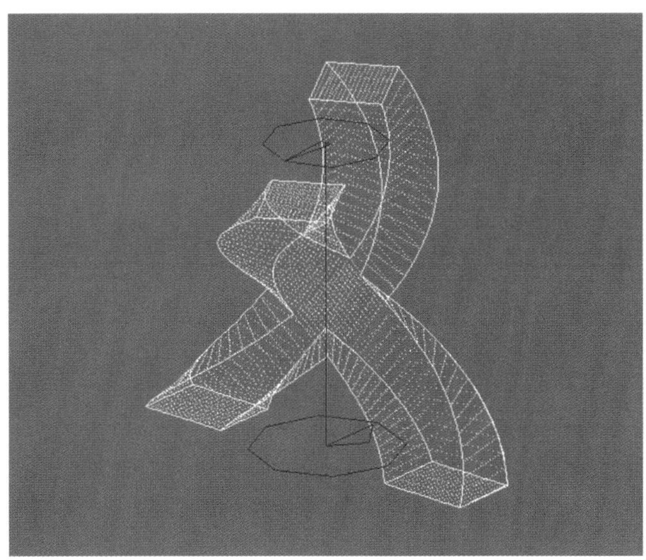

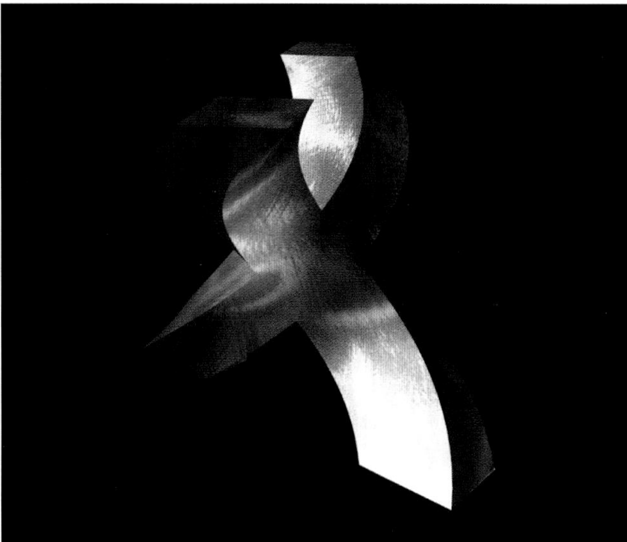

Wireframe [Ta]t [P]3

120° Twist [Te]o [Td]ccw [B]0

Twist uses a template (shown in red) to produce a clockwise or counterclockwise twist in a single 3D object or series of morphable 3D mesh objects.

VIEW

Yost Group \view VIEW_I.PXP

Summary

View is a simple shaded mesh viewer that enables you to select an object and then quickly see a shaded view of it. This is similar to 3D Studio Release 4's Fast Preview function. You can interactively rotate the object while it is shaded by moving your cursor around in the view window. View will display wireframe, flat shaded, and Gouraud shaded views of your object. It doesn't show texture mapping or the lighting from your scene. The view of the object is not a perspective view and you cannot zoom or pan the image. Still, View's capability to easily rotate a shaded object (even in 3D Studio Release 3) makes it well suited to checking the form of an object and the integrity of its surface.

The View dialog box.

View Parameters

Shade mode [S] g, f, w (Gouraud, Flat, Wire) — Sets one of three shading modes. Gouraud is a smooth shaded mode. Flat shaded is shaded but without smoothing. Wireframe is similar to 3D Studio's wireframe render mode.

Dismiss — Exits the program.

WAVES

WAVES_I.PXP **\waves** **Autodesk**

Autodesk 3D Studio Object Wave Generator
by Tom Hudson, Version 1.0

Amplitude axis: Top Front Right All

WAVE 1:
Period: 10 Wavelength: 120 Amplitude: 12
WAVE 2:
Period: 5 Wavelength: 12 Amplitude: 6

# of morphs: 1 Hide >0? YES NO Name prefix: wave

OK Cancel

The Waves dialog box.

Summary

Included with 3D Studio Release 4, Waves applies a linear sine wave deformation to any 3D mesh object. You can apply the effect through any individual object axis or all axes simultaneously, and you can specify wave period, wavelength, and amplitude, which combine to shape and vary the deformation. Waves also produces morph targets and can be used to produce cyclic animated waves.

Waves Parameters

Amplitude axis [Aa] t, f, r a (Top, Front, Right, All) — Specifies the axis to which the waves will be applied. Top applies the waves parallel to the XZ plane, front applies the waves parallel to the XY plane, and right applies the waves parallel to the ZY plane. All applies the waves through X, Y, and Z combined.

Period Wave 1 and 2 [P1] [P2] — The time in frames for the waves to complete one cycle. The period must be greater than 1 for animation.

Wavelength Wave 1 and 2 [W1] [W2] — The radius of a single wave for one period.

Amplitude Wave 1 and 2 [A1] [A2] — The height of the waves.

# of morphs [M] — Specifies the number of morph objects that will be created. This enables you to apply the deformation in stepped increments or to animate waves.

Hide >0 (yes, no) — Hides all but the first morph object.

Name prefix — Sets the name prefix for the morph objects produced by Waves.

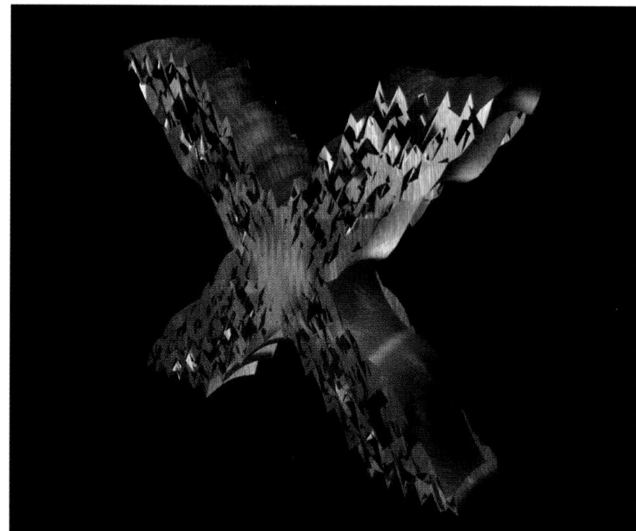

[Aa]t [W1]8 [W2]4 [A1]12 [A2]6

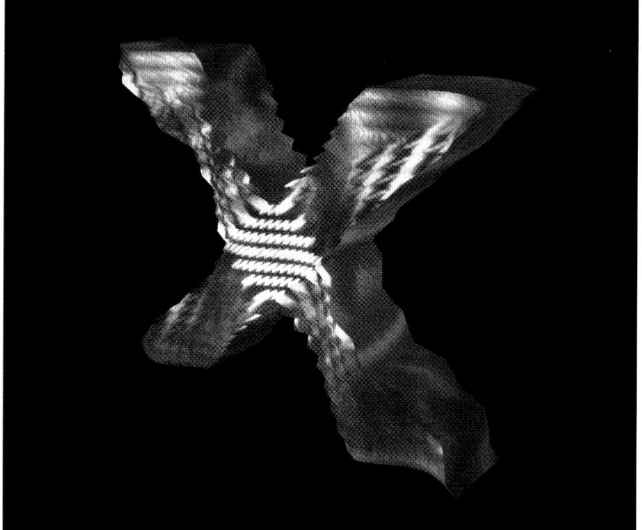

[Aa]f [W1]120 [W2]4 [A1]12 [A2]6

Waves applies a concentric wave function to a 3D mesh object.

Summary

YUV is a combination of a bitmapped files used with broadcast video systems. The control module enables you to change the operation of the BXP module. The BXP adds a new file type that 3D Studio can read from and write to. After YUV is installed, you can render to the new file type by typing the name of the file you want to render to followed by the YUV extension. 3D Studio will find the YUV.BXP and use it to write the file. Reading a YUV file works the same way.

YUV Parameters

Chroma filter [C] e, d (Enabled, Disabled) — Enables or disables YUV chroma filtering. The default is chroma filtering enabled.

Generate alpha channel [A] s, o, n (Separate, Only, No) — Controls the generation of alpha channel files. Separate writes alpha channels to separate files, Only writes only the alpha channel to the YUV file, and No (the default) doesn't write any alpha channel.

The YUV dialog box.

amoeba_i.sxp
ball_i.sxp
beaded_i.sxp
beaded_i.sxp
ccube_i.sxp
check_i.sxp
cubic_i.sxp
dents_i.sxp
earth_i.sxp
earth_i.sxp
flameo_i.sxp
granit_i.sxp
granit_i.sxp
layers_i.sxp
marbl_i.sxp
marbl_i.sxp
mottle_i.sxp
noise2_i.sxp
planet_i.sxp
planet_i.sxp
rocks_i.sxp
smoke_i.sxp
speckl_i.sxp
splat_i.sxp
squigl_i.sxp
stucco_i.sxp
tornad_i.sxp
trihex_i.sxp
turb_i.sxp
turb_i.sxp
vary_i.sxp
water_i.sxp
wipe_i.sxp

Three-Dimensional Textures

Solid Pattern External Processes (SXP) plug-ins create static and animated three-dimensional textures that can be used to create an enormous variety of photorealistic materials and patterns. These textures can include corroded metals, naturalistic stones, rippling water, and swirling smoke, as well as numerous surrealistic materials that defy description.

Most SXP plug-ins can be used as any of the Material Editor's maps or masks (see figure) except reflection maps, although they can be used as reflection map masks. SXP plug-ins can also be used singly or in any combination for multiple map materials.

SXP maps differ from bitmap-based image maps in that they are procedural. In other words, each SXP is actually a program that calculates a texture on-the-fly at render time.

Understanding SXP plug-ins begins with a brief review of how 3D computer graphic objects are made to appear wooden, smoky, or metallic. *Image mapping,* commonly known as *texture mapping,* is one of the longest-standing methods of assigning complex textures and patterns to 3D geometry. It consists of projecting or wrapping two-dimensional color or grayscale bitmaps around three-dimensional models. Several such image maps are often used to impart not only texture, but variable opacity, bumpiness, or shininess.

Image mapping produces imagery of excellent quality, is simple to use, and renders quickly. Image mapping does, however, suffer from several disadvantages. Perhaps the most common of these is the seam that can occur at the boundaries of an image map where the image runs out. This can result in an obvious jump in a planet's terrain or undesirable tile-like breaks in an otherwise smoothly textured plane.

Another problem with image maps is that they are tied to a single resolution, such as 640x480. This might work well within a specific camera range; however, the bitmap can lack detail for close-up views and can make for needlessly slow rendering for distant views.

Procedural shading using SXP plug-ins solves these problems handily while offering uncommon flexibility and variation to boot. First, because SXP plug-ins are created mathematically, the level of texture detail available is not fixed. This means that each surface is created "to order" at the resolution requirements of the scene at hand, which makes it possible to move very close to SXP materials with little or no degradation in the image quality.

Another SXP advantage is that they occupy considerably less disk space than their bitmap counterparts, with most requiring a mere 20–60 KB per texture. This is downright demure when compared to a typical 640x480 24-bit file at over 1 MB.

Yet another advantage is that SXP plug-ins act like real-world solid textures in that they run through the inside, as well as on the surface, of the geometry. This enables you to achieve the look of carved objects that are composed of solid materials having interior textures that match their surface textures.

But, as the saying goes, there's no such thing as a free lunch—and so it is with SXPs. They can take a good deal longer to render than bitmaps, for instance, and render time increases very quickly when working with multiple SXP materials.

Another issue is that SXP plug-ins act like infinite virtual 3D textures that encase each 3D object. The texture is linked to a 3D object's bounded area rather than its geometry, so the texture gets its scale information from the entire object. This means that if you transform an object in the 3D Editor at an Element, Face, or Vertex level, the result appears as though it had moved through the texture, instead of the texture scaling with the object as expected. Animating SXP-mapped objects in the Keyframer works as expected with the exception of morphs, which have the same effect as an element-, face-, or vertex-level edit in the 3D Editor.

Note: *Remember that SXP plug-ins do not require you to assign mapping coordinates to the 3D model unless you have used a bitmap along with an SXP.*

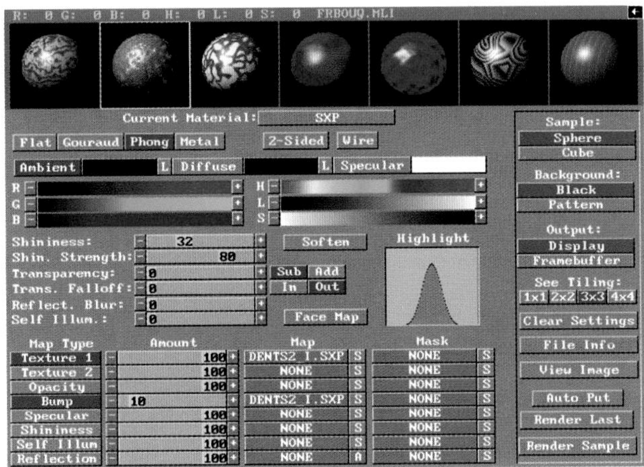

This view in the Materials Editor shows DENTS2 being used as both a texture map and a bump map. The result is rendered as a multicolored and mottled sphere shown in the highlighted sample window second from left.

Using SXP Plug-Ins

In spite of their faults, SXP plug-ins offer amazing flexibility and variation, literally at the touch of a button. They are assigned in the Materials Editor using the same process used to assign any image map.

Before using any SXP plug-in, verify that it has been placed in your primary maps directory or any Map-Path directory such as C:\3DS4\MAPS. You can check this using Info\Configure\Map-Paths, which brings up the Map Paths dialog box. To add a map path, highlight the Add button and click anywhere in the path list. Then, using the Add Map Path dialog box, select the drive and path name that contains your SXPs.

Note: *If you are network-rendering a scene that uses multiple occurrences of the same SXP plug-in, keeping the parameter and color settings the same for each SXP occurrence can save considerable memory*

To use an SXP, first clickSXPs on the map assignment slot next to the texture, opacity, bump, specular, shininess, or self-illumination map types. Select and load a file with an SXP file extension, which causes the file name to appear in the assignment slot.

To adjust the plug-in, click on the S button next to the assignment slot. This displays an SXP dialog box such as that shown in the following figure. These dialog boxes range in complexity from those consisting of only an OK button to dialog boxes that contain multiple sliders, buttons, and numeric fields as well as additional dialog boxes. You can make any number of adjustments, then click on OK to return to the Materials Editor. Click on the Render Sample button to see the result.

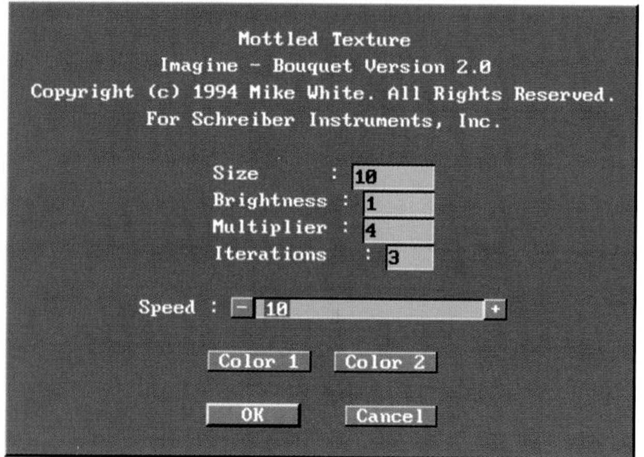

A typical SXP dialog box, showing a slider, buttons, numeric fields, and color selection buttons.

As you make edits, it is useful to remember that SXP plug-ins use numerous interdependent variables and that many also use fractal algorithms, which are based on the mathematics of chaos. This means that for all their variation, it is also possible to make significant changes in one or more SXP parameters, only to get essentially the same look.

For instance, if you are working with several variables, each with ranges of .0001–10,000, and have one or more set to their extremes, you might notice little effect as you vary a given parameter from 10,000 to 10. If this happens, try returning one or more parameters to a more central value. In general, most SXP plug-ins have a sweet spot or range of adjustment that provides maximum texture variation, which often tends to be toward the center of a given parameter range.

Remember too that the SXP scale, typically the size parameter, is critical to assure that a texture in the 3D Editor and Keyframer will look similar to its sample displayed in the Materials Editor. The best approach here is to make frequent use of the Materials Editor's Render Last button, located at the lower right in the Command column. This enables you to check your textures on the actual model and to take into account other important scene conditions such as lighting.

Color selection for SXP plug-ins is typically limited to two colors—occasionally three. Remember that the color you select has a varying impact on the final effect depending on the map type to which you have assigned the SXP. Remember also that color is an additional interdependent variable that can be used to mask as well as enhance SXP attributes such as contrast and fine detail. Experimenting with hue, saturation, and value can make an average SXP material astounding.

For any texture map or texture map mask, the SXP colors influence or replace the diffuse object color. For any specular map, the SXP influences or replaces the specular object color. The degree to which an object color is replaced depends on the Amount Slider setting for that map.

A given material's color palette might also be influenced by SXP variables. A good example of this is Autodesk's Dents Function. As the strength parameter increases, the material's pattern becomes brighter until a complementary color and finally white is gradually added to the color mix.

For opacity, bump, shininess, or self-illumination maps, the luminance of the colors specifies the degree of opacity, bumpiness, shininess, or specularity. Opacity maps range from black (0,0,0 RGB) for transparency or holes to white (255,255,255 RGB), which specifies opacity. Varying degrees of transparency are created using the range of grays between black and white.

Another example of SXP color selection is bump maps where black specifies recessed areas and white (255,255,255) specifies raised areas. This same idea applies to the remaining map types, with white setting maximum specularity, maximum shininess, and maximum self-illumination.

Note: *When creating specular maps, you must set the Material Editor's Shininess and Shin. Strength sliders to see the effect.*

The SXP Reference

The SXP plug-ins described in this chapter are listed alphabetically by their product names, which are in bold type and at the top of each plug-in section. The color bar below the plug-in name lists the plug-in file name, such as WATER_I.SXP. In addition, the path name for the *3D Studio IPAS Plug-In Reference* CD-ROM and the product vendor are shown. The CD-ROM subdirectory contains any sample files along with demonstration versions of the plug-ins where possible.

The text is divided into two areas: a summary and a parameter listing. The summary provides a look at the plug-in's characteristics and capabilities. The parameter listing displays the name of each parameter in bold type along with its corresponding abbreviation in brackets. Where applicable, there is an adjustment range in parentheses and a description of the parameter function.

Each plug-in is illustrated with a screen capture of its dialog box and up to eight example textures. The textures are applied to a simple circular form, approximately 570 units in diameter with a wedge-shaped section removed (see the following figure). This provides a combination of rounded and flat areas to demonstrate texture attributes. The project file used to create the sample images is in the *3D Studio IPAS Plug-In Reference* CD-ROM in the \SXP directory.

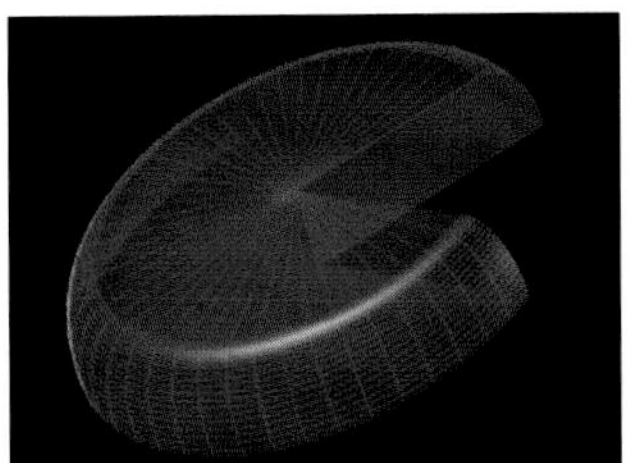

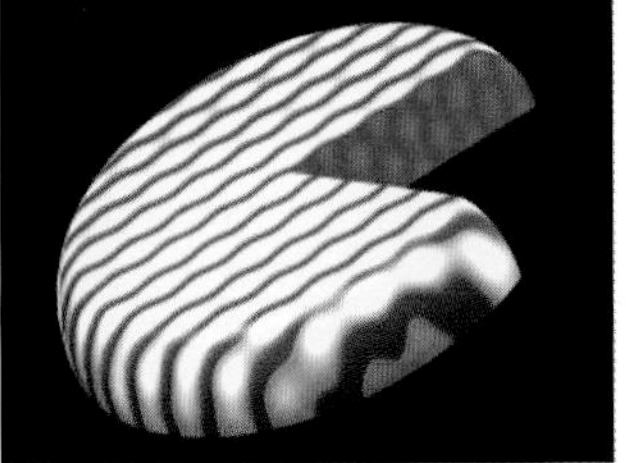

A simple rounded form with a wedge removed was used as a subject for the textures.

Each figure has the parameter abbreviation along with the value used to create that texture. If a map type other than texture was used, it is also shown under the illustration, or a note appears in the parameter listing. The specific texture variations shown were chosen to represent as broad a selection of surface attributes as space permitted. They were also chosen on the basis of providing SXP plug-in users shortcuts to creating unique, interesting, and useful materials as quickly as possible.

The color choices used for each texture were selected largely on the basis of providing an interesting overall color variation with some consideration given to the SXP type, such as marble or smoke. Because color choice is such a subjective area, no effort was made to provide specific color information except where the texture's color palette was directly affected by a plug-in variable. The selected sample images are provided in their final rendered form. These images are located on the *3D Studio IPAS Plug-In Reference* CD-ROM in the directory specified in the information bar at the beginning of each plug-in.

AGATE TEXTURE

AGATE_I.SXP | **\agate** | **Schreiber Instruments**

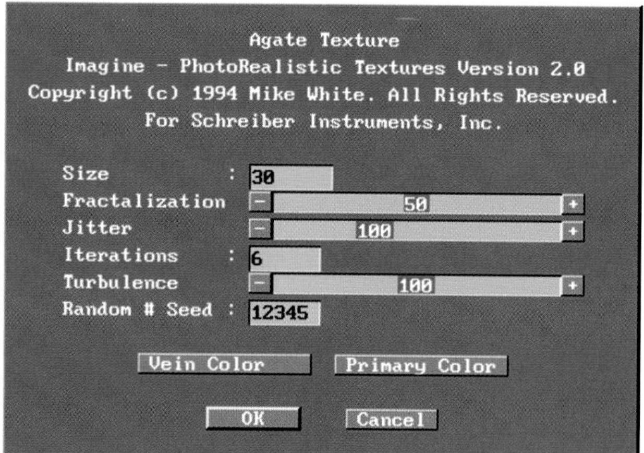

The Agate Texture dialog box.

Summary

Agate is available as part of Schreiber Instruments' Imagine Photorealistic Textures bundle. It produces a range of solid patterns using computations based on fractal geometry or the mathematics of chaos. This technique is capable of producing a broad range of layered textures that vary from smooth, regular stripes through complex, natural-looking patterns to fine, granular textures.

You can control Agate's look using several interdependent variables including fractalization, jitter, and turbulence. For all the variation possible, this interdependence can result in near identical or identical textures being created from dramatically different settings. For the same reason it is also possible to change a variable with no apparent result. Generally, this occurs while working with two variables with one or both set to an extreme value. Though this approach can produce some useful results, working in a range around the middle or default range increases Agate's responsiveness. Agate's textures are horizontally oriented.

Agate Texture Parameters

Size [S] (.0001–100,000.0) — Sets the texture's overall scale.
Fractalize [F] (0–100) — Sets the texture's randomness or chaos.
Jitter [J] (0–300) — Sets the vein width variance and knots.
Iterations [I] (0–99,999) — Sets the number of times the algorithm is applied. Higher numbers create more detail.
Turbulence [T] (0–200) — Sets the overall noise added to the veins. Turbulence is needed for Fractalize or Jitter to have an effect.
Random Seed [R] (0–999,999) — Sets the algorithm's start point with an arbitrary number. Each number produces a unique pattern.
Vein color [C1] — Sets the RGB or HSL values for the secondary color.
Primary color [C2] — Sets the RGB or HSL values for the main color.
Note: *Bump maps are duplicates of SXP's given settings.*
Note: *[C1]RGB 27,0,27 [C2]RGB 241,134,133 for all textures.*

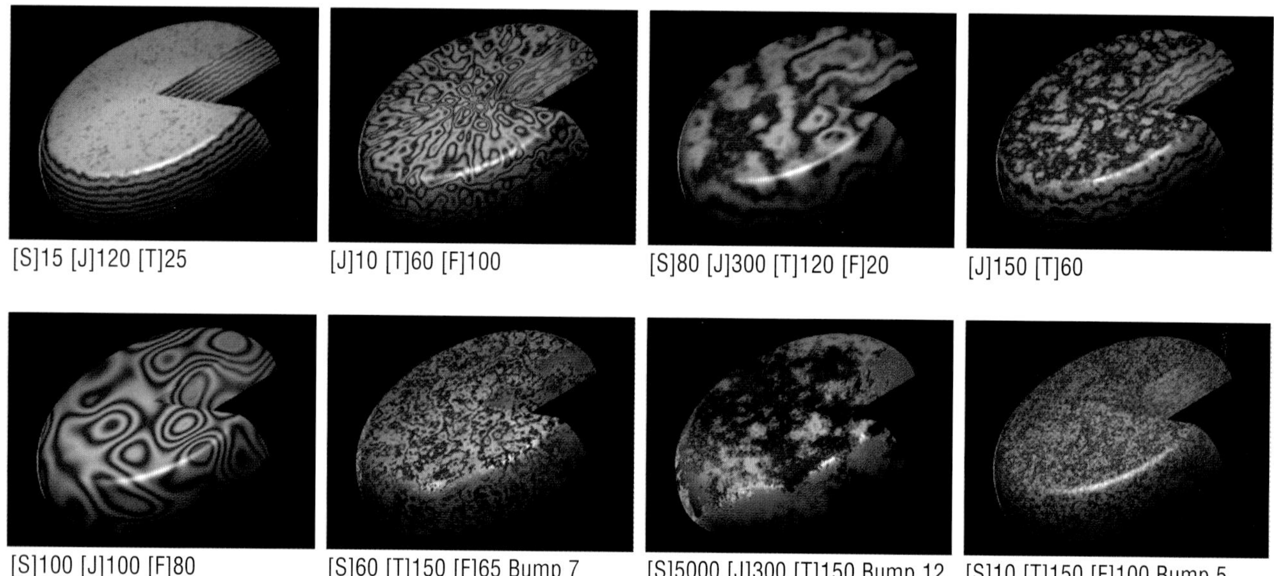

[S]15 [J]120 [T]25 | [J]10 [T]60 [F]100 | [S]80 [J]300 [T]120 [F]20 | [J]150 [T]60

[S]100 [J]100 [F]80 | [S]60 [T]150 [F]65 Bump 7 | [S]5000 [J]300 [T]150 Bump 12 | [S]10 [T]150 [F]100 Bump 5

Summary

Amoeba is available as part of Schreiber Instruments' Imagine Fractal Bouquet bundle. It produces three-color, plasma-like, animated textures consisting of non-uniform blobs. The Size parameter provides scale adjustment, and Offset in X,Y, and Z controls the animation.

Color variation as well as pattern is controlled by the first and second colors, their associated level settings, and the added color settings. These parameters combine to provide animated color patterns from subtle to garish.

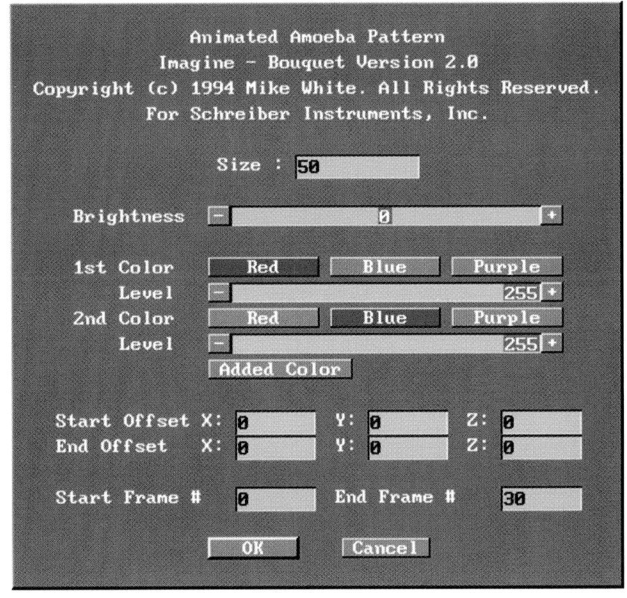

The Amoeba Pattern dialog box.

Amoeba Pattern Parameters

Size [S] (.0001–10,000) — Sets the texture's overall scale.
Brightness [B] (.0001–10,000) — Controls the overall pattern brightness as well as the interaction between colors.
1st and 2nd Color [C1]rbp [C2]rbp — Sets the first color and second color as either red, blue, or purple.
1st and 2nd Color Level [C1l] [C2l] (0–255) — Sets the range of the selected colors.
Added Color [Ac] — Sets the third pattern color using RGB.
Start Offset X, Y, Z [SoX] [SoY] [SoZ] — Sets the starting offset values for the pattern animation.
End Offset X, Y, Z [EoX] [EoY] [EoZ] — Sets the ending offset values for the pattern animation.
Start frame and End frame [Sf] [Ef] — Sets the starting and ending frames for the pattern animation.

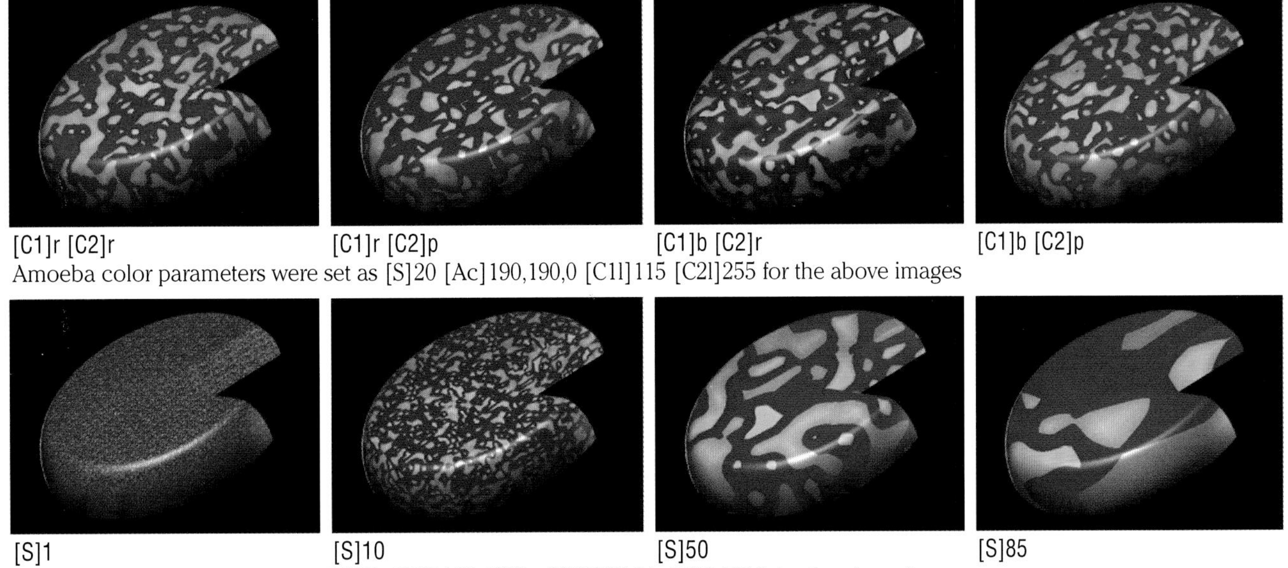

[C1]r [C2]r [C1]r [C2]p [C1]b [C2]r [C1]b [C2]p

Amoeba color parameters were set as [S]20 [Ac]190,190,0 [C1l]115 [C2l]255 for the above images

[S]1 [S]10 [S]50 [S]85

Amoeba parameters were set as [C1]b [C1l]128 [C2]p [C2l]255 [Ac]190,190,0 for the above images.

BALL FUNCTION

BALL_I.SXP \ball **Autodesk**

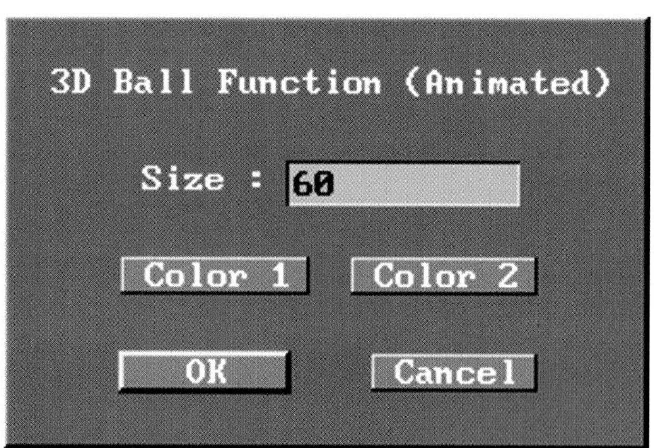

The Ball Function dialog box.

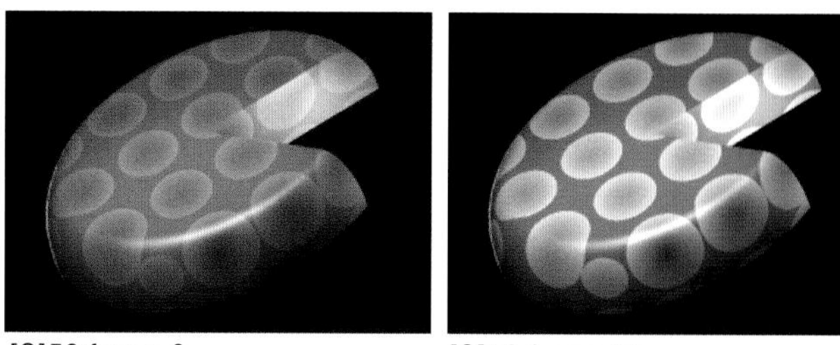

[S]56 frame 0 [S]56 frame 20
Ball color cycles the dots between [C1] and [C2].

Summary

Ball is included with 3D Studio Release 4. It produces a grid of dots consisting of a two-color radial gradient. The gradient color is set using [C1] and [C2]. The resulting texture appears on a medium gray background and color cycles between the colors at a preset rate.

Ball Function Parameters

Size [S] (0–10,000) — Sets the size of the dots.
Color 1 and Color 2 [C1] [C2] — C1 sets the outside and C2 the inside color for the dots.

BEADED TEXTURE

BEADED_I.SXP \beaded **Schreiber Instruments**

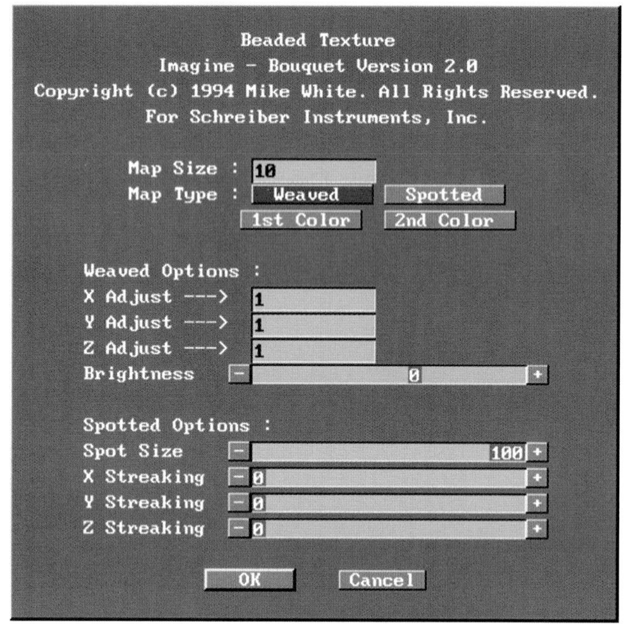

The Beaded Texture dialog box.

Summary

Beaded is included in Schreiber Instruments' Imagine Fractal Bouquet bundle, and produces three-color, striped, woven, and spotted patterns based on a grid of 3D dots or rings. In addition to pattern size and color choices, Beaded provides adjustment over scale of its pattern elements independently in X, Y, and Z.

Beaded Texture Parameters

Map Size [S] (.0001–10,000) — Sets the texture's overall scale.
1st and 2nd Color [C1] [C2] — C1 sets the foreground element or spot color and C2 the background color.
Map Type Weaved or Spotted [M] — Selects between weaved or spotted patterns.
Weave Adjust X, Y, Z [Ax] [Ay] [Az] (.0001–100,000) — Sets the scale independently in X, Y, or Z, with higher values producing larger pattern elements.
Brightness [B] (.0001–10,000) — Controls the overall pattern brightness as well as the interaction between colors.
Spot Size [Ss] (0–100) — Controls the size and coarseness of the spots.
Streaking X, Y, Z [Stx] [Sty] [Stz] — Sets the spot scale independently in X, Y, or Z, with larger values increasing spot contrast.

BEADED TEXTURE cont

Schreiber Instruments \beaded **BEADED_I.SXP**

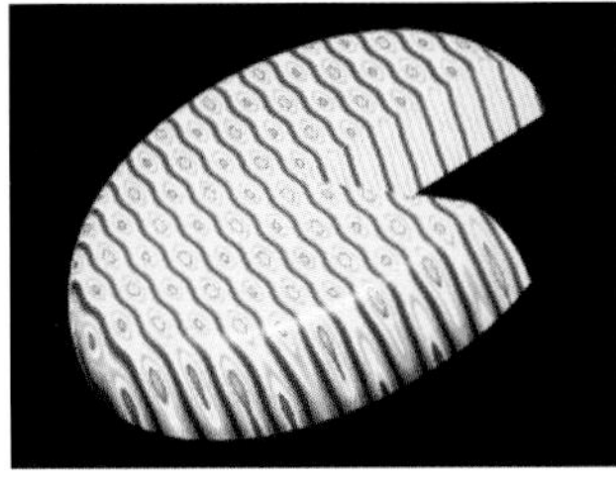
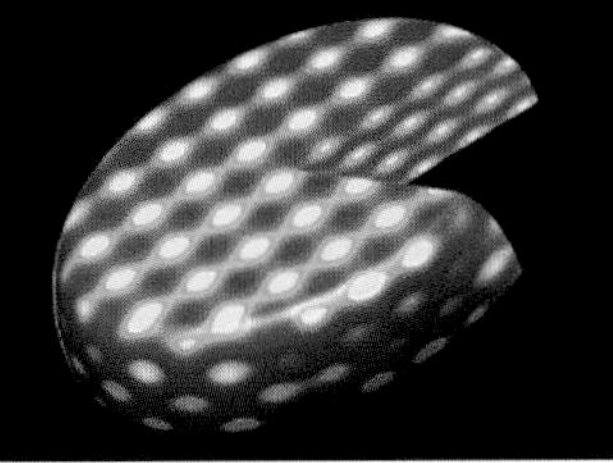
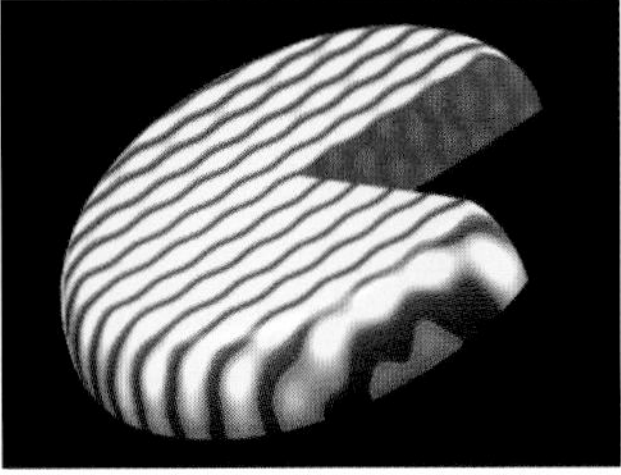
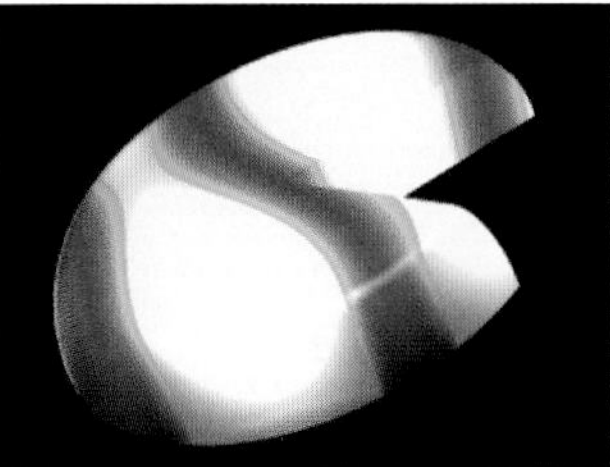

[S]10 [M]wea [Ax]25 [Ay]5 [Az]1 [S]10 [M]wea [Ax]2 [Ay]3 [Az]7 [S]10 [M]wea [Ax]3 [Ay]15 [Az]1 [S]75 [M]wea [Ax]15 [Ay]5 [Az]1
Woven patterns with variations in Map Size and X,Y, and Z scale.

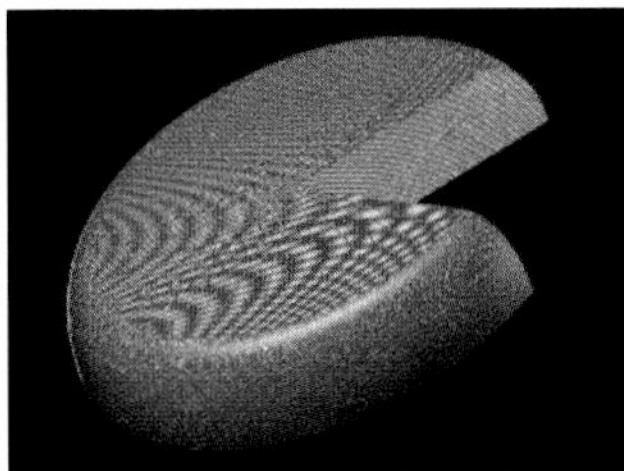
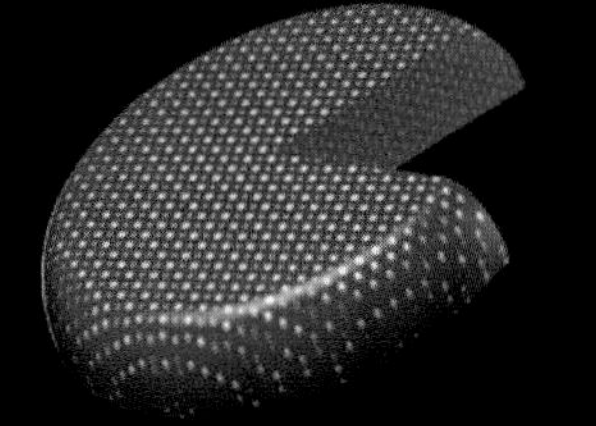
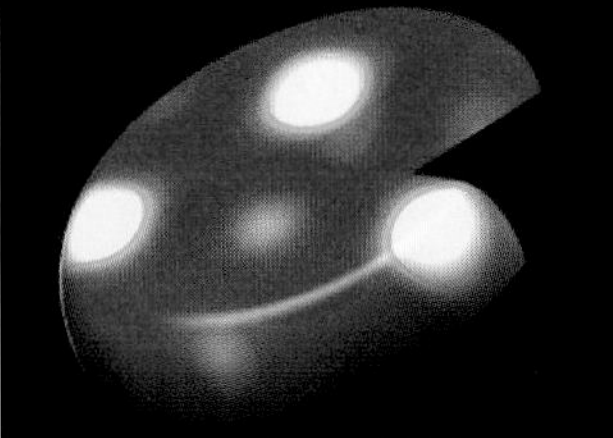
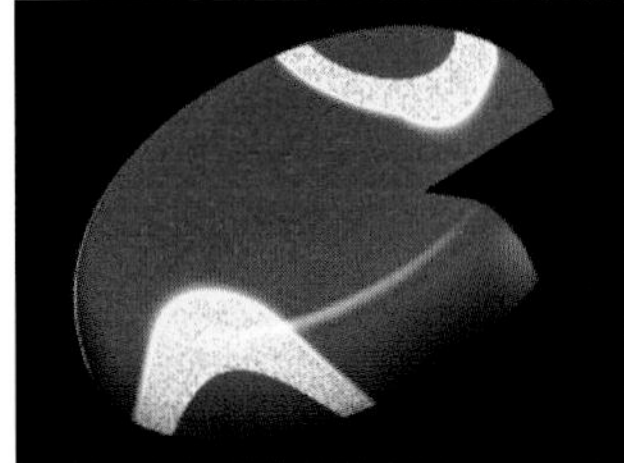

[S].1 [Ss]100 [Stx]0 [Sty]200 [S]3 [Ss]100 [Stx]200 [Sty]200 [S]43 [Ss]100 [Stx]143 [Sty]143 [S]115 [Ss]45
Spotted patterns with variations in Map Size, Spot Size, and X,Y, and Z Streaking.

CHECKER PATTERN

Autodesk \check **CHECK_I.SXP**

Summary

Checker is included with 3D Studio Release 4. It creates a checker pattern with variable size, colors, and offset, which enables placement of the pattern relative to a mesh object.

Checker Pattern Parameters

Check size [S] (0–10,000) — Sets the size of the checker pattern.
Offset X, Y, and Z [Ox] [Oy] [Oz] — Sets the pattern offset.
Color 1 and Color 2 [C1] [C2] — Sets the pattern colors.

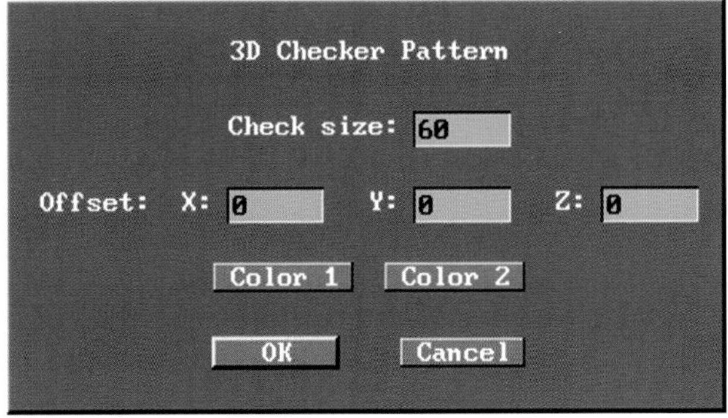

The Checker Pattern dialog box.

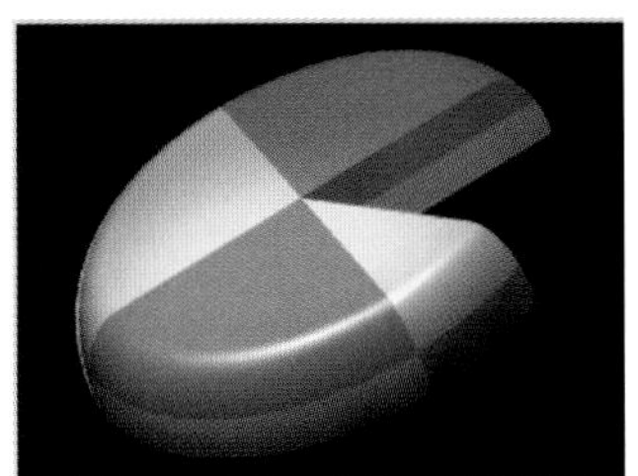
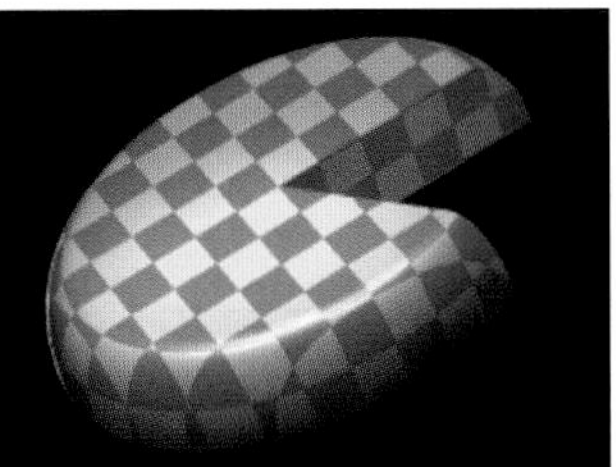
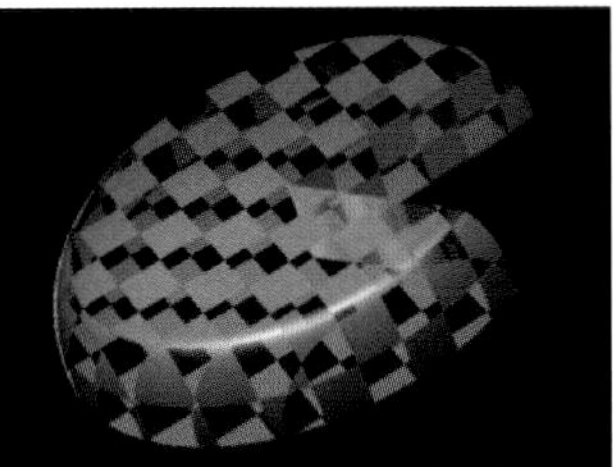
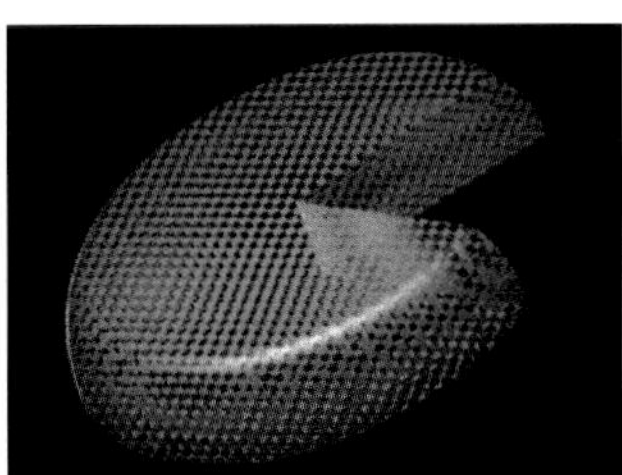

[S]500 [S]50 [S]50 opacity 100 [S]10 opacity 100
Varying the size parameter produces cloth-like patterns. Images 3 and 4 were used as two-sided materials.

COLOR CUBE

CCUBE_I.SXP | **\ccube** | **Autodesk**

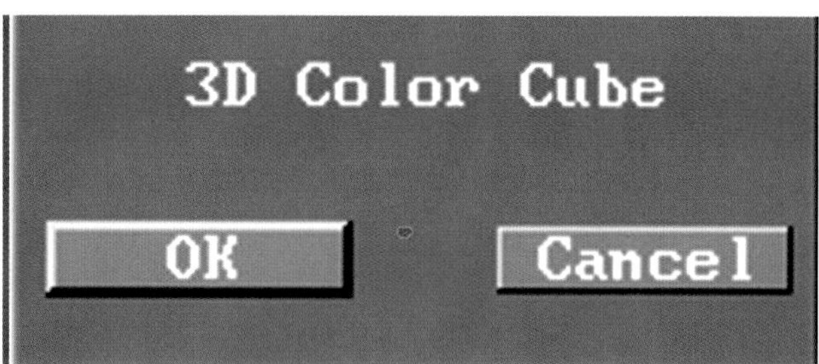

The Color Cube dialog box.

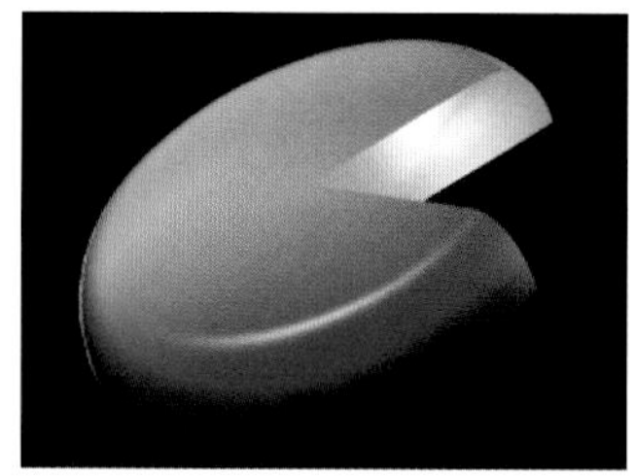

Color Cube produces a scalable color map.

Summary

Color Cube is included with 3D Studio Release 4. It produces a scalable smooth color map and is provided as a demonstration program with no parameters.

CUBIC FRACTAL FUNCTION

CUBIC_I.SXP | **\cubic** | **Schreiber Instruments**

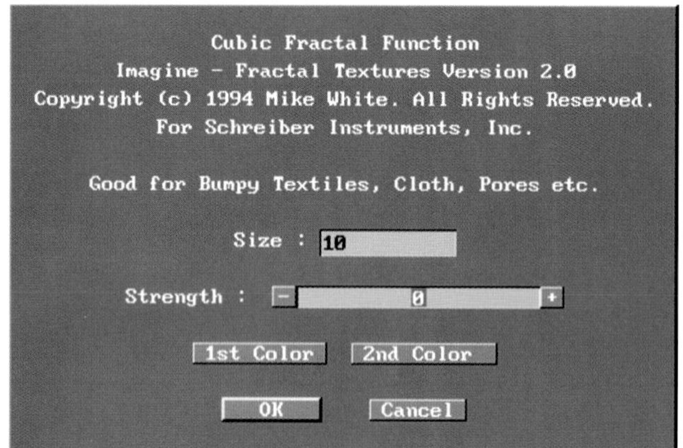

The Cubic Fractal Function dialog box.

Summary

Cubic is included with Schreiber Instruments' Imagine Fractal Textures bundle. Cubic produces tiled square solid patterns using computations based on fractal geometry. This technique is capable of producing a broad range of textures that vary from large gradient tiles to fine, granular textures.

You can control Cubic's look using size, strength and color. The effect of strength is very subtle—only slight shifts in color can be perceived.

Cubic Fractal Function Parameters

Size [S] (.0001–100,000.0) — Sets the texture's overall scale.
Strength [St] (–99–99) — Sets the texture's color strength.
1st and 2nd Color [C1] [C2] — Sets the RGB or HSL values for the foreground and background colors.
Note: *Bump maps are duplicates of SXP's given settings.*

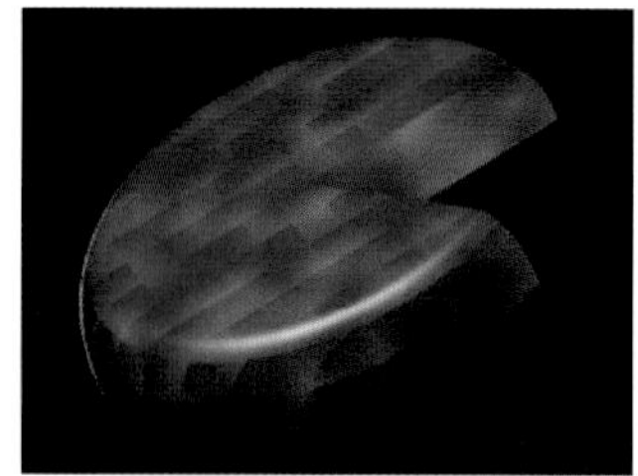

[S]40 [St] 99

[S]20

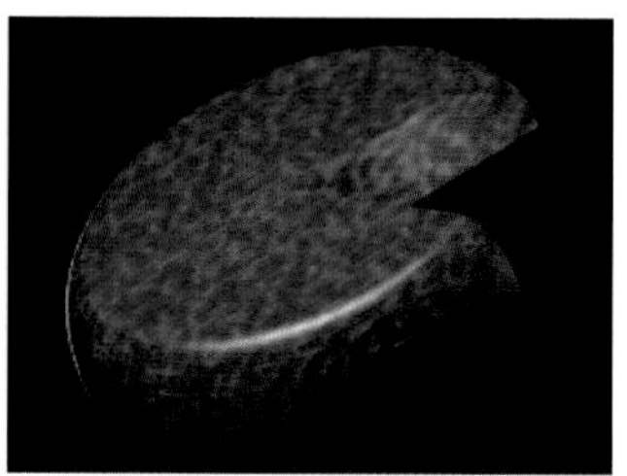

[St]99

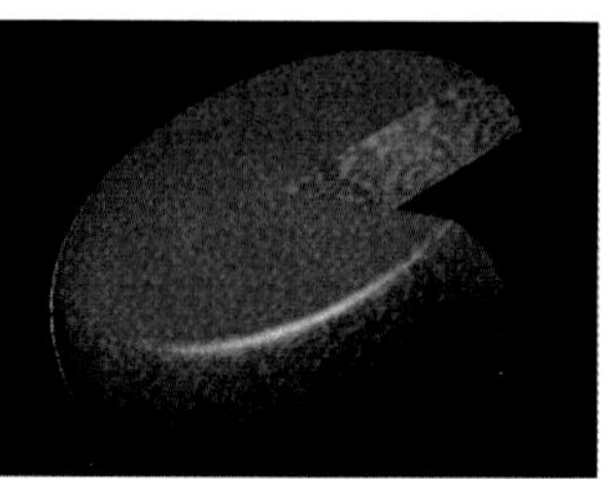

[S]5 Bump 10

DENTS FUNCTION

Summary

This product is packaged with 3D Studio Release 4 and in the Yost Group's Special Effects disk. It produces dented, dimpled, and complex patterned surfaces that are calculated using a fractal noise function. Dents are particularly useful when used in combination to create multimapped materials. Applying a bit of self-illumination to the resulting material enhances the effect.

The Strength parameter produces some interesting color effects that, depending upon the setting, can add C2's complementary color to the surface.

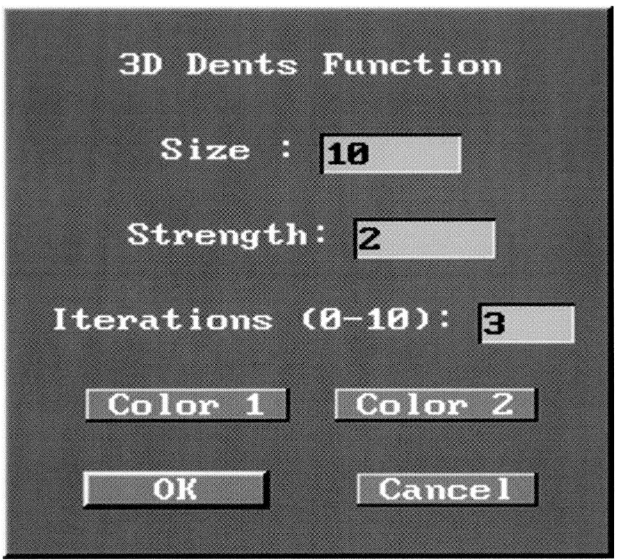

The Dents Function dialog box.

Dents Function Parameters

Size [S] (0–10,000) — Sets the size of the dents.
Strength [St] (0–10,000) — Controls the depth of the dents and also can add a complementary color gradient.
Iterations [N] (0–10) — Specifies the number of times the fractal noise is calculated per pixel.
Color 1 and 2 [C1] [C2] — C1 sets the background color and C2 sets the dent color.

[S]30 [St]10 [I]3 Bump 75

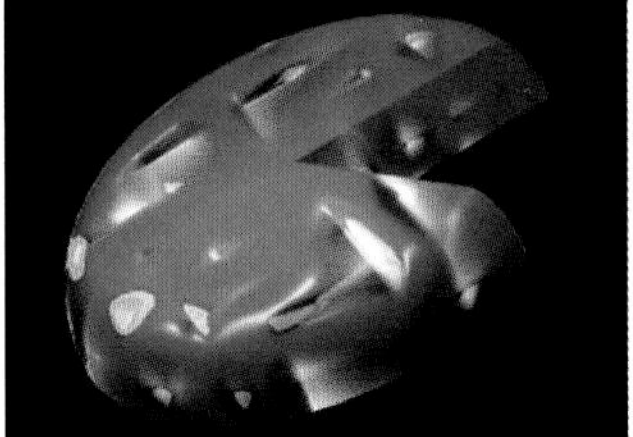
[S]60 [St]20 [I]1 Bump 80

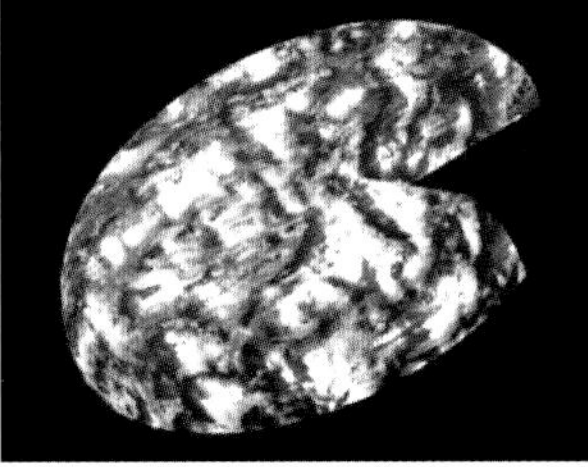
[S]50 [St]50 [I]5 Bump 100

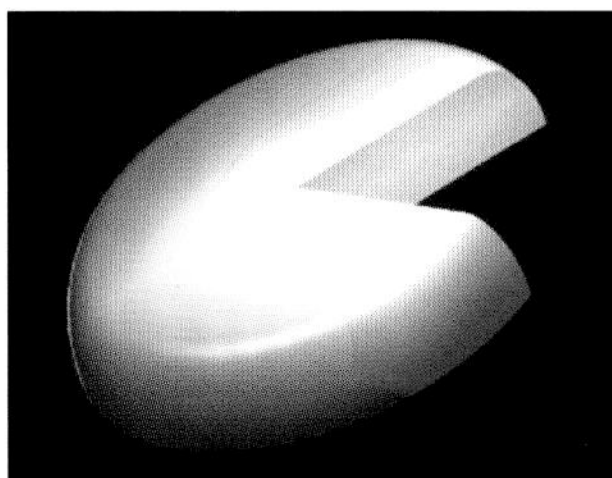
[S]750 [St]30 [1]1

Dents is excellent for multimapped materials that mimic moldy and eroded materials.

EARTH PLANET GENERATOR

Summary

Earth Generator is included with Schreiber Instruments' Imagine Photo-Realistic Textures bundle. Earth produces a range of planet-like solid patterns using computations based on fractal geometry. Earth is controlled with Size and Fractalization variables, which scale and set the chaos of the pattern to produce a wide range of patterns. Contrast between land colors and water colors controls the amount of blending. Black and white and shades of gray work well for bump, transparency, and specular maps.

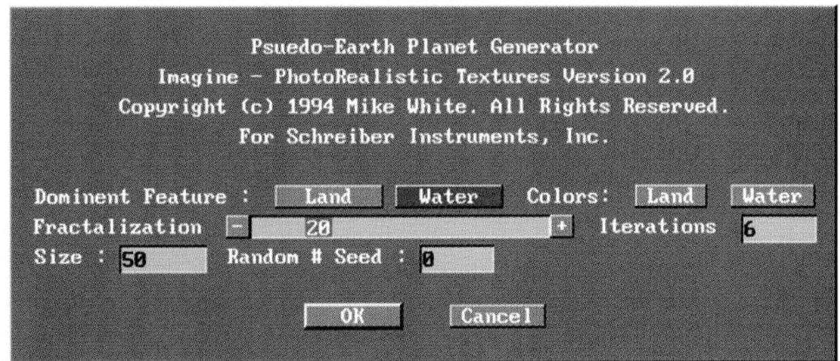

The Earth Planet Generator dialog box.

Earth Planet Generator Parameters

Dominant Feature [D] — Sets the texture's primary color area.
Land Color, Water Color [Cl] [Cw] — Sets the RGB or HSL values for the pattern colors.
Fractalization [F] (0–100) — Sets the texture's randomness or chaos.
Iterations [I] (0–10) — Sets the number of times the algorithm is applied. Higher numbers create more detail.
Size [S] (.0001–999,999.9) — Sets the texture's overall scale.
Random Seed [R] (0–999,999) — Sets the algorithm's start point with an arbitrary number. Each number produces a unique pattern.
Note: *Bump maps are duplicates of SXP's given settings.*

EARTH PLANET GENERATOR cont

EARTH_I.SXP \earth **Schreiber Instruments**

[D]land [F]50 [S]50 Bump 5

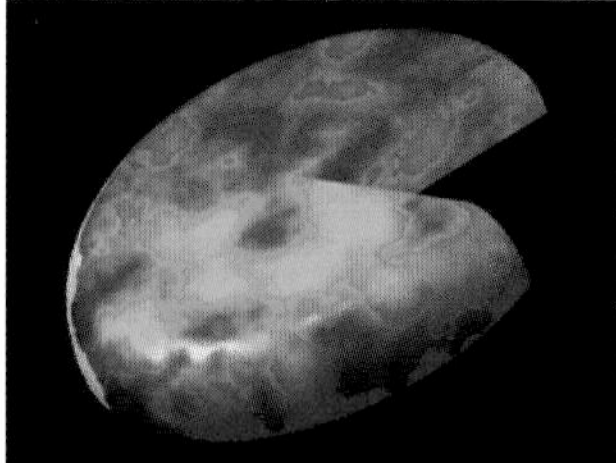
[D]wat [F]20 [S]70 Bump 5

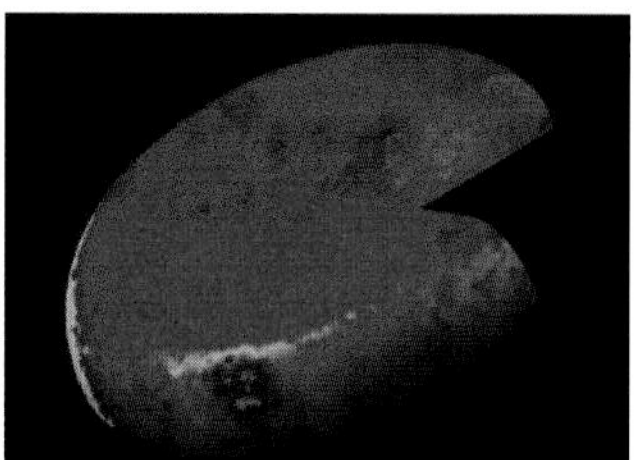
[D]land [F]80 [S]80 Bump 5

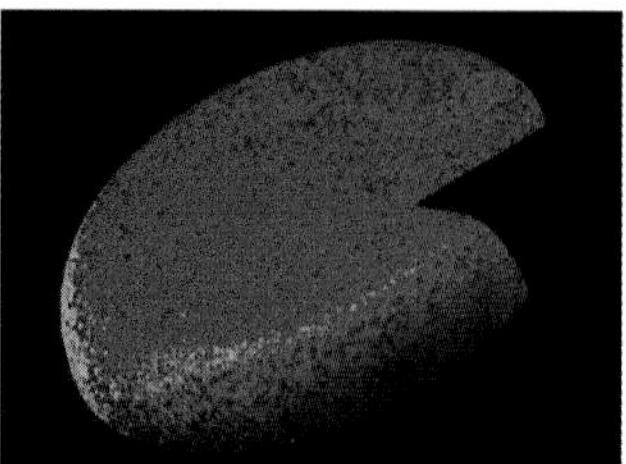
[D]land [F]10 [S]5 Bump 10

FLAME

FLAMEO_I.SXP \flamemsk **Yost Group**

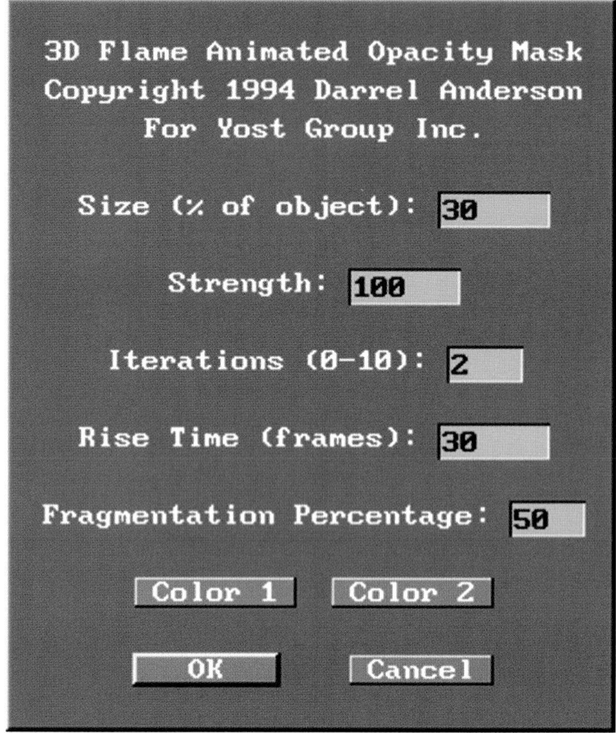

The Flame dialog box.

Summary

Flame is available with Yost Group's IPAS3 disk 6. Although it was designed to be used as an opacity map in conjunction with the Flame AXP, the flame mask itself is capable of creating a variety of wispy and feathery animated textures.

Flame Parameters

Size [S] (.0001–10,000) — Sets the texture's overall scale.
Strength [St] (0–10,000) — Controls the intensity of the blobs.
Iterations [I] (0–10) — Sets the level of detail.
Rise Time (frames) [Rt] (0–99,999) — Specifies the time an element takes to move from the bottom to the top of the object.
Fragmentation Percentage [F] (0–100%) — Controls the cutoff point of a white gradient that is mixed with the pattern. A setting of 40 allows the upper 40 percent of the object to render at full contrast.
Color 1 and 2 [C1] [C2] — C1 sets the foreground element and C2 the background color.

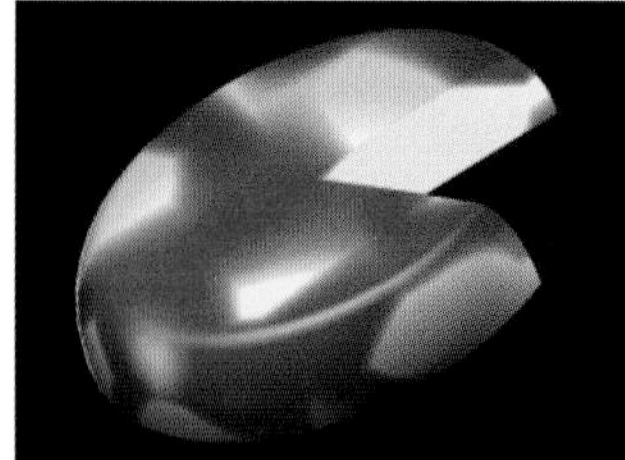
[S]300 [St]2,000 [I]1 [F]100

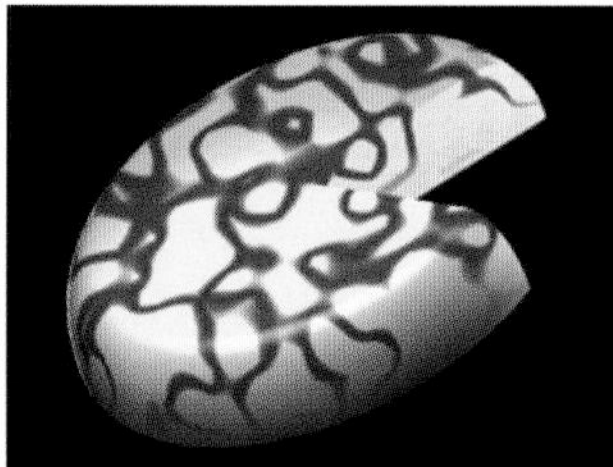
[S]90 [St]3,000 [I]1 [F]50

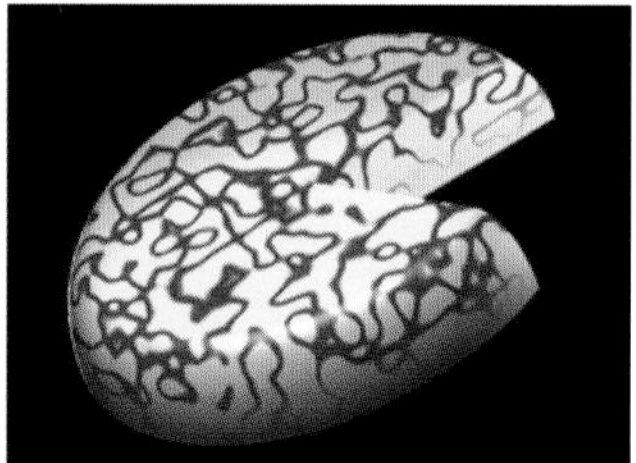
[S]45 [St]3,000 [I]1 [F]50

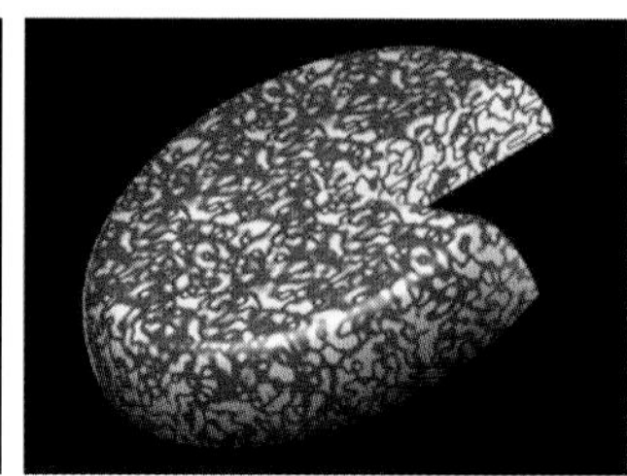
[S]20 [St]500 [I]1 [F]50

Summary

Fractal Layers is available as part of Schreiber Instruments' Imagine Fractal Textures bundle. Fractal Layers produces solid patterns using computations based on fractal geometry. This technique is capable of producing a range of naturalistic stony, moldy, and eroded animated textures. Its patterns are similar to the Turbulence pattern generator.

You can control the look of Fractal Layers using several interdependent variables including size, brightness, and detail. Raising the multiplier value not only controls which color is dominant, but also controls color clipping, enabling you to suppress one of the chosen colors or change the stripe width.

Animation is controlled by Start and End Phase settings, which cause the textures to move and swirl through the mesh object.

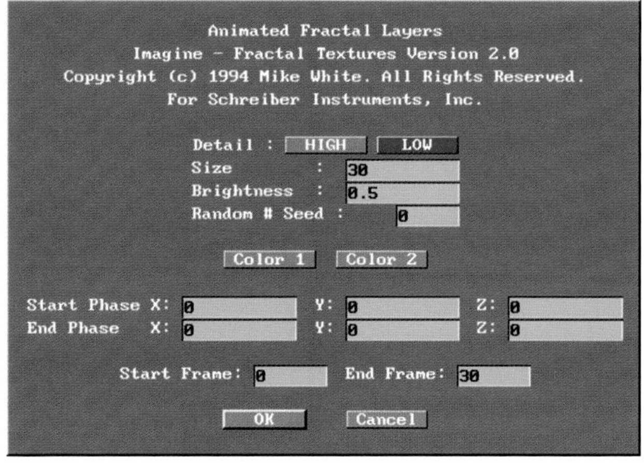

The Fractal Layers dialog box.

Fractal Layers Parameters

Detail [D] l, h (low, high) — Sets the texture's detail level.
Size [S] (.0001–100,000) — Sets the texture's overall scale.
Brightness [B] (0–10,000) — Sets the texture's overall brightness. Also acts to control color dominance and proportion.
Color 1, Color2 [C1] [C2] — Sets the RGB or HSL values for the Fractal Layers and background colors.
Start and End Phase (–1,000–1,000) — Sets the texture's start point on the X, Y, and Z axis.
Start and End Frame (0–32,000) — Sets the first and last frames for the texture animation.
Note: *Bump maps are duplicates of Layer's settings.*

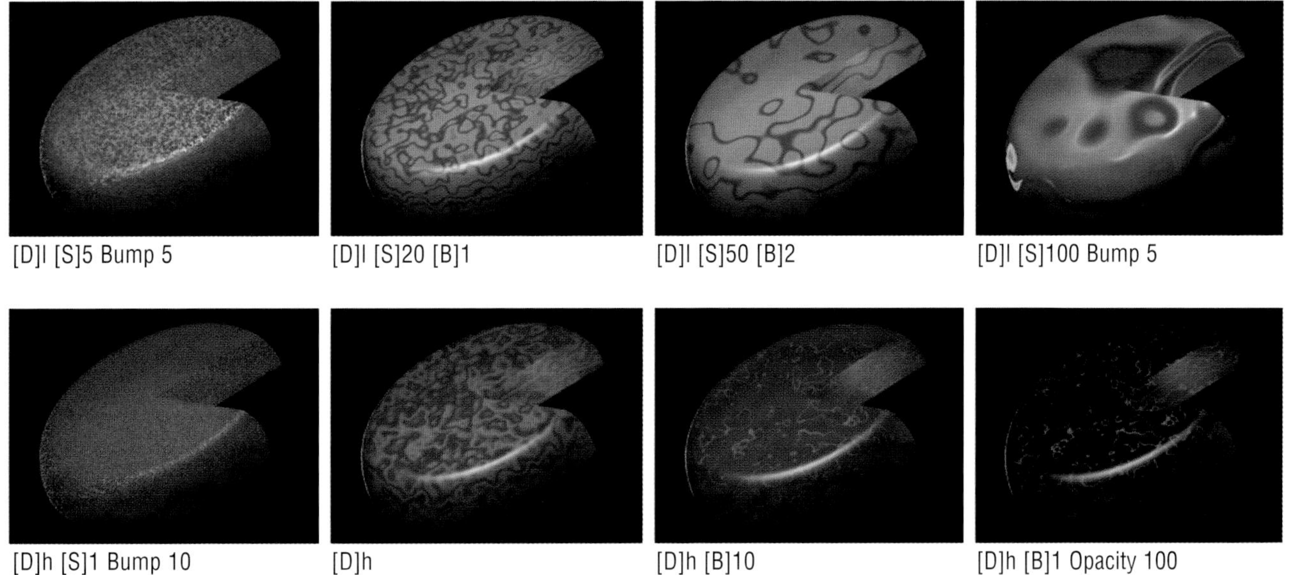

[D]l [S]5 Bump 5 | [D]l [S]20 [B]1 | [D]l [S]50 [B]2 | [D]l [S]100 Bump 5

[D]h [S]1 Bump 10 | [D]h | [D]h [B]10 | [D]h [B]1 Opacity 100

FRACTAL STRIPES

STRIPE_I.SXP \fstripe **Schreiber Instruments**

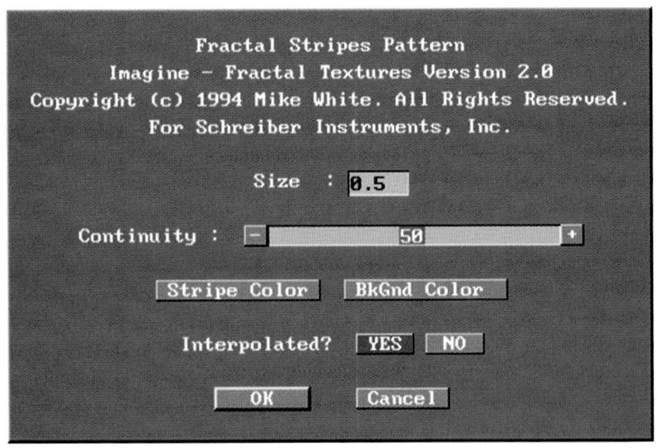

The Fractal Stripes dialog box.

Summary

Fractal Stripe is included with Schreiber Instruments' Imagine Fractal Textures bundle. Fractal Stripe produces smooth and jagged stripe patterns using computations based on fractal geometry. This technique is capable of producing a range of layered textures that vary from sharp stripes to irregular faded bands.

Fractal Stripes Parameters

Size [S] (.0001–1,000.0) — Sets the texture's overall scale.
Continuity [C] (0–100) — Sets the stripe's noise level, from straight to jagged.
Stripe Color, BkGnd Color [C1] [C2] — Sets the RGB or HSL values for the Fractal Stripe and background colors.
Interpolated [I] y,n (yes, no) — Sets the amount of blending between stripes.
Note: *Bump maps are duplicates of SXP's given settings.*

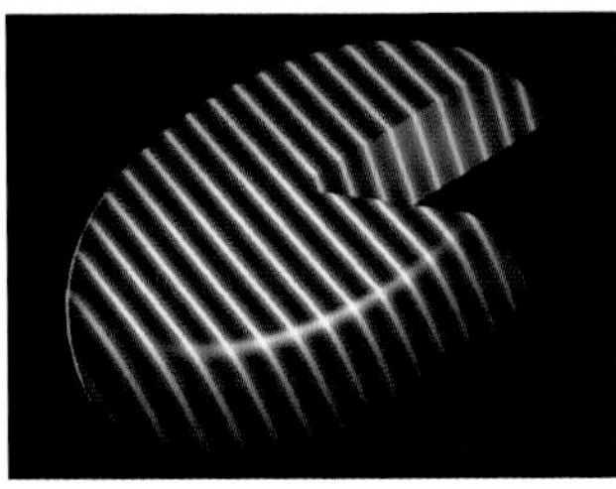

[S].6 [C]100 [I]y

[S].6 [C]1 [I]y Bump 10

[S]1 [C]10 [I]n

[S]1 [C]1 [I]n

GRANITE TEXTURE

GRANIT_I.SXP \granite **Schreiber Instruments**

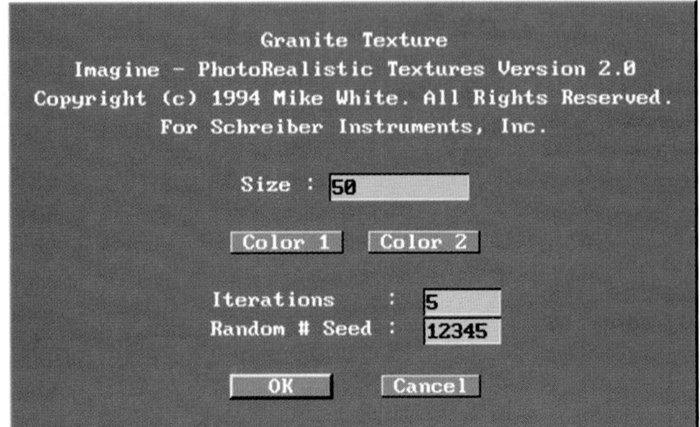

The Granite Texture dialog box.

Summary

Granite is part of Schreiber Instruments' Imagine Photo-Realistic Textures bundle. Granite produces a range of solid patterns using computations based on fractal geometry. This technique is capable of producing a range of layered textures that vary from rough, random splotches to puffy, cloud-like blobs to fine, granular textures.

Granite is controlled with a Size variable, which scales the pattern to produce a range of patterns. Contrast between C1 and C2 controls the amount of blending. Black and white and shades of gray work well for bump, transparency, and specular maps.

Granite Texture Parameters

Size [S] (.0001–100,000.0) — Sets the texture's overall scale.
Iterations [I] (0–99,999) — Sets the number of times the algorithm is applied. Higher numbers create more detail.
Random Seed [R] (0–999,999) — Sets the algorithm's start point with an arbitrary number. Each number produces a unique pattern.
Color 1 and Color 2 [C1], [C2] — Sets the RGB or HSL values for the pattern colors.
Note: *Bump maps are duplicates of SXP's given settings.*

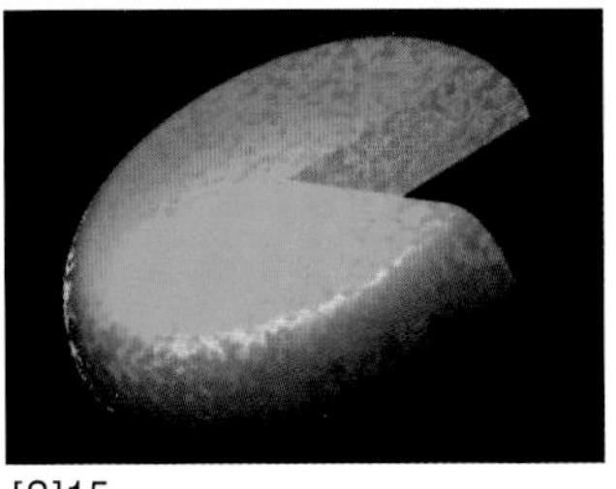
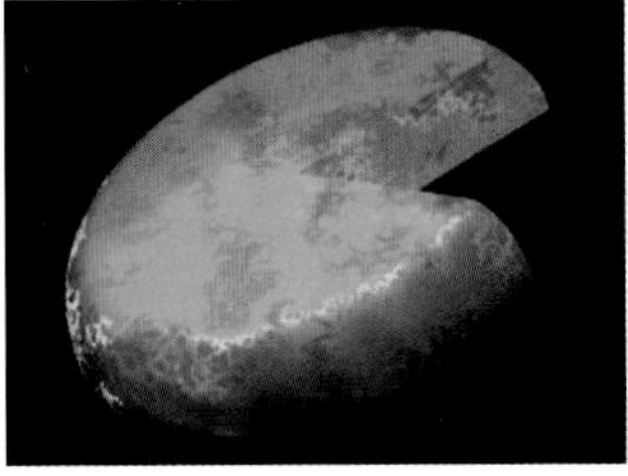
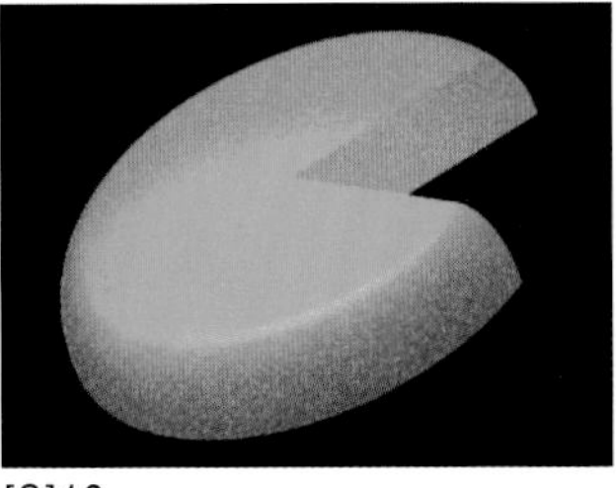
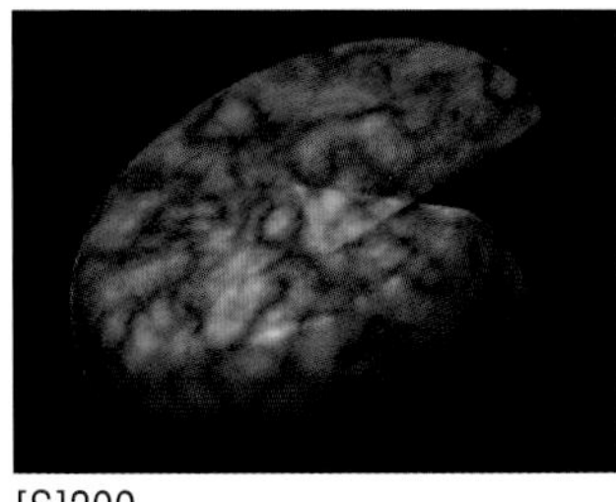

[S]15 [S]50 [S]10 [S]200

A range of patterns can be produced by varying the scale parameter, particularly toward the smaller values. These images use the same values applied as a 15% bump map, a 10% bump map, 100% specular/self-illumination maps, and 100% opacity/shininess maps, respectively.

HEXAGONAL PATTERN

Schreiber Instruments \hexagonl TRIHEX_I.SXP

Summary

Creates a tri-colored, solid hexagonal pattern which is projected through either the XY, XZ, or YZ plane. The color for each hexagon group is set using RGB and HLS color models via a color definition dialog box.

The Size parameter is essential in producing a surprising range of noisy, moiré textures and simulated refractive and interference patterns. The use of color and value is key to controlling the resulting effect.

The Axis parameter is useful for specifying how the hexagon pattern cuts through a given 3D mesh object, and the Phase parameters provide a means of aligning the pattern or specifying its starting point.

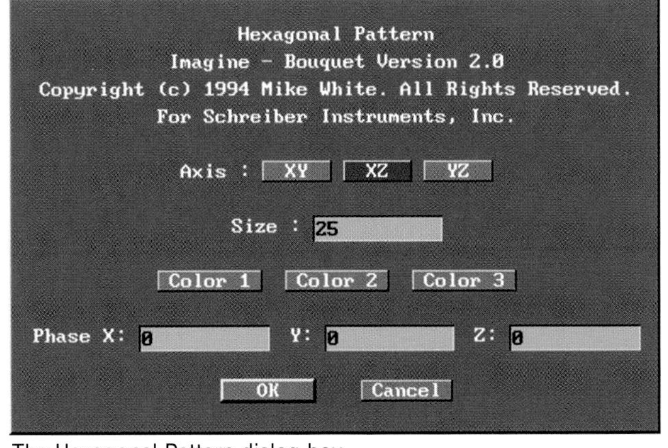

The Hexagonal Pattern dialog box.

Hexagonal Pattern Parameters

Axis XY, XZ, and YZ — Sets the projection plane for the hexagonal texture

Size [S] (0001–10,000) — Sets the texture's overall scale.

Color 1, 2, and 3 — Sets the color for the first, second, and third order hexagons which make up the pattern.

Phase X, Y, and Z (–1,000–1,000) — Specifies position offset for X, Y, and Z axes.

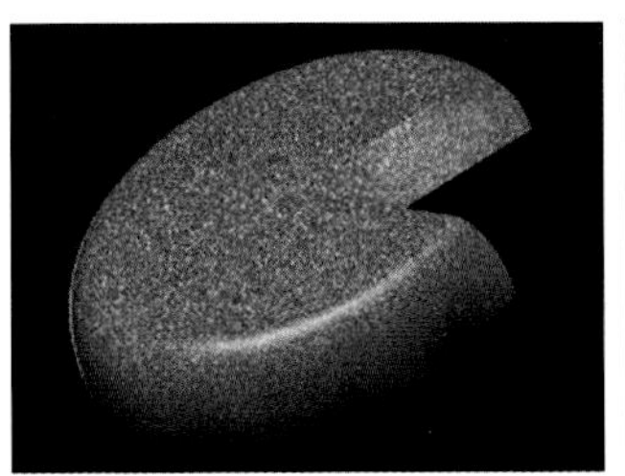
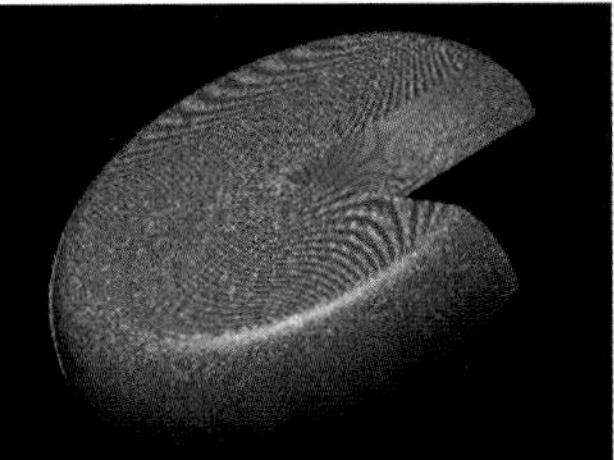
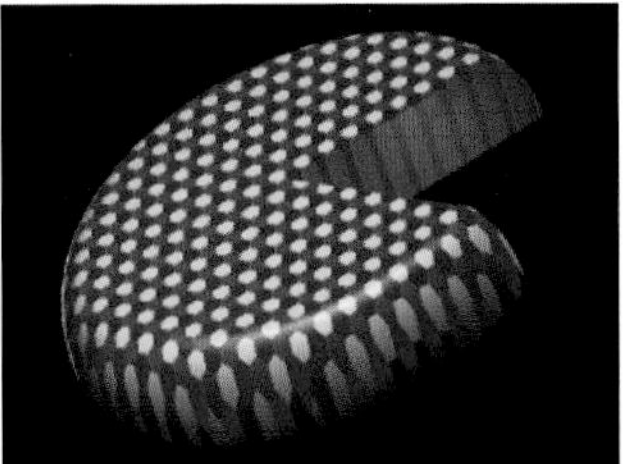

[S].0001 [S].1 [S] 10 [S] 100

A range of patterns can be produced by varying the scale parameter, particularly toward the smaller values.

MARBLE FUNCTION

MARBL_I.SXP \marble4 Autodesk

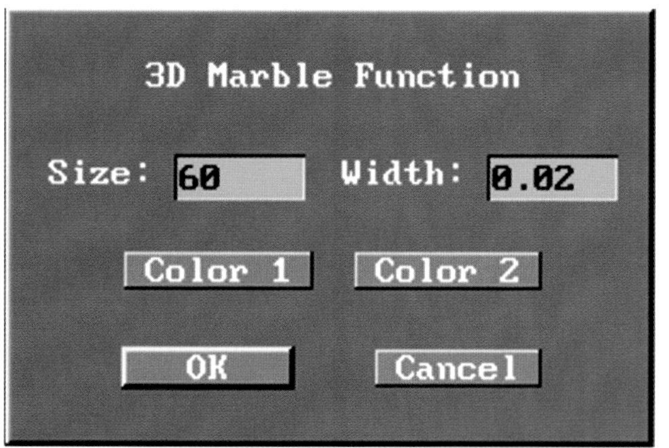

The Marble Function dialog box.

Summary

This product is packaged with 3D Studio Release 4 and in the Yost Group's Special Effects disk. Marble renders turbulent streaks and variegated and blobby patterns. The Size and Width parameters work together to set the scale and thickness of the color pattern produced by Color 1 and Color 2.

The resulting textures have a subtle opalescent character produced by the stepped blending that occurs between the selected colors.

Marble Function Parameters

Size [S] (.0001–10,000) — Sets the scale of the streak pattern.
Width [W] (.0001–10,000) Specifies the frequency of streaks.
Color 1 and 2 [C1] [C2] — C1 sets the foreground or streak color and C2 sets the background color.

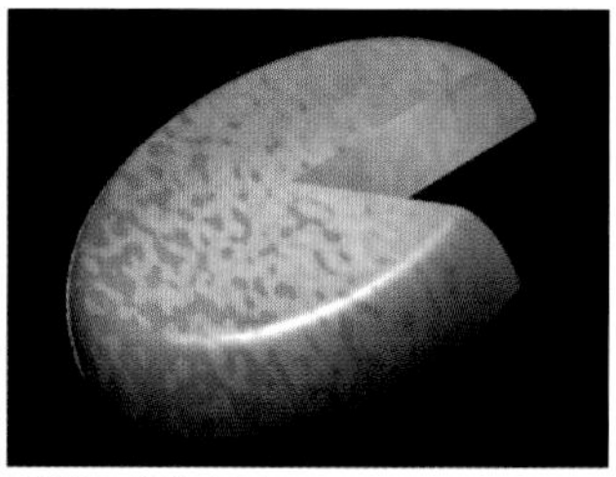

[S]60 [W].001 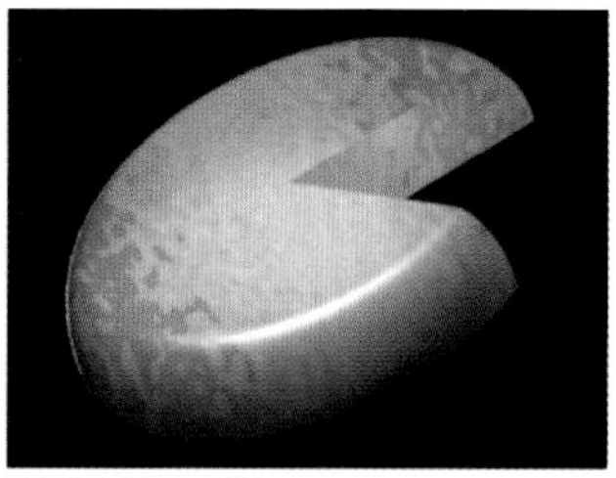 [S]60 [W].005 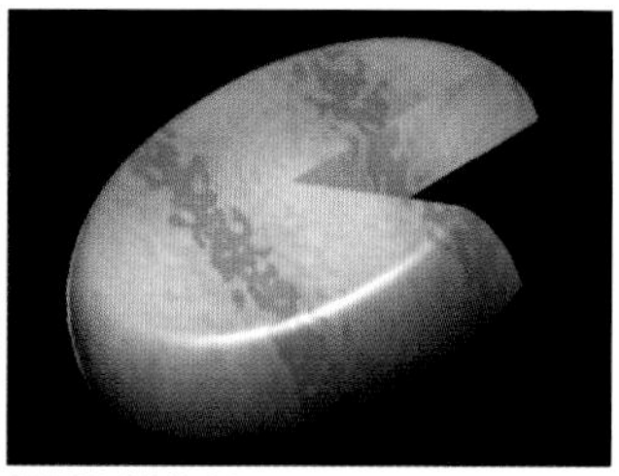 [S]60 [W].01 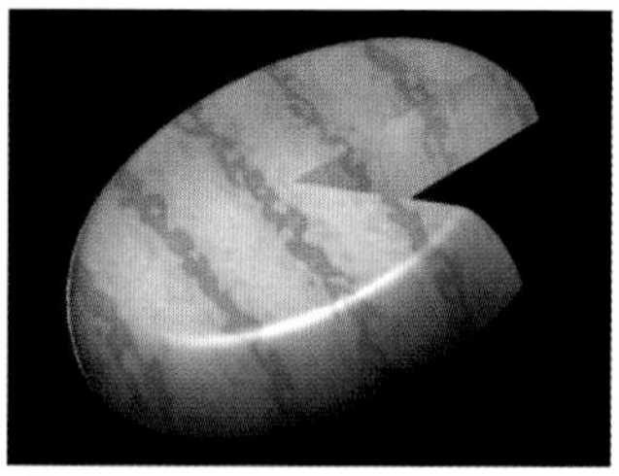 [S]60 [W].02.

The Width variable controls the frequency and distribution of the streak pattern.

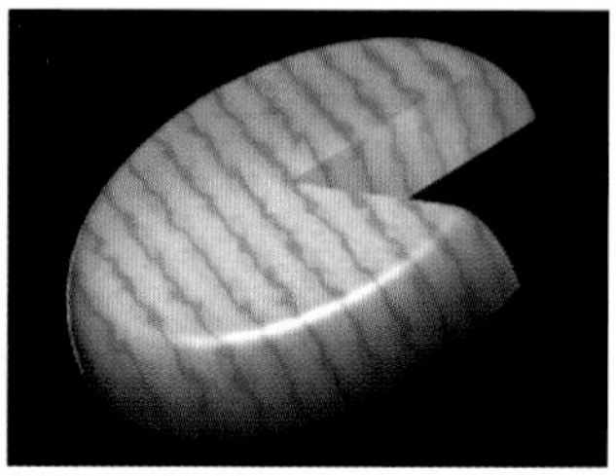

[S]60 [W].05 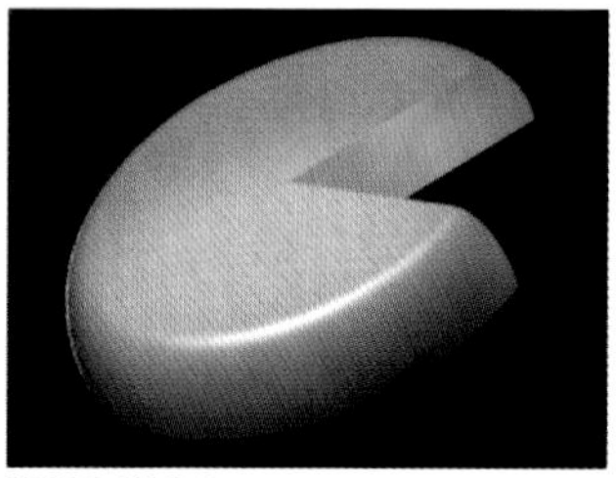 [S]60 [W].3 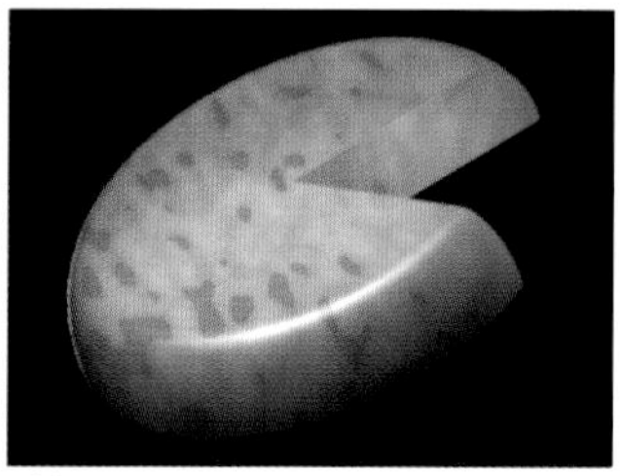 [S]120 [W].001 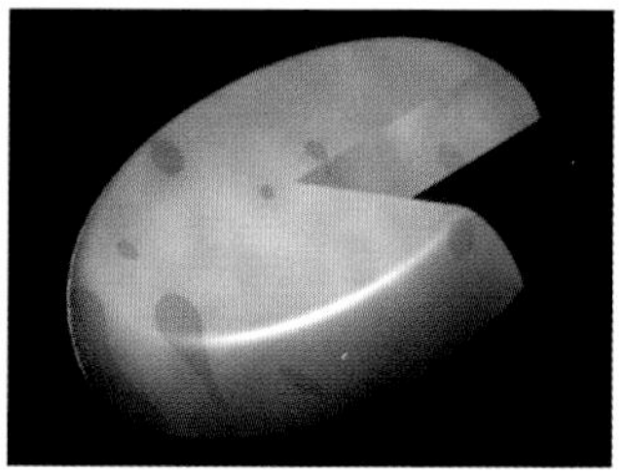 [S]240 [W].001

Size works with Width to scale and distribute the texture.

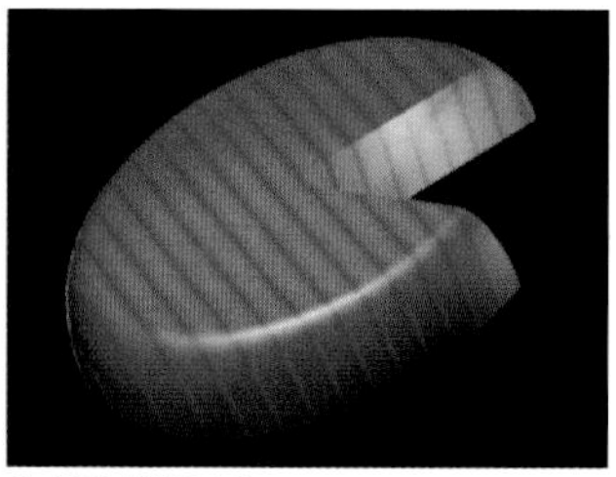

5,000 [W]5.2 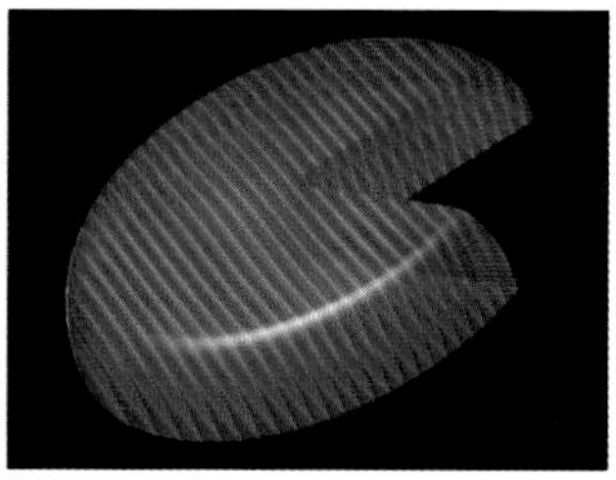 [S]500 [W]1 opacity 100 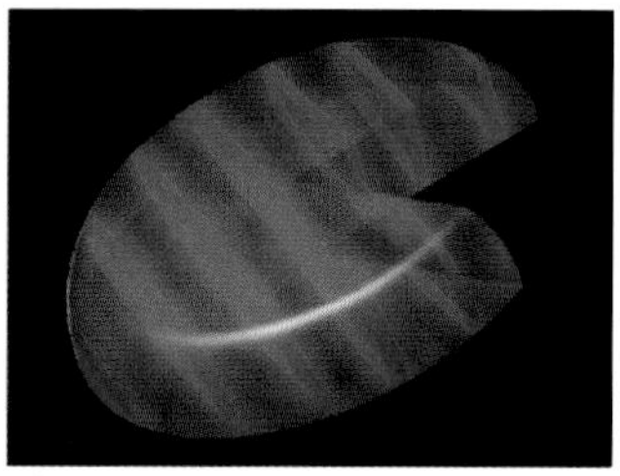 [S]500 [W].2 opacity 100 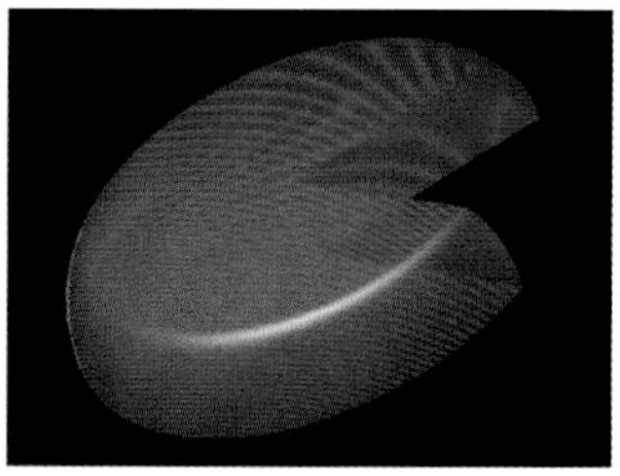 [S]515 [W].5 opacity 100

Summary

Marble Texture is included with Schreiber Instruments' Imagine Photo-Realistic Textures bundle. Marble produces a range of patterns using computations based on fractal geometry. This technique is capable of producing a broad range of layered textures that vary from smooth, regular stripes to complex, natural-looking patterns.

You can control Marble's look using several interdependent variables including fractalization, jitter, and turbulence. For all the variation possible, this interdependence can result in near-identical or identical textures being created from dramatically different settings. For the same reason it is also possible to change a variable with no apparent result.

Generally, this occurs while working with two variables with one or both set to an extreme value. Though this approach can produce some useful results, working in a range around the middle or default range increases Marble's responsiveness. Marble's textures are oriented vertically.

Marble Texture Parameters

Size [S] (.0001–100,000.0) — Sets the texture's overall scale.
Fractalization [F] (0–100) — Sets the texture's randomness or chaos.
Jitter [J] (0–300) — Sets the vein width variance and knots.
Iterations [I] (0–99,999) — Sets the number of times the algorithm is applied. Higher numbers create more detail.

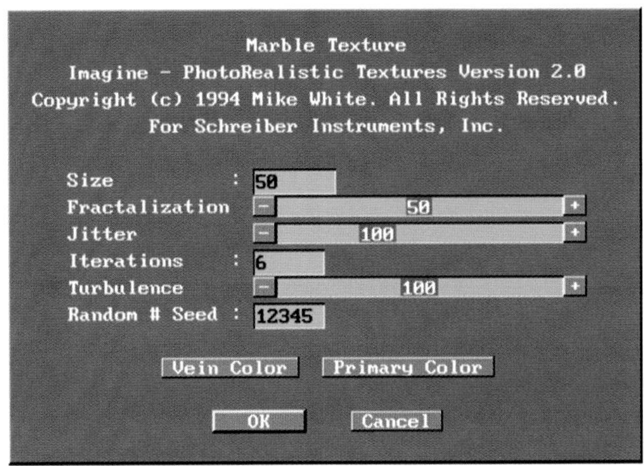

The Marble Texture dialog box.

Turbulence [T] (0–200) — Sets the overall noise added to the veins. Turbulence is needed for Fractalization or Jitter to have an effect.
Random Seed [R] (0–999,999) — Sets the algorithm's start point with an arbitrary number. Each number produces a unique pattern.
Vein Color [C1] — Sets the RGB or HSL values for the secondary color.
Primary Color [C2] — Sets the RGB or HSL values for the main color.
***Note:** Bump maps are duplicates of SXP's given settings.*

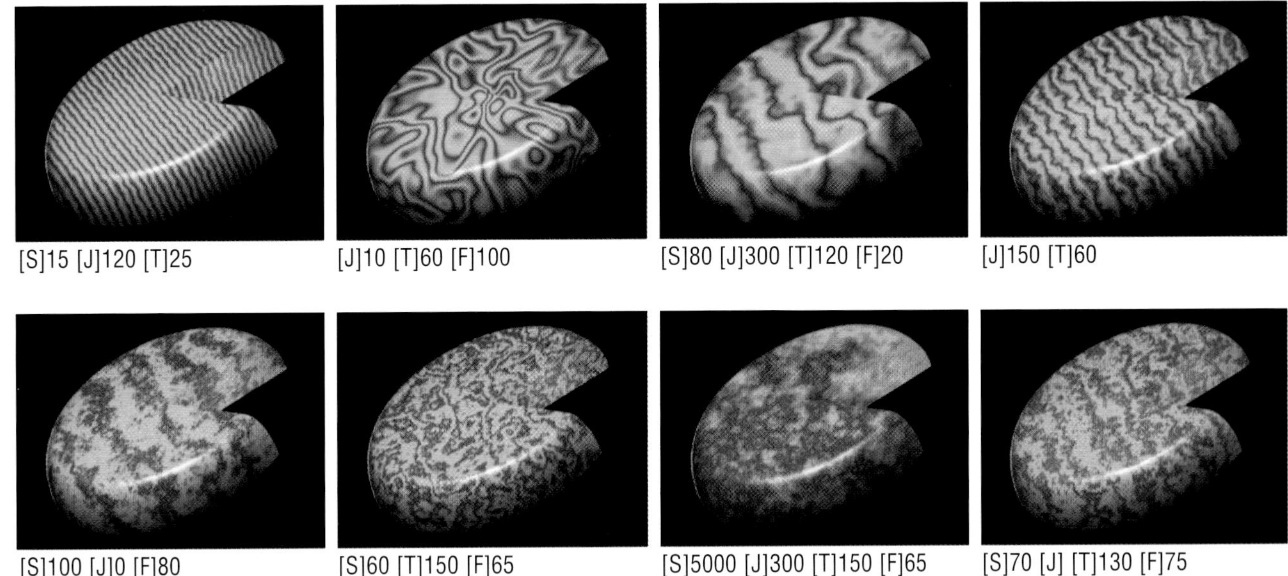

[S]15 [J]120 [T]25 | [J]10 [T]60 [F]100 | [S]80 [J]300 [T]120 [F]20 | [J]150 [T]60

[S]100 [J]0 [F]80 | [S]60 [T]150 [F]65 | [S]5000 [J]300 [T]150 [F]65 | [S]70 [J] [T]130 [F]75

The 6th, 7th, and 8th images use bump maps of 7, 12, and 5, respectively.

MOTTLED TEXTURE

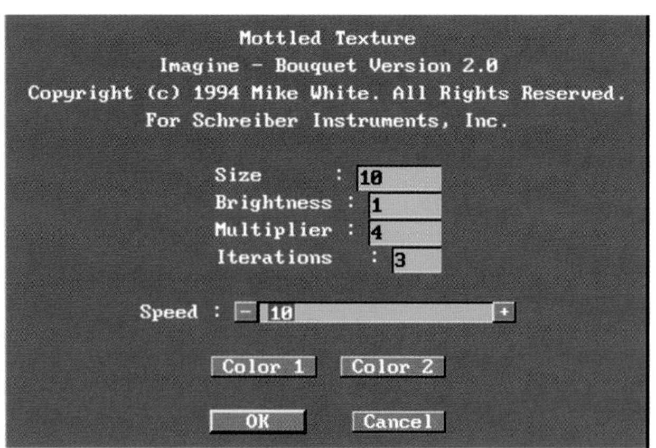

The Mottled Texture dialog box.

Summary

Mottled Texture is included with Schreiber Instruments' Imagine Fractal Bouquet bundle. It produces a range of streaked and blotchy solid patterns using computations based on fractal geometry. Mottle's variables, particularly Size, Brightness, and Multiplier, produce numerous color distortions, often adding the complementary color of [C1] to the color palette.

Mottled Texture Parameters

Size [S] (.0001–100,000.0) — Sets the texture's overall scale.

Brightness [B] (0–10,000) — Sets the texture's overall brightness and can produce useful color distortions.

Multiplier [M] (0–10,000) — Varies texture complexity.

Iterations [I] (0–99,999) — Sets the number of times the algorithm is applied. Higher numbers create more detail.

Speed [Sp] (0–200) — Sets the step value for the iterations parameter.

Color 1 and Color 2 [C1] [C2] — Sets the RGB or HSL values for the mottle and background colors.

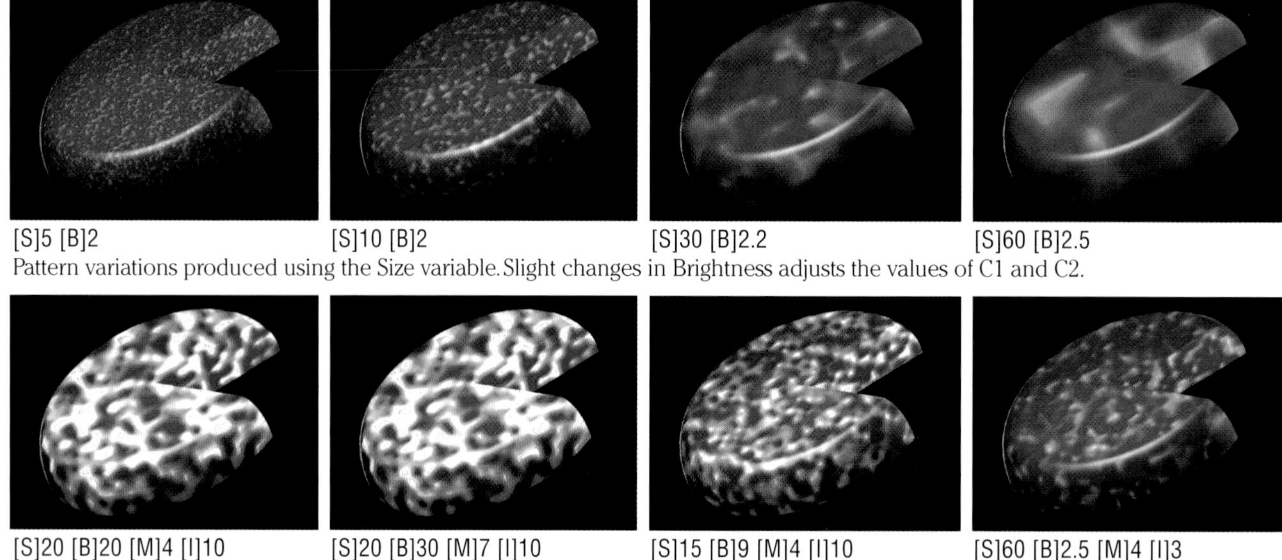

[S]5 [B]2 | [S]10 [B]2 | [S]30 [B]2.2 | [S]60 [B]2.5

Pattern variations produced using the Size variable. Slight changes in Brightness adjusts the values of C1 and C2.

[S]20 [B]20 [M]4 [I]10 | [S]20 [B]30 [M]7 [I]10 | [S]15 [B]9 [M]4 [I]10 | [S]60 [B]2.5 [M]4 [I]3

The same color settings were dramatically altered, adding pink and white to the color mix by varying the [B] and [M] parameters.

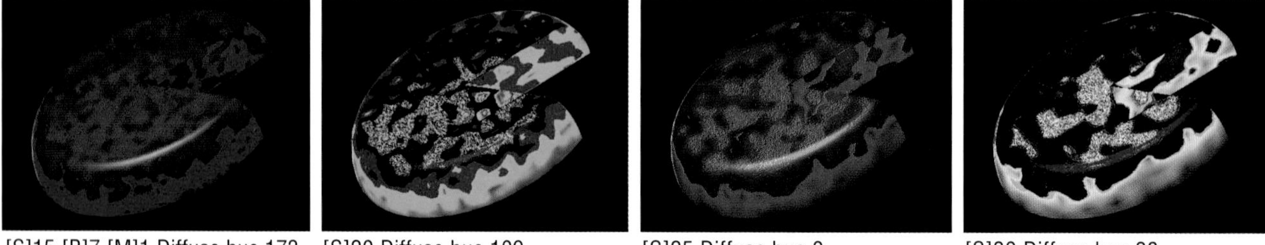

[S]15 [B]7 [M]1 Diffuse hue 173 | [S]20 Diffuse hue 109 | [S]25 Diffuse hue 0 | [S]30 Diffuse hue 38

Mottle was used as a 100% opacity map. Diffuse color values were set to Luminance 128 and Saturation 255 for each sample.

NOISE FUNCTION

Summary

This product is packaged with 3D Studio Release 4 and in the Yost Group's Special Effects disk. It produces random patterns ranging from smooth blotches to specks with Color 1 setting the foreground and Color 2 the background color.

The X,Y, and Z Offset parameters provide control over various animation effects such as frenetic, gritty, or slowly rolling soft-featured surfaces. The Noise Function works best on materials where the same Size settings are applied as both texture and bump maps.

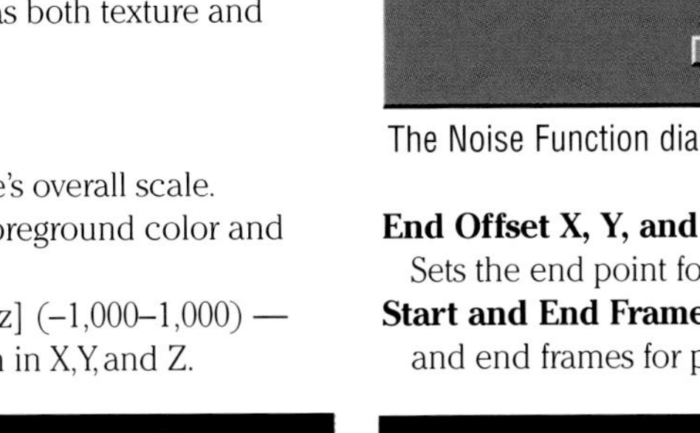

The Noise Function dialog box.

Noise Function Parameters

Size [S] (.0001–10,000) — Sets the texture's overall scale.
Color 1 and 2 [C1] [C2] — C1 sets the foreground color and C2 the background color.
Start Offset X, Y, and Z [Sox] [Soy] [Soz] (–1,000–1,000) — Sets the start point for pattern animation in X,Y, and Z.
End Offset X, Y, and Z [Eox] [Eoy] [Eoz] (–1,000–1,000) — Sets the end point for pattern animation in X,Y, and Z.
Start and End Frame [Sf] [Ef] (0–32,000) — Sets the start and end frames for pattern animation.

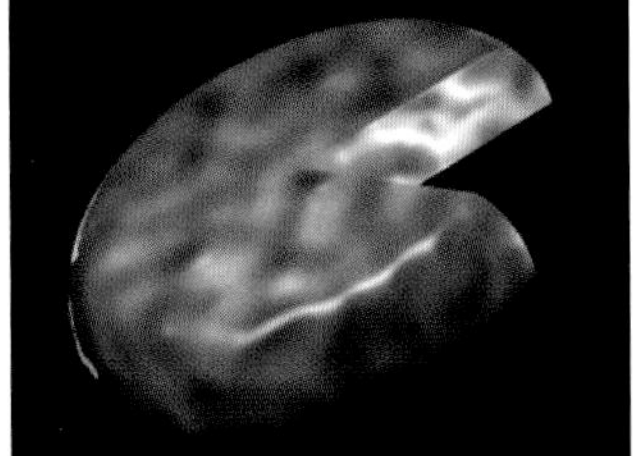

[S]100 bump 30

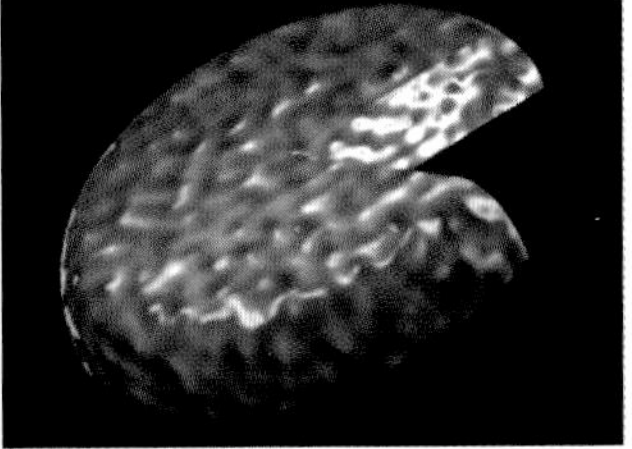

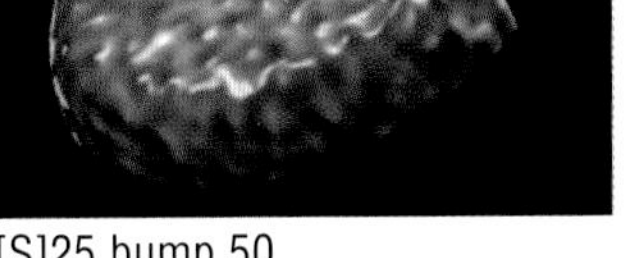

[S]25 bump 50

[S]12 bump 60

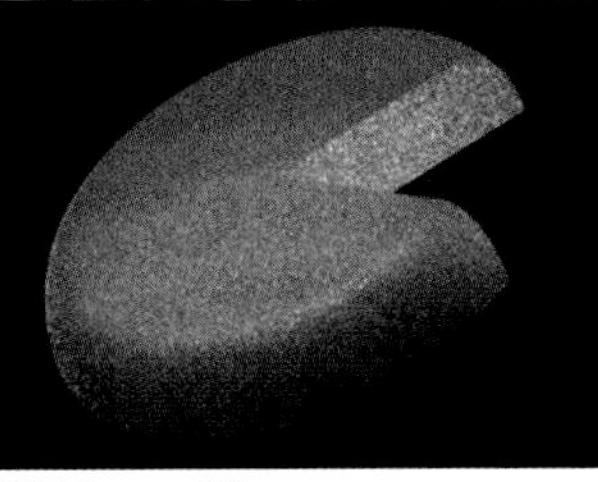

[S]1 bump 80

When also applied as both a texture and bump, Noise's Size variable provides textures from gooey to gritty.

PLANET FUNCTION

Summary

Planet is available as part of Yost Group Special Effects disk #7. It produces simulated planet textures with variable ocean size, continent size, and island factor. It uses fractal noise and palette files created in Autodesk Animator Pro for the pattern and color range.

Planet Function Parameters

Continent Size [S] (0–10,000) — Sets the texture's overall scale.
Island Factor [Is] (0–10,000) — Controls the roughness of land mass edges and mountains.
Ocean Percentage [O] (0–100%) Controls the proportion of ocean to land.
Blend water/land? [B] y,n (yes or no) — Optionally blends the ocean and land areas.
Palette File (*filename*.COL) — Specifies the name of an external color palette file.
Random Seed [Rs] (0–99,999) — Sets the initial starting point for the pattern.

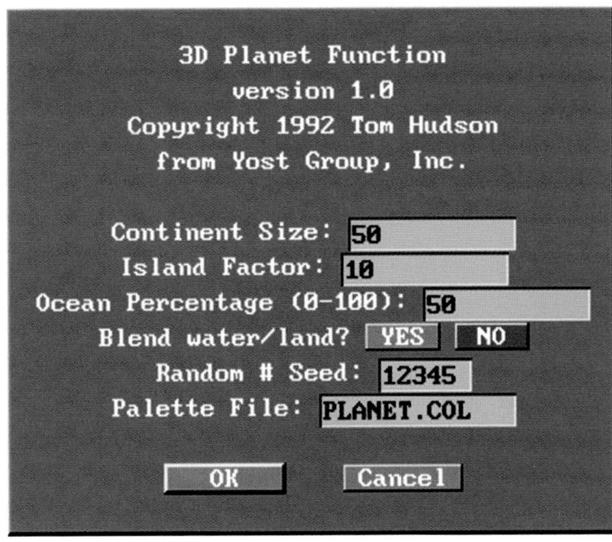

The Planet Function dialog box.

PLANET FUNCTION cont

PLANET_I.SXP | **\planet** | **Yost Group**

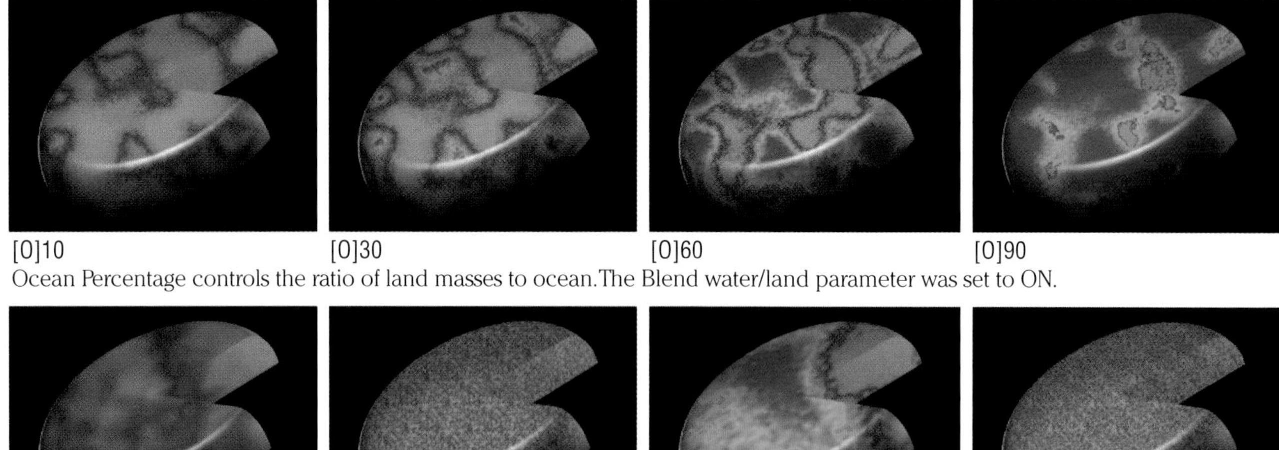

[O]10 [O]30 [O]60 [O]90

Ocean Percentage controls the ratio of land masses to ocean.The Blend water/land parameter was set to ON.

[S]300 [O]10 [S]5 [O]30 [S]120 [O]60 [S]5 [O]60

Planet also is useful for producing numerous multicolored fractal-based textures.

RAINBOW

RAINBW_I.SXP | **\rainbow** | **Pointer Digital Graf/x**

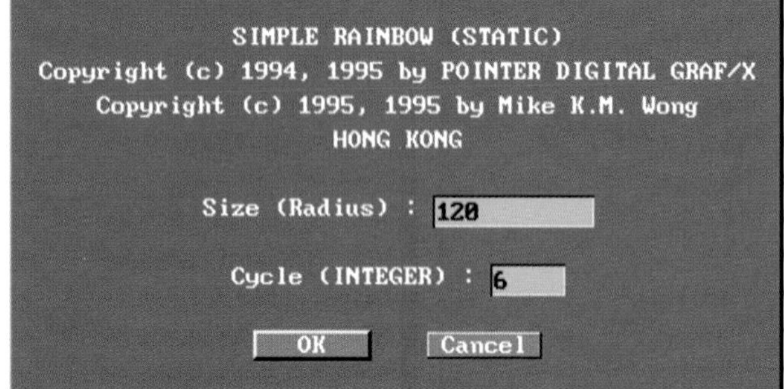

The Rainbow dialog box.

Summary

Rainbow projects a radial rainbow pattern through the XY plane of the object.Some interesting pattern distortions and spatter effects can be produced by setting both the Size and Cycle to their extreme values.

Rainbow Parameters

Size (Radius) [S] (.1–10,000) — Sets the size of the rainbow relative to the mesh object.

Cycle [Cy] (0–1,000) — Specifies the number of rainbow cycles.

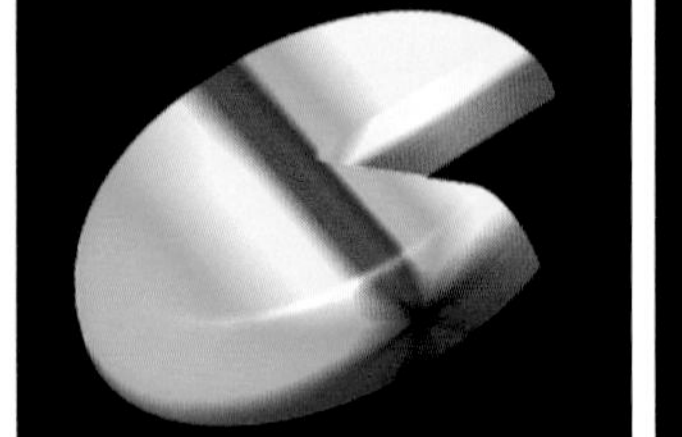

[S]60 [Cy]3 [S]60 [Cy]60

Adjusting [S] and [Cy] produces a range of color variation.

Summary

Rock Textures is included with Schreiber Instruments' Imagine Fractal Bouquet bundle. Rocks produces a range of rock-like solid patterns using computations based on fractal geometry. The results range from fine-grained uniform patterns to loopy, veined patterns.

Controls include color, size, width, differentiation, and perturbation, which vary the pattern scale and randomness. There also are presets for several common pattern groups: marble, agate, slate, and porcelain.

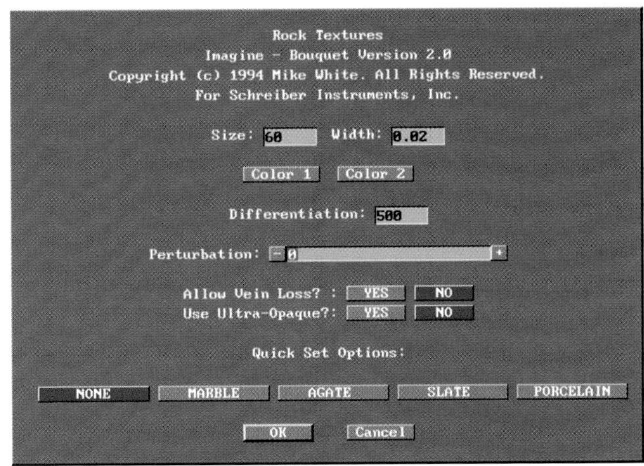

The Rock Texture dialog box.

Rock Textures Parameters

Size [S] (0.001–100,000) — Sets the texture's overall scale.
Width [W] (0.0–10,000) — Sets the width of veins or surface bumps.
Color 1 and Color 2 [C1] [C2] — Sets the RGB or HLS values for the vein and background colors.
Differentiation [D] (0.0–99,999.0) — Sets the frequency of the surface pattern. Smaller numbers give a finer grain to the texture.
Perturbation [P] (0–100) — Sets the amount of chaos in the pattern.
Allow Vein Loss? [VL] (yes or no) — Determines whether veins can disappear as a result of chaos in the pattern.
Use Ultra-Opaque? [UO] (yes or no) — Determines whether the dimmest colors in the pattern are set to black for use in opacity maps.
Quick Set Options [QS] (none, marble, agate, slate, porcelain) — Preset variable groups to quickly select common pattern types. These options override some of the manual settings.

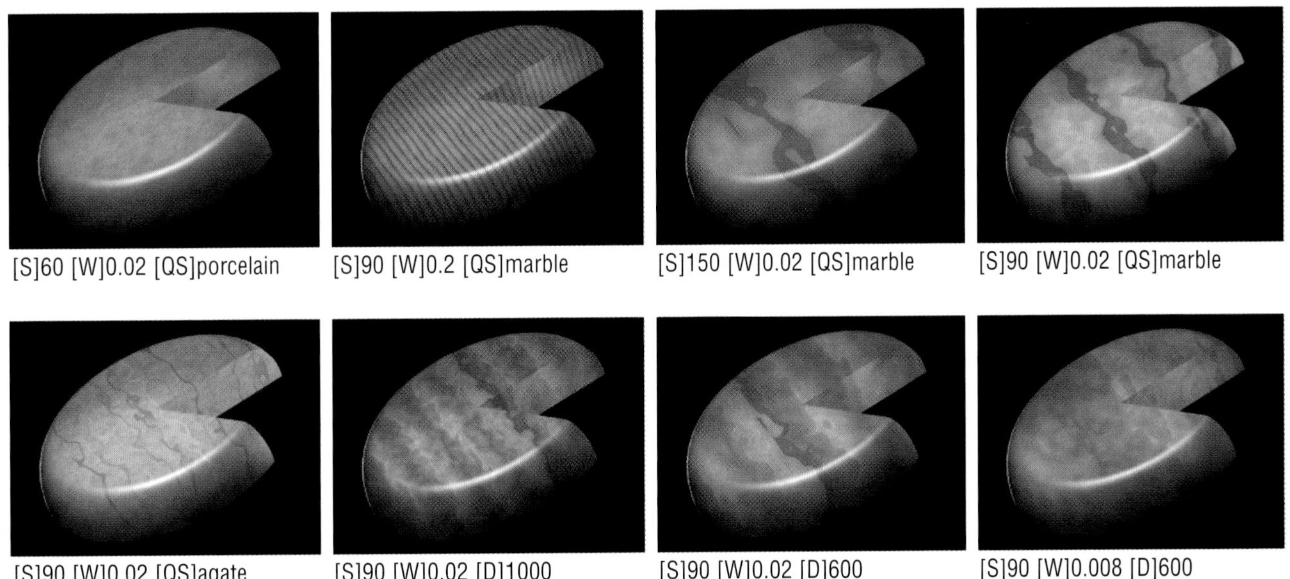
[S]60 [W]0.02 [QS]porcelain — [S]90 [W]0.2 [QS]marble — [S]150 [W]0.02 [QS]marble — [S]90 [W]0.02 [QS]marble

[S]90 [W]0.02 [QS]agate — [S]90 [W]0.02 [D]1000 — [S]90 [W]0.02 [D]600 — [S]90 [W]0.008 [D]600

The main changes between samples were size, vein width, and Quick Set pattern types.

SMOKE FUNCTION

SMOKE_I.SXP \smoke Yost Group

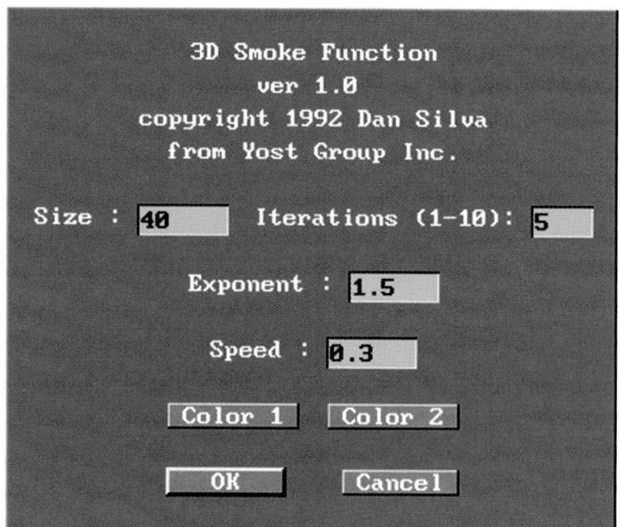

The Smoke Function dialog box.

Summary

Smoke is included with Yost Group's Special Effects IPAS package #2. It produces turbulent smoke-like patterns that can be animated using a speed parameter. Smoke is particularly useful as an opacity map in producing effects such as smoke swirling through a beam of light.

Smoke also is capable of a range of intricate curvilinear patterns of varying weights along with grainy patterns. Exponent is used to control the proportion of C1 to C2, and with that the contrast of the pattern, particularly when set to values less than 1. As Iterations decrease, the pattern becomes softer and more linear.

Smoke Function Parameters

Size [S] (.0001–10,000) — Sets the texture's overall scale.
Iterations [I] (1–10) — Sets the level of detail within the smoky pattern, with higher values increasing both detail and render time.
Exponent [E] (.01–10) — Higher values make the pattern sharper and cause Color 1 to expand.
Speed [Sp] (0–100) — Controls the rate of turbulence, with higher numbers increasing speed.
Color 1 and 2 [C1] [C2] — C1 sets the background color and C2 the smoke color.

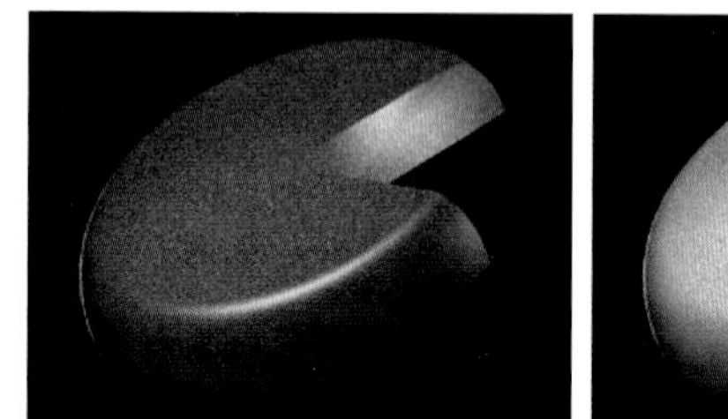
[S].1 [I]1 [Ex]1.5

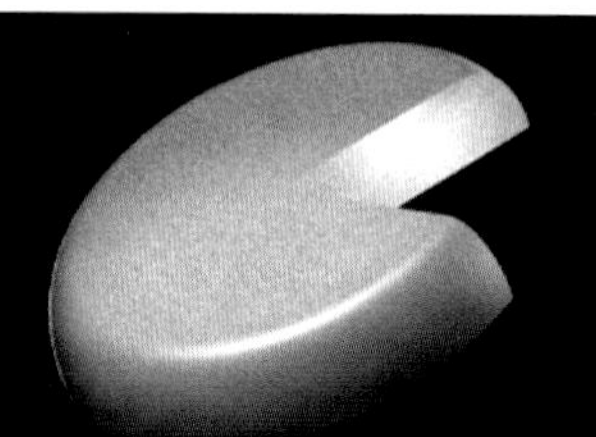
[S].1 [I]5 [Ex].5

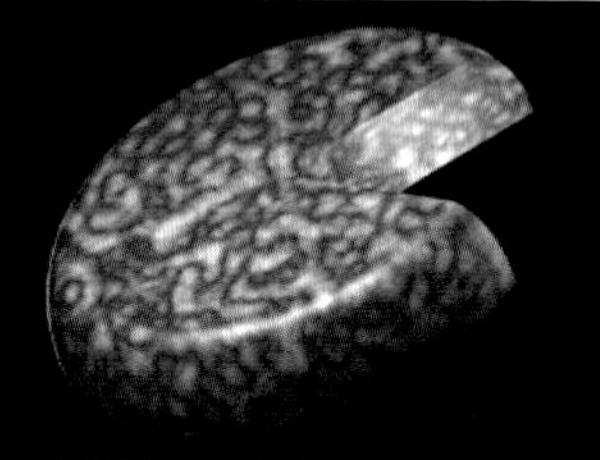
[S]30 [I]10 [Ex]1.5

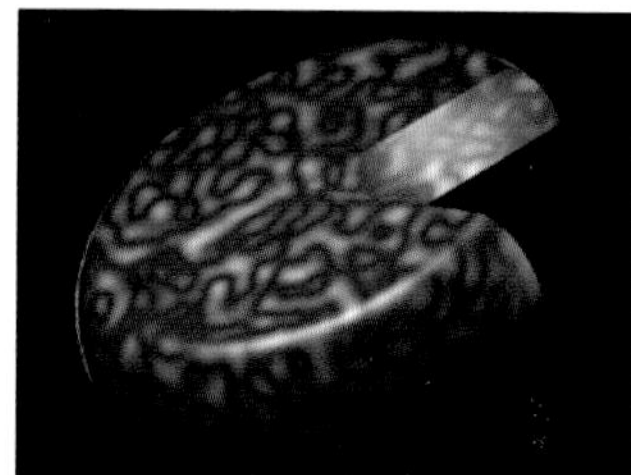
[S]30 [I]1 [Ex]1.5

Size values less than one produce noise patterns, and Iterations controls the pattern's detail level.

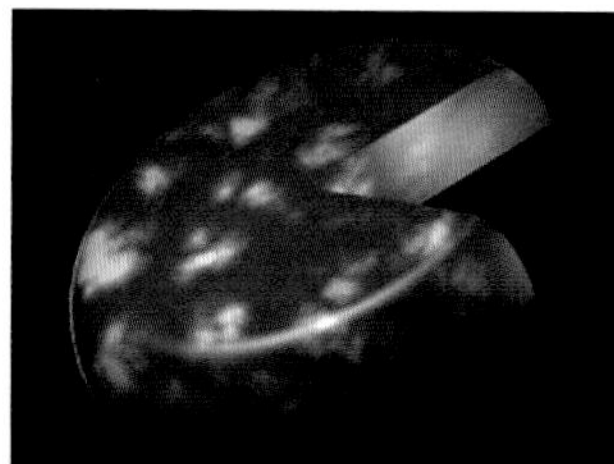
[S]90 [I]10 [Ex]4.5

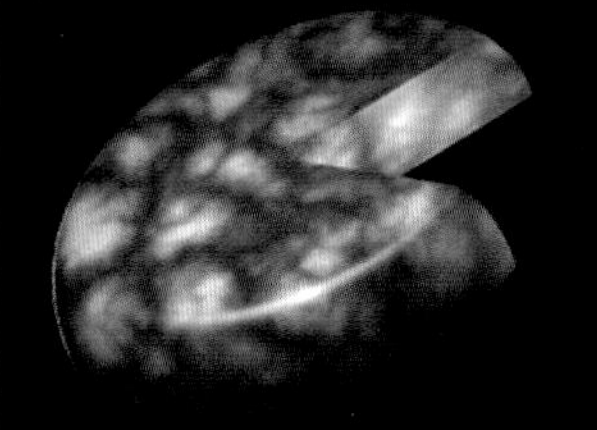
[S]90 [I]10 [Ex]2

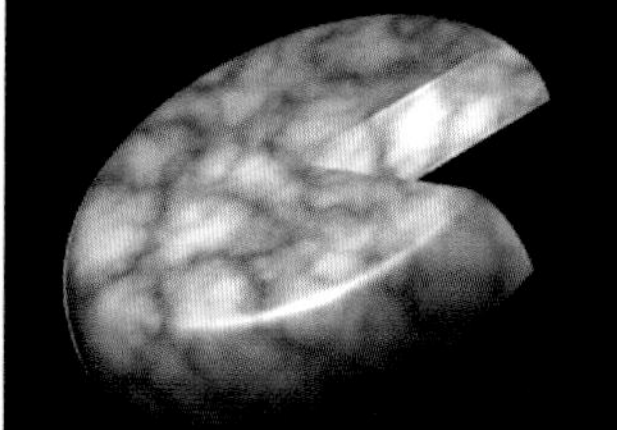
[S]90 [I]10 [Ex].75

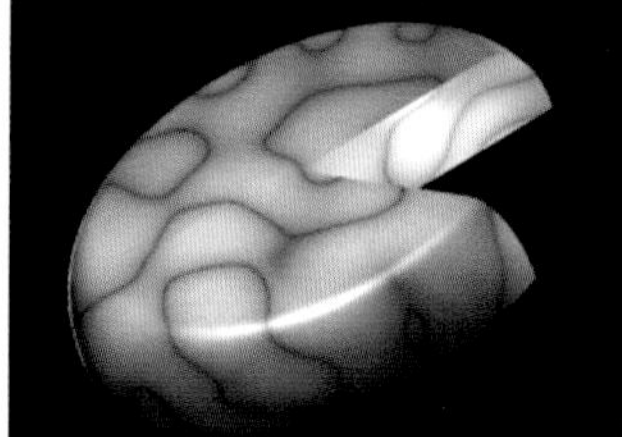
[S]90 [I]1 [Ex].3

Exponent controls the proportion of C1 to C2; in the range of .01–1, Exponent can produce subtle pattern variations.

SPECKLE FUNCTION

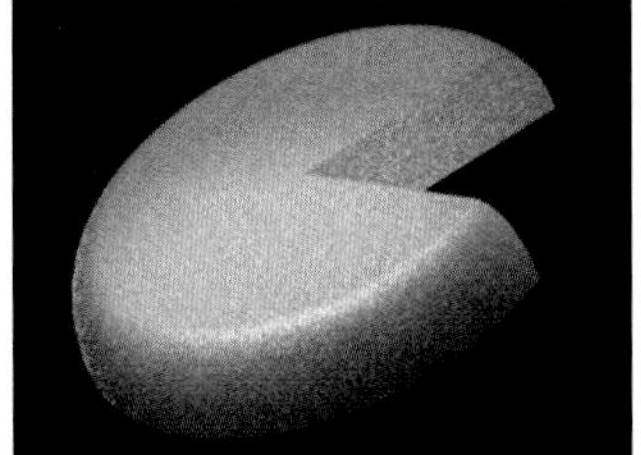

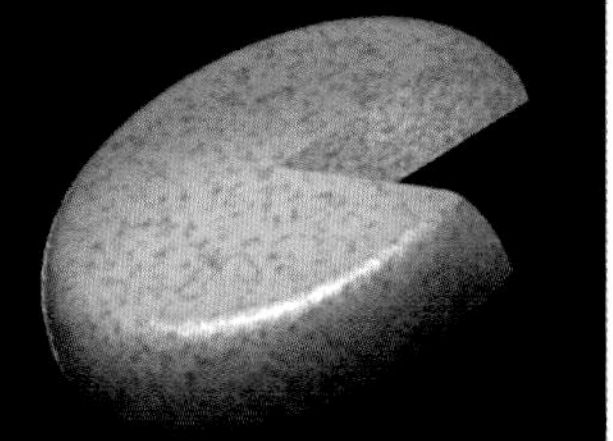

[S] 10 Bump 30 [S] 100 Bump 80
Speckle SXP was used for a mix of texture, bump, and opacity maps.

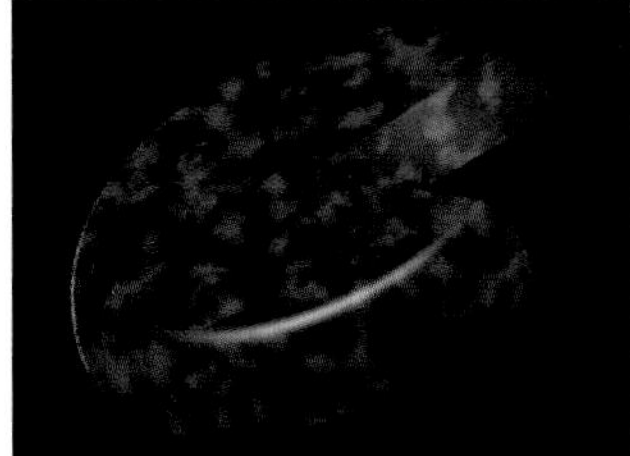

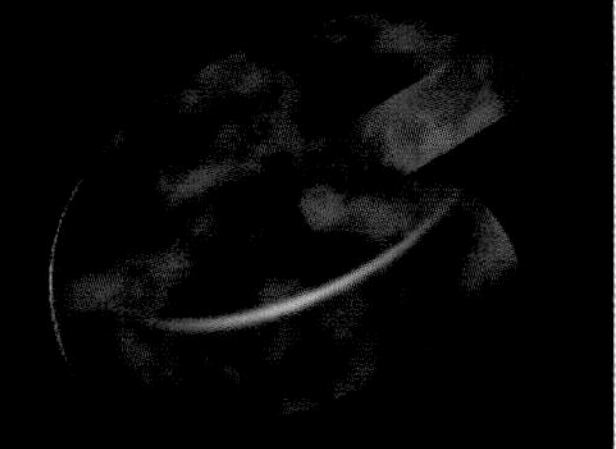

[S] 350 Opacity 100 [S] 750 Opacity 100
Colors were set to black and white for bump and opacity maps.

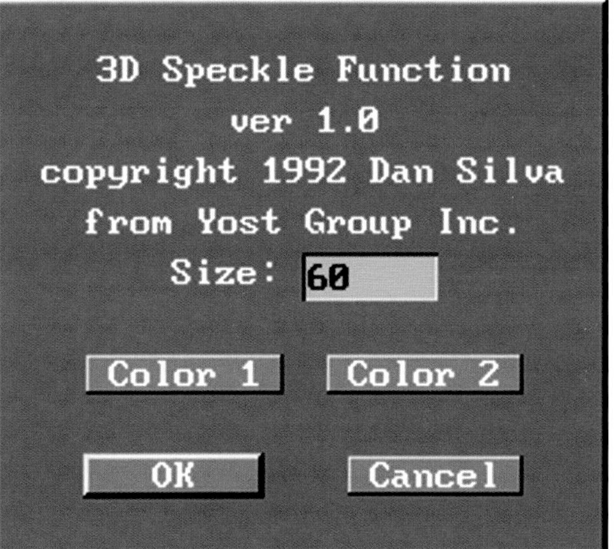

The Speckle Function dialog box.

Summary

Speckle produces speckled or spattered textures. Color is set using RGB and HLS color models via a color definition dialog box with Color 1 specifying the speckle's color and Color 2 the background color. The Size variable can be used to produce a range of texture from sharp and stippled to diffuse or smoky.

Speckle Function Parameters

Size [S] — Sets the speckle size relative to the 3D object.
Color 1 and 2 — Sets the speckle and the background colors.

SPLATTER FUNCTION

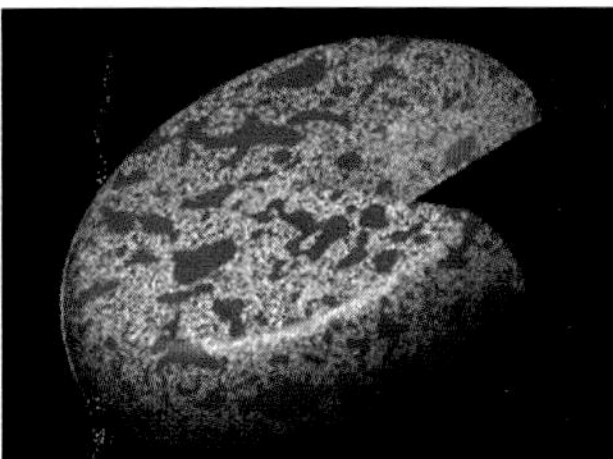

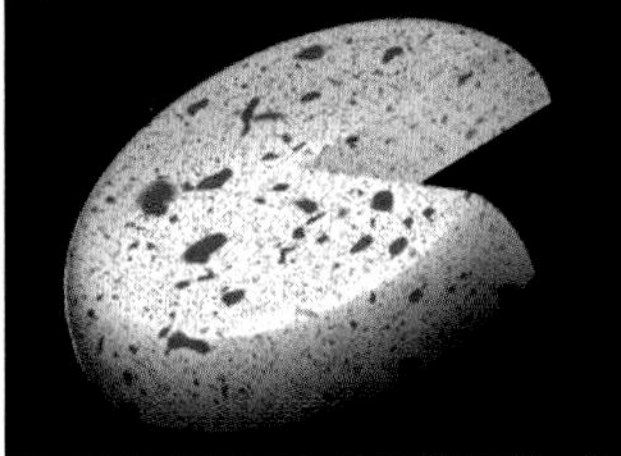

[S]60 [I]10 [T].3 [S]125 [I]10 [T].2
[T] works best at .5 or less, and [N] controls the level of detail.

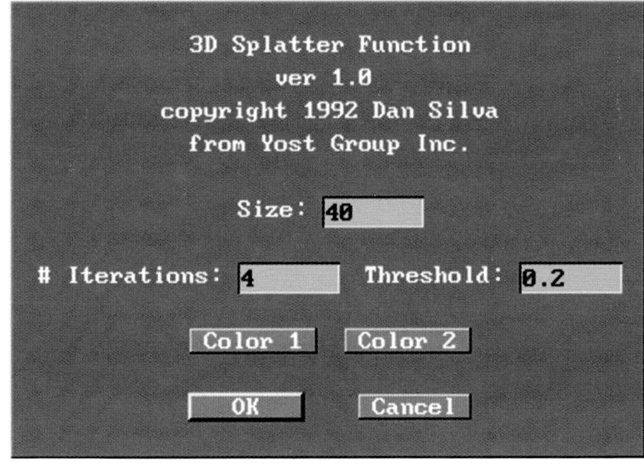

The Splatter Function dialog box.

Summary

The Splatter Function is included in Yost Group's Special Effects IPAS package #2. Splatter produces paint splatter and stipple patterns that are computed using a fractal noise function. Threshold specifies how Color 1 is mixed into Color 2.

Splatter Function Parameters

Size [S] (0–10) — Sets the size of the color.
 # Iterations [N] (0–10) — Specifies the number of times the fractal noise is calculated per pixel.
Threshold [T] (0–1) — Controls the proportion of C1 to C2.
Color 1 and 2 [C1] [C2] — C1 sets the background color and C2 the splatter color.

SQUIGGLE PATTERN

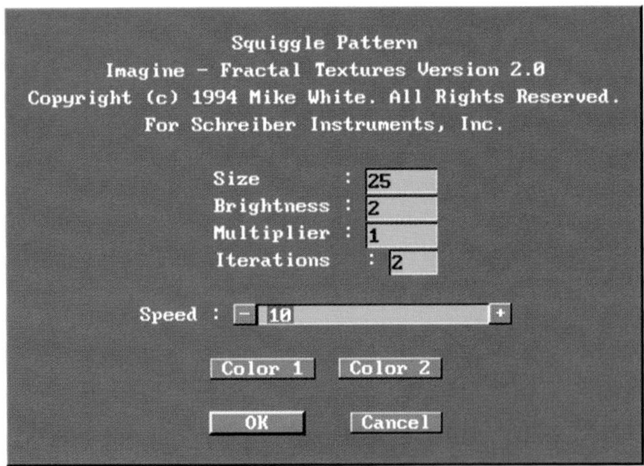

The Squiggle Pattern dialog box.

Summary

The Squiggle Pattern is included in Schreiber Instruments' Imagine Fractal Textures package. Squiggle produces a range of stone-like solid patterns using computations based on fractal geometry. This technique is capable of producing a broad range of layered textures that vary from flowing stripes to tight, irregular spots to fine, granular textures.

Squiggle is controlled using several interdependent variables including size and brightness. As the Multiplier value is increased, Brightness must be increased correspondingly.

Squiggle Pattern Parameters

Size [S] (.0001–100,000.0) — Sets the texture's overall scale.
Brightness [B] (0–10,000) — Sets the texture's overall brightness. Also acts to control color dominance and relation.
Multiplier [M] (0–10,000) — Sets the texture's complexity.
Iterations [I] (0–99,999) — Sets the number of times the algorithm is applied. Higher numbers create more detail.
Speed [Sp] (0–200) — Sets the step value for the iterations parameter.
Color 1, Color2 [C1] [C2] — Sets the RGB or HSL values for the squiggle and background colors.

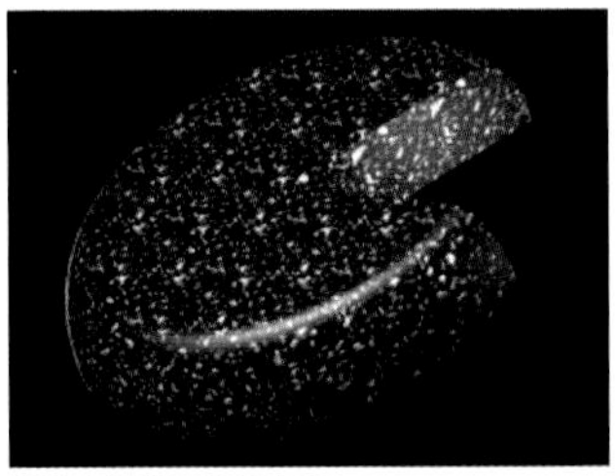

[S]5 [B]500 [M]5

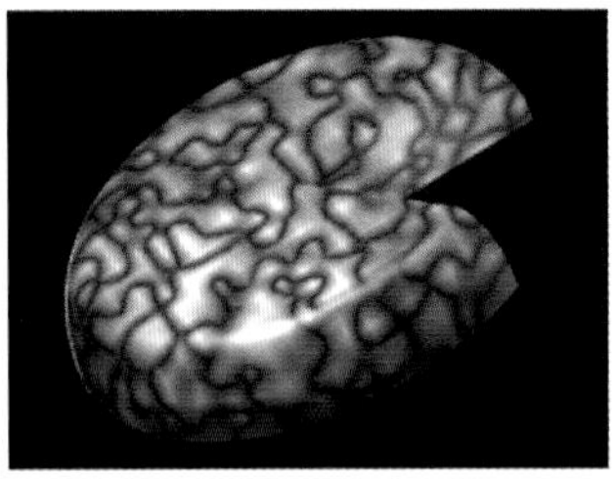

[M]4

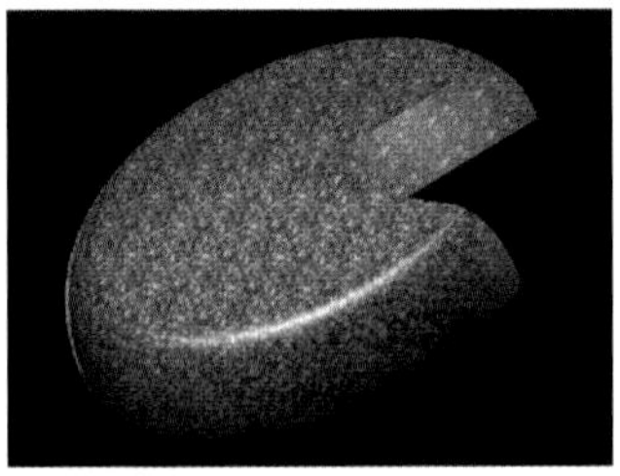

[S]3 [B]3

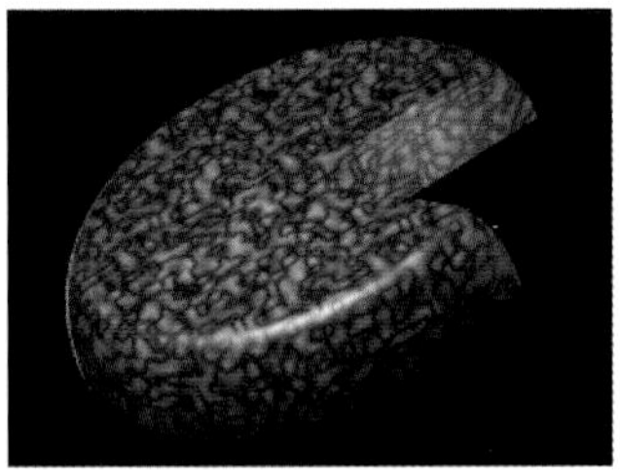

[S]10

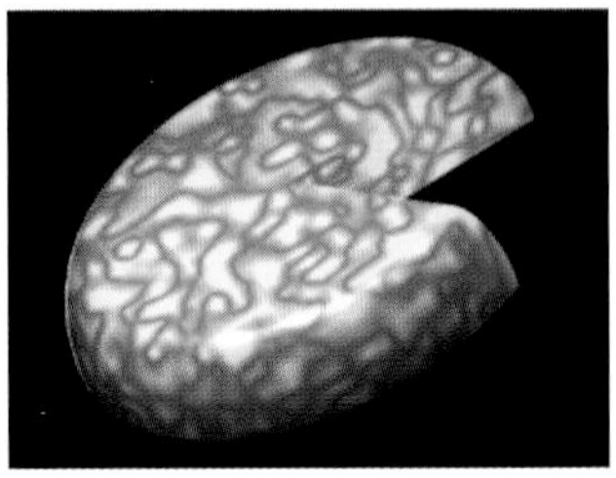

[S]10 [B]2 [M]1

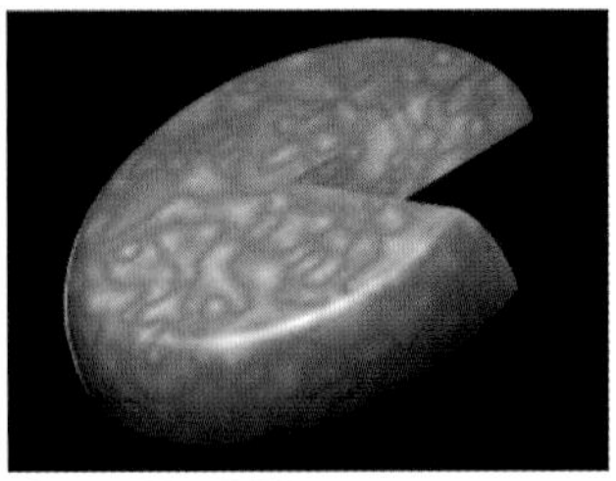

[S]20 [B]2 [M]1

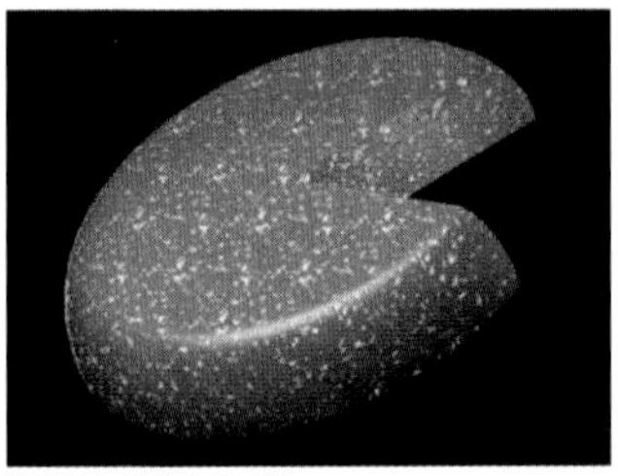

[S]50 [B]2 [M]1

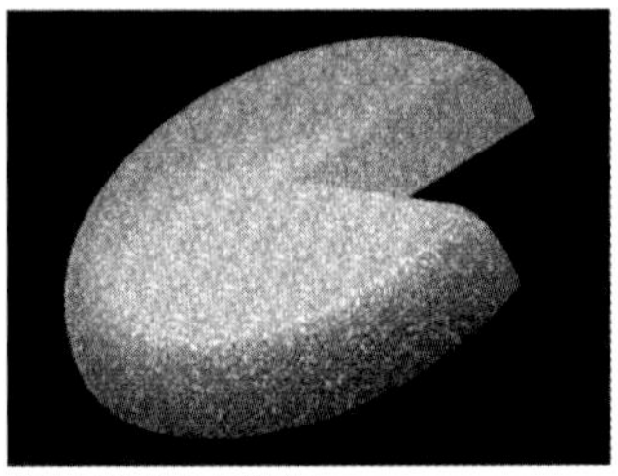

[S]100 [B]2 [M]1

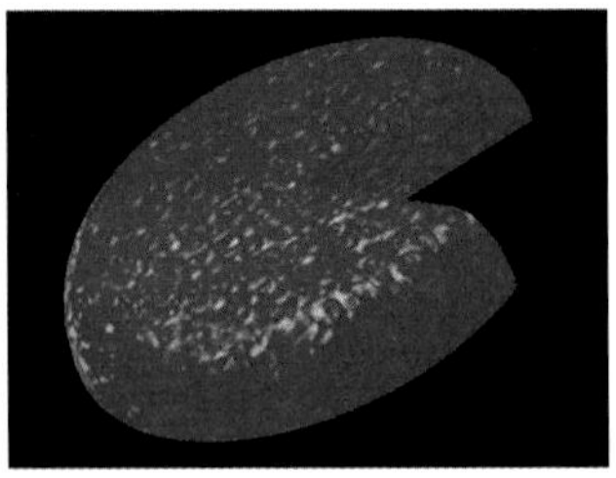

[S]20 [B]6 [M]6

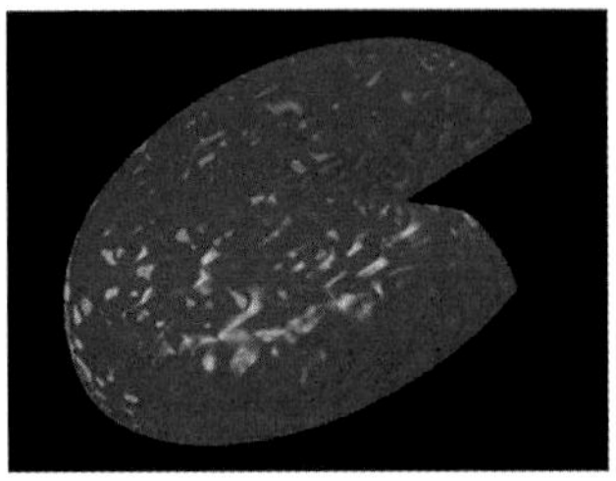

[S]20

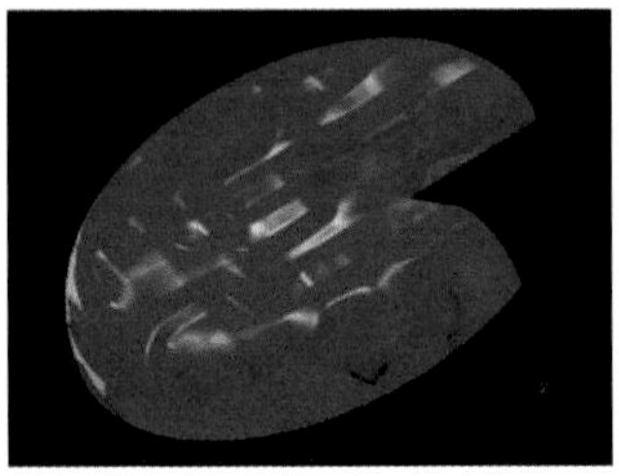

[S]5 [B]500 [M]5 Bump 10

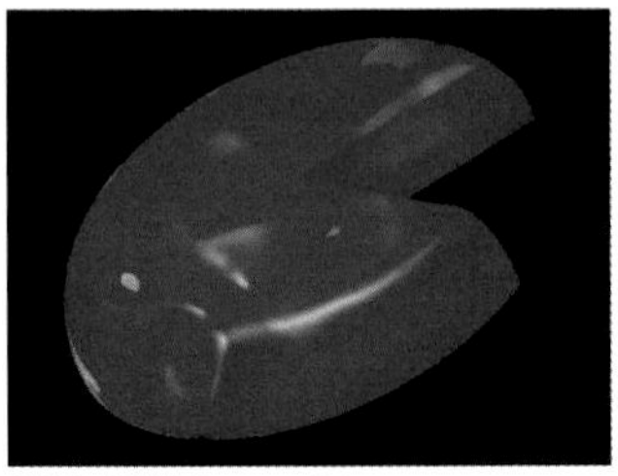

[S]3 [B]6 Bump 20

Squiggle was used as a bump (50%) and self-illumination map (100%). Diffuse settings of 172, 135, 255 provided the blue color.

Summary

Stucco is included with 3D Studio Release 4. It creates patterns consisting of randomly dispersed and interlocking globs to sharply defined stucco-like textures. Colors 1 and 2 can be optionally linked by a soft color gradient or separated by a sharply defined edge.

Stucco Function Parameters

Size [S] (.0001–10,000) — Sets the texture's overall scale.
Threshold [Tr] (0–1) — Sets the proportion of C1 to C2 so that as threshold decreases, C2 expands.
Thickness [Th] (0–1) — Controls the transition between C1 and C2 so that as thickness decreases, edge sharpness increases.
Color 1 and Color 2 [C1] [C2] — Specifies the two colors for the pattern.

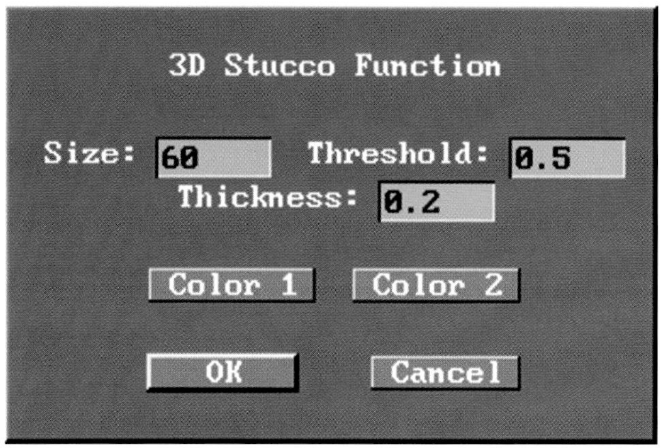

The Stucco Function dialog box.

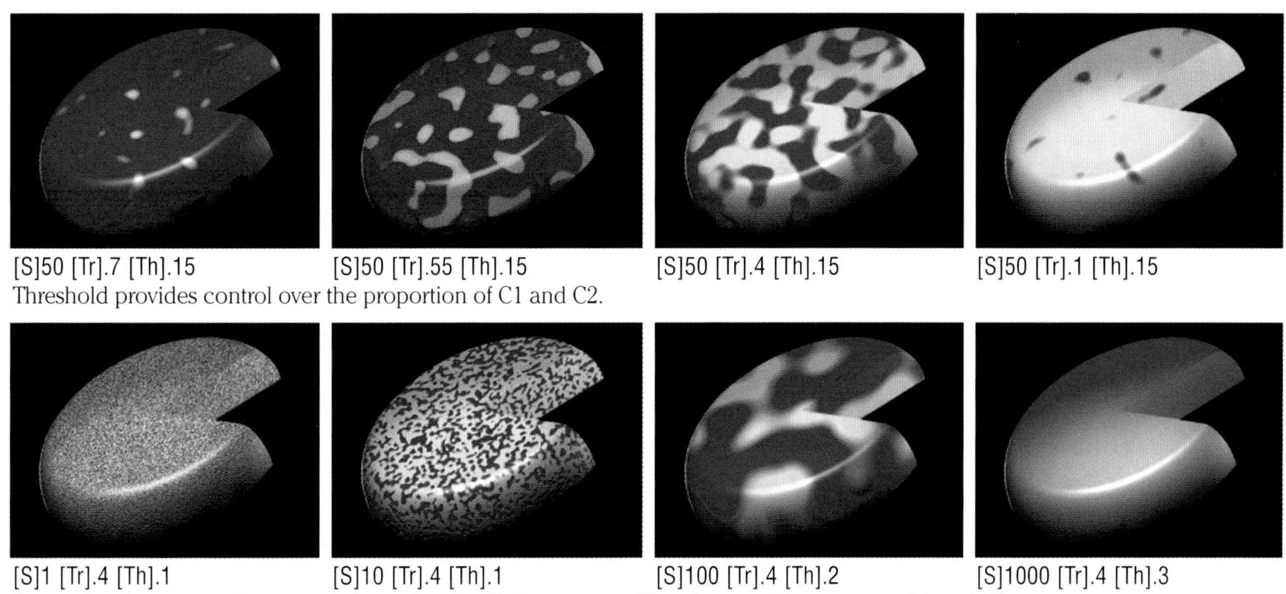

[S]50 [Tr].7 [Th].15 [S]50 [Tr].55 [Th].15 [S]50 [Tr].4 [Th].15 [S]50 [Tr].1 [Th].15

Threshold provides control over the proportion of C1 and C2.

[S]1 [Tr].4 [Th].1 [S]10 [Tr].4 [Th].1 [S]100 [Tr].4 [Th].2 [S]1000 [Tr].4 [Th].3

Size scales the pattern from stippled to soft, with thickness controlling the transition between C1 and C2.

TORNADO NOISE FUNCTION

TORNAD_I.SXP \tornado **Pointer Digital Graf/x**

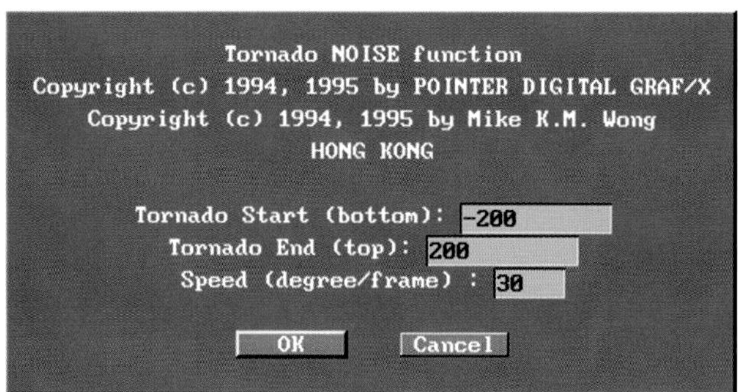

The Tornado Noise dialog box.

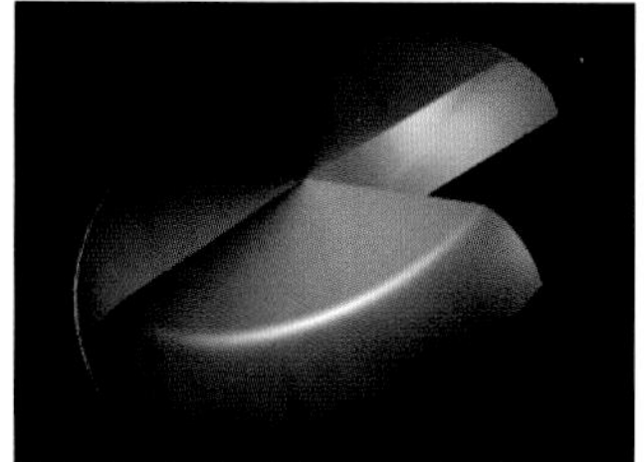

[Ts]-2000 [Te]2000 frame 0

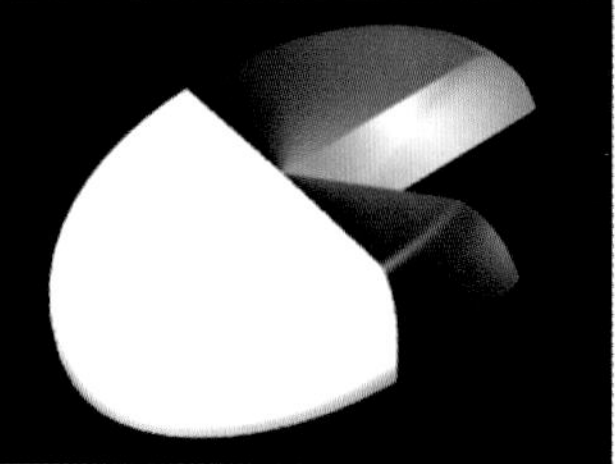

[Ts]-2000 [Te]2000 frame 15

Tornado begins as a gray wedge that expands to a spinning, white, 180-degree section through the object.

Summary

Tornado simulates spinning objects by applying a rotating aliased wipe to the object's XZ plane. The wipe travels through the object beginning as a subtle wedge that expands to approximately 180 degrees as it passes through the object in Z. It produces both color and value distortions, particularly in mapped objects when used as an opacity map.

Tornado Noise Parameters

Tornado Start and End [Ts] [Te] (–10,000–10,000) — Sets the starting and ending points and the scale for the effect.

Speed [S] (1–9,999) — Sets the effect's rotation speed in degrees per frame.

TURBULENCE FUNCTION

TURB_I.SXP \turbulnc **Schreiber Instruments**

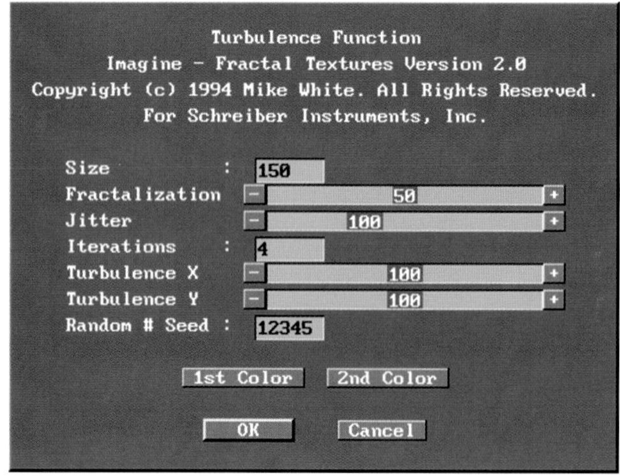

The Turbulence Function dialog box.

Summary

The Turbulence Pattern is included in Schreiber Instruments' Imagine Fractal Textures bundle. Turbulence produces solid patterns using computations based on fractal geometry. It can produce a range of naturalistic textures including mossy, moldy, and eroded looks. It also is capable of unique geometric patterns and oily effects.

Turbulence is controlled by several interdependent variables including fractalization, jitter, and turbulence. For all the variation possible, this interdependence can result in near identical or identical textures being created from dramatically different settings. In general, Turbulence is most responsive when its variables are set around the middle of their working ranges.

Turbulence Function Parameters

Size [S] (.0001–99,999.9) — Sets the texture's overall scale.

Fractalization [F] (0–100) — Sets the texture's randomness or chaos.

Jitter [J] (0–300) — Sets the vein width variance and knots.

Iterations [I] (0–99,999) — Sets the number of times the algorithm is applied. Higher numbers create more detail.

Turbulence [T] (0–200) — Sets the overall noise added to the veins. Turbulence is needed for Fractalization or Jitter to have an effect.

Turbulence X, Turbulence Y [Tx] [Ty] (0–200) — Independently sets the noise added on the X and Y axes.

Random Seed [R] (0–999,999) — Sets the algorithm's start point with an arbitrary number. Each number produces a unique pattern.

1st Color, 2nd Color [C1] [C2] — Sets the RGB or HSL values for the main and secondary colors.

Note: *Bump maps are duplicates of SXP's given settings.*

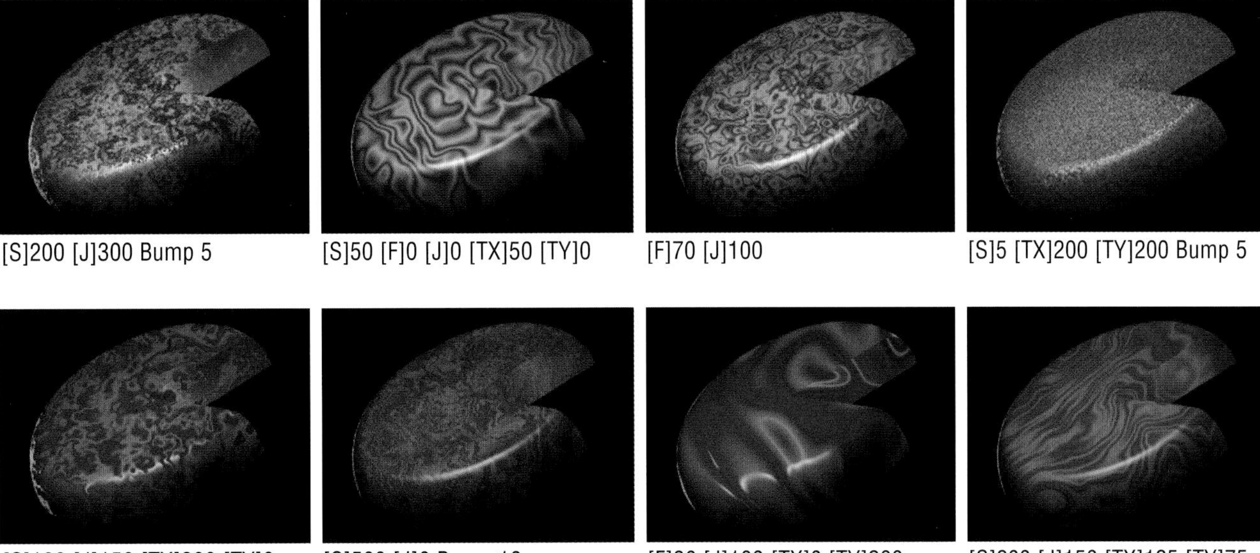

[S]200 [J]300 Bump 5 | [S]50 [F]0 [J]0 [TX]50 [TY]0 | [F]70 [J]100 | [S]5 [TX]200 [TY]200 Bump 5

[S]100 [J]150 [TX]200 [TY]0 | [S]500 [J]0 Bump 10 | [F]30 [J]100 [TX]0 [TY]200 | [S]200 [J]150 [TX]125 [TY]75

VARY

Autodesk \vary VARY_I.SXP

Summary

Vary is included with 3D Studio Release 4. It is an animated texture that varies the color or shininess (Release 3 only) of an object over a specific number of frames. Vary can be useful for making objects disappear and reappear at specified times, assuming that either the shininess of the material is minimal or that the object need not be made completely invisible.

Vary Parameters

Start Color and End Color [Sc] [Ec] — Sets the start and end colors or opacity using either an RGB or HLS color model.

Start Shine and End Shine [Ss] [Es] — Sets the starting and ending values for the material shininess. This does not work in 3D Studio Release 4.0.

Start Frame and End Frame [Sc] [Ec] — Sets the start and end frames for the effect.

Note: *3D Studio Release 4.0 ignores Vary's shininess settings.*

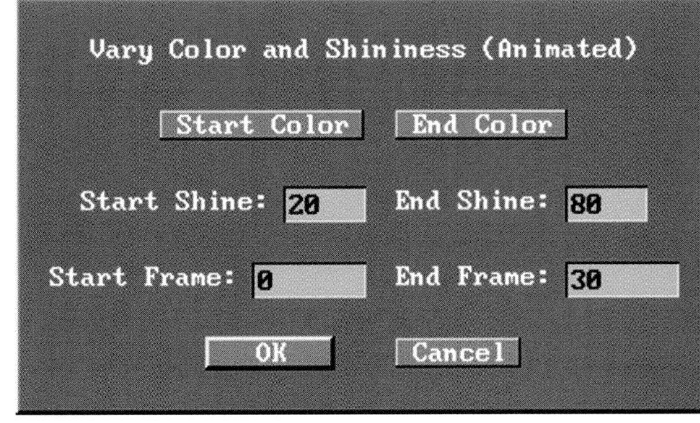

The Vary dialog box.

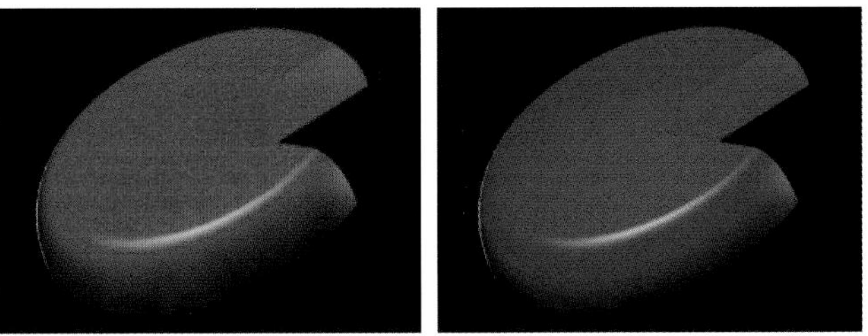

Frame 0 | Frame 15

Vary changes color or opacity over a specified range of frames.

WATER FUNCTION

WATER_I.SXP | **\water** | **Yost Group**

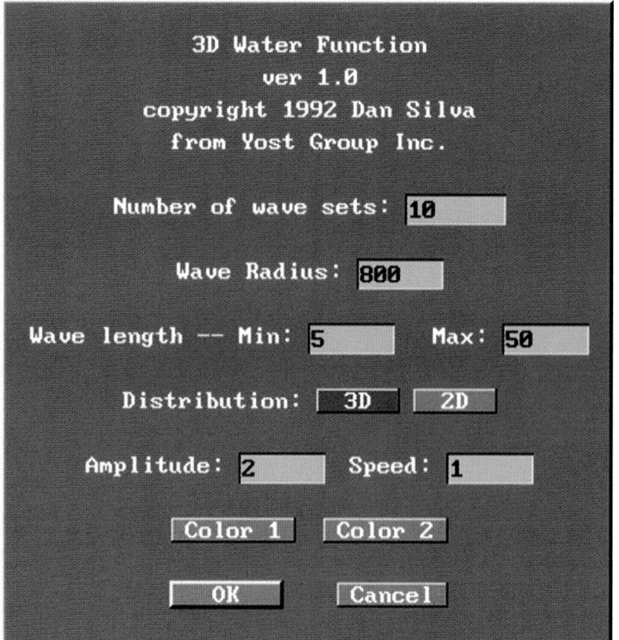

The Water Function dialog box.

Summary

Water is available as part of the Yost Group's Special Effects disk #2. It produces animated wave patterns suitable for simulating various watery effects, and is controlled by parameters for wave length, amplitude, and 2D or 3D distribution.

2D distribution applies the waves on a horizontal circular plane, making it a good choice for surfaces such as oceans. 3D distribution affects all sides of a three-dimensional object.

The watery effects are particularly effective when used together as texture, opacity, and bump maps.

Water Function Parameters

Number of wave sets [W] (1–50) — Sets the number of sets or "sources" from which the wave originates.

Wave Radius [Wr] (1–10,000) — Sets the size of the wave rings.

Wave length—Min, Max [L1] [L2] (0–1,000) — Sets the distance between wave crests or valleys.

Distribution 2D, 3D [2d] [3d] — Applies the wave pattern along two or three axes.

Amplitude [A] — Sets the depth of the waves.

Speed [Sp] — Controls the speed of wave motion.

Color 1 and 2 [C1] [C2] — Sets the color for the wave peaks and valleys.

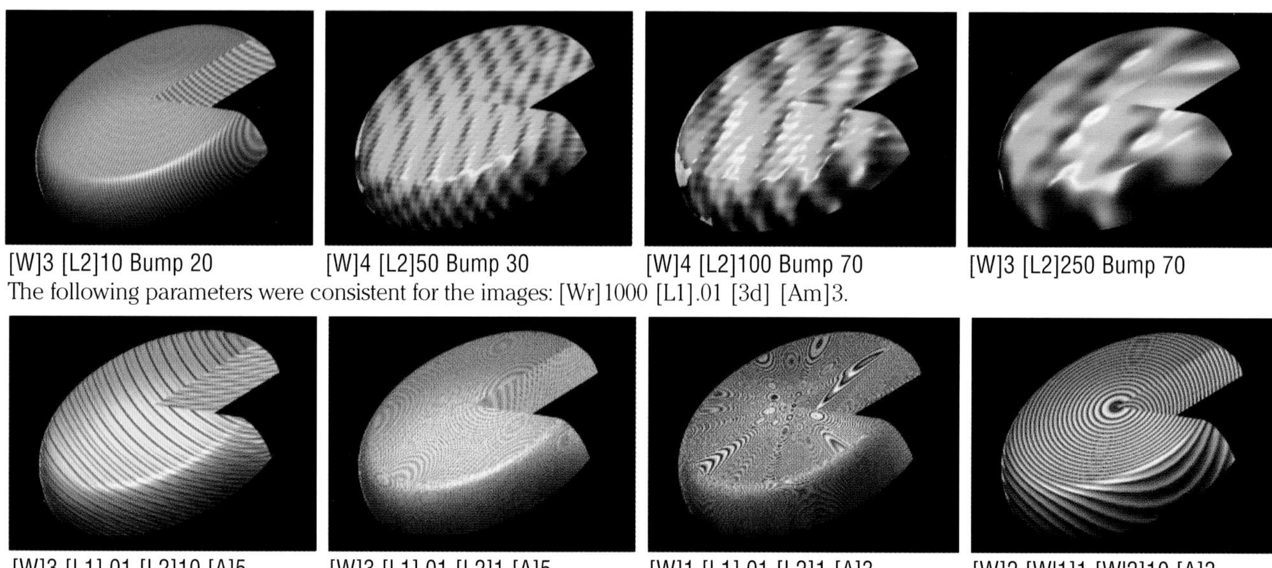

[W]3 [L2]10 Bump 20 | [W]4 [L2]50 Bump 30 | [W]4 [L2]100 Bump 70 | [W]3 [L2]250 Bump 70

The following parameters were consistent for the images: [Wr]1000 [L1].01 [3d] [Am]3.

[W]3 [L1].01 [L2]10 [A]5 | [W]3 [L1].01 [L2]1 [A]5 | [W]1 [L1].01 [L2]1 [A]3 | [W]2 [Wl1]1 [Wl2]10 [A]3

2D Distribution produces an range of linear patterns. These images all had the same settings applied as a 25 percent bump map.

WIPE

Digital Graf/x \pointer\wipe WIPE_I.SXP

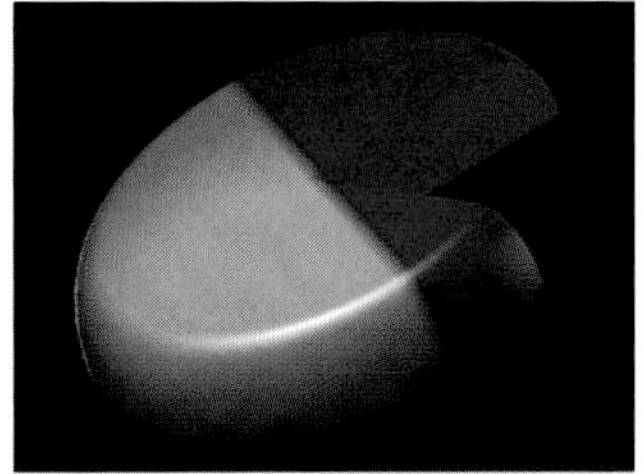

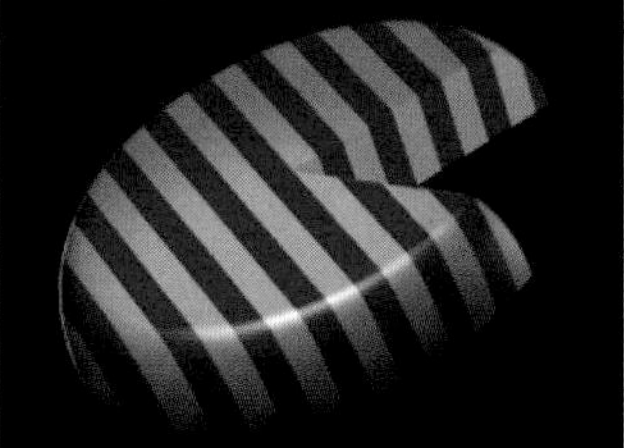

[Ns]1 frame 15 [Ns]10 frame 15

The Wipe effect can range from a single element to multiple stripes and intricate moiré patterns.

Summary

Wipe produces a white wipe that moves across the object as a solid transition or series of stripes that pass through either the XY, XZ, or YZ object plane. Specifying a number of strips can provide some interesting textural and moiré effects.

Wipe Parameters

Contracting Color [Cc] — Sets the contracting color using RGB or HLS color models.

Expanding Color [Ec] — Sets the expanding color using RGB or HLS color models.

Wipe along axis X, Y, and Z [Wx] [Wy] Wz] — Sets the projection plane for the effect with X setting the ZY, Y setting XY, and Z setting the XZ plane.

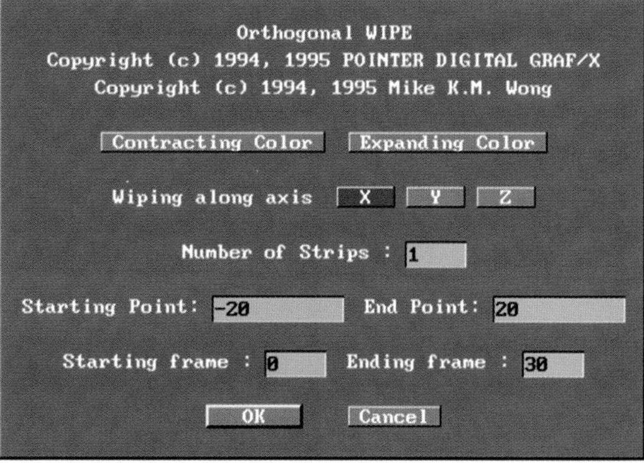

The Wipe dialog box.

Number of Strips [Ns] (1–9,999) — Sets the number of strips, with higher numbers producing textural effects.

Starting Point and End Point [Sp] [Ep] — Scales the effect to the specific object.

Starting frame and Ending frame [Sf] [Ef] — Sets starting and ending frames for the effect.

Note: *Set anti-aliasing off to improve pattern depth at high [Ns] settings.*

WOOD

Autodesk \wood WOOD_I.SXP

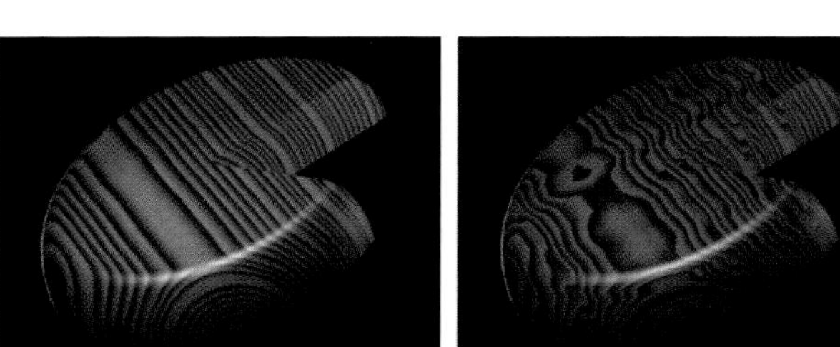

[S]10 [R1].1 [R2].1 [S]10 [R1]1 [R2]1

R1 controls the uniformity around the concentric pattern and R2 controls it along the pattern.

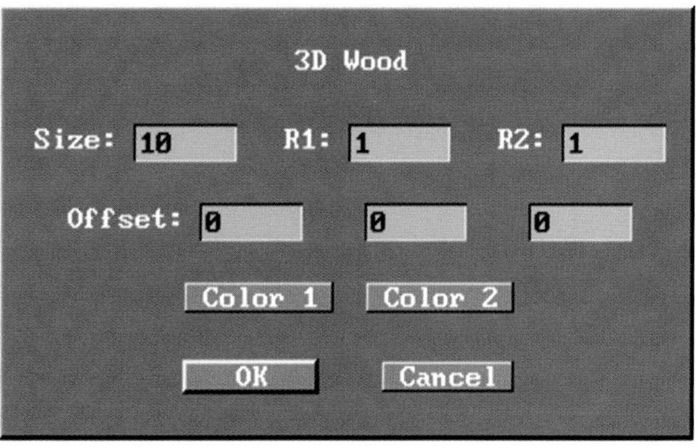

The Wood dialog box.

Summary

Wood is included with 3D Studio Release 4. It produces a solid wood texture with knot-like structures and concentric bands resembling wood edge grain. Wood provides two colors that define the grain pattern and a size parameter that scales the pattern to the object. R1 and R2 provide control over the pattern in the XY and XZ planes.

Wood Parameters

Size [S] (.0001–10,000) — Sets the texture's overall scale.

R1 [R1] — Affects the pattern around the concentric rings that form the knots. As R1 increases the rings become more chaotic.

R2 [R2] — Affects the pattern created along the concentric rings as they pass through the object. As R2 increases the grain pattern becomes less uniform.

bounce_i.kxp
calc_i.kxp
dmm_i.kxp
ik_i.kxp
keydxf_i.kxp
keyman_i.kxp
kfbnc_i.kxp
kfdup_i.kxp
kfpick_i.kxp
mrph_i.kxp
quick_i.kxp
script_i.kxp
solar_i.kxp
stereo_i.kxp
tempo_i.kxp
bones_i.kxp
bounce_i.kxp
calc_i.kxp
dmm_i.kxp
ik_i.kxp
keydxf_i.kxp
keyman_i.kxp
kfbnc_i.kxp
kfdup_i.kxp
kfpick_i.kxp
mrph_i.kxp
quick_i.kxp
script_i.kxp
solar_i.kxp
stereo_i.kxp
tempo_i.kxp
bones_i.kxp
bounce_i.kxp

A Procedural Animation Suite

Keyframe External Processes (KXP) plug-ins automate the control of keyframes for objects, lights, and cameras. KXP plug-ins provide access to motion dynamics and skeletal animation tools, along with the capability to program or script any 3D Studio entity.

Dynamics such as gravity, wind, and collision can be used to produce complex animations that automatically set keyframes based on these properties. This saves the time and tedium associated with setting up the numerous tweaks for realistic object interaction. A classic example of how keyframe dynamics works is demonstrated by the break shot in a pool game. There are 15 object balls and a cue ball placed on a surface that is framed by bumpers. Using any one of several KXP plug-ins, such as Key Factory, Dynamic Motion Module, or Keyscript (which is included with 3D Studio Release 4), you can create the interaction of the pool balls and bumpers. This automatically produces the keyframes necessary to animate the effect of the balls bouncing off of each other and the bumpers.

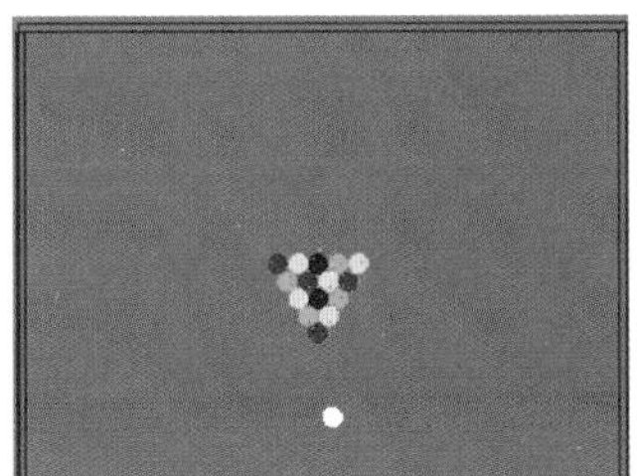

The break shot

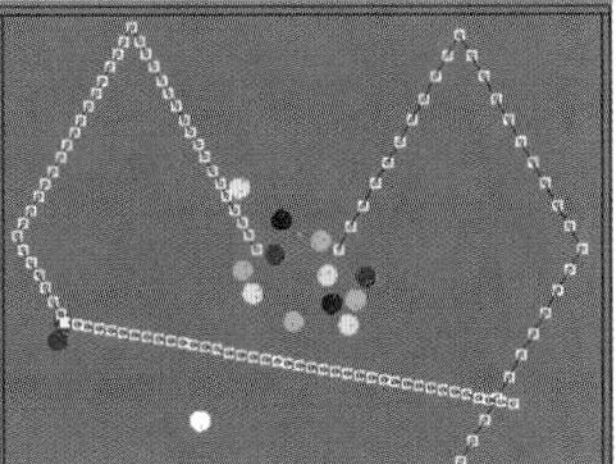

Dynamic object interaction

Keyscript was used to automate the motion paths of the pool balls based on collision detection.

Some KXP plug-ins are controlled using one or more dialog boxes, whereas others use a custom programming language similar to BASIC. KXP dialog boxes are similar to other plug-in types, and enable you to specify essential issues such as the type of effect—like collision, wind, or gravity—along with the degree of the effect.

The Keyscript KXP enables you to control many 3D Studio Keyframer events by scripting or programming them from 3D Studio's text editor. The Script Extensions expand on Keyscript to provide program control of IXP, SXP, PXP, and AXP plug-ins. Keyscript and the Script Extensions use an interpreted programming language that is maintained in its original text format and executed from within the scripting program. This enables you to not only control 3D Studio entities, but to set up useful amenities such as custom dialog boxes as well. 3D Studio Release 4 ships with several scripts that demonstrate this use, such as LIGHTMAN.K3D, which enables you to manipulate 3D Studio lights using a time envelope, and MORPH.K3D, which demonstrates lip-sync animation. These are useful for getting a basic feel for the process. Learning to write effective scripts, though certainly accessible to nonprogrammers, is nonetheless demanding and requires careful, systematic approach. However, the results, which amount to no less than control over a complete procedural animation studio, are well worth the effort.

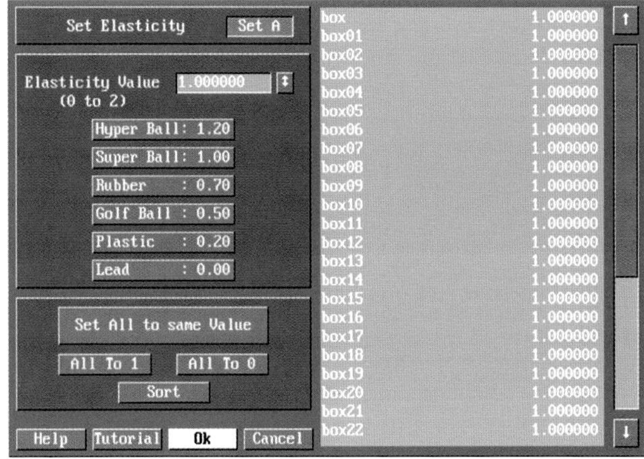

KXP plug-ins enable you to adjust various dynamics parameters such as the direction of a gravity force and the amount of elasticity in a given object.

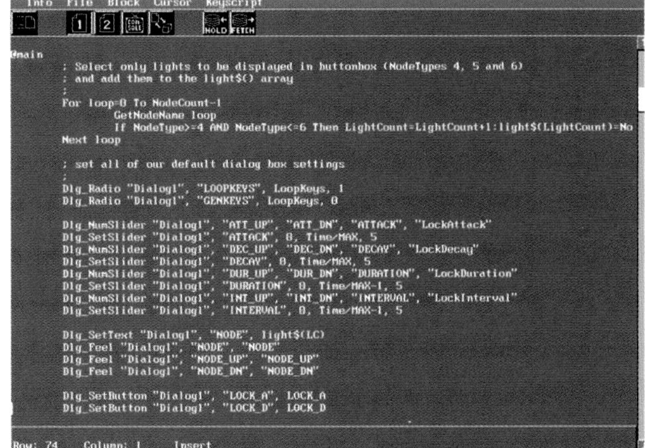

Scripting is accomplished in the 3D Studio text editor using a custom programming language similar to BASIC.

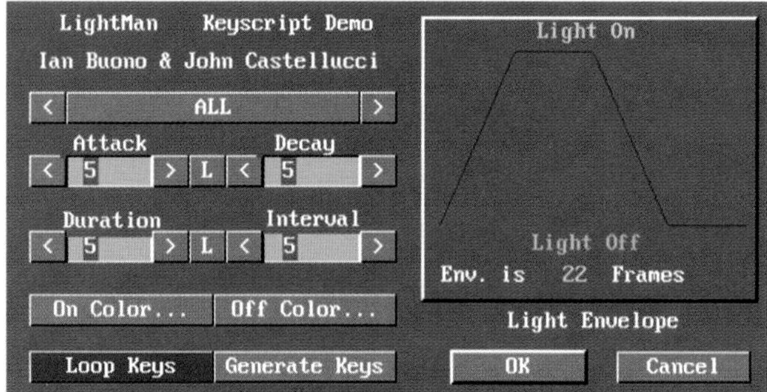

The scripting process enables you to create any number of special purpose programs, such as LightMan, which choreographs on-time and off-time for selected 3D Studio spotlights.

Along with dynamics and scripting, KXP plug-ins also simplify the process of producing complex choreography and character animation. To conventionally animate the legs of a woman walking, for example, you begin by building a hierarchy of the woman's foot linked to her lower leg, her lower leg to her upper leg, and her upper leg to her pelvis. Here, each successive element is the parent of the previous element, so that if you rotate the upper leg, for instance, the linked lower leg and foot will follow. This makes the process of defining each footstep one of performing numerous manual moves and rotations to keyframe the walk.

In contrast, the Inverse Kinematics plug-in, which is included with 3D Studio Release 4, enables you to easily manipulate complex groups of hierarchically linked objects. Using Inverse Kinematics and given the preceding hierarchy, you need only move the foot; in so doing, you automatically set all the essential keyframes for the remainder of the linked chain. From within the Inverse Kinematics plug-in you can interactively set joint parameters for each member of the selected hierarchy and see the result in your choice of viewports. By setting Joint Limits you can add reality to your model by specifying the range of motion or rotation for the given joint; this can prevent the woman's knee from hyperextending, for instance. From here you need only link the end of the kinematics chain—the foot in this case—to a Follow Object and animate the Follow Object to create the walking woman's gait.

KXP plug-ins such as BonesPro enable you to produce intricate character moves using skeletal animation. This process is surprisingly direct. Skeletal animation consists of moving or deforming a 3D mesh object using an internal skeleton that is assigned to the mesh. The skeleton consists of multiple hierarchically linked geometric elements called bones which, when rotated, translated, or scaled, automatically create all keyframes needed to cause the 3D mesh to move or distort accordingly. At render time the skeleton is hidden, leaving a smoothly animated object.

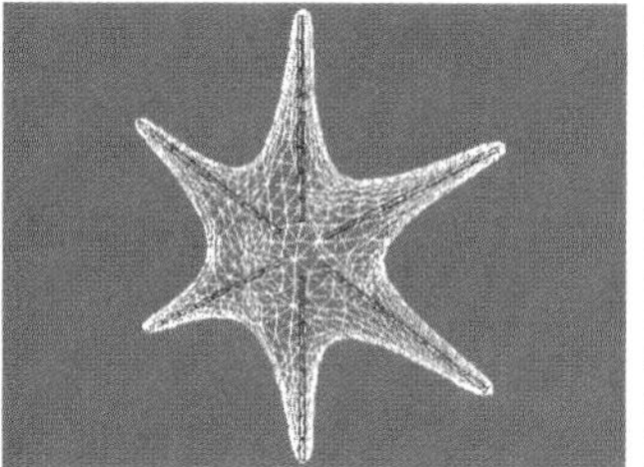

3D mesh and skeleton

Animated 3D mesh

Skeletal animation with BonesPro enables you to assign a mesh to a skeletal structure that, when moved, produces a smoothly animated mesh.

Additional examples of KXP functionality are the various plug-ins that enable you to easily manage morph targets and perform explicit keyframe calculations.

Using KXP Plug-Ins

Before you use a KXP plug-in, be sure that it is properly installed using its installation program or instructions. Furthermore, be sure to read and follow any accompanying instructions exactly. Attempting to shortcut this process, particularly with complex plug-ins, is a mistake. At the least you will likely receive regular error messages as the plug-in attempts to find its resource files, or the plug-in could either cause a crash or simply fail to run.

For those times where there is no installation program or documentation, copy the plug-in—*XXXXXX*_I.KXP—into your 3D Studio \Process directory.

KXP plug-ins can be applied and adjusted from either the Keyframer or the 3D Studio Script Editor. To apply a KXP, access the KXP Selector from the Program pull-down menu or by pressing F12. Scroll through your installed KXP plug-ins and click on the name of the KXP you want to use. This loads the selected KXP for adjustment.

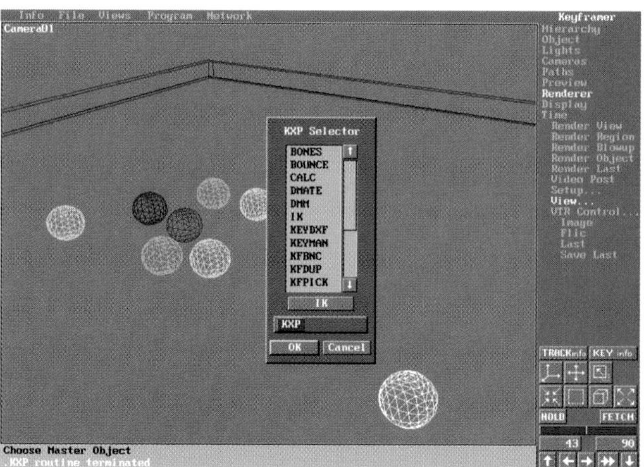

KXP plug-ins are accessed from the KXP Selector in the 3D Editor.

With all your plug-in parameters set, exit the KXP dialog box by clicking on OK. This returns you to the Keyframer. To see the results of your KXP edits, choose a render method from the command column and the view you want to render. Then set up the render parameters using the Render Still Image or Render Animation dialog boxes and click on Render.

Alternatively, you can work with an existing script or create a new one from scratch using Keyscript. Keyscript is accessed the same as any KXP; however, selecting SCRIPT brings up the 3D Studio Script Editor. You can then load any script by selecting Load from the File pull-down menu. A script can be executed by clicking on Keyscript/Execute, pressing F1, or clicking on the execute icon located at the left of the icon bar. To return to the Keyframer, select Exit from the File menu or press Ctrl+Q.

The KXP Reference

The KXP plug-ins are listed alphabetically with the product name in bold type at the beginning of each plug-in's section. The color bar below the plug-in name lists the plug-in file name, such as BOUNCE_I.KXP, the *3D Studio IPAS Plug-In Reference* CD-ROM path name, and the vendor. The CD-ROM subdirectory contains any sample files and demonstration versions of the plug-ins where possible.

The text is divided into two areas: a summary and a parameter listing. The summary provides a look at the plug-in's characteristics and capabilities. The parameter listing displays the name of each parameter in bold type along with its corresponding abbreviation in brackets. For example:

Horiz Edge Effect [He] p,s (plain, striated) (0–100%) — Specifies a sharp or ragged edge for the transition. The sliders control the width of the striated edge.

The bracketed abbreviations are followed by any parameter modifiers, their abbreviations, and an adjustment range in parentheses, whenever applicable. A description of each parameter function follows.

Each plug-in is illustrated with screen capture of its dialog box or boxes and one or more sample images when appropriate.

Many of the project files used to create the sample images are available on the CD-ROM in the directory specified in the information bar at the beginning of each plug-in entry.

Sample images show the parameter abbreviations along with the essential values used to create that effect. The specific effect variations shown were chosen to represent as broad a range of variation as space permitted. They were also chosen on the basis of providing KXP plug-in users shortcuts and starting points for creating unique, interesting, and useful effects.

Selected KXP sample images are provided in their final rendered form. These files are located on the CD-ROM in the directory specified in the information bar at the beginning of each plug-in or in the \KXP directory.

BONES

BONES_I.KXP **\bonespro** **Digimation**

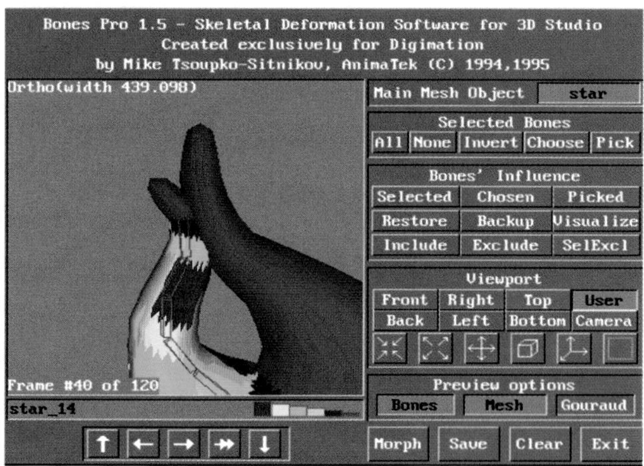

The Bones dialog box.

Summary

Bones is part of the Bones Pro package, which also includes SMOOTH.PXP and BONES.AXP. Bones uses an internal skeletal structure to smoothly deform geometry over a series of frames. Simple objects, usually elongated boxes, are placed inside the geometry to be deformed. As the internal skeleton is manipulated, the surrounding mesh deforms accordingly. This process is invaluable for producing character animation, and is a natural to use with Inverse Kinematics.

The first step in using Bones is to apply the BONES.AXP to the Main Mesh Object. The Main Mesh object must consist of a solid mesh with welded vertices or individual objects joined using Boolean operations. SMOOTH can be used to even out inconsistencies in meshes that have been joined using Boolean Union. If lofted objects are used they must be constructed with endcaps. Bones does not add vertices to the Main Mesh Object as it is distorted, so the mesh must be dense enough that it can bend and twist smoothly. This can be accomplished by lofting with a large number of steps and detail set to high, or by tessellating the object using the 3D Editor or OPTIMIZE.

Next, boxes are created, scaled, and rotated to represent the deformation bones. The bones should fit entirely inside the mesh object, and the ends of adjacent bones should be close but not touching. (An exception to this rule is if an external bone was used to poke an object and create a depression.) This technique enables the bones to be used as modeling tools to selectively push and pull the mesh into shape. All bones must begin with the same prefix as the main mesh object; if the MMO is named "star", for example, then all bones would begin with the star prefix, as in "star_arm01". Because Bones uses the skeletal objects bounding box to determine the area of influence, each object must be created individually, instead of copying or mirroring objects, as this will distort the bounding box. If the bounding box becomes skewed or does not match the orientation of the object, it can be corrected by rotating the object back to square and choosing Modify/Object/Reset Xform.

In the Keyframer, the bones are assigned pivot points and are hierarchically linked together. Linking the bones is not necessary for Bones to work, but this usually simplifies the animation process. At this point, the bones can be traditionally keyframed, or 3D Studio's Inverse Kinematics plug-in can be used to animate the skeleton. After the animation of the skeletal objects is set, the Bones KXP is activated. After choosing the Main Mesh Object, the area of influence and multiplier of the bones can be set individually. This data can be saved for each bone and recalled later or used in other animations. A preview window shows the deformation of the mesh object in wireframe, flat, or Gouraud shading. The preview window is also used with the visualize option, which shows a given bones area of influence as a range of six colors. Visualize can also be used to show only the maximum area of influence of a particular bone. An exclusion feature allows areas of the mesh to be affected only by their respective bones. For example, exclusion would be used to prevent the bones in a hand from pulling at adjacent digits and skin when the fingers were clenched in a fist.

Once the skeletal deformation is satisfactory, the Bones data is saved and the program is exited. The bones are then hidden and animation is rendered in the keyframer. Morph targets can also be generated within Bones to create the animation. Because Bones is a KXP, the frame-by-frame deformation cannot be seen outside the plug-in except when morph targets are used.

Bones Parameters

Main Mesh Object [Mmo] — Sets the mesh object to be deformed

Selected Bones [S] (All, None, Invert, Choose, Pick) — Selects individual or groups of bones.

Bones' Influence [I] (Selected, Chosen, Picked) — Selects a bone to edit zone and multiplier values.

Zone % [Z] — Sets the area that a selected bone will affect. The value is either doubled or halved as it is raised or lowered. Larger numbers increase the area of the mesh object that the bone affects.

Multiplier [M] — Sets the intensity of a selected bone's effect. The value is either doubled or halved as it is raised or lowered. Larger numbers increase the intensity or pull of the bone on the mesh.

Restore, Backup [R, B] — Saves or recalls zone and multiplier information as a proprietary PRX file.

Digimation | \bonespro | **BONES_I.KXP**

Visualize [V] — Shows the color-coded area of affect of a selected bone on the Main Mesh Object. The Control key can be held down to show only the area of maximum influence.

Include, Exclude [In,Ex] — Allows or prohibits the effect of selected bones on the maximum influence area of a picked bone.

SelExcl [Se] — Selects bones that are excluded from affecting the picked bone.

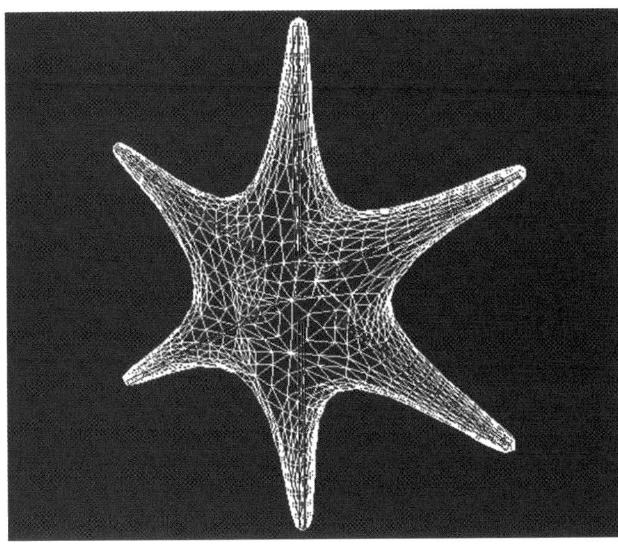

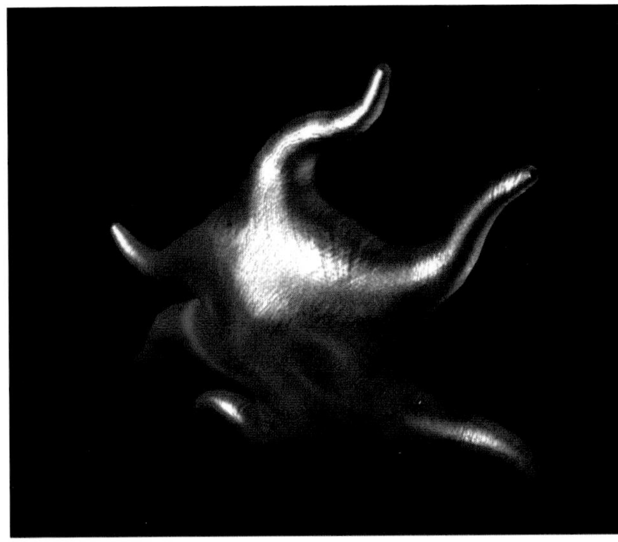

Elongated boxes are placed inside the geometry and used as bones to smoothly deform and animate the mesh object.

BOUNCE

Autodesk | \bounce | **BOUNCE_I.KXP**

Summary

Part of the 3D Studio Release 4 package, Bounce automatically creates position keys for an object to simulate a bouncing effect, with the option to decay the motion (150–200 frames are required for a convincing decay effect). The routine prompts the user to select the object to bounce, then the surface.

Note: *A position key is created on every frame, making some key editing necessary after Bounce is applied.*

Bounce Parameters

Click On Node To Bounce — Selects the object to bounce.

Click On Object For Surface — Selects the bounce plane for the effect.

Decay Bounce [D] y, n (yes, no) — Chooses whether the selected object has a decayed or continuous bounce.

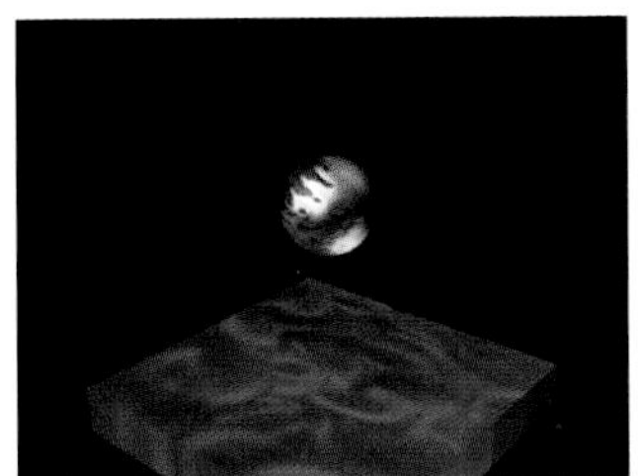

Frame 15

Frame 94

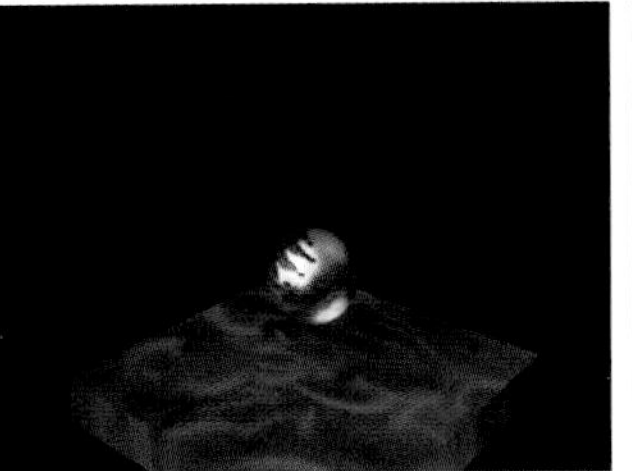

Frame 148

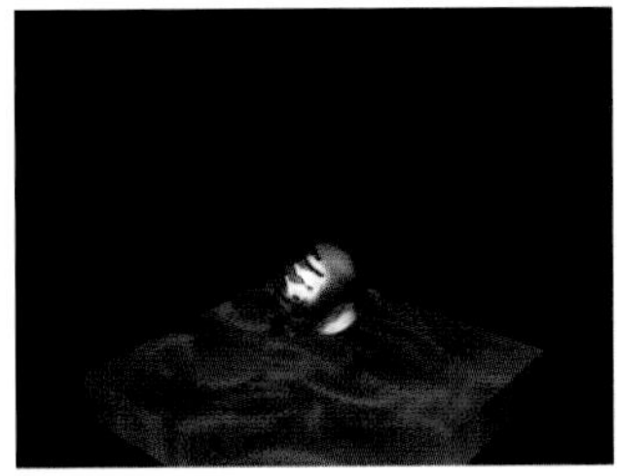

Frame 200

Bounce creates position keys for an object, simulating a bounce effect. All four sample images show the ball at the top bounce position.

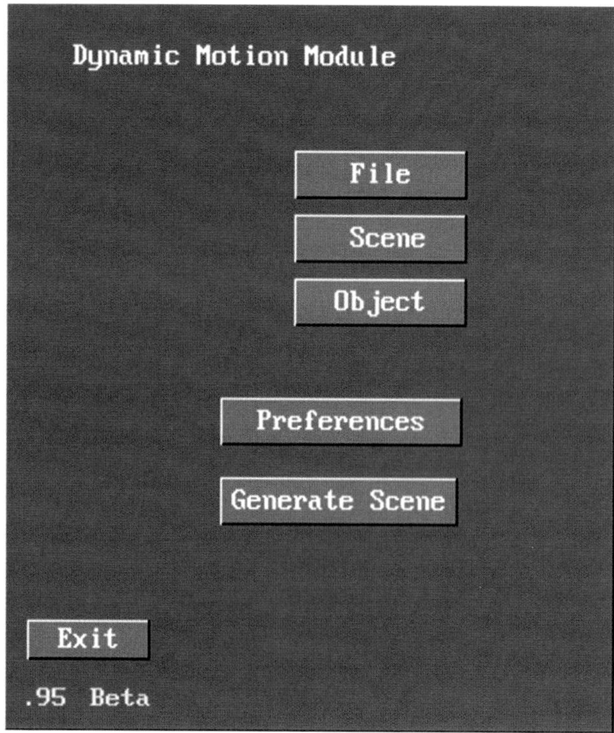

The main Dynamic Motion Module dialog box.

Summary

Dynamic Motion Module (DMM) animates the movement and collision of multiple objects in a scene.You give each object a position and initial motion, and DMM projects their motion, calculating collisions and bouncing objects off of each other.You can set an object's mass, elasticity, drag, rotation, velocity, and acceleration. Global settings for gravity and wind are applied to all objects. Collisions are accurately calculated for objects by checking for collisions between vertices and faces rather than just bounding boxes or spheres. DMM calculates the object interactions and then generates new keys for each object.

This summary is based on a prerelease version of the software.

Dynamic Motion Module Parameters

File [F] — Displays a dialog box for loading and saving settings.
Scene [S] — Displays a dialog box for setting scene parameters.
Object [O] — Displays a dialog box for setting object parameters.
Preferences [P] — Displays a dialog box for setting preferences.
Generate Scene [G] — Generates keys for the objects in the scene using the current settings.

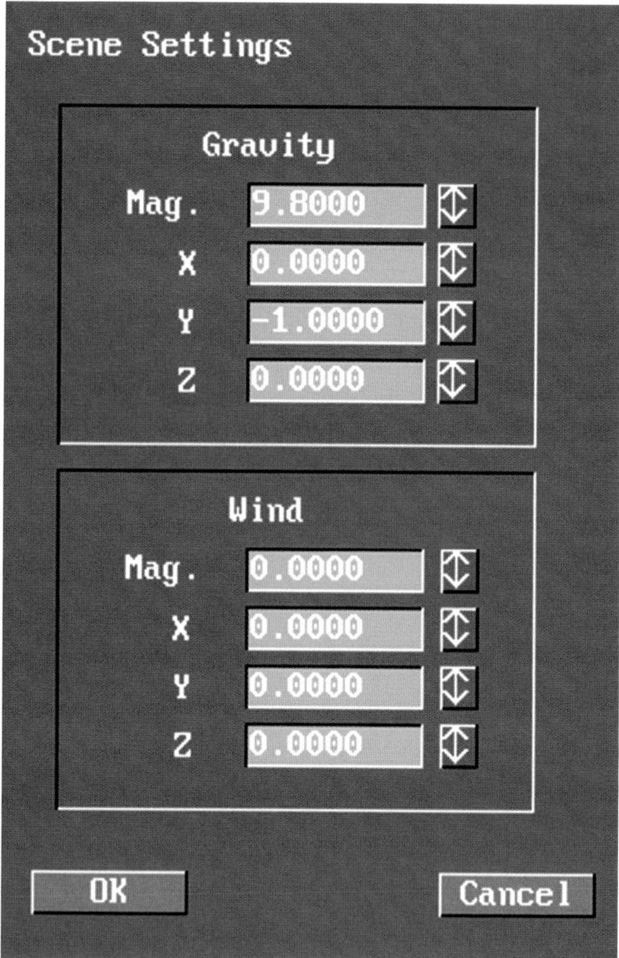

The Scene Settings dialog box.

Scene Parameters

Gravity magnitude [G] — Sets the strength of gravity in meters per second per second.
Gravity direction X, Y, Z [Gx] [Gy] [Gz] — Three coordinates that define the gravity direction.
Wind magnitude [W] — Sets the strength of wind in meters per second.
Wind direction X, Y, Z [Wx] [Wy] [Wz] — Three coordinates that define the wind direction.

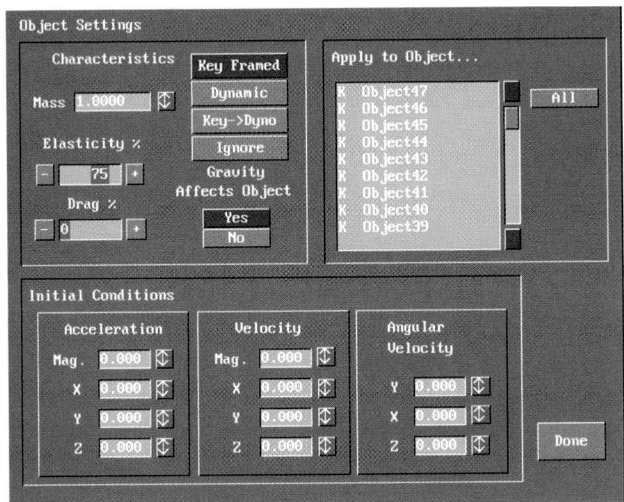

The Object Settings dialog box.

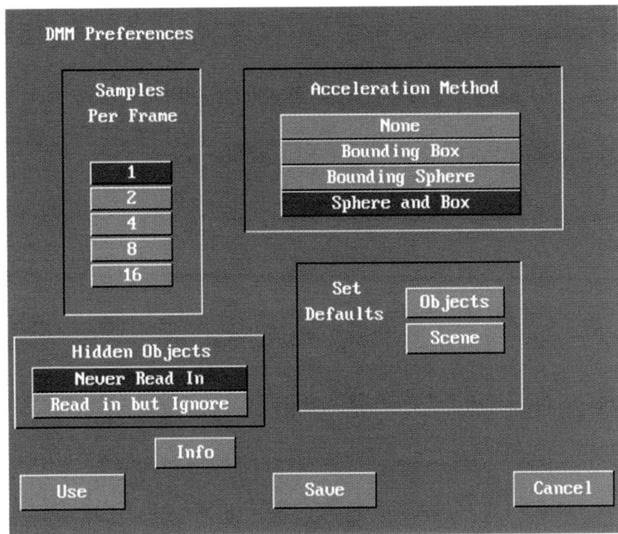

The DMM Preferences dialog box.

Object Parameters

Detection mode [Dm] k, d, kd, i (Key Framed, Dynamic, Key->Dyno, Ignore) — Selects how keys are treated and generated for an object. Key Framed means that DMM does not change any keys, and for collisions treats the object as if it had infinite mass. This is appropriate for unmovable objects such as ground planes. Dynamic generates keys based on dynamics settings in DMM. Key->Dyno uses the existing keys for an object until it collides with another object, after which keys are created using dynamics.

Mass [M] — The mass of the object in kilograms.

Elasticity [E] — The bounce elasticity in collisions for the object.

Drag [D] (0–100) — Sets the drag on an object. This is the percentage of velocity lost per second.

Gravity Affects Object [Ga] y, n (yes, no) — Determines whether an object is affected by gravity.

Apply to Object [Ao] — A scrolling list of objects in your scene. Click on the object to apply the current settings to it. Shift-click on an object to acquire its settings.

All [Am] — Applies the current settings to all object on the list.

Acceleration magnitude [Am] — Sets the initial acceleration of the current object in meters per second per second.

Acceleration direction X, Y, Z [Ax] [Ay] [Az] — Three coordinates that define the acceleration direction. You will normally set either acceleration or velocity, not both.

Velocity magnitude [V] — Sets the initial velocity of the current object in meters per second.

Velocity direction X, Y, Z [Vx] [Vy] [Vz] — Three coordinates that define the velocity direction.

Angular Velocity X, Y, Z [Avx] [Avy] [Avz] — Three values that define the rotation around each axis.

Preference Parameters

Samples Per Frame [S] (1, 2, 4, 8, 16) — Sets the number of times per frame that DMM will check an object for collision.

Acceleration Method [A] n, bb, bs, sb (None, Bounding Box, Bounding Sphere, Sphere and Box) — When checking for collision, DMM first performs a quick check on two objects to see if they could collide, and then performs a more detailed check to see where they collide. This setting sets the method that DMM uses on the first quick collision check. None checks the entire mesh. The other methods use a bounding box, a bounding sphere, or both.

Hidden objects [H] n, i (Never Read In, Read in but Ignore) — Determines whether DMM reads in keys for hidden objects. This affects only memory usage.

Set Defaults Object [So] — Displays an object settings dialog box to set object defaults.

Set Defaults Scene [Ss] — Displays a scene settings dialog box to set scene defaults.

DYNAMIC MOTION MODULE cont

DMM_I.KXP \dmm **Positron Publishing**

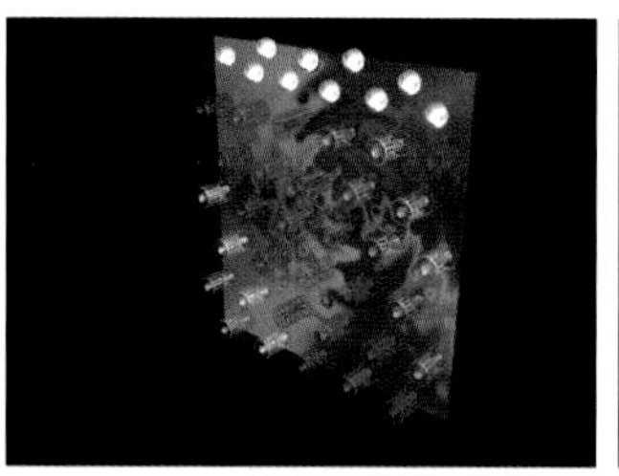
Frame 0

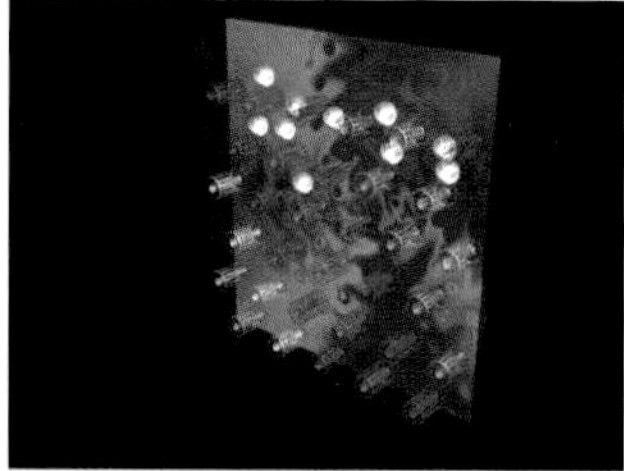
Frame 100

Frame 200

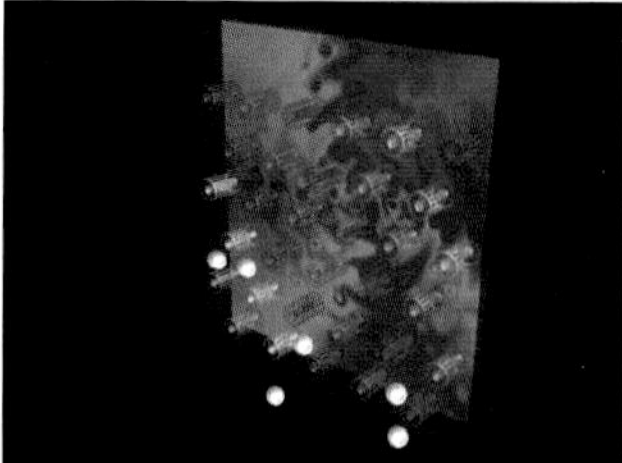
Frame 600

An animation of falling pinballs produced by Dynamic Motion Module.

INVERSE KINEMATICS

IK_I.KXP \ik **Autodesk**

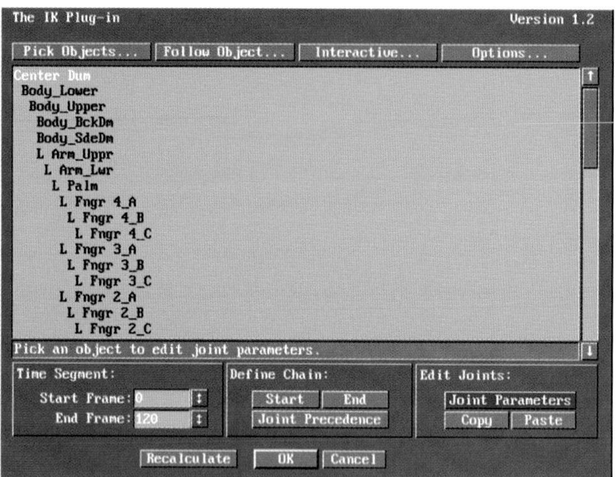

The Inverse Kinematics dialog box.

Summary

Inverse Kinematics (IK) is included with 3D Studio Release 4. IK uses hierarchically grouped objects that are linked together to simplify the animation process. After limits are selected for each joint's range of movement, any object in the chain can be manipulated and the surrounding objects will follow. An entire arm, for example, can be positioned by simply moving a finger, the leaf object, to the desired location on any given frame. IK "solves" for the placement of each of the objects in the chain based on each joint's limiting parameters and precedence, or weight, in the chain.

IK uses two methods for creating animations: automatic and interactive. The first step in both modes is to construct a scene consisting of a series of linked objects with appropriate pivot points. Next, this hierarchical structure is loaded into IK using the Pick Objects command. Parameters for each joint are then defined by setting the limits of the joint's rotation or movement on each of the three axes. Precedence enables objects to produce more or less overall movement in the chain, and damping slows the object as it approaches the limit of its range. Setting the joint parameters for each joint in a complex model can be a daunting process, but is vital for producing an accurate IK model.

The automatic mode mimics the motion and optionally the orientation of *follow objects*—dummy objects that follow a previously defined motion path. A kinematic chain, part of the linked object hierarchy, is selected and a follow object is designated for a particular object contained in the chain called the *end effector*. To define a kinematic chain, the start object must be above the end object in the hierarchy and the end effector must be in the same branch as the start of the chain. Follow objects are chosen for each chain in the hierarchy, and IK automatically computes the position of each object in the chain.

The interactive mode enables any object in the chain to be interactively positioned so that the object can be posed for each frame of the animation. The time slider is moved to the desired frame, and the object to be moved is selected using the IK button. As the object is moved, its kinematic chain is updated based on the joint parameters and precedence. The inverse kinematic keyframes, which optionally can be reduced within IK, are saved automatically when the plug-in is exited.

IK Parameters

Pick Objects [Po] — Selects an object from the keyframer for IK editing or animation.

Follow Object [Fo] — Selects an object from the scrolling list to use as a follow object for the selected kinematic chain.

Interactive [I] — Sets IK to the interactive mode for animation posing or previewing.

Options [O] — Sets the user preferences, resets changes, and saves or resets IK joint data.

Start and End Frame [Sf] [Ef] — Sets the beginning and ending frame of the IK animation.

Start and End [St] [En] — Sets the beginning and ending objects in the selected kinematic chain.

Joint Precedence [Jpr] — Displays the Joint Precedence dialog box, which sets the order of joint precedence.

Joint Parameters [Jpa] — Displays the Joint Parameters dialog box, which sets the linking parameters of the selected object.

Copy, Paste [Co] [Pa] — Copies and pastes from the Joint Parameters dialog box.

Recalculate [Re] — Sets IK to recalculate the animation of the current kinematic chain.

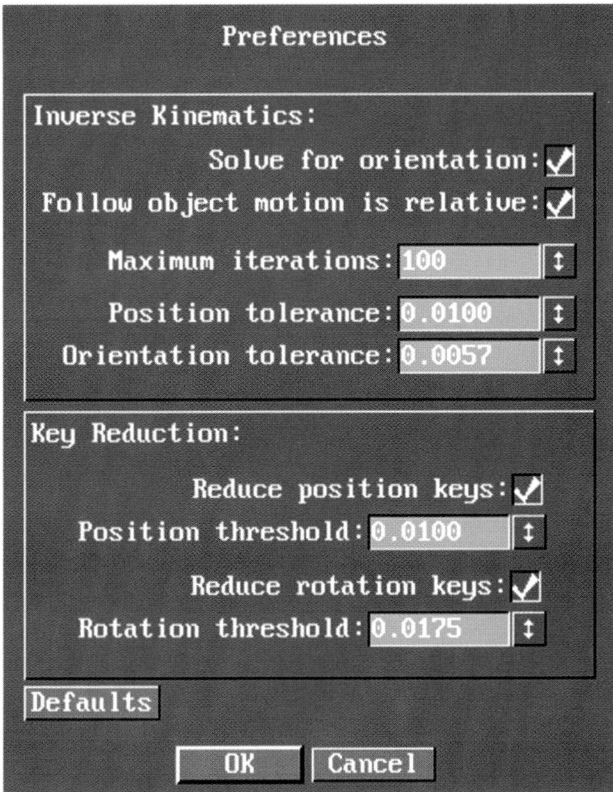

The IK Preferences dialog box.

Preferences Parameters

Solve for orientation [So] — Sets IK to make follow-object calculations using orientation as well as position.

Follow object motion is relative [Mr] — Sets IK to make follow-object calculations using object motion rather than absolute position.

Maximum iterations [Mi] (1–99,999) — Sets the maximum number of attempts per frame that IK will make to complete the animation.

Position tolerance [Pt] (0–9,999,999) — Sets the amount of variance in position allowed between the end effector and the follow object.

Orientation tolerance [Ot] (0–9,999,999) — Sets the amount of variance in orientation allowed between the end effector and the follow object.

Reduce position keys [Rpk] — Sets IK to reduce the number of position keys created when solving for an animation.

Position threshold [Pth] (0–9,999,999) — Sets the amount of variance allowed in position keys created using reduce position keys.

Reduce rotation keys [Rrk] — Sets IK to reduce the number of rotation keys created when solving for an animation.

Rotation threshold [Rth] (0–1,000) — Sets the amount of variance allowed in rotation keys created using reduce rotation keys.

Defaults [Def] — Sets all Preferences parameters to default values.

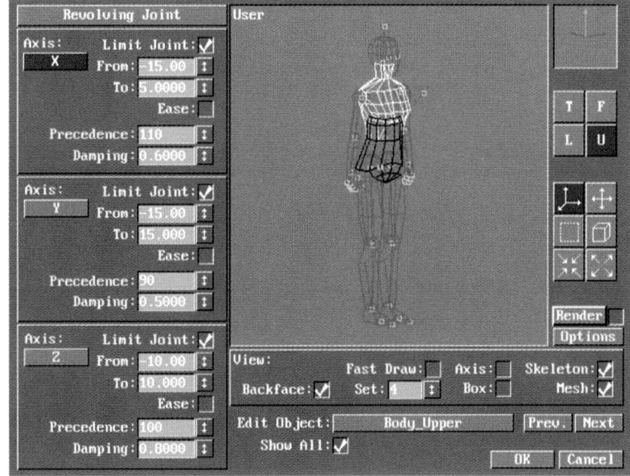

The Joint Parameters dialog box.

Joint Parameters

Revolving, Sliding [Rev] [Sli] — Sets the joint type to either a sliding joint or a revolving joint.

Axis [Ax] (x,y,z) — Sets the joint to rotate or slide on the given axis when turned on, and freezes the given axis when turned off.

Limit Joint [Lj] — Limits the joint to the settings in From and To.

From, To [Fr] [To] (–9,999–99,999) — Sets the limits of rotation in degrees or slide distance in units.

Ease [Ea] — Sets the object's movement to slow as it reaches the limits of its range.

Precedence [Pre] (–9,999,999–9,999,999) — Sets the joint to have more or less importance relative to the kinematic chain. Objects with higher precedence contribute more motion to the chain.

Damping [Da] (0–1) — Enables joints with lower precedence to contribute a larger amount of motion to the chain.

Backface [Bac] — Sets the preview window to display only those faces that point towards the viewer.

Fast Draw [Fd] — Sets the preview window to display only every *N*th face based on the value in Set.

Set (1–999) — Sets how many faces will be displayed in Fast Draw mode.

Axis — Sets the preview window to display axes of rotation for each joint.

Box — Sets the preview window to display all objects as bounding boxes.

Skeleton — Sets the preview window to display the hierarchical skeleton of the object.

Mesh — Sets the preview window to display or hide the object geometry.

Render — Sets the preview window to render the object mesh. Placing a check in the check box enables the window to be updated continuously.

Options [Opt] — Sets the object shadow and highlight color when Render is turned on. Sets the shading mode to wire, flat, or Gouraud.

Edit Object [Eo] — Selects the current object for editing from a scrolling list.

Show All [Sa] — Sets the preview window to display the entire hierarchy.

Prev., Next [Pre] [Nxt] — Selects the previous or next object in the kinematic chain for editing.

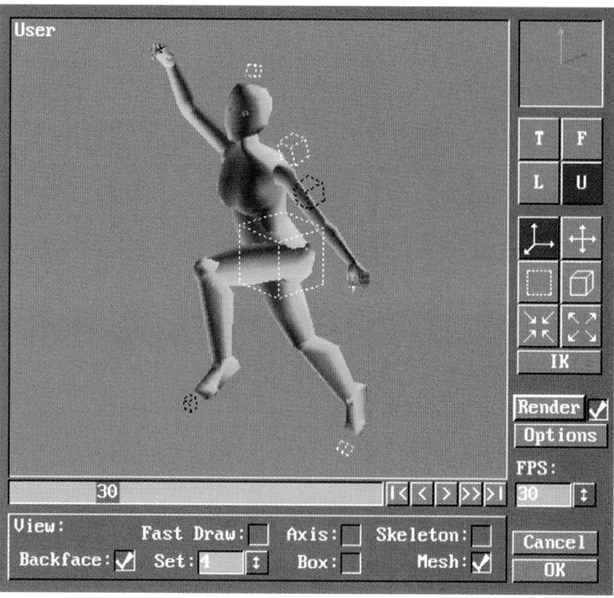

The IK Interactive dialog box.

Interactive Parameters

IK [Ik] — Selects objects in the display window to be interactively positioned.

Backface [Bac] — Sets the preview window to display only those faces that point towards the viewer.

Fast Draw [Fd] — Sets the preview window to display only every *N*th face based on the value in Set.

Set (1–999) — Sets how many faces will be displayed in Fast Draw mode.

Axis — Sets the preview window to display axes of rotation for each joint.

Box — Sets the preview window to display all objects as bounding boxes.

Skeleton — Sets the preview window to display the hierarchical skeleton of the object.

Mesh — Sets the preview window to display or hide the object geometry.

Render — Sets the preview window to render the object mesh. Placing a check in the check box enables the window to be updated continuously.

Options [Opt] — Sets the object shadow and highlight color when Render is turned on. Sets the shading mode to wire, flat, or Gouraud.

KEY DXF

CompuServe | **\keydxf** | **KEYDXF_I.KXP**

Summary

Key DXF generates a DXF file from motion path data in the keyframer. This enables lofting paths to be generated within the actual scene. Key DXF uses the same name each time it generates a new path, so objects must be renamed or moved to avoid overwriting previous files.

KEYDXF_i.KXP ver 1.0
Public Domain IPAS by Enthed Animation
CIS : M Enthed 100277,1272
FAX : +46+455+82311
PHONE : +46+455+28980
ABOUT EXIT

The Key DXF dialog box.

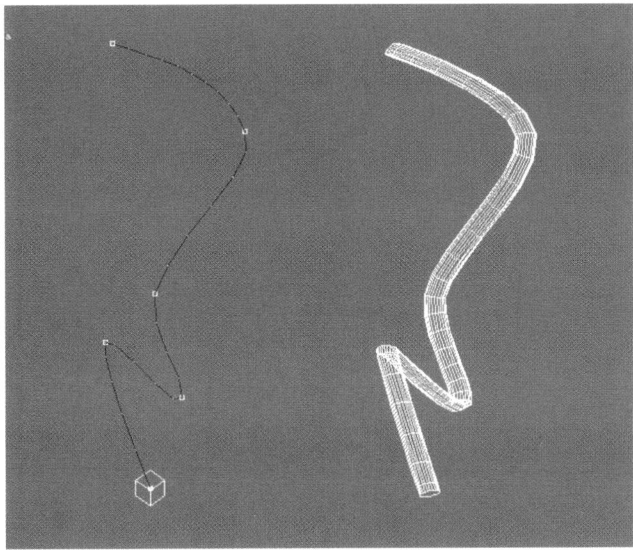

Object with path and lofted object
Key DXF generates a DXF file from motion path data in the keyframer.

KEY FACTORY

Schreiber Instruments | **\keyfacto** | **KFBNC_I.KXP, KFDUP_I.KXP, KFPICK_I.KXP**

Summary

Imagine Key Factory is a suite of KXP plug-ins that work together to provide motion dynamics from within 3D Studio. You can set up physical properties such for mass, elasticity, and friction and assign them to selected 3D mesh objects. Furthermore, you can apply physical forces including gravity, wind, explosion, implosion, and Brownian motion to groups of objects. Key Factory then computes the interaction and thus the motion paths between objects using several collision detection methods. The result is that Key Factory automatically produces all the keyframes needed to animate all the assigned object interaction and motion.

Key Factory uses three assignment levels for its various properties, forces, motion, and effects: by object, by set, and globally. A *set* is a specific subset or group in the Keyframer scene; for example, elasticity is applied at an object level, collision detection is applied at a set level, and wind magnitude is applied globally.

The process begins as with any animation, with all objects created and the scene built as desired. From the Keyframer, Key Factory then enables you to assign objects to unique sets, each with a specific behavior. Then physical properties such as mass and elasticity are assigned at the object level. You can then choose and assign the motion type and desired effects for each set and select Proceed, which calculates the necessary keyframes and creates a preview. Previews can be played back from within Key Factory and appear in wireframe, flat-shaded, or Gouraud-shaded views.

You can subdivide your Keyframer scene into up to four sets, which is useful for excluding objects from specific effect types. This can keep computation to a minimum by, for instance, limiting collision detection to only those objects that are required. There are 11 classes of set-level effects, including gravity, wind, drag, collision, and collision acceleration.

Key Factory also supports 9 different types of motion control, including linear, random linear, Brownian, and explode or implode. Most motion types provide speed and direction control, which is accessed by clicking the associated setup button.

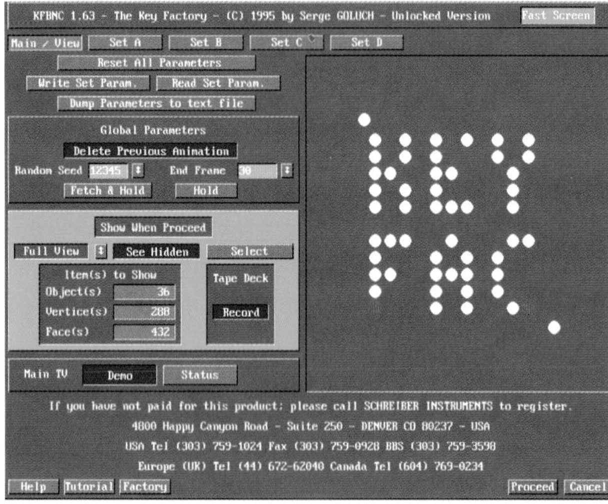

The Main/View dialog box.

Main/View Parameters

Main/View [Mvw] — Sets the interface to the main screen.

Set [SA,SB,SC,SD] (set a, set b, set c, set d) — Sets the object group to edit motion parameters.

Reset All Parameters [Rap] — Resets previous parameters within Key Factory.

Write/Read Set Parameters [Wp] [Rp] — Writes or reads Key Factory settings to and from a file.

Dump Parameters to text file [Tx] — Writes a text file of Key Factory settings.

Global Parameters

Delete Previous Animation [Dpa] — Deletes the keyframes and preview data from previous Key Factory animation.

Random Seed [Rs] — Sets the algorithm's start point with an arbitrary number. Each number produces a unique animation.

End Frame [Ef] — Sets the last frame of dynamic effects.

Fetch & Hold / Hold [Fe] [Ho] — Hold temporarily writes parameters to disk. Parameters can be recalled using Fetch.

View [Vw] (no view, 1/4 view, half view, full view) — Sets the animation preview window size.

See Hidden [Sh] — Enables objects hidden in the keyframer to be visible in the Key Factory animation preview.

Select [Sel] — Selects objects to include in the preview animation.

Record [Rec] — Turns on the record function in the preview animation. This enables animation playback and frame step functions in the preview window.

Main TV [MTV] demo, status — Sets the main window function. Demo runs a looping ball collision animation, and status lists set objects and their parameters.

Motion Type Parameters

Motion Type [Mt] zs, l, rl, rr, ex, o, b, h, pre (zero speed, linear, random linear, random random, explode or implode, orbit, brownian, helix, pre-existing) — Sets the type of motion that is applied to the object set. Objects set to zero speed are static, and pre-existing motion uses the objects existing position keys. Linear motion enables independent control of direction and speed for each object in a set, whereas object sets that use random linear motion allow independent control of direction and speed for the entire group of objects. Random Linear motion maintains the direction vector between frames, whereas Random Random motion varies the directional vector each frame. Explode / Implode creates spherical motion relative to a center point, and the center point can be an object in motion. Negative speeds are used to create implosions. Orbital motion creates orbital paths for each object in the set relative to a center object, which can be static or in motion. In object sets that use Brownian motion, individual objects within the set change direction according to a user-specified probability. Helical motion moves objects in a spiral path around a specified axis.

Setup [Set] — Calls the Motion Setup dialog box for the selected motion type.

Effects and Tags Parameters

Collide [Col] — Turns on global collision detection for the selected object set.

Rotation [Rot] — Turns on rotational motion for the selected object set.

Start Frame [Sf] — Turns on object start frame for the selected object set.

Drag [Dr] — Turns on object drag for the selected object set and displays the Drag dialog box.

Gravity [Gr] — Turns on global gravity for the selected object set and displays the Gravity dialog box.
Scale [Sc] — Turns on object scaling for the selected object set and displays the Scale dialog box.
Speed Limit [Sl] — Turns on object speed limits for the selected object set and displays the Speed Limit dialog box.
Lock [Lok] — Turns on individual axis locking for the selected object set and displays the Lock dialog box.
Wind [W] — Turns on global wind for the selected object set and displays the Wind dialog box.
Hide [Hid] — Turns on hidden objects for the selected object set and displays the Hide dialog box.
Frame 0 Pos [F0] — Turns on frame 0 position for the selected object set and displays the Frame 0 Position dialog box.

Globals Parameters

Collide [Col] — Displays the Global Collision Settings dialog box. Collision sets the accuracy and number of calculations used with collision detection.
Gravity [Gra] — Displays the Global Gravity Settings dialog box. Gravity applies a uniform directional force to the selected set. Objects are not affected by mass or size.
Wind [W] — Displays the Global Wind Settings dialog box. Wind applies a second uniform directional force to the selected set.

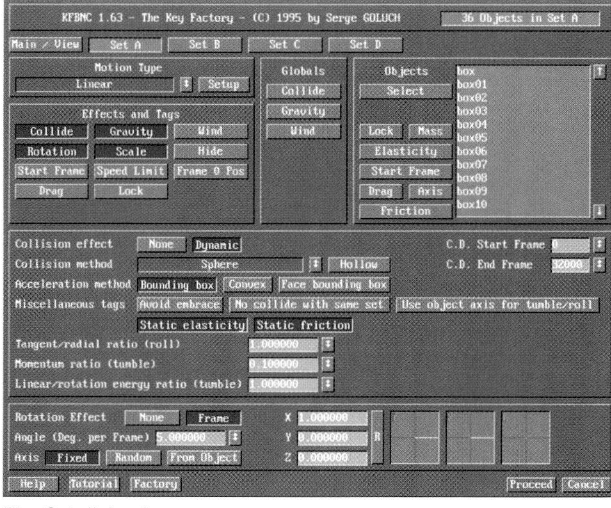

The Set dialog box.

Objects Parameters

Select [Sel] — Selects objects for object parameter assignment.
Lock [Lok] — Displays the Set Lock dialog box. Lock prevents object movement on the specified axes.
Mass [Ma] — Displays the Set Mass dialog box. Mass controls an object's reaction when using collision detection. Specifying huge mass enables an object to remain static in a collision.
Elasticity [El] — Displays the Set Elasticity dialog box. Elasticity controls the amount of momentum transferal or rebound when objects collide.
Start Frame [Sf] — Displays the Set Start Frame dialog box. Individual start frames can be specified for each object to create staggered object motion.
Drag [Xy] [Dr] — Displays the Set Drag dialog box. Drag creates a resistance force in the opposite direction of the object's motion, effectively slowing the object's movement over time.
Axis [Xy] [Ax] — Displays the Set Axis dialog box. Axis sets the rotation axis for individual objects.
Friction [Fri] — Displays the Set Friction dialog box. Friction is used to determine how objects roll when they obliquely strike a surface.

Collision Effect Parameters

Collision effect [Ce] — Turns on global collision detection for the selected object set.
Collision method [Cm] s, ef, fmv (sphere, edge to face, fast moving vertex) — Sets the method of collision detection. Sphere is the fastest method of calculation. It measures from the center of the first object to the center of the second object, and if the distance is less than the sum of both sphere radii, calculates a collision. Edge to face is the most accurate and slowest method of collision detection. Each face of an object has three edges, and a collision is calculated if an edge crosses through a face. This method can fail if fast-moving objects are used, as an edge can pass through a face before a calculation is made. Fast moving vertex connects the position of each vertex from frame to frame and calculates a collision if the path intersects a face.
Hollow [H] — Sets the collision calculations to be made as if object interiors were hollow.
Acceleration method [Am] bb, c, fb (bounding box, convex, face bounding box) — Sets the method of collision detection acceleration. Bounding box uses the object's bounding box for collision detection using the edge to face method. Convex encloses concave surfaces of an object to reduce calculation time. Face bounding box calculates collision by constructing a bounding box for each face and using the edge to face technique.
Miscellaneous tags [Mt] ae, ss, oa (avoid embrace, no collision with same set, use object axis for tumble/roll) — Sets the collision detection options. Avoid embrace prevents objects with similar directional vectors from becoming stuck and oscilating when they collide over a period of frames. No collision with same set prevents objects from colliding with objects belonging to the same set. Use object axis uses the object axis set in the object parameters for tumble and roll.

Static elasticity [Se] — Sets the collision calculation to use static object elasticity when calculating dynamic-static collisions, and dynamic elasticity when calculating dynamic-dynamic collisions.

Static Friction [Sf] — Sets the collision calculation to use static object friction when calculating dynamic-static collisions, and dynamic friction when calculating dynamic-dynamic collisions.

Tagent/radial ratio (roll) [Trr] — Sets the ratio of tangential speed relative to a dynamic object's speed when it collides with a static object.

Momentum ratio (tumble) [Mr] — Sets the transfer of rotational kinetic energy when two dynamic objects collide.

Linear/rotation energy ratio (tumble) [Lrr] — Sets the way in which kinetic energy is divided between rotational and linear motion during a collision.

C.D. Start/End Frame [Cds] [Cde] — Sets the frames to start and end collision detection.

Rotation Effect Parameters

Rotation Effect [Re] n, f (none, frame) — Turns the rotational effect on and off.

Angle (Deg, per Frame) [Ra] — Sets the amount of rotation per frame in degrees.

Axis [Ax] f, r, o (fixed, random, from object) — Sets the type of rotational axis. Fixed uses the axis set in rotational X,Y,Z; random selects an axis randomly for each object; and from object uses the axis specified in the object axis settings.

X,Y,Z [X,Y,Z] — Sets the axis of rotation when using fixed rotation.

Linear Motion Parameters

All parameters are contained in Random Linear Motion.

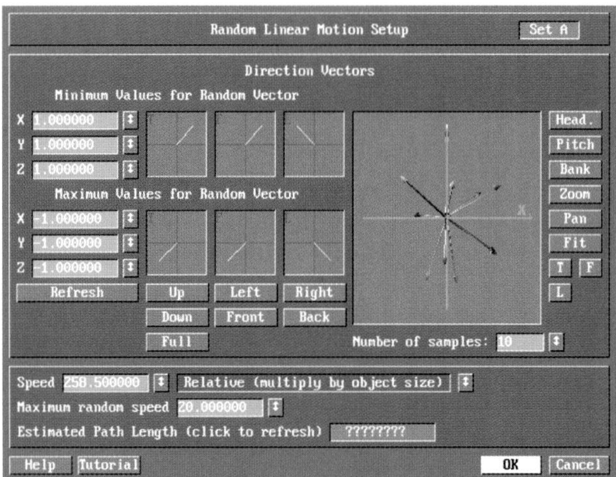

The Random Linear Motion dialog box.

Random Linear Motion Parameters

Minimum Values For Random Vector [Mi] x, y, z (x direction, y direction, z direction) (0–1,000) — Specifies three minimum direction values for applying random motion.

Maximum Values For Random Vector [Ma] x, y, z (x direction, y direction, z direction) (0–1,000) — Specifies three maximum direction values for applying random motion.

Preset Direction Buttons u, d, f, l, fr, r, b (up, down, full, left, front, right, back) — Automatically aligns the direction vector(s) along a given axis.

Number Of Samples [Ns] (0–1,000) — Sets the number of vector samples displayed in the 3D viewport.

Speed Value [Sv] (0–1,000) — Sets the speed of the linear motion in world units per frame.

Speed Type [St] f, r, rm, rd (fixed, random, relative multiply, relative divide) — Selects the speed type, which determines how the speed value is applied.

Maximum Random Speed [Mr] (0–1,000) — If Random Speed is selected, sets a random speed (between Speed and Maximum Random Speed values) for each selected object.

Estimated Path Length [Ep] Displays the estimated length of the object's path.

Random Random Parameters

All parameters are contained in Random Linear Motion.

Explode or Implode Motion Parameters

Center [C] o, f (object, fixed center) — Sets the explosion or implosion center either to an object or a specified point in 3D space.

Scale Factor [Sc] x, y, z (x direction, y direction, z direction) — Sets a scale factor for the three direction vectors. A zero value creates a planar explosion.

All additional parameters are identical to Random Linear Motion.

Note: *Setting a positive Speed value creates an explosion, and setting a negative value creates an implosion.*

Orbit Motion Parameters

All parameters are contained in Helix Motion.

Brownian Motion Parameters

All parameters are contained in Random Linear Motion.

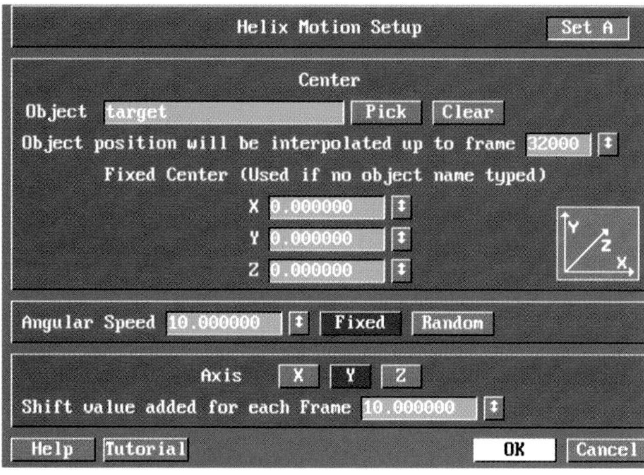

The Helix Motion dialog box.

Helix Motion Parameters

Center [C] o, f (object, fixed center) — Sets the center of the helical path to either an object or a specified point in 3D space.

Angular Speed [As] f, r (Fixed, Random) (0–1,000) — Specifies the speed of orbital motion in degrees per frame. Selecting Fixed applies the same speed to all the objects, Selecting Random applies different but constant speeds to each object.

Axis [Ax] x, y, z (x axis, y axis, z axis) — Sets the axis of rotation for the helical path.

Shift value added for each frame [Sv] Sets the amount of directional shift in units that is applied to the rotational movement to create the helical path. Lower values produce condensed coils, larger values produce elongated coils.

Global Collision Detection Parameters

Accuracy [Ac] (1–1,000) — Sets the number of steps that object motion is divided into between each frame. Values between 1 and 5 are generally acceptable. Large values can significantly increase collision computation time.

Minimum Absolute value for linear motion [Mlm] — Sets the minimum speed an object can be traveling before it is considered to have stopped.

Gravity Parameters

Gravity [Xy] — Sets the amount of gravitational pull in the vector direction.

Values For Gravity Vector [Gv] x, y, z (x direction, y direction, z direction) — Sets the direction of gravitational pull.

Preset Direction Buttons u, d, f, l, fr, r, (up, down, full, left, front, right) — Automatically aligns the direction vector along a given axis.

Wind Parameters

Wind [W] — Sets the amount of wind force in the vector direction.

All additional parameters are contained in Gravity.

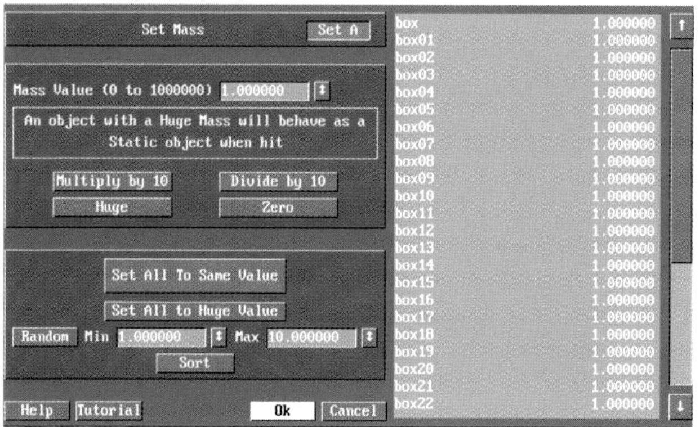

The Mass dialog box.

Mass Parameters

Mass value [M] (0–1,000,000) — Sets the object mass, which affects collision behavior. Setting mass to the maximum value makes an object immovable.

Mass shortcuts [Ms] m, d, h, z (multiply by 10, divide by 10, huge, 0) — Shortcuts for setting and changing mass. Huge sets the mass to the maximum value.

Set all to same value [S] — Sets all objects in the list to the current mass setting.

Set all to huge value [H] — Sets all objects in the list to the maximum value, essentially fixing the objects in place.

Random [R] — Sets each object in the list to a random number that falls between the Min and Max settings.

Sort [So] — Sorts the object list by object name.

Elasticity Parameters

Elasticity value [E] (0–2) — Sets the elasticity value for an object.

Elasticity shortcuts [Es] h, s, r, g, p, l (hyper ball, super ball, rubber, golf ball, plastic, lead) — Sets the current elasticity settings to common preset values.

All to 1 [A1] — Sets the elasticity of all objects in the list to 1.

All to 0 [A0] — Sets the elasticity of all objects in the list to 0.

Start Frame Parameters

Start Frame Value [Sfv] — Sets the frame on which an object will begin its motion sequence

Multiply Value by number found in name [Xv] — Sets the start frame to the number at the end of the object name multiplied by 10. For example, an object named Ball12 would start moving on frame 120 (12x10).

Add Value to number found in name [Av] — Sets the start frame to the number at the end of the object name plus 1. For example, an object named Ball12 would start moving on frame 13 (12 + 1).

All additional parameters are contained in Mass Parameters.

Drag/Acceleration Parameters

Drag value [D] (–1–1) — Sets the drag/acceleration value for an object. Positive values set the drag for an object. Negative values produce an acceleration effect (negative drag). Frictionless motion is produced by a value of 0, and a value of 1 produces objects that won't move.

All to -0.1 [A1] — Sets the drag of all objects in the list to –0.1.

All to 0.0 [A2] — Sets the drag of all objects in the list to 0.

All to 0.1 [A3] — Sets the drag of all objects in the list to 0.1.

All to 1.0 [A4] — Sets the drag of all objects in the list to 1.

Axis Parameters

Axis value X,Y,Z [Ax] [Ay] [Az] — Sets the rotation axis vector for an object. You can set individual values for X, Y, and Z, or you can use your mouse to graphically move the vectors in the three display areas.

All to 0,0,0 [A0] — Sets the drag of all objects in the list to 0,0,0. This has the effect of turning off an axis of rotation. The object then defaults back to the rotation axis set in the main dialog box.

Friction Parameters

Friction value [F] (0–2) — Sets the friction value for an object. This friction only come into play when an object is rolling on an incline surface. Its range is normally from 0 to 1.0 but can be set as high as 2.0

Friction shortcuts [Fa] mx, mn, a, l (maximum, minimum, average, low) — Maximum sets the friction value to 1.0, Minimum sets it to 0.0, Average sets it to 0.9, and Low sets it to 0.5.

All to 1 [A1] — Sets the friction of all objects in the list to 1.

All to 0 [A0] — Sets the friction of all objects in the list to 0.

Drag/Acceleration Effect Parameters

All parameters are contained in the Scale Effect parameters.

Gravity Effect Parameters

All parameters are contained in the Scale Effect parameters.

Scale Effect Parameters

None [N] — Turns the effect off for all frames.

All [A] — Sets the effect to be used for all frames.

After [Aft] — Sets the effect to be applied only after the start frame.

Before [Bef] — Sets the effect to be applied only before the start frame.

Hit [H] — Sets the effect to be applied only after the first collision.

Hit Pulse [Hp] — Sets the effect to be applied for the number of frames set in frame 1 after the first collision.

Hit Any [Ha] — Sets the effect to be applied for the number of frames set in frame 1 after the Any collision.

Between [Btw] — Sets the effect to be applied only between frames 1–2.

Frame1/Frame2 [F1/F2] — Sets the frame numbers to start and end the effect.

Fixed [Fxd] — Sets a linear scale effect between the settings in Scale1 and Scale2.

Random [Ran] Sets a random scale for each node in the Scale1 to Scale2 range.

Sine [Si] — Sets the scale transition to a sine wave between Scale1 and Scale2.

Jitter [Jit] — Sets a random scale for each node and frame in the Scale1 to Scale2 range.

Scale 1/Scale 2 [Sc1] [Sc2] x, y, z (x scale, y-scale, z-scale) — Sets the object start and end scale.

Sine period [Sip] — Sets the number of frames for the sine effect.

Sine decay [Sid] — Sets the sine damping over time as a value the sine value is multiplied by each frame. Enables objects to be deformed as they collide when used in conjunction with Hit.

Order with speed [Ows] — Sets the x scale to the largest speed axis, y to the middle speed axis, and z to the smallest speed axis.

Speed Limit Effect Parameters

Maximum absolute value for speed [Mfs] — Sets the maximum speed an object can attain after physical forces are applied.

Minimum absolute value before stop [Mbs] — Sets the minimum speed an object can be traveling before it is considered to have stopped.

All additional parameters are contained in the Scale Effect parameters.

Lock Effect Parameters

All parameters are contained in the Scale Effect parameters.

Wind Effect Parameters

All parameters are contained in the Scale Effect parameters.

Hide Effect Parameters

Frame [F] — Sets keys at frame 1 and 2. A value less than 0 will not set a key.

Random [R] — Sets a key at a random frame between frames 1 and 2.

SFrame [Sfr] — Sets keys at the start frame + frame 1 and start frame + frame 2.

Hit [H] — Sets a key at the first collision.

Frame1/Frame2 [F1] [F2] — Sets the frame numbers to start and end the effect.

Frame 0 Position Effect Parameters

No Change [Nc] — Leaves all objects at their present location.

Origin [Or] — Sets all objects to align at point 0,0,0.

Origin (pivot) [Orp] — Sets all object pivots to align at point 0,0,0.

Object [O] — Sets all object pivots to align at the center object location.

Object (pivot) [Op] — Sets all object pivots to align at the center object location.

Center Object [Co] — Sets the center object by name.

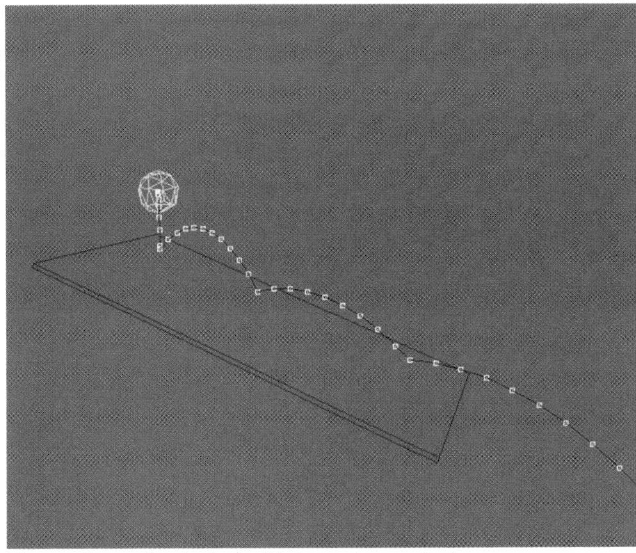

The motion path of a ball with dynamics applied

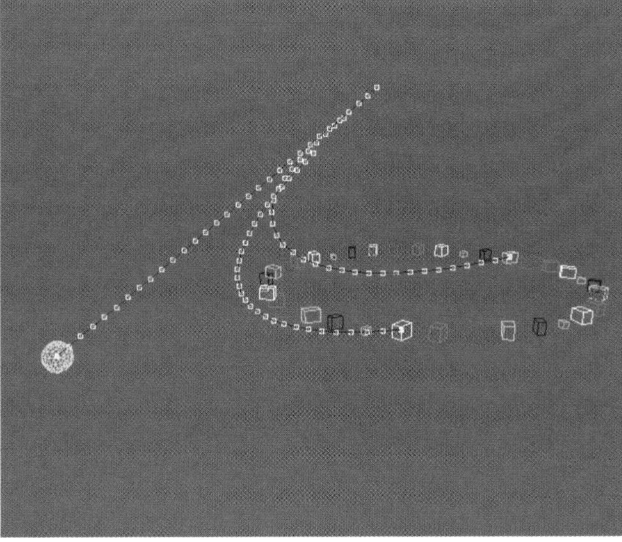

Motion objects chase a target object

Imagine Key Factory sets physical properties for properties including mass, elasticity, and friction to selected 3D mesh objects. Physical forces including gravity, wind, explosion, implosion, and Brownian motion can be applied to groups of objects.

KEY MANAGER

Yost Group \keyman KEYMAN_I.KXP

Summary

Key Manager (Keyman) is part of the Yost Group Disk #7 package. It enables you to store multiple sets of position and rotation keys inside an object. You can then recall and use those key sets at a later time. Keyman can also reduce the number of position and rotation keys based on threshold values. A preview window enables you to see the animation for an object in wireframe mode.

The main dialog box lets you select the object you want to use by picking it on the screen or selecting it from a list. You then can embed the current keys in the object as a named set, which displays the Embed Key dialog box. Here you can enter a name under which to save a set of keys. You can save

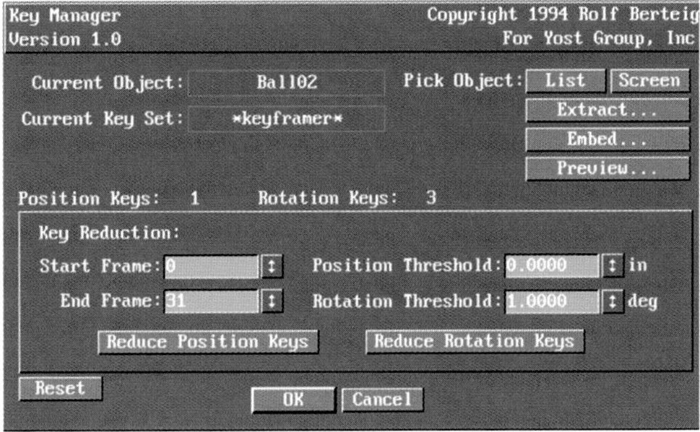

The Key Manager dialog box.

position data, rotation data, or both in a set. When you want to retrieve a saved set of keys, you display the Extract Key dialog box and select a key set name from the list. You can extract position, rotation, or both from a key set.

Keyman can reduce the number of keys for either position or rotation. You set the thresholds and Keyman removes any keys that produce changes less than the threshold values.

Keyman Parameters

Pick Object [Po] l,s (List, Screen) — Select the object to work with by either selecting from a list or picking from the screen.
Extract — Displays the Key Set Extraction dialog box.
Embed — Displays the Embed Key Set dialog box.
Preview — Displays a preview window for the current object's keys.
Start Frame [Sf] — Sets the starting frame for key reduction. Keyman will reduce keys starting at this frame and ending at the End frame.
End Frame [Ef] — Sets the ending frame for key reduction.
Position Threshold [Pt] — Sets the threshold for position key reduction.
Rotation Threshold [Rt] — Sets the threshold for rotation key reduction.
Reduce Position Keys [Rp] — Reduces position keys.
Reduce Rotation Keys [Rr] — Reduces rotation keys.

Embed Key Parameters

Key set list [Sl] — A scrolling list of embedded key sets.
Key Set Name [Sn] — Sets the name of the key set to embed.
Delete — Deletes the currently selected key set.
Preview — Displays a preview dialog box for the currently selected key set.
Key type [Kt] p, r, pr (Position, Rotation, Position and Rotation) — Sets the type of key saved in the current key set.

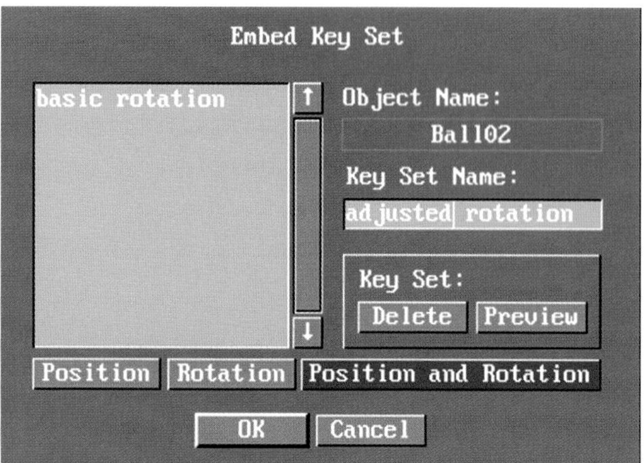

The Embed Key Set dialog box.

Preview Parameters

Display controls — Enable you to change your viewpoint on the object.
Frame Rate [Fr] — Sets the desired frame rate.
Current frame [Cf] — A slider that sets and displays the current frame.
Play — Plays the current animation keys at the current frame rate.

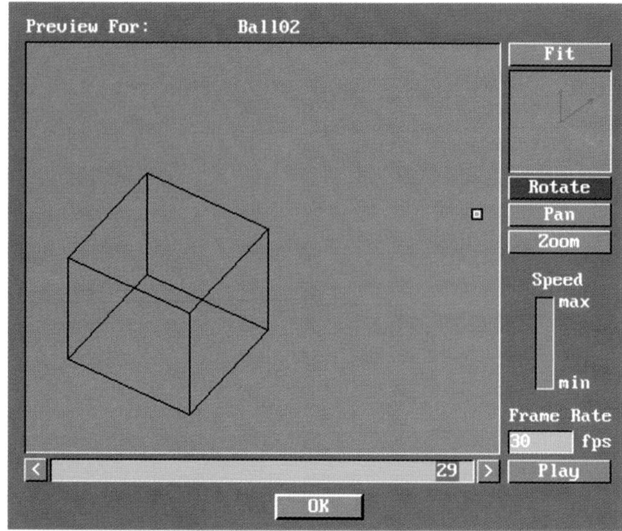

The Preview dialog box.

Summary

Keyframe Calculator is a programmable calculator for Keyframer keys. Using this plug-in you can create keys based on calculations and on keyboard entry of coordinates. You can apply these precise operations to a single object or to a group of objects.

Keyframe Calculator uses RPN notation for all its operations. There are eight levels in its entry stack. Four levels are visible at any one time, and you can shift stack levels up and down, or you can swap values between levels.

You can create keys for Position, Rotation, Scale, Hide, Color, Hotspot, FOV, Roll, and Falloff. Position and Rotation keys can be specified using either relative or absolute coordinates. You can enter coordinates using rectangular, polar, cylindrical, or spherical notations. There is an extensive range of functions available for use in calculations, including sqrt, abs, exp, get_object_xform, integer_portion, fractional_portion, tens_cont_bias, delete_keys, get_position_key, and get_scale_key, along with trigonometric functions and basic arithmetic functions. Nearly any button in the interface can be called as a function.

This last item is most useful in the scripting language that is built into the calculator. It reads text files with lists of functions and parameters (including object names), executing them in turn. You can develop a set of scripts that can be reused on any object with only minor editing. In addition to the scripting language, this plug-in enables you to define keyboard macros that can be saved and reused inside Keyframe Calculator.

A unique feature of Keyframe Calculator is the capability to assign a macro to a mouse gesture. Each time you reproduce the gesture (using the right mouse button) the macro is executed. These gestures are based on mouse movements across coarse grid coordinates on the screen and can be edited and saved for later use.

Keyframe Calculator includes an extensive system of on-screen help. Alt+clicking on any button displays help on the function for that button. Clicking on the Help button displays a series of general help screens. This plug-in requires at least 800x600 resolution for its dialog boxes.

The Keyframe Calculator dialog box.

Keyframe Calculator Parameters

Quit (icon in upper left corner) [Q] — Quits the plug-in.

Hide dialog box(icon in upper right corner) [Hd] — Hides the dialog box and shows the Keyframer screen. Any mouse click redisplays the dialog box.

Stack level display 1, 2, 3, 4 [S1] [S2] [S3] [S4] — Displays the data in four stack levels out of eight total. You can scroll the data trough the stack levels to see the remaining data. Clicking on a stack level swaps its data with the level below it.

Keyframe coordinate type [Kc] r, a (Relative, Absolute) — Determines whether coordinate data will be interpreted as a relative offset or as absolute coordinates.

Keyframe type [Kt] p, s, r, hi, c, ho, fo, r, fa (Position, Scale, Rotate, Hide, Color, Hotspot, Fov, Roll, Falloff) — Selects the type of key that will be created or changed.

Function operators [Fo] (+, -, *, /) — Selects a basic arithmetic operator.

List [Li] — Enables you to select a function from a scrolling list of all the available functions.

Again [Ag] — Reinvokes the most recently selected function.

Coord [Co] — Displays a dialog box enabling you to retrieve the coordinates of the bounding box of an object.

Size [Sz] — Displays a dialog box enabling you to retrieve the size of the bounding box of an object.

Area [Ar] — Displays a dialog box enabling you to retrieve the surface area of an object.

%Ch [Ch] — Retrieves the difference between level 2 and level 1.

Help — Displays a series of general help screens.

Read Script [Rs] — Reads and executes a script file.

File Notes [Fn] — Switches to the 3D Studio text editor, enabling you to create and edit project notes that are embedded in the mesh file or project file.

Clear [Cl] — Clears the contents of all stack levels.

Last [La] — Restores the most recent contents of all stack levels.

Choose Obj [Co] — Displays a dialog box enabling you to select a single object on which to operate.

Tag SelSet [Ts] — Displays a dialog box enabling you to select, by tagging on a list, one or more objects on which to operate.

Pick SelSet [Ps] — Displays a dialog box enabling you to select, by picking from the Keyframer screen, one or more objects on which to operate.

R-up, R-down [Ru] [Rd] — Scrolls the stack levels up and down.

1<>2, 1<>3, 2<>3, 2<>4 [S12] [S13] [S23] [S24] — Swaps data between levels on the stack. The numbers refer to the level numbers.

Display units [Du] d, f (Decimal, Feet & Inch) — Selects the display mode for distance values.

View Level 1 [V1] — Displays the entire contents of stack level 1. This is for cases in which the data string is too long to display in the normal Stack Level display area.

Coordinate display mode [Ce] r, c, s (Rec, Cyl, Sph) — Sets the mode for coordinate display. Rec sets the display mode to rectangular, by which coordinates are displayed as sets of X,Y,Z values. Cyl sets the display mode to cylindrical, by which coordinates are displayed using distance, angle, and height. Sph sets the display mode to spherical, by which coordinates are displayed using distance, angle in plan, and angle from plan.

Decimal display [Dd] (0–6) — Sets the number of decimal places displayed.

Fractional display [Fd] (1/256–1/1) — Sets the maximum denominator for fractional display. Denominators are factors of 2.

Object Filtering Parameters

Type list [Tl] m, d, ol, sl, st, c, ct (Mesh Object, Dummy Object, Omni Light, Spotlight, Spotlight Target, Camera, Camera Target) — Sets the types of objects that will be displayed in the Object Tagging list. You can set one or more types.

Type tagging [Tt] a, i, n (All, Invert, None) — Tags and untags object types. All tags all types, None untags all types, and Invert swaps the tag status of all types.

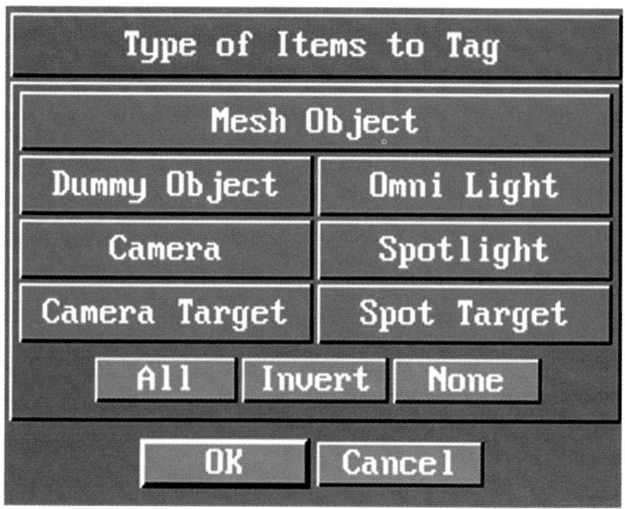

The Object Filtering dialog box.

Object Tagging Parameters

Object list [Ol] — A scrolling list of objects. Double-click on an object to tag or untag it.

All, None [A] [N] — These buttons tag or untag all objects.

Tag, Untag [T] [U] — These buttons tag or untag the highlighted object.

Invert [I] — Inverts the tagged status of all objects.

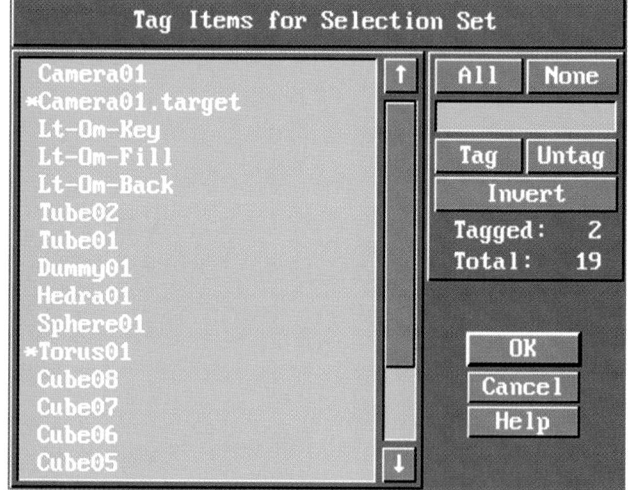

The Object Tagging dialog box.

Coordinate Filtering Parameters

Width Min, Cen, Max [Wmn] [Wc] [Wmx] (on, off) — Retrieves the width coordinate from the minimum, maximum, or center of the object's bounding box.

Depth Min, Cen, Max [Dmn] [Dc] [Dmx] (on, off) — Retrieves the depth coordinate from the minimum, maximum, or center of the object's bounding box.

Height Min, Cen, Max [Hmn] [Hc] [Hmx] (on, off) — Retrieves the height coordinate from the minimum, maximum, or center of the object's bounding box.

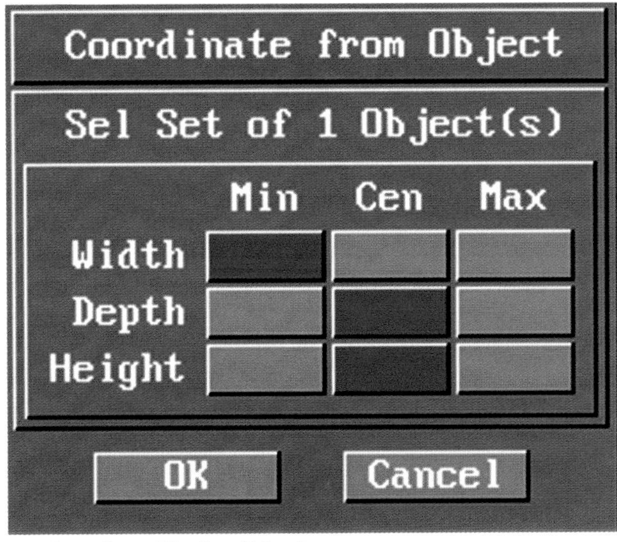

The Coordinate Filtering dialog box.

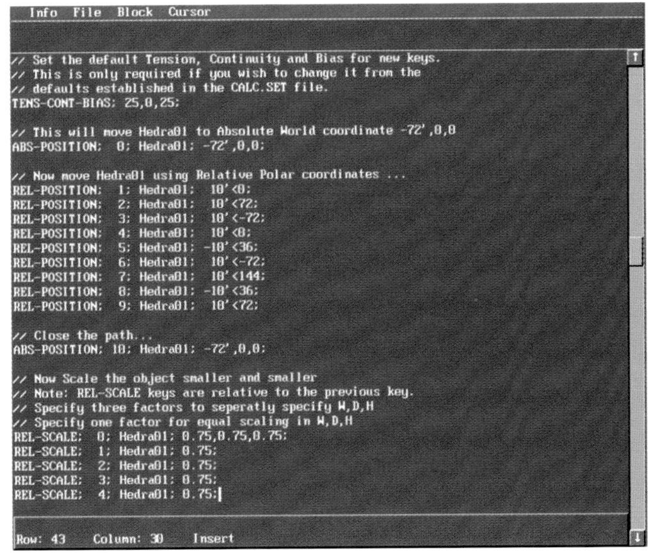

A script creating position and scale keys
Keyframe Calculator includes a script execution function.

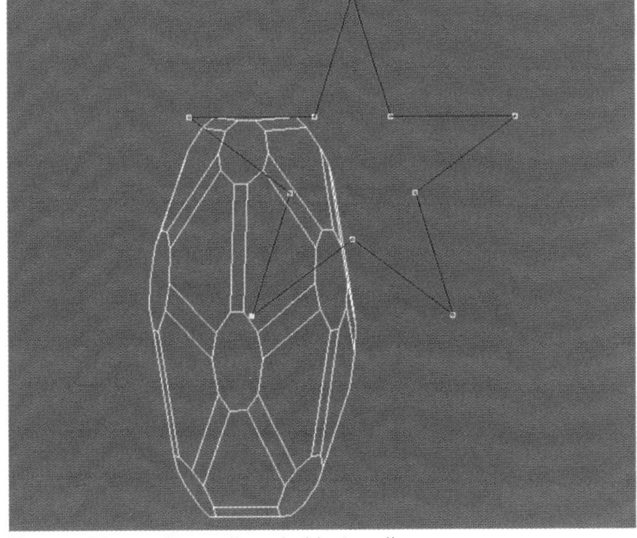

The resulting motion path and object scaling

KEYSCRIPT

Autodesk \kscript SCRIPT_I.KXP

Summary

Keyscript is a scripting language bundled with 3D Studio Release 4 that enables you to control events in 3D Studio's Keyframer. It gives you the ability to write your own programs that can create and modify animation keys in the Keyframer.

The Keyscript language is an interpreted language based on BASIC with extensions for dealing with object keys and for interacting with users. You can create user-defined data types that work like records in languages such as C and Pascal for dealing with the variety of data that 3D animations require.

Scripts are text files that you work with by calling the Script KXP plug-in. This displays an editor based on 3D Studio's text editor. From here you can create or load a script and execute it. Scripts switch to the Keyframer to run and return to the script editor when finished. They can display simple dialog boxes for user interaction and data entry. You can use complex dialog boxes that are produced by the 3DE resource editor. This is a separate program available on CompuServe that enables you to create dialog boxes by drawing them on-screen. These dialog boxes can then be saved and called by Keyscript.

Keyscript scripts are flexible and can automate almost any task in the Keyframer. Keyscript comes with some sample scripts that manage groups of lights, adjust motion paths, and create morph objects for simulated mouth movements during speaking. Keyscript includes a built-in function to detect collision between objects. You then can write a subroutine that decides what happens to the objects after the collision.

Keyscript only functions inside the Keyframer. It does not work in the 3D Editor or in video post and cannot create new objects. The Script Extensions is a separate product that extends the Keyscript language to the 3D Editor, video post processing, SXP materials, and AXP procedural surfaces.

```
 Info  File  Block  Cursor  Keyscript
                                   HOLD FETCH
; MORPH.K3D
; Morph Target Manager
; 3DStudio R4
; 940926
; Martin Doudoroff
;
; Note: This script is formatted to be viewed with Tab Length set to 8 characters.

GFX_Redraw

; Setup

        ' Constants
        Frames= 1 : TimeCode = 2
        Edit  = 1 : Add  = 2 : Delete   = 4
        Black = 0 : Cyan = 3 : LightGray= 5 : DarkGray = 6 : Gray = 8 : Yellow = 14 : White = 15

        ' Setup general variables
        NumFrames
        TotalFrames    = Time
        MaxAliases     = 200      :' Arbitrary max.
        FrameRate      = 30       :' Currently only works for video/30fps
        TotalAliases   = 0        :' Tallies number of aliases
        D2S1Index      = 0        :' Slider position indexes
        D1S2Index      = 0
        D1S1Index      = 0

Row: 8     Column: 1     Insert
```

The Keyscript Editor screen.

Common Script Editor Parameters

Info menu [I] — Commands for general status and editor configuration.

File menu [F] — Basic file commands such as new, load, save, and merge, and an exit command for leaving the editor.

Block menu [B] — Text-block editing command such as copy, cut, paste, and undo.

Cursor menu [C] — Help, search, and replace commands along with parenthesis matching commands.

Keyscript menu — Script management commands for switching between the two file buffers, embedding scripts, and executing scripts. These commands are duplicated in the icon bar.

Execute icon [E] — Runs the script.

Script buffers 1, 2 [S1] [S2] — Switches between the two available script file buffers. This enables you to edit two scripts at one time.

Console icon [Co] — Switches to the text output window.

Embed icon [Em] — Displays the embed/extract dialog box for embedding scripts in objects.

Hold, Fetch icons [H] [F] — These are the same as the Hold and Fetch buttons in the Keyframer. They save and restore the current state of the scene, enabling you to try out a script and restore the scene after it executes.

Morph Target Manager Parameters (sample script)

Object [O] — Selects the morph object.

Alias list [Al] — A scrolling list of aliases for morph target objects. The aliases are defined to make it easier to work with morph objects.

Track window [Tw] — Next to the Alias list, this grid enables you to specify a morph target at each point in time for the morph object. Just click on a point in time for a particular morph target to assign it to the morph object.

Aliases [A] — Displays a dialog box enabling you to edit object aliases.

Preferences [P] — Displays a dialog box enabling you to set preferences for the Morph Target Manager script.

Load, Save [L] [S] — Lets you load and save predefined lists of aliases and morph settings.

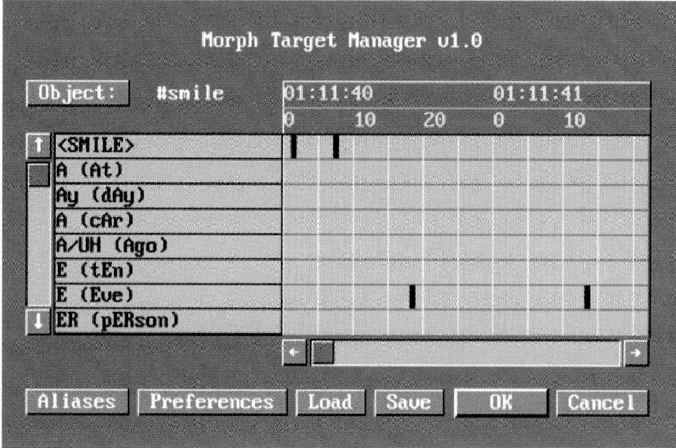

The Morph Target Manager dialog box (sample script and dialog box).

KEYSCRIPT cont

Autodesk | **\kscript** | **SCRIPT_I.KXP**

Selected Keyscript Functions

For/next — An incremental control loop.
If/then — Conditional control loop.
Gosub/return — Branch to a subroutine.
Arrays — You can define arrays with from one to three dimensions. Each dimension can be up to 32,767 integers long.
PickObjects — Displays a scrolling object selection list.
Collision — Tests for collision between two objects over time.
CreateKey — Creates a new Keyframer key.
GetBoundBox — Returns the bounding box of an object.
GetKey — Returns the key data for an object.
SetPivot — Sets the coordinates for the pivot point of an object.

Frame 0

Frame 10

Frame 15

Frame 25

An animated face created from morphs using the Morph Target Manager sample script.

MORPH ALCHEMY

Schreiber Instruments | **\alchemy** | **MRPH_I.KXP**

Summary

Morph Alchemy is part of the Imagine Morphology package. Morph Alchemy quickly assigns morph target objects to a master object in ascending or descending order, making the process much easier than using 3D Studio's sometimes tedious Object/Morph/Assign command. The Ease To, Ease From, Tension, Continuity, and Bias sliders can be adjusted globally in the main dialog box, or individually in the Morph Key Assignment dialog box, accessed by clicking in the Object Name field. The Update, Insert, Slide, and Delete buttons are the same as found in 3D Studio's Track Info dialog box. Morph Alchemy also provides an Undo Last/Redo Last toggle button, and the option to show the Morph Key Assignment parameters listed beside each object.

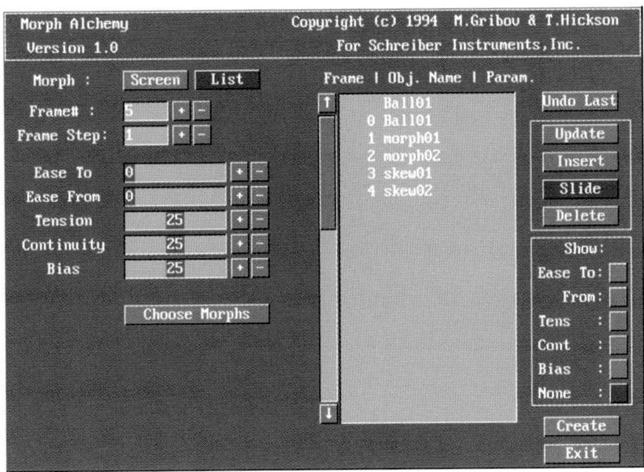

The Morph Alchemy dialog box.

Morph Alchemy Parameters

Morph [M] s, l (Screen, List) — Enables you to choose morph targets either from a list or by clicking on the object(s) in the scene.
Choose Master, Choose Morphs — Accesses the Master Object Selector and Morph Key Selector dialog boxes.
Show [S] et, ef, t, c, b, n (Ease To, Ease From, Tens, Cont, Bias, None) — Displays the Morph Key Parameter values for the selected parameters in the Parameters column of the Object Name field.

MORPH ALCHEMY cont

MRPH_I.KXP \alchemy Schreiber Instruments

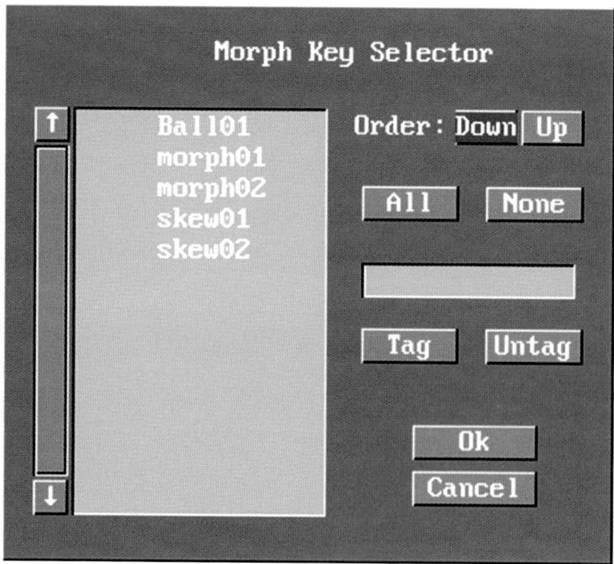

The Morph Key Selector dialog box.

QUICK MORPH

QUICK_I.KXP \qmorph Schreiber Instruments

Summary

Quick Morph is part of the Imagine Morphology package. Quick Morph quickly assigns morph target objects to a master object in ascending or descending order by accessing a Morph Objects Selector dialog box, making the process much easier than using 3D Studio's sometimes tedious Object/Morph/Assign command. After the targets are assigned, the morph keys can be manipulated by accessing 3D Studio's Track Info and Key Info dialog boxes.

Quick Morph Parameters

Order [O] d, u (Down, Up) — Chooses the order of selection of the target objects.

Note: *The All, None, Tag, and Untag buttons have the same function as their 3D Studio counterparts.*

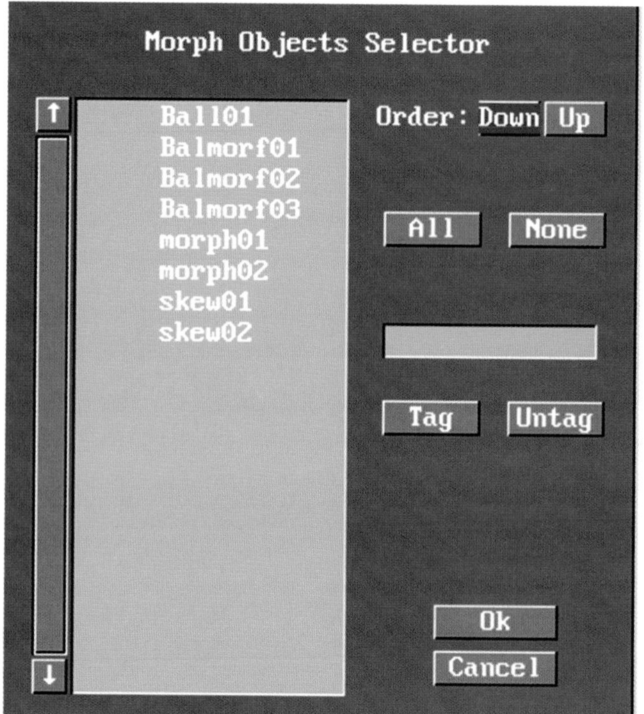

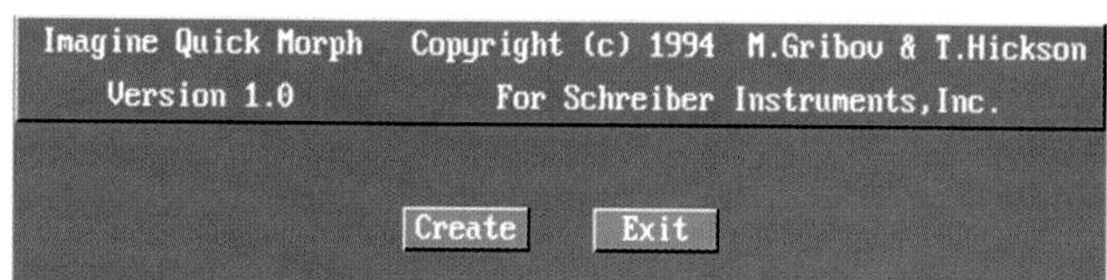

The Quick Morph dialog boxes.

Quick Morph quickly assigns morph targets to a master object.

Summary

Stereo KXP orients right and left cameras for generating stereo pair images. Two cameras are added to the scene for the left and right eye views. Stereo then allows the offset between the two views, or inter-camera distance, to be specified to generate the stereo pairs. Stereo automatically generates camera position, target position, and camera roll based on the original camera. The stereo views can be generated for an entire animation or for a limited number of frames. Rendered images can be processed for viewing with polarized or red/blue glasses, or spatially multiplexed into a format that can be viewed on VRex stereoscopic display systems.

Stereo Parameters

Physical Screen Width [Ps] — Sets the width at which the final image will be displayed.

Inter Pupil Distance [Ipd] — Sets the distance between the viewer's eyes. The distance for most adults is 2.5 inches.

Screen Pixel Width and Height [S] w, h — Sets the height and width in pixels of the final image.

Aspect Ratio [A] — Sets the aspect ratio of the final rendered image.

ICD Mode [Icd] f, t, d, 1 (Fixed, Target, Data File, 1st Target) — Sets the method used to calculate the inter camera distance. Fixed uses the value in the fixed ICD field; Target uses the camera target to set the middle of the depth of field; 1st target is similar to target, but uses only the camera target from the first frame; Data File uses a data file to generate the camera spacing, but is not currently implemented.

Fixed ICD [Fx] — Sets a fixed distance of camera separation.

Start and End Frame [Sf] [Ef] — Sets the frame to start and end the stereo camera effect.

Use All Frames [Af] (yes, no) — Sets the effect to be applied over all the frames in an animation.

Save Info File [Si] (yes, no) — Saves a text file that specifies the required rendering parameters of all frames.

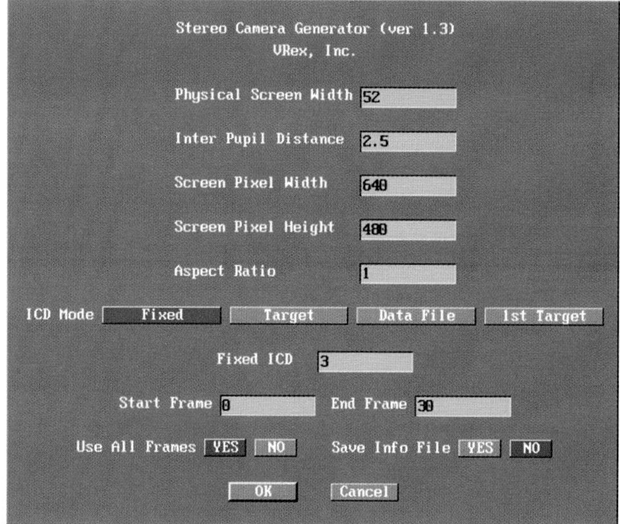

The Stereo dialog box.

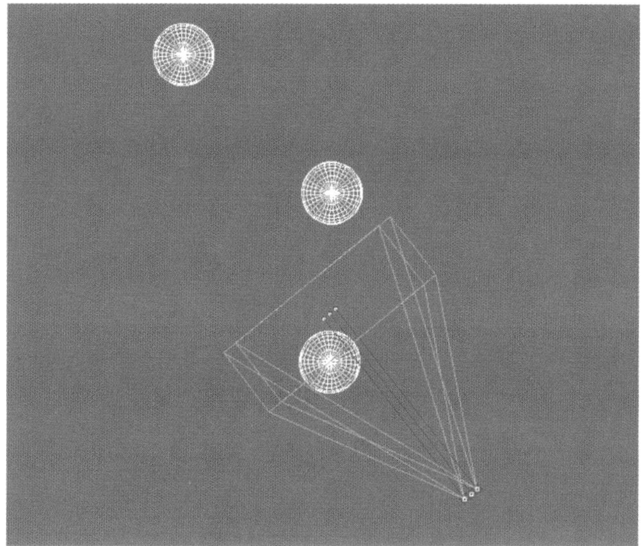
The left and right cameras

Post-processed red/blue stereo image

Stereo KXP orients right and left cameras for creating true stereo-pair images with variable depth of field focusing.

SOLARTRACK

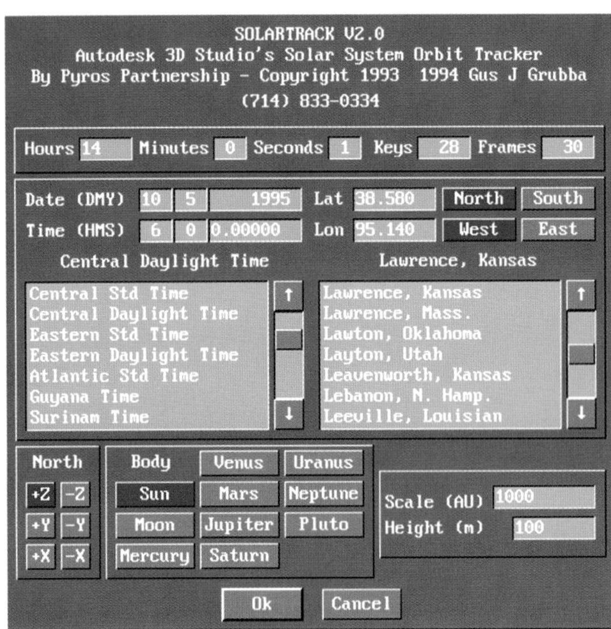

The Solartrack dialog box.

Summary

Solartrack is a plug-in that calculates the apparent movement of the sun and other celestial bodies from a specific location on the earth. The main use for this is to calculate the position and angle of the sun to illustrate lighting and shadows.

You begin by setting up your scene, adding an object to be the focal point of movement, and adding another object to represent the sun (these can be dummy objects). You then create a spotlight, link it to the sun object, and link the spotlight's target point to the focal point object. You can set the number of frames, the number of keys to be set, and the time period that the keys span. You then can set the date, time of day, and location. Numerous locations are listed from around the world. If your particular location is not listed you can enter latitude and longitude values. Settings for scale and height enable you to set the distance from the sun object (and spotlight) to the focal object, enabling you to adjust for shadow problems that can arise from very distant spotlights. Besides the sun, you can track the motion of the moon and the planets.

Solartrack Parameters

Hours, Minutes, Seconds [H] [M] [S] — Sets the time span for the animation sequence.

Keys [K] — Sets the number of keys that will be generated.

Frames [F] — Sets the total frames in the animation sequence.

Date [D] — Sets the date that will be simulated.

Time [T] — Sets the starting time for the simulation.

Lat [La] — Sets the latitude for the location.

Lon [Lo] — Sets the longitude for the location.

Time zone [Tz] — Selects the time zone for the current city. This will automatically be set based on your city selection.

City [Ci] — Selects a city for the location. This automatically sets the latitude and longitude.

North [N] (+Z, -Z, +Y, -Y, +X, -X) — Selects the direction of north for this simulation.

Body [B] s, mo, me, v, ma, j, s, u, n, p (Sun, Moon, Mercury, Venus, Mars, Jupiter, Saturn, Uranus, Neptune, Pluto) — Selects the celestial body whose movement will be tracked.

Scale [Sc] — This sets the distance from the focal point to the celestial body. If this distance is too large in relation to your scene, it can cause problems with shadows.

Height [He] — Height of the focal point above sea level in meters.

7:00 a.m.

9:30 a.m.

1:30 p.m.

6:00 p.m.

Frames from a solar shadow study in Lawrence, Kansas on 5/11/95.

Summary

Tempo is part of the Yost Group Disk #7 package.

Tempo Parameters

Pick Object [Po] l, s (List, Screen) — Select the object to work with by either selecting from a list or picking from the screen.
Preview — Displays a preview window for the current key settings.
Preferences — Displays the Preferences dialog box.
Track Type [Tt] p, r (Position, Rotation) — Selects the type of keys to be displayed and modified.
Graph window [Gw] — Displays a graph of the current keys.
Graph Scale Time [Gs] (0.01–1.0) — Sets the time scale of the graph. This changes the display of the keys, not key values.
Graph scale value [Gv] — Sets the scale for the value axis of the graph. The label can be velocity, acceleration, or position depending on the graph type.
Graph scale fit [Gf] — Scales the entire graph to fit in the window.
Graph Type [Gt] v, a, p (Velocity, Acceleration, Position) — Selects the type of graph to be displayed.
Velocity Curve [Vc] — Displays a dialog box to adjust the velocity of the key curve.
Constant Velocity [Cv] — Displays a dialog box to set a specified range of keys to a constant velocity.
Constant Acceleration [Ca] — Displays a dialog box to set a specified range of keys to a constant acceleration.
Fractal [Fr] — Displays a dialog box to apply a fractal noise pattern to a specified range of keys.
Reset [Re] — Resets all changes to the key settings.

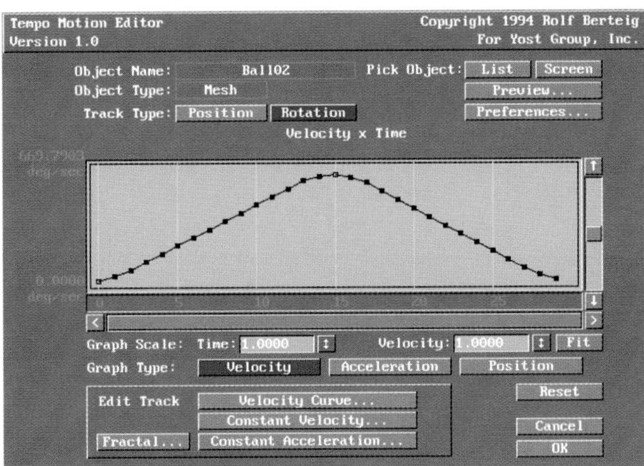

The Tempo dialog box.

Preview Parameters

Display controls — These controls enable you to change your viewpoint on the object.
Frame Rate [Fr] — Sets the desired frame rate.
Current frame [Cf] — A slider that sets and displays the current frame.
Play — Plays the current animation keys at the current frame rate.

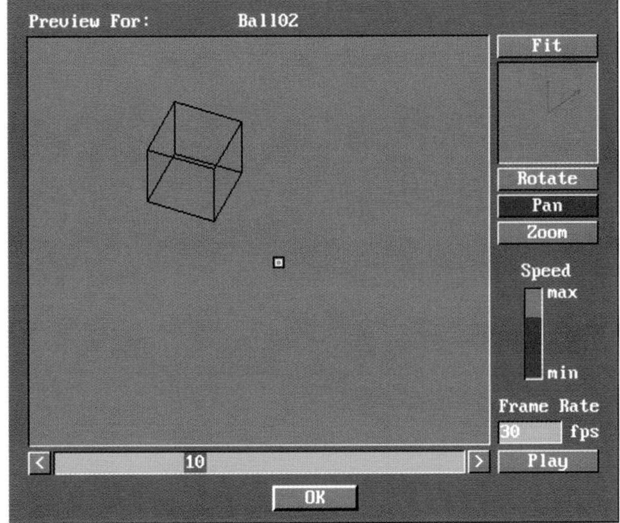

The Preview dialog box.

Velocity Curve Parameters

Curve graph — Displays a graph of the velocity using a Bézier spline. You can add, delete, move, and adjust points on the curve.
Graph Scale Time [Gs] (0.01–1.0) — Sets the time scale of the graph. This changes the display of the keys, not key values.
Graph Scale Velocity [Gv] — Sets the scale for the velocity of the graph.
Graph scale fit [Gf] — Scales the entire graph to fit in the window.
Active Segment Start and End [As] [Ae] — Sets the start and end of the current active segment in frames.
Reset [Re] — Resets the velocity curve to a straight segment with two points.
Sample [Sa] — Samples the velocity of the current object and generates a curve based on that.
Edit Mode [Em] mp, ma, aj, s, ad, d, f (Move Point, Move All, Adjust, Scale, Add, Delete, Fit to Track) — Sets the current curve editing mode. Move Point enables you to move a single point. Move All moves the entire curve. Adjust enables you to change the spline values for a point. Add and Delete work on single points. Fit to Track adjusts a curve to fit to fit within the specified segment.

Auto Fit To Track [Af] (on, off) — When selected, this automatically performs a Fit to Track when you exit.

Embed [Eb] — Enables you to embed curve a curve in an object for later use.

Extract [Ex] — Enables you to extract an embedded curve from an object.

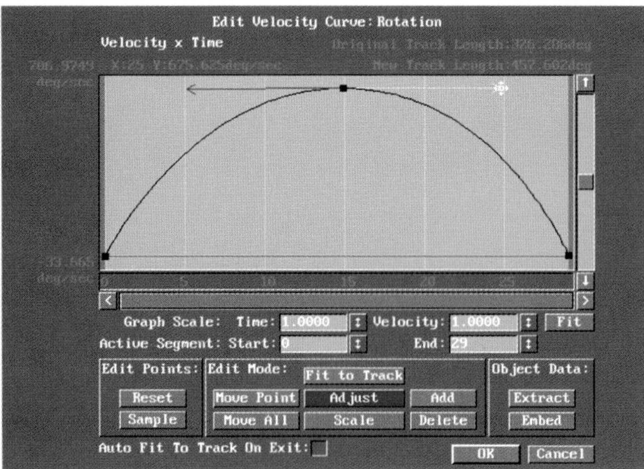

The Velocity Curve dialog box.

Constant Velocity Parameters

Start Frame [Sf] — Sets the starting frame of the active segment. Movement between this and the end frame will be set to constant velocity.

End Frame [Ef] — Sets the ending frame of the active segment.

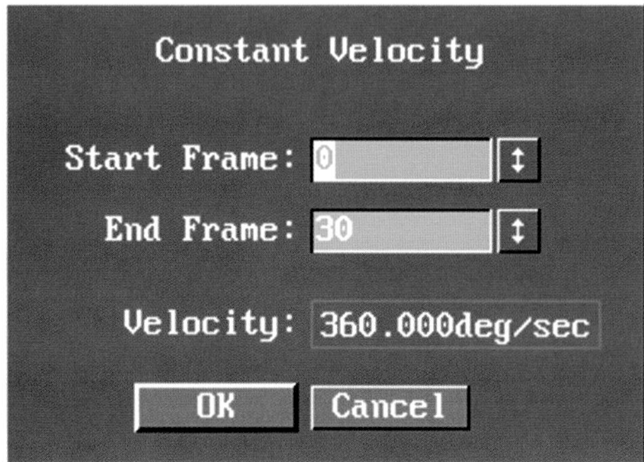

The Constant Velocity dialog box.

Constant Acceleration Parameters

Start Frame [Sf] — Sets the starting frame of the active segment. Movement between this and the end frame will be set to constant acceleration.

End Frame [Ef] — Sets the ending frame of the active segment.

Initial Velocity [Iv] — Sets the velocity at the beginning of the segment.

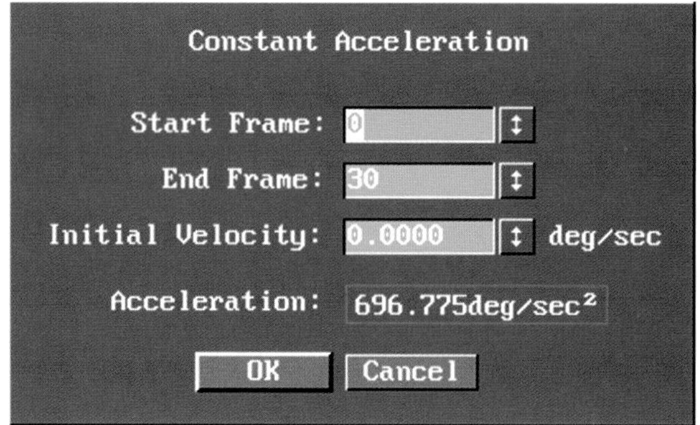

The Constant Acceleration dialog box.

Fractal Noise Parameters

Variation [V] — Sets the maximum amount of deviation of the fractal waveform from a straight line.

Power [P] — Changes the degree of irregularity in the Variation.

Decay [D] — Smooths the fractal waveform.

Random Seed [R] — Sets the seed value for a random number controlling the fractal noise.

Start Frame [Sf] — Sets the starting frame of the active segment.

End Frame [Ef] — Sets the ending frame of the active segment.

Axis Rotations X, Y, Z [Ax] [Ay] [Az] — Sets the axis on which the fractal waveform is applied. This is a two-dimensional effect. To get a fractal noise effect in three dimensions, you need to apply the effect a second time on another axis.

Fit [F] — Scales the graph to fit in the display window. This does not change any curve values.

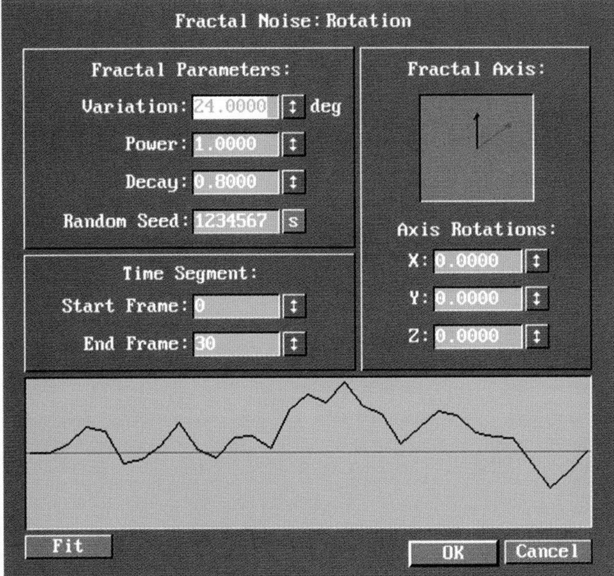

The Fractal Noise dialog box.

Using the *3D Studio IPAS Plug-In Reference* CD-ROM

The CD-ROM contains demonstration versions of a number of IPAS plug-ins, selected sample images from the book, FLIC animations for selected plug-ins, and numerous 3D Studio project files and Video Post files. There also are several catalog FLICs that were designed to provide a visual reference of the plug-ins. These consist of multiple arrays of sample images from the book that are labeled by plug-in family and name.

The CD File Structure

All sample images, FLIC animations, project files (PRJ) and Video Post files (VP) that pertain to specific plug-ins are located in their associated plug-in directories. Each plug-in CD-ROM directory is shown at the center of the horizontal color bar below the plug-in name. To find any example files that were created using Yost Group's Displacement Map Modeler, for example, look in the \DISPLACE directory.

Any sample images or FLIC animations that pertain to an IPAS family are located in that family's directory: \AXP, \IXP, \KXP, \PXP, \SXP, \OTHER. This includes, for instance, the IPAS plug-in catalog FLICs.

All the plug-in demonstration programs are sorted by vendor name or a vendor name abbreviation. The subsequent file structures will vary depending upon the installation requirements for each plug-in.

Please be sure to check the README.TXT and PLUG_IN.TXT files for any information added after the book's printing deadline.

index

Symbols

A

B

INDEX

G

H

I

J

K

L

M

N

O

P

Q

R

S

GET CONNECTED
to the ultimate source of computer information!

The MCP Forum on CompuServe

Go online with the world's leading computer book publisher! Macmillan Computer Publishing offers everything you need for computer success!

Find the books that are right for you!

A complete online catalog, plus sample chapters and tables of contents give you an in-depth look at all our books. The best way to shop or browse!

- Get fast answers and technical support for MCP books and software
- Join discussion groups on major computer subjects
- Interact with our expert authors via e-mail and conferences
- Download software from our immense library:
  - Source code from books
  - Demos of hot software
  - The best shareware and freeware
  - Graphics files

Join now and get a free CompuServe Starter Kit!

To receive your free CompuServe Introductory Membership, call **1-800-848-8199** and ask for representative #597.

The Starter Kit includes:

- Personal ID number and password
- $15 credit on the system
- Subscription to *CompuServe Magazine*

Once on the CompuServe System, type:

GO MACMILLAN

for the most computer information anywhere!

3D Studio IPAS Plug-In Reference

Name ______________________ Title ______________________

Company ______________________ Type of business ______________________

Address ______________________

City/State/ZIP ______________________

Have you used these types of books before? ☐ yes ☐ no

If yes, which ones? ______________________

____

How many computer books do you purchase each year? ☐ 1–5 ☐ 6 or more

How did you learn about this book? ______________________

Where did you purchase this book? ______________________

Which applications do you currently use? ______________________

____

Which computer magazines do you subscribe to? ______________________

____

What trade shows do you attend? ______________________

____

Comments: ______________________

____

____

Would you like to be placed on our preferred mailing list? ☐ yes ☐ no

☐ **I would like to see my name in print!** You may use my name and quote me in future New Riders products and promotions. My daytime phone number is: ______________________

New Riders Publishing 201 West 103rd Street ◆ Indianapolis, Indiana 46290 USA

Fax to **317-581-4670** Orders/Customer Service **1-800-653-6156** Source Code **NRP95**

Fold Here

NO POSTAGE
NECESSARY
IF MAILED
IN THE
UNITED STATES

BUSINESS REPLY MAIL

FIRST-CLASS MAIL PERMIT NO. 9918 INDIANAPOLIS IN

POSTAGE WILL BE PAID BY THE ADDRESSEE

NEW RIDERS PUBLISHING
201 W 103RD ST
INDIANAPOLIS IN 46290-9058

NRP REGCARD